Understanding Social Inequality

Intersections of Class, Age, Gender, Ethnicity, and Race in Canada

Julie McMullin

OXFORD
UNIVERSITY PRESS

1904 ✦ 2004

100 YEARS OF
CANADIAN PUBLISHING

OXFORD
UNIVERSITY PRESS

70 Wynford Drive, Don Mills, Ontario M3C 1J9
www.oup.com/ca

Oxford University Press is a department of the University of Oxford.
It furthers the University's objective of excellence in research, scholarship,
and education by publishing worldwide in

Oxford New York
Auckland Bangkok Buenos Aires Cape Town Chennai
Dar es Salaam Delhi Hong Kong Istanbul Karachi Kolkata
Kuala Lumpur Madrid Melbourne Mexico City Mumbai Nairobi
São Paulo Shanghai Taipei Tokyo Toronto

Oxford is a trade mark of Oxford University Press
in the UK and in certain other countries

Published in Canada
by Oxford University Press

Statistics Canada information is used with the permission of the Minister of Industry,
as Minister responsible for Statistics Canada. Information on the availability of the wide range of data from
Statistics Canada can be obtained from Statistics Canada's Regional Offices, its World Wide Web site at
http://www.statcan.ca,
and its toll-free access number 1-800-263-1136

Every effort has been made to determine and contact copyright owners. In the case of any omissions,
the publisher will be pleased to make suitable acknowledgement in future editons.

National Library of Canada Cataloguing in Publication

McMullin, Julie Ann, 1965–
Understanding social inequality: intersections of class, age, gender, ethnicity and
race in Canada/Julie McMullin.

Includes bibliographical references and index.
ISBN 0-19-541734-8

1. Equality–Canada–Textbooks. 2. Social classes–Canada–Textbooks. 3. Canada–Social
conditions–1991–Textbooks. I. Title.

HN110.Z9S6 2004a   305'.0971   C2003-907335-1

Cover Design: Brett Miller

Cover Image: PhotoDisc

1 2 3 4 - 07 06 05 04

This book is printed on permanent (acid-free) paper ∞.
Printed in Canada

Contents

Preface   vii
Acknowledgements   ix

PART I   1

Chapter 1   **Introduction**   3

[handwritten: Week 1]
Defining Social Inequality   6
Defining Social Structure   9
Structures of Inequality   10
Human Agency: Connecting Individuals to Social Structures   13
Social Time   14
Sites of Inequality   14
Glossary   16
Questions for Critical Thought   16
Recommended Reading   17

Chapter 2   **Class and Inequality**   18

[handwritten: Week 2 Marx]
Introduction   18
Marx: Class as a Productive Social Relation   19
Neo-Marxism: Issues of Exploitation, Authority, and Credentials   21
[handwritten: Week 3/4 Durk Weber + Stratifica.]
Weber: Class, Power, and Distribution   24
Neo-Weberian Approaches: Frank Parkin   27
Neo-Weberian Approaches: Edward Grabb   29
A Note on Stratification Approaches   31
Conceptualizing Social Class in a Framework of Inequality   34
Glossary   39
Questions for Critical Thought   40
Recommended Reading   41

Chapter 3   **Gender and Inequality**   *[handwritten: I–Stasiulis]*   41

[handwritten: Week 5]
Introduction   41
Explanations of Gender-Based Inequality   42

	Bringing It All Together	53
	Conceptualizing Gender in a Theory of Inequality	54
	Glossary	56
	Questions for Critical Thought	57
	Recommended Reading	57

Chapter 4   Race, Ethnicity, and Inequality   58

	Introduction	58
	Conceptualizing Race/Ethnicity and Racism/Ethnicism	64
	Racism in Everyday Life	75
	Conceptualizing Race and Ethnicity in a Theory of Inequality	77
	Glossary	80
	Questions for Critical Thought	80
	Recommended Reading	81

Chapter 5   Age and Inequality   82

	Introduction	82
	Explanations of Age-Based Inequality	84
	Conceptualizing Age in a Theory of Inequality	100
	Glossary	101
	Questions for Critical Thought	102
	Recommended Reading	102

Chapter 6   Actors and Agency   103

	Introduction	103
	Actors and Human Action	103
	Agency	106
	Intersections of Agency and Structure	108
	Glossary	118
	Questions for Critical Thought	118
	Recommended Reading	119

Chapter 7   Actors and CAGE(s)   120

	Introduction	120
	Social Time	123
	Social Processes	127
	Social Structure	128
	Agency and Structure: Actors and CAGE(s)	130
	Structure, Agency, and Anna's Life	131
	Social Inequality	134
	Glossary	135
	Questions for Critical Thought	135
	Recommended Reading	135

PART II   137

Chapter 8   **CAGE(s), Families, and Unpaid Labour**   **138**
Introduction   138
Defining Families   140
Domestic Labour   141
Violence in Families   151
Sexuality   159
Explaining Inequality in Families   161
Beyond Statistics: Agency and Experience within Families   162
Conclusions   165
Glossary   166
Questions for Critical Thought   166
Recommended Reading   167

Chapter 9   **CAGE(s) and Paid Work**   **168**
Introduction   168
Canada's Class and Occupational Structure   171
Unemployment   179
Income and Poverty   182
Alienation and Skill   191
Explaining Inequality in Paid Work   192
Beyond Statistics: Agency and Experience in Paid Work   195
Conclusion   195
Glossary   198
Questions for Critical Thought   199
Recommended Reading   199

Chapter 10   **CAGE(s) and Education**   **201**
(Tammy Duerden Comeau and Julie McMullin)
Introduction   201
Focusing on Class: Historical Notes and Existing Patterns   203
Focusing on Race/Ethnicity: Historical Notes and Existing Patterns   210
Focusing on Gender: Historical Notes and Exisiting Patterns   216
Focusing on Age and Life Course   222
Beyond the Statistics: Agency and Experience in Education   229
Conclusion   233
Glossary   233
Questions for Critical Thought   234
Recommended Reading   235

Chapter 11   CAGE(s) and Health   **236**

(Tammy Duerden Comeau and Julie McMullin)

Introduction   236

Inequality in Health: Some Current Perspectives and Critiques   238

Mortality, Morbidity, and Mental Health   240

Understanding Inequality in Health   261

Conclusion   274

Glossary   275

Questions for Critical Thought   276

Recommended Reading   276

Chapter 12   CAGE(s) and the State   **278**

(Tammy Duerden Comeau and Julie McMullin)

Introduction   278

Focusing on Class: Making Citizens, Making 'Class'   280

Focusing on Race: Making Citizens, Making 'Race'   287

Focusing on Gender: Engendering Citizens   294

Focusing on Age: Citizenship over the Life Course   301

Conclusion   306

Glossary   306

Questions for Critical Thought   307

Recommended Reading   308

Chapter 13   Epilogue   **309**

Appendix A   318

References   325

Index   353

Preface

When I was five years old I decided that I wanted to visit a friend who lived quite a distance away. When I asked my mother and father if I could go to Susan's house, they said no. When I asked why, they said, 'Because we said so.' At this point I became aware of the fact that I was young and that being young didn't seem fair. I remember this incident because when my parents couldn't give me a good reason for not visiting my friend, I decided to run away from home. Luckily, as I was hitch-hiking down the street with my hand open wide (my version of the one thumb up pose), a friendly woman picked me up and told me she'd take me home. I couldn't remember where I lived, so the woman drove me up and down many streets until we found one that I recognized as my own. When I was 16 years old, I worked as a waitress, but I was paid less per hour than my 18-year-old friend. This too seemed unfair.

When I was eight, my younger brothers and I were playing outside on a very hot day. My mother took off my brothers' shirts for relief from the heat. When I started to take off my shirt, my mother told me that girls must keep their shirts on. 'Why?' I asked. 'Because,' she said. I couldn't understand this at all; my brothers and I looked the same. I thought to myself, being a girl isn't fair.

When I went to university I discovered I was a member of the working class. My professors told me that capitalists employed workers at relatively low wages to ensure high levels of profit for themselves. They told me about the social and cultural disadvantages of being from a working class background. Gradually my university experience began to make some sense. I couldn't figure out why my grades were only average despite my considerable effort. Part of it was that I didn't know how to play the game—that is, how to ask my professors for help, how to use a big library, how to study effectively—and no one I knew could coach me. This seemed unfair.

It wasn't until I was in my late twenties that I discovered I was white. This awareness came as I was reading Patricia Hill Collin's book, *Black Feminist Thought* (1990). Of course, at some level I knew I was white, but I wasn't fully aware of the privilege associated with the colour of my skin until then. This too seemed unfair.

Structures of inequality in Canada are organized along age, class, gender, ethnic, and racial lines. The preceding stories, as trivial as they may seem, show some of the ways in which this occurs. They show that this involves power, the ability of individuals or groups to impose their will, with or without resistance, on others. They show that ideology is an important dimension of inequality; that societal beliefs about what is appropriate for people to do on the basis of their sex, class, race, or age creates advantage for some and disadvantage for others. The stories show that inequality is about the distribution of material, cultural, and social resources. And they show that the meaning people attribute to sex, class, race, and age is shaped by experience. These are some of the complex issues that I will consider throughout this book.

Acknowledgements

As I wrote this book, I often reflected upon my life as an academic and thought about how privileged I am. Part of what makes my life so privileged is that I am surrounded by wonderful colleagues, family, and friends, to whom I owe much gratitude for the help and support that they graciously give me. When I didn't know how to begin to write this book, James Teevan, Michael Gardiner, Edward Grabb, Victor Marshall, and Ingrid Connidis read my proposal and provided me with valuable feedback. To Ed, I am especially grateful because he suggested that I send my proposal to Megan Mueller, the then acquisitions editor for Oxford University Press. Megan liked my proposal and pursued the book project with vigour. Although Megan persuaded me to write this manuscript much more like a text than I had originally intended, I thank her for her welcome and very positive encouragement along the way.

The Academic Development Fund at the University of Western Ontario supported the writing of this book by providing me with the resources to hire research assistants. Katherine Pendakis and Erin Demaiter did literature searchers, tracked down references, and combed the Internet for stories that could be used in the boxed inserts. Thanks, Kate and Erin, for your excellent work. I am particularly indebted to Tammy Duerden Comeau, who also worked as a research assistant on this book. Tammy saved my sanity by agreeing to co-author chapters 10, 11, and 12, with me. Tammy, you have no idea how grateful I am. Merci beaucoup!

Parts of this book have been adapted from some of my previously published work. Chapter 5 is a revised version of my article 'Diversity and the State of Sociological Aging Theory', which appeared in volume 40 of *The Gerontologist*, and bits of chapters 9 were taken from 'Social Class and Inequality' which appeared as chapter 14 in *Sociology: A Canadian Perspective*, edited by Lorne Tepperman and Jim Curtis and published by Oxford University Press. Other parts were read by my colleagues Tracey Adams and Lorraine Davies, who took the time away from their own work to comment on mine; for that, I thank them. My thanks also go to two anonymous reviewers for their helpful suggestions; to Phyllis Wilson, managing editor of Oxford University Press for answering all of my silly questions; to Freya Godard for excellent editorial suggestions; and to Sharon Sabourin for helping me compile and format my list of references. Although I can't possibly convey thanks to all of the many friends and colleagues who have helped me, given me advice, or inspired me over the years, Tracey Adams,

Danièle Belanger, Michael Gardiner, Ed Grabb, Victor Marshall, and Kevin McQuillan deserve special thanks for never telling me to get lost when I was rambling on about an idea or complaining about departmental happenings.

As I was writing this book, Ingrid Connidis, Lorraine Davies, and I shared many moments of joy, sadness, anger, and frustration owing to both our work and our personal lives. It is impossible to imagine my life without having Ingrid and Lori to celebrate the good times with and to lean on when the times are tough. What an honour it is to have them as friends, collaborators, and colleagues!

I am very fortunate to have a wonderful family who serve as an important diversion from my work. I am grateful to my father-in-law, Peter Arnold, for his baby-sitting services and his fine Sunday dinners. Thanks to my brother Rick, my sister-in-law, Louanne Provost, and their children Malcolm and Makayla for many fun cottage days and to my brother Rob and his wife Kristi Adamo for their constant support. My mom and dad made many sacrifices for their children, and for that we cannot thank them enough. Whenever I have needed them they have been there for me. To them, I give my love and deepest thanks.

When I was writing this book I went to work everyday between 6:30 and 7:00 am, shut my office door, and wrote until about noon. For my husband, Scott Arnold, that meant caring for our daughter in the mornings on his own. For our daughter, Emma McMullin Arnold, that meant waking up and asking her dad where I was. Scott would say, 'Mommy is writing a book', to which Emma would reply, 'Why?' Why indeed. Emma and Scott are the loves of my life, and without them my work, and this book, would be for naught. Thank you both.

For Emma and Scott
and in memory of my mother-in-law and friend, Donna Arnold.

The first objective of Part I is to discuss and assess theories of class, age, gender, ethnicity, and race that have been used to explain inequality. Of course, it would be impossible to discuss all of the theories; instead, the first part of this book considers theories that have made influential contributions to our understanding of class, age, gender, ethnicity, and race in relation to inequality, especially in Canada. Furthermore, theories that consider the structural nature of these factors are prioritized. However, because structures do not exist outside of the individual interaction that creates them, some symbolic interactionist perspectives are discussed. In particular, there has been some very good work done on gender and race from a symbolic-interactionist perspective and to ignore it would be remiss.

The second objective of Part I is to examine human agency and the relationship between social structure and human agency. Although most of the work on social inequality is at the macro, structural level, sociologists recognize that to understand social life better, assessments of the intersection between individual agency and social structures are required. However, there is very little agreement regarding the specific relationship between agency and structure.

The third objective of Part I is to integrate ideas from the various perspectives on class, age, gender, ethnicity, race, and human agency into a cohesive conceptual framework. The aim of this exercise is to provide an organizational tool that will enable us to explore social inequality without giving *a priori* emphasis to any of class, age, gender, ethnicity, or race. In doing so, we will be able to examine how structures of inequality are produced and reproduced through human agency and interaction.

Chapter 1

Introduction

This is a book about social inequality, and to begin it describes the life of a woman I know. Anna was born to white, English-speaking parents of British descent, just after the First World War began (in 1915); she grew up on a farm in Ontario with her mother, father, and two brothers. Although it was only a small farm, Anna's father and mother worked hard and were able to provide their family with the essentials of life. Anna graduated from high school, which was unusual for a rural girl in that day, and although she had the opportunity to go on to teachers' college, as her mother did before her, she decided to marry John Warner, a local man who was seven years her senior. She married well. John's family were well-to-do small business owners, and with their help, Anna and John began their marriage in the late 1930s in relative financial stability. They moved to town and had two daughters, one in 1941 and the other in 1943.

Anna was always a homemaker, and John never had a stable job. His older brother, who was married and childless, inherited his father's business and John worked for him occasionally. John also bought houses, restored them, and sold them for a profit. Money was tight in the Warner household, but no one seemed to want for anything. There was food on the table, they had paid for the house in full when they bought it, and they had a few good clothes.

In 1970, John died suddenly in a car accident. He was 62 and Anna was 55. John's estate consisted of some savings and his house. His will stipulated that Anna could draw $200 per month from his estate until she either remarried or died, at which time the estate would be divided equally among her daughters. Suddenly, Anna was poor. Her income was well below the qualifying cut-off for social assistance, but she refused to apply for it and was too young for the old age pension. The will stipulated that she could not sell John's house. Aside from a brief stint in business college, Anna had no training, no work experience, and no marketable skill. Besides, at 55 she was unlikely to find work. Her daughter hired her to babysit her grandchildren, and for the next 10 years she made do with the clothes she already owned, shopping at yard sales and eating anything that she could buy for next to nothing in the grocery store—old bread, dinted canned food, and so on. After 10 years Anna turned 65 and began receiving old-age security. Though she was still poor, she was no longer destitute. Five years later her sister-in-law, the widow of John's childless brother who had inherited the family business, died, leaving Anna one-third of her quite large estate. Suddenly, at 70, Anna was better off financially than she had ever been before.

A central aim of this book is to develop a conceptual framework that will help explain the ebb and flow of poverty that Anna experienced throughout her life. We often think of the conditions of inequality, such as poverty (see Box 1.1) or homelessness (see Box 1.2), as inescapable fixed states, and indeed there is ample evidence that for many this is true. However, the description of Anna's life demonstrates that

---

Box **Working Definitions of Poverty**

Canada–like most countries, but unlike the United States–has no 'official' definition of poverty. Different agencies and organizations in Canada measure poverty in different ways, and this chapter describes several working definitions:

- Statistics Canada Low Income Cut-offs (LICO), calculated using both pre- and post-tax income;
- Statistics Canada Low Income Measure (LIM);
- Lines of income inequality developed by the Canadian Council on Social Development (CCSD);
- Market Basket Measure (MBM) under development by the federal, provincial and territorial governments;
- Fraser Institute poverty lines;
- Montreal Diet Dispensary guidelines;
- Social Planning Council of Metropolitan Toronto Budget guides;
- The Cost of Living Guidelines developed by the Social Planning Council of BC.

For a benchmark comparison with the above working definitions, this chapter also provides estimates of: average and median incomes; the basic income levels provided by provincial social assistance rates; and minimum income levels suggested by Gallup public opinion.

None of these definitions of poverty is exhaustive or precise. They are designed as working measures, and as such they are all founded on various simplifying assumptions. Given the immense complexity of the problem–the fact that what constitutes poverty varies from place to place, from decade to decade, and even from household to household–it can be argued that the only alternative to an inadequate definition is no definition at all. Nevertheless, some working definitions are more inadequate than others. This chapter describes the various prevailing definitions of poverty, and then explores their shortcomings.

Because poverty is based on the deficit of income compared to essential expenditures, disagreements over how poverty should be defined can be reduced conceptually to two questions. First, how is income defined? Second, what are legitimate necessary expenditures–and necessary for what purpose? Of course, the answers to these questions depend on place, time, and household circumstances.

Source: Ross et al. (2000: 13–14). Reprinted by permission of the Canadian Council on Social Development.

Box 1.2   'People Who Slipped thru the Cracks'

Julia Vinograd is a street poet who lives in Berkeley, California. In her poem 'People Who Slipped Thru the Cracks', Vinograd presents a conversation with a man living on the streets and trying to stay safe and sane.

People Who Slipped thru the Cracks
I talked to a man who wasn't there.
'Well, that's not exactly fair', he said,
'the cold still gets to me
and I only go invisible when the cops come
and I can't keep it up for long.
Its like holding your breath
to hold light away from your skin,
you just have to know how.
But I'm not like those imaginary people
crazies are always losing arguments with,
at least not yet.'
He sounded a little wistful.
'Would you like that?' I asked.
'Dunno', he shrugged. 'It'd be easier.
I always have to check the back of my knees
I keep leaving them behind.
Not fingerprints, they were easy.'
He held up his hand and the lines spun for me.
Like a child's whirligig in the wind.
'Imaginary people don't get cold
but they're stuck with their crazies.
I suppose I'll just go on like this
till I'm hit by a truck that didn't see me.'
He laughed, the sound low in his throat
like a beaten dog, afraid to come close enough
to a fire.
I wondered how old he'd been before
and how many other people weren't there
And no, it isn't fair.

Source: Vinograd (1997).

for others, experiences of inequality may be more complex, involving multiple transitions in and out of relative states of deprivation (see Davies, McMullin, and Avison 2001; Leisering and Leibfried 1999). To understand inequality in this way requires a definition of it that considers durable patterns of advantage and disadvantage, the capacity of individuals to act toward change, and time.

Defining Social Inequality

Sociologists argue that inequality is *not* caused by innate personality flaws. People are not poor because they are lazy or because they lack motivation or ambition. They are poor because opportunities are distributed differentially in society on the basis of things such as class, age, gender, ethnicity, and race. Sociologists are interested in why social inequality exists, what factors contribute to social inequality, how and through which processes it is maintained, and what changes need to be made to create a more equal society. A unifying assumption in much of the contemporary sociological work on social inequality is that it is a social problem. Few sociologists would argue that we need higher rates of poverty, more hungry malnourished people in the world, or more disparity in wealth between the rich and the poor. Indeed, many sociologists search for ways in which problems of inequality can be alleviated and, in doing so, they specify policies and programs that would help to eradicate it. This line of inquiry is as old as the discipline itself, for Karl Marx and Max Weber both considered these issues (see Grabb 2002 for a detailed account).

At a very basic level inequality is a condition or situation that is not equal. This suggests that inequality does not simply refer to differences among individuals but rather reflects differences that matter, differences that result in unfairness and disadvantage for some and privilege for others (see Box 1.3 for an example). In Canada, class, age, gender, race, and ethnicity are differences that matter; colour or texture of hair do not. **Social inequality**, as it is usually defined, refers to relatively long-lasting differences among individuals or groups of people that have implications for individual lives, especially 'for the rights or opportunities they exercise and the rewards or privileges they enjoy' (Grabb 2002: 1–2; see also Pampel 1998). So, for example, compared to people from the middle and upper classes, people who are a part of the working class do not have the same educational opportunities and they tend to have worse health. Women and members of racial and ethnic minority groups tend to work in bad jobs while good jobs are reserved for men and members of privileged racial and ethnic groups. And, compared to middle-aged adults, older and younger people suffer longer bouts of unemployment and earn less money. In these examples, class, gender, race, ethnicity, and age are social structures of inequality that result in outcomes that matter. These **structures of inequality** are patterns of advantage and disadvantage that are durable (Tilly 1998), but penetrable.

At an individual level the experience of inequality refers to the meaning that is attached to unequal life conditions as well as the things that people do to manage or penetrate the structures of inequality. These issues reflect human agency or the capacity of individuals to interpret their situation and act to change it. However, the experience of inequality is at odds with the experience of privilege by which those in positions of power act to maintain their advantage and reproduce the structures of inequality (see Box 1.4). Furthermore, the experience of inequality must be examined within the context of social time. For our purposes,

Box 1.3   Poverty Statistics Tell Startling Truth

One of the easiest ways to dismiss the hard, cold numbers of the just-released United Way study on poverty in Toronto is to quote Mark Twain quoting Benjamin Disraeli, 'There are three kinds of lies: lies, damned lies, and statistics.'

In this case, the tactic won't work.

For *A Decade of Decline: Poverty and Income Inequality in the City of Toronto in the 1990s* confirms a trend the United Way has been tracing for years, one that will jump up and bite us in the butt if we don't pay attention.

Regardless of one's definition of poverty, its causes or cures, and who's to blame for the high incidence of citizens straining to make ends meet, this is irrefutable:

Despite a robust economic recovery in the last half of the past decade, Torontonians got poorer while the rest of Canada marked time.

The numbers are numbing enough.

The median incomes of single-parent families dropped 18 per cent to $24,600 from $29,900 over the decade.

Single persons are earning just $20,300, down from $23,200 in 1990.

And if you think that's par for the course—that single parents made their beds and must lie in it; and that singles have to pay their dues—explain this: The median income of Toronto husband-and-wife families dropped 13 per cent to $51,300 from $59,000 at the start of the decade.

There were 14,310 more Toronto children living in poverty at the end of the decade than in 1995. Poor seniors in the city increased by 11,300 over the same time, a 40 per cent hike.

Even if you believe the poverty line, ($17,780 for a single-parent family with one child; $25,400 for a two-parent family with two children) is too high, consider this: Half the one-parent families deemed to be living in poverty had incomes of $10,100 or less.

Translated, that means their entire monthly income was $82 less than the average rental cost of a two-bedroom apartment in Toronto in 1999.

The middle-class is shrinking. Middle-income earners now make up 57 per cent of all Toronto families, compared to 65 per cent in 1990. Meanwhile, the gap between rich and poor grows. High-income (more then $100,000) jumped to 23 per cent from 18 per cent; and low-income families (earning less $30,000) increased to 20 per cent from 18 per cent.

The median incomes of Toronto's 12 poorest neighbourhoods fell to $36,800 in 1999 compared to $43,600 in 1990. Conversely, the median incomes in the 12 most affluent neighbourhoods increased to $125,600 from $114,200.

All this is happening in Toronto. In boom times. Even as the rest of Canada holds its own.

Source: Royson (2002). Reprinted with permission – Torstar Syndication Services.

social time refers to issues of generation and the life course. The experience of inequality in this context is understood as a dynamic process that evolves throughout one's life and is influenced by the generation in which one is born.

Box **Toronto's Tent City Sealed Off, Squatters Ejected**
By Wallace Immen and James Rusk

A shantytown that had become a civic embarrassment for Toronto was cleared yesterday in an operation Mayor Mel Lastman praised and poverty activists condemned.

About 100 people looked dishevelled, dazed and angry as security officials hired by the landowners, Home Depot Canada, rousted them from the camp in a rubble-strewn field near the harbour.

Some wept and others yelled in contempt as a police cordon kept them from retrieving their belongings from the makeshift shanties that had been home to some for as long as two years.

'Shame on you, You don't have the right to destroy people' s houses', one yelled.

Mr Lastman defended the action, telling reporters that the eviction was at Home Depot's, not the city's, initiative.

'Home Depot has the same right as you or I to move trespassers from their land', he said.

No one has claimed the collection of cobbled shelters that became known as Tent City would ever be a permanent solution to Toronto's lack of housing for the poor. There was no running water and no electricity, and the soil of the former industrial site on the shore of Lake Ontario is tainted with toxic wastes.

The camp had attracted a growing population of homeless men and women who refused to use the city's shelters, many of whom have drug and alcohol addictions or mental illness.

Home Depot Canada had warned the squatters repeatedly that they must leave the crime-plagued, litter-strewn site or be moved out.

First, security officials in flak jackets marched through openings in a chainlink fence that surrounded the site in an industrial zone on the city's eastern harbour. A large number of Toronto police stood by.

When the people and their pets had been moved out, trucks moved in carrying front-end loaders while teams went into action to install more secure chainlink fencing.

Meanwhile squads of workers wearing white coveralls and face masks used chain saws and weed whackers to clear-cut a patrol zone around the entire perimeter of the site.

Police arrested two people, including a woman who was handcuffed and held in a van during the eviction.

The eviction shocked Sam Rosen, who said he was sitting in a latrine when he heard an announcement that everyone had 10 minutes to leave the site.

'They told me if I left peacefully they would arrange food and shelter. But now there's nobody doing anything for us', said Mr Rosen, who moved into a wooden shack in Tent City this summer after eight years of using shelters. He said he had to leave behind his clothes, pots and pans and books and was allowed to return only to get medication for his diabetes.

Those evicted were handed pink notices that resembled traffic tickets. A box checked on each said they were charged with trespassing and faced a fine of up to $2,000.

. . .

After the operation, advocates for the homeless held protests at City Hall and the Tent City site. A press conference Home Depot had planned was cancelled when a large angry group gathered to protest. Some of those evicted and their supporters briefly broke up a meeting of Toronto Council's planning and transportation committee, which was conducting a hearing on the new official plan.

The meeting recessed for about 10 minutes while they shouted slogans such as 'The people's homes cannot be bulldozed,' but resumed after a meeting was arranged between the protesters and the city's chief administrative officer, Shirley Hoy.

Source: Immen and Rusk (2002). Reprinted with permission from the Globe and Mail.

In short, the perspective developed in this book suggests that to understand social inequality we need a framework that integrates social structure, human agency, and social time. Hence it is important to define each of these terms carefully and to discuss the assumptions made about them in this book.

Defining Social Structure

If we acknowledge the assumptions that sociologists make about social structures in their work we can understand better why certain research questions are asked in the first place and we can interpret research in context. **Social structures** generally refer to relatively long-lasting, patterned relationships among the elements of society (Abercrombie, Hill, and Turner 2000). Although this broad definition holds true regardless of one's sociological perspective, there is little agreement in sociology about what social structures precisely are and even less agreement about their relationship to individuals. In general, however, there are two dominant and counter views of the social structure; one has its intellectual roots in structural functionalism, the other in critical theory.

Following the work of Talcott Parsons, structural functionalists conceive of society as an all-encompassing social structure that may be decomposed into several specialized substructures. Examples of these substructures are the economic, the political, and the educational systems of society. From this point of view, the elements of social structures include social institutions (e.g., work organizations and political institutions) and patterns of social roles (Parsons 1951). Roles are the building blocks of institutions, which are, in turn, the building blocks of society (Parsons 1951; Riley 1971). Structural functionalists tend to overemphasize the degree to which individuals conform to the values and norms established in the social structure and the degree to which society is based on consensus (Layder 1994). Furthermore, structural functionalism de-emphasizes the possibility of conflict in society or the possibility that individual choices are constrained by the forces of social structures.

Stratification approaches to the study of inequality tend to make assumptions about social structures that are in line with structural functionalist thought (see Grabb 2002: 106–10). According to stratification theory, individuals can be ranked hierarchically according to socially desirable characteristics such as income, education, occupation, status, or prestige. This hierarchical procedure groups individuals together in discrete categories or social strata (Turner 1988). Because social structures are thought to comprise patterns of social roles which are acted out by individuals, much of this work focuses on the characteristics of individuals rather than on relationships among people. This led Tilly (1998: 34) to suggest, 'Instead of reducing social behavior to individual decision-making, social scientists urgently need to study the relational constraints within which all individual action takes place.' The idea of 'relational constraints' points to the importance of adopting a more critical view of social structures when studying inequality.

Critical approaches to studies of inequality and social structures are sometimes informed by Marxist sociology; and they assume that social relations, especially class relations, are the fundamental elements of the social structure. Of course there are many definitions of social class, the details of which will be discussed in chapter 2. Put simply, however, class relations reflect the relative rights and powers that people have in production processes (Wright 1997). The structural significance of class relations is the manner in which they produce durable and patterned systems of inequality; central to this process is the conflict embedded in class relations. According to these approaches, inequality results largely from class structures, and thus explanations of inequality are reduced to issues of economic subordination. Yet, to understand inequality better, the structures of age, gender, ethnicity, and race must also be considered.

Structures of Inequality

In studies of inequality, scholars make different assumptions about which social structures are important. Some emphasize class, social gerontologists focus on age, feminist researchers concentrate on gender relations, and still others consider race or ethnic relations as the central element of social inequality. This is not to say that there has been no overlap. Many have considered at least two of these dimensions, but few have examined each of them in relation to the others. This book begins with the assumption that researchers should consider all of these factors and that neglecting one or more of them may distort descriptions and explanations of social inequality. Consider, for example, the following discussion of age, social inequality, and social policy.

The importance of age relations in the analysis of social inequality is crucial, particularly in the current climate of policy reform and social welfare cutbacks. Some of the recent political solutions for deficit reduction have targeted public pensions. For instance, the former Reform Party proposed taxing back 100 per cent of Old Age Security (OAS) benefits for households with incomes above $54,000 a year, and there continues to be talk of raising the age of eligibility for OAS by several years (Myles and Street 1995).

The fact that Canada's population is aging is well known. At the beginning of this century 6 per cent of the Canadian population were aged 65 and over (Marshall and McPherson 1994), and by 1991 this had almost doubled to 11.6 per cent. Denton and Spencer (1995) predict that by 2041 the proportion of the population aged 65 and over will double again, to 23.2 per cent. The proportion of the population aged 80 and over is growing even faster. Between 1971 and 1991 the percentage of the population in this age group had increased from 1.6 per cent to 2.4 per cent, and by 2041 it is expected to reach 7.9 per cent, or more than triple the 1991 figure (Denton and Spencer 1995). Although demographic predictions about the aging of the population vary depending on the assumptions made about future immigration, mortality rates, and fertility rates, most agree that, barring disaster or unforeseen circumstances, the trend is real and significant.

The economic strain that an aging population may impose on Canada cannot be ignored. However, the crisis ideology that often frames political and media discussions of this topic serves to create a sense of urgency about Canada's financial problems while downplaying the economic needs of disadvantaged people. Thus, the emphasis is placed on Canada's fiscal well-being rather than on the 16.4 per cent of Canadians who are poor (National Council of Welfare 2000).

These discussions also create an environment of competition over the distribution of limited resources between younger and older adults. Although debates over generational equity have been slow to evolve in Canada (Marshall, Cook and Marshall 1993), with health care and pension reform at the anterior of the political agenda, politicians started to make proposals in the 1990s that fuelled such debates. For instance, in 1994 Lloyd Axworthy, then human resources minister of Canada, suggested that a portion of the money spent on old age security should be redirected toward job retraining for young people (*The Globe and Mail*, 9 March 1994, cited in Myles and Street 1995). Yet one might ask why these

monies could not be redirected toward older people who are economically disadvantaged, particularly when the poverty rate among Canadians aged 65 and over is 17.5 per cent, similar to the poverty rate among Canadians under the age of 18 (18.8 per cent) (National Council of Welfare 2000).[1]

Part of the problem with policy directives like the ones mentioned above is that the population is categorized into the old and the young without taking gender, class, race, ethnicity, or further age distinctions into account. Close examinations of poverty rates do not support the simple bifurcation of the population according to age. For instance, the poverty rate among people aged 55 to 64 is 14.5 per cent for men but 16.8 per cent for women. This gender difference is more pronounced among those aged 85 and over, where the poverty rate for women is 37.5 per cent compared to 20.7 per cent for men. Marital status also differentially affects the poverty rate for men and women 65 and older. In 1998, the poverty rate for unattached women in this age group was 39.4 per cent and for unattached men of the same age it was 28.9 per cent for men (National Council of Welfare 2000).

Poverty rates also vary by occupation (which is often used as a measure of social class) among those under age 65. Family heads and unattached individuals employed in managerial occupations have the lowest poverty rate, while those employed in services have the highest. The year of immigration to Canada is another important consideration. For unattached persons who arrived in Canada between 1946 and 1960 the poverty rate is 29.9 per cent. For those who came to Canada in the 1960s, 1970s, and 1980s respectively, it is 37.2 per cent, 32 per cent, and 55.9 per cent. For those who arrived after 1989 the poverty rate is 42.1 per cent. Heads of family have much lower poverty rates, ranging from 6.6 per cent if the immigration years were between 1946 and 1960 to 18.9 per cent if one immigrated in the 1980s. Interestingly, poverty rates are similar and quite high for immigrants who arrived in Canada after 1989, regardless of whether they are unattached persons or family heads (National Council of Welfare 2000).

These figures provide useful information about economic inequality in Canada, but they are limiting because they do not take more than two factors into account at the same time. This narrow type of analysis, which is typical of the analyses conducted by governments, is somewhat misleading because only two factors are considered at once. One of the key assumptions that the analysis in this book makes clear is that class, age, gender, ethnicity, and race must each be considered in studies of inequality. Scholars have attempted to integrate two or three of these factors with varying success. The challenge here is to give equal theoretical weight to each of these factors in order to understand social inequality. To do this I will argue that a framework must evolve that considers at least three interconnected processes of social life—production, reproduction, and distribution—processes that are central to the survival of individuals and societies. In chapter 2, I define these processes, and in chapter 7, I elaborate upon how they are structured by the power relations that are assumed among class, age, gender, and ethnic and race relations.

Class, age, gender, ethnicity, and race are conceptualized here as sets of **social relations** that are characterized by power and that are fundamental structures or organizing features of social life (Calasanti 1996).

Power relations, which are essential to Weberian approaches to inequality, are determined by the ability of individuals in social relationships to impose their will on others regardless of resistance (Weber [1922] 1978). Conceptualizing class, age, gender, ethnicity, and race as social relations characterized by power suggests that conflict is present more often than consensus in these sets of relations (McMullin and Marshall 1999: 308–9). Indeed, a relational understanding of class, age, gender, ethnicity, and race requires an emphasis on 'structured forms of power, organization, direction, and regulation that exist in modern societies and through which ruling groups maintain and reproduce their dominant positions' (Layder 1994: 159; see also Smith 1987). These structured forms of power are established and reproduced through daily experiences as individuals and groups interact with one another (Grabb, 2002; McMullin, 2000; Smith, 1987).

These views of social structures and power fall more in line with critical approaches to social inequality than with those found in stratification theory or structural functionalist approaches. It is assumed that social relations are composed of social structures and that conflict and power are fundamental characteristics of these relations. This does not mean that social relationships are in a state of constant conflict or that people engage in daily power struggles. It does suggest, however, that the possibility of conflict and power struggle in these relations is omnipresent. In chapters 2 to 5, I expand on these ideas by providing an overview of the principal theories of social class, gender, race and ethnicity, and age.

Chapter 2 considers sociological debates about the conceptualization of social class. It begins with a discussion of Karl Marx's and Max Weber's theories of social class. It then considers the elaboration and extension of these classics by leading neo-Marxist and neo-Weberian thinkers and briefly discusses stratification approaches to social class. Chapter 2 concludes with a working definition of social class that will be used in this book.

Chapter 3 explores the relationship between gender and social inequality. It discusses various feminist approaches to social inequality, including radical feminism and socialist feminism. In particular, this chapter considers how the combination of patriarchy and capitalism leads to gender inequality. The chapter moves on to examine the pervasiveness of gender inequality in daily life; it concludes with a discussion of the approach to gender that will be used in this book.

Chapter 4 examines conceptualizations of race and ethnicity in relation to inequality. Beginning with the contentious debate about whether the term race should be used at all, chapter 4 outlines and contrasts various points of view about this issue. Chapter 4 considers the relationship between the concepts of race and ethnicity, although the emphasis is more on the former than the latter. The chapter also examines some theoretical work that has considered the experience of everyday racism. It concludes with a discussion of how race and ethnicity will be conceptualized in this book.

Chapter 5 considers various approaches to the study of age relations and the conceptualization and social construction of age. This chapter discusses how age is a structure of inequality in society and considers the stratification approaches and political economy approaches to age relations in this regard. Chapter 5 concludes with a working definition of age relations that will be used in the conceptual framework presented in chapter 7.

Human Agency: Connecting Individuals to Social Structures

Too often, research and theory on inequality concentrate either on structure or on individuals rather than combining the two. The framework in this book highlights the importance of agency and its relationship with social structures. Agency expresses the idea that individuals do not passively conform to the circumstances of their lives. Rather, they are active participants in social relationships. They sometimes rebel or, on the other hand, choose to follow the crowd, and so on. In this regard, I make two related assumptions about social life. First, 'social structures do not stand outside of the human, social behaviour that produces them, yet, they nevertheless take on properties that transcend the behaviour of those who construct it'; and second, 'while these properties of durability constrain and limit the agency of the individual they never do so completely' (McMullin and Marshall 2001: 114). In this light, although I assume that analyses of social inequality cannot be reduced to issues of individual motivation, ambition, and the like, individuals nonetheless make choices and decisions that influence their lot in life.

In Chapter 6, I discuss how actors are conceptualized in this book by drawing on key works in several different theoretical traditions. In particular, I argue that we need to clarify and specify what is meant by structuration theory (Giddens 1984) by focusing on how individuals and structures are connected to one another. Thus, I place emphasis on how individuals negotiate real social structures, the mechanisms through which they do so, the constraints placed on individual negotiation by social structures, and how social structures gradually change or are reproduced through individual negotiations.

Social Time

As noted above, social time refers to life course and generation issues. The life-course perspective allows us to examine how individuals manage social change and how their past experiences affect their ability to cope. It also considers transitions and trajectories involving school, work, parenthood, retraining, job exit and re-entry, and retirement and the timing of them, all of which influence inequality. Generation reflects the idea that people are born into groups that have meaningful significance. For instance, individuals who were born between 1910 and 1915 were coming of age during the Depression and their lives have been similarly shaped by that experience.

In chapter 7, I discuss the life-course perspective and the concept of generations and integrate them into a conceptual framework of inequality that also considers the intersections between agency and structure. I revisit Anna's life and show how the conceptual framework developed in part I of this book is a useful tool in explaining the ebbs and flows of social inequality she experienced.

Sites of Inequality

The second part of this book considers empirical research on social inequality in various domains. In sociological research, studies of social inequality often consider the gap in earnings, income, and assets between advantaged and disadvantaged groups of people (Casper, McLanahan, and Garfinkel 1994; Grabb 2002; Langton and Pfeffer 1994; Morris, Bernhardt, and Handcock 1994). To restrict analyses of social inequality to economic issues is limiting because inequality encompasses all differences between people that become embedded in the social structure and that influence social relations (Grabb 2002). Hence, among the other issues that are important to consider when examining social inequality are education, health, and unpaid labour.

Chapters 8 to 12 examine the ways in which the factors considered in the conceptual framework developed in Part I influence outcomes of inequality in families (chapter 8), labour markets (chapter 9), schools (chapter 10), health (chapter 11), and states (chapter 12). These chapters show how class, age, gender, ethnicity, and race affect outcomes of inequality through the processes of production, distribution, and reproduction. Each chapter concludes with policy implications and directions for further research.

Chapter 8 examines inequality in families. In particular it considers how the processes of reproduction are organized in such a way as to assign the unpaid labour responsibility of housework and caring disproportionately to women and when these tasks are paid for, to women in ethnic and racial minorities. The relationship between these issues and the processes of production and distribution are also explored. Finally, this chapter considers the power imbalances in families and the violence that occurs there.

Chapter 9 outlines aspects of inequality in labour markets. It considers changes in Canada's class structure, the polarization of income and issues with respect to skill and alienation in the workplace. Each of these points and related issues that classify jobs as good or bad are examined. Chapter 9 also examines how the social organization of production processes and the relationship between production, distribution, and reproduction leads to inequality in various working conditions and in the intrinsic and extrinsic rewards of paid work.

Chapter 10 considers educational attainment in Canada. In particular, it examines the barriers to education and how they are influenced by social class, race, ethnicity, gender, and age. It also examines the influence that each of these factors has historically had on educational attainment, how they affect educational attainment today, and the relationship between these factors and the returns on education achieved through labour markets.

Chapter 11 considers inequality in health in Canada. It critiques current theoretical perspectives that focus too little on how health experiences are structured by class, age, gender, ethnicity, and race. It moves on to consider the relationships between class, age, gender, ethnicity, and race and each of mortality, morbidity, mental health, life-style behaviour, and access and use of health care services.

The state is ubiquitous; it weaves through all aspects of our lives and determines who is a deserving recipient of state benefits. The 'deservingness' of Canadians revolves around the concept of citizenship, the central topic of chapter 12. Chapter 12 discusses unemployment insurance, parental benefits and maternity leave, social welfare, pensions, and old age security and shows how they reproduce existing inequalities and shore up long-standing advantages among privileged groups. Chapter 12 also considers the role that states play in social regulation and how the law works to the advantage of some and the disadvantage of others.

Chapter 13 begins by summarizing the main points and findings of this book. Next, it discusses the ways in which research and policy would be improved by adopting an inclusive and integrated approach to inequality, such as the one outlined here. For instance, feminist scholars have long argued that much social policy, although seemingly gender-neutral, is not and that this has harmful effects for women. I argue that the same can be said for age, ethnicity, and class and that when the four are considered together, the effects are particularly troublesome. The same is true of research. I argue that to understand social inequality, we must understand better how the bases of inequality are connected and how actors negotiate these structures in day-to-day life. Until we do so, our assessments of inequality will remain both biased and inaccurate.

Notes

1   Notably, while the poverty rate among older adults and children is about the same, since 1980 it has decreased by 16 per cent among those aged 65 and over and has increased by 4 per cent among children under the age of 18.

Glossary

Critical approaches, critical theory Approaches to the study of social inequality that: (1) assume social relations are the essential elements of social structures; (2) assume that social relations are characterized more by conflict than consensus. Commentators sometimes reserve the term critical theory to refer to the work of scholars associated with the Frankfurt school of sociology. These theorists, however, have strong intellectual roots in Marxist and Weberian thought and were certainly not the first to think 'critically' about social life.

Social inequality The existence of advantages and disadvantages in many aspects of social life, including income, education, health, opportunities for paid work, unpaid work responsibilities, and so on. The study of social inequality involves an examination of the factors that contribute to meaningful differences in the rights, resources, and privileges of individuals and groups of people.

Social relations Fundamental elements of the social structure. Social relations do not refer to interpersonal relations. Rather they are structural and reflect power differences among groups of people. Examples of structured sets of social relations are class, age, gender, ethnic, and race relations.

Social structures Well-established patterns of social organization among the elements of society. Sociologists disagree over which elements of society are of most concern.

Stratification An approach to the study of social inequality that ranks individuals in a hierarchy on the basis of socially desirable characteristics such as income, status, wealth, or occupation. These approaches often draw on structural-functionalist thought and assume that social roles are the principal elements of the social structure.

Structures of inequality Durable patterns of social organization that influence social inequality.

Questions for Critical Thought

1. Some people argue that social welfare recipients are lazy, that they don't want to work, and that governments should not contribute to the 'cycle of poverty' by providing these people with monetary assistance. These arguments focus on individual attributes in explanations of poverty. Discuss the alternative, structural explanation of poverty.

2. Julia Vinograd's poem 'People Who Slipped through the Cracks' is reproduced here in Box 1.2. In this poem, Vinograd discusses the invisibility of homelessness. In contrast, the visibility of homelessness is made evident in the newspaper article which discusses the eviction of homeless squatters (see Box 1.4). From a social-structural point of view, how can homelessness be both visible and invisible?

3. What are the structural factors that contributed to the ebb and flow of poverty in Anna's life? How did agency affect the ebb and flow of poverty in Anna's life? What role does social time play in explaining Anna's relative advantages and disadvantages throughout her life?

4. Is it possible to understand and explain poverty in Canada by considering only social class? Why or why not?

5. What are the advantages and disadvantages to stratification approaches to social inequality?

Recommended Reading

Curtis, James E., Edward G. Grabb, and Neil L. Guppy (eds.) (1999). *Social Inequality in Canada: Patterns, Problems, and Policies.* Scarborough: Prentice Hall Allyn and Bacon Canada. This is *the* information source book on various aspects of social inequality in Canada.

Davies, Lorraine, Julie Ann McMullin, and William R. Avison (2001). *Social Policy, Gender Inequality and Poverty.* Ottawa: Status of Women Canada. A study that uses both qualitative and quantitative data to examine how the social policy changes in Ontario in the mid-1990s affected poverty among women.

Leisering, Lutz, and Stephan Leibfried (1999). *Time and Poverty in Western Welfare Studies.* Cambridge: Cambridge University Press. One of the very few books that take a life-course approach to poverty and emphasize agency in the transitions on to and off social assistance.

National Council of Welfare. (2000) *Poverty Profile: A Report.* Ottawa: Minister of Works and Government Services Canada. An excellent source book with lots of data and information about poverty in Canada.

Ross, David P., Katherine J. Scott, and Peter J. Smith (2000). *The Canadian Fact Book on Poverty.* Ottawa: Canadian Council on Social Development. This book provides a comprehensive overview of poverty in Canada.

Chapter 2

Class and Inequality

When I look back on my childhood I wonder how I survived at all. . . . People everywhere brag and whimper about the woes of their early years, but nothing can compare with the Irish version: the poverty; the shiftless loquacious alcoholic father; the pious defeated mother moaning by the fire; pompous priests; bullying schoolmasters; the English and the terrible things they did to us for eight hundred long years (Frank McCourt, *Angela's Ashes*, 1996: 11).

Introduction

The quotation above is from *Angela's Ashes*, Frank McCourt's touching and funny yet disturbing memoir. Indeed, as one reads this book one wonders how Frank did survive his childhood. He did not have enough clothes to keep him warm, proper shoes for his feet, enough food, or much of a roof over his head. The neighbourhoods where he lived were decrepit and unsanitary. Frank's father was an alcoholic who couldn't hold down a job; his mother was chronically depressed and thought it improper for women to work. In reading this book one also wonders why Frank's parents didn't do something to change their lives; if only Mr McCourt had stopped drinking and held down a job, and if only Mrs McCourt had got a job instead of 'moaning by the fire'. But to blame the

McCourts' poverty on an individual's alcoholism or mental health ignores the complex reality of the social structures in which the McCourts were embedded. Class, gender, and ethnic structures in Ireland during McCourt's childhood (the 1930s) were pervasive. English imperialism over Ireland produced and reproduced economic and other hardships for the Irish. Advanced education was essentially unavailable to the poor, women, and minorities. Labour laws did little to protect workers, and as a result, the conditions of the 'working man' were deplorable. And, on top of it all, because Frank's parents came of age during the Depression, paid work was hard to come by.

The conditions of Frank McCourt's childhood may be explained by his class position, which, in turn, negatively affected his family relations, education, and health. The McCourt family was in a state of constant conflict. Frank's mother and father either fought or did not speak, and the children were often ignored and neglected. Education, beyond the state-required minimum, was unattainable. The children had various health difficulties, the most severe of which culminated in the death of Frank's baby sister.

Although the effects of the McCourts' class position are evident, a more complex question is what accounts for their lower-class position? Is it because they had no money and little food? Is it because Mr McCourt rarely had a job and when he did it was a bad one? Is it because his family had too little power or authority to impose their will on others? Is it because Mr and Mrs McCourt were poorly educated? These are among the questions that are asked by sociologists who study class.

There is considerable disagreement among sociologists over how to conceptualize social class, how many classes there are, the extent to which class conflict exists, and how classes are formed. These points of contention stem from the analysis of social class that was put forth by Karl Marx and then critiqued and expanded upon by Max Weber. Volumes have been written about these issues, and it is certainly beyond the scope of this chapter to engage in all of these debates. Instead, the ensuing discussion will focus on the question of how to conceptualize social class and will venture into other areas of debate only if they are important to the argument being presented.

Marx: Class as a Productive Social Relation

In the *Communist Manifesto*, Marx ([1848] 1983: 203–4) wrote:

> The history of all hitherto existing society is the history of class struggles. Freeman and slave, patrician and plebeian, lord and serf, guild-master and journeyman, in a word, oppressor and oppressed. . . . Our epoch, the epoch of the bourgeoisie, possesses, however, this distinctive feature: It has simplified class antagonisms. Society as a whole is more and more splitting up into two great hostile camps, into two great classes directly facing each other—bourgeoisie and proletariat.

In these few lines Marx emphasizes the importance of class and class conflict in his work and implies that a distinctive feature of capitalism is the division of society into two central classes. But what is left unsaid here and in much of Marx's work is a precise definition of class, of what distinguishes capitalists from workers, and whether the polarization of the classes assumes that the petite bourgeoisie and others in the middle classes will become extinct. Ambiguity around these issues has led to various interpretations of who belongs to what class, how many classes there are, and what distinguishes the middle class from the others (Poulantzas 1975; Wright 1985).

Marx began what appears to be a systematic analysis of social classes in the last chapter of *Capital III* ([1893–4] 1956: 178–9) but wrote only a few paragraphs before the project was interrupted. In the first two paragraphs Marx writes that the three classes of modern capitalist society are the owners of **labour-power**, the owners of capital, and the landowners, but he suggests that this is the pure form of class distinctions. 'Intermediate and transitional strata obscure the class boundaries' even in the case of England, where the 'economic structure of modern society is indisputably the most highly and classically developed'. However, Marx dismisses strata distinctions as immaterial to his analysis because of the tendency of capitalism to transform labour into wage-labour, the means of production into capital, and landed property into a form that corresponds with the capitalist mode of production.

In the next paragraph of this last chapter of *Capital III*, Marx suggests that the answer to what constitutes a class can be determined by answering the question 'what constitutes wage-labourers, capitalists and landlords as the three great social classes?' For Marx, the answer to this question does not come from examining differences in income or status. Rather, the key is the means by which people derive their income, that is, from the use of their labour-power, capital, or landed property. In the concluding paragraph, Marx's analysis breaks off just as he suggests that this distinction is not complete.

On the basis of the scattered references to class throughout Marx's work, researchers generally agree that, in principle, Marx believed that society is divided into classes that are defined by their relationship to the principal means of production in society (Giddens 1971; Zeitlin 1990). Put simply, in capitalism those who own the means of the production (the **bourgeoisie**) exploit labourers (the **proletariat**), who have no choice but to sell their labour-power to the bourgeoisie in order to survive. The emphasis in Marx's work, then, is on relationships between those who appropriate the labour of others to make a profit and those who need to sell their labour-power. Hence, Marx is less concerned with how resources are distributed within capitalism and instead places the emphasis on the relationships among people who engage in economic systems of production.

According to Giddens (1971: 37), Marx developed a dichotomous conception of two antagonistic classes. These classes 'are constituted by the relationship of groupings of individuals to the ownership of private property in the means of production.' Marx recognized that historically, class societies were more complex than this theoretical dichotomy revealed (Giddens 1971; Zeitlin 1990). He was also aware that in bourgeois society, classes were divided into strata and

that there were individuals who were located at the margins of the class system (e.g., lumpenproletariat and a reserve army of labour) (Giddens 1971).

Two themes emerge from Marx's work on social class that help us define what is meant by class in Marxist sociology. These ideas are summarized as follows:

1. Social class is based in productive relations. That is, individuals who engage in production processes have various rights and powers over the resources that are used in production processes (see also Wright 1999).
2. Social class is conceptualized in relational terms. Unequal access to the rights and powers associated with productive resources (which by definition is relational) is thought of as class relations (Wright 1999). Ownership of the tools that are required in production processes is a necessary but not sufficient condition for being a member of the bourgeoisie class. Thus, the issue is not simply the fact that capitalists own machines, but that they 'deploy those machines in a production process, hire owners of labor power to use them, and appropriate the profits from the use of those machines. A collector of machines is not, by virtue of owning those machines, a capitalist' (Wright 1999: 5).

The preceding discussion also shows that there is a great deal of uncertainty in Marx's work about how many classes there are (although most agree that Marx believed that as capitalism developed, society would become polarized into two central classes) and how we are to conceptualize social classes that do not fall neatly into either the capitalist or working-class categories. Indeed, these are two crucial issues for present-day Marxists.

Neo-Marxism: Issues of Exploitation, Authority, and Credentials

More than two decades ago, Alfred A. Hunter (1981: 12) observed that 'contemporary Marxism is a growing and several-headed beast which defies simple, summary description.' This observation still applies today. Some rather orthodox Marxists, who believe that Marx got it right, stray very little from his ideas and theories (Braverman 1974; Rinehart 1996). Others, while maintaining the basic premises of Marx's work, elaborate, modify, and extend his theories with the belief that social life has changed too much since Marx's time to leave his theories unchanged (Poulantzas 1975; Wright 1997). Into this latter category falls the work of Erik Olin Wright.

Although many neo-Marxists have rethought Marx's ideas of social class, I will focus on Wright's class analysis because it has arguably been the most influential neo-Marxist approach to class issues, at least in North American sociology. Shortly after completing his doctoral dissertation in 1976, Wright began his international research on class structure and class consciousness. Since that time he has written an impressive amount of work on Marxist conceptualizations of social class and has rethought his original ideas of class several times.

Exploitation is a central dimension of Wright's latest approach to class analysis. He argues that the following principles form the basis of class exploitation:

(a) The inverse interdependence principle: The material welfare of one group of people causally depends upon the material deprivations of another.

(b) The exclusion principle: The inverse interdependence in (a) depends upon the exclusion of the exploited from access to certain productive resources, usually backed by property rights.

(c) The appropriation principle: Exclusion generates material advantage to exploiters because it enables them to appropriate the labor effort of the exploited (Wright 1997: 10; Wright 1999: 11).

According to Wright, if the first of these two conditions are met, 'non-exploitative economic oppression' occurs but it is not technically a situation of class exploitation per se. Exploitation only exists when all three principles are operating simultaneously.

Note the relational component in each of these exploitation principles. Explicit in these statements is the idea that class exploitation involves social interaction and that this interaction is structured by sets of productive social relations that serve to bind exploiter and exploited together (Wright 1997: 12). Following Marx, Wright's conceptualization of class exploitation also highlights the presence of inherent conflict in class relations. Put simply, a profit-driven capitalist system requires that owners want workers to work longer and harder than the workers would freely choose to. Hence, class conflict results, not simply over wage levels but also over how much 'work effort' is expected (Wright 1997: 18).

To deal with the problem of 'middle classes', Wright (1997) integrates two key concepts, authority and skill, into his ideas of exploitation. For Wright, authority involves domination and is one axis upon which employees in capitalist systems are differentiated. If owners of capital relinquish control over the production process to managers or supervisors, then people in these positions have various degrees of authority and are able to dominate their subordinates in the workplace. Furthermore, managers and supervisors earn wages that are higher than the costs of producing and reproducing their labour power. Hence, managers and supervisors are in contradictory class locations because (1) they earn higher wages than what makes sense under the logic of capitalism; (2) they help to exploit the workers they manage; and (3) their labour is exploited by the capitalists they work for (Wright 1997: 20–1).

The second axis of class differentiation in Wright's scheme is skill. As is the case with authority, there is an emphasis here on the wage. Because certain skills or credentials are scarce resources in certain labour markets, people who possess them are able to command a wage that is higher than the costs of producing and reproducing their labour power. Furthermore, when workers have control over knowledge or skill sets their labour is hard to monitor or control (Wright 1997: 22–3).

In the end, Wright comes up with a class typology that is outlined in Figure 2.1. Here we see that people are cross-classified according to their relation to the means of production, their relation to scarce skills, and their relation to authority. Also included in this scheme is the number of employees. This latter classification category refers to the number of people that are under the authority of each particular class location. For example, managers tend to have many employees over which they have authority and dominance, whereas non-managers have authority over no one. Owners are separated from employees in this scheme. Owners are only differentiated from one another on the basis of whether they have employees and how many. Hence, owners who have only a few employees are thought to be different from those who have many or those who have none. Employees, on the other hand, are differentiated on the basis of number of employees, skills, and authority. Expert managers, then, have high levels of authority and high levels of skill and tend to supervise many employees. They stand in most stark contrast to non-skilled workers, who have no authority and no skill and supervise no employees.

In this typology, the cells do not represent classes as such; rather, they refer to class locations within the capitalist class structure. The distinction here is a subtle but important one that allows Wright to cover all his bases. Unlike an earlier version of this framework, in which he refers to the various groupings in this model as classes (Wright 1985), in his most recent work, Wright makes it clear that these cells represent class locations within an overriding framework of class relations.[1] In doing this, Wright can stay true to a Marxist version of class relations in which exploitation is at the core, while at the same time identifying contradictory places within class relations that individuals occupy.

Wallace Clement and John Myles also take a Marxist approach to the study of social class. Through their work on Eric Olin Wright's Comparative Project on Class

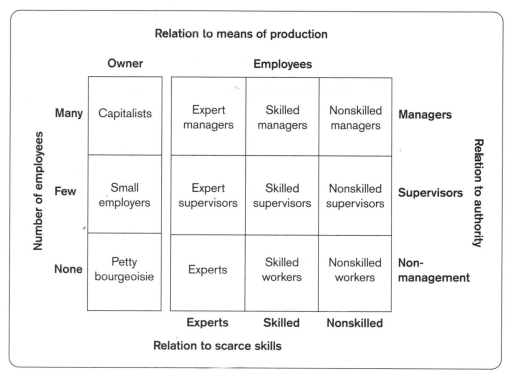

Figure 2.1 Wright's Class Typology

Source: Wright (1997: 25).

Structure and Class Consciousness, Clement and Myles (1994) developed a four-category, class-classification scheme. As Table 2.1 shows, the capitalist-executive class controls both the labour power of others and the means of production. The old middle class, the petite bourgeoisie in Marxist terminology, commands the means of production but not the labour power of others. The 'new' middle class controls the labour power of others but not the means of production. The advantage of this approach lies in its parsimony. It accurately explains the 'relations of ruling' in Canada while at the same time eliminating the unnecessary and often tedious class-location distinctions in

Table 2.1 Clement and Myles's Class Typology

	Command Labour Power of Others	
Command Means of Production	Yes	No
Yes	Capitalist-executive	Old middle class
No	New middle class	Working class

Source: Clement and Myles (1994: 16). Reprinted by permission of McGill-Queen's University Press.

Wright's approach. Notably, however, embedded within the seeming simplicity of Clement and Myles' typology is a complex set of criteria for inclusion and exclusion in the various cells. Box 2.1 outlines these criteria.

Weber: Class, Power, and Distribution

Some scholars argue that Weber's assessment of social class is in fundamental opposition to that of Marx (Parsons 1929; Turner and Beeghley 1981). Others suggest that it is more likely that Weber attempted to develop Marx's thought, agreeing with some of his points, disagreeing with others, and elaborating upon his ideas in a way that corresponded to recent developments in the capitalist system (Zeitlin 1990). Indeed, some of the concepts that are central to Marx's analysis—class consciousness, class conflict, and class interest—are employed by Weber as well (Zeitlin 1990). Weber also agrees with Marx regarding the importance of property ownership in the assessment of class (Giddens 1971; Zeitlin 1990).

For Weber, classes are groups of people who share a common class situation. In *Economy and Society* Weber defines class situation as the

> typical chances of material provision, external position, and personal destiny in life which depend on the degree and nature of the power, or lack of power, to dispose of goods or qualifications for employment and the ways in which, within a given economic order, such goods or qualifications for employment can be utilised as a source of income or revenue. (Weber [1922] 1978: 57)

Weber argued that there are three types of classes—property classes, income classes, and social classes. A property class is one in which differences in property ownership determine the class situation. An income class is one in which 'the chances of utilising goods or services on the market determines the class situation' (Weber [1922] 1978: 57). A social class is a combination of the class situations created by property and income, and one where mobility between the social classes is a typical occurrence within either an individual lifetime or over successive generations.

Weber identified four main social classes: (1) the working class as a whole; (2) the petite bourgeoisie; (3) propertyless intellectuals, technicians, commercial workers, and officials who are possibly different from one another socially depending on the cost of their training; and (4) classes privileged because of property or education. Although these social-class distinctions are similar to those proposed by Marx (except in the emphasis on education and the cost of training), Weber employs a different method in assigning groups of individuals to each class. For Weber, the emphasis is on the distribution of resources (see definition of class situation above), whereas Marx is mainly concerned with the social relations of production.

Parties and **status groups** are other pillars of social power according to Weber. By party, Weber means voluntary associations that organize for the collective pursuit of interests such as political parties or lobbying groups. A status group consists of a number of individuals who share a common status situation. Although members of a particular class may not be aware of their common situation, members of a status group usually

Box **2.1** **Criteria for Operationalizing Class Categories in the Clement and Myles Typology**

Capitalist-Executive   (A) If self-employed *or* has paid employees *and* number of permanent employees is three or more;

OR (B-1) respondents make decisions about such things as the products or services delivered, the total number of people employed, budgets, and so forth;

and are personally involved in decisions to increase or decrease the total number of people employed in the place where they work;

or about policy decisions to change significantly the products, programs, or services delivered;

or the policy concerning the routine pace of work or the amount of work performed in the work place as a whole;

or about policy decisions to significantly change the basic methods or procedures of work used in a major part of the workplace;

or deciding the overall size of the budget;

or in general policy decisions abut the distribution of funds within the overall budget of the workplace;

AND (B-2) if for any of these, the respondents make the actual decisions themselves or make the decisions as voting member of a group;

AND (B-3) respondents are located within the organization as top, upper, or middle managers.

New Middle Class   (A) If, as an official part of their main jobs, the respondents supervise the work of other employees;

and decide how fast they work, how long they work, or how much work they have to get done;

or grant a pay raise or promotion to a subordinate;

or prevent a subordinate from getting a pay raise or promotion because of poor work or misbehaviour;

or fire or temporarily suspend a subordinate;

or issue a formal warning to a subordinate;

OR (B) if, as in B-1 above, and for any of B-1, the respondents make the actual decisions, as voting members of group.

or make the decisions subject to approval.

Old Middle Class   If self-employed and not more than two people are employed by the respondents on a permanent basis.

Working Class   If employed by someone else or work without pay and not included above.

Note: The logic of this operationalization requires that each set of requirements occur in succession, so if the requirements for capitalist-executive are met, the person is not eligible for the new middle class, and those meeting these conditions are not eligible for the old middle class and, finally, the working class.

Source: Variable construction' from Clement and Myles (1994: 257–8). Reprinted by permission of McGill-Queen's University Press

are (Giddens 1971; Grabb 2002). Classes, status groups, and parties sometimes overlap, but not always. Thus, each is analytically distinct and central to any class analysis (Weber [1922] 1978; see also Giddens 1971; Grabb 2002).

Weber's assessment of status groups and parties and the analytical importance that he attaches to these multiple bases of **power** point to the fundamental difference between his analysis of class and Marx's. According to Weber, although status groups and parties are analytically distinct from classes, they are central to class analysis (Giddens 1971; Grabb 2002). For Weber ([1922] 1978), 'status situations', although related to class situations, are distinct from them and refer to the social status, prestige, and esteem that are associated with a social position. Unlike Marx, who believed that power is held by those who own the means of production, Weber felt that certain people in high-status groups derive power by virtue of their social position rather than through economic control.

The analytical importance that Weber attaches to the concept of power is evident in the preceding discussion. Unlike Marx, who believed that power relations are structural and cannot be separated from class relations, Weber ([1922] 1978: 38) defines power as 'every possibility within a social relationship of imposing one's own will, even against opposition, without regard to the basis of this possibility.' Weber clarified this broad definition of power by introducing the concept of domination. Domination exists in social relationships when one person (or group) comes to expect that their orders will be followed by the other person (or group) (Weber [1922] 1978: 38–9).

Domination is a specific power relation in which 'regular patterns of inequality are established whereby the subordinate group (or individual) accepts that position in a sustained arrangement, obeying the commands of the dominant group (or individual)' (Grabb 2002: 60). Weber states that, although relations of domination are usually at work in associations or in cases where an individual has an executive staff, other non-economic situations are also characteristic of relations of domination. One of the examples that Weber mentions is that the head of the household exercises domination over the members of the household 'even though he does not have an executive staff' (Weber [1922] 1978: 39).

Although Weber recognized that subordinate groups or persons accept domination for a host of reasons, his analysis focuses on three pure types of legitimate domination, or authority. Traditional authority refers to a dominating relationship that is based on the acceptance that those in charge should be in charge because of traditional right. In other instances, individuals are in dominant relationships that are based on legal authority, in which case subordinates accept the legal right of those in charge. Finally, charismatic authority refers to the situation in which leaders have control of others because of their appealing or charming characteristics (Weber [1922] 1978).

Three themes in Weber's concept of class separate his work from that of Marx. First, Weber's insistence that classes, class situations, parties, and status groups must all be considered if we are to understand the class structures of societies differs significantly from Marx's view. Second, and related to the first is Weber's emphasis on power. Marx felt that power was derived from an economic base and was largely structural. Weber, on the other hand, saw power as a multifaceted concept that could be derived from many sources and that has both structural and individual dimensions. And third, rather than adopting the social-relational approach to class in Marxist sociology, Weber focuses far more on distributional issues. For Weber, the ability of people to gain access to scarce resources such as income and education is central to any analysis of class. Indeed, these three central themes of Weber's work lie at the heart of its appeal.

Neo-Weberian Approaches: Frank Parkin

In the tradition of Weber, power is a central component of Frank Parkin's approach to class analysis. But Parkin takes a rather different view of power than Weber, and indeed suggests that Weber's definition is unhelpful (Parkin 1979). Instead, Parkin discusses power in relation to the idea of social closure. Social closure, as discussed by Weber, refers to processes through which collectivities restrict access to resources and opportunities to those inside the group. According to Parkin, classes should not be defined in relation to the means of production, but rather in relation to their modes of social closure.

Parkin argues that the classes of the bourgeoisie are formed and continue through two means of social closure, one involving property and the other involving credentials. Regarding property ownership, the issue here is the exclusionary powers that certain groups have on the basis of whether they own property that can be used in production processes. The legal, exclusionary property rights that come with this ownership are critical for class analysis to

the extent that they have 'important consequences for the life chances and social condition of the excluded' (Parkin 1979: 53). The crucial issue in this exclusionary process of social closure is not exploitation, but whether property owners can legally exclude people from making a living. Hence, the role of the state in legitimizing social closure is central in Parkin's framework.

The second means through which social closure is invoked is credentialism, which is the 'inflated use of educational certificates as a means of monitoring entry to key positions in the division of labour' (Parkin 1979: 54). Credentialism allows high-status occupations to limit entrance to their ranks by making the credentials for entrance into the occupation increasingly onerous. Professional occupations thereby limit the supply of their labour, thus heightening its value and status. Credentialism also masks variations in skill among the members of a professional group and in that way protects the least skilled among them from the sanctions that might otherwise come their way (e.g., less pay, demotion, or firing). As was the case with exclusion on the basis of capital ownership, the state is important in legitimizing the exclusionary practices of credentialism. States legitimize exclusionary strategies by issuing professional licences only to members of professional organizations who have achieved the credentials that the professional organization requires.

Recall that Parkin argues that social classes should be defined in relation to the modes of social closure. The two central modes of closure for Parkin are exclusion on the basis of property and exclusion on the basis of credentials. Both modes of closure use exclusionary rules to confer rights and privileges on some while denying those rights and privileges to others. Hence, according to Parkin, 'the dominant class under modern capitalism can be thought of as comprising those who possess or control productive capital and those who possess a legal monopoly of professional services' (Parkin 1979: 58).

That said of the dominant classes, the question that remains is how Parkin deals with subordinate class boundaries. If exclusionary practices are power tactics that dominant classes use to maintain social closure, then, for Parkin, usurpation strategies refer to countervailing uses of power mobilized by subordinate classes to gain access to scarce resources or to achieve 'distributive justice' (Parkin 1979: 75). Members of subordinate classes have no legal property rights and have limited credentials. However, subordinate classes vary in the extent to which they can activate usurpation strategies. For instance, if a group of workers is unionized they have considerably more usurpation power to achieve distributive justice than do groups of workers who are not unionized (Parkin 1979). The middle classes, for Parkin, consist of persons who tend not to have legal property rights but who do have certain credentials. There is also variation among semi-professionals in the power they have to encroach on the privileges of professional groups. Such power depends, in large part, upon how successful the semi-professional group has been in gaining legitimate authority in the eyes of the state and their clients. Semi-professionals are not, however, completely aligned with the 'working class', for they use both usurpation strategies to gain privilege and exclusionary strategies to maintain the privilege they already have. Parkin refers to

this as a dual-closure strategy (Parkin 1979).

Several well-founded criticisms are levied against Parkin for his emphasis on the legal bases of power to the neglect of other dimensions of power (see Grabb 2002). But what is particularly problematic about Parkin's approach is his use of the term power to refer to the strategies that subordinate classes use for gaining access to scarce resources and privileges. This lies at the heart of Parkin's argument regarding class boundaries. Notably, Parkin sees usurpation as a mechanism of closure that is less powerful than exclusion, but does it really make sense to discuss this as an issue of power? I think not. Power is held by dominant groups in society and is structural in form. Individuals may draw on the power they have by virtue of being a member of a dominant group in order to get what they want. However, as Parkin points out, power is much more than the ability of an individual to exercise his or her will over someone else. To be sure, subordinate groups act; they struggle to get higher wages, more prestige, or more status. They mobilize themselves and lobby to do so. But do they use power in doing so? No. At best, they use mechanisms such as resistance, influence, or persuasion to gain distributive justice.

The idea that subordinate groups do not hold real power is worth pursuing here. Parkin is certainly not the only scholar who argues that subordinate groups or individuals have power (see Giddens 1979). More radical thinkers such as Wright (1997) argue that workers have power because they control their labour and can therefore use that control to struggle for their interests. Although it is true that collectively, workers can generate opposition to capital because they control their labour, to suggest that they are in a position of power in doing so is misplaced. Further, although it is also true that a worker could choose not to work, the alternative to working for a wage is rather bleak in contemporary capitalism. Is this then a true choice that confers power upon the labourer? Imagine this rather extreme analogy. A man is being held at gunpoint in a secluded area by another man who is demanding that the first man hand over his wallet. The victim in this case has two choices: he can either hand over the wallet or not. Suppose he chooses not to and is shot. The victim acted, he made a choice, and he used his agency; but did he use power in this situation? No. This analogy demonstrates that clear distinctions need to be made between power and agency, and this is true even in situations that are far less extreme.

Ironically, though, the strength of Parkin's approach lies in this criticism of his concept of power. In Parkin's model, the importance of human action, both collective and individual, is evident. Hence, his model effectively considers the intersection of individual action and social structure, and on this score it is an improvement over most theoretical and empirical accounts of social inequality.

Neo-Weberian Approaches: Edward Grabb

In Edward Grabb's work on social inequality and social class, power is of central importance. According to Grabb (2002: 224–5) power is the 'differential capacity to command resources, which gives rise to structured asymmetric relations of domination and subordination among social actors'. In an elaborate scheme of power, domina-

tion, and social inequality, Grabb (2002: 224) suggests that there are three means of power—control of material resources, control of people, and control of ideas—that correspond primarily with economic structures, political structures, and ideological structures respectively (see Figure 2.2). These structures of power are crossed by class and non-class bases of inequality that represent the 'human content' of power relations. Hence, like Parkin, Grabb should be commended for rightly emphasizing the dualism between structure and human agency.

Grabb defines class on the basis of ownership, education, and occupation. For Grabb, these factors represent a synthesis of the key concepts in class analysis that are discussed by other influential class analysts such as Wright and Parkin. Ownership includes ownership of property but also material possessions and income. Education comprises credentials and knowledge. Occupation involves distinctions such as manual versus non-manual labour but also includes issues of skill. Grabb (2002: 226–7) suggests that, although classes should not be considered in static terms because they vary over time and space (i.e., historically and in different regions and countries), there tend to be three main class categories in modern capitalist systems: an upper class, a heterogeneous central category, and a working class. Like Wright and Parkin, Grabb defines the working class as those who do not own capital, have no special skills or credentials, and sell their labour to make a living. The upper class consists mostly of the capital owners, although persons with significant political or ideological power fall into this category as well. The middle class is a diverse group that may or

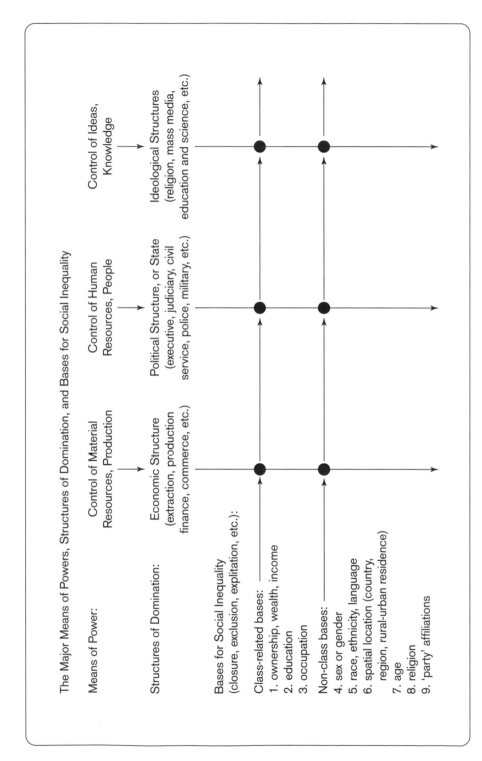

Figure 2.2 Grabb's Conceptual Framework

Source: Grabb (2002: 224).

may not have limited ownership but is mostly distinguishable from the working class on the basis of their credentials.

According to Grabb, the means of power (economic, political, and ideological) are differentially distributed along class lines. Of course, people in the upper classes control the means of material production or the economic structure by virtue of their ownership of the means of production. The middle classes may have some economic power depending on whether their incomes are sufficient to purchase desirable consumer goods and to the extent that their occupation confers upon them a certain amount of authority or autonomy. And the working classes tend not to have economic power at all. In Grabb's scheme, class crosses political and ideological structures of power as well. Hence, those in the upper class, by virtue of their capital, high levels of education, and good occupations, tend to control political and ideological institutions such as the judiciary and educational systems. Those in the working class tend not to have ideological or political power, and those in the middle class vary in the extent to which they hold such power, again on the basis of class-related factors.

Assuming that social inequality is a multi-faceted phenomenon that involves many bases of inequality (as most researchers and theorists now acknowledge), then both Grabb and Parkin's work represent significant conceptual contributions to understanding inequality. Why? Because the emphasis in both frameworks is on power and not class. The inherent problem with theories of inequality that begin with class is that other bases of inequality, such as gender, race, ethnicity, and age, carry less theoretical significance. Notably,

in both Grabb's and Parkin's work, class takes a certain primacy, but there is nonetheless room for conceptual development in each approach across the other significant bases of social inequality.

There is one minor point in Grabb's framework that needs to be addressed. This is the underlying tendency in his approach toward a reification of the structures of power. According to Grabb the organizations and collectivities that compose the power structures operate in complex ways and 'together they largely determine the nature and extent of inequality in society, what the social bases for inequality will be and how much they will matter' (Grabb 2002: 226). Thus, although Grabb discusses a 'dualistic view of power', it is unclear whether or how people act within power structures to either resist or maintain them (see chapter 6 for an in-depth discussion of agency).

A Note on Stratification Approaches

It would be remiss to discuss social inequality without paying heed to social-stratification research. Indeed, stratification approaches to social inequality have been very influential, particularly in American sociology. As noted in chapter 1, stratification approaches conceptualize inequality as a hierarchal order (Davis and Moore 1945), in which individuals are grouped into strata on the basis of their income, education, occupation, prestige, or status. Inequality, then, tends to be conceptualized at the level of individual difference rather than relational terms or on the basis of class structures (Grabb 2002: 121; Tilly 1998: 27–31). Traditionally, stratification approaches have assumed that the rank ordering of people into socially defined strata is a universal and functionally necessary dimension of society (Davis and Moore 1945). In other words, an ordering of people according to their worth, variously defined, is required for the smooth functioning of society. Certain positions in society are more valued than others because of the high level of skill that is attached to them. Only a few people can attain the skill required to fulfill these positions, and such attainment requires significant time for the appropriate training. People who choose to invest the time in such training deserve higher-status positions in society and the resultant rewards attached to these positions. Furthermore, there is general agreement among the members of society that such stratification systems are acceptable (Davis and Moore 1945).

Nonetheless, there are two common underlying assumptions in contemporary stratification research that set it apart from Marxist or Weberian approaches to inequality discussed in this chapter. The first is the tendency to overemphasize the extent to which society operates on the basis of consensus. The second, which is related to the first, is the underemphasis in stratification research on issues of power and exploitation (see Grabb 2002 for an extensive discussion of these issues). These are the crucial problematic assumptions of stratification research that scholars have taken issue with for decades and that are highlighted by Melvin Tumin's (1953) response to Davis and Moore's (1945) seminal article 'Some Principles of Stratification' (see Table 2.2).

The identification of problematic assumptions in stratification research has not, however, led to its demise. Instead, it remains influential in studies of inequality and informs much empirical research on the

Table 2.2 Some Principles of Stratification

Davis, K., and W.E. Moore (1945). 'Some principles of stratification'. *American Sociological Review* 10: 242–9.	Tumin, M. (1953). 'Some principles of stratification: a critical analysis'. *American Sociological Review* 18: 378–94.
(1) Within any society certain positions are functionally more important than others and require special skills for their operation.	(1) There is no clear understanding of what is meant by 'functionally important'; rather judgements are usually arbitrary, based upon the dispensability and replaceability of a particular division of skills in the population.
(2) There are a limited number of individuals who have the particular talent to be trained in the skills required for the functionally more important positions.	(2) The range of talent within any society is not known within stratified systems, as there are obstacles to the exploration of available talent. This is true of societies where the opportunity to discover talent is dependent upon the resources of the parent generation. In addition, the unequal distribution of rewards of the parent generation results in the unequal distribution of motivation in the succeeding generation.

(continued)

Table 2.2 (continued)

(3) A period of training is necessary for the conversion of talent into skill, during which sacrifices are made.	(3) The two sacrifices are said to be a loss of earning power and the cost of training. However, the latter is usually assumed by parents, and the former becomes inconsequential as those with training acquire much higher wages than their untrained counterparts once they are employed.
(4) In order that an individual may be persuaded to endure these sacrifices, positions must contain inherent value in the form of privileged access to scarce rewards.	(4) There are an assortment of alternative motivational mechanisms that could be institutionalized and used effectively, such as the 'joy of work' inherent in a position.
(5) These scarce goods consist of rights and advantages attached to or built into the positions and can be organized into those things which contribute to (a) sustenance; (b) humour and diversion; (c) self-respect and ego expansion.	(5) There are alternative rewards that could be used but Davis and Moore's analysis does not allow for this.
(6) The consequence of differential access to rewards is the differential of the prestige and esteem which various strata acquire. This, along with the rights and privileges, constitutes institutionalized inequality, or social stratification.	(6) There has been no demonstration that it is unavoidable that differential prestige and esteem shall accrue to positions which command differential rewards in power and prestige.
(7) Therefore, social inequality in the amounts of scarce goods, and the amounts of prestige and esteem individuals receive, is functional and inevitable.	(7) The only things that must be distributed unequally are the power and property necessary to accomplish particular tasks. If this differential power and property are deemed merely to correspond to the differential responsibilities, and to be resources, rather than rewards, then it is not necessary that differential prestige and esteem follow.

subject. Grimes (1991: 212) argues that many researchers apply stratification measures to the study of class inequality either because they remain committed to certain aspects of functionalist thought or because stratification measures are often used in large surveys. It is important to clarify that stratification researchers do not suggest they are studying class, and class researchers, although they sometimes do stratification research, make the distinction between the two. The point that Grimes makes is nonetheless an important one, which stems, perhaps, from a more general observation that researchers whose primary interest lies outside of class and stratification analysis tend to confound the two approaches. This propensity is most likely a result of the significant overlap among the social factors that are examined in these approaches. For instance, occupation, defined in various ways, tends to be at the core of research on social inequality regardless of theoretical perspective. Further, there is a general, albeit varied, concern in all conceptual frameworks over the distribution of scarce resources such as income, education, and skill. Hence, the tendency to use stratification measures as indicators of inequality likely stems from the continued use of traditional measurements in survey research and also from the fact that the indicators of social inequality are quite similar, regardless of theoretical perspective.

Conceptualizing Social Class in a Framework of Inequality

The preceding discussion highlights several issues that are central to the conceptualization of social class—power, exploitation, oppression, property ownership, education, and so on. All of these approaches contribute in one way or another to the working definition of social class presented here. Thus, in this section I draw on approaches discussed above to develop a concept of social class that is compatible with the view that gender, age, ethnic, and race relations are equally important structural dimensions of inequality.

One way to approach our understanding of social inequality is to consider how social processes are shaped by structured sets of social relations such as class, age, gender, ethnicity, and race. Three such processes that are critical for individual and societal survival are production, distribution, and reproduction. According to Marx, processes of production are the ways by which raw materials are converted into useful and valuable objects (Allahar 1995). Processes of distribution are the ways in which material resources change hands in society (Acker 1988, 1989; Weber [1922] 1978). Distributive processes include wage, state, personal, and marital transfers (Acker 1988). Processes of reproduction refer to the ways in which life is maintained both daily and from one generation to the next; they include 'how food, clothing, and shelter are made available for immediate consumption, the ways in which the care and socialization of children are provided, the care of the infirm and elderly, and the social organization of sexuality' (Laslett and Brenner 1987: 382).[2] The mere fact of these social processes does not necessarily imply an outcome of social inequality. However, understanding the historical context and the nature of the social relations that structure these processes is of fundamental importance to understanding and explaining social inequality (McMullin 2000).

A central problem in traditional class analysis is that it has focused far too much on production to the neglect of reproduction and to a lesser extent, distribution. Yet, class relations are social relations that extend beyond the arena of production, and Marxist approaches that conceptualize social class simply as a relation of production are too restrictive. This is true, in part, because traditional class analysis excludes far too many people who are not directly linked to production processes, such as homemakers and retired individuals. Notably, scholars have tried to reconcile this problem by attributing the social class of husbands to homemakers and by assigning a class to retired persons based on their pre-retirement status. However, none of these approaches is satisfactory because they do not capture important distributive and status differences between housewives and their husbands or between a retired auto worker and her employed counterpart (see Acker 1988; Estes 1999).

How then do we conceptualize social class in such a framework? At the outset, it is important to point out that there are many indicators of social class—occupation, education, status, wealth, ownership—all of which tell us something about class-based inequality. However, these indicators cannot fully capture the view of social class presented in this book. Instead, as I suggested above, a relational understanding of social class is necessary. Such an understanding follows a long tradition in Marxist sociology which suggests that class is not merely an economic matter. Rather, social class manifests itself as people from various classes interact with one another. On the shop floor, employers and employees interact with one another in production processes, and it is through that interaction that social class is produced and reproduced (Reiter 1996). In school yards, working-class children interact with middle-class children and their social class is realized in relation to the other (Willis 1977).

Second, material oppression is a primary organizing principle of social class in this framework. This view stands in contrast to Marxist approaches that focus on exploitation (see Wright 1997). Modifying Wright's account of 'non-exploitive economic oppression',[3] material oppression occurs if (1) the material welfare of one group of people depends upon the material depriva-

tions of another and (2) the material deprivations of the oppressed group depends upon the exclusion of the oppressed group from access to productive resources, backed by *ownership of the means of production, occupation, or some combination of the two* (italics indicate modification to Wright's principles).

Much research and theoretical effort has been devoted to trying to establish elaborate and conclusive typologies or categorizations of social class. Although this work is valuable, I do not plan to add to that dialogue here. For the purposes of this book, I assume that, in Canada, three broad classes can be distinguished from one another on the basis of their ownership of the means of production and their occupation. Of course, there will be important variation within these classes with respect to income, status, power, relative oppression, and so on.

Members of the upper class own the means for production and/or control the work process. Hence, company presidents and CEOs are part of the upper class, not necessarily because they own the means of production (although most have a stake in it) but because they are ultimately in control of how work gets done. Working and middle classes are distinguished from one another largely on the basis of occupational characteristics. Working-class jobs are highly oppressive, and workers have very little control over the work process. Hence, assembly-line workers are part of the working class because (1) the material welfare of one group (their employers) depends on the material deprivation of the workers; (2) their material deprivation depends upon their exclusion from access to productive resources (note that 1 and 2 are the conditions of material oppression listed above);

and (3) they have little say about how they do their work. Middle-class jobs may be characterized by similar levels of oppression but more control over the work process, as is the case in many middle-management positions. Alternatively, middle-class jobs may not be oppressive in the preceding sense, but individuals employed in these jobs have relatively little control over how they do their work. This is true for nurses, elementary and high-school teachers, social workers, and other similar-status service occupations.

At first glance, the self-employed and professionals seem not to fall anywhere in this schema. Members of each group tend to have control over their work, and their material well-being seems not to rely on the material welfare of another group. Nonetheless, the self-employed are thought to fall into this middling category because their ability to make a living is often contingent upon whether large conglomerates actively seek to monopolize their markets (see Box 2.2).

Box **War of Independents: Battle of the Bookstores**
By Elizabeth Renzetti

You can't hear the sound of the war drums in Different Drummer Books, Richard Bachmann's elegant store in Burlington, ON, but they're there. In the battle between the independent booksellers and the chain superstores, where words are weapons and no prisoners are taken, the rattle and hum gets louder every day.

Although the store has remained in its 19th-century brick mansion for more than 20 years, today it features the kind of enticements needed to compete in a brutal retail market: it's open Sundays; it has a new book club. A brand of beer, named for the store, is brewed at the pub down the road. Like hundreds of independent bookstores across Canada, Different Drummer has been forced to gussy itself up or lose fickle clients to the big superstores, such as Chapters and Indigo, which are flaunting their wares nearby.

For many customers, the main draw is the intimacy of a store where everybody knows your name. Nick Petruzzella, shopping with his wife and four-year-old daughter at Different Drummer, has chosen his side in this battle. 'As nice as it is to walk into Chapters and get a café au lait, this is a much better place to buy books. I'm not a big fan of the "big lump stores", I can see the walls here.'

Burlington, an affluent bedroom community located southwest of Toronto on the shores of Lake Ontario, was the natural starting-place for these big stores. Its wealthy and white-collar citizens were served by just one high-end bookstore, Different Drummer. Chapters opened its first superstore here at the end of 1995, followed closely by Indigo Books and Music.

Bachmann, a bearded, reflective fellow whose cutting pronouncements about the superstores belie a calm manner, called the invasion 'a backhanded compliment. They were going to look for the best independent bookstore around, and try to run us out.'

Bachmann, and his wife and business partner Jane Irwin, bought the store in the mid-eighties. It's still open—in fact, last night it was named independent bookstore of the year by the Canadian Booksellers Association. Sales, however, have suffered; some clients, less loyal than Petruzzella or in the market for a better bargain, are stretching their book-buying dollars at Chapters and Indigo.

'People talk about the retailing climate,' said Bachmann. 'Well, this is El Niño.'

Dire predictions about the future of independent bookstores swirled in the wake of the Chapters tornado, but only a handful of prominent bookstores across the country have closed (Ottawa's Food for Thought and Toronto's Book Cellar among them). Many others, however, have seen their sales dip.

Chapters continues to grow at a blistering pace: It currently has 34 superstores in major centres across the country and plans an additional 40 in the next two years. In addition, it owns more than 300 mall stores, and the McGill University bookstores, the first in its college division. The Chapters flagship store, on Toronto's Bloor Street West, carries 127,000 titles plus hundreds of magazines on three airy levels. That's at least twice as many titles as most good-sized independents. With Indigo also reported to be expanding, it's little wonder booksellers act as if all four horsemen have arrived with news of their doom.

As representatives from the Canadian Booksellers Association's 1,300 member stores—usually a placid, crunchy-granola lot—gather this weekend in Toronto for their annual conference, the air will be filled with unusually martial phrases: 'carpet bombing', 'when the dust clears', 'the war is in the store'. But the talk will also be about counteroffensives and pre-emptive strikes, about how to make best retail use of the Internet, a business that's evolving at a pace that makes book people's heads spin. About how, in the end, they hope to survive.

They should worry: a recent study from the Canadian Publishers' Council revealed that customers at superstores and independents, while similar in educational background and income, differ in one key way. Shoppers at superstores are younger.

How have the independents been fighting back? In a variety of hard-scrabble ways. Richard King's Paragraph Books in Montreal has a partnership with a Second Cup coffee shop, and a conference room that it makes available to anyone who wants to use it (the store also has Brian Mulroney as a customer).

Most independents have stepped up the number of readings and signings in their stores, and some have tried to compete with Chapters' discount policy on bestsellers. Although for most bookstores, living on paper-thin profit margins, a price war is a dangerous thing.

Taking a cue from the booming coffee business, many stores now offer frequent-buyer discount cards. The stretch to retain customers ranges from the ordinary—specializing inventory to a particular neighbourhood—to the mildly heroic. Bryan Prince, a bookseller from Hamilton, ON, has been known to drive his customers downtown so they won't miss the shuttle to the airport.

But other stores have taken the bigger-is-better mantra to heart. Both the Duthies and McNally Robinson mini-chains have expanded the size and number of their stores in Vancouver and Winnipeg, respectively. Last year, Duthies bought the flagship Vancouver location of the failed regional superstore chain Bollum's, which also had an outlet in

Calgary. McNally Robinson's superstore in Saskatoon, scheduled to open 1 Oct., has raised hackles of independent booksellers there, who wonder why their colleagues have to out-super the superstores in order to survive.

'Size is certainly an issue,' says Celia Duthie, whose new main location will soon compete with two Chapters stores. 'I prefer the smaller store, but the public perception out there is that bigger is better.'

Her soon-to-be rival, who can afford to be magnanimous, gives Duthie the home-field advantage. Said Chapters CEO Larry Stevenson, 'She's going to stand up—and if I were her I'd do the same thing—and say, 'They're the bad people from Toronto, and I've been here committed to Vancouver my entire life. They're the bad people from the East.' I think that's an effective strategy because by and large people want to support—and they should want to support—local enterprise.'

The Quebec-born Stevenson, as his competitors never fail to point out with some derision, is both a former paratrooper and Not From The Book Business (he is, moreover, a Harvard MBA). With Chapters' most recently reported revenues at $456,611,000, up from $389,766,000 the previous year, he can afford to absorb the rocks that all these little Davids throw his way. The rivals also sling rumours, like the one about Chapters not meeting sales targets in certain stores.

Yes, Stevenson concedes, it's not easy playing Goliath, but if you ask him, he's only giving the people what they want: lots of choice, including back-list titles; discounts on bestselling titles; convenient hours and locations; author events; educational programs; enough mocha-cappa-latte to float an armada.

Its rivals aren't buying, however. To them, Chapters is a 'predatory' market which is oversaturating the book market with stores (Stevenson believes Canada can hold 125 to 150 superstores, both Chapters and rivals). They say, darkly, that Chapters is building up a chain of superstores that it will one day sell to a foreign buyer.

This would necessitate a change in federal regulation: the last time a foreign chain tried to colonize Canada, it was Heather Reisman's partnership with the giant US chain Borders, and initiative that was rebuffed by Investment Canada. Barnes and Noble, the other giant US chain, owns a minority share of Chapters.

Source: Renzetti (1998). Reprinted with permission from the Globe and Mail.

It is difficult to think of professionals (e.g., physicians, professors, or lawyers) as an oppressed group, and for the most part, they also control their work processes. How then do they fall into the middle? Professionals are not part of the upper class because their access to productive resources is restricted. Professionals tend not have the exploitive capabilities of the upper class, and access to productive resources is generally outside of their reach. Thus, professionals fall between the upper and working-class groups.

One important issue that is missing from the preceding discussion is the effect of social class on identity formation and everyday interaction, issues that are of particular concern to scholars such as Anthony

Giddens and Pierre Bourdieu. These are issues that will be discussed in chapter 6. For now, it is important to recognize that the conceptualizations of class presented here do not take into account how class identities and inequalities are produced and reproduced through daily interaction. Indeed, the view of social class presented in this chapter does not stray very far from more estab-

lished structural approaches. However, as the next chapters show (see especially chapter 7), the subtle differences in the conceptualization of social class presented here merge nicely with conceptualizations of gender, ethnicity, race, and age to form an integrated and coherent framework of structural social inequality. With that in mind, I now turn to a discussion of gender relations.

Notes

1   Wright has vacillated on this issue since his earliest work. In the late 1970s he referred to these groups as class locations; then in his 1985 publication *Classes*, he called them classes. In *Class Counts* (1997), however, he makes it quite clear that these are class locations but not classes per se.

2   This view of reproduction is generally held by socialist feminist scholars and should not

be confused with reproduction in the Marxist sense of the term.

3   Recall that Wright argues that if appropriation of labour power does not exist, neither does exploitation. He suggests, however, that if the inverse interdependence and exclusion principles were fulfilled, 'non-exploitive economic oppression' occurs.

Glossary

Bourgeoisie   The class that owns the means of production; the ruling class.

Exploitation   At the heart of Marxist sociology, exploitation refers to the situation under capitalism in which the bourgeoisie take advantage of the proletariat. Class-based exploitation occurs when the bourgeoisie appropriate the labour effort of the proletariat to create their own material advantage.

Labour-power   Marx argued that labour is work and labour-power is the capacity to work. According to this view, the only 'real' power that the proletariat has under capitalism is the power to choose whether to work.

Parties   Voluntary associations, such as political parties or lobbying groups, that organize for the collective pursuit of interest. Common in Weberian scholarship.

Petite bourgeoisie   In Marxist sociology the petite bourgeoisie refer to those who own the products of their labour and who do not

exploit the labour power of others. Members of the petite bourgeoisie are self-employed and are also referred to as the old middle class.

Power   In Marxist sociology power is essentially a social relationship that has a material base. Those who own the means of production have the power to exploit workers through the appropriation of their labour efforts. In Weberian sociology, where the term is more broadly defined, power can mean an individual's or group's capacity to impose their will on others.

Proletariat   The working class, the members of which sell their labour-power to the owners of the means of production in exchange for a wage.

Status groups   Status groups are organized groups comprising people who have similar social-status situations.

Questions for Critical Thought

1. Some researchers have argued that social class is becoming insignificant to issues of inequality in contemporary Western nations. Do you agree or disagree with this view? Why?

2. How does Wright's view of social class differ from that of Karl Marx? Is Marx's approach to social class useful in present-day Canadian society? In what ways?

3. What are the chief differences between Marxist accounts of social class and Weberian accounts? Which view of social class is more helpful for understanding class-based inequality in Canada?

4. Compare and contrast Wright's view of social class with Grabb's view. Which is more helpful for understanding class-based inequality in Canada?

5. What are the advantages of defining class in terms of material oppression as opposed to exploitation? What are the disadvantages?

Recommended Reading

Clement, W., and J. Myles (1994). *Relations of Ruling: Class and Gender in Postindustrial Societies.* Montreal: McGill-Queen's University Press. Applies Wright's conceptualization of social class in an analysis of class and gender inequality. Although it is concerned primarily with Canada, there are also comparisons with the United States, Norway, Sweden, and Finland.

Edgell, Stephen (1993). *Class: Key Ideas.* London: Routledge. Provides an excellent overview of the key themes in class analysis.

Grabb, Edward (2002). *Theories of Social Inequality.* 4th edn. Toronto: Harcourt Canada. An excellent overview and analysis of classical and contemporary theories of social inequality.

McCourt, Frank (1996). *Angela's Ashes: A Memoir.* New York: Touchstone. An autobiography that tells a heart-wrenching story of what it is like to grow up poor.

Wright, E.O. (1997). *Class Counts: Comparative Studies in Class Analysis.* Cambridge: Cambridge University Press. A comprehensive book that outlines Eric Olin Wright's ideas on social class.

Gender and Inequality

Introduction

In 1998 I met Beth, a 64-year-old mother of seven children, who agreed to be a part of my three-generation family study. One of the things we asked the study participants was how they had managed to combine employment, domestic labour, and child care when their children were young. Beth had married when she was 18 years old and had seven children in the next eight years. Although it was not what she would have preferred, her husband John insisted that she work for pay. Beth was also responsible for all of the housework and child care when their children were young. Indeed, John, who worked the day shift in a manufacturing company, spent most of his free time with his friends at the pub.

To manage her family responsibilities, in combination with her factory job, Beth worked the night shift. When she was pregnant with her seventh child, she would arrive home from work at 8:00 a.m., get the three oldest children ready for school, and spend the rest of the day caring for her two pre-school age children:

> I would come home [from the factory] and get the kids off to school and then tend to the younger kids. And do what had to be done [housework]. And the older kids would come home for lunch. . . . I'd look after them [the two youngest children] through the day and just sleep when I could get them down together. When they got up, I got up. . . . The younger kids went to bed at 7 o'clock at night, I'd lay down from 7 to 10 before going back to work. . . . I didn't have the energy to even think that it wasn't fair.

Gender affects almost every aspect of social life and is often the basis of differential access to resources and power in Canada and in other Western societies. Usually, although not always, men as a group benefit from such patterns of gender. Beth's situation is somewhat extreme because she had a large family and an absent husband. However, the fact that she was responsible for unpaid work in the home and needed to combine that responsibility with paid labour is a typical experience for women. Indeed, research on families and unpaid labour shows that women are disproportionately responsible for household labour, child care, emotion management in families, and caring for older relatives (see chapter 8).

Beth's story also demonstrates gendered disadvantage in labour markets. In fact, industries, labour markets, occupations, and jobs are segregated on the basis of gender (see chapter 9). Compared to women, men tend to be concentrated in industries, labour markets, occupations, and jobs that are characterized by higher salaries, more benefits, greater autonomy, and higher status. Women are sometimes subjected to discrimination and sexual harassment in their work places (Welsh 1999), and they often encounter the 'glass ceiling', or invisible barriers to promotion, in their careers (see Krahn and Lowe 2002 for overview). Alternatively, if men are employed in occupations that are typically seen as female, they are often given a ride on the glass escalator and promoted early and often (Williams 1992).

Explanations of Gender-Based Inequality

Scholars disagree about how to explain gendered inequality, and they emphasize different factors in understanding the role that gender plays in individuals' lives. Unlike social class, gender relations were not generally studied before the 1970s. Although there were various statements about sex differences before that time (Parsons 1942), these were not generally framed in relation to inequality. Research over the past few decades has evolved so that gender relations are now widely recognized as a ubiquitous

pillar of inequality. Yet, as was the case with social class, there is much disagreement in the literature over how gender should be conceptualized and what lies at the root of gender-based inequality.

Before we turn to various conceptualizations and explanations of gender based inequality, the distinction between sex and gender must be addressed. The term gender was introduced in sociology as a way of avoiding biological essentialist views that were associated with the term 'sex'. Essentialist perspectives reinforced beliefs that biological differences between men and women determine their disparate positions in society. Gender, on the other hand, was used to express the view that there is nothing innate about men or women that makes one sex more suitable for performing a particular task than another. Gender, then, refers to the social construction of difference that is largely organized around biological sex. This view of gender is widely held in sociology and in feminism (Nicholson 1994). Yet some feminist scholars argue that biological sex is also socially constructed (see Box 3.1).

 Box 3.1   Biology as Ideology

Until the eighteenth century, Western philosophers and scientists thought that there was one sex and that women's internal genitalia were the inverse of men's external genitalia: the womb and vagina were the penis and scrotum turned inside out. Current Western thinking sees women and men as so different physically as to sometimes seem two species. The bodies, which have been mapped inside and out for hundreds of years, have not changed. What has changed are the justifications for gender inequality. When the social position of all human beings was believed to be set by natural law or was considered God-given, biology was irrelevant; women and men of different classes all had their assigned places. When scientists began to question the divine basis of social order and replaced faith with empirical knowledge, what they saw was that women were very different from men in that they had wombs and menstruated. Such anatomical differences destined them for an entirely different social life from men.

. . . .

Neither sex nor gender are pure categories. Combinations of incongruous genes, genitalia, and hormonal input are ignored in sex categorization, just as combinations of incongruous physiology, identity, sexuality, appearance, and behaviour are ignored in the social construction of gender statuses. Menstruation, lactation, and gestation do not demarcate women from men. Only some women are pregnant and then only some of the time; some women do not have a uterus or ovaries. Some women have stopped menstruating temporarily, others have reached menopause, and some have had hysterectomies. Some women breastfeed some of the time, but some men lactate. Menstruation, lactation, and gestation are individual experiences of womanhood, but not determinants of the social category 'woman', or even 'female'. Similarly, 'men are not always sperm producers, and in fact, not all sperm producers are men. A male-to-female transsexual, prior to surgery, can be socially a woman, though still potentially (or actually) capable of spermatogenesis.'

When gender assignment is contested in sports, where the categories of competitors are rigidly divided into women and men, chromosomes are now used to determine in which category the athlete is to compete. However, an anomaly common enough to be found in several women at every major international sports competition are XY chromosomes that have not produced male anatomy or physiology because of a genetic defect. Because these women are women in every way significant for sports competition, the prestigious International Amateur Athletic Federation has urged that sex be determined by simple genital inspection. Transsexuals would pass this test, but it took a lawsuit for Renée Richards to play tournament tennis as a woman, despite his male sex chromosomes. Oddly, neither basis for gender categorization—chromosomes nor genitalia—has anything to do with sports prowess.

In the Olympics, in cases of chromosomal ambiguity, women must undergo 'a battery of gynecological and physical exams to see if she is "female enough" to compete. Men are not tested'. The purpose is not to categorize women and men accurately, but to make sure men don't enter women's competitions, where, it is felt, they will have the advantage of size and strength. This practice sounds fair only because it is assumed that all men are similar in size and strength and different from all women. Yet in Olympics boxing and wrestling matches, men are matched within weight classes. Some women might similarly successfully compete with some men in many sports. Women did not run in marathons until about twenty years ago. In twenty years of marathon competition, women have reduced their finish times by more than one-and-one-half hours; they are expected to run as fast as men in that race by 1998 and might catch up with men's running times in races of other lengths within the next 50 years because they are increasing their fastest speeds more rapidly than are men.

The reliance on only two sex and gender categories in the biological and social sciences is as epistemologically spurious as the reliance on chromosomal or genital tests to group athletes. Most research designs do not investigate whether physical skills or physical abilities are really more or less common in women and men. They start out with two social categories ('women', 'men'), assume they are biologically different ('female', 'male'), look for similarities among them and differences between them, and attributes what they have found for the social categories to sex differences. These designs rarely question the categorization of their subjects into two and only two groups, even though they often find more significant within-group differences than between-group differences. The social construction perspective on sex and gender suggests that instead of starting with the two presumed dichotomies in each category—female, male; woman, man—it might be more useful in gender studies to group patterns of behaviour and only then look for identifying markers of the people likely to enact such behaviours.

Source: Lorber (2000). *Gender and Society* 7,: 568–81. Reprinted by permission of Sage Publications, Inc.

One significant point that feminist sociologists identified in their critique of sex research is that it is difficult, if not impossible, to address structural aspects of gender through empirical research. Framed in a more general critique of positivist science that privileges hegemonic knowledge, feminists argued that multivariate, empirical models can take our understanding of gender only so far because the interpretation of these models tends to be reduced to individual difference (Smith 1987). Most sociologists now dismiss arguments that treat such differences as innate. Yet, there still remains a tendency to interpret these sex and gender differences as individual characteristics rather than as structural features of social life.

Structural accounts of gender inequality generally address how various social institutions such as states, families, and labour markets are 'gendered'. In other words, feminist researchers have shown that women and men have different experiences and opportunities in most institutions. For example, labour markets are structured such that women have fewer opportunities for promotion than men which, in turn, is related to women's primary responsibility for

domestic labour within families. Although studies that consider the gendered nature of social structures have advanced our understanding of gender inequality, they fall short of assessing the full nature of gender inequality because they tend not to treat gender itself as a social structure (Risman 1998). To suggest that gender is a social structure means that it is a central organizing feature of social life. What we do, who we are, how we interact with others, our opportunities and constraints, our advantages and disadvantages are all patterned by gender (Chafetz 1990; Lorber 1994). Patterns of gender, in turn, are made manifest through human interaction (West and Zimmerman 1987) in our productive, reproductive, and distributive activities.

In summary then, although the conceptualization of gender may at first seem straightforward—there are women and there are men—the seeming simplicity of this exercise adds to its complexity. Gender relations are historically variable, cultural, ideological, biological, sexual, political, and material (see Marshall 2000). Gender involves identity, power, exploitation, and oppression. The debate among feminist scholars and others about which of these matters lies at the heart of gendered inequality is long-standing and continues today. In the sections that follow, these issues will be considered as they pertain to the processes of reproduction, production, and distribution.

Social Relations of Reproduction: Patriarchy as a System of Domination

Whereas the social relations of production are an essential element of social-class analysis, assessments of gender inequality are often grounded in the relations of social reproduction and sexuality. **Radical feminists**, for instance, generally assume that gender inequality is a function of men's control of women's reproduction and sexuality (Firestone 1971; O'Brien 1981). This produces an inherently unequal *gendered power relationship* that determines the sexual division of labour, is perpetuated by the nuclear family, and makes women economically dependent upon men. Hence, radical feminists suggest that gender inequality is distinct from other forms of oppression, that sex-based inequality is the original and most basic form of oppression, and that the dominance of women by men is universal (Firestone 1971; Millett 1969; O'Brien 1981).

According to Shulamith Firestone (1971), women's subordinate position in relation to men is rooted in the human 'biological family'. Biological families are characterized by four universal features: (1) women's biological capacity to reproduce made them dependent on men for their survival; (2) children take a long time to become independent compared to the young of other species; (3) bonds between

mothers and children are universal, and these bonds determine the psychology of all women and children; and (4) the reproductive biological capacity of women led to the first categorical division of labour. According to Firestone (1971) these characteristics of biological families and the sexes lead to a power imbalance between men and women that needs to be overcome. She argues that if women are to be emancipated, there must be a revolution in which women gain control over their reproduction in much the same way as a working-class revolution would lead to the control of the means of production. She argues that, to free 'women from the tyranny of their reproductive biology', natural reproduction must be replaced by the use of new reproductive technologies.

In *The Politics of Reproduction*, Mary O'Brien (1981) also argues that the root of women's oppression lies with their biology, but unlike Firestone, she suggests that the reproduction process is dialectical and has changed throughout history. Men need to control reproduction because, unlike women, they are 'alienated from their seed of reproduction' through the act of sexual intercourse. Thus, to compensate for this alienation men seek to control women through patriarchal order.

Although radical feminists differ in their explanations of how and why men have come to control reproduction, they agree that it is, in part, through this process that gendered subjectivities, defined as psyches, personalities, or levels of self-conscious awareness, are born (Firestone 1971; O'Brien 1981). Furthermore, gendered ideologies about love, sexuality, and motherhood perpetuate gender inequality by keeping women unaware of their subordinate status

(Burton 1985). For instance Firestone (1971) argues that the joy of giving birth is a patriarchal myth. Instead, she argues that pregnancy is barbaric and that natural childbirth is 'at best necessary and tolerable' and at worst 'like shitting a pumpkin'.

Explanations of gender inequality have benefited from radical feminist thought, in particular the importance it places on the relations of reproduction, gendered ideology, power, and control. However, radical feminist thought has been criticized on several counts. For our purposes, the most important criticism is that it treats the system of male dominance or **patriarchy** as a 'universal, trans-historical and trans-cultural phenomenon; women were everywhere oppressed by men in more or less the same ways' (Acker 1989: 235). Moreover, conceptualizing patriarchy tends to reduce male oppression of women to biological essentialism and is limiting because it does not consider historical or contemporary variations in women's situations (Acker 1989; Fox 1988). Moreover patriarchy in this way leads to assessments of men as having an 'innate desire for power' (Fox 1988: 165).

Another problem with radical feminist thought is its rather limited focus on the procreative aspect of social reproduction. Missing in these accounts is an assessment of social reproduction as a material relation that includes 'the activities and attitudes, behaviours and emotions, responsibilities and relationships directly involved in the maintenance of life on a daily basis, and intergenerationally' (Laslett and Brenner 1987: 382). Hence, social reproduction is work, and how social reproductive labour is divided is critical to social organization. Finally, in its emphasis on social reproduction, radical feminist thought tends to neglect the relationship between gender and the processes of production.

Social Relations of Production and Reproduction: Capitalism and Patriarchy as Intersecting Systems of Domination

Socialist-feminist accounts of gender inequality consider the relations of production and reproduction in their work. Influenced by Marxism, socialist feminists have united the relations of production and reproduction in their work by linking the systems of patriarchy and capitalism in an integrated theory (Young 1981). **Dual-system theorists**, for instance, suggest that patriarchy and capitalism are two distinct systems that intersect in relation to the oppression of women. Heidi Hartmann (1981) developed one of the most prominent and most debated dual-systems theories in her paper 'The unhappy marriage of Marxism and feminism: Towards a more progressive union'. Hartmann (1981: 14) defines patriarchy as 'a set of social relations between men, which have a material base and which, though hierarchical, establish or create inter-dependence and solidarity among men that enable them to dominate women.' The material base of patriarchy, she suggests, is the control of women's labour power by men. Men control women by restricting their economic and sexual activity. According to Hartmann (1981), women work for men by raising their children and doing their housework. These social relations are perpetuated ideologically through the systems of patriarchy and capitalism, in part, by equating male characteristics with capitalist values and female characteristics with social reproduction (Hartmann 1981: 28).

According to Hartmann (1981: 24), capitalism and patriarchy are systems with competing interests that adjust to and reinforce one another. Capitalism is not an 'all-powerful' system of inequality; rather it is responsive and flexible to contradictions that stem from patriarchy. This is the crux of Hartman's argument, and to illustrate this point she relies on a historical analysis of women's labour power and the development of the family wage during the nineteenth century in the United States. During this time, working-class men, women, and children were working in factories; this kept the supply of labour large and wages low. Wages were based on what would be required for individual, not family, subsistence. Hence, many members in working-class families were required to work in factories for their very survival. Male workers and unions opposed women's factory work, recognizing, first, that the excess supply of labour lowered wages and, second, that if women worked for pay, there was no one left to tend to the home. According to Hartmann (1981: 21), rather than organizing the labour of women and children, a tactic that would have solved the first problem, working-class men fought for the family wage, a solution that would allow them to maintain patriarchal power in the home as well as obtain higher wages. Hence, 'family wages may be understood as a resolution of the conflict over women's labour power which was occurring between patriarchal and capitalist interests' (Hartmann 1981: 22).

According to Hartmann, although women's labour-force participation has increased dramatically since the Second World War, this does not signify the emancipation of women, as Marxist scholars might argue. Rather, the family wage is still institutionalized in capitalism because men continue to be primarily responsible for earning a living, women remain primarily responsible for maintaining families, and women earn lower wages in labour markets than men do (Hartmann 1981: 25). Hence, Marxist analyses of women's oppression are flawed because they do not fully acknowledge the strength of patriarchy in maintaining a system of disadvantage for women.

Responding to Heidi Hartmann's article and other dual-system approaches, some feminists argue that it is a mistake to treat patriarchy and capitalism as separate systems of oppression (Young 1981). This is largely because dual-system theories tend to relegate patriarchy to one level of analysis, usually the ideological, which organizes women's unpaid work and capitalism to another, the material, which organizes women's paid work (Hartmann 1981; Young 1981). Although Hartmann avoids this specific problem by giving patriarchy a material base, it is unclear how the analytic separation between patriarchy and capitalism can be maintained. Others, most notably Sylvia Walby, suggest that dual-system theorizing is appropriate but that it must be further developed, conceptualizing patriarchy as a multi-dimensional structure.

In several publications in the late 1980s and early 1990s, Sylvia Walby developed a theory of patriarchy that attempted to correct the shortcomings of the concept by (1989: 214) defining patriarchy as 'a system of social structures and practices in which men dominate, oppress, and exploit women' (Walby 1989: 214). According to Walby, considering the social-structural nature of patriarchy corrects the problems of biological essentialism and the idea that all individual men dominate all individual women (Walby 1989, 1990).

In order to understand the structural nature of patriarchy, Walby (1989: 214) argues that it should be considered at different levels of analysis. Most abstractly, patriarchy is a system of social relations that exists alongside capitalism and racism. At the next level there are six patriarchal structures: the patriarchal mode of production (i.e., household production), patriarchal relations in paid work, patriarchal states, male violence, patriarchal relations in sexuality, and patriarchal culture. Finally, in each of the patriarchal structures, patriarchal practices establish or reinforce systems of patriarchy (Walby 1989, 1990). Walby (1989: 220) argues that these patriarchal structures are not sites of oppression but are rather defined 'in terms of the social relations in each structure'. These structures 'represent the most significant constellations of social relations which structure gender relations' (220). This statement leads to some difficulty in understanding Walby's work because she does not define what is meant by 'constellations of social relations'. Farther on in both her 1989 article and her 1990 book, *Theorizing Patriarchy*, Walby suggests there are characteristics of gender relations that are crucial in every patriarchal structure. In paid employment these characteristics are a sex-segregated labour force, sex-based wage discrimination, and the fact that women engage in the paid labour force at lower rates than men; in household production the domestic division of labour, reproductive capabilities, and household compositions more generally are the key features of gender relations. What remains unclear is how 'constellations of social relations' shape these features of gender relations and what these social relations are.

Nonetheless, Walby, in identifying six structures of patriarchy, addresses another of the central criticisms of the concept, namely, the tendency among those who use it to locate women's oppression in one or possibly two domains of social life (Acker 1989; Fox 1989). As shown above, radical feminists most often discuss patriarchy in relation to women's domestic responsibilities, their reproductive capacity, or 'compulsory' heterosexuality (Firestone 1971; O'Brien 1981; Rich 1980). The problem with such approaches is that the oppression of women occurs outside the home as well, most notably for Walby, in paid labour, culture, and the state. Furthermore, variations in women's experiences, both historically and cross-culturally, are difficult to capture if assessments are limited to one domain. Hence, Walby suggests, and rightly so, that she rescues patriarchy from one of its essential pitfalls by considering six structures of the oppression of women (Walby 1990).

In her work, Walby (1989, 1990, 1997) is concerned primarily with patriarchy and capitalism although she does acknowledge that these systems vary by other dimensions such as race and age. Hence, she favours a dual or plural-system theoretical approach and conceptualizes patriarchy as a system of oppression that is separate from capitalism, racism, and ageism. In dual-system theories, the roots of patriarchy are generally thought to be located within the reproductive sphere of the family, whereas the roots of the political-economic system are located in the mode of production (Hartman 1981). Walby argues that patriarchy infiltrates both and that over time women's oppression and inequality have come to be based less on 'private' patriarchy and more on 'public'

public + private patriarchy

patriarchy (Walby 1989, 1990). Private patriarchy is centred in the home and is distinguished by the exclusion of women from public roles and by the appropriation of women's domestic labour by men. Public patriarchy, on the other hand, is centred in the economic and political spheres of social life and is characterized by the segregation of women into less powerful positions than men (Walby 1989, 1990).

Walby (1990: 243) concludes *Theorizing Patriarchy* by stating bluntly that patriarchy is an essential concept for understanding gender inequality. Interestingly enough, Walby is less inclined to use the term patriarchy in her 1997 book, *Gender Transformations*, and instead favours the term gender relations. Yet her theoretical premises have changed only slightly, and she continues to insist on a separate-system approach.

Combining the Relations of Production and Distribution

Taking issue with dual-system theory and the concept of patriarchy, Acker (1988, 2000) sets out to develop a single-system theory of social relations that places equal emphasis on gender and social class. According to Acker, this requires 'broadening class' and 'the economic' (Acker 2000: 59). She argues that one way to do this is to consider both the *social relations of distribution* and the *social relations of production* in conceptualizing class, an idea that she introduced in her 1988 article 'Class, gender, and the relations of distribution'.

The relations of distribution 'are sequences of linked actions through which people share the necessities of survival' (Acker 1988: 478). According to Acker, the

fact that there has always been a sexual division of labour suggests that in all known societies the relations of distribution are influenced by gender and take on a gendered meaning. Gender relations of distribution in capitalist society are rooted in history and are transformed (like the relations of production) as the means of production change.

Acker suggests that the wage, which is rooted in the relations of production, is the essential component of distribution in capitalist society. The wage has developed historically as a gendered phenomenon because women have always been paid less than men and gendered job segregation is typical. Thus, 'the wage and the work contexts within which it is earned are gendered in ways that re-create women's relative disadvantage' (Acker 1988: 483).

Personal relations, marital relations, and state relations are the gendered processes through which distribution occurs. According to Acker, *personal relations of distribution* are held together by emotional bonds, usually between blood relatives, and are dependent upon the wage. Resulting from both the sex-based division of labour and the ideology of the family wage, gender serves to organize the personal relations of distribution. In its simplest form, this system requires that at least part of the male wage be distributed to women, who then redistribute it to the dependents in their families. The personal relations of distribution often extend beyond the household. In instances where economic hardships are typical, women often maintain extensive kinship networks in which survival is ensured through the allocation of resources between households. Among the economically advantaged, gender-based personal relations of distribution also occur, thereby helping to ensure the stability and reproduction of class (Acker 1988).

Marital relations are the central component of distribution for married women who do not work for pay and are thus dependent upon their husbands for their wage. According to Acker, unwaged housewives are connected to the production process through their husbands' wages. Although they share common standards of living with their husbands, they do not assume the same class because their situations, experiences, and activities are different. Unwaged wives have little control over their economic situation, although Acker suggests that this control likely varies by the men's and women's class.

State relations of distribution are the final type of distribution arrangement that Acker considers. The state relations of distribution are based on laws and governmental policies that have historically been developed in gendered ways. Policies and laws established to alleviate the financial burden of the working class when the market fails are based on gendered ideologies supporting the 'male breadwinner/dependent housewife' ideal. This renders some groups of women—those who remain unmarried, single mothers, poor working women—particularly disadvantaged. Women are further disadvantaged by the gendered nature of entitlement regulations because many social security programs are based on the labour-force experiences of men.

For Acker, the cumulation of these gendered relations shapes social class (Acker 1988: 495). Conceptualizing class in this way allows unwaged persons to be included in the class structure. Thus, in order to fully understand the

links between gender and class, divisions must be changed. One way to do this is to see class as rooted in relations of distribution (as well as in relations of production) that necessarily embed gender, both as ideology and material inequality (Acker 1988: 496).

Besides 'broadening class and "the economic"', Acker (2000: 57) draws on the work of E.P. Thompson (1963) and Dorothy Smith (1987) to argue that class should be conceptualized as social relations that take into account the 'processes that produce contradiction, conflict, and different life experiences' (Acker, 1988: 496) and that are understood from the 'standpoints of a multiplicity of women' (Acker 2000: 59). This view stands in contrast to those that argue for categorical conceptualizations of class; instead it emphasizes the things people do to manage their day-to-day lives. Furthermore, when class is understood from the standpoint of women, activities that may seem irrelevant in traditional class analysis, such as housework, become subjects worthy of analysis.

Finally, Acker argues that to understand fully the intersections between gender and class, scholars must understand that each mutually constitutes the other (Acker 2000). In other words, the experience of being a woman or man is fundamentally shaped by her or his social class but their class experience is also fundamentally shaped by their gender. Acker points out that this applies to intersections between class, race, and gender as well, and although underdeveloped in her work, the mutually constitutive nature of gender, race, and class has been taken up by multicultural feminist scholars, notably Evelyn Nakano Glenn and Patricia Hill Collins.

class
+ location

What is missing in feminist scholarship, however, is a systematic assessment of the relationships between age relations and gender, class, ethnicity, or race.

'Doing Gender':
Issues Agency and Identity

Also missing in the preceding discussion is an assessment of how gender is produced and reproduced, or socially constructed, in daily interaction and how **gendered identities** are formed. Candace West and Don Zimmerman's (1987) seminal article 'Doing Gender' deals with these issues. As Table 3.1 shows, West and Zimmerman argue that to understand gender, a distinction needs to be made between sex, sex category, and gender. Sex refers to the biological criteria that are widely accepted in society to signify whether one is a man or a woman. Sex category is defined as the 'socially required identificatory displays' that help to determine whether one is a man or a woman (see Table 3.1 for examples). Gender is 'the activity of managing situated conduct in light of normative conceptions of attitudes and activities appropriate for one's sex category' (West and Zimmerman 1987: 127).

According to West and Zimmerman, if we are to understand the social significance of gender, consideration needs to be given to

Table 3.1 Sex, Sex Categorization, and Gender

	Definition	Example of Agnes: A transsexual, raised as a boy who developed a female identity at age 17.
Sex	Biological criteria: genitalia at birth (i.e., penis or vagina) or chromosomal typing (i.e., XX or XY).	Agnes had a penis. She thought it was a mistake and had sex reassignment surgery (several years after she developed a female identity) to correct it.
Sex Categorization	Socially required identification that determine one's membership in a sex category (i.e., style of hair or dress; mannerisms, etc.)	At age 17 Agnes began looking like a woman by dressing 'appropriately', wearing make-up, etc.
Gender	Configurations of behaviour and activities involved in 'being' a woman or man.	Agnes began acting like a woman by learning appropriate and inappropriate gendered behaviours. This behaviour was learned, in part, through interactions with her fiancé, who would comment on whether other women were acting appropriately. For instance, she learned that it was 'offensive' for a woman to sunbathe on her front lawn because 'it put her on display to other men'.

Source: West and Zimmerman (1987).

both sex category and gender. Sex is less important because we rarely scrutinize the genitals or chromosomes of individuals. Rather, sex is assumed on the basis of sex categorization. Yet, 'socially required identificatory displays' in and of themselves are not sufficient explanations of gender. Rather, we must understand that individuals 'do gender' and it is through doing so that sex categorization is reproduced:

> Doing gender involves a complex of socially guided perceptual, interactional, and micropolitical activities that cast particular pursuits as expressions of masculine and feminine 'natures'. . . gender is an emergent feature of social situations: both as an outcome of and a rationale for various social arrangements and as a means of legitimating one of the most fundamental divisions of society. (West and Zimmerman 1987: 126)

Unlike the preceding discussions in which gender inequality is largely considered a structural issue, West and Zimmerman draw on **symbolic interactionism,** arguing that gender inequality is realized and socially constructed through our daily activities in interaction with others. Gender is 'the activity of managing situated conduct in light of normative conceptions of attitudes and activities appropriate for one's sex category' (West and Zimmerman 1987: 127). It is through social interaction that we develop gendered identities (i.e., masculinity and femininity) that come to be seen as 'natural'.

Although West and Zimmerman make occasional references to social structures in their work, the relationship between gender as an activity and the social structure remains ambiguous. This is, in part, due to

the fact that they never define what they mean by social structure itself. Early in the article they seem to suggest that gender is a social structure when they note that Agnes's situation (see Table 3.1) 'demonstrates how gender is created through interaction and at the same time structures interaction' (131) and that 'doing gender' is institutional in character (137). But in their concluding discussion of gender, power, and social change, they suggest that 'if we do gender appropriately, we simultaneously sustain, reproduce, and render legitimate the institutional arrangements that are based on sex category' (146). Hence, rather than gender being a structure in itself, West and Zimmerman argue (1987: 147) that

> Doing gender furnishes the interactional scaffolding of social structure. . . . Gender is a powerful ideological device, which produces, reproduces, and legitimates the choices and limits that are predicated on sex category. An understanding of how gender is produced in social situations will afford clarification of the interactional scaffolding of social structure and the social control processes that sustain it.

Here, doing gender seems to reflect the interactional activities that are temporarily attached to an evolving social structure that is based on sex category.

In short, West and Zimmerman seem to vacillate between an approach that conceptualizes gender as a social structure and one that locates it as part of what Goffman (1983) has referred to as the 'interaction order'. It is likely that West and Zimmerman intended to develop a conceptualization of gender that encompassed both structural and interactional components. However, their lack of clarity about what social structure is and about the relationship between structural and interactional orders leaves the reader rather confused about their assessment of gender. Nonetheless, their article is one of the few conceptual papers on gender that explicitly consider agency and interaction (see McMahon [1995] for an excellent example of this approach with respect to motherhood).

Bringing It All Together

In an effort to incorporate macro- and micro-assessments of gender, Barbara Risman develops an instructive conceptual framework that treats gender itself as a social structure. As Figure 3.1 shows, Risman argues that to conceptualize gender as a structure in its own right one must consider three levels of analysis. At the individual level, socialization processes and iden-

tity formation are at issue. The interactional level of analysis considers cultural, taken-for-granted expectations about behaviour, whereas the institutional level of analysis considers processes of distribution, organizational rules, and ideological discourse. For a full understanding of the structural nature of gender, Risman (1998: 26–9) argues, the relationship between all three levels of analysis must be considered. Risman (1998: 28) says that 'Gender itself must be considered a structural property of society. . . . Gender is deeply embedded as a basis for stratification, differentiating opportunities, and constraints.' The idea that gender is a structural property of society aligns well with the conceptual development of gender presented in this book. Yet, because Risman does not discuss gender in relational terms, the gender structure seems rather unconnected from individual experience. This idea is developed further in the next section.

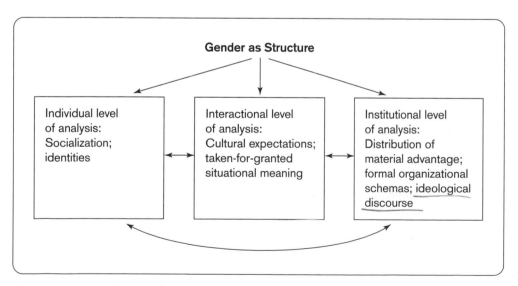

Figure 3.1 Risman's Structure Framework

Source: Risman (1998: 29). Copyright © 1998. Reprinted by permission of Yale University Press.

Conceptualizing Gender in a Theory of Inequality

An essential task for the present analysis is to develop gender as a concept that can be well integrated with class, ethnic, race, and age relations. To do so, some argue that the gendered division of labour must be at the core of the analysis (Chafetz 1990; Young 1981). Indeed, my emphasis on the processes of production, reproduction, and distribution suggests that I am sympathetic to such calls. However, it is a mistake to place the 'gendered' division of labour at the forefront of such work because the division of labour in society, in the family, and at work, is simultaneously organized around the structures of gender, class, race, ethnicity, and age. What we need to ask is how labour and distribution processes are racialized, gendered, class-based, and age-based. In other words, we need to know how these fundamental processes of social life are structured by the intersections of class, gender, age, race, and ethnic relations.

A relational understanding of gender assumes that it is through our interactions with others that the structure of gender is realized. This view is similar to West and Zimmerman's view of gender in its emphasis on interaction. As West and Zimmerman point out, the structure of gender is not something that acts upon people. Rather, as individuals engage in interactive processes of production, reproduction, and distribution, they reinforce and sometimes modify existing masculine and feminine identities and structures. Structure does not exist outside of the individuals who produce it. However, unlike West and Zimmerman's view of gender as an activity, gender as a structured social relation is conceptualized

as a 'deep' social structure (Sewell 1992). Deep social structures underlie all of the activities of everyday life, and they are often invisible. In other words, a deep social structure such as gender is so pervasive in its influence that it is often 'unconscious' and reflects 'taken-for-granted mental assumptions or modes of procedure that actors normally apply without being aware that they are applying them' (Sewell 1992: 22). These taken-for-granted mental assumptions reflect the formal and informal cultural rules of behaviour (Sewell 1992) that influence the actions of women and men. It is important that assumptions about gendered behaviour are not thought to emerge from biological sex differences. Rather, these gendered structures refer to socially constructed differences that reinforce inequality on the basis of one's membership in a particular sex category (Gerson and Peiss 1985; Glenn 2000; Tilly 1998).

As is the case in most structural accounts of gender (see especially Acker and Walby above), a relational understanding of gender focuses on how oppression is implicated in relations among women, among men, and between women and men. Hence, like social class, oppression is also an organizing feature of gender relations. For gender relations however, material oppression is extended to include all types of oppression. Oppression occurs if (1) the welfare of one group of people depends upon the deprivations of another; and (2) the deprivations of the oppressed group depend upon the exclusion of the oppressed group from access to resources, rewards, and privileges. In this sense, gendered oppression can be both material and non-material and it can take place in various settings, including families, labour markets, states, and the education and health systems.

Charles Tilly (1998) argues that exploitation and opportunity hoarding are two mechanisms through which categorical inequality is produced. These mechanisms are especially helpful in explaining the relationship between oppression and structured gender relations. Unlike Wright's view of exploitation (see chapter 2), Tilly's (1998: 10) definition does not depend on the appropriation of labour but rather sees exploitation as a mechanism 'which operates when powerful, connected people command resources from which they draw significantly increased returns by coordinating the effort of outsiders whom they exclude from the full value added by that effort'.

Opportunity hoarding is a second mechanism through which categorical inequality is produced. Tilly (1998: 10) defines opportunity hoarding as a mechanism that 'operates when members of a categorically bounded network acquire access to a resource that is valuable, renewable, subject to monopoly, supportive of network activities, and enhanced by the network's modus operandi.'

Although these definitions are abstract, if we consider housework as a concrete example we can see how gendered oppression is produced through exploitation and opportunity hoarding. When applied to this situation of housework, the assumption of power in Tilly's definition of exploitation suggests that men have the power and resources available to have women do their housework for them. Power, in this instance, stems from many sources, including the ideological and cultural schemas that guide gendered behaviour. In twenty-first-century Western civilizations our ideology

and culture suggest that housework, for the most part, is women's work and responsibility. These ideologies combine with the material advantages that most men have over most women in creating a situation where men can exploit the unpaid labour of women. Men, then, benefit from increased returns on their material advantages by coordinating the unpaid work efforts of women, 'whom they exclude from the full value added by that effort.' (See Box 3.2.)

In the case of housework, opportunity hoarding works to men's advantage in dyadic relationships in which women have more material resources. In these situations, women are still generally responsible for the housework and men tend not to labour for their wives (Davies and McAlpine 1998). This happens because men are members of 'a categorically bounded network' who have access to unearned resources, (i.e., traditional authority) simply by virtue of their group membership.

According to Tilly (1999), categorical inequality is maintained through emulation and adaptation. That is, we learn from our interaction in social relations in one place, such as the family, and transpose that knowledge to another one, such as labour markets and adapt accordingly. Continuing with the example of gendered oppression in unpaid work, the experiences of women labouring for men in the home may be transposed to other settings, thereby reinforcing and reproducing gendered oppression. Consider, for instance, a secretary getting her boss a cup of coffee or the segregation of women in undervalued nurturing-type jobs such as nursing or elementary-school education. Both examples reproduce a structure of gender relations that privileges men at work and at home.

Box 3.2   Why Married Men Earn More: A New Study Says It Solves the Puzzle
By Gene Koretz

What explains the so-called marriage premium—the fact that married men tend to earn more than single men of similar backgrounds and educations? Economists have been divided on the issue.

Some believe that married men earn more because women tend to select mates with good earnings prospects. Others credit the institution of marriage itself, arguing either that it makes men more responsible and diligent or that it boosts their productivity by freeing them from housework and allowing them to focus more on their jobs.

In a new study in the journal *Economic Inquiry*, Hyunbae Chun, of Queens College in New York, and Injae Lee, of New York University, claim to solve the puzzle. Analyzing 1999 survey data covering nearly 2,700 men, they find that married men earn an average of 12.4 per cent more per hour than never-married men, after adjusting for age, work experience, education, and other factors that may affect both wages and marriage prospects.

The two researchers find no evidence that the marriage premium reflects the better economic prospects of men who tend to get hitched. Rather, it appears related to the state of being married—and specifically to the likelihood that wives shoulder household tasks.

Chun and Lee report that the wage gap declines as wives put in more hours working outside the home. While married men whose wives aren't employed earn about 31 per cent more per hour than never-married men, for example, men married to women with a full-time job earn only 3.4 per cent more.

Thus, having a wife who devotes most of her time to raising the kids and other housework evidently pays off for dad in his work on the job. All of which implies that the marriage premium will inevitably shrink as more wives spend longer hours at outside jobs.

Source: Koretz (2001).

While the concepts of exploitation, opportunity hoarding, emulation, and adaptation account nicely for the depth of structured gender relations, they shed very little light on how the structure of gender relations has changed and how it continues to evolve. The challenge, then, is to tie the insights gained from 'doing gender' to more structural accounts of gender relations so that social change and the significance of human agency are accounted for (see Gerson and Peiss 1985). Structure and agency will be discussed in chapter 6, but before I do so, the structures of race, ethnicity, and age will be examined.

Glossary

Dual-system theorists   Socialist feminists who consider patriarchy and capitalism simultaneously as they interact with one another. The problem with dual-system theorists is that they do not acknowledge how capitalism and patriarchy mutually constitute one another.

Gendered identities   The feelings, meanings, and subjective experiences that are attached to a particular gender. Such meanings are developed as we interact with others and are shaped by dominant gender ideologies.

Patriarchy   As discussed by Weber, a form of traditional authority which reflected the relations between men and the power that men had over women, children, and often slaves. Feminists consider patriarchy as a system of inequality in which men dominate women.

Radical feminism   A branch of feminism that places emphasis on the relations of reproduction and the disadvantages that women face as a result of how reproduction is organized in society. Traditionally, this branch of feminism tended to reduce explanations of women's inequality to their capacity to give birth.

Socialist feminism   A branch of feminism that explains gender inequality by considering both gender relations and class relations or patriarchy and capitalism simultaneously.

Symbolic interactionism   A sociological approach that bases its understanding of social phenomona in daily interpersonal interactions. One important criticism of this approach is that it emphasizes individual behaviour to the neglect of social-structural issues.

Questions for Critical Thought

1. What does it mean when someone says that sex is socially constructed?
2. Discuss the 'problem with patriarchy'. How can patriarchy be reconceptualized as a useful theoretical tool?
3. Choose an activity that you regularly engage in. How does that activity reflect the idea of 'doing gender'? Try to think of a social activity that is not gendered. Now, show how gender may influence that activity.
4. How was Beth's life shaped by gender? Discuss the processes of production and reproduction in this regard.
5. How does the concept of opportunity hoarding apply to gender relations? Use two examples (not housework) to discuss your points.

Recommended Reading

Acker, J. (1988). 'Class, gender, and the relations of distribution'. *Signs* 13, no. 8: 473–97. A seminal article that tackles the complexities of integrating gender and class into a single system of inequality.

Fox, Bonnie J. (1988). 'Conceptualizing "patriarchy"'. *Canadian Review of Sociology and Anthropology* 25: 163–83. This article provides a good overview of the debates in feminism about the problems with the concept 'patriarchy'.

Marshall, Barbara L. (2000). *Configuring Gender: Explorations in Theory and Politics*. Peterborough, ON: Broadview Press. In this book, Marshall explores the concept 'gender', how it has changed, and how it has been used politically in various contexts.

Walby, Sylvia (1997). *Gender Transformations*. London: Routledge. Sylvia Walby is an ardent supporter of the 'patriarchy' concept. This is one of her latest and best books on how gender structures many domains of social life.

West, Candace, and Don Zimmerman (1987). 'Doing Gender', *Gender and Society* 1: 125–51. This is perhaps the most widely cited theoretical article on gender. Using a symbolic interactionist perspective, it is a theoretical account of how gender is reproduced in everyday life.

Race, Ethnicity, and Inequality

Introduction

The following quotation is from the end of an influential book by Michael Omi and Howard Winant (1994: 158–9), *Racial Formation in the United States*:

> In the US, race is present in every institution, every relationship, every individual. This is the case not only for the way society is organized–spatially, culturally, in terms of stratification, etc.—but also for our perceptions and understandings of personal experience. Thus as we watch the videotape of Rodney King being beaten, compare real estate prices in different neighbourhoods, select a radio channel to enjoy while we drive to work, size up a potential client, customer, neighbour, or teacher, stand in line at the unemployment office or carry out a thousand other normal tasks, we are compelled to think racially, to use the racial categories and meaning systems into which we have been socialized.

Although there are notable differences between the historical processes of racial formation and racism in Canada and the United States, it is nonetheless clear that racial issues of social inequality are omnipresent in Canada as well. In Canada, we need only be reminded of Darrell Night, a First Nations man who was dumped by the police on the outskirts of Saskatoon on a freezing February night in 2000 and of the numerous other instances of police brutality toward First Nations peoples that have occurred across Canada (see Box 4.1). We need only remember how First Nations children were taken from their homes, placed in residential schools, and often abused in the last century. We need only remember Oka. As Valerie Bedassigae Pheasant's narrative in Box 4.2 shows, the experience of racism is devastating in its social and psychological consequences.

Of course, the history and extent of white privilege and racism in Canada extends beyond the First Nations/white racial dichotomy. During the early part of the 1900s, Chinese immigrants were required to pay an exorbitant $500 'head tax' for entry to Canada; according to one government spokesperson, this tax 'so effectually restricted the inflow from China that it ceased to be a cause for alarm' (Craig 1968, cited in Knowles 1992: 48). Furthermore, during the Second World War, Japanese Canadians were moved to internment camps simply because of their ancestry. They have since received compensation and a formal apology from the federal government for the injustices they suffered, but similar class action suits arguing that the Chinese head taxes were discriminatory and racist have not been successful

(Makin 2002). Although these events appear to be part of a distant past, the racialized persons and their families who were affected by these events still suffer the social, economic, and health effects (Ujimoto 1994).

Those are some examples of the blatant racism that occurs in Canada. More subtle forms of racism and racial discrimination also exist in our schools, families, labour markets, health systems, and in the state. These issues will be discussed in the second part of this book. The purpose of this chapter is to assess several approaches to race that have been proposed in the literature. The relationship between ethnicity and race will also be discussed. The chapter will conclude with a discussion of the conceptualization of race that will be used in this book.

Thus far in this discussion I have taken as given the concept of race. Some sociologists argue that using the concept race without being critical of it is misleading, analytically incorrect, and politically dangerous (Loveman 1999; Miles and Torres 2000; Satzewich 1998). They argue that if scholars use the concept of race without problematizing it, race becomes reified. Sociologists use the term **reification** to refer to processes in which abstract concepts become real. Usually, processes of reification involve a generally held acceptance of the concept as immutable and somehow grounded in nature. Although most sociologists now accept that the character of race varies historically and temporally and that there is no biological basis for race, the problem is that these are not universally held views. By using the concept race, it is argued, sociologists reinforce and reproduce commonly held assumptions about the 'nature' of race. Hence, scholars who see reification as a problem argue that race as a category of

sociological analysis should be abandoned. Debates about this issue are rampant and contentious. It is to these debates that I now turn.

Abandoning the Concept of Race

The dangers of reifying race, combined with ambiguities about the concept itself have led some to argue that the concept should not be used at all in social scientific analysis (Loveman 1999; Miles and Torres 2000; Satzewich 1998). Arguments of this sort emerged in the social sciences in the early 1900s when scholars such as Max Weber, W.E.B. Du Bois, and Franz Boas rejected biological assessments of race (Omi and Winant 1994). Ashley Montagu was perhaps the first physical anthropologist to adopt this view in his controversial and bold book called *Man's Most Dangerous Myth: A Fallacy of Race* (see Reynolds 1992). In this book Montagu argued against the use of mainstream classifications of race that relied on biological or physiological criteria. Since then, social scientists have disputed the scientific 'evidence' which suggests that *homo sapiens* can be neatly divided and classified into different racial categories on the basis of some physical characteristic (phenotype, e.g., skin colour) or genetic difference (genotype, e.g, identification of a 'race' gene). Historical research outlining how the meaning of race has changed over time and place (Miles 1989) add support to the idea that 'race' categories are fluid. Most sociologists who study race are persuaded by these arguments and view race as a **social construction** rather than a biological essence. Notably, however, there is still a tendency among physical and developmental psychologists either to endorse the existence of

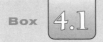

Box **4.1** **Canada's Apartheid Part 1: Welcome to Harlem on the Prairies**
By John Stackhouse

Here in Saskatoon, the police are vilified as racists who run drunks out of town and leave them to freeze. But it is also home to the nation's highest crime rate and a native population that accounts for more than half of all arrests. What's it really like to uphold the law in this ghetto? Let's spend 12 hours on patrol with the cowboy and the Indian.

The toughest cops on the Indian beat know what they will find even before they kick in the door. Hair Spray Jerry is there, slouched against a wall, and in the basement apartment's bedroom is his girlfriend, Diane, on a bare mattress, contorted in pain. Her face is bruised, her mouth badly swollen, her blood moist on the floor.

Diane is often in this state on 'payday Friday', the day Saskatoon is flooded with welfare cheques and its jagged-edged native neighbourhood on the west side turns violent. 'I called 911 because he was being a shit,' she says as tears stream across her cuts.

Nearby sit a half-finished bottle of Extra Gold beer (9 per cent alcohol) and a 7-Eleven Big Gulp container. Constables Ernie Louttit and Dean Hoover know that it holds the last of the couple's preferred cocktail: one part hair spray to six parts water.

. . .

In recent years, Saskatchewan's biggest city has come close to a racial explosion after allegations of rampant police abuse and police complaints that they cannot cope alone with a crime-ridden native community.

In February, 2000, a native man named Darrell Night accused the police of dumping him, while he was intoxicated, on the outskirts of town on a freezing cold night. Two officers, Ken Munson and Dan Hatchen, were fired from the force in September after being found guilty of unlawful confinement. At a hearing this week, they asked to have a traditional community sentencing circle decide their punishment—a request so bizarre that it prompted laughter in the courtroom and anger on the part of the natives, who felt they were being mocked. The judge said he will rule on the request on Nov. 30.

But there seems to be no end to the friction between a largely non-native judicial system and aboriginal people, who account for about one-fifth of the local population—and more than half of those arrested on a typical night.

Coroner's inquests are looking into the deaths last year of two native men who may have been abandoned like Night. Then there is the Melvin Bigsky case.

On April 27, an RCMP officer shot and killed Bigsky, a long-time criminal, when he rammed his vehicle into a police car and allegedly attacked the driver. Three weeks later, local police shot and killed another native man, Keldon McMillan, after he gunned down a police dog during an attempt to arrest him on weapons charges.

So strong is the community's antipathy that the city fired police chief, David Scott, last June in part to soothe growing public anger.

With Canada's highest crime rate last year, many residents blame an aboriginal population that they say can't cope with the transition from isolated reserves to a multicultural city, where universal laws and independent police and courts are supposed to prevail.

Many natives, on the other hand, believe that they are victims of a white majority that refuses to address their chronic social problems, except with the blunt end of a police force.

Valid or not, the accusations have sent a chill through Saskatoon's native population—and through police ranks. In private, some members of the force say they are reluctant to respond to native calls.

'You have a segment of the population afraid of the police,' says Mayor Jim Maddin, himself a former cop, 'and a segment of the police afraid of the population.'

. . .

No end of social agencies have tried to break the west side's vicious and unyielding cycle of welfare, drinking, and jail. The Saskatoon Tribal Council has built a big community centre next to the bingo hall. Out on 20th Avenue, a posse of missionary groups runs soup kitchens, prayer clubs and clothing depots, as they have for years.

Every evening, the Hands On Ministry provides a haven for about 150 children, with games and a free loaf of bread to take home. When the ministry closes at 10 or 11, the kids, many of then preschoolers, can be seen walking home in small groups, their loaves tucked under their arms.

It's the sort of scene that infuriates many people impatient with the lack of progress, among them the police who keep having to arrest the kids' parents. 'Police can get frustrated with an individual when they deal with him repeatedly, whether he's aboriginal or not—the revolving door,' Mayor Maddin says.

Would they go so far as to dump drunk people on the edge of town in sub-zero temperatures?

The mayor, remembering his policing days, admits that the infamous 'starlight tours' aren't 'an unknown phenomenon'.

'It's happened. Should it happen? I don't think so. Will it happen again? I would hope not.'

Source: Stackhouse (2001a). Reprinted with permission from the Globe and Mail.

a biologically grounded race concept or to be ambivalent about it (Reynolds 1992). Outside of academia there is a general acceptance that clearly demarcated 'races' do exist. The persistence of these beliefs and the limited academic endorsement of biological race is one of the central reasons that critics of the term call for it to be abandoned (Miles and Torres 2000; Satzewich 1998).

A second argument against the use of the concept of race reflects the complexity and ambiguity associated with the term (Small 1998). If we accept, for instance, that phys-ical characteristics and biological differences cannot accurately classify races of people, then what does? Country of birth? Nationality? Mother tongue? Some combination of these things? Does the colour of one's skin matter at all? Further confusion arises when one considers the relationship between race and ethnicity. Is race different from ethnicity? If so, how?

Notably, scholars who condemn the use of the race concept in the social sciences do not dispute that white privilege, racism, and inequality on the basis of what many refer to

Box 4.2   My Mother Used to Dance
By Valerie Bedassigae Pheasant

She was graceful and light. Her movements made the room disappear. There was only her. Every shift and swirl of her warp caused the air to move so that I could see the patterns in the air. I looked at her face. It was my mother's face, but it was possessed by a spirit that I had not seen before. She kept moving, without touching the floor. She smiled and danced. Her face radiated—my mother was free.

I sat on the banister railing for what felt like an eternity watching my mother. As silently as I crept to watch, I left. I wondered why she did not dance for us. That was the first and only time I saw my mother dance with abandon. What I did see was a gradual freezing of her emotions and a treacherous walk with silence. Her metamorphosis had happened before our eyes and we were unable to stop it. Why didn't she yell at them? Why didn't she tell them—no? Where did the fire go? When was it that the dancing stopped?

The cocoon that encased my mother was woven by inside thoughts that constricted her more strongly than anything tangible in the human world. Inside thoughts reacting to outside action generated towards our family's Nativeness. Blatant racist remarks and statements by women who did not care to know us. Each word, each comment diminished her capacity to speak—she moved slower and slower.

. . .

I have to accompany my mother to the school for parent-teacher interviews. We go from teacher to teacher. My mother glances at the report cards and listens to the teacher pass information to her about her children. Each in succession. We are almost finished. It is time for her to see the grade three teacher. I am instructed to wait outside the door. My mother is alone. In the stillness I can hear everything that my mother hears. I am afraid to move. The voice grows loud in my ears, telling her that her son doesn't know what to do. How can he pass? He has trouble reading. The voice grows louder, trying to convince her. I hear no response. Pages are being torn out of a workbook. The voice burns in our ears. . . . 'He cheated. He could not have done this. This work will not count!' More pages being ripped. I feel the shame and the guilt. It grows quiet. A chair moves. The door opens. My mother walks out. I am waiting. I see the humiliation and the pain. My anger ignites, recedes, and begins to smoulder. My mother is exhausted. We go to the next teacher.

More pressure is put on the older children to help the younger ones with their homework. We do it because we cannot allow people to think that we are 'stupid Indians'. I detest these people I do not know. How can they make a judgement about Native people without knowing or caring to know about us?—judgements made in ignorance. I decided that someday I would tell them about things they did not want to hear, about things they were afraid to ask. I decided to talk back. There was nothing to lose. People hated us anyway.

. . .

Parent-teacher interviews for my daughter. I go alone. I am afraid. Each time, I am afraid. I recognize the fear—we have met before. Now I am the mother. There is no child outside the door. I will not let her come along. The meeting is between adults—both trained in the same Bingo Palace. Only this time one of us refused to be a player.

We meet. Cordial greeting. Forced pleasantries. I am asked what the problem is. Why is it that your daughter will not participate? Why does she think she can get away with this? How come she didn't finish her project on the family unit? I cut in. I willed my voice to an even tone. There are explosions in my brain. I refuse to have this woman speak to me in a condescending fashion. I inquire about my daughter's lack of participation; about the model of family structure that is being recognized and rewarded in class. Ours does not fit the mould. I explain. My words are vaporized. I ask about forms of resistance being demonstrated by other girls. None. I ask about the manner in which questions are directed at my daughter. The teacher's voice rises by several decibels. She yells, 'I am sick and tired of hearing Athena this and Athena that. She is not that special. What's all the fuss about?'

I breathe in. I stare in disbelief. I refuse to accept the blame, and feel the guilt and shame this woman, this teacher, is trying to place on me. Sparks are flying. I must remain in control. I refuse to speak. I can only stare. She stops to catch her breath. She demands to show me her proof. I move the chair and stand up. She steps back. I look at her with disgust. I start towards the door. She yells out at me, 'I am not finished yet!' I am overwhelmed by her bile. I begin to smile, the images of long ago play themselves out, and the anger subsides. The spectre of my younger self shadowed in the doorway looks on, lips upturned and eyes strong and steady. I turn and distinctly reply, 'Yes, but I am.' My smile grows. I walk out on shaky legs. Somewhere music—and my spirit starts to dance.

Tears? Yes, there are tears. I cry for my mother, myself, and my daughter. I cry because our children's spirits are still being assaulted—not educated. My tears (I am reminded) are good. They help us to heal. They return to Mother Earth. They cleanse us, help us grow.

My anger is still in me. It is mine. I earned it. I share it. It belongs to all of us, collectively. The forces of religion, education, society, the judiciary, the media, make it a real, everyday occurrence. At times I do not realize there is a difference between being happy, being angry, and being alive. I have had to make friends with anger. We are together when people continue to say—you sound so angry when you speak about the education system. Yes I am, because it continues to perpetuate inaccuracies. I am angry when Aboriginal peoples are labelled 'Indians'. I am angry when a person is devalued by the colour of their skin. Yes I am, when children are victimized. Yes I am, when I am patronized. Yes I am, when teachers continue to tell us that we were discovered out of our own savage chasm of non-sentience. Yes, I am angry when people are silenced. Yes I am, when people try to use me to justify their theories. Yes, I am angry.

Who says we can't dance? 'Whoever pays the piper, calls the tune'—well, we've paid the piper for half a millennium. It's time to call the tune. It's time to dance.

Source: Pheasant (2001). Reprinted by permission of Between the Lines.

as race exists. And indeed arguments that call for us to abandon 'race' in our scholarship are meritorious. However, just as using the concept race is risky business, so too is abandoning it. This is especially true in an era where academic work is increasingly subjected to scrutiny by politicians, members of the media, and the public and where the potential exists for a conservative misinterpretation of 'race' as insignificant (Omi and Winant 1994). In fact, others argue that because race is real in its consequences, it should not be abandoned as a category of sociological analysis (Omi and Winant 1994; Bonilla-Silva 1997). Indeed, Omi and Winant go so far as to say that it is only

> by noticing race [that] we can begin to challenge racism, with its ever-more-absurd reduction of human experience to an essence attributed to all without regard for historical or social context. By noticing race we can challenge the state, the institutions of civil society, and ourselves as individuals to combat the legacy of inequality and injustice inherited from the past. By noticing race we can develop the political insight and mobilization necessary to make the US [and Canada] a more racially just and egalitarian society. (1994: 159)

Race is *not* rooted in biology. It is *not* a natural category of distinction. Race *is* socially constructed. And the social construction of race *does* matter. Although the use of the term race is unfashionable, I am convinced by Omi and Winant's argument and hence I use the term here. The challenge lies in conceptualizing race in a way that (1) does not disregard the complex social processes that lead to racialized outcomes of inequality (e.g., differences in income or occupational status) and (2) does not lead to a legitimation of the 'essence' of race by either academics or non-academics (see Miles and Torres 2000).

Conceptualizing Race/Ethnicity and Racism/Ethnicism

Although the preceding discussion has focused on race, both race and ethnicity have historically been significant structures of inequality in Canadian society (see Kalbach and Kalbach 2000). Not surprisingly, in light of some of the questions posed above, in the empirical literature on race and ethnicity there is considerable conceptual confusion between the two terms. Indeed, one cannot understand race without understanding ethnicity, and yet distinguishing between the two terms is a complex issue.

Ethnicity: Issues of Culture and Identity

There is a decided emphasis in ethnic studies on culture, ideology, and descent as determinants of ethnic group and ethnic identity. Such accounts probably stem, at least in part, from Weber's ([1922] 1978) assessment of ethnicity in *Economy and Society*. For Weber, ethnicity is socially constructed because *beliefs* about group differences serve to exclude individuals from certain associations while including them in others. Actual group differences need not have considerable social consequences. The social consequences of group differences only emerge when people begin to believe that they are significant. For Weber, ethnicity is constructed around several dimensions, including differences in language, customs, religion, ancestry, and physical characteristics. Again, however, these differences have social significance only when they serve as the basis for labelling people as members of one ethnic group or another (Weber [1922] 1978). Weber argued that the reason for this labelling is not to identify groups of people with a common ancestry or nation. Rather, it is a way of excluding some groups from the rights and privileges that other groups enjoy. Social exclusion is thus a crucial concept in

Weberian scholarship on ethnic-based inequality.

Similarly, Allahar and Côté (1998: 72) rely on social exclusion, or what they refer to as an 'in-group/out-group dynamic' in their definition of ethnicity. In their view, ethnic-group identification and membership involve both subjective and objective assessments about whether the following characteristics apply to an individual or group:

(a) a common history with a set of shared values and customs, language, style of dress, food, music, and other cultural attributes
(b) a myth of common descent
(c) national or territorial claims to sovereignty

(d) an assumed inherited racial marker such as skin colour, hair texture, or facial features
(e) some degree of economic or occupational specialization (Allahar and Côté 1998: 72)

Using one or more of these criteria, most Canadians engage in subjective assessments about whether they belong to a particular ethnic group and to which ethnic group others belong. We often interpret each other's names and physical characteristics and either ask questions such as: Are you Italian? What am I? or assign some sort of ethnic identity (e.g., Scottish, Greek, Italian) to ourselves and others. As Table 4.1 shows, Canadians use ethnic and racial markers to

Table 4.1 Percentage of Canadians Who Have High Levels of Comfort Being around Persons from Various Ethnic Groups

Origin Being Evaluated	Respondents Indicating the Highest Comfort Levels Towards	
	Immigrant Ethnic Group (%)	Canadian-Born Ethnic Group (%)
British	83	86
Italian	77	83
French	74	82
Jewish	74	78
Ukrainian	73	79
German	72	79
Portuguese	70	76
Chinese	69	77
Native Canadian	–	77
West Indian Black	61	69
Moslem	49	59
Arab	52	63
Indo-Pakistani	48	59
Sikh	43	55

Source: Angus Reid (1991: 51). Reproduced in Li (1998: 121).

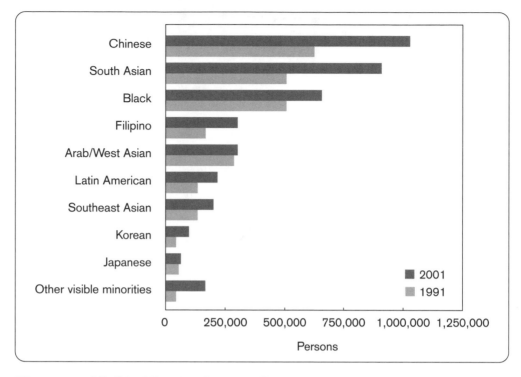

Figure 4.1 Visible Minority Groups, Canada, 1991 and 2001

Source: Statistics Canada, (2003). Catalogue 96F0030 available at: <http://www12.statcan.ca/english/census01/products/analytic/companion/etoimn/canada.cfm>

assess others and their level of comfort with people of 'other' ethnic and racial backgrounds (Li 1998). Researchers examine ethnicity on the basis of these self-assessments as well (see Figure 4.1 and Table 4.2 for description of the racial and ethnic composition of Canada's population).

Furthermore, in a recent compilation on ethnicity in Canada (Kalbach and Kalbach 2000), self-reported survey items indicating nation of origin, language, and process of citizenship (by birth or immigration) were commonly used to assess ethnicity. Studies of ethnicity tend to be concerned with assimilation (the extent to which ethnic groups are integrated into communities), cultural pluralism (the extent to which eth-

nic groups have maintained their ethnic identity), and whether certain ethnic groups are socially disadvantaged compared to other ethnic groups (see Kalbach and Kalbach 2000; Satzewich 1998). Although all of these issues are related, the focus in this book is on the last of those issues.

Notably, certain characteristics that are usually associated with 'race', such as colour of skin, are included as one component of ethnicity in Allahar and Côté's definition. Indeed, in sociological research, race is often subsumed under the broad rubric of ethnicity (Anthias 1992; Loveman 1999). For instance, Anthias (1992) argues that race categories 'belong to the more encompassing category of ethnic collectivity' because

Table 4.2 Top 10 Ethnic Origins, Based on Total Responses, Canada, 2001 and 1996

	2001			1996	
	Number	%		Number	%
Total population	29,639,030	100.0	Total population	28,528,125	100.0
Canadian	11,682,680	39.4	Canadian	8,806,275	30.9
English	5,978,875	20.2	English	6,832,095	23.9
French	4,668,410	15.8	French	5,597,845	19.6
Scottish	4,157,215	14.0	Scottish	4,260,840	14.9
Irish	3,822,660	12.9	Irish	3,767,610	13.2
German	2,742,765	9.3	German	2,575,140	9.7
Italian	1,270,369	4.3	Italian	1,207,475	4.2
Chinese	1,094,700	3.7	Ukrainian	1,026,475	3.6
Ukrainian	1,071,055	3.6	Chinese	921,585	3.2
North American Indian	1,000,890	3.4	Dutch (Netherlands)	916,215	3.2

Note: Table shows total responses. Because some respondents reported more than one ethnic origin, the sum is greater than the total population or 100%.

Source: Statistics Canada (2003: 45).

'race' is only one of many ways in which exclusion is perpetuated on the basis one's ethos or origin (either socially constructed or real). Similarly, Loveman (1999: 895) argues against the separation of race and ethnicity as categories of analysis because she questions whether there is anything 'unique about the operation or consequences of 'race'. On the other hand, Omi and Winant (1994) argue that processes and consequences of racial formation are very different from processes and consequences of ethnic formation. For example, the social construction of 'native' or 'black' in Canada and the United States, rooted in processes of genocide and slavery, is very different from the ethnic formation and discrimination experienced by Irish immigrants in North America in the nineteenth century. What is needed, Omi and Winant argue, is a structural approach to race that does not reduce it to issues of ethnicity.

Toward a Structural Account of Race and Racism

In the Marxist tradition, race and ethnicity 'are the masks behind which actors conceal their class position both from each other and from themselves' (McAll 1990: 70). Marxist accounts of social inequality examine the role that race and ethnicity play in maintaining class boundaries. According to these perspectives, owners in certain manufacturing industries have traditionally hired immigrant workers at low levels of pay in order to maintain or increase their profit margins. Because they have little choice but to work for low wages, these immigrant workers are considered a threat by the established and higher-paid working class. Race and ethnicity become divisions within the working class. This process is useful for capitalism because hostilities that would normally be directed toward the owners of the means of production are now contained among the workers themselves (Miles 1989; and see also McAll 1990). As Miles (1989: 111) argues,

Benadict

> racism became a relation of production because it was an ideology which shaped decisively the formation and reproduction of the relation between exploiter and exploited: it was one of those representational elements which became historically conducive to the constitution and reproduction of a system of commodity production.

The main problem with Marxist approaches to race and ethnicity is that their analysis is reduced to issues of social class; ethnicity and race do not warrant investigation in their own right (Bonilla-Silva 1997). Taking issue with approaches to race that focus on class (or ethnicity or nation), Omi and Winant (1994: 55) define race as 'a concept which signifies and symbolizes social conflicts and interests by referring to different types of human bodies.'

Racial Formation

According to Omi and Winant (1994: 55) racial formation is a 'sociohistorical process by which racial categories are created, inhabited, transformed, and destroyed'. The theory of racial formation centres on two related social phenomena: (1) historically situated *racial projects* and (2) the evolution

of *hegemony*. **Hegemony**, a concept Omi and Winant borrow from the work of Antonio Gramsci, refers to the achieving and maintaining of rule both by political coercion and ideological consent (Gramsci 1971). Hence, Omi and Winant emphasize the role that political structures play in racial formation, arguing that 'race is now a preeminently political phenomenon' (1994: 65) maintained through hegemonic forms of racial rule (67).

According to Gramsci (1971), hegemonic forms of rule evolve in modern societies as the force and coercion necessary for a ruling class to achieve dominance gives way to consent. Consent does not replace coercion in hegemonic forms of rule, but it takes on a more central role in modern systems of domination. Consent is achieved through the assimilation of crucial interests of subordinate groups with the interests of dominant groups, often to the disadvantage of the dominant groups themselves. It is maintained through an ideological system that is controlled by the ruling group but that subordinate groups accept as legitimate. Such ideological systems are perpetuated in practice through institutions such as the family, religion, education, and the media.

With respect to racial formation in the United States, Omi and Winant note that the use of extreme force in a racial dictatorship through African slavery and the mass murder and expulsion of First Nations peoples gave way to consent in what might now be referred to as a racial democracy. Crucial to this process were efforts of the subordinate racial groups to usurp, and later embrace, the religious and philosophical ideas of their oppressors. In reference to African slaves Omi and Winant (1994: 67) write:

In their language, in their religion with its focus on the Exodus theme and on Jesus's tribulations, in their music with its figuring of suffering, resistance, perserverance, and transcendence, in their interrogation of a political philosophy which sought perpetually to rationalize their bondage in a supposedly 'free' society, the slaves incorporated elements of racial rule into their thought and practice, turning them against their original bearers.

Besides hegemony, Omi and Winant argue, racial formation also relies on racial projects. Racial projects are processes through which 'human bodies and social structures are represented and organized'. They link everyday experiences with social structures. In other words, racial projects 'connect what race means in a particular discursive practice and the ways in which both social structures and everyday experiences are racially organized, based on meaning' (Omi and Winant 1994: 56). Hence, racial projects occur at both the structural level and as individuals interact with one another. Racial projects are historically situated, and conventional understandings of race vary accordingly (Omi and Winant 1994). In

other words, what is meant by 'race', 'black', 'white', or 'aboriginal' today is very different from what these words meant 100 years ago. And the meanings of these words are different depending on where one lives (e.g., Canada as opposed to South Africa).

Structural racial projects occur in social, political, and economic domains, and examples of structural racial projects appear in Canada's newspapers nearly daily. For instance, in 2001 the government of British Columbia attempted to resolve native land claim disputes and other 'native' issues by conducting a survey of its residents to assess their views on these issues. The questions were worded in such away that the answers would favour right-wing government action. Aboriginal groups and human-rights advocates argued that the questions were biased against First Nations peoples. The use of the survey by the government of British Columbia and the negative response to it by some groups are examples of politically structured racial projects. In labour markets, the failure of management or unions to take claims of racism seriously is another example of a structural racial project (see Box 4.3)

Box **Ontario's Black Jail Guards Want Probe Into Workplace Racism. Complaints Taken Seriously, Minister Says, But No Inquiry Planned.**
By Colin Perkel

The day Anthony Weekes started working as a corrections officer in Toronto, the racist response from fellow guards stunned him.

'You mean they hired another effin' nigger?' Mr Weekes remembers one saying. 'That was my greeting on the first day of the job,' he told a news conference yesterday.

Seventeen years later, rampant and systemic racism persists, Mr Weekes and other black corrections workers say, and neither the government nor their own union has done much to stop it.

They want a public inquiry, saying it's the only way to shed light on what they describe as an ugly environment for members of visible minorities working in Ontario's prison system.

From racial slurs and Ku Klux Klan signs scribbled on prison walls to denials of promotions, the workers say they've paid a price for the colour of their skin, and a dearer price for speaking out.

'Our careers are done,' said Anthony Simon, 54, another guard who says his car was smashed after he complained.

'This is the reality of the society that we live in . . . that when we speak up for our own, when we speak up for our rights and justice, we pay the price.'

Correctional Services Minister Rob Sampson says the government takes the complaints 'quite seriously' but immediately refused a public inquiry, saying a process is in place to deal with them.

Liberal Alvin Curling says Mr Sampson has 'failed miserably'.

'Nothing has been done. People continue to be harassed and discriminated against.'

Mr Curling believes a public inquiry is required because the complaints processes aren't effective. Recommendations for the Human Rights Commission and labour board rulings have been ignored, he says.

The officers say their own union has failed them as well.

Leighton Hope, 46, who works at the Maplehurst Correctional Complex, says he filed a grievance in 1989 through the Ontario Public Service Employees Union after being denied a promotion.

His case remains unresolved more than a decade later.

'I have resigned myself that not much will change,' Mr Hope said.

OPSEU officials could not be reached for comment.

Anthony Garrick, 41, who started working at the Toronto youth detention centre in 1986, has been active on the ministry's antiracism committee and represented the union on race issues.

'It's very difficult because you're addressing the problem while being victimized,' Mr Garrick said.

The managers who are supposed to implement anti-racism policies in the workplace are among those who either overlook the racism or practise it themselves, Mr Garrick said.

For Mr Weekes, the situation at the probation office where he now works got so bad he took stress leave last August to escape the 'poisoned environment'. When his vacation and sick time expired, Mr Weekes says he was forced to return to work against his doctor's orders.

'It clearly shows there is no hope for any improvement in this ministry unless the public gets involved.'

Source: Perkel (2000). Reprinted by permission of The Canadian Press.

Racial projects also occur at the individual level as people interact with one another. People make assumptions about others on the basis of their race and interact with them accordingly. Box 4.4 provides many examples of interactional racial projects. In it is the story of Crystal Samms, an aboriginal 14-year-old who recently transferred to a Toronto high school that takes pride in its diversity. One of Crystal's racial projects becomes clear early in the article when she notes that she is 'not racist, but there's a certain race that causes trouble [speaking of the Caribbean girls in her class]'. And the racial projects of others in her class emerge when Crystal recounts how she was mistaken for

Box **4.4**   **Canada's Apartheid Part 2: Crystal's Choice: the Best of Both Worlds**
By John Stackhouse

Beneath the west flight path into Toronto's international airport sits a swath of portable classrooms, unheated and dimly lit, and each one resounding with a medley of accents.

On a field that was part of an Indian village before it was plowed by British settlers, converted to subdivisions and finally jammed with apartment blocks full of new immigrants, St Francis Xavier Secondary School in central Mississauga has become the image of a new Canada.

In a Grade 9 portable, a couple of Jamaicans talk about a coming track meet and plans for a weekend party. Italian, Ecuadorean and Chinese kids join in, ignoring their math assignments as they jabber in some of the 16 languages known to the school, and then revert as easily to English.

After a while, the conversations weave through each other so much that any inflection or slang becomes indistinguishable from the next. It seems as though the students and their families have always been here.

Except for one girl. She looks a bit uncomfortable as she sheds her nylon jacket and settles at the back of the classroom, but she knows that even though she is new to the school, her people always have been here.

At 15, Crystal Samms bubbles with the pride and confusion of someone trying to find her way in a foreign land. St Francis Xavier's 1,000 students list 90 countries as their homelands, but she is the only native Canadian among them. 'When you speak of Canada, I am Canadian,' she says. 'This is my country.'

Which is why, in Grade 9, she represents the biggest emerging challenge for native Canadians. Once segregated and forgotten on remote reserves, Aboriginal people are fast becoming urban people. But in the ethnic sprawl of Toronto or Vancouver, or even Edmonton, Winnipeg, and Ottawa, they are finding a very new Canada that is not very white, not very homogenous and not very interested in their concerns.

For Crystal, there is an age-old struggle here to preserve her native identity as she grows more distant from her ancestral reserve in Southwestern Ontario. But there is also that new challenge: how to forge an identity as one minority among many.

Inside the main building at St Francis Xavier (which relies on portables to keep up with local population growth), the hallways are a river of colours and torrent of international concerns. There are posters denouncing Third World sweat shops, coffee slaves and sugar slaves, as though the school were preparing for a Naomi Klein convention. By the entrance, there are also sacks and sacks of clothes, toys, and cooking utensils, collected by students as part of a drive to help families in Zambia and Malawi.

Soon after she transferred here in September, 2000, Crystal discovered that most students hang out with kids of their own race or colour. The school is proud of its diversity, even in the face of emerging ethnic gangs. ('I'm not racist, but there's a certain race that causes trouble,' Crystal says of the Caribbean girls in her class.)

At first, many kids took her for Hispanic, with her lip gloss, long nails and dark hair slicked back into a ponytail. When she told them she was Aboriginal, most of them stared blankly, which angered her more.

Didn't the students understand, she wondered, that there is a Third World just down the highway, a place where she once lived?

'I want them to focus on our world,' Crystal says as her teacher interrupts his lesson to listen to her. 'This is our land. The Spanish people, their land is in Ecuador. The Jamaican people, their land is in Jamaica. The English, their land is London. Our land is right here and we had it taken away.'

By the time math class ends, Crystal has calmed down and turned her attention to another conversation, to find out where the weekend party will be. She also needs to collect her books and hurry to the main building to find her friend Amber. They need to talk about lunch.

While Crystal may have to shout to express her native identity, she also has to cope with the struggle of every teenager, to find herself in a world her parents do not understand. On the reserve, it might have been dictated by elders and traditional mores. But in the city, she has only herself, in an ocean of choices.

As Crystal goes in search of her best friend, she passes through the crowded school atrium, slipping by the taunts of a thuggish Hispanic gang. She hopes to find Amber at the entrance to the cafeteria, which is licensed to Harvey's, but the doorway is blocked by a group of black kids.

Crystal pushes past them too, as if she were at Square One, Mississauga's nearby shopping centrepiece. She's in a hurry, and afraid of no one.

When she was introduced at an assembly as the school's only Aboriginal student, jokers began to call her 'Running Water' and ask if she parked her canoe in the school lot. Others showed reverence. 'I wish I could be native, it's the coolest culture,' she remembers one girl saying to her. 'It's so spiritual.'

Those who knew anything about natives seemed to get their images from television, from Hollywood stereotypes and shocking nightly news clips, like the ones last year that showed children sniffing gasoline in Sheshatshui. At the time, someone asked Crystal why the Labrador gasoline sniffers did it. She said she didn't know. They weren't her kids. She said she was 'disgusted' with the media for focusing on one negative image of native life.

'I had friends come up to me and ask me, "So what's that all about?"'

'I said, "How am I supposed to know?"'
'"You're native."'
'I said, "Because I'm native, I'm supposed to know all the answers?"'
'Then an Italian friend said, "Is it like that on your reserve?"'
'"Like what?"'
'"I heard there's lots of drugs and drinking on reserves."'
'I was disgusted. I told her to walk away. Then I said, "Oh, yeah, I heard Italians are fat and eat a lot of pasta. Is that true?"'

Source: Stackhouse (2001b). Reprinted with permission from the Globe and Mail.

Hispanic and when she corrected this misconception her friends stared at her blankly not knowing how to respond.

The preceding examples of racial projects point to the importance of distinguishing racist racial projects from non-racist racial projects. Omi and Winant argue that 'a racial project can be defined as racist if and only if it creates or reproduces structures of domination based on essentialist categories of race' (Omi and Winant, 1994: 71). The BC government's survey can be defined as a racist project because it meets both of these criteria. However, mistaking Crystal for Hispanic does not contribute to creating or reproducing a structure of domination and hence it is not likely 'racist'. As Omi and Winant (1994: 71) conclude, 'to attribute merits, allocate values or resources to, and/or represent individuals or groups on the basis of racial identity should not be considered racist in and of itself.'

Paying close attention to the ways in which social structures and individual experiences intersect, Omi and Winant (1994) argue that it is through structural and interactional racial projects that race becomes 'common sense' (Omi and Winant 1994), conventional (Giddens 1993), or a deep structure (Sewell 1992). Through our experiences with racial projects we internalize racial classification schema and make assessments about our own racial identity and that of others. For Omi and Winant then, racial projects connect social structures with individuals and are simultaneously interactional and structural.

Omi and Winant's racial-formation theory has been most strongly criticized for their use of the concept of race (Loveman 1999; Miles and Torres 2000; Satzewich 1998). As noted above, while I am sympathetic to arguments in favour of abandoning 'race', I remain convinced of the utility of studying it as a social structural, relational, and socially constructed concept. Eduardo Bonilla-Silva's (1999: 905) comments in defence of his use of the concept of race are telling in this regard:

As long as 'reified' blacks in the United States are still lynched by individual whites (as in the recent case in Jasper, Texas) and are 4.3 times more likely than whites to receive the death sentence; insofar as 'reified' white Brazilians are 8.5 times more likely than black Brazilians and 5 times more likely than *pardos* to receive a college education; and as long as black Puerto Ricans have little access to political, economic, and social resources, I, a 'reified' black-looking Puerto Rican, will continue to study racial structurations throughout the world.

Although agreeing with Omi and Winant's use of the concept race, Bonilla-Silva (1997) is critical of them for not placing enough emphasis on the structural component of race and racism.

Structural Racism

Dissatisfied with Omi and Winant's work, as well as Marxist and ideological accounts of race and racism, Bonilla-Silva argues that a structural view of race and racism is necessary. Recognizing that races are socially constructed, Bonilla-Silva (1997) nonetheless feels that we need to understand that the social relations that emerge through these constructions are real in their consequences. In particular, racial classifications require analysis because they limit the life chances and status of certain racial groups in relation to others.

Bonilla-Silva (1997) develops a conceptual framework of racialized social systems to understand various racial phenomena. He argues that many societies experience a process of racialization as racialized groups oppose one another at all societal levels. Such societies are racialized social systems 'in which economic, political, social, and ideological levels are partially structured by the placement of actors in racial categories or races' (469) where 'races' are socially constructed categories usually identified by phenotypes. The placement of actors in racial categories corresponds with a hierarchy of social relations in which 'superior races' have advantages that 'subordinate races' do not have. According Bonilla-Silva (1997: 470), subordinate races are in positions in society that limit their access to valuable resources. These resources are both material (e.g., lower-status occupations) and ideological (e.g., superior races are considered smarter or better looking), and 'the totality of these racialized social relations and practices constitutes the racial structure of society.' Furthermore, the dynamics of everyday life in racialized social systems 'always include[s] a racial component' (Bonilla-Silva 1997: 473).

Bonilla-Silva argues that in racialized social structures, races come to define their interests collectively, not individually, according to relations between racial groups. Race relations are rooted in power struggles where power is defined as a 'racial group's capacity to push for its racial interests in relation to other races' (Bonilla-Silva 1997: 470). Racial power struggles lead to racial 'strife', or what Bonilla-Silva refers to as 'racial contestation' (473). Racial contestation is the 'struggle of racial groups for systematic changes regarding their position at one or more levels' where levels refer to economic, social, political, and ideological domains (473). Hence, it is through the processes of racialization and racial contestation that 'a set of social relations and practices based on racial distinctions develops at all societal levels' (474).

The crucial distinction between Bonilla-Silva's perspective and other views of race and racism is his focus on the structural nature of race relations rather than on their ideological character. In his view, although ideology plays a significant role in determining how various races are treated and viewed, the structure of race relations extends to social, political, and economic realms as well. In short, race also has a material base. Race relations are deep structures that are taken for granted and that inform individual interaction every day. Race structures everything.

Despite Bonilla-Silva's view that his approach differs significantly from Omi and Winant's, the two seem more similar than different. It is true that Omi and Winant focus somewhat more on ideology than Bonilla-Silva, but that does not necessarily mean that their view of race and racism is not structural, as Bonilla-Silva implies. Indeed, Bonilla-Silva recognizes that ideology is one of several structural dimensions of race that need to be acknowledged. Further, by focusing on the structural nature of race and racism, Bonilla-Silva underemphasizes human agency and its relationship to structure in the process of racialization. Hence, one advantage of Omi and Winant's perspective is their conceptualization of racial projects as a link between structure and agency. However, neither of these approaches theorizes the relationship between social structure and agency fully enough for us to understand the everyday experience of racism.

Racism in Everyday Life

In her book *Understanding Everyday Racism*, Philomena Essed (1991) formulates a theory of race and racism which starts with the assumption that to understand the experience of racism we must consider both macro- and micro-issues, or the relationship between structure and agency. On the question of 'race', Essed uses the term in quotation marks and refers to it as both an ideological and a social construction. Her ideas about the social construction of 'race' are

similar to those of Omi and Winant and Bonilla-Silva, but her approach differs in its emphasis on the ideological construction of race. According to Essed, race is an ideological construct because the 'idea of race has never existed outside of a framework of group interest . . . in which whites rank higher than non-whites' (1991: 43–4).

Essed's view of the structure of race is also very similar to those of both Omi and Winant and Bonilla-Silva. She argues, for instance, that 'racism is a system of structural inequalities and a historical process, both created and recreated through routine practices' (Essed 1991: 39). In her definition of racism, Essed uses the term 'system', which follows Anthony Giddens's use of the term, (see chapter 6) meaning the 'reproduced social relations between individuals and groups organized as regular social practices' (Essed 1991: 39). The term social relations does not refer to interpersonal relations between two people; rather, it is a structural term that refers to the rights, privileges, and rewards that define relationships among groups. Hence, the term race relations highlights the fact that access to resources and political, economic, and social rights are critical attributes of in-group–out-group dynamics.

Essed differs from Omi and Winant and Bonilla-Silva in her emphasis on micro-sociological processes. She argues that, at a micro-level, we must pay attention to the intentional and unintentional practices and consequences of human agency. In short, 'structures of racism do not exist external to agents—they are made by agents—but specific practises are by definition racist only when they activate existing structural racial inequalities in the system' (Essed 1991: 39).

Racism, for Essed, is at once an ideology, a structure, and a process in which power, prejudice, and meaning are central elements. Relying on the work of Hannah Arendt and Steven Lukes, Essed defines power as a macro-process in which certain groups (not individuals) maintain their position of power by drawing on ideologies that suggest there are innate differences between the powerful group and others. Furthermore, power 'over other people affects them, through action or inaction, in a manner contrary to their interests, whether or not those who exercise power are aware of the success or consequences of their practices and whether or not the other party is aware of the power being exercised over him or her' (Essed 1991: 41). According to Essed, the idea that inaction is a form of power is especially important in understanding racism. This is particularly evident when individuals from dominant racial groups do not speak out against racism and instead are passively tolerant of it.

According to Essed (1991: 44), racism is a process whose structures and ideologies are produced and reproduced through **prejudice** and **discrimination.** The central components of prejudice are feelings of superiority, perceptions of intrinsic group differences, feelings of 'propriety claim' to privileges and resources, and fear or suspicion that the subordinate race may take privileges away from the dominant race. Whereas prejudice is an attitude, discrimination refers to acts of behaviour with 'intended or unintended negative or unfavourable consequences for racially or ethnically dominated groups' (Essed 1991: 45).

Finally, Essed argues that meaning is central to understanding the process of everyday racism. From a micro-sociological point of view, the meaning that is assigned to everyday events and interpersonal interaction is critical to the existence of society. Through processes of socialization, we learn to take the rules and norms of social behaviour for granted and attribute meaning to them accordingly. Although individuals engage in heterogeneous activities, there are underlying patterns of uniformity and acceptable modes of behaviour that we rely on in our everyday encounters with others. Hence, everyday racism is defined as a process in which

> (a) socialized racist notions are integrated into meanings that make practices immediately definable and manageable, (b) practices with racist implications become in themselves familiar and repetitive, and (c) underlying racial and ethnic relations are actualized and reinforced through these routine or familiar practices in everyday situations. (Essed 1991: 52)

Essed elaborates upon her theory of everyday racism as she recounts the intensive interviews that she conducted with well-educated, professional black women who live in the United States and the Netherlands. The story of Rosa N. that Essed describes is particularly telling. Summarizing the experiences of everyday racism that she has experienced as a doctor at a hospital in the Netherlands, Rosa discusses how difficult it is to acknowledge racism in an environment where it is not supposed to be tolerated:

> I can never in my life bring up the subject of racism. That just can't be, because they'll only trip me up. If you want to say anything about racism, you've got to state your case very well. Otherwise . . . they tackle you and lay down a thousand

pieces of evidence to prove the opposite, and they make you ridiculous. (Essed 1991: 155)

Hence, the subtle nature of everyday racism exists in part because people of dominant groups are reluctant to acknowledge and address their own racist behaviour. With this in mind, Essed develops a theoretical framework, shown in Figure 4.2, that outlines the structure, ideology, and process of everyday racism. Here we see that culture and structure serve to rationalize and legitimize racial hierarchies that are defined by meaning (definitions of reality), norms and values, and access to resources. Structure and culture influence, and are influenced by, processes of exclusion and subordination. Exclusion can be both blatant and subtle. Examples of blatant exclusion include racial- and ethnic-based labour-market segmentation and the banning of certain racial- and ethnic-minority groups from organizations such as golf clubs. Examples of subtle exclusion are passive tolerance and ignoring racism. Both forms of exclusion lead to a reproduction of the dominant views of the status quo. Examples of subordination include patronizing as well as other forms of racist behaviour and attitudes; subordination is influenced by tolerance, including a reluctance to take a stand against racism.

The strength of Essed's approach is its theoretical emphasis on the relationship between structure and agency and its acknowledgement of the intended and unintended consequences of human action, including the decision not to act at all. However, Essed's emphasis on ideology as the structural base on which race relations are organized is unfortunate. As Omi and Winant and Bonilla-Silva point out, race relations have historically had and continue to have a material base, which is characterized by exploitive labour practices. Although this oversight may be somewhat justified because of Essed's analysis of professional black women, her neglect of the material base of the social structure becomes problematic when one considers other occupational groups.

Conceptualizing Race and Ethnicity in a Theory of Inequality

If we are to understand inequality in Canada, both race and ethnicity must be addressed. Although some argue that race and racism must be given priority to fully appreciate inequality (Dei 1996), the approach taken here is that class, age, gender, ethnicity, and race must all be given equal weight. Some will be critical of such an approach and will question the right of a white woman to make such claims. Though I empathize with such views, I agree with Daiva Stasiulis (1999: 391), who says, 'No one gender, race, or class should have the monopoly on intersectional theorizing'.

Markers of race and ethnicity, such as colour of skin, mother tongue, and country of birth, may be identified for the purpose of empirically analyzing various outcomes of inequality. Such markers do not tell us much about the historical processes of racial and ethnic formation (Omi and Winant 1994) or about the everyday experiences of racism (Essed 1991). Nevertheless, they are important for descriptive assessments of various outcomes of inequality, such as educational attainment, income, and health. Hence, in Part II of this book such markers will be used as indicators of race and ethnicity,

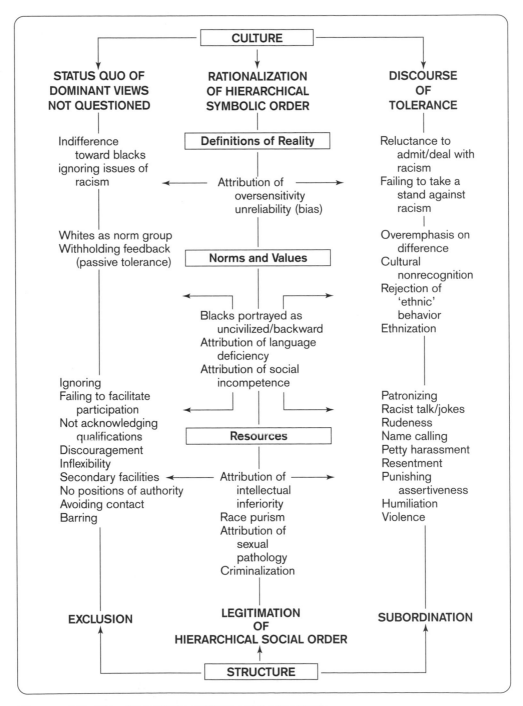

Figure 4.2 The Structure of Everyday Racism

although it will be noted simultaneously that race and ethnicity are social and ideological constructions that cannot be understood fully by being reduced to variables.

The challenge that remains is to conceptualize race and ethnicity within the theoretical framework of inequality that has slowly been evolving in this book. Recall that the processes of production, reproduction, and distribution are at the core of such a framework. Race and ethnicity, like gender and class, are consequential to these processes (Acker 2000). For instance, racial and ethnic minority groups face discrimination in production processes, and they are often in positions in production processes that are less autonomous and more alienated than positions held by dominant-group members (Das Gupta 1996). Dominant racial and ethnic groups have and continue to exploit the reproductive labour of subordinate racial groups (Glenn 1992), and processes of reproduction vary considerably among racial groups (Collins 1990). Processes of distribution are also structured by race and ethnic relations, as is evident in 'racially and ethnically neutral' state unemployment insurance policies that model entitlement on the typical employment patterns of white middle-class men.

As was the case with gender and class, a relational understanding of race and ethnicity that focuses on how oppression is implicated in relations among various racial and ethnic minority groups is necessary for this framework. Although the theories discussed in this chapter do not elaborate upon issues of racial and ethnic oppression, they all mention its importance. Recall that oppression occurs if (1) the welfare of one group of people depends on the deprivations of another; and (2) the deprivations of the

oppressed group depend upon the exclusion of the oppressed group from access to resources, rewards, and privileges. As with class and gender, racial and ethnic oppression is both material and non-material and can take place in various settings. Exploitation, opportunity hoarding, emulation, and adaptation as Tilly (1998) discusses them and as they are discussed in relation to gender in chapter 3 are also important considerations in assessments of race and ethnic relations.

Clearly, **ideology** is a central concept in assessments of race relations, and although it was discussed in relation to class and gender, I have yet to provide a working definition of it. This is, in part, because it is used in many diverse ways, making it an elusive concept in sociological theory. At a very basic level, ideology refers to the ideas, attitudes and beliefs, and norms and values that are held by members of a particular social group. With respect to race and ethnicity, ideology encompasses, for instance, ideas of racial and ethnic inferiority and attitudes towards inclusion or segregation. In theories of inequality, ideology is important to the extent that it serves to reproduce the rewards and privileges of certain groups in relation to others. Hence, when ideology is used to legitimize the inferior position of members of racial and ethnic minority groups in social hierarchies, it becomes a central issue in studies of inequality. Indeed, recall from chapter 2 that Grabb (2002) considers the control of ideas to be one of three constituent elements of power (the other two are control of material resources and control of people).

The difficulty with integrating the concept of ideology into a theory of inequality is the relative emphasis that it is given in the framework. In Marxism, it is often thought that ideology stems from the economic relations of production and that dominant belief systems exist only to serve the interests of capitalists and capitalism more broadly. On the other hand, radical feminists, as well as some of the theorists discussed in this chapter, tend to think of ideology as systems of ideas (e.g., patriarchy and racism) in their own right that have little to do with the relations of production. Neither of these approaches is sufficient for a theoretical framework of inequality that assesses the intersection of class, age, gender, ethnicity, and race. Hence, for the purpose of the theoretical framework presented in this book, I view ideology as systems of ideas and beliefs (sexism, racism, ageism, individualism, elitism, etc.) that are dialectically intertwined with one another and with the structures of gender, class, age, race, and ethnicity. Hence, as Omi and Winant (1994: 74) put it, 'ideological beliefs have structural consequences and social structures give rise to beliefs'.

Glossary

Discrimination   Prejudicial treatment of a person or group. Although related to prejudice, discrimination refers to behaviour rather than to subjective feelings. Discrimination results when individuals or groups carry through with their prejudice and preclude members of other groups from gaining access to resources, rewards, or privileges.

Hegemony   Refers to the dominance of one group over another. It expresses the idea that dominance is achieved and maintained through both ideological and coercive processes.

Ideology   Generally held beliefs, ideas, attitudes, or opinions about social life that significantly influence human behaviour. These ideas are not viewed simply as a product of thought but are based on economic and social realities. Some argue that people who hold power in society actively construct a dominant ideology that will allow them to maintain their control (see also Hegemony above).

Prejudice   Feelings of superiority often resulting from beliefs in intrinsic differences among racially classified groups.

Reification   Social processes through which social phenomena or characteristics become naturalized and thereby considered immutable.

Social constructionism   The process through which meaning is attributed to social rather than to biological or genetic factors. Closely connected to ideas associated with reification. Although much sociological work does just this, the social construction of sex and race are more controversial in this regard.

Questions for Critical Thought

1. What are the advantages and disadvantages of using the concept of race in sociological research? In light of these advantages and disadvantages construct an argument in favour of one approach or the other.

2. Discuss a racialized project that you've read about in the news or heard about on radio or television. Is this racial project racist?

3. Assume that two people who had equal qualifications applied for a job. One of

these people was black, the other white, and all else was equal. The place of employment had an equal-opportunity hiring policy, and the black person was hired. According to Omni and Winant, is this a racial project? Is this racist? Why or why not?

4. Choose an activity that you regularly engage in. How does that activity reflect the idea of 'doing race'? Try to think of a social activity that is not racialized. Now, try to show how race or ethnicity may influence that activity.

5. Compare and contrast the concept of race with the concept of ethnicity.

Recommended Reading

Bonilla-Silva, Eduardo (1997). 'Rethinking racism: Toward a structural interpretation'. *American Sociological Review* 62 (June): 465–80. This is a controversial, theoretical article that acknowledges race as a socially constructed category and works toward developing a structural conceptualization of race with respect to inequality.

Essed, Philomena (1991). *Understanding Everyday Racism: An Interdisciplinary Theory*. Newbury Park: Sage. This research monograph is based on a qualitative study of black women. The quotations and analyses in this book provide valuable insight into the experience of racism.

Kalbach, Madeline A., and Warren E. Kalbach (eds) (2000). *Perspectives on Ethnicity in Canada*. Toronto: Harcourt Canada. This is a collection of articles on race and ethnicity in Canada. Topics include ethnic identification, ethnic diversity, and intersections of gender, race, and ethnicity.

Omi, Michael, and Howard Winant (1994). *Racial Formation in the United States from the 1960s to the 1990s*. 2nd edn. New York: Routledge. This is a very influential book on the formation of race in the United States. The authors argue in favour of using race as an analytic concept.

Satzewich, Vic (ed.) (1998). *Racism and Social Inequality in Canada*. Toronto: Thompson Educational. This is a comprehensive collection of articles on racism in Canada. It covers both theoretical and empirical issues and includes discussions of education, immigration, and justice.

5

Age and Inequality

Privacy is a privilege not granted to the aged or the young. Sometimes very young children can look at the old, and a look passes between them, conspiratorial, sly and knowing. It's because neither are human to the middling ones, those in their prime, as they say, like beef.

(Margaret Laurence, *The Stone Angel*, 6)

Introduction

In this short quotation from *The Stone Angel,* Hagar Shipley, the 90-year-old protagonist, laments that her son and daughter-in-law have not complied with her request to put a lock on her bedroom door. In doing so, she astutely recognizes several issues that will be discussed in this chapter. First, Hager recognizes that certain privileges in society are distributed on the basis of age. Second, she notes that age distinctions are made between the old, the middle-aged, and the young. And third, Hagar observes a connection between the young and the old because of their relationships to the more privileged 'middling ones'.

Margaret Laurence's choice of the word 'middling' to refer to those who are neither young nor old is interesting. At first one is struck by how much the word 'middling' sounds like 'meddling', which means interfering in other people's lives. The Oxford English Dictionary illustrates this use of the word with the following quotation: 'A meddling government, a government which tells them what to read, and say, and eat, and drink, and wear.' This meddling government bears a striking similarity to Hagar's perceptions of the roles that her son and especially her daughter-in-law play in her life. Second, and ironically in the context of the above quotation, the word 'middling' may refer to 'a person who or a thing which is mediocre or second-rate' (OED). Hence, Laurence may also use the phrase 'middling ones' to express Hager's contempt for those who, because of their age, occupy a more privileged position in society than she does.

Indeed, privileges that are distributed on the basis of age relations extend far beyond that of privacy. In Canada in the early twenty-first century, very rarely are young children or teenagers afforded higher levels of status and power than middle-aged adults. Regardless of maturity, dexterity, or intellectual ability, teenagers who live in North America must reach a certain chronological age before they can legally drive a car, vote, or drink alcohol. Wage scales are established for teenagers, not on the basis of what they do, but on their chronological age. Hence, a 17-year-old working at the same job as a 20-year-old could legally be paid less for doing the same work. All of this suggests that the status and power of younger people in North America lags far behind that of middle-aged or older persons.

Yet, as Hagar Shipley knew, this age-based assessment of status and power is far too simple because it does not account for the decline in status and power that older adults experience. How does this happen? In North American culture there is a 'cult of youth' which favours young over old and suggests that to be young is to be vibrant, beautiful, and happy whereas to be old is to be tired, unattractive, and grim (see Box 5.1). These cultural views do little to take away from the status and power of middle-aged people. However, for older adults these views are especially detrimental because combined with the loss of their youthful appeal is their loss of the power and status associated with middle-aged activities, such as working for pay and raising families (see Calasanti and Slevin 2001).

Box **5.1**   **Ageism and Old Bodies**

The discussion above focuses on the way in which power relations result in some groups being more likely to become 'dependent' than others. However, this is not the only source of ageism, of designating someone as 'old' and 'other'. Another critical source of ageism is physical appearance, and this too varies by the intersection of social locations.

Bodies serve as markers of age. Gray hair, wrinkles, brown spots—each of these denotes 'old'. Yet if we think about it, these traits are not universally judged to signify someone is old. Not all gray-haired people are seen to be old, nor are all who exhibit wrinkles. Most of us have heard of the 'double standard' of aging, by which we usually mean that women are seen to be old at an earlier age than men. Recent attitude polls confirm that the gray hair and wrinkles a woman experiences mark her as old sooner. Why is this the case? How and why ageism based on physical appearance occurs is very much related to power relations. We begin with a focus on gender to make this clearer.

Why would people see an old woman wearing a miniskirt as deviant? Part of the reaction, and the rationale for regarding women as old earlier in their lives, arises from the fact that their value is based on their attractiveness to men and their reproductive abilities. Thus the old woman in the miniskirt is deviant for appearing sexual beyond her fertile years. By contrast, men's attractiveness stems from other sources not as quickly diminished. Indeed, sometimes age enhances men's attractiveness, especially if they are associated with public achievements, money, and power. Women even 'age' more quickly than men in the workplace, where they do deal with money, power, and public achievement. This is particularly true if they are engaged in jobs where 'attractiveness' matters—such as jobs dealing with the public or working for (predominantly white) male supervisors. For instance, when airline attendants in this country were almost exclusively women, their unions fought the airlines on a number of occasions where women were removed from their jobs because they were seen as 'too old' (in other words, no longer attractive). However, as we have noted, such issues are shaped differently in different societies. Thus, for example, we find that in Finland youthfulness and attractiveness are not as important for women as they are in the United States.

Having said this, however, we must note that the preceding scenario is too simplistic. What women are we talking about? Do physical signs of aging result in ageism for all women in similar ways? If we accept the fact that people see employed women as old sooner than men, and that this hinges at least in some part on their attractiveness to White men, we must question what this means for the aging of Black women, for example, in the labour force. Are they sexualized in the same way as White women, earlier or later in life? How about women who live openly as lesbians? Or working-class women?

Class plays an important role in another way as well. As was apparent in our discussion of dependence, class—through economic resources—can play a critical role in denying or providing resources that allow the old to choose the ways in which they will manage growing old. To the extent that outward signs of aging can be forestalled by such physical transformations as face-lifts, the well-to-do enjoy an obvious advantage. 'Remaking' aging bodies is expensive and time consuming and, hence, beyond the reach of the working-class or poor. At the same time, which women do the remaking, and how, tells us about racial and ethnic relations. Not all women feel the 'need' to hide gray hair or diminish wrinkles.

Although earlier studies on gay men suggested that the influence of age on one's appearance is critical, and even more so or earlier than among heterosexual men, more recent research has failed to corroborate this assertion. Adam's recent study suggests that age preferences of homosexual men are as similar to and as complex as those among heterosexual men. Similarly, despite assertions that lesbians' changes in appearance with age appear to be more 'acceptable', old lesbians still report feeling like outcasts and age still plays a role in the organization of gay and lesbian communities.

Source: Calasanti and Slevin (2001: 24–5). Reprinted by permission of AltaMira Press, a division of Rowman & Littlefield Publishers, Inc.

Explanations of Age-Based Inequality

Age is the fifth dimension of inequality that is considered in this book, and it may well be the most understudied among them. This is curious in light of the fact that the Canadian population is aging and that changes to the population age structure have led to considerable discussion of the challenges facing public pension schemes such as the Canadian Pension Plan. As Table 5.1 shows, 13 per cent of Canada's population is aged 65 and over, compared to 26 per cent in the age 19 and younger category. This represents a 10 per cent increase in the number of people aged 65 and over since 1996 and a 1 per cent decline in the number of persons aged 19 and under. While there are obvious challenges that will result from the aging of populations, if we place too much emphasis on older adults and the elderly, we are liable to ignore the difficulties that face younger adults and to fuel intergenerational equity debates. Indeed, age relations are important in assessments of inequality regardless of chronological age. Unfortunately, most of the conceptual work on age in relation to inequality has been conducted by researchers who concentrate on the elderly. Of necessity that will be the emphasis here.

Table 5.1   Age Distribution, Canada, Provinces, and Territories, 2001

	Age Group			
	0–19 (%)	20–64 (%)	65+ (%)	Total (%)
Canada	25.9	61.1	13.0	100.0
Newfoundland and Labrador	25.0	62.7	12.3	100.0
Prince Edward Island	27.3	59.0	13.7	100.0
Nova Scotia	25.0	61.1	13.9	100.0
New Brunswick	24.8	61.7	13.6	100.0
Quebec	24.2	62.5	13.3	100.0
Ontario	26.3	60.8	12.9	100.0
Manitoba	28.1	58.0	14.0	100.0
Saskatchewan	29.2	55.8	15.1	100.0
Alberta	28.3	61.4	10.4	100.0
British Columbia	25.0	61.4	13.6	100.0
Yukon Territory	29.0	64.9	6.0	100.0
Northwest Territories	35.0	60.7	4.4	100.0
Nunavut	46.5	51.2	2.2	100.0

Source: Statistics Canada (2001l). <http://www12.statcan.ca/english/census01/products/highlight/AgeSex/HighlightsTables.cfm?Lang=E>.

Age Stratification Theory

The development of a formal statement of age-stratification theory was foreshadowed in the late 1950s and early 1960s by Leonard Cain and Bernice Neugarten (Marshall 1995), but Matilda White Riley and her colleagues are responsible for the formalization and subsequent elaborations of the theory. Riley now refers to her work as 'the aging and society paradigm', which expresses her concerns about the overly static nature of the term stratification (Riley 1994). However, the basic premises of age-stratification theory have changed little since its conception, although recent statements of this approach are perhaps more succinct and clearer (Riley et al. 1988; Riley and Riley 1994b).

Riley and her colleagues conceptualize age as both a process and a structure. At the structural level, similar-aged individuals form strata that may be defined on the basis of either chronological age or biological, psychological, or social stages of development (Riley et al. 1972: 6). Age strata differ from one another in size and composition as well as in the relative contributions that each makes to society. Age is also established in the social structure as a 'criterion for entering or relinquishing certain roles' (Riley et al. 1972: 7), and thus it is used as a marker by which age-appropriate behaviour is gauged.

Riley uses the concept of structure without providing a concise definition of the term (Dowd 1987). Functionalist leanings are, however, clearly present in her discussions of social structures. Elements of the social structure are viewed either as social institutions (i.e., families, schools, work organizations, and nations) (Riley 1994; Riley and Riley 1994a; Riley and Riley 1994b) or as patterns of social roles (Riley et al. 1972). People (population structure) and roles (role structure) are differentiated by an age structure (Riley et al. 1972: 6), the elements of which are age strata, age-related acts, age structure of roles, and age-related expectations and sanctions.

The fundamental processes in age stratification theory (Riley et al. 1972) are cohort flow, individual aging, allocation, and socialization. Figure 5.1 documents how these processes influence the age-related social structures discussed above. In describing this figure Riley and her colleagues. (1972) suggest that **cohort** flow is the

essential process underlying the changing size and composition of the age strata [and] consists of the formation of successive cohorts, their modification through migration and the gradual reduction and eventual dissolution of each cohort through the death of individual members. (Riley, et al. 1972: 8)

The aging process is conceptualized as a **biopsychosocial** process (Riley 1994), thus capturing psychological and biological development as well as the experience of entering and exiting social roles (Riley et al. 1972). According to this theory, the aging process influences the structure of age-related acts or capacities (see Figure 5.1). **Allocation** and **socialization** are the processes that intervene between the social structures relating to people (persons of given ages or age strata and age-related acts or capacities) and those relating to roles

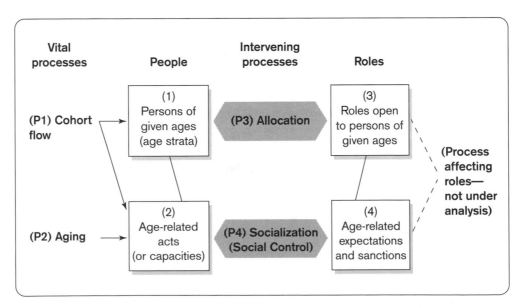

Figure 5.1 Processes Related to Structural Elements: Age Stratification Perspective

Source: Riley et al. (1972: 9). © 1972 Russell Sage Foundation, 112 East 64th Street, New York, NY 10021. Reprinted with permission.

(roles open to persons of given ages and age-related expectations and sanctions) (see Figure 5.1). Allocation is the process by which individuals are continually assigned and reassigned to particular roles; socialization is the process of teaching individuals how to perform new life-course roles (Riley et al. 1972).

To disentangle issues related to aging from those related to cohort succession, Riley and her colleagues (1972) developed another conceptual scheme that incorporates time. Figure 5.2, which presents this scheme, shows that as cohorts age they move through time and through age strata (represented by the vertical lines). Thus, differences in age strata reflect a culmination of the effects of individual aging as well as dif-

ferent patterns of cohort composition (Riley et al. 1972: 11).

The difference between the models and theory Riley used in 1972 and those she uses now lies more in clarity than in content. She now presents the first model (Figure 5.1) as a **synchronic** view of the 'paradigm' and expands it by enveloping it in social values and the physical environment. The second model now represents a **diachronic** view of the 'paradigm'. The conceptual clarity of this model is greatly improved; it is reproduced here in Figure 5.3. The vertical axis represents aging, which is conceptualized as changes in individual lives and the age criteria for entering and leaving roles. The horizontal axis represents time or history and refers to political,

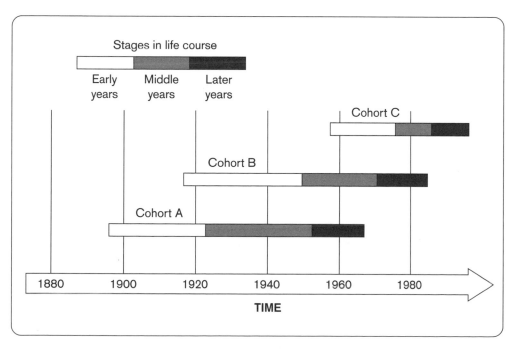

Figure 5.2 Processes of Cohort Formation and Aging Showing Selected Cohorts over Time: Age Stratification Perspective

Source: Riley et al. (1972: 10). © 1972 Russell Sage Foundation, 112 East 64th Street, New York, NY 10021. Reprinted with permission.

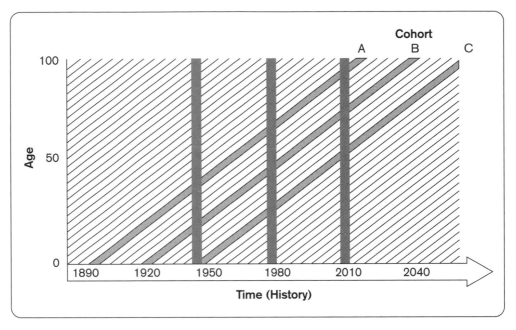

Figure 5.3 The Age-Stratification System: A Schematic View

Source: Riley et al. (1988: 245). Copyright © 1998. Reprinted by permission of Sage Publications, Inc.

economic, and cultural changes in society over time. The letters A, B, and C, representing cohorts, are placed on the diagonal to show the simultaneous processes of cohort flow and aging. The vertical bars represent the people and associated roles that constitute age-related structures, such as families, schools, and work organizations. Finally, the cross-sections show 'how many people who are at different stages of their lives and involved in different social roles and institutions, are organized roughly in socially recognized age divisions or strata' (Riley et al. 1988: 244). The addition of age-related structures and the clarity of this model make it different from its predecessors. It does not, however, represent a significant change in the perspective because its components and their specification are the same.

Nonetheless, subtle changes in the terminology used to describe the theory came with the elaboration of the model, not least of which was the change of name to 'aging and society paradigm'. In the mid- to late 1980s the word dynamism appeared, which encompassed both process and change (Riley 1988). Riley describes the evolution of the paradigm when she says that the 'distinction between people and roles led us to focus directly on the central theme of the paradigm: the two dynamisms—changes in lives and in structures' (Riley 1994: 438). Each dynamism is a distinct and separate process, they are interdependent, and both are asynchronous (different in timing) (Riley et al. 1988; Riley and Riley 1994b) and as a result, they produce a structural lag because human lives change faster than the social structure (Riley and Riley 1994b).

The models that make up the age-stratification theory were primarily established to organize a large body of data and to dispel several fallacies that were common in the aging literature before 1972 (some persist today). The *life-course fallacy* refers to the assumption that cross-sectional age differences capture the process of aging. *Cohort centrism* is the error of assuming that other cohorts age in the same way as one's own. *Age reification* treats chronological age as *the* life-course variable and does not take into account other factors that influence aging. Finally, *reifying historical time* places emphasis on historical change rather than drawing attention to the particular aspects of change that are central to an understanding of variations in age structures or processes (Riley et al. 1988: 248).

By recognizing these misinterpretations, the **age and society paradigm** seeks to explain the processes that underlie the movement of age cohorts through time and age-related social structures. Exploring the asynchrony between individual and structural change, it attempts to resolve issues of conflict related to this 'structural lag'. The theory also strives to understand the interdependence between age cohorts, social structures, and individual aging processes (Bengtson, Parrott, and Burgess 1994).

Age Strata

In age-stratification research the age system of inequality is generally conceptualized in terms of the differences between older, middle-aged, and younger age strata. Although there is some recognition that inequalities arise as age strata are constructed and reformulated through the changes in society and age-related processes (Riley et al. 1988: 268),

age tends to be treated in static rather than dynamic terms. Thus, the processes and changes that are captured in the diachronic view of age stratification theory (see Figure 5.3) are generally absent in assessments of social inequality. Instead, there is a tendency to start with the assumption that **age strata**, with clearly defined roles and consequential rewards and expectations, exist and that they constitute a system of age-based inequality (Foner 1974, 1986; Riley et al. 1972; Riley et al. 1988). Hence, these theories of inequality are generally framed within the synchronic model of age-stratification theory (see Figure 5.2) and focus on the process of allocation and the structure of roles and age-related expectations and sanctions.

Literature on the cultural meanings that individuals attribute to age casts doubt on the assumption that there are clearly defined age norms for different age strata. For instance, Neugarten, Moore, and Lowe (1965) show that the importance individuals assign to age norms in determining appropriate behaviour is a function of the age of the respondent (see also Elder and Rockwell 1976; Fallo-Mitchell and Ryff 1982). Compared to younger and middle-aged respondents, older adults tend to hold stronger convictions about age norms. Compared to older women, younger women prefer later ages for the onset of family events and earlier ages for educational and occupational events (Fallo-Mitchell and Ryff 1982). Assumptions about widely held age norms are also tenuous in the face of anthropological evidence showing that there are variations in the meanings attributed to age both within a given society and cross-culturally (Fry 1976, 1980, 1985, 1986). For instance, Christine Fry (1976) asked a group of American adults to sort pictures that depicted people in different life situations into as many age categories as they deemed necessary. The respondents created between two and fifteen age categories and used more than 100 terms to describe them. The average number of age categories chosen was between five and six, depending on other variables such as gender or marital status. Indeed, some argue that boundaries between culturally specified age categories are becoming increasingly blurred as active lifestyles, related consumer products, and the promotion of never-ending sex through medicalization (e.g., Viagra) are being marketed to aging baby-boomers (Katz and Marshall 2003; Marshall and Katz 2002).

The preceding findings suggest that there are problems with the underlying assumptions about age strata as used in the age-stratification approach. Nonetheless, the usefulness of this conceptualization comes from the idea that age distinctions are fundamental in our society and that they influence patterns of resource distribution.

Cohorts

The process of cohort flow is considered in age-stratification discussions of inequality. In fact, Riley (1985: 386) goes so far as to suggest that age may predominate over other bases of inequality,[1] largely because cohort differences in education have strengthened the age-stratification system. Here, the concept of cohort flow is discussed within the confines of the synchronic model. Historical, time-related issues, such as the experience of the Depression or the Second World War, are left unmentioned, even though their influences on an individual's life chances have been demonstrated (Easterlin 1987; Elder 1985).

The relative neglect of temporal issues in this approach suggests that the conceptualization of cohort in age-stratification theory may be problematic. Riley defines a cohort according to the definition Norman Ryder (1965) proposed in his seminal article 'The cohort as a concept in the study of social change'. For Ryder (1965: 845), a cohort is an aggregate of individuals who experienced the same event within the same time interval; birth cohorts are only a special case of this more general definition. Notably, Ryder's conceptualization allows for individuals to be grouped according to any significant event. In practice, however, year of birth tends to be the event that is assigned the greatest significance. Thus, Riley views cohorts as aggregates of individuals who are born in the same time interval.

Conceptualizing cohorts in arbitrarily defined single- or five-year age categories reifies chronological age as the basis of inequality and ignores more subjective dimensions of age that may be relevant (Marshall 1983; Passuth and Bengtson 1988). By assuming that one-year or five-year age cohorts take on meaningful significance, this approach masks qualitative differences in personal experience that are related to age (Marshall 1983).

Age Stratification Theory and Inequality

Age-stratification theory has been applied to a large gamut of substantive research, including inequality in labour markets and families. According to age-stratification theory, paid employment and family membership are considered socially valued roles because they function to maintain order in society. Older and younger age strata are relatively disadvantaged because they tend not to take part in the productive roles that are highly valued in modern society. Labour-force entries and exits are allocated by age, both directly through labour laws and indirectly by educational criteria for entering jobs, and by the perceived age-related performance abilities for job exit (see Box 5.2). There are age differences in the kinds of jobs people hold and in the age distribution of the work force. These age-related roles and expectations for labour force participation lead to different rewards according to age. Thus, compared to labour-force participants, retired workers and young people tend to be less powerful and are economically disadvantaged (see Box 5.3 for a narrative on the

experience of inequality in later life). In labour markets, older workers assume more power and tend to make more money than younger workers, especially in well-established firms (Foner 1986; Foner and Schwab 1981; Riley et al. 1972; Riley et al. 1988). However, when older workers lose their job, they are unemployed longer than younger workers (McMullin and Marshall 2001).

Age-stratification discussions of the family have concentrated on the age-graded nature of the family, its changing structure, its functions, and the roles and norms associated with different types of membership in families (Foner 1986). Inequality in families is generally assessed through economic dif-

---

Box **Job Ghettoization**

Young workers not only are paid less and participate in the workforce less, they are also becoming less well represented in all job categories except customer services. Indeed, it is in the subordinate service occupations that their (cheap) labour is most in demand.

Betcherman and Morissette tell us that between 1981 and 1989, the proportion of service sector jobs held by young workers aged 16 to 24 rose from 69.7 per cent to 75.8 per cent, while in the goods sector it dropped from 30.3 per cent to 24.2 per cent. The two most common service sector jobs held in 1989 were retail trade (22.7 per cent) and accommodation and food (13.7 per cent). Statistics Canada noted from these trends a 'substantial absolute decline of youth employment in the goods sector and in public administration, health, social services, and education' and concluded that for 'earlier generations of young people, these industries typically offered good entry-level opportunities.' When broken down by gender, over 84 per cent of employed females between the ages of 15 and 19 worked in the service sector, compared with about 60 per cent of their male counterparts.

A clear picture emerges here: the jobs available to the young are increasingly unskilled, poorly paid, subordinate dead-end jobs, with little chance for advancement. At the same time, these are also the most common jobs available. Two-thirds of the new jobs created in the Canadian labour force are in sales and services, suggesting a long-term trend that many young people will be confronted with throughout their working lives.

Source: Allahar and Côté (1998: 132–6).

Box   **A Window Full of Sky**

A few blocks away from the roominghouse where I live is an old people's home. 'Isle of the Dead', I used to call it. But one day, after a severe attack of neuritis, I took a taxi to that house of doom from which I had fled with uncontrollable aversion for years. Cripples in wheelchairs and old men and women on benches stared into vacancy—joyless and grief-less, dead to rapture and despair. With averted eyes I swept past these old people, sunning themselves like the timbers of some unmourned shipwreck.

The hallman pointed out a door marked 'Miss Adcock, Admissions'. I rapped impatiently. Almost as though someone had been waiting, the door opened, and there was Miss Adcock trimly tailored with not a hair out of place. Just looking at her made me conscious of my shabbiness, my unbrushed hair escaping from under my crumpled hat, the frayed elbows of my old coat. She pulled out a chair near her desk. Even her posture made me acutely aware of my bent old age.

The conflict, days and nights, whether to seek admission to the home or die alone in my room, choked speech. A thin thread of saliva ran down from the corner of my mouth. I tried to wipe it away with my fingers. Miss Adcock handed me a Kleenex with a smile that helped me start talking.

'I've been old for a long, long time,' I began, 'but I never felt old before. I think I've come to the end of myself.'

'How old are you?'

'Old enough to come here.'

'When were you born?'

'It's such a long time ago. I don't remember dates.'

Miss Adcock looked at me without speaking. After a short pause she resumed her probing.

'Where do you live?'

'I live in a roominghouse. Can anyone be more alone than a roomer in a rooming-house?' I tried to look into her eyes, but she looked through me and somehow above me.

'How do you support yourself?'

'I have a hundred dollars a month, in Social Security.'

'You know our minimum rate is $280 a month.'

'I've been paying taxes all my life. I understood that my Social Security would be enough to get me in here. . . .'

'It can be processed through Welfare.'

I stood up, insulted and injured: 'Welfare is charity. Why surrender self-respect to end up on charity?'

'Welfare is government assistance, and government assistance is not charity,' Miss Adcock calmly replied. 'I would like to explain this more fully when I have more time. But

---

Source: From *The Open Cage* by Anzia Yezierska. Copyright © 1979 by Louise Levitas Henriksen. Reprinted by permission of Persea Books, Inc., New York.

right now I have another appointment. May I come to see you tomorrow?'

I looked at Miss Adcock and it seemed to me that her offer to visit me was the hand-clasp of a friend. I was hungry for hope. Hope even made me forget my neuritis. I dis-missed the thought of a taxi back to the roominghouse. I now had courage to attempt hob-bling back with the aid of my cane. I had to pause to get my breath and rest on the stoops here and there, but in a way hope had cured me.

The prospect of Miss Adcock's visit gave me the strength to clean my room. Twenty years ago, when I began to feel the pinch of forced retirement, I had found this top-floor room. It was in need of paint and plumbing repairs. But the afternoon sun that flooded the room and the view across the wide expanse of tenement roofs to the Hudson and the Palisades beyond made me blind to the dirty walls and dilapidated furniture. Year after year the landlord had refused to make any repairs, and so the room grew dingier and more than ever in need of paint.

During my illness I had been too depressed to look at the view. But now I returned to it as one turns back to cherished music or poetry. The sky above the river, my nourishment in solitude, filled the room with such a great sense of space and light that my spirits soared in anticipation of sharing it with Miss Adcock.

When Miss Adcock walked into my room, she exclaimed: 'What a nice place you have!' She made me feel that she saw something special in my room that no one else had ever seen. She walked to the window. 'What a wonderful view you have here. I wonder if it will be hard for you to adjust to group living—eating, sleeping, and always being with others.'

'I can no longer function alone,' I told her. 'At my age people need people. I know I have a lot to learn, but I am still capable of learning. And I feel the Home is what I need.'

As if to dispel my anxiety, she said, 'If you feel you can adjust to living with others, then of course the Home is the place for you. We must complete your application and arrange for a medical examination as soon as possible. By the way, wouldn't you like to see the room we have available right now? There are many applicants waiting for it.'

'I don't have to see the room,' I said in a rush.

She pressed my hand and was gone.

About two weeks later, Miss Adcock telephoned that I had passed the medical exam-ination and the psychiatrist's interview. 'And now,' she said, 'all that is necessary is to establish your eligibility for Welfare.'

'Oh, thank you,' I mumbled, unable to conceal my fright. 'But what do you mean by eli-gibility? I thought I was eligible. Didn't you say . . . ?'

In her calm voice, she interrupted: 'We have our own Welfare man. He comes to the Home every day. I'll send him to see you next Monday morning. As soon as I can receive his report, we can go ahead.'

The Welfare man arrived at the appointed time.

'I'm Mr Rader,' he announced. 'I am here to find out a few things to complete your application for the Home.' The light seemed to go out of the room as he took possession of the chair. He was a thin little man, but puffed up, it seemed to me, with his power to give or withhold 'eligibility'. He put his attaché case reverently on the table, opened it, and spread out one closely printed sheet. 'Everything you say,' he cautioned, 'will of course be checked by the authorities.' He had two fountain pens in his breast pocket, one red and one black. He selected the black one. 'How long have you lived here?'

'Twenty years.'

'Show me the receipts.' He leaned back in his chair and looked around the room with prying eyes. He watched me ruffling through my papers.

'I must have last month's receipt somewhere. But I don't bother with receipts. I pay the rent . . . they know me,' I stammered. I saw him make rapid, decisive notations on his form.

'What are your assets?' he continued.

My lips moved but no words came out.

'Have you any stocks or bonds? Any insurance? Do you have any valuable jewelry?'

I tried to laugh away my panic. 'If I had valuable jewelry, would I apply to get into the Home?'

'What are your savings? Let me see your bankbook.' I stopped looking for the rent receipts and ransacked the top of my bureau. I handed him my bankbook. 'Is that all your savings?' he asked. 'Have you any more tucked away somewhere?' He looked intently at me. 'This is only for the last few years. You must have had a bank account before this.'

'I don't remember.'

'You don't remember?'

Guilt and confusion made me feel like a doddering idiot. 'I never remember where I put my glasses. And when I go to the store, I have to write a list or I forget what I came to buy.'

'Have you any family or friends who can help you?' He glanced at his watch, wound it a little, and lit a cigarette, puffing impatiently. 'Have you any professional diplomas? Do you go to a church or a synagogue?'

I saw him making quick notes of my answers. His eyes took in every corner of the room and fixed on the telephone. He tapped it accusingly.

'That's quite an expense, isn't it?'

'I know it's a luxury,' I said, 'but for me it's a necessity.'

He leaned forward. 'You say you have no friends and no relatives. Who pays for it? Can you afford it?'

'I use some of my savings to pay for it. But I have to have it.'

'Why do you have to have it?'

'I do have a few friends,' I said impulsively, 'but I'm terribly economical. Usually my friends call me.'

I could feel my heart pounding. My 'eligibility', my last stand for shelter, was at stake. It was a fight for life.

'Mr Rader,' I demanded, 'haven't people on Social Security a burial allowance of $250? I don't want a funeral. I have already donated my body to a hospital for research. I claim the right to use that $250 while I am alive. The telephone keeps me alive.'

He stood up and stared out the window; then he turned to me, his forehead wrinkling: 'I never handled a case like this before. I'll have to consult my superiors.'

He wrote hastily for a few minutes, then closed the attaché case. 'Please don't phone me. The decision rests in the hands of my superiors.'

When the door closed, there was neither thought nor feeling left in me. How could

Miss Adcock have sent this unseeing, unfeeling creature? But why blame Miss Adcock? Was she responsible for Welfare? She had given me all she had to give.

To calm the waiting time, I decided to visit the Home. The woman in charge took great pride in showing me the spacious reception hall, used on social occasions for the residents. But the room I was to live in was a narrow coffin, with a little light coming from a small window.

'I do not merely sleep in my room,' I blurted out. 'I have to live in it. How could I live without my things?'

She smiled and told me, 'We have plenty of storage room in the house, and I'll assign space for all your things in one of the closets.' 'In one of the closets! What earthly good will they do me there?' I suddenly realized that it would be hopeless to go on. Perhaps the coffin-like room and the darkness were part of the preparation I needed.

Back in my own place, the sky burst in upon me from the window and I was reminded of a long-forgotten passage in *War and Peace*. Napoleon, walking through the battlefield, sees a dying soldier and, holding up the flag of France, declaims: 'Do you know, my noble hero, that you have given your life for your country?'

'Please! Please!' the soldier cries. 'You are blotting out the sky.'

ferences and power imbalances between parents and their younger children. In families of procreation, parents have more power and economic control than their children because they assume the socializing and care-giving roles. In some of the worst cases power imbalances in families cause children to run away from home, quit school, and live on the streets. The emphasis in discussions of later-life families is on whether older parents are neglected by their adult children (Riley et al. 1988). Although these discussions tend not to be framed within the context of power, an imbalance is implied in which the power shifts from parents to children.

In summary, age-stratification researchers believe that people and roles are differentiated by an age structure, the elements of which are cohorts, age strata, age-related acts, age structure of roles, and age-related expectations and sanctions (Riley et al. 1972; Riley 1994). Although this approach has made the theory accessible to large audi-

ences of gerontologists (Dowd 1987), it has led to an over-simplification of the inequalities that are associated with age. Age strata with their related roles, expectations, and sanctions are assumed and are considered necessary to the functioning of society. Hence, this approach neglects the conflict that occurs when normative, in this case, age-based roles are violated.

The Political Economy of Aging

In the late 1970s and early 1980s social gerontologists began to critique the normative and highly individualistic theories that were prominent in aging research (Marshall and Tindale 1978; Tindale and Marshall 1980). Responding to these critiques and the calls for a more radical and critical approach, several scholars from different countries began to assess old age from a political-economy perspective (Estes 1979; Estes, Swan, and Gerard 1982; Guillemard 1982, 1983; Myles 1980, 1981, 1984;

Phillipson 1982; Townsend 1981; Walker 1981).

Political-economy theorists seek to explain the relative situation of older individuals by examining the relationship between the economic, political, and ideological structures that these systems of domination construct and reconstruct. Rather than explaining the problems that older people face as a result of their inability to adjust to retirement or aging, or to their naturally diminishing physical or mental capacities, political economists attribute the problems of older people to structural characteristics of the state and the economy and to inequalities in the distribution and allocation of resources that these institutions create (Estes 1979; Guillemard 1983; Myles 1984, 1989; Townsend 1981; Phillipson 1982; Walker 1981).

The following are among the topics that political-economy-of-aging scholars have examined:

1. How social policy has structured dependency in old age (Phillipson 1982; Townsend 1981; Walker 1981).
2. How the commodification of the needs of older adults benefits capital and creates an 'aging enterprise' (Estes 1979, 1991).
3. How old age is dependent on the division of labour in society as well as upon the distribution and allocation of resources. Related to this is how the institution of retirement creates a 'social death' that serves to define old age (Guillemard 1982, 1983).
4. The contradiction between the principles of democratic citizenship and the principles governing the capitalist system of allocation. In other words, the contradictions that arise in a social welfare state that assumes primary financial responsibility for its older population in a market economy that eliminates older people from the work force (Myles 1980, 1984, 1989).

To a greater or lesser extent, these studies consider the socially constructed nature of aging, old age, and dependency, the influence of ideology in this construction, the legitimation of social interventions pertaining to the elderly, the influence of state, capital, and labour relations on aging and old age, and the effects of social policy for the elderly (Estes 1991; Estes et al. 1996). Although it is beyond the scope of this chapter to discuss the specifics of each of these arguments, it is important to consider the role of the state in political-economy research.

Although the state comprises many institutions (such as those concerned with education, criminal justice, and health care), research from a political-economy-of-aging perspective generally equates the state with the governing bodies responsible for the policies related to social welfare. Social welfare in studies of aging most often refers to social security and health benefits (Estes et al. 1996). The importance of the state in this research stems from the power that it has over resource allocation and distribution because of its relations with capital and labour and its ultimate responsibility for the survival of the economic system (Estes et al. 1996; Myles 1989, 1995). From the political-economy perspective, the state is thought to represent the interests of the most powerful members of society and the existing social order is thought to be the result of power struggles in which the state participates (Estes 1991; Estes et al. 1996). Unlike consensus models, where the state is considered a 'neutral entity, operating in the universal interests of all members of society' (Estes 1991: 22), political-economy scholars generally believe either that the state acts to maintain its own bureaucratic control (Offe and Ronge 1982, in Estes 1991) or that power struggles within the state represent class struggles (Myles 1989).

Important advances in the study of social inequality and aging have come from the political-economy analysis of state policies regarding retirement and pensions. For instance, Myles (1980, 1984, 1989) shows that income inequality in older age is a function of both the overall levels of inequality in a society and the way pension systems alter or reproduce that inequality. Although inequalities in pre-retirement years persist after retirement, an understanding of income inequalities among older people and between the old and the young requires an analysis of public-pension structures. Traditionally, public pensions have been based either on pre-retirement incomes or on the idea of a national minimum benefit. In the first instance, pensions perpetuate class-, gender-, and ethnicity-based inequalities in older age by graduating pension incomes according to pre-retirement income. In the second instance, income equality among older people is achieved because the same sum of money is paid to everyone (this is known as flat-benefit structure) (Myles 1980, 1984, 1989).

Most Western capitalist nations have pension structures that combine flat and graduated pension schemes (Myles 1980). In Canada for instance, the Canada Pension Plan/Quebec Pension Plan (C/QPP) represents a graduated scheme whereby employ- ees and employers pay into the plan according to the employee's pre-retirement income. However, these plans have an upper contribution limit that renders the pension scheme graduated at the bottom and flat on top (Myles 1980). Old Age Security (OAS) is a Canadian pension scheme that traditionally guaranteed a flat, per month benefit to all people aged 65 and over. There are also several provincial and federal programs that, based on income tests, provide income supplements to low-income pensioners.

The interplay of the C/QPP and OAS highlights a contradiction in modern, liberal-democratic states between the rights attached to the ownership of property and the rights afforded to persons in their capacity as citizens (Myles 1984, 1989). According to Myles (1989), the strategies that different countries use to come to terms with this contradiction determines the relative pension benefits of older people and is a reflection of class struggles within the state. Thus, Myles (1989) suggests that the quality and quantity of pension benefits are largely a function of the political mobilization of the working class and the election of working-class parties.

This brief summary of Myles' work illustrates the power that the state has in determining the economic status of older adults. Few researchers who study aging would dispute this point, although there is some disagreement among political economists over the precise conceptualization of the state (see Estes 1991; Estes et al. 1996) and the relative emphasis that should be placed on the state relations (Myles 1989) as opposed to the relations of production (Guillemard 1982, 1983) in assessments of inequality. Most would also agree that old age and aging are socially constructed, in part, through these and other state policies.

Crucial to the political-economy-of-aging approach is the concept of social class. It is in discussions of social class that the Marxian influence in this perspective is most evident. Like Marx ([1867] 1967; Marx and Engels [1848] 1970), political-economy-of-aging researchers emphasize the relations of production in their conceptualization of social class and specifically the relations between those who own the means of production and those who do not (Guillemard 1982, 1983; Myles 1980, 1984, 1989; Phillipson 1982 ; Townsend 1981; Walker 1981). Thus, according to Guillemard (1982: 228), 'the traditional Marxist definition, which analyzes the class structure of the capitalist mode of production by basically contrasting the two antagonistic classes—capitalist and proletarian—must be upheld.'

The emphasis on the relations of production in the political economy of aging approach is paradoxical because most older people are no longer directly engaged in socially defined productive relations (Dowd 1980; Estes et al. 1982; Estes 1991). One strategy used by political economists to deal with this paradox is to use a life-course framework to assess the class relations of older adults according to their pre-retirement social class (Guillemard 1982, 1983; Phillipson 1982; Walker 1981). Aware of life-course processes, these political economists believe that power relations and resources in later life are shaped by people's earlier location within the social structure or their class position. Missing in these accounts is an analysis of the relationship between age relations and class relations as they structure inequality in later life. As others point out (Kohli 1988; Myles 1980), the

economic and social locations of older people result not only from class inequalities in early life but also from unique processes that are structured by age relations.

Estes deals with the contradiction between the Marxist emphasis on productive labour and assessing the social location of older people by turning to a more Weberian view of class. Drawing on Ehrenreich and Ehrenreich (1979: 11), she suggests that a social class is 'characterized by a coherent social and cultural existence; members of a class share a common life style, educational background, kinship networks, consumption patterns, work habits, and beliefs' (Estes 1991: 25). This definition of social class, Estes (1991; Estes et al. 1982) argues, is analytically appropriate for older people because it does not necessarily reflect productive relations and can capture the dynamics involved with aging and social inequality.

Another way of dealing with this paradox is to assume that more than one structure of domination influences social inequality. Myles (1989), who employs this approach, argues that inequality in older age is shaped by two structures of domination in Western capitalist societies. One is based on the productive relations by which power is given to those who control economic resources. The other is based in the polity where power is maintained by those who control political resources. The interplay between these power sources determines, both in principle and in practice (these do not often converge), the value of old-age pensions and hence, structures economic inequality in later life.

According to Myles (1989), negotiations between the polity and the economy over old-age benefits are framed in contradictions because the principles of democratic politics are inconsistent with the principles of a capitalist economy. Public pension systems represent the compromise between these sets of principles that have been negotiated in the political arena. Thus, Myles (1989) argues that income inequality in old age is structured by the state rather than being controlled by the market's invisible hand. However, a critical factor determining the extent of pension entitlements is the political mobilization of the working class (defined in Marxist terms), for Myles believes that power struggles within the state are essentially class conflicts.

The Social Construction of Old Age

Theorists who study age from a political-economy perspective tend to conceptualize age in terms of **age groups**. Thus, from this perspective Western capitalist societies are thought to be organized on the basis of whether one is old, middle-aged, or young. Political economists are, however, critical of these divisions, for they question how a particular chronological age becomes the marker by which one is defined as old and how the polity and the economy legitimize old age by defining it as a problem and then by developing solutions to deal with the problem (Estes 1979; Guillemard 1982, 1983; Myles 1989; Phillipson 1982; Walker 1981). Several political economists have argued that the transformation of old age into a social category based on chronological age was made possible by the establishment of a set of age-based pensions administered by the state and that old age has come to be defined in terms of retirement (Guillemard 1982, 1983; Myles 1989; Phillipson 1982; Walker 1981).

Estes describes an 'aging enterprise' that comprises 'programs, organizations, bureau-cracies, interest groups, trade associations, providers, industries, and professionals that serve the aged in one capacity or another' (Estes 1979: 2). The interests of those that constitute the aging enterprise are realized by making the elderly dependent upon the services they offer. In this way, the aged are processed and treated as a commodity (Estes 1979; Estes et al. 1982). The social construction of old age is especially fuelled by the medical profession, which has transformed aged bodies into sick bodies (Katz 1996). Further, this 'socially constructed problem, and the remedies invoked on the policy level, are related, first, to the capacity of strategically located interests and classes to define the problem and to press their views into public consciousness and law and, second to the objective facts of the situation' (Estes et al. 1996: 349).

The crisis ideology perpetuated by the state and the media regarding the aging of the population and social welfare is another example of how old age becomes socially constructed as a problem (Gee, 2000a). The message put across is that with the increasing number of seniors will come a financial burden too large for Canada to bear (the emphasis is usually on the baby-boom generation reaching old age). However, as Myles (1980, 1995) and others have demonstrated, although the structure of state spending, ownership, and control will probably change, it is unlikely that population aging will 'break the national bank'.

The political-economy approach has advanced the state of theorizing in gerontological research over the last 20 years by examining issues relating to older age through a critical lens. Nonetheless, the conceptualization of age by political economists is problematic on several counts. First, although this approach places emphasis on the structural characteristics that frame the aging experience and older age, age relations themselves are often considered secondary to issues of social class. Second, political economists of aging have been critical, and rightly so, of gerontological work that seeks to explain older age by 'naturalizing' the biological conditions of aging. In doing so, the tendency in this school of thought has been to understate the significance of the biological aging process. Rather than examining the subtle institutional procedures that discriminate on the basis of age (Charness et al. 1995), understating biological aging has the effect of rendering the aging process insignificant. Third, the emphasis in this approach on social structure leads to a neglect of human agency. This serves to depict older people as powerless and exploited without paying attention to the meaning older adults attribute to the aging experience and the strategies that they might use in dealing with some of their difficulties.

Conceptualizing Age in a Theory of Inequality

The way in which age is conceptualized depends a lot on what it is that people want to study. Age strata, biopsychosocial processes, cohorts, and age groups are the four views of age that emerge from the theories discussed above. Age-strata and stratification research stems from the economic-stratification research that was discussed in chapter 2 and for similar reasons is discarded here. More useful in studies of inequality are conceptualizations of age that consider biopsychosocial processes, cohorts, and age groups. The importance of biopsychosocial processes and cohorts are discussed in

greater detail in the conceptual framework presented in the chapter 7. For now, we must consider how age groups are viewed in this approach.

The idea from the political-economy approach that Western societies are loosely organized or structured according to socially constructed age groups is correct as long as we emphasize the social construction of age and recognize that the chronological ages associated with such groupings depend on the specific social context. There are old workers, middle-aged workers, and young workers, and there are old family members, middle-aged family members, and young family members; the chronological ages associated with age groups at work are different from the chronological ages associated with age groups in families.

According to the political-economy perspective, age groups structure social life in large part because an age structure serves the interests of the dominant social classes (Estes 1999; Myles 1989). Power does not seem to be derived from relations among age groups but rather from relations among classes. Yet, to understand age and inequality better, age relations must be conceptualized as oppressive relations in their own right. What then are age relations, and what distinguishes age relations from age groups?

In this book I argue that age is a relational and structural basis of inequality in Canada. On the one hand it is relational because people define their various positions in society according to their membership in an age group as it relates to other age groups. It is relational in a second sense because various rights and privileges are assigned on the basis of age-group location.

A relational understanding of age requires an emphasis on forms of oppression and power that are structured on the basis of membership in age groups. Recall that oppression occurs if (1) the welfare of one group of people depends upon the deprivation of another; and (2) the deprivation of the oppressed group depends upon the exclusion of the oppressed group from access to resources, rewards, and privileges. In this sense, age-based oppression, like gender-, race-, and ethnicity-based oppression can be both material and non-material, and it can take place in various settings including families, labour markets, states, and the education and health systems. The most obvious example of age-based oppression for older adults is the mandatory retirement that exists in most provinces in Canada and, for younger adults, it is the fact that the minimum wage varies with age.

Besides the economic power differences that result from material oppression, ideological power varies on the basis of age (Calasanti and Slevin 2001). Recall that the dominant ideology in North American culture favours youth and suggests that to be young is to be vibrant, beautiful, and happy whereas to be old is to be tired, unattractive, and grim. People are judged on the basis of whether they act their age, look their age, and are aging well. Yet, there is no linear relationship between age and ideological power, for while it is considered a great compliment to be told one looks young, an older woman who wears a mini-skirt may be scolded for not acting her age (see Calasanti and Slevin 2001).

Note

1. Notably, Riley may be overstating the significance of age here. In fact, Neugarten (1970; Neugarten and Hagestad 1976) has argued that the potential exists for an age-irrelevant society because the cohorts that are currently becoming old are like the young in terms of health, educational attainment, income security, and social values.

Glossary

Age group   In Canada, adults are often categorized as being old, middle-aged, or young. These are social constructions of age categories that are referred to as age groups.

Age and society paradigm   A modified and more dynamic version of Matilda White Riley's original approach. Known formally as the age stratification perspective.

Age strata   Recognizing that all societies are organized on the basis of age and the associated rites of passage, age strata and related terms such as age set refer to the stratification of societies along these lines. The assumption is that there are specific sets of roles and responsibilities attached to membership in a particular age stratum and that status varies accordingly.

Allocation   Processes through which individuals are assigned and reassigned to social roles.

Biopsychosocial process   The intersections of social, psychological, and biological factors that contribute to processes of aging and development.

Cohorts   Aggregates of individuals who are born in the same time interval.

Diachronic   Changing, in reference to states.

Socialization   Processes through which individuals learn how to engage in appropriate social roles. This involves learning and conforming to normative rules of behaviour.

Structural lag   The gap between the activities individuals engage in and the ability of structures to adapt to people's behaviour. Recall that in age stratification theory structures refer to institutions. The idea here is that institutional arrangements need to be modified to catch up with behaviour. For example, although women's rates of labour-force participation are higher than they ever have been, institutional family and work arrangements have not kept up with these changes. As a result, women (and some men) find it difficult to balance work and family responsibilities.

Synchronic Static, in reference to states.

Questions for Critical Thought

1. Discuss the social construction of age in the following domains: work, sport, health. How old does one have to be to be considered old in each of those domains? What factors influence the social construction of age in each domain?

2. Many provinces in Canada require their employees to retire at age 65. Yet, the human rights codes in these same provinces state that it is unlawful to discriminate on the basis of age. Using what you have learned about the social construction of age answer the following question: Is mandatory retirement discriminatory?

3. Age strata, age groups, and cohorts are related but distinct categories of analysis. Compare and contrast each of these terms in relation to the chronological age markers that are used to demarcate categories within these concepts.

4. Increasingly, consumer products are being developed for older adults. Using a political-economy perspective, apply the aging-enterprise concept to critically assess this marketing strategy.

5. Drawing on what you know about class, age, gender, ethnicity, and race, discuss why there has been less research on age structures of inequality than on the class, gender, ethnicity, and race.

Recommended Reading

Calasanti, Toni M., and Slevin, Kathleen E. (2001). *Gender, Social Inequalities, and Aging.* Walnut Creek, CA: Altamira Press. An excellent book that examines the intersections between age and gender as they frame social inequality throughout life and especially in old age. A particularly useful part of this book is its discussion of the body, which is rare in assessments of inequality.

Estes, C.L. (1999). 'The new political economy of aging: introduction and critique'. Chapter 1 in M. Minkler and C. Estes (eds.), *Critical Gerontology.* Amityville, NY: Baywood. In this article, Estes elaborates upon her previous work by including gender in her critical assessment of aging and later life.

Katz, Stephen (1996). *Disciplining Old Age: The Formation of Gerontological Knowledge.* Charlottesville: University Press of Virginia. A theoretically rich account of the 'social, political, organization, and epistemological conditions' that made the study of aging and old age possible.

Myles, J.F. (1984). *The Political Economy of Public Pensions.* Boston: Little Brown. A classic, Marxist account of how the state and economy intersect in creating situations of relative advantage and disadvantage in later life.

Riley, M.W., A. Foner, and J. Waring (1988). 'Sociology of age', in N.J. Smelser (ed.) *Handbook of Sociology.* Newbury Park, CA: Sage, 243–90. One of the most comprehensive accounts of how age is conceptualized from a sociological perspective.

Chapter 6

Actors and Agency

Introduction

As the preceding chapters show, sociological theories of inequality usually highlight social structures as key explanatory mechanisms of advantage and disadvantage in social life. In chapter 2 for instance, we saw how Frank McCourt's childhood poverty may be understood on the basis of his social class rather than on individual characteristics of his father or mother. Chapter 3 showed how the structure of gender can explain the various hardships that women such as Beth experience. Chapter 4 showed how racial projects structure the everyday experiences of individuals such as Crystal Samms, and chapter 5 outlined how age structures Hagar Shipley's experiences with her family. The preceding chapters also illustrate how structures of class, age, gender, ethnicity, and race constrain the choices of individuals who are disadvantaged as a result of these structures. Hence, individuals are poor not because they are stupid, unambitious, or lazy, but because they have had limited opportunities to be anything other than poor. However, if we take these structural explanations to the extreme there would be no room in society for the social mobility demonstrated by Frank McCourt.

Studies of **social mobility** are common in sociology. Some of this work characterizes countries on the basis of how much opportunity each has for social mobility. Studies of intergenerational mobility examine the characteristics of parents and assess the likelihood that children will attain higher-status occupations or educational levels than their parents. According to this research, children are constrained by their parents' education and occupation but in some countries there is more opportunity for ambitious and able children to do better than their parents. In explaining Frank McCourt's situation then, social mobility researchers might argue that McCourt's ambition and ability led him to move to a country that offered more opportunity than his homeland and as a result he was able to live a better life than his parents. But here lies a tension in sociology between structural and individual explanations of inequality. How do we explain the lives of McCourt's peers who did not do as well as he? The logic in social-mobility studies suggests that these children were less ambitious and less able to succeed than McCourt was. Although I do not dismiss the importance of ambition and ability in one's life, such explanations oversimplify the processes through which individuals either challenge or comply with the structural circumstances of their lives.

Unlike proponents of theories that emphasize the social structure over and above the actor, I do not start with the assumption that structure ultimately determines individual action. Individuals are not passive objects who conform to structural forces in their day-to-day lives. Nor do I start with the assumption that individuals act freely in a world that is untouched by structural pressures. Indeed, the range of options that are available to individuals vary, and they are constrained by a host of structural factors, including gender, class, ethnicity, race, and age. The theories of inequality presented in the preceding chapters vary in the extent to which they put emphasis on individuals, social structures, or some combination of the two. Indeed, we see glimpses of actors in even the most structural of these theories. As Marx suggested, 'men make their own history.' Yet, Marx did not focus as much on the human action that was required in doing this, but on the idea that while people make their own history 'they do not make it just as they please; they do not make it under circumstances chosen by themselves, but under circumstances directly encountered, given, and transmitted from the past. The tradition of all the dead generations weighs like a nightmare on the brain of the living' (Marx 1969: 398). The task ahead is to develop an approach to inequality that considers the intersections between social structures and individual actors. Before considering such intersections, however, I consider what is meant by actors and action in sociology.

Actors and Human Action

When sociologists discuss actors and social action they are examining social life at the level of the individual. Most of the sociological insight we have regarding individuals comes from the symbolic-interactionist tradition. **Symbolic interactionism** is, however, a diverse field of inquiry, and action is only one small component of it. Although in the symbolic-interactionist tradition, action is related to other individual-level concepts, such as self and identity, it must not be confused with them.

The sociological understanding of actors and action stems, in large part, from the work of Max Weber. In Weber's conceptions of social life and social theory, unlike those of Marx, actors and action were central. Indeed, according to Weber ([1922] 1978: 4), the objective of sociology is to interpret social action through causal explanations. Put simply, actors or agents are individuals who take part in action that is meaningful or intentional. Most of us, then, are actors in the sociological sense, most of the time.

Weber ([1922] 1978: 4) distinguished between **action** and **social action**. He considered that action is meaningful human behaviour from the point of view of the actor or actors involved. Action could be internal behaviour, as is the case when individuals justify or rationalize spending money on something that they don't really need. Action could also be external behaviour, including decisions either to act or not. Thus, action is implied in both sending flowers to someone on their birthday or deciding not to send them. Weber also suggests that action can refer to the act of having something done to you. For instance, whether you receive flowers on your birthday from someone, or not, is action because this act is subjectively meaningful to you.

Whereas action is behaviour that is individually meaningful, social action according to Weber refers to action that is meaningful only in relation to another person's behaviour. To explain this point, Weber ([1922] 1978: 23) discusses two cyclists who collide with each other. The fact that the cyclists collide is not social action but merely an event. Social action involves the negotiations that transpire after this event, whether it is a fight, an argument, or a peaceful resolution. Notably, and as with action, social action also includes deciding not to act or being acted upon.

Weber ([1922]1978: 24–6) distinguishes four **ideal types** of action and social action: traditional, affectual, instrumental (zweckrational), and rational (wertrational). Traditional action refers to actions that take place because they are habitual and have taken place in the past; affectual actions are the things people do to display emotion. The latter two types of action can be categorized as rational action and were of most concern to Weber. Zweckrational, or instrumental, action, refers to appropriate actions that individuals engage in while deciding how they can attain something and whether it is worth attaining. It also refers to meaningful assessments about what is required to achieve this goal. For example, if a woman decides that she wants to go to law school by carefully assessing what she is required to do, what she may have to give up, what the consequences of these actions is likely to be, and whether attaining a law degree is worthwhile, she is acting rationally in the zweckrational sense. Wertrational action, or value-rational action, refers to action performed to attain a goal rather than the means through which the goal must be attained. The actor does not compare different means to an end or evaluate the consequences of the action but rather acts out of conviction. A mother who is committed to breastfeeding her premature baby and does so against her doctor's orders and without regard for the possible conse-

quences of disregarding the status quo is acting in the wertrational sense.

Drawing on Weber, Talcott Parsons developed a theory of social action in which motivation and values determine action (Parsons 1951). Parsons believed that people are naturally capable of making choices and that they behave rationally to attain goals. Action is constrained by social systems, but it also conveys the idea that actors make conscious decisions to attain goals (Parsons 1949). Values and motives determine the type of action individuals engage in. Parsons identified three types of action—instrumental, expressive, and moral. Instrumental action, which is similar to the rational action of Weber's framework, refers to action that allows people to achieve a particular goal efficiently. Expressive action, which is similar to Weber's affective action, is the things people do to attain emotional satisfaction. Moral action, which is not found in Weber's framework, is behaviour that is concerned with standards of right and wrong (Parsons 1951: 45–51).

Whereas Weber acknowledged that an individual's behaviour could consist of more than one type of action simultaneously, Jürgen Habermas (1984) makes this point central to his theory of action. According to Habermas, there are different kinds of action, and what distinguishes them from one another has nothing to do with the act itself but rather with how agents are oriented to the act. The task for theory is to determine the various ways in which individuals may be compelled to act. In this vein, Habermas identifies five kinds of action: instrumental, strategic, normatively regulated, dramaturgical, and communicative (Habermas 1984: 273–337). Individuals engage in instrumental and strategic action when they are striving for success in the physical world (instrumental action) or success that takes the social context into account (strategic action) (Habermas 1984: 285–6). Normatively regulated action occurs when individuals take norms into account before acting. An individual who is concerned about how he or she appears to others and who acts accordingly is acting dramaturgically. Finally, communicative actions align with needs for mutual understanding and refer to actions people engage in to make themselves understood (Habermas 1984: 333–4).

To illustrate Habermas's views on action, let us consider the act of sitting down in a chair. This act cannot be classified as normatively regulated, instrumental, or dramaturgical unless we know what prompted the individual to sit down. The kind of action that this act reflects depends on whether it was in response to being tired or a reaction to someone saying 'please sit down.' If an employee enters an employer's office and chooses to stand until asked to sit down, this behaviour is normatively regulated action and probably involves some component of dramaturgical action as well. If the employee chooses to remain standing after the invitation to sit down, he or she is probably acting strategically as well.

Several key ideas from the work of Parsons, Weber, and Habermas have informed most sociological views on actors and action. First, part of being human is the capacity to make intentional choices. Second, action is not simply the act of doing, but also the act of not doing and having something done to you. Third, there is a rational component to action. In other words, people calculate the potential rewards and sanctions of their actions and

behave accordingly. Fourth, there is also a non-rational component to action. In other words, people act in traditional, normative, and affectual ways without rationalizing their behaviour. Fifth, any particular act may represent more than one kind or type of action. Sixth, people act within a social structure that constrains and orients action. This last point has been most contentious among sociologists and has led many to use the term agency in their work.

Agency

In an effort to avoid overly deterministic views of social life in which actors are like puppets being manipulated and constrained by social structures, scholars began using the term agency. Thus, in contrast to Parsons's theory of action, which emphasizes structure over and above action, the term agency stresses the idea that structures are composed of individuals who engage with social structure and can initiate structural change (Barnes 2000: 45–9). It is on this point that the similarities in theories of agency end. Indeed, there is little theoretical consensus over what agency means (Barnes 2000: 49) and whether or how it is different from the concept of action. In this section I will discuss two central views of agency, one put forth by Anthony Giddens and a second that Margaret Archer developed in reaction to Giddens.

Since the mid-1970s, Anthony Giddens has been arguing for a conceptualization of social structure that is inextricably bound to human action, and arguably, it is through his work that agency has become a fashionable term in sociology. In developing his theory, Giddens, claiming that agency and structure 'presuppose one another' (Giddens 1979:

53), develops a theory of structuration that involves

> the duality of structure which relates to the fundamentally recursive character of social life, and expresses the mutual dependence of structure and agency. By the duality of structure I mean that the structural properties of social systems are both the medium and the outcome of the practices that constitute those systems. (Giddens 1979: 69)

As Figure 6.1 shows, for Giddens, agency refers to a continuous flow of conduct by an actor or the activities of an agent and captures the ideas of progress, intentionality, and responsibility in the actions of human beings. Another central feature of agency is the capacity of actors to have acted differently, either by doing something else or by not acting at all. Involved in action are issues relating to its purposive or intentional processes, its human accountability, its unintended consequences, and the unacknowledged conditions under which it takes place.

Clearly, there are many similarities between Giddens's view of agency and the views of action espoused by Weber, Parsons, and Habermas. Indeed, Giddens uses the terms agency and action, and agent and actor interchangeably in his structuration theory; this has led Margaret Archer to be critical of his work and to theorize the distinctions between the two.

Unlike Giddens, who views structure and agency as part of the same thing, Archer favours analytic dualism in her approach to sociology. In other words, she believes that structure is analytically distinct and temporally separate from agency, yet 'intimately intertwined' with it (Archer 1995: 65–75). And, for Archer (1995: 252–3), agency and structure must be separated if we are to understand the processes through which both are transformed over time. This is the crux of Archer's response to Giddens, and it is a point that I return to below. For now, I will focus on Archer's conception of agency, keeping in mind that she makes a distinction between agency and social structure.

According to Archer (1995: 248–9) there is a fundamental difference between action and agency and between human beings, social actors, and social agents. Archer (2000: 261) defines agents as 'collectivities sharing the same life-chances' and suggests that all persons are agents because all persons occupy a position in relation to

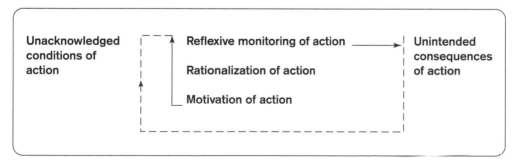

Figure 6.1   Action and Agency in Giddens's Framework

Source: Cassell (1993: 92).

the distribution of resources in society. Hence, agents are not individuals but rather groups of individuals who have in common their privilege or disadvantage in society. When Archer refers to an agent, she is referring, not to an individual, but rather to a single group of people who share the same life chances. People are born into pre-determined structures and are hence 'involuntarily situated beings' (Archer 2000: 262). Thus, according to Archer (2000: 262), 'humanity enters society through the maternity ward doors and we immediately acquire the properties of Primary Agents through belonging to particular collectivities and sharing their privileges or lack of them—as males/females; blacks/whites; foreigner/indigenous; middle class/working class.'

Social agency, then, refers to relations or interactions between groups and can affect social change and stability. It is 'reflective, purposive, promotive, and innovative' (Archer 1995: 249) and it often operates under 'unacknowledged conditions of situated action [that] lie beyond the ken of time-and-space-bound agents' (Archer 1995: 250).

According to Archer (1995, 2000), time links agents with actors and agency with action because we are born agents and grow into mature actors. Individuals have no choice about their agent status or what social collectivity they are born into. One is either male or female, white or black, middle-class or working-class, and so on. Choice, is however, implied in Archer's view of social actors. Social actors are defined as 'role incumbents' (Archer 2000: 283). Action, which seems to be synonymous with choice in Archer's view, is exercised as individuals decide which roles they will take and which they will reject. Agents vary, however, in the options and opportunities that are available to them, and therefore action is conditioned by agency.

This rather confusing view of agents and agency is Archer's critical response to approaches to inequality that view categorical distinctions (between women and men or blacks and whites, for instance) as individual characteristics. It is also a critical response to Giddens, who in Archer's view, does not allow for collective action in his theory. According to Archer, by conceptualizing agents as collectivities and actors as role incumbents, we eliminate both problems.

Intersections of Agency and Structure

As the preceding discussion shows, there is little agreement in sociology over what is meant by agency and action. Indeed, the two concepts are often used to mean the same thing. For the time being, then, let us think of the terms agency and action as interchangeable and as referring to the capacity of humans to make choices and to behave in meaningful, thoughtful ways. That being said, the next issue to consider is the relationship between agency and structure. Approaches to this topic fall into two broad camps. In the first 'enmeshed' camp, scholars consider structure and agency to be part of the same thing. In the second, 'analytic dualism' camp, scholars treat structure and agency as separate, yet related features of social life.

Enmeshed Approaches

One of the best-known enmeshed approaches was described by Peter Berger and Thomas

Luckmann in their book *The Social Construction of Reality*. Berger and Luckmann (1967) approach the relationship between structure and action in dialectic terms. According to Berger and Luckmann (1967: 18), reality is socially constructed through three dialectical processes in which 'subjective meanings become objective facticities'. The first of these processes is externalization. In this process individuals create their social worlds through their own actions. Social order is the result of past human activity, and the reproduction of this social order is only possible through this action. The second, objectivation process, involves the views that individuals share about social reality. In this process individuals come to understand that everyday life is ordered and prearranged. The third process is called internalization. Social order is legitimized and reinforced in this stage. Elements of socialization are apparent in this stage as individuals learn what is expected of them and behave accordingly. When individuals engage in this process by conforming to the existing social order they are also reproducing that social order. Reification of the social order occurs when individuals forget that human activity created the social order in the first place.

In Berger and Luckmann's (1967) approach to social life, individuals are treated as active participants. Individuals are able to evaluate the social structure and respond critically to it. However, the assumption is that individuals are on a level playing field in their ability to oppose any aspect of the social order. Furthermore, although this approach recognizes that many actors feel that their choices are limited, the responsibility for perceptions of limited choice lies in the hands of the individual. If individuals perceive that they have no choice, the dialectical processes that create and recreate the social structure disappear and the actor is only acted upon. This analysis underemphasizes the fact that it is in the interests of some individuals or groups to maintain the existing social order and to limit the choices available to others. Hence, by assuming that individuals are on a level playing field and by locating limited choice within the realm of individual responsibility, this approach neglects to consider power relations as fundamental elements in social life and in an explanation of inequality.

Perhaps the best-know enmeshed approach is Anthony Giddens's structuration theory. According to Giddens, structure is composed of rules and resources that are organized as properties of social systems. Rules are the norms and practices of a society, and resources are bound to power relations. In fact, resources are the bases of power that make up the structures of domination. Social systems are systems of social interaction that reproduce relations between actors or collectivities and have structural properties. The theory of structuration seeks to explain 'the ways in which that [social] system, via the application of generative rules and resources, and in the context of unintended outcomes, is produced and reproduced in interaction' (Giddens 1979: 66).

According to Giddens, structure is involved in the production of action, but structure is not thought to place limits on action. Giddens (1979: 71) suggests that 'rules and resources are drawn upon by actors in the production of interaction but are thereby also reconstituted through such interaction. Structure is thus the mode in which the relation between moment and totality expresses itself in social reproduction'. (See Box 6.1 for a conversation with Anthony Giddens on structuration theory.) Accordingly, the assumption that structure is involved in the production of action stands in opposition to the view that structure places limits on action. However, one might argue that to adhere to the assumption that structure is involved in the production of action is not to oppose the view

---

Box **Conversations with Anthony Giddens**

Interview Three

Structuration Theory

Christopher Pierson *The relationship between agency and structure and, paralleling that, between voluntarism and determinism is amongst the most ubiquitous and difficult issues in all social theory. In a number of texts in the late 1970s and early 1980s, culminating in the publication of* The Constitution of Society *in 1984, you developed your own distinctive resolution of this issue under the rubric of the theory of structuration. Perhaps I could begin by asking how you understand the traditional problem of structure and agency in social theory.*

Anthony Giddens It isn't a 'traditional problem', at least expressed in these terms. In the past it was usually seen as a dualism between individual and society, or the actor and the social system. Thinking about this traditional question of the relationship between the individual and society lay at the origin of the idea of structuration. I felt these were all unelaborated notions. People would speak of the individual as though it was obvious what 'the individual' was and quite often the same was true of 'society'. I wanted to break them down and give them more substance. The term 'structuration' I originally borrowed from French— I don't think it was used in English before I appropriated it. I wanted to place an emphasis on the active flow of social life. We should see social life not just as 'society' out there or just the product of 'the individual' here, but as a series of ongoing activities and practices that people carry on, which at the same time reproduce larger institutions. That was the original thought and from there I tried to elaborate each of the key terms, precisely by speaking of 'agency' and 'structure'. I put the idea of recurrent social practices at the core of what social sciences are about, rather than either starting with 'the individual' or starting with 'society'.

The Constitution of Society *is not necessarily the easiest book. Could you give some indication, in fairly straightforward terms, of how the theory of structuration resolves the dualism between structure and agency?*

This depends on two things really. The first is rethinking the notion of structure. I wanted to get away from the characteristic Anglo-Saxon way of conceptualizing structure, where structure is some given form, even a visible form of some sort. But I also sought to get away from the idea that agency is just contained within the individual. I wanted to see it as more of a flow of people's actions and to connect it with attributes of self-consciousness. Within certain limits, speaking a language shows us something about what the relationship between them might be. In other words, language has structure, language has form, but it isn't visible and it is only 'there' in so far as it actually forms part of what people do in their day-to-day use of it. That is what I call the recursive quality of language. I didn't claim that society 'is like a language', as the structuralists used to say; but language gives us key clues as to how recursiveness happens. 'Society' can be understood as a complex of recurrent practices which form institutions. Those practices depend upon the habits and forms of life which individuals adopt. Individuals don't just 'use' these in their activity but these life practices constitute what that activity is.

You talk in some places about structural effects and these being a better way of describing the impact of structure. Are 'structural effects' simply a euphemism for some kind of structure which is observable or has some existence other than through these perceived effects?

The structural properties of societies and social systems are real properties, but at the same time they have no physical existence. They are real properties in the sense in which they depend upon the routine qualities of people's actions and they can be very fixed or 'hard'. I don't want to discard the Durkheimian point that society is a structured phenomenon and that the structural properties of a group or a society have effects upon the way people act, feel, and think. But when we look at what those structures are, they are obviously not like the physical qualities of the external world. They depend upon regularities of social reproduction. Language has this incredibly fixed form. You can't go against even the most apparently minute rules of the English language without getting very strong reactions from other speakers. But at the same time, language doesn't exist anywhere, or it only exists in its instantiations in writing or speaking. Much the same thing is true for social life in general. That is, society only has form and that form only has effects on people in so far as structure is produced and reproduced in what people do. This to me applies right through from the most trivial glance you might give someone to the most globalized of systems.

Source: Giddens and Pierson (1998).

that structure places limits on action; the distinction is more subtle, and it lies more in language than in philosophy.

In fact, Giddens's discussion of power points to the differences, not the opposition, of the distinction between a structure that produces action and one that confines it. Giddens rejects views of power that treat it as a phenomenon of intended action. He also rejects views of power that locate it within the social structure as a medium by which group interests are realized. According to Giddens, Lukes comes closest to the correct consideration of power. Lukes (1974) suggests that

a person or party who wields power could have acted otherwise, and the person or party over whom power is wielded, the concept implies, would have acted otherwise if power had not been exercised. 'In speaking thus, one assumes that, although the agents operate within structurally determined limits, they none the less have a certain relative autonomy and could have acted differently.' (Cited in Giddens 1979: 91)

However, Giddens (1979: 91) argues that by suggesting that structure places limits on agency this approach is 'unable satisfactorily to deal with structure as implicated in power relations and power relations as implicated in structure'. This problem can be alleviated only 'if the resources which the existence of domination implies and the exercise of power draws upon, are seen to be at the same time structural components of social systems. The exercise of power is not a type of act; rather, power is instantiated in action, as a regular and routine phenomenon.' For Giddens it is important to consider the dialectic between action and structure in discussions of power: 'Resources are the media whereby transformative capacity is employed as power in the routine course of social interaction; but they are at the same time structural elements of social systems as systems, reconstituted through their utilisation in social interaction' (Giddens 1979: 92). Thus the subtle difference between the view that structure limits action and that structure produces action lies in Giddens' dialectical assumption that one mutually creates the other.

Arguably, a more accurate view of social life lies within the combination of these two approaches. Structure produces action, but the particular action that is produced lies within the realms of structure itself. Only under exceptional circumstances does human agency push structural barriers to the extent that structure itself is changed. Yet agents have a certain relative autonomy and could have acted differently even

though they operate within structurally determined limits. This view of social life challenges enmeshed approaches to social structure by considering agency and structure as distinct yet related social phenomena, as do theorists in the analytic-dualism camp.

Analytic Dualism

Scholars who favour analytic dualism suggest that enmeshed approaches are problematic because they conflate issues of structure and agency (Archer 1995, 2000; Layder 1994). Analytic dualists argue that agency and structure are two distinguishable, yet related features of social life (Archer 1995: 65). The task of sociologists, according to analytic dualists, is to examine how structure and agency are related and to analyze the processes and mechanisms that bind them together (see Box 6.2 for an example of an analytic dualist approach).

Although Erving Goffman (see Box 6.2) was much more concerned with the interactional order that the structural order, in his undelivered presidential address to the American Sociology Association, published after his death, he discusses the relationship between the two. In this paper, Goffman (1983) argued that there are social membranes that act like filters to determine which structural influences are let through and whether they are transformed in the process. Goffman (1983) argues that the relationship between structure and agency is fluid or 'loosely coupled' and that the membranes that connect them will vary depending on the empirical and historical reality that encompasses them. One example that Goffman (1983: 11) mentions is 'precedence through a door'. Door-opening rituals are

Box 6.2   Creative Knowledge You Can Put in Your Pocket™
CARD [6]: ERVING GOFFMAN

THEORY.ORG. UK TRADING CARD
Erving Goffman

American sociologist, 1922–1983, whose readable classic *The Presentation of Self In Everyday Life* (1959) saw social interaction as 'performances' by individuals, which vary according to context, usually intended to please the current 'audience'. Not merely micro-level social psychology, this book suggests how identities and ideologies are reproduced on a grand scale (see Giddens and structuration, card #1).

for more, see www.theory.org.uk/goffman   [Card 6 of 12]

STRENGTHS: New model of social action, fully explored

WEAKNESSES: May be too cynical. Is any behaviour 'real'?

SPECIAL SKILLS: Accidentally invented postmodernism?

Note: In fact, Goffman died in November 1982.

Source: <www.theorycards.org.uk/card06.htm>. Cards produced by David Gauntlett: see www.theory.org.uk. Reprinted by permission.

situated within the interaction order and 'at best they are likely to have only loosely coupled relations to anything by way of social structures that might be associated with them'. Indeed, Marilyn Frye (1983) quite convincingly discusses the practice of men opening doors for women as an expression of women's structural oppression in relation to men. But we know from our experiences that this 'act' is only loosely coupled with structural realities. There are men who hold doors open for painfully long periods of time for women who are 10 yards away from the door. Yet women hold doors open for men and some men do not hold doors open for women. A membrane is at work here such that 'social structures don't 'determine' culturally standard displays [but] merely help select from the available repertoire of

them' (Goffman 1983: 11). Although Goffman did not explain precisely how these membranes work, he does point us to the mutual and reciprocal constuitive processes between the structural and interactional orders.

In a similar vein, Pierre Bourdieu (1977) argues that structure and agency are linked through 'habitus'. Habitus refer to relatively stable sets of attitudes and beliefs that social actors hold and that reflect their social circumstances, such as their class background, gender ethnicity, race, and so on. They are 'generative principles of distinct and distinctive practices' (Bourdieu 1998: 8) that influence the behaviour of individuals as well as their preferences and choices. Habitus is the mechanism through which the structural circumstances of individual lives play out in the actions of individuals; what and how they eat, what activities they engage in, and how they are engaged in them. Individuals can act only on the basis of what they know, and past experience crucially influences action. Members of different classes or different ethnic or racial groups eat and play differently, not because of innate differences between them, but because their habitus informs their behaviour and distinctions get reproduced. Distinctions in behaviour among groups take on a certain value status, and here we see a striking similarity to Goffman's idea of loose coupling. Acts tend to be judged by members of society as good or bad, distinguished or vulgar, and so on. But the very same act can be perceived in many ways depending on the structural circumstances of both the actor and the perceiver. In sum, habitus is embodied in individuals as links between social structural circumstances and actions while they simultaneously serve to distinguish among groups of people (Bourdieu 1998).

A central problem in Bourdieu's work on structure and agency is that social change seems unlikely (Sewell 1992). Habitus influences behaviour but in a unidirectional way; it tends to constrain individual actions because people can only act on the basis of what they know and within the limits of their social structural constraints. This is, in part, because Bourdieu does not engage in a discussion of time, an issue which is at the heart of Margaret Archer's theory of structure and agency.

The problem of structure and agency is a 'vexatious fact of society' according to Archer; neither society nor social interaction can be discussed in isolation from the other, and yet there are properties of both that transcend the other (Archer 1995, 2000). In

fact, Archer takes issue with theorists in the enmeshed tradition, and much of her work serves as a useful critique of these perspectives. Archer elaborates upon her critique by developing a theory that relies on the notions of **morphogenesis** and **morphostasis**. The former means the processes that 'elaborate or change a system's given form, state, or structure' (Archer 1995: 166). The latter means 'processes in complex system-environmental exchanges which tend to preserve or maintain a system's given form, organization or state'. Put simply, Archer is referring here to the transformation and reproduction of social systems or the processes through which social systems change or remain the same. Hence, unlike Goffman and Bourdieu's views, one advantage of Archer's theory is that it explicitly considers social change.

According to Archer (1995: 193), problems with both practical theorizing and **realist social ontology** can be overcome by creating bridges between the two. To do so, Archer conceives of three related morphogenetic/static cycles that refer to structures, cultures, and agency (see Figure 6.2). Regarding the structural and cultural morphogenetic/static cycles, at time one (t_1), individuals are faced with structural and cultural conditioning. Between times two (t_2) and three (t_3), social interaction transpires. The result, at time four (t_4), is structural and cultural elaboration. In the morphogenesis of agency, time one is characterized by the socio-cultural conditioning of groups. Recall that, in Archer's view, agents are groups of people born in similar structural and cultural circumstances. Between times two and three group interaction occurs until at time four when there is group elaboration. All of these cycles intersect

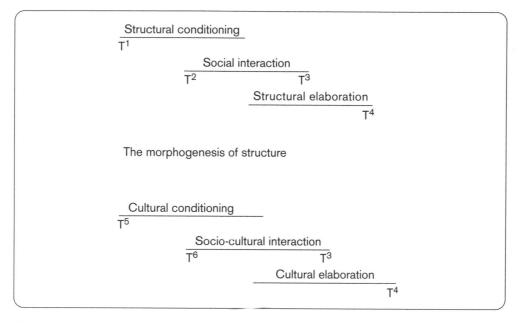

Figure 6.2 Archer's Morphogenesis of Structure and Culture

Source: Archer (1995: 193). Reprinted by permission of Cambridge University Press.

because they have as a common thread, social interaction which is the middle component in each of them.

One important component of Archer's theory is her distinction between corporate agents and primary agents. Corporate agents are more able than primary agents to affect social change because corporate agents are born into structural circumstances that better enable them to do so. In other words, 'corporate agents maintain/re-model the socio-cultural system and its institutional parts: primary agents work within it and them' (1995: 265). Social change occurs when the lives of primary and corporate agents are altered by the other group; it is 'the resultant of aggregate effects produced by primary agents in conjunction with emergent properties generated by corporate agents and thus does not approximate to what anyone wants' (1995: 265). In other

words, for social change to take place, agents with different amounts of power and resources enter into a state of conflict, and to resolve the conflict change occurs. A double morphogenesis is possible whereby 'agency leads to structural and cultural elaboration, but is itself elaborated in the process' (Archer 2000: 258). It is important to note that agents are not actors in Archer's view. Social actors only embrace sets of social roles and in as much as Archer is concerned with large-scale social change, social actors then have very little influence.

Archer's work is dense, complex, and overly complicated for the purpose of research on inequality. It is unclear, for instance, why Archer feels the need to distinguish agents from actors on the basis of what social circumstances individuals are born to. Individuals are born into lives that vary on continua of advantage and disad-

116 Understanding Social Inequality

vantage. This has much more to do with structure than with agency. Indeed, referring to groups of people who share similar life circumstances as agents who vary in terms of whether they can initiate social change serves to conflate structures and agents. Ironically, this is the very problem that Archer was trying to avoid in her work.

Nonetheless, it is clear from Archer's work (and from Goffman's and Bourdieu's) that there are advantages to analytic dualism. Primarily, analytic dualism allows us to study properties of structures and individuals that do not transcend one another. Empirically, this is a very useful strategy. And to the extent that sociologists are concerned with the practicalities of social inequality as much as abstractions of it, such approaches are worthwhile. However, these theories usually end up favouring structure (Archer and Bourdieu) or agency (Goffman), unlike enmeshed approaches. What is required then is a perspective that bridges enmeshed and analytic dualism approaches, a framework that gives equal theoretical weight to structure and agency while at the same time noting their distinctiveness.

A View in the Middle

William Sewell's (1992) account of structure and agency, which straddles the enmeshed and analytic-dualist positions, represents the best statement on the relationship between structure and agency. Notably, Sewell wants to retain Giddens's idea of the duality of structure, and he rethinks certain categories that are central to Giddens's structuration theory in this light. Simultaneously, he relies quite heavily on Bourdieu's notion of habitus, specifies nicely what is meant by agency and structure, and discusses how the

two are linked. Hence, his theory is best described as lying somewhere between analytic dualism and enmeshed approaches.

To begin, Sewell (1992) takes Giddens to task for the idea that structures are virtual and composed of rules and resources. To do so, he first explains what he means by rules. In line with Giddens, Sewell suggests that rules are things that people draw on when they engage in social interaction. They are the taken-for-granted informal schemas that guide individual action. This, of course, stands in opposition to a more common definition of rules as being formally stated regulations, such as laws, about how one should behave. To resolve the possible confusion about these two very different views of rules, Sewell suggests using the term schemas to refer to 'generalizable procedures' that apply to a variety of social interactions. Schema are generalizable in the sense that individuals draw on them in various contexts. Some examples of schema are etiquette, aesthetic norms, or the assumptions about how people should act on the basis of categorical distinctions such as female and male. Such 'recipes' for behaviour can be applied to both old and new situations and it is because of their 'transposability' that they may be understood as virtual. Hence, schema are virtual because they are generalizable and cannot be specifically located in any particular social interaction or in any particular place and time. In other words, they exist but they cannot be empirically specified.

Resources for Sewell are of two types, human (authorization for Giddens) and non-human (allocation for Giddens). Human resources are things such as physical strength, emotional commitments, and knowledge; and nonhuman resources are animate or inanimate objects; both can be deployed in power relations. Unlike Giddens, Sewell argues that whereas schema are virtual, resources are actual. Here lies a contradiction between Giddens and Sewell that Sewell must reconcile before moving on. If structures are virtual then they cannot be composed of both schema and resources as Sewell has defined them. If both are included, structures cannot be considered virtual. To solve this conundrum, Sewell argues that we should think of resources as the effect of schemas and schemas as the effect of resources. This is similar to Bourdieu's idea of habitus whereby a dialectic process occurs such that structures are formed through the mutual constitution of schemas and resources.

Having defined structure, Sewell goes on to describe how agents intersect with social structures, thereby potentially changing them. According to Sewell (1992: 20) 'To be an agent means to be capable of exerting some degree of control over the social relations in which one is enmeshed, which in turn implies the ability to transform those social relations to some degree.' Sewell conceptualizes agency as the human capacity to be intentional, creative, and ambitious, but he suggests that people develop different levels of this capacity depending on the structural circumstances they are faced with.

Because societies are characterized by a 'multiplicity of structures' that intersect one another, for example, the class, age, gender, ethnicity, and race structures that are discussed in this book, social actors are required to draw on a range of schemas and resources in their social interactions with others. This creative capacity allows for the possibility that actors may transpose the schemas that they draw upon from one

structure to another. Furthermore, because of the intersection and multiplicity of structures, individuals may attribute different meanings and interpretations to resources and schemas. The various meanings that may be attached to one structure or another by different actors depending on the array of schemas and resources at their disposal, signify the possibility of social change.

Finally, according to Sewell, there is a certain 'unpredictability of resource accumulation' that allows for the transformation of social structures. Because social actors attribute different meanings to structures, have the creative capacity to transpose schema from one to another, and are located across a wide array of structural positions, 'the resource consequences of the enactment of cultural schemas is never entirely predictable' (Sewell 1992: 18). What Sewell seems to be referring to here is the unintended consequences of one's actions: 'If the enactment of schemas creates unpredictable quantities and qualities of resources, and if the reproduction of schemas depends on their continuing validation by resources, this implies that schemas will in fact be differentially validated when they are put into action and therefore will potentially be subject to modification' (Sewell 1992: 18). Thus, according to Sewell, if the unintended consequences of one's action affect one's resources, then structural change is likely to occur (see also, Archer 1995, 2000).

In short, although Sewell suggests that his approach modifies and expands on Giddens's idea of the duality of structure, he veers away from the heart of this approach by discussing the intersections of structure and agency rather than their presuppositions. In other words, he discusses the unique characteristics of agency, agents, and structures in a way that Giddens does not, while at the same time recognizing their influences on one another. Furthermore, his approach avoids the problems with Bourdieu's tendency toward structural determinism and Archer's view that agents are only collectivities that share similar structural backgrounds. Although I quibble with some of the specifics of Sewell's approach to structure and agency (more on that in the next chapter), it is, in my mind, the best statement on the topic.

This chapter has examined various sociological meanings of action and agency and theoretical views on the links between agency and structure. In the next chapter, a conceptual framework is developed that specifies how the concepts introduced in the preceding chapters come together. Also clarified in the next chapter is the relationship between structure and agency. In particular, several mechanisms are introduced that link structure and agency in relation to social inequality.

Glossary

Action   Meaningful human behaviour from the point of view of the actor or actors involved.

Ideal types   Theoretical abstractions of a particular social phenomenon. Observations that are exaggerated and used as a methodological tool to provide insight into the observed phenomena and for assessing variations from the abstraction. Introduced by Weber.

Morphogenesis   Processes that elaborate or transform an existing system or structure.

Morphostasis   Processes that work at maintaining a system's organizational structure.

Realist social ontology   Philosophical assumptions about the realism of unobservable social phenomena. Realism is the idea that abstract ideas are real in their consequences. Social structures, for instance, are not directly observable but their social influence is real. Ontology refers to the philosophical beliefs about the nature or essence of being.

Social action   According to Weber, action that is meaningful only in relation to another person's behaviour.

Social mobility   The process of moving between status positions in society. Studies of social mobility sometimes examine country variations in opportunities for occupational or educational mobility. Other social mobility studies examine intergenerational mobility and whether children have surpassed the occupational status or educational attainment of their parents.

Symbolic interactionism   An approach to sociological study that situates analysis within interaction. People evaluate and define themselves on the basis of how they think others view them. And we imagine ourselves in other social roles and through role playing we learn appropriate and inappropriate forms of behaviour.

Questions for Critical Thought

1. Critically assess the views of action put forth by Weber, Parsons, and Habermas. Evaluate an action that you do every day according to each of these perspectives.

2. Consider the decision that you made to attend university. What role did structure play in that decision? What role did agency play? Which theory of structure

and agency best explains your decision-making process?

3. Compare and contrast the theories of structure and agency put forth by Giddens and Sewell. Why is Sewell's theory more applicable than Giddens's structuration theory to the study of social inequality?

4. Does Sewell's theory improve upon the work of Berger and Luckman? If so, how? If not, why not?

5. In chapter 3, housework and child care were discussed in relation to the oppression, exploitation, and opportunity hoarding that characterize the structure of gender relations. Continue with that discussion by evaluating how Goffman's idea of membranes relates to the negotiation of childcare and housework in families.

Recommended Reading

Bourdieu, Pierre (1998). *Practical Reason: On the Theory of Action*. Stanford: Stanford University Press. A collection of Bourdieu's lectures that cover his key ideas, including that of habitus.

Giddens, A. (1984). *The Constitution of Society: Outline of the Theory of Structuration*. Berkeley: University of California Press. This book develops Giddens's seminal work on structuration theory.

Goffman, Erving (1983). 'The interaction order'. *American Sociological Review* 48, February: 1–17. This is Goffman's presidential address to the American Sociological Association, which was published shortly after his death. Notwithstanding the title, this paper considers the relationship between the interaction order and social structures.

Layder, D. (1994). *Understanding Social Theory*. Thousand Oaks, CA: Sage. This book focuses on the agency/structure dualism in sociology. It covers theorists ranging from Dorothy Smith to Michel Foucault.

Sewell, William H.J., Jr (1992). 'A theory of structure: Duality, agency, and transformation'. *American Journal of Sociology* 98: 1–29. In this excellent, clearly written article on agency and structure, Sewell draws heavily on Giddens and Bourdeau to develop his own ideas about the production and reproduction of social life.

Chapter 7

Actors and CAGE(s)

Introduction

The preceding chapters have outlined many of the elements of inequality that are included in the conceptual framework that is developed in this chapter. This chapter brings these elements together in a coherent whole. As a first step it is important to acknowledge the general assumptions that guide this approach. These assumptions are informed by several branches of critical theory and are summarized by Connidis and McMullin (2002: 559) as follows:

1. The social structure of Western nations is comprised of interlocking sets of social relations that privilege certain groups of people over others. Key sets of social relations include those that are based on class, gender, age, race, and ethnicity (Acker 1988; Collins 1990; Glenn 1992; McMullin 1996; Tilly 1998).
2. Individuals, though constrained to varying degrees by the social structure, attempt to exert control over their lives. They act with agency (Dannefer 1984; Habermas 1987; Lukes 1974; Marshall 1995; Weber [1922] 1978).
3. Social life is negotiated through interaction. It is constituted by and constitutive of interaction (Berger and Luckman 1967; Dannefer 1984; Giddens 1979; Marshall 1995).

4. Society is more accurately characterized as based on conflicting interests than on consensus. Different placement in the social structure creates conflicting interests and investments in the status quo (Marx [1848] 1983). There is an essential conflict or tension between the constraints placed on individuals by social structure and the desire of individuals to act with agency (Habermas 1987). Such an approach recognizes that conflicts are not episodic and unpredictable but rather are patterned features of relationships (Morgan 1985).

Although theoretical assumptions influence all sociological work, they are often left unacknowledged. Yet, to understand theoretical frameworks, the assumptions that guide them must be recognized. The assumptions are listed for readers to keep in mind as they consider the conceptual framework developed here. To develop the framework, this chapter begins by revisiting Anna's life (the woman discussed in Chapter 1). It then discusses social time and the life-course perspective and in doing so introduces the substantive-birth-cohort concept. Next, the concepts discussed in earlier chapters are integrated into the framework throughout this chapter. Finally, the conceptual framework is used to analyze Anna's life.

Figure 7.1 depicts Anna's life graphically. As shown on the far left of Figure 7.1 and as mentioned in Chapter 1, Anna was born to white, English-speaking parents of British descent, in 1915 during the First World War. She grew up on a farm in Ontario with her mother, father, and two brothers. Although it was only a small farm, Anna's father and mother worked hard and were able to provide their family with life's essentials. The arrow at the bottom of Figure 7.1 maps out the timing of some life events and transitions that Anna experienced. Anna graduated from high school, an unusual achievement for rural girls in that day, and although she had the opportunity to go on to teacher's college, as her mother had done before her, she decided to marry John Warner, a local man who was seven years her senior. She married well. John's family were well-to-do farmers, and with their help, Anna and John began their marriage in the late 1930s in relative financial stability. John and Anna moved to town and had two daughters, one in 1941 and the other in 1943.

Located in the centre of Figure 7.1 are the central activities that Anna engaged in to maintain her life and the life of her family. Anna was always a homemaker, and John never had a stable job. His older brother, who was married and childless, inherited his father's farm, and John worked for him occasionally. John also bought houses, restored them, and sold them for a profit. Money was tight in the Warner household, but no one seemed to want for anything. There was food on the table, John had paid for the house in full when he bought it, and the family had a few good clothes.

John died suddenly in 1970, when he was 62 and Anna was 55. His estate comprised some savings and his house. He had stipulated in his will that Anna could draw $200 per month from his estate until she either remarried or died, at which time the estate would be divided equally among her daughters. Suddenly, Anna was poor. Though her income was well below the qualifying cut-off for social security, she refused to apply for it and was too young to receive old age security. The will stipulated that she could not sell the house. Other than a brief stint in business college, Anna had no training, no work experience, and no marketable skill. Besides, at 55 she was unlikely to find work. Her daughter hired her to babysit her grandchildren and for the next 10 years she made do with the clothes she already owned, shopping at yard sales and eating anything she could buy for next to nothing in the grocery store—old bread, food in dinted cans, and so on. After 10 years Anna turned 65 and began receiving the old age pension. She was still poor but no longer destitute. Five years later Anna's sister-in-law, the wife of John's childless brother who inherited the family business, died and left Anna one-third of her quite large estate. Suddenly, at age 70, Anna was better off financially than she had ever been before.

In chapter 1, I noted that a central aim of this book was to develop an understanding of inequality that would help us to explain the ebb and flow of poverty that Anna experienced. In the preceding chapters class, age, gender, ethnicity, and race have mostly been considered as static structures that constrain opportunity. Yet, as was noted in chapter 1, social inequality, as it is experienced by individuals, is dynamic, and to understand it we need to take social time into account.

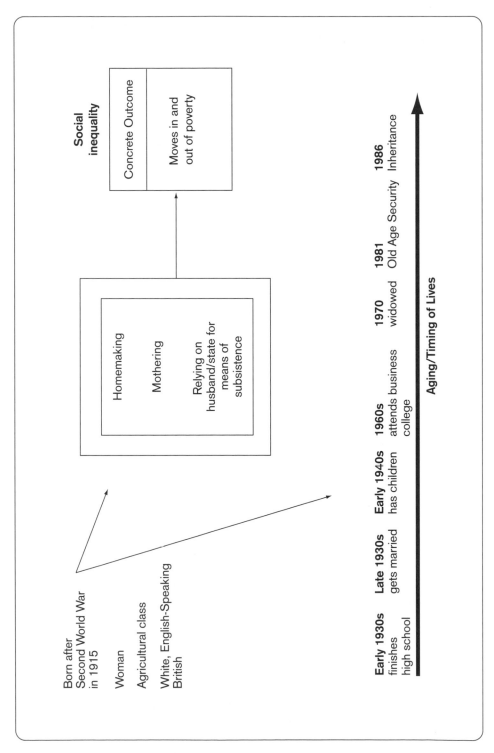

Figure 7.1 Anna's Life

Social Time

Structural accounts of gender and race or ethnicity rarely take social time into account. This is partly because gender, race, and ethnicity are usually considered to be ascribed and static individual characteristics. Yet, historical sociology shows us the importance of the social context to variations in gender, race, and ethnic inequality (Adams 2000; Laslett and Brenner 1987). Moreover, the individual experiences of gender, race, and ethnic inequality may vary throughout one's life. Social time is, however, considered in studies of social mobility (see chapter 6) that examine whether social class changes across generations. It is also considered in studies of aging that assess the biopsychosocial processes associated with the passage of time. Indeed, Anna's life shows that to understand the structural inequalities that individuals face throughout their lives, we must address the intersection of individual and historical time. The life course approach, as outlined by Glenn Elder (1974, 1995), provides useful insight into how issues of time might be considered in an integrated framework.

The Life-Course Perspective

The life-course idea that people progress through life by taking on different roles and statuses at various ages is not new. Among the earliest depictions of the life course is the fifteenth-century Dutch painting by an anonymous artist entitled *The Stairway of Life* (see Figure 7.2). In this picture we see a boy who ascends in his life until he reaches a peak at age 50 and then descends thereafter until his death at age 100. The various roles and statuses this boy takes on are con-veyed through his clothes, the objects he holds, and his posture on each step of the stairway. Until recently, Europeans for centuries were given stairways made in various media that they would hang on the walls in their homes as gifts to mark life transitions such as birth or marriage (Dekkers 2000).

The life-course perspective develops the ideas represented by *The Stairway of Life* and theoretically guides research in problem identification and formulation (Elder 1995; Elder and O'Rand 1995). In particular, it has 'made time, context, and process more salient dimensions of theory and analysis' (Elder 1995: 104). Life-course research conceptualizes social time by recognizing and attempting to understand (1) that individuals begin the dynamic and contextual aging process at birth; (2) that historical time, period, and cohort influence the aging process; (3) that aging is a biopsychosocial process which is related to and is shaped by social contexts, cultural meanings, and social structural locations; and (4) that age-related life transitions and trajectories are heterogeneous and are marked by sequences of events and social transitions (Elder 1995; Elder and O'Rand 1995; Hagestad 1990; Hagestad and Neugarten 1985; Passuth and Bengtson 1988; Bengtson et al. 1994).

According to Elder (1994, 1995), the timing of lives and lives in time and place are two of the central principles of the life-course paradigm. Issues related to the **timing of lives** include historical time, the social timing of transitions across the life course, the synchrony (or asynchrony) of individual careers, and one's life stage at the point of social change (Elder 1995). Thus, 'social timing refers to the incidence, duration, and sequence of roles; and to related age expectations and beliefs' (Elder 1995: 114).

The Stairway of Life, c. 1640

Figure 7.2 The Stairway of Life, Anonymous c 1640—

The **lives in time and place** principle refers to the effect of contextual change, caused by a particular historical event, on individual life trajectories, noting that historical changes do not uniformly occur in different places. This is conceptually distinct from other life-course work that either studies birth cohorts in their relevant historical context (as in age-stratification theory—see chapter 5) or examines individual life courses as they are framed and constrained by a social system (see Mayer and Muller 1986). Instead, Elder's research starts with the properties of social change and then moves to an assessment of how this change affects individual life trajectories (Elder 1995), taking into account the age of individuals at the time of the historical event that led to social change. Thus, Elder (1974, 1995) suggests that the effects of the Depression (with its resultant social changes) once traced through individuals and families, shows that children of the Depression developed individual characteristics, such as a 'sense of industry and responsibility from the required helpfulness experience of needy households' (Elder 1995: 110).

Figure 7.3, which depicts my conceptual framework, illustrates the influence of the life-course perspective (Elder 1995) in my

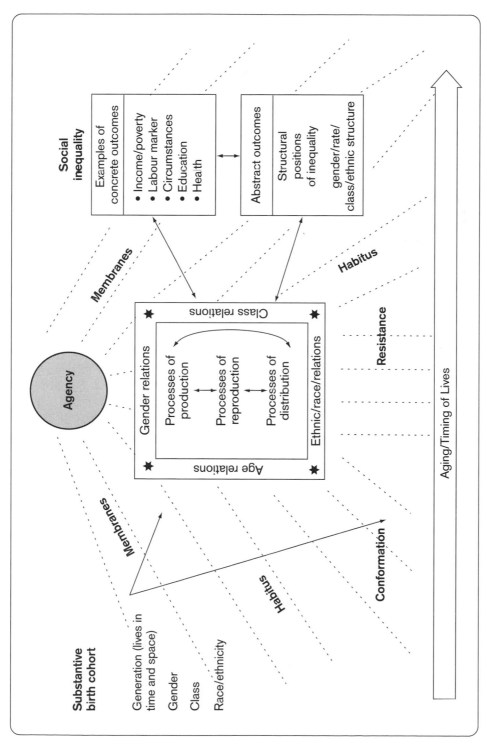

Figure 7.3 The Coalescence of Class, Age, Gender, and Ethnicity

work. The lives-in-time-and-place principle is located on the far left of the diagram under the umbrella term **substantive birth cohort**. Substantive birth cohorts also represent the generation, gender, ethnicity, race, and class positions in which people are born through no choice of their own. This concept takes social time into account, which Margaret Archer (see also chapter 6) alludes to when she says, 'We are all born into a structural and cultural context which, far from being of our own making, is the unintended resultant of past interaction among the long dead' (Archer 1995: 253). The social structures and experiences of gender, ethnicity, race, and class have been discussed in previous chapters, but it is their relationship to the generation concept and the ideas of social time that require introduction here.

The term **generation**, as used here, is similar to the lives-in-time-and-place concept in Elder's life-course perspective. The term generation is used in various ways in the literature. Some scholars refer to generations as age-based locations within families. Hence, four generation families are those comprising great-grandparents, grandparents, parents, and grandchildren. Others, however, use the concept of generation to mean time-specific social locations that are similar to social-class locations and that might give rise to group conflict and consciousness (Mannheim [1928] 1952; Marshall 1983). It is the latter understanding of generation that I use here.

In his classic article 'The Problem of Generations', Karl Mannheim ([1928] 1952) generalized Marx's conception of class to demonstrate the sociological significance of generations. Mannheim criticized previous assessments of generations, arguing that they relied too much on chronological age or the biological fact that generations reproduce themselves. Hence, past treatments of generations neglected the true sociological importance of generational relations. According to Mannheim, although it is true that the sociological phenomenon of generations is based on the biological rhythm of birth and death, 'Were it not for the existence of social interaction between human beings—were there no definable social structure, no history based on a particular sort of continuity, then generations would not exist as a social location phenomenon' (Mannheim [1928] 1952: 290–1).

Thus, in the first place Mannheim believes that a generation represents a unique type of social location based on the dynamic interplay between being born in a particular year and the socio-political events that occur while a birth cohort comes of age. Generational location is an objective fact similar to that of class position. Hence, all individuals, whether they acknowledge it or not, belong to a particular generational location within a given society.

According to this view of generations, its importance lies, not in the fact that one is born in a particular year, but in the sociological relevance of being born at a particular historical time in a given society. It reveals that belonging to the same generation

> endow[s] the individuals sharings in them with a common location in the social and historical process, and thereby limit[s] them to a specific range of potential experience, predisposing them for a certain characteristic mode of thought and experience, and a characteristic type of historically relevant action. Any given location, then, excludes a large number of possible modes of thought, experi-

ence, feeling, and action, and restricts the range of self-expression open to the individual to certain circumscribed possibilities (Mannheim [1928] 1952: 291).

The significance of substantive birth cohorts may be illustrated with a simple example. The life choices available to a white English woman born into a working-class family in 1920 are not the same as they are for a white English woman born into a working-class family in 1965. For the first woman the likelihood of finding work in the manufacturing sector (particularly because she was probably looking for work during the Second World War) is much greater than it is for the second woman, who is likely to find work in the service sector. The Second World War, while significantly influencing the first woman's life will only indirectly influence the second woman's life. Likewise, the second woman will be influenced by the women's movement in a much different way than the first. Not only are the relations of production, reproduction, and distribution different, but the way they are shaped by gender, age, and racial, and ethnic processes is considerably different. In turn, all of these processes influence and are influenced by the timing of lives.

The timing-of-lives concept and aging are dimensions of social time (which are represented along the bottom of Figure 7.3) and both are influenced by substantive birth cohorts. The timing-of-lives concept mirrors the life-course perspective's conceptualization of it (see above). Thus the substantive birth cohort that one is born into shapes the incidence, timing, duration, and sequencing of various life course events and transitions such as marriage, parenthood, retirement, and so on. For instance, people who were

born in the generation that came of age during the Depression were more likely to delay marriage than the generation that followed them, in part because of the macro-economic situation in which members of each generation were required to make decisions.

The process of aging, which is also shown along the bottom of Figure 7.3, is the final dimension of social time that is considered in this framework. Aging refers to the experiences that come with the passage of time, as well as the biopsychosocial processes that alter one's body and physical capabilities. The substantive birth cohort into which one is born influences aging processes to the extent that physical decline can be reduced by certain social habits that have changed over time such as eating, smoking, and exercising. Such processes are also influenced by the generation, gender, ethnicity, race, and class in which one is born, as is evident from the different life expectancies of these various groups at birth.

Social Processes

Located in the centre of Figure 7.3 are the interrelated processes of production, reproduction, and distribution. These three processes refer to the organization and nature of the activities that are required for the survival of individuals and species. Recall from chapter 2, that processes of production are the ways by which raw materials are converted into useful and valuable objects. Processes of distribution are the ways in which material resources change hands in society (Acker 1988 1999; Weber [1922] 1978). Distributive processes include wage, state, personal, and marital transfers (Acker 1988). Processes of reproduction are the ways in which life is maintained both daily and intergenerationally (Laslett and Brenner 1987). Social processes of production, reproduction, and distribution are interrelated. People who have indirect relationships with a particular social process tend to be more directly involved with another. A retired worker, for instance, has no direct relationship to production processes but is indirectly linked to them through the distributive processes by which he or she receives a company pension. A divorced father may not have a direct relationship with the processes of reproduction but may be linked to those processes through the distribution of money to his children and former wife.

Processes of production, distribution, and reproduction become sociologically significant when we recognize that they are carried out by individuals in interaction with others. In other words, it is the social relations of production, distribution, and reproduction that are of primary concern to sociologists. In the literature on social inequality, researchers generally emphasize one set of social relations as it relates to a specific social process. For example, social-class relations are often seen as the root of inequality in production processes, and indeed the terms 'social class relations' and 'relations of production' are often used interchangeably. Similarly, gender relations are most often considered at the heart of inequality in processes of reproduction. However, there is ample evidence to suggest that the rewards, privileges, and resources associated with one's relationship to the processes of production, distribution, and reproduction are affected by a complex interplay of class, age, gender, ethnic, and race relations. Class, for instance, does not account for all of the power differentials that

occur as a result of production processes. Hence, it is unacceptable to suggest, as Wright does, that gender-based worker exploitation is simply a specific kind of class relation; this privileges class in the analysis of inequality and ignores the uniqueness of other forms of disadvantage (Wright 1997). What is needed is a theoretical shift in which the relations of production will assume not only class relations but gender, ethnic, racial, and age relations as well.

Social Structure

The existence of the social processes discussed above does not necessarily imply an outcome of social inequality. Rather, understanding how these processes are structured is of fundamental importance to understanding and explaining social inequality (McMullin 2000). Figure 7.3 shows that class, age, gender, race, and ethnic relations frame the interrelated processes of production, reproduction, and distribution. Here, the connections (indicated by the stars in Figure 7.3) among class, age, gender, race, and ethnic relations, and the power and rewards associated with one's position within these structures, shape the ways in which production, reproduction, and distribution are organized.

As noted in the previous chapters, class, age, gender, and ethnicity or race are conceptualized as sets of *social relations, characterized by power*, which are fundamental structures or organizing features of all aspects of social life, including the processes of production, distribution, and reproduction (Ng 1993). Embedded in these social relations (or structures) are the taken-for-granted informal schema (see Sewell 1992, and chapter 6) that guide individual action (e.g., ideas about appropriate behaviour) and various human resources (e.g., physical strength and knowledge) and non-human resources (e.g., money and property). Structures of class, age, gender, ethnicity, and race are formed through the mutual constitution of such schemas and resources (see Sewell 1992, and chapter 6).

Although the processes of class, race, ethnic, age, and gender formation are unique, several interrelated theoretical constructs have been identified in preceding chapters that apply, in varying degrees, to all of them: oppression (see chapters 2 to 5), power (see especially chapter 2), exploitation, and opportunity hoarding (chapter 3 and Tilly 1998). Recall that oppression occurs if (1) the welfare of one group of people depends upon the deprivation of another; and (2) the deprivation of the oppressed group depends upon the exclusion of the oppressed group from access to resources, rewards, and privileges. As we have seen in the preceding chapters, in contemporary Canadian society both conditions of oppression apply to class, age, gender, race, and ethnic relations.

Oppressive relations are produced and reproduced through power. Power results from the control that certain groups have over economic, political, and ideological resources (Grabb 2002). It is through these systems of control that certain groups exclude others from gaining access to resources, rewards, and privileges. Thus, certain groups are deprived vis à vis others through mechanisms of power. Notably, there is a recursive relationship between power and oppression that is actualized in class, age, gender, ethnic, and race relations, and through which patterns of inequality are produced and reproduced.

This recursive relationship is fostered through two mechanisms of control. First, exploitation produces oppressive relations when individuals and groups control resources (economic, political, ideological) and use those resources to their advantage by mobilizing the efforts of others for their own gain (Tilly 1998). Opportunity hoarding is a second mechanism through which oppressive relations are produced and reproduced. Here, members of a particular group obtain a valuable resource that reinforces the group's privilege and status. The group then acts in ways that will ensure the maintenance of their monopoly over that resource (Tilly 1998).

When the disadvantage of certain groups depends on the advantage of others the oppression that results is relational. It is in this sense that class, age, gender, ethnic, and race relations were discussed above. Relationality takes on a second meaning when it is positioned within a structure and agency framework. Here, a relational understanding of class, age, gender, ethnic, and race relations takes into account the meaning that is attributed to these categories of inequality based on relative positioning within social hierarchies (Stasiulis 1999; Glenn 2000). Meaning is derived through the assessment of difference by which 'oppositional categories require the suppression of variability within each category and the exaggeration of differences between categories' (Glenn 2000: 10). Hence, even though men and women are more physiologically similar than different (Lorber 1994), small differences are exaggerated and problematized. Men appear genderless, and the inequalities that women face are assigned meanings that are derived from these differences (Glenn 2000).

The graphical depiction of class, age, gender, ethnicity, and race relations surrounding the processes of production, reproduction, and distribution resembles a picture in its frame. This representation illustrates that these structured sets of social relations are not thought to be causally linked, in any linear sense, to the processes of production, distribution, and reproduction. Rather, they mediate these processes and cannot be separated from them. This approach allows for considerable latitude in assessing both the independent and combined effects of these sets of relations on the processes of inequality. This suggests, following Wright's (1997) discussion of the connections between gender and class, that some of what is consequential about each of these sets of relations occurs independently of the others, and yet an assessment of inequality would be incomplete without consideration of the intersecting influences as well.

However, this does not imply that one can pick and choose among the components of the framework that one deems worthy of study. Rather, the issue of coalescence in this approach suggests that inaccurate assessments of social inequality will result from such strategies. Although one can examine both the independent and interlocking effects of the components of this, the processes and sets of relations contained within it must be considered as a whole if we wish to understand the nature of social inequality. To examine one component without the other will present a distorted picture of social reality. It will also miss the fact that social life is mutually constituted by gender, class, race, age, and ethnicity (Glenn 2000). Thus, the coalescence represented in this approach might be visualized as a colourful and tightly woven fabric; the threads may be discernable from one another, but the removal of any one of them distorts the overall pattern.

Interestingly, the first letters of class, age, gender, and ethnicity or race form the word CAGE. There is a lot of imagery that comes to mind when one hears the word CAGE, and much of it is relevant to studies of inequality. I use this acronym to depict images of the social-structural constraints that individuals and groups often face. However, to make too much use of this acronym would diminish the significance of individual agency in systems of inequality and in everyday life.

Agency and Structure: Actors and CAGE(s)

In Figure 7.3, agency flows throughout the diagram in a way that represents its omnipresence in social life. Recall that agency is the ability to exert some control over the social relations in which one is enmeshed (Sewell 1992). Agency includes decisions to act and not to act, and discussions of agency and structure must take into account both the intended and unintended consequences of one's action or non-action. The location of agency at the top of the diagram does not imply that it has a superior status to social structure. Rather, it is meant to capture the idea that agency runs through social structures and that 'social structure does not stand outside of the human, social behaviour that produces it yet, it nevertheless take on properties that transcend the behaviour of those who construct it' (McMullin and Marshall 1999: 309)

As argued in chapter 6, this approach favours analytic dualism over enmeshed accounts of the relationship between structure and agency. Recall that analytic dualism suggests that there is something unique about agency and about social structure, even though both are intricately connected. Notably, the theories presented in chapter 6 were not established primarily as explanations of social inequality but were concerned with explaining the relationship between structure and agency in relation to social change. Although social change is a central topic in the study of inequality, it is not the subject of this book. However, the organizational and conceptual framework developed here will help us to understand social inequality as it exists in Canada in the early part of the twenty-first century. A remaining challenge is to explain the mechanisms that link structure and agency in relation to inequality.

Habitus (Bourdieu 1977) and membranes (Goffman 1983) represent two linking mechanisms that apply generally to daily interactions. Recall that habitus is the cumulative embodied experiences that are shaped by structural realities. Individuals rely on their habitus in their daily interaction with others. Recall also that membranes are meant to represent Goffman's idea of the loose coupling of social orders. According to Goffman, membranes determine which aspects of the social structure influence an individual's behaviour and which do not. Both habitus and membranes work simultaneously in everyday life as individuals negotiate the social-structural realities of their lives.

Two other mechanisms, **conformation** and **resistance**, pertain more specifically to inequality. Conformation refers to the processes through which individuals comply with and accept the various schemas and resources that structure society. Conformation

captures Sewell's (1992) idea of transposability (see chapter 6) and Tilly's notions of adaptation and emulation. Thus, schemas are learned in one setting and used in others, thereby reinforcing the social structure itself. Alternatively, resistance is the processes through which individuals reject and act against established social structures. Resistance can be subtle (e.g., a wife ignores her standards of cleanliness so that her husband will continue to clean the bathroom) or blatant (e.g., protesting discrimination on Parliament Hill), and it can be chronic (e.g., being an ongoing and active member of the Grey Panthers) or acute (e.g., taking part in one activist march). Although conformation and resistance are set up here as the antithesis of each another, no one ever completely conforms or resists. Rather, a complexity of resistance and conformation emerges as individuals negotiate their interests within the various domains of social life. Conformation and resistance are acted out by individuals, but the choice to conform or resist as well as the specific strategies one uses in these processes are influenced by the structured sets of social relations described above. Furthermore, tensions, contradictions, and paradoxes result from the complexities of resistance and conformation. Individuals then act to negotiate the ambivalence created by these tensions, contradictions, and paradoxes in everyday life (see Connidis and McMullin 2002).

Structure, Agency, and Anna's Life

The discussions of social time, social processes, structure, and agency presented above are necessarily abstract. To demonstrate how they work in real life we turn back to Anna's life and superimpose Figure 7.1 (Anna's life) onto Figure 7.3 (the coalescence framework), the result of which is depicted in Figure 7.4.

The substantive birth cohort in which Anna was born structurally affected her life chances. Even though women's rights and opportunities were expanding during the early twentieth century, women who were born during this time were still not encouraged to be economically self-sufficient, especially if they lived in rural areas. Instead, they were expected to marry a man who would be able to provide for them and their families. English common law, which suggested that property be passed on to the eldest son, was still well established in practice. Hence, Anna by virtue of the fact that she had been born a girl, had little hope of inheriting any property from her family. The fact that Anna's family worked in agriculture meant that there was little money to spare and that all family members needed to work on the farm and in the home in order to make ends meet. Anna helped her mother with household chores, gathering eggs, gardening, and making meals for her family and the boarders they took in.

Like many other farmers of British descent, Anna's mother and father embraced white, middle-class ideologies of family and work; a woman's place was in the home and good men provided for their families. Anna's parents also embraced the middle-class idea that their children should pursue post-secondary education. For Anna, these two sets of ideals created a tension. Why go to teacher's college if it is not needed to be a wife and a mother? A complexity of resistance and conformation emerged in Anna's life when she was caught between the structure of gender, which suggested that she

didn't need post-secondary education in order to fulfill her social role, and middle-class ideals that encouraged higher education. Anna resolved this complexity by completing high school but marrying instead of going on to teacher's college. This complexity was negotiated not only through Anna's actions and the meaning that she attributed to the structures of class and gender but also by her parents' actions and their understanding of white, middle-class values. Anna did not regret this resolution but rather interpreted it as a 'proper' course of events.

Anna became a full-time homemaker and mother who relied for her means of subsistence on the money her husband distributed to her (see centre of Figure 7.4). Indeed, her life progressed in a typical fashion after she completed high school. She was married in her mid-twenties, which was considered 'on time' for women who were coming of age during the Depression. Anna and John had two children shortly after they married. Their daughters were born 'on time' and it was typical for people who came of age during the Depression to have only two children.

The ways in which the processes of distribution, production, and reproduction were organized in Anna's life are a direct result of the gender, age, ethnic, and class relations in which she was enmeshed. Anna and her family of procreation were no longer farmers. John occasionally worked for his older brother in the family business but earned his living mostly by buying and selling property. They had little money, but John did own the house in which his family lived. The Warners tried very hard to achieve the white, middle-class standards that were typical of the times, especially regarding education, the appropriate gen-

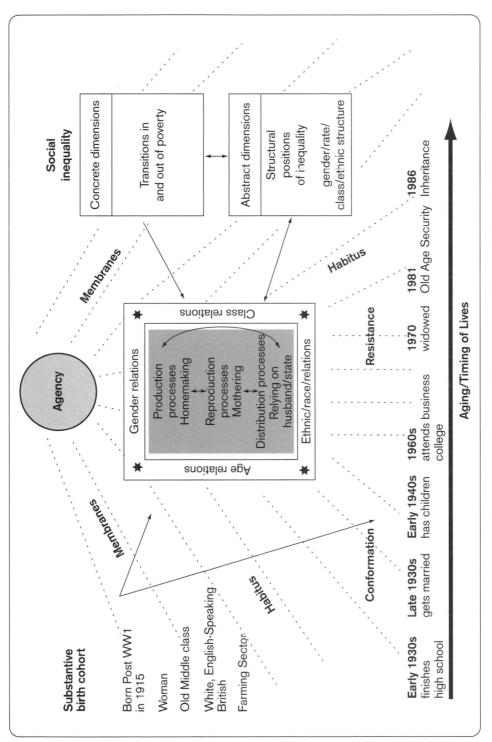

Figure 7.4 The Coalescence of Class, Age, Gender, Ethnicity, and Race in Anna's Life

dered division of labour in the family, and religious morality. The fact that Anna chose not to rely on social assistance after the death of her husband is linked to the pressures that she felt to continue to maintain these standards. Paid work may have been an option for her, but the structures of gender and age stood in her way.

Clearly, the choices that Anna made during young adulthood and through the middle years of her life fall much more toward the conformation end of the conformation-resistance continuum than the resistance end. But these choices must also be seen in light of the habitus that Anna developed through her early experiences; a habitus that was shaped by rigid gendered expectations, middle-class ideals of work and family, and the hardships that many faced during the Depression. Anna would probably not view the choices she made as choices at all but rather just as 'the way things were meant to be'. Hence, for Anna, the membranes that linked social structure and agency during this time were very thin; structural constraints were adhered to, not challenged.

Given the circumstances and habitus of Anna's life, it is difficult to make sense of her decision to go to business college. One possible explanation, however, is linked to her daughters' decisions to pursue post-secondary education (one attended business college and the other enrolled in a university secretarial science program). Perhaps she decided that if her daughters could further their education she could too, especially since her daughters needed less of her time by now. The idea that the decisions and circumstances of others in our social networks influence our choices and life circumstances is an important consideration. This idea is captured by the term 'linked lives' (see Elder

1995). Indeed, there are several times at which the circumstances and choices of people who were close to Anna affected her life and the ebb and flow of her poverty. Her husband decided to invest his wealth rather than leaving it to her, so that when he died, she became poor. Her brother and sister-in-law did not have children, they both died, and, at a time quite late in her life, Anna became rich.

Social Inequality

Recall from chapter 1 that social inequality refers to relatively long-lasting differences among individuals or groups of people, and that these differences have considerable implications for individual lives, especially 'for the rights or opportunities they exercise and the rewards or privileges they enjoy' (Grabb 2002: 1–2; Pampel 1998). Thus, social inequality has both abstract and concrete dimensions. Rights and opportunities are shaped by one's position in structured social hierarchies. As Figure 7.3 shows, the interplay between agency and structure organizes the processes of production, reproduction, and distribution, the combination of which leads to abstract outcomes of inequality. These abstract outcomes are the structural hierarchy of inequality in which categorical differences between sexes, races, ethnic groups, age groups, and classes are reinforced and, in some cases, modified. There is a reciprocal relationship between objectively defined structural positions of inequality and the organization of the processes of production, reproduction, and distribution—the two mutually constitute one another.

The second dimension of social inequality is more concrete, representing the advantages and disadvantages experienced by members of society. Hence, the ways in which the processes of production, reproduction, and distribution are organized shape, in Anna's case, transitions in and out of poverty. More broadly, the organization of

production, reproduction, and distribution influences the rewards, privileges, and resources that are accrued in various social domains, such as families, labour markets, states, education, and health. These issues are discussed in Part II of this book.

Glossary

Conformation The processes through which individuals comply with and accept the various schemas and resources that structure society.

Generation The subjectively meaningful cohort into which one is born. This concept is similar to the lives in time and place concept in Elder's life course perspective but reflects Mannheim's ideas involving the sociological relevance of being born at a particular historical time in a given society.

Lives in time and place The effects of contextual change, caused by a particular historical event, on individual life trajectories.

Resistance The processes through which individuals reject and act against established social structures.

Substantive birth cohort An umbrella term that includes the ideas captured by 'lives in time and place' while also representing the generation, gender, ethnicity, race, and class positions into which people are born through no choice of their own.

Timing of lives An umbrella concept that captures issues relating to social time, the timing of significant transitions (e.g., transition to parenthood), historical time, and the duration and sequencing of life events.

Questions for Critical Thought

Map the life course of either your mother or father on the conceptual framework presented in Figure 7.3, and consider their paid- and unpaid-labour circumstances.

1. What structural conditions influenced these circumstances in your mother's or father's life?
2. Did your mother or father act with agency in determining these circumstances? What are the choices they made that influenced their paid and unpaid labour? Were these truly choices?

3. What role did your mother's or father's substantive birth cohort play in influencing her or his paid and unpaid labour circumstances?
4. What role has aging and the timing of lives played in your mother's or father's paid- and unpaid-labour circumstances?
5. What other factors influenced your mother's or father's paid- and unpaid-work circumstances? Where do they fit in the framework (i.e., structure, agency, linking mechanism)?

Recommended Reading

Elder, G.H., Jr. (1974). *Children of the Great Depression: Social Change in Life Experience.* Chicago: University of Chicago Press. A classic study of how substantive cohorts and historical time influence inequality and other life experiences.

Elder, G.H., Jr., and A.M. O'Rand (1995). 'Adult lives in a changing society', in K. Cook, G. Fine, and J.S. House (eds) *Sociological Perspectives on Social Psychology*. New York: Allyn and Bacon, 452–75. A clearly written article that lays the foundations of Elder's life-course perspective.

Laslett, B., and J. Brenner (1987). 'Gender and social reproduction: Historical perspectives'. *Annual Review of Sociology* 15: 381–404. Perhaps the best historical account of the processes of reproduction and the social construction of gender and gender relations.

Mannheim, K. ([1928]1952). 'The Problem of generations'. In P. Kecskemeti (ed.), *Essays on the Sociology of Knowledge*. London: Routledge and Kegan Paul. In this essay, Mannheim applies Marxist theories of social class to the study of 'generations'.

Tilly, Charles (1998). *Durable Inequality*. Berkeley: University of California Press. A comprehensive account of categorical inequality. In this book, Tilly argues that some categories of inequality have more depth than others depending on how and whether various mechanisms, such as opportunity hoarding, are implemented by the dominant group.

Part II

Part II reviews the Canadian literature on social inequality in five
domains of social life: unpaid work, paid work, health, education, and states.
The conceptual framework presented in Part I is used as an organizational tool
for presenting the information in Part II. Although efforts were made to find literature that considered the intersections of class, age, gender, ethnicity, and
race, few, if any, studies examined all of these factors simultaneously. And even
fewer explicitly considered the links between structure, agency, and social time.
As a result, the goals of Part II are modest. It provides a partial picture of various
outcomes of inequality as they play out in families, paid work, health, education,
and the state in Canada.

Each chapter in Part II begins with an example or case study. Through these
examples the ideas presented in the conceptual framework are most easily
observed. Second, an overview of the literature on each domain of social
inequality is presented. This will enable the reader to gain an understanding of
the structure of social inequality in Canada. Finally, each chapter concludes
with a brief section on the general policy implications that may be derived from
the existing research.

8

CAGE(s), Families, and Unpaid Labour

Introduction

In 1998 and 1999, I worked on a project that involved collecting life-history interviews with 60 low-income mothers (see Davies, McMullin, and Avison 2001). Part of this research examined the extent to which mothers' family responsibilities influenced their poverty. Using life-history analyses, we found that the processes through which women became mothers influenced their experiences of poverty. Mothers faced barriers in continuing their education and in securing gainful employment (see chapter 10). One of the most significant barriers for these mothers was finding suitable and affordable child care, but there were also ideological barriers. One of the mothers in our study told us that she quit high school after she became pregnant because of the attitudes of the teachers and principal. In fact, the principal told her she could not take her physical education class because he feared that someone from the board of education would come to the school and see a 'big fat blimp running around the gym' (Davies, McMullin, and Avison 2001: 63).

Beginning in early childhood, beliefs about motherhood and family are instilled in us. For some of the study participants, these beliefs acted as barriers to education and employment. One mother had this to say:

'Girls were raised to think they had to grow up and get married and I thought that was the be-all and end-all and the only way that I was ever going to be independent was to be married. It didn't even enter my mind to think well I could go to school and get a job and I don't have to be married.'

And another said: 'I wasn't getting a lot of support or encouragement at home [regarding her schooling]. In fact, I was basically told by my parents that it wasn't as important for me to succeed as it was for my brothers.' These ideological beliefs about families and women's roles within them were best summarized by the comments of a third study participant:

> I had two or three [career] goals, lawyer, nurse, airline stewardess, but my parents said don't go into that, just get a job, get married, and you know you're going to get married and you're going to have a husband that looks after all that. Like you're so wrapped up in what you want but you're going to get married and you're going to have kids, so there's no sense even setting a goal like that, just do well in school and get yourself a job. . . . So that's what I did.

Such traditional belief systems 'place girls on trajectories of low income because they often emphasize the importance of marriage and family at the expense of economic self-sufficiency' (Davies, McMullin, and Avison 2001: 63).

Traditional family belief systems, combined with family violence or insidious poverty, made life especially difficult for some of the mothers in our study. In these cases, physical or sexual abuse, neglect, or parental alcoholism in their families of origin often led them to leave home when they were young teenagers. In the case of Mary (one of our study participants), her mother helped her leave home when she was 14 so that Mary could escape her mother's abusive partner. Unable to support Mary for very long outside of the home, Mary's mother encouraged her to become pregnant so that she could collect social assistance and mother's allowance. Mary did as her mother said, had a baby when she was 15 years old, and continues to struggle with poverty.

Among the low-income mothers in this study, 87 per cent had received social assistance at least once in their lives, but 60 per cent of these women were not receiving social assistance at the time of the interviews. This allowed us to assess the pathways by which women move from social assistance to economic self-sufficiency. For the mothers in this study, the most common pathway off welfare was marriage or a common-law relationship with an employed man (Davies, McMullin, and Avison 2001: 72).

The preceding discussion points to the importance of the intersections between the processes of production, distribution, and reproduction in systems of inequality. It shows that women provide for families and children and that the ideologies that shape this care (reproduction) limit their opportunities for education and paid work (produc-

tion). As a result, distributive processes vary accordingly, with women often relying on spouses or the state for their means of subsistence. Furthermore, the findings from the poverty study discussed above suggest that families are one of the principal domains in which the processes of reproduction, distribution, and production are organized.

Over the last several decades there has been considerable debate among academics and policy makers regarding the status of families in Canada and the United States. Some commentators argue that contemporary families are in a state of crisis. The American sociologist David Popenoe (1993) argues that between 1960 and 1990 the family was in a state of decline. According to Popenoe, families do not provide the functions, such as procreation, socialization, caring, economic support, and sexual regulation as effectively as they once did. He argues that families have lost their social power and control over their members, in part because they are smaller and less stable, and do not last as long as they used to. In a move toward individualism, American families are less willing to invest time, money, and energy in family life.

For Popenoe, who uses statistics about American families to support his claims, the most significant trends since the 1960s have been the following: (1) considerable fertility decline; (2) 'marital role erosion' with more women working for pay and fewer taking full responsibility for the care of their children; (3) increases in divorce rates, step-families, and lone-parent families; and (4) increases in singlehood and non-family living. As a result of these trends, Popenoe concludes that families are in a state of decline. Family members are less bound to one another because women are more economically self-sufficient than they used to be. Families are less willing and able to carry out their traditional functions (see above), and they have transferred their power to other institutions such as schools and states. According to Popenoe, families are also in a state of decline because family values are eroding. Family identification, loyalty, mutual assistance, and concern for the perpetuation of family have given way to values of self-fulfilment and egalitarianism. The consequences of such decline are alarming to Popenoe because the family is the most fundamental unit of society and 'breaking up the nucleus of anything is a serious matter' (Popenoe 1993: 539). He considers the most serious consequence of family decline is that fewer children are living in nuclear families and he believes that children cannot become successful adults without proper socialization within families. Popenoe advocates a return to traditional, Ozzie-and-Harriet-style families in which mothers, fathers, and children live together in perfect harmony, families in which mothers care and clean and fathers work for pay.

The American trends that Popenoe uses in support of his argument are indisputable and are similar to those in Canada (see Johnson, Lero, and Rooney 2001: 17–19). In 1961, the **fertility rate** in Canada was 3.85; by 1995 it had fallen to 1.64. More Canadian women and mothers are working for pay now than ever before (see chapter 9). Canadian divorce rates are higher now than they were 30 years ago, and there are fewer **nuclear families** now than there were in the past. Higher proportions of Canadians are remaining single or living in non-traditional families, such as same-sex unions (Gee 2000b). However, Popenoe's interpretation of these trends may be criticized on at least

two counts. First, because he uses a very conservative and limited conceptualization of family, he underestimates how central families are to many people in contemporary American and Canadian societies. Second, he ignores the fact that 'the family' is a primary site of oppression of and violence against women, children, and the elderly.

Defining Families

Popenoe defines family as 'a group of people who typically live together in a household and function as a cooperative unit, particularly though the sharing of economic resources in the pursuit of domestic activities' (Popenoe 1993: 529). On the surface there is nothing particularly troubling about that definition. Yet, because he argues that there are fewer families today than in the past and is critical of lone-parent families, his ideal 'group of people' is narrowly defined. Although it is true that the number of nuclear families has declined over the years, the majority of Canadians live together as 'a group of people'. According to the 1996 census, 76 per cent of Canadians lived in a household with two or more people. However, only 72 per cent of these are considered 'families' according to the census definition. The Canadian census definition of family is 'a husband and wife (either legally married or in a common-law union) with or without children who are never-married, regardless of age, or a lone parent with one or more children who are never-married regardless of age' (Gee 2000b: 82). Hence, siblings who live together, parents who live with their divorced child, and same-sex partners who live together, are not families according to the census definition.

Indeed, the 'nuclear family' is a middle-class construct that reproduces white privilege and ideology and neglects racialized families (Dua 1999), older families (Connidis 2001), and working-class families (Gardiner-Barber 2003). Historically, white, middle-class men and women took an especially active role in promoting such ideologies. So too did the Canadian state, which has continued to reproduce white, middle-class views of family through discriminatory immigration and family-welfare policies (see Das Gupta 1995, and chapter 12).

Useful and inclusive definitions of families have been elusive in the family-sociology literature. Table 8.1 shows how the definitions of family have evolved. The restrictions in Murdock's definition are obvious, but they resemble the definitions of family proposed by some vocal and conservative organizations in Canada, such as Focus on the Family. Margrit Eichler's discussion of family, which is in reaction to Murdock's and other conservative definitions, concentrates on who comprises families. Unlike the other definitions, that of the Vanier Institute of the Family concentrates more on what families do (points 1–6) than on who comprises them (e.g., two or more people who are 'bound together by ties of mutual consent, birth and/or adoption/placement). Finally, Fox and Luxton focus exclusively on what families do, equating family with the relations of social reproduction as they are defined in this book. Hence, a family comprises anyone who is involved in the processes of reproduction. The obvious advantage to this definition is that it includes those who have traditionally been excluded in definitions of family. Fox and Luxton (2001) argue that in all social systems there is a relationship between the

processes of production and reproduction. Before industrialization both productive and reproductive work were organized in the household. These processes were separated by the development of industrial capitalism as more and more men were required to work for a wage so that their families could make ends meet. Processes of reproduction were privatized in a way that they had not been in the past, and the division of labour between men and women became increasingly stringent (Fox and Luxton 2001). Also during this time, ideologies evolved that reinforced the relegation of women to domestic duties and of men's responsibilities for paid labour (Cott 2001; Margolis 2001; May 1993). As the findings from the poverty study discussed above show, these ideologies still exist. The next section of this chapter considers how reproductive processes of care and housework are organized in Canada in ways that create and recreate systems of advantage and disadvantage for various groups of people.

Domestic Labour

There are three main elements of domestic labour: maintaining the household; caring for adults and children; and the processes involved in consumption or making ends meet (Luxton and Corman 2001). Cleaning, cooking, gardening, shovelling snow, and mowing lawns are examples of the activities required to maintain a household (Luxton 1980). Caring includes both 'caring about' and 'caring for' others. Hence, caring refers to 'feelings of affection and responsibility combined with actions that provide responsively for an individual's personal needs or well-being' (Cancian and Oliker 2000: 2). Economic support for caring comes in the

Table 8.1 Definitions of Family

George Murdock (1949). *Social Structure*. New York: MacMillan, p. 1.

'. . . a social group characterized by a common residence, economic cooperation and reproduction [including adults of both sexes, at least two of whom maintain a socially approved sexual relationship] and one or more children, own or adopted, of the sexually cohabiting adults.'

Margarit Eichler (1988). *Families in Canada Today*. Toronto: Gage, p. 4.

'. . . a family is a social group which may or may not include adults of both sexes (i.e., lone-parent families), may or may not include one or more children (i.e., childless couples), who may or may not have been born in wedlock (i.e., adopted children or children by one adult partner of a previous union). The relationship of the adults may or may not have its origin in marriage (i.e., common-law couples), they may or may not share a common residence (i.e., commuting couples). The adults may or may not cohabit sexually, and the relationship may or may not involve such socially patterned feeling as love, attraction, piety and awe.'

Vanier Institute (2003). <www.vifamily.ca>.

'. . . any combination of two or more persons who are bound together over time by ties of mutual consent, birth and/or adoption/placement and who, together, assume responsibilities for variant combinations of some of the following:

- physical maintenance and care of group members
- addition of new members through procreation or adoption
- socialization of children
- social control of members
- production, consumption, and distribution of goods and services
- affective nurturance—love

Census definition (2001). <www.statcan.ca>.

'Refers to a married couple (with or without children of either or both spouses), a couple living common-law (with or without children of either or both partners) or a lone parent of any marital status, with at least one child living in the same dwelling. A couple living common-law may be of opposite or same sex.'

Fox and Luxton (2001: 26).

The study of family involves 'the maintenance of life on a daily and generational basis'. Families are 'the social relationships that people create to care for children and other dependants daily and to ensure that the needs of the adults responsible for these dependants also are met.'

form of wages, social assistance, retirement pensions, or some combination of these distributive mechanisms. Individuals and families use the money gained through these distributive mechanisms to purchase clothes, food, shelter, and other necessities of life. Low-income families, which usually do not have enough money to buy these things, often use creative and strategic methods to make ends meet.

In Canada, domestic labour is usually organized in families and households. Yet, for the 24 per cent of Canadians who live alone (and probably for many others), the processes of domestic labour transcend household boundaries. This is particularly true for people 65 and over, who are more likely to live alone as a result of widowhood, and for younger people, who are more likely to be childless and unmarried. For older people, members of other households or paid workers often help with household maintenance, while the labour of caring for and about them is often (but not always) undertaken by close relatives (Connidis and McMullin 1994). Although research tends not to consider how domestic labour is organized among younger, unmarried, and childless Canadians, we can speculate that they either purchase these services or do it on their own. Their care is likely provided by close family ties, with friends also being instrumental in providing support. Unfortunately, most of the research on domestic labour has used the household as the unit of analysis, and hence this chapter must do the same.

Gender is a crucial structural determinant of who does what for whom in families, regardless of age (Connidis 2001). As Table 8.2 shows, women spend more time doing *housework* than men do. According to the 1990 Canadian general social survey, 78.4 per cent of men did less than half (42.9 per cent) or none (35.5 per cent) of the meal preparation, 72.7 per cent did less than half (38.6 per cent) or none (34.1 per cent) of the dish washing, and 82 per cent did less than half (35.5 per cent) or none (46.5 per cent) of the washing and cleaning. Men did the majority of the household maintenance (45.3 per cent did all of it, and 37.8 per cent

did half or more of it). Furthermore, when asked who is primarily responsible for particular tasks, meals, dishes, and washing and cleaning are said to be women's responsibilities (77.7 per cent, 66.9 per cent, and 79.5 per cent respectively), whereas the majority of men in families are primarily responsible for household maintenance (Beaujot 2000). Of course, making meals, cleaning dishes, and general housecleaning are done every day, whereas household maintenance is done much more sporadically. Hence, it is no surprise that, compared to men, women spend more time doing housework (Gazso-Windle and McMullin 2003; Marshall 1993a, 1993b). This overall pattern in the gendered division of labour in the home intensifies when couples have children, and it remains the same as couples age. But when husbands and wives retire, husbands increase the masculine tasks that they perform (Askam 1995).

These findings are generally supported by Rod Beaujot's (2000) comprehensive overview of over a dozen Canadian community studies that were conducted between the early 1970s and the late 1990s. In each of the studies Beaujot reviewed, women spent more time doing housework than did men. Notably, however, in all studies men did more housework if their wives were employed. Indeed, the amount of household work that men and women do seems to vary according to employment and parental status. For instance, the amount of housework husbands and wives do increases with the number of hours their partners spend engaged in paid labour (Gazso-Windle and McMullin 2003). The more hours women work for pay, the fewer hours they spend doing household labour (Luxton and Corman 2001). Among younger and mid-

Table 8.2 Average Weekly Hours of Unpaid Work by Demographic Groups, Canada, 1986 and 1992

	1986		1992	
	F	M	F	M
All Persons 15+	28.3	14.0	28.5	16.0
Employed	23.2	13.0	21.6	14.7
Not employed	33.3	16.3	33.9	18.5
Wifes and husbands	34.5	16.3	33.9	19.3
Employed	27.0	14.4	27.3	17.2
with children	31.9	16.0	32.5	20.1
Not employed	42.3	22.6	42.4	24.7
with children	49.2	25.5	52.3	26.9
Lone Parents	30.9	19.2	34.0	19.5
Employed	25.1	18.6	26.8	18.8
Not employed	36.5	20.6	41.3	20.9
Children 15+ with parents	12.8	7.3	13.0	7.6
Employed	14.5	7.2	13.4	7.4
Not employed	11.2	7.4	12.6	7.8
Persons living alone	22.2	14.1	22.4	16.0
Employed	17.7	12.5	17.8	12.9
Not employed	25.0	16.7	25.2	20.3
Other persons	16.9	11.1	19.1	10.0
Employed	14.0	11.4	13.8	8.6
Not employed	19.6	10.5	24.4	12.2

Source: Statistics Canada, no. 13-603, 3: 67. General Social Survey, 1986, 1992. Reproduced in Beaujot (2000: 190).

dle-aged men, married fathers do twice as much unpaid work (includes child care and volunteer work) as unmarried, childless men and one and a half times as much unpaid work as married, childless men. Similarly, married mothers do twice as much unpaid work as childless women regardless of marital status. Women who are employed full-time do less unpaid labour than do those who are either not employed or work part-time regardless of how many children

they have living at home. Furthermore, compared with all families, higher proportions of men in two-earner families do half or more of the main household tasks (e.g., cooking and cleaning) and take primary responsibility for them (Beaujot 2000).

Caring within families transcends household boundaries more than housework does. Many of us care about our mothers, fathers, grandchildren, brothers, sisters, aunts, uncles and so on, even if we do not live with them. Grandparents often care for their grandchildren when parents need help with child care. Similarly, aunts and uncles sometimes care for their siblings' children. Children sometimes care for their older parents, especially if they are ill and unable to care for themselves. Husbands and wives often care for one another, and with increasing age and illness are often required to provide much more physical care for one another.

The obligations that family members have to care for and about one another are structured by class, age, gender, ethnicity, and race. The extent and nature of family care one provides will vary depending on how one is situated within these social structures (Finch 1989). Among the many caring relationships within families, the most widely studied is the relationship between younger parents, especially mothers, and their young children. One of the most consistent findings in the family sociology literature is that women are primarily responsible for *child care,* and compared to men, they spend more time providing care. This is still the case even though many more women are working in the paid labour force now than in the past (see chapter 9). However, the nature of how and by whom children are cared for has evolved over the past few generations. Compared to past generations of children, more pre-school aged children are being cared for by babysitters and licensed care facilities. This is, in large part, because labour-force participation by women has increased substantially. As a result, mothers and fathers make child-care arrangements with one another, with child-care providers, with their employers, and with other family members more so now than in past generations.

However, parenting and the care involved does not end when children leave home, but the nature of the care relationship changes significantly. Yet, with a few notable exceptions, mainstream family studies rarely consider how processes of caring evolve throughout the life course or the experiences of caring and parenting in mid-life. Unlike the mainstream family literature, the gerontology literature has paid some attention to issues of life-long parenting. Early research on mid-life families, for instance, identified a stage in life after children left home that was coined the **empty nest**. It was thought that because women in their middle years disengage from their active parenting role, these women would experience the 'empty nest syndrome' and have various social and psychological problems as a result. Later research, however, found that, in fact, many women enjoyed their lives after their children had left (Black and Hill 1984). More recently the term **cluttered nest** has surfaced to refer to families whose children, after having left home and living elsewhere for a period, return to live with their parents (Mitchell 2000; Mitchell and Gee 1996). Research has shown that parents provide more support to these children, both financially and with respect to domestic services, than they receive from the children (Mitchell 2000).

When we consider the links between production and reproduction, it is important to note that most working-age mothers work for pay and most mothers in the labour force work full-time (Johnson, Lero, and Rooney 2001). Yet the labour-force participation rate among working-aged mothers is still much lower than it is for working-aged fathers. Barring unemployment or disability, almost all working-aged fathers work for pay and almost all of the fathers in the labour force work full-time. Indeed, compared to fathers, mothers are more likely to have discontinuous paid-work histories and more tenuous attachments to the labour market, largely because of their family responsibilities. A substantial number of younger mothers forgo a wage to stay at home and raise their children, making them economically dependent on either their partners or the state. Women who work for pay take primary responsibility for the care of their children by making arrangements for child care and taking time off from work when the children are ill or when child care is unavailable (see Johnson, Lero, and Rooney 2001). This, however, places women at a labour-market disadvantage because very few workplaces offer child care or dependant care for their employees (see Box 8.1). Because domestic labour is undervalued in Canada, such patterns of paid and unpaid labour result in long-term financial disadvantages for women in relation to men—lower pay, fewer promotional opportunities, and smaller pensions (see chapter 9).

Because gender so deeply structures our ideas about who does what in families and homes, there is little opportunity for indi-

Box **8.1**   **Balancing Work and Family**
Firms Still Struggling with How to Help Workers
Who Care for Others
By Elizabeth Church

A new study by the Conference Board of Canada has some good news and some not-so-good news if you're struggling to keep your head above water when it comes to balancing work and family.

As you race to pick up the kids or hurry home to make dinner for an aging relative, you'll be happy to learn that compared with 10 years ago, more companies understand how your situation may be increasing your stress level and hurting your morale.

Better still, the board says, the majority of employers feel they have a role to play in helping you achieve some kind of balance on the home and work front.

But if you are expecting help from your employer with child care or support for an elderly relative, chances are you are going to be disappointed.

'Organizations do realize they have a role to play. I just think a lot of them are still struggling with what that role is and how to make it work within the organization,' says Kimberley Bachmann, author of the study *Work-Life Balance, Are Employers Listening*?

While the report finds generally the answer is yes, it says that in some areas such as child care and dependent care benefits, most organizations have a long way to go.

The finding is based on a survey of 220 public- and private-sector organizations, in which they were asked about the benefits offered to non-union staff. The research, conducted in 1999, replicates in many areas work that was done a decade earlier by the board, providing a look at how attitudes and practices have changed during that time.

The report finds a broad and growing acceptance among employers for programs such as flexible scheduling (88 per cent offer it, compared with 49 per cent in 1989), job sharing (52 per cent, up from 19 per cent) and telecommuting (50 per cent, up from 11 per cent).

More employers also offer workers a compressed workweek option (48 per cent, up from 28 per cent) and some form a part-time work arrangement with a variety of benefit options.

But when it comes to child care and dependant care benefits, companies offering programs are still in the minority. According to the study, only 15 per cent of organizations have a day care on site or near their offices. That's up from 5 per cent a decade ago. Four per cent have before-school or after-school programs, up from 1 per cent.

Ten per cent of companies offer employees emergency care for elderly relatives or elder care case management services.

About half the organizations that do not offer any of these benefits say they have never even considered it, about the same number as in 1989.

The largest increase is in referral services for obtaining help. About one-third of companies offer these for elder care, child care, and care of relatives with disabilities. That's up from 10 per cent or less in these categories a decade ago. Ms Bachmann explains that such services have become part of many organization's employee assistance programs. But she adds that with the country's aging population, she expects to see growth in this area.

'A lot of these programs haven't taken off as much as we would have liked to see, especially in the area of elder care,' she says. 'That's an area that employers are going to have to move on quickly.'

As well, while most companies are now on the record as offering programs such as flexible scheduling, the study finds that the use of many alternative work arrangements are often left to the discretion of management.

Front-line managers, Ms Bachmann says, may be faced with a balancing act of their own. With pressure from superiors to improve performance and produce results, they may be reluctant to accommodate employees who want to cut back hours or work in a way that does not fit the status quo.

'They are getting squeezed from both sides,' she says.

The study found only one-third of companies offered education to managers on work-life balance issues; 27 per cent encourage them to share experiences in this area; and less than one-quarter recognize and reward supportive managers.

'That's key because [middle managers] are the ones who have to implement policy,' Ms Bachmann says. 'A lot of work has to be done in terms of how the organization is run and how management works out people issues.'

Source: Church (2000). Reprinted with permission from the Globe and Mail.

vidual men to take on the role of full-time domestic worker. Men are even less likely than women to get support from employers when they request alternative work arrange- ments, and very few men take parental leave (Hochschild 1997). This robs some men of the opportunity to experience the some- times fulfilling and gratifying aspects of caring for children (see Box 8.2) that many women share. Indeed, the proportion of stay-at-home dads among two-parent families is still very low, even though it increased from 2 per cent in 1976 to 6 per cent in 1997 (Johnson, Lero, and Rooney 2001: 19). Nonetheless, the fact that men are not given the opportunity to look after their children should not be interpreted as structural inequality. Recall that social inequality refers to unequal access to resources and privileges in society. Domestic labour is not yet considered a valuable resource or privilege in the same way that paid work is. Hence, the restrictions that the gender structure places on men's involvement in housework and child care do not create disadvantage for men in the same way that the restricted access to paid work does for women.

Box **Lessons from Stay-at-Home Dads**
Take Tips from Men Who Turned Parenting into their Full-time Profession
by Darlene Ryan

Six years ago Glen Daniels turned in his computer, and gave up his job at an engineering firm, to be a stay-at-home father. Now the father, of Julianne, 4, and seven-year-old twins Josh and Joey, can often be seen surrounded by a herd of preschoolers at the local library.

He confesses it was a bit of an adjustment to make the switch to home life. 'We're talking about a drastic change,' he says. '[I'd] never changed a diaper until I changed the boys' diapers when they came along.'

Mick Noftall, dad to Luke, 4, and Sarah, 9, had a similar lack of experience when he gave up his job in fitness and recreation to take care of the kids. 'With Sarah, before three months, I found I was afraid to touch her,' he says. 'Afraid to change her diaper. Afraid she was going to break. Afraid I was going to break something.'

For dads who wish to swap their briefcase for a diaper bag, Daniels and Noftall offer the following tips:

Don't try to be Mom
Be yourself. Daniels says, 'They get different things from me, and different things from their mother. And that's good for them.'

Make an effort to meet other parents
Introduce yourself to the moms and dads in the library or at the playground. Being an at-home parent can be isolating. 'I find if you don't interact with people, you're lost,' says Noftall.

Get creative
Daniels explains, 'You've got to think like a six year-old, or a four year-old.' One of his children's favourite excursions was a trip to the airport. 'We went down into the tower and watched a plane come in. It was great.'

Be prepared

Kids can get bored, tired, or hungry quickly. 'When we go out I have cars, books, [and] four or five different types of food,' says Noftall.

Stay organized

Both men agree life runs more smoothly when they have a routine. Daniels relies on a big calendar. Noftall uses the planning skills he developed while working in recreation.

Delegate

Work out, in advance, with your partner which jobs around the house you'll be responsible for. 'I do the laundry and Lori comes home to the smell of cooking,' Daniels says. 'Supper's ready because it makes sense. Especially when there's stuff going on at night.'

Take some pointers

If possible, talk to someone who is or was a stay-at-home dad. Full-time parenting takes lots of patience. 'It can be very stressful when a child is upset,' Noftall says. 'You don't know what they want, they don't know what they want sometimes.'

Make time for yourself

Noftall exercises regularly at the YMCA. Daniels unwinds by working on his home.

Both Daniels and Noftall conclude that they are happy with the decision to be stay-at-home dads and content about the close relationships they have with their children. 'If a father can financially stay at home,' says Daniels, 'if he can be dedicated and jump into it with both feet and not want to change it for anything else—and have patience—do it!'

Source: Ryan (2003).

Although women still spend significantly more time doing housework and child care than men, some evidence suggests that men are sharing, or at least willing to share, domestic labour more now than they were in the past (Fox 1997; Sullivan 2000). In 1986, Canadian fathers aged 25 to 44 did an average of two and a half hours of unpaid work a day. In 1998, that figure had risen to three and a half hours a day. Although women also seemed to be doing more household work in 1998 than in 1986, the increase was smaller than for men. Canadian mothers aged 25 to 44 spent an average of 5.8 hours per day doing unpaid labour in 1996 compared to 6.1 hours per day in 1998 (Fast et al. 2001).

Research on caring has proliferated in the gerontological literature, with a typical focus on the difficulties facing adult children, usually daughters, in caring for elderly parents (Aronson 1992). Much of this research emphasizes the stress of combining paid work with care or support for older parents. Early work in this regard noted that this stress was particularly acute for women because they formed a **sandwich generation** that had to combine work, caring for older parents, and childcare. Although subsequent research showed that the proportion of women who are 'sandwiched' is actually quite small (Martin-Matthews 2000; Rosenthal, Matthews, and Marshall 1989), the proportion of employees who care for older family members and have children living at home has risen from 9.5 per cent in the late 1980s to about 15 per cent today (MacBride-King and Bachmann 1999). As is the case with child care, research shows that children who provide support and care to older parents often make alternative work arrangements to facilitate their supportive role. And, compared to sons, daughters are more likely to make such arrangements (see Connidis 2001 for an overview).

Women take responsibility for housework, and they do more housework and provide more care than do men regardless of social class. Yet, if we use income as a proxy of class, we note that income influences the amount of housework, meal preparation, and child care that Canadians do. On average, high-income Canadians (i.e., those with a household income of more than $80,000 a year) do 20 minutes less housework, 12 minutes less meal preparation, and 12 minutes less child care per day than low-income (household income of less than $30,000 a year) (Williams 2002). Working-class women often turn to their mothers for help with baby-sitting and housework (McMullin, 2002). Although often viewed within the context of the love grandmothers feel for both children and grandchildren, we should not lose sight of the labour that is involved. This 'labour of love' is grounded in a strong gendered ideology that limits the responsibility that fathers and grandfathers have in care of children and grandchildren (Fox 2001). Alternatively, middle- and upper-class women often pay other women for child care and housework. This process reproduces white and middle-class privilege because middle-class white women usually hire working-class, racialized, and immigrant women to do this work (Arat-Koc 2001; Glenn 1992).

Class and gender structure the division of housework and child care among black Canadian families. Black women tend to be responsible for most of the housework, and among the working class, they take responsibility for making ends meet (Calliste 2001). In addition, compared to white women, black women do disproportionately more housework and child care. This is because black families are more likely than white families to be working-class, and because there are three times as many female, lone-parent families among black Canadians as among all ethnic groups (Calliste 2001).

Intersectional research on families (i.e., research that simultaneously considers class, gender, ethnicity, and race) has been less concerned with the division of domestic labour in families than with how the institution of the nuclear family has reproduced white privilege in Canada. As an institution, the nuclear family has served to promote the morality of the white middle-class and the colonialization and nation building projects of the state. As Enakshi Dua (1999: 255) points out,

> White women were racially gendered as mothers of the nation whose participation in the nuclear family was crucial for the (re)production of the nation. In contrast, women of colour were racially gendered as posing a triple threat to the racialized nation as they could not reproduce a white population, allowed for the possibility of interracial sexuality, and challenged, by their presence within the nation state, the very racialized

moral order that the nuclear family was to protect.

Such research has also been critical of feminist research on families for concentrating too narrowly on the family experiences of white women. Rather than being oppressive, families, for women of colour, are often seen as a place where they can escape from the oppression they experience in paid work, and they have striven to live in nuclear families, a privilege often denied them (see Dua 1999 for an overview).

The transformation of wages into food and other necessities of life is a second dimension of domestic labour. Although the work of making ends meet has received relatively little research attention in Canada, Meg Luxton's work stands out as exceptional. Luxton's work on domestic labour, which spans three decades, examines the processes of domestic labour in white working-class families in Flin Flon, Manitoba (Luxton 1980), and Hamilton, Ontario (Luxton and Corman 2001). According to Luxton and Corman (2001: 172), transforming wages into the necessities of life involves 'allocating the available income to the various needs and choices of household members, from paying the mortgage and buying groceries to purchasing luxury goods and services'. Luxton and Corman (2001) find that the shopping involved in making ends meet is mostly done by women in families, but that the paying of bills is evenly divided among men and women. Both studies showed that shopping for the supplies necessary to run a household without breaking one's budget required considerable skill (see also Luxton and Corman 2001). This involved searching for the best deals, clipping coupons, being frugal if money was tight owing to lay-offs

or unemployment, and coming up with creative ways to make a dollar go farther.

Even though the responsibility for making ends meet usually falls to women, Luxton and Corman's (2001) research shows that men often control the money in the household. Because wages are the legal property of the person who earns them, there are no guarantees that the wage will be redistributed among the members of a family. Hence, most wives are economically dependent upon their husbands because they either do not work for pay or because they earn significantly less than their spouse. Unfortunately, there is no Canadian research that assesses the work of making ends meet in middle- and upper-class families, in ethnic and racial-minority-group families, or on whether this process varies across the life course.

Violence in Families

According to the World Health Organization (1996), violence is 'the intentional use of physical force or power, threatened or actual, against oneself, another person, or against a group or community, that either results in or has a high likelihood of resulting in injury, death, psychological harm, maldevelopment, or deprivation.' Gender and age structure the likelihood of experiencing violence at the hand of an intimate partner or parent. Hence, women, children, and the elderly are at risk of experiencing violence within families (Krug et al. 2002).

Although the violence that men experience is most often perpetrated by strangers, intimate partner violence (IPV) is the most common form of violence against women (Krug et al. 2002; Statistics Canada 2002b). IPV refers to intentional, controlling, and

systematic behaviour in intimate relationships that causes physical, sexual, or psychological harm (Krug et al. 2002;
Middlesex-London Health Unit 2000;
Tjaden and Thoennes 2000). Power and
control are central dimensions of IPV. Figure
8.1 identifies many of the tactics that men
(mostly) use to maintain power and control
in intimate relationships. These tactics

include physical, sexual, and emotional
abuse, isolation, economic deprivation,
intimidation, and the use of social status to
reinforce power and control within an intimate partnership.

IPV is a serious public health issue.
Considering women-abuse only, IPV is estimated to cost Canadians $408 million annu-
ally (Greaves, Hankivsky, and Kingston-

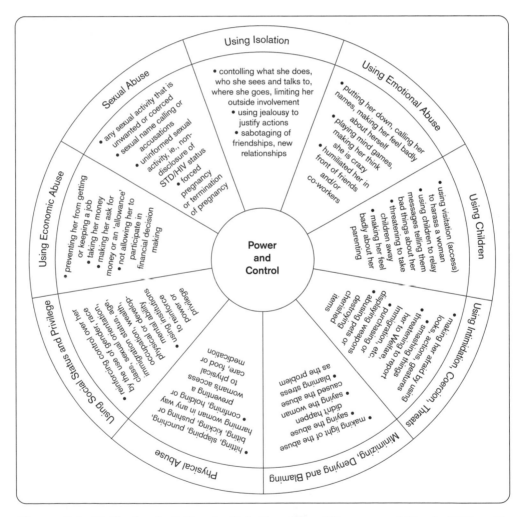

Figure 8.1 Battering in Intimate Relationships "Power and Control Wheel"

Source: Originally developed by the Domestic Abuse Intervention Project, Duluth, MN, further adapted by the
London Battered Women's Advocacy Centre, London.

Riechers 1995). Data from the 1993 Violence Against Women Survey show that 29 per cent of Canadian ever-married women, aged 18 and older, have experienced some type of violence at the hand of an intimate partner at some point in their lives (Johnson 1996; Johnson and Sacco 1995). As Table 8.3 shows, the severity of IPV ranges from threats of being hit (25 per cent), to being beaten up (9 per cent), to the threat or use of a gun or knife (5 per cent). For 38 per cent of these women, the experience of IPV led them to fear for their lives (Statistics Canada 2002b).

Similar proportions of Canadian men (7 per cent) and women (8 per cent) report that they experienced some form of IPV in the five years preceding the 1999 General Social Survey of Canada (Statistics Canada 2002b). Although these figures indicate that more research needs to be done on intimate violence against men, they may also be misleading because they do not take into account who instigated the violence and whether it was an act of self-defence. Furthermore, the violence inflicted on women is more severe than that inflicted on men. Compared with husbands, wives are

Table 8.3 Number and Percentage of Ever-married Women 18 Years and Over Who Reported Violence by a Marital Partner[a], by Type of Assault

Type of Assault	Number in millions	Current or previous (%)	Current partner (%)	Previous partner (%)
Total ever-married women[a]	**9.06**	**100**	**100**	**100**
Total victims of wife assault[a]	**2.65**	**29**	**15**	**48**
1. Threatened to hit her with his fist or anything else that could hurt her	1.69	19	7	35
2. Threw something at her that could hurt her	1.02	11	4	21
3. Pushed, grabbed or shoved her	2.22	25	12	40
4. Slapped her	1.36	15	4	30
5. Kicked, bit, or hit her with his fist	.96	11	2	22
6. Hit her with something that could hurt her	.51	6	1	12
7 Beat her up	.79	9	1	19
8. Choked her	.61	7		14
9. Threatened to or used a gun or knife on her	.42	5	1	10
10. Forced her into any sexual activity when she did not want to by threatening her, holding her down, or hurting her in some way	.73	8	2	17

[a]Includes common-law partners

Figures do not add to totals because of multiple responses.

Source: Violence Against Women Survey. Statistics Canada, 1993. Reproduced in Johnson and Sacco (1995: 295).

two to seven times more likely to have been beaten, choked, physically injured, or sexually assaulted (Statistics Canada 2002b). Although the number of spousal homicides is declining, at least four times as many wives as husbands are killed each year in Canada (Statistics Canada 2002b). Whereas wife killings are most often the end result of long-term wife-battering, husband killings are most often committed by abused wives in an act of self-defence (Johnson 1996: 179).

Age and socio-economic status influence the likelihood of IPV. Women who are involved with young men (under the age of 25) in common-law unions are much more likely to have experienced IPV within the last year than are women who are married to their partners and whose partners are older. Wives are more likely to be abused when they live in poor families than in middle- or high-income families. They are also more likely to be abused if their partners have not graduated from high school or are unemployed (Johnson 1996). Of course, all of these factors are highly correlated. Taken together, however, these findings suggest that women who are involved with men who have relatively little power on the basis of their age or class are more likely to experience IPV. Some commentators argue that men make up for their lack of power in the public sphere by dominating in the private sphere and that this occasionally results in IPV (see Johnson 1996 for an overview of the explanations of IPV).

Power imbalances on the basis of age make children vulnerable to abuse in families. Unfortunately, there is no data available on the prevalence of child abuse in Canada. Instead, researchers have relied on a combination of police records and reports of child welfare agencies to assess the extent of child abuse. There is little doubt that this approach underestimates the extent of child abuse and neglect in Canada, especially within families. To assess these shortfalls, the Canadian Incidence Study of Reported Child Abuse and Neglect (CIS) was conducted in 1998. This study examined the cases 'reported to, and investigated by, child welfare services during a three month period, from October to December 1998' (Statistics Canada 2001a: 4). Of course, focusing on 'reported and investigated cases' still misses the less severe instances of child abuse and maltreatment that may remain hidden within families. Furthermore, violence in families that is defined as punishment is not reported as abuse. Although Canadians disagree about whether corporal punishment such as spanking should be defined as abuse, the fact that it is unacceptable to spank adults if they misbehave says a lot about power relations between parents and children (see Box 8.3).

Nonetheless, data from the CIS provides more information about child abuse and neglect in Canada than was previously the case. These data suggest that there were an estimated 135,573 child maltreatment investigations in Canada in 1998. Of these investigations, 45 per cent were substantiated by child welfare workers, 22 per cent were suspicious but unsubstantiated, and in 33 per cent of the cases the investigation revealed that the child was not maltreated. Most of the substantiated cases involved neglect (40 per cent). Physical abuse accounted for 31 per cent of the substantiated cases, sexual abuse for 10 per cent, and emotional maltreatment for 19 per cent (Statistics Canada 2001a). In 1998 there were 5,958, 537 children between the ages

Box **8.3**   **Spanking Puts Power over Safety, Court told**
By Graeme Smith

Corporal punishment laws value parents' authority above the safety and well-being of their children, an appeals court heard during the first day of a controversial spanking case.

The arguments in the Ontario Court of Appeal in Toronto yesterday were just the latest salvos in a five-year court battle to quash section 43 of the Criminal Code, which lets parents and teachers discipline children by hitting them.

The Attorney-General's lawyers will offer their rebuttal today. Arguments are expected to finish tomorrow, through observers say the dispute could end up in the Supreme Court of Canada.

Lawyers for the Canadian Foundation for Children, Youth and the Law, which is challenging the law, told a panel of three judges that a decision by a lower court that supported spanking had mistakenly valued parents' 'protected sphere of activity' over children's rights.

'This section denies children equal protection under the law,' said lawyer Paul Schabas. 'We submit it does so in an unjustifiable, stereotypical manner, based on the notion that it [corporal punishment] is good for kids.'

On the contrary, Mr Schabas said, most experts agree that corporal punishment—hitting, slapping, and spanking—harms children's physical and emotional development.

Mr Schabas added that the vague wording of section 43 which endorses any 'reasonable' punishment, allows too many cruel acts such as beatings with rulers, belts, and even horse harnesses.

'At the end of the day, we're left with the personal opinions of the judge [in each case],' said Cheryl Milne, another lawyer for the foundation.

'Because the law presumes hitting is okay, it's based on a false premise. It's completely anathema to our modern, twenty-first-century conception of children's rights.'

The arguments were met with vigorous questioning from the appeal judges, who often interrupted the lawyers' presentations. Mr Justice Stephen Goudge in particular defended the law's inclusion of the word 'reasonable', which is used in many other laws.

'At the heart of this vagueness argument is an attack on our reasonableness standard,' Judge Goudge said. 'If that's not valid, we [judges] would be out of work, not just in this case but in every case.'

Besides criticizing the law as being too vague, the foundation said it violates children's right to proper judicial process because caregivers are granted authority to punish them arbitrarily.

Judge Goudge interrupted again: 'How could you have a quasi-judicial hearing before a spanking?'

'You can't,' Ms Milne replies. 'And that is another reason to strike the section altogether.'

On another occasion, Judge Goudge voiced a concern that outlawing spanking would intrude on citizen's personal lives.

Source: Smith (2001). Reprinted with permission from the Globe and Mail.

of 0 and 14 years (Statistics Canada 2001b). Hence, approximately 0.4 per cent of Canadian children were physically or sexually abused to the point that child welfare agencies intervened. Another 0.4 per cent were neglected, and 0.2 per cent suffered emotional maltreatment. According to these data, girls and boys were equally likely to experience maltreatment in families. Boys were more likely than girls to have been physically abused, and girls were more likely than boys to have been sexually abused in families. Older boys and girls are more likely to experience abuse than are younger girls and boys. Among girls the likelihood of sexual assault is highest among those aged 4–7 and 12–15 (Statistics Canada 2001a). Higher incidents of abuse and neglect are found in families that are more likely to be at risk of poverty (e.g., lone-mother families) (Statistics Canada 2001a), and a direct relationship between poverty and child abuse has been found in other countries around the world (Krug et al. 2002).

The above data only take into account the cases of child abuse that are reported to child-welfare agencies, yet the most severe cases of child abuse are usually handled by police. Police records from 2000 show 23 per cent of the victims of physical and sexual assault are children or young people, a figure that corresponds with the percentage of children and young people in the population of Canada. These data show that the majority of child and youth victims of crime were assaulted by strangers or acquaintances rather than relatives. Family members were the perpetrators in 23 per cent of the cases, and of these, parents were most likely to be the abusers. However, there is some variation on the basis of age. Children aged five and under are more likely to be assault-

ed by relatives, whereas children six and older are more likely to be assaulted by someone who is not related to them. In the case of homicide, infants are more likely to be killed by their mothers, and older children and young people by their fathers. With the exception of homicide, the risk of abuse increases with age (Statistics Canada 2002b).

Elder abuse is defined as an intentional or unintentional act of commission or neglect. It may be physical, psychological, financial, or material (McDonald et al. 1991; Podnieks 1992; Krug et al. 2002). Data from the 1999 General Social Survey (GSS) show that physical or sexual abuse perpetrated by a spouse, adult child, or caregiver over the last five years was reported by only 1 per cent of non-institutionalized Canadians aged 65 and older. Although these numbers were too small to allow for subsequent analyses, this 1 per cent figure may represent wife abuse 'grown old' (Phillips 1986: 212). Because of the structural intersections between age and gender, Aronson, Thornewell, and Williams (1995) argue that it is important to consider 'wife assault in old age' as distinct from either wife assault or elder abuse. In doing so, they document the story of Eve, a woman who, at age 75, left an abusive relationship (see Box 8.4). Indeed, there are continuing debates in the literature about whether elder abuse is a problem unique to old age or whether it represents a continuation of life-long family violence (McDonald and Wigdor 1995).

Data from the 1999 GSS shows that approximately 7 per cent of older Canadians reported that a spouse, adult child, or caregiver had financially (approximately 1 per cent) or emotionally (approximately 7 per cent) abused them over the last five years. In

Box **8.4** **Eve's Story**

At the time that Eve participated in this project, she was 79 and living in a retirement home. She had left her husband four years earlier, at 75, after being married for almost 50 years. A year after her marriage in 1940, she give birth to a son, whom she described with great fondness and pride. Her husband went overseas with the Canadian forces in 1942 and, by the time he returned, she had accumulated enough money from her own earnings and her 'soldier's pay' to buy a house. She described how, after that, her husband's actions increasingly isolated and silenced her; for example, he bought all the groceries and clothes for the household, she seldom went out and he would not let her talk with company so that, eventually, their friends stopped visiting. When their son left home and moved to the west coast, her husband's mental, emotional and physical abuse escalated:

> If he had to pass by me, like in the hallway, he would move as far away from me as possible in order to avoid touching me. He couldn't stand to be near me. He began to slap and choke me. I don't remember the times in hospital. You don't, you know. I was told that I had received shock treatments. I can't recall how long or how many times I was on the psychiatric ward, but I think it went on for years.
>
> The worst part was the women. Young girls—he paid them . . . I couldn't do anything about it. In our bedroom we had twin beds. One night he brought a woman into bed with him while I was sleeping in the next one and I woke up . . .
>
> I think it was during my second last hospitalization my psychiatrist drew me out—they can do that, get you to talk about things. He asked me if there was anywhere else I could go for a few months when I left the hospital. I think he knew something was wrong. I did go to my sister's for a couple of weeks but then I had to go back home. Things were worse then than ever.
>
> The last time I came home from the hospital, my doctor ordered home care and a VON for me. The VON nurse came every day to bathe and dress me. She looked after my personal needs on a daily basis. Frank did not want this. He said we didn't need the nurse or the home care worker. The nurse and I would find him listening outside the bathroom door. She noticed that he never let me speak when he was around. She said she wouldn't put up with that and that I shouldn't have to either. I told her this was normal for Frank. She got to know what was happening.
>
> It wasn't long before the VON and I planned my escape. She helped me pack my bag and she made arrangements with the local women's shelter. I couldn't bring myself to leave that night but the next morning I called a cab and left . . .
>
> I didn't mind it at the shelter, but they told me that it was too noisy for me to have all the kids around and I was moved to another shelter. There, I was given clothes and a worker from a family agency visited me. She was just won-

derful. I don't know what I would have ever done without her. I had no help from my family you know. My sisters, nobody believed me—they all believed Frank. I was still really not well and don't remember much about that time. My worker really helped me. It was she that found this retirement home for me and helped me through the adjustment period. I've been here four years now.

Ever since I've been here I have never again 'gone mental' or been hospitalized. I am on my own and, for the most part, look after my own affairs. It isn't easy because I never had to do these things before—banking, taxes, government pensions—all those details. Do you know, I had never been to a grocery store? Now I go to the mall and marvel at all the food . . .

As you know, I've been concerned that I'm not the best woman to talk about this because I had my own money. Most women don't, and the women in the shelters with children had nowhere to go. It was terrible for them. After a long and difficult court process, I have money to live on but it dwindles every year. It worries me because it's so expensive to live here and my bank account is going down all the time. It's a scary feeling.

The thing that really makes me mad is that Frank is living in *my* house. I try not to think about it. I paid for that home and he lived there rent-free all those years because of me. All the gifts and possessions I accumulated over fifty years are still there. I had to fight even to get my clothes.

Source: Aronson et al. (1995: 79–80).

the majority of these cases the abuser was a spouse (or ex-spouse) (Statistics Canada 2000b). Older men were somewhat more likely than older women to report emotional or financial abuse (9 per cent versus 6 per cent), and divorced older adults (13 per cent) were more likely than those of other marital status groups (4 per cent among widowed and 8 per cent among married) to report such abuse (Statistics Canada 2000b).

At an individual level, victims of familial abuse have limited agency to deal with violence because of the excessive control and power that husbands, parents, or adult children have over them. Nonetheless, agency among the victims of family violence is revealed in the strategies that they use to curtail it or escape from it. In violent families, wives, children, and the elderly pay

attention to the things that trigger acts of violence from the abuser and actively seek ways in which they can avoid such things. Wives sometimes flee abusive relationships, often taking their children with them, and teenagers sometimes run away from home. Yet the intersecting structures of gender, age, race, ethnicity, and class limit the options that are available to victims of abuse and severely restrict their ability to leave abusive families. Besides differences in physical strength, women, children, and the elderly are often financially and otherwise dependent on family members.

This structured dependence, combined with ideologies regarding familial love, make it difficult to leave abusive families. For instance, only 43 per cent of abused wives leave their husbands, and three-quarters of those who leave return. Among those who returned, a third did so 'for the sake of their children', one-quarter wanted 'to give the relationship another chance', 17 per cent felt that their partner would change, and 9 per cent lacked the money or housing to live on their own[1] (Rodgers 1994). Although there is no survey evidence that indicates that violence resumes after women return to their partners, the systemic nature of family violence, combined with qualitative data that demonstrate recurring abuse (Davies, McMullin, and Avison 2001), suggests that this is likely. Hence, romanticized ideals of family may perpetuate family violence even among women who have once left the abusive situation. Further, remaining separated from a partner does not guarantee the end of IPV. Husbands sometimes find their estranged wives and continue to threaten, abuse, and sometimes even murder them (Statistics Canada 2001c).

Compared to individual agency, collective action has been a much more effective means of dealing with family violence. Indeed, the recognition of the abuse of women, children, and elderly people as serious social problems throughout the 1970s and 1980s was a direct result of the collective lobbying of feminist and other activist groups (e.g., National Advisory Council on Aging). Through these efforts, community services have been put in place, especially for women and children, that help victims of family abuse leave abusive relationships and otherwise cope.

Sexuality

Sexuality is a central dimension of the social relations of reproduction. Sexuality has different meanings in dif-

ferent situations. In some ways it is an expression of human need, of pleasure and of the social togetherness of lovers. In other ways it is an oppressive and repressive relationship which grinds the tenderness and love out of people, leaving behind the frustration, bitterness, and violence. (Luxton 1980: 55)

Indeed, some argue that heterosexuality itself is a repressive patriarchal institution. For instance, in a seminal article, Adrienne Rich (1980) argued that heterosexuality is not natural but is a mechanism through which men maintain their powerful and privileged status in society. To truly have control over one's sexuality, Rich argues that one needs to be able to choose heterosexuality freely. Yet, in contemporary Western societies heterosexuality is not questioned, but is taken for granted. According to Rich, the organization of productive relations in capitalism reinforces **compulsory heterosexuality** because: (1) women's success at work is often tied to their degree of femininity (which implies acting in an overtly heterosexual manner); (2) women often endure sexual harassment to keep their jobs; (3) women are economically dependent upon men because they earn less.

In Canada, sexuality is often organized in families and is structured by class, age, gender, ethnicity, and race. Indeed, colonized peoples in North America have had to endure centuries of sexual regulation and abuse by Europeans (Stasiulis 1999). Heterosexual teenage sex, especially for girls, is subjected to excessive moral regulation, and in most nursing homes, elderly residents are not permitted to have sexual relations.

When teenagers and adults date, processes of production, reproduction, and distribution are evident in the rules of exchange that frame the dating experience. Even though there has been movement toward more equality in dating, boys and men (who are often older than their dating partners), tend to pay for meals, movies, and other forms of entertainment in exchange for kissing, petting, and intercourse. We do not often think about dating in these terms because our assumptions about love and family suggest that this behaviour is both normal and traditional (Luxton 1980). Yet, if women do not submit to a man's advances after he has paid for the date, she is at risk of 'losing' him (Luxton 1980) or in more extreme cases she is at risk of sexual abuse. Although determining the prevalence of sexual abuse among dating couples (i.e., 'date rape') is fraught with methodological difficulties, Canadian data suggest that 28 per cent of women attending college and university had been sexually abused within the past year (DeKeseredy and Schwartz 1998). The fact that, on average, men earn more than women (see chapter 9), also reinforces the idea that men 'should' pay for entertainment on dates and links inequality in processes of production to sexuality. Indeed, because women are at a disadvantage in the labour market, they are more likely than men to consider the earning potential of their dating partners in making decisions about marriage (Coltrane 2000).

One of the functions that marriage continues to play in Canadian society is the regulation of sexual relations. This remains true regardless of Popenoe's claim that this function is eroding. Indeed, monogamy within marriage is the expectation in Canada. Although most Canadians report that they have never had an extramarital affair, the proportion of men who report such affairs is higher than it is for women. This suggests that there is a power imbalance in the control that men and women have over each other's sexuality within marriage. The fact that men often believe that marriage gives them the right to have sex with their wives on demand and that sex should revolve around a man's pleasures and needs, is evidence of this gendered power imbalance in families (Luxton 1980). At the extreme, this gendered power imbalance leads to sexual assault. According to 1999 Canadian GSS data, 20 per cent of women had experienced sexual assault at the hand of a spouse (Statistics Canada 2001a). Wives often feel obligated to fulfill the sexual desires of their husbands either because they fear the physical and emotional response or they are afraid of losing their husbands to other women. Although the feelings of love and attachment that wives have toward their husbands are related to these fears, such fears are also augmented by the economic insecurity wives face. If their husbands leave, many wives would have economic difficulties. This is because wives are primarily responsible for domestic labour and consequently are connected only tenuously to the labour market (see chapter 9). Hence, sexual relations between husbands and wives are at some level economic relations as well (Luxton 1980).

Even though men control women's sexuality both inside and outside of marriage, the regulation of pregnancy and childbirth is usually the woman's responsibility. Furthermore, the consequences of poorly timed pregnancies severely affect women's economic well-being, but not men's. Teenage girls who get pregnant reduce the risk of a lifetime of financial struggle if they marry the father of their child. Yet, even if a marriage does take place, there is no guarantee that it will last. Furthermore, among women who work for pay and who get pregnant when they are older, careful timing is often also required so that they get the most out of public and private maternity leave benefits. If, for instance, a woman who is working for pay gets pregnant before she has been employed with a company for six months, she is most often ineligible for either company or government benefits. In such instances, a woman would not even be guaranteed her job if she took a leave. Of course, men tend not to have to deal with these issues at all.

Explaining Inequality in Families

The preceding discussion shows that families are sites of considerable conflict and inequality. Because so many people view families in romanticized ways as places in which love and harmony abound, less emphasis was placed on this topic here. And there is little doubt that many families provide comfort, love, and nurturing for its members; for racialized women, families may act as protection from oppression in paid work and other social institutions. Moreover, in some families the division of labour is organized in relatively equal ways (Risman 1998). Hence, explanations of inequality within families must simultaneously consider both the harmony and conflict that characterizes family life.

Many of the models that have been put forth to explain inequality within families have focused on inequities in the division of household labour and child care. For instance, some researchers have focused on

power imbalances within marriage to explain the unequal division of unpaid labour in families. In this literature, marital power is often conceptualized as the relative resources (e.g., income or education) that husbands and wives have within a marriage. Hence, the more income or education a wife has compared to her husband, the less household work and care she will perform. In this model, this hypothesis is generally supported; couples who have relatively equal levels of resources tend to have a more equitable division of household labour than those who do not (Kamo 1988; Gazso-Windle and McMullin 2003). Other models have analyzed the views that partners hold about gender equality and correlate these views with the relative time that husbands and wives spend doing household labour. Still other models focus on time availability. A serious problem with these models is that the researchers who use them tend not to contextualize them within the structures of gender, class, ethnicity, race, and age. As a result, these analyses tend to place too much emphasis on individual differences to the neglect of social structure. Furthermore, such research usually avoids discussions of the struggle and conflict that often take place as families try to struggle through the work of maintaining households and caring for children.

More fruitful approaches to studies of inequality within families would take both structure and agency into account and recognize that through these structures families are often oppressive institutions. In this regard, Connidis and McMullin (2002) have worked to develop a structural concept of sociological ambivalence that characterizes family ties. Their summary of ambivalence is worth quoting at length:

Ambivalence is created by the contradictions and paradoxes that are imbedded
in sets of structured social relations (e.g.,
class, age, race, ethnicity, gender)
through which opportunities, rights, and
privileges are differentially distributed.
Individuals experience ambivalence
when social structural arrangements collide with their attempts to exercise
agency when negotiating relationships,
including those with family members.
Managing ambivalence in daily life
shapes the very social structures that
produce ambivalence in the first place.
(2002: 565)

To explain what is meant by ambivalence I
will use a personal example. Gender, class,
and race structure my experiences at paid
work and as a mother. As a professor of sociology in a department and university that
have traditionally been very conservative,
there are rigid expectations about what
makes a 'good' scholar, and these expectations are classed, gendered, and racialized in
the ways that one would expect. One must
be articulate, show little emotion, work long
hours, and so on. These expectations often
clash with the gendered, classed, and racialized expectations of me, particularly of me
as a mother. This clash results in a structurally based ambivalence that I must negotiate and try to resolve within my family and
at work. This requires me to actively rene-
gotiate the expectations of me as a mother
and as a professor.

Beyond Statistics: Agency and Experience within Families

The preceding sections illustrate structured
patterns of inequality that persist in

Canadian families. Within these structures,
individuals negotiate their lives and, in the
process, conform or resist these structures of
dominance. In doing so, individuals are
active in the production and reproduction of
these social structures. Although concentrating primarily on white middle-class mothers, Bonnie Fox (2001) has explored how
parenthood in heterosexual families socially
constructs gender. This study shows that
new mothers actively negotiate child care
and housework with their partners, but that
because mothers must take responsibility
for their children and become more dependent upon their partners when they do so,
fathers have more 'bargaining' power in the
negotiations that take place. Using Janet
Finch's terminology, partners and fathers
have 'legitimate excuses' for not looking
after the children. A particularly telling finding from this study is that structures of gender inequality in the division of housework
are reproduced through these negotiations.
New mothers feel that their partners should
be involved in the care of their children and
'prioritized daddy's time with the baby'
while they did the housework. As a result,
'one product of women's agency in drawing
men into active fathering may be a more
conventional division of housework' (Fox
2001: 385).

Within the context of class, gender, age,
ethnic, and racial structures, even the most
structurally disadvantaged individuals make
choices about how they should best live
their lives. Looking from the outside in, and
until you hear the stories, these choices are
often considered irrational among those
who have never experienced extreme disadvantage. Box 8.5 presents an excerpt from
the life-history narratives from the poverty
study that introduced this chapter. Pam

Box **8.5** **Pam's Family Experiences**

From what I remember from about seven, seven up, I don't remember a lot of traumatized stuff. A lot of abuse obviously. Strict, upper hand, you don't talk back, kids are supposed to be seen not heard. There's a lot of violence, 14 years she [Pam's mother] put up with abuse and stuck it. People say you can leave but it's not as easy as said.

I left home at fourteen, moved here, lived on the streets. Ate out of the garbage bins. I don't know, there was lots of abuse. There was alcohol in my family, left and right. Drugs and, see, my brother he was, started young, he was about eleven when he started drugs. My mom acknowledged it but she was so messed up she really, you know, she didn't do nothing about it. It was rough.

My dad was always in jail so to speak, and she met this guy. This guy was very stiff, upper hand, you know you don't talk back, you do as I say. He used to make us, as kids you know when you run down the stairs and that and you creak the stairs or something, he would think we were banging. So we would have to go up and down the stairs 150 times or more. And if we made one creak, we would have to start all over again. Well to this day I can't walk up stairs properly. Like I can't walk flat, always on the tippy toes. You know, just something like that. There was like dishes, he used to make us do dishes real young. And as kids you don't worry about every little spot on them, and if we had one we had to do them all over again. And we'd do them like five or six times, yeah, in a day. There was little things here and there that he would make us do. School, I wasn't good in school because I was, I had other problems to worry about. You know, more or less taking care of my mom when she was all drunk, and cleaning up the house and doing whatever.

We used to get hung out, we lived in a two storey house, he'd hang us upside down by our feet out the window. A lot of physical abuse. Later on the down the road, when my mom finally did leave this guy, there were two men that raped and molested me, and I told her. She was like, no they wouldn't do that kind of thing, right. So that's when I said that's it, I've had enough. And my brother was the only one who believed me. I just left it.

I lived in the park for the longest time. I cleaned up from the water fountains there. I cleaned up the best I could. Just carried a back pack with me. At night we would have to watch. I met a couple of friends in the park and they would watch for police because at that time they would come through the park and see if anybody was sleeping on the benches and that's where we slept. Then if my friends seen them or whatever, wake me up and we'd just sit there and talk, and then go back to sleep. So it was really rough, I looked like a bag of crap. Not the proper hygiene of it all, I was fairly clean considering some of them, they were really gross. Towards the end of the night we'd just go, like there was a doughnut shop downtown at the time, and we used to go into their dumpsters and get their doughnuts and whatever garbage there was there to eat. We'd go to the Salvation Army, we'd get one meal there, so we'd do that.

And I didn't even panhandle or nothing, so whatever I could get, and it was hard. I did that for about six months and I couldn't take it no more. I was just on the verge of committing suicide and everything. It was all going downhill. I heard about this place that would help so I went there. And they weren't going to take me because I was fifteen and they don't usually, they need a consent and all this. And I explained to them there is no consent, there has never been a consent. I've been my own person for a long time. And I've been feeding myself for a while. OK the food might have been in the cupboards or whatever, but I'd be making it. So they took that into consideration.

I hated it because people would steal what little stuff I had, and there was like fights. And they would say there is different walks of life and you're going to face that. I didn't agree with that 100 per cent, I said I understand there's different people with different problems, but leave my stuff alone that's all I want. I don't got much. Eventually I got privileges to get my own room, private room. So I enjoyed that. I stayed there for the longest time, I stayed about eight months there. So I was happy about that and when I did finally say OK, I'm out of here, I got my own apartment downtown.

And then I met my husband, well boyfriend at the time. We lived together and stuff like that, my mom was not good about that. First time I ever got a welfare cheque, and it was cool, because I saved money. I didn't really spend nothing because I wasn't in a spending mode, I just wanted to save everything I could get. So every time I'd get my welfare cheque I'd go out and hang around the café, doughnut café and stuff like that, and my mom would say well you can't do that. Well why can't I? I pay my own rent, it's my place. I'm still your mother and you can't do this and you can't do that, I'm going to send you to a girls' home. She used to threaten me with that all the time. And I just lost it, you want to send me, go for it, try it, see what happens. You're not going to get anywhere, they're going to laugh at you because I'm out on my own. You got nothing to do with me. She hated it, we fought for a while there too.

I wouldn't even tell her, because I didn't want to tell her that, my husband now, was living with me. She knew, I knew she knew because she'd seen men's stuff here and there. I just said no, its just my friend's stuff or whatever. But she knew and I didn't want to hurt her feelings or whatever, you know.

Eventually we, me and my husband, we moved to a bigger place, it wasn't much bigger but it was bigger. We ended up being superintendents cleaning out the garbage. We had to deal with the clientele there so to speak, it was rough. There was a lot of drugs going through there. I didn't like it because I wanted to get away from that situation.

We finally made it. I was sixteen when we moved again over top of a bar and there are nice places there, really, really nice places. I ended up being a superintendent there for like five buildings. They hemmed and hawed about it too because I'm sixteen being a superintendent, not mature. Well they later on realized that it was a good decision because I got rid of a lot of the drug addicts that were in there. It was hard to deal with because you kind of sleep not knowing if they would break into your apartment and do something to you because you phoned the police on them. So we had lots of difficulties with that but eventually it panned out into a nice place to live.

And then I ended up getting pregnant with my daughter, because we were doing that for a while and I was eighteen when I got pregnant. And I decided to leave [my job]. I gave the landlord proper notice and whatnot and said I can't be bringing my daughter up here in a downtown area, over top of a bar, no. There's no play land or anything for them. He kind of understood but he was disappointed because I had been there for so long. And then we moved over here, like that was a two bedroom, this is a three, and we've been here ever since. Its been not bad, I don't want stay here long because there's so to speak, people call them 'lifers' here. Been here 20, 26 years. I've been here six and when I do move its going to be to a house. I'll stay a long time, length of time you need and I'll never come back again. This is public housing, eh, so and there's different walks of life here. They don't like the fact that my husband works, because a lot of them are on mother's allowance or welfare.

Source: Davies and McMullin.

grew up in a white, poor family with a physically abusive stepfather and a mother who drank. Poverty, combined with gender- and age-based power relations forced Pam onto the streets when she was 14. Pam used various survival strategies and made choices within the context of debilitating structures of age, gender, and class to get off the streets. Although she only had a grade 8 education when she left home, when we talked with her, she was 26 years old, was a married mother of two children, had nearly finished high school, was earning a living as a part-time apartment-building superintendent and was learning a trade. Notably, Pam makes sense of her life by contrasting her life and what she has made of it with her observations of her neighbours' problems. Throughout her teenage years, her mother tried to enforce middle-class family and gender values upon her and she resisted. Yet now, she struggles to maintain a happy family life with an unfaithful husband so that her children will have what she didn't and so that she does not 'become a statistic'.

Conclusions

Although Popenoe and other neo-conservative commentators interpret changes in

women's lives and families negatively, those interested in eradicating inequality view them positively. Indeed, Anthony Giddens (2002: 65), in speaking about the relationship between families and globalization goes so far as to suggest that

the persistence of the traditional family—or aspects of it—in many parts of the world is more worrisome than its decline. For what are the most important forces promoting democracy and economic development in poorer countries? Well, precisely the equality and education of women. And what must be changed to make this possible? Most importantly, the traditional family.

Yet, as Bonnie Fox points out (2001: 388), and as this chapter shows, irrespective of the positive changes that have occurred for women in families, 'the division of household work and responsibility in heterosexual couples has stubbornly resisted significant change. This absence of change suggests that gender divisions in intimate relations are deeply embedded in social structures.' Added to this is the persistence of physical and sexual violence against women, children, and older adults in families. Clearly, although power imbalances may make families 'a haven in a heartless world' for men, for many women, children, and older adults the structure and experience of families may be characterized as much by ambivalence and conflict as by love and harmony.

Compared to gender and age, there has been very little Canadian research on race and ethnic inequality in families and unpaid work. The work of Tania Das Gupta, Enakshi Dua, and Agnes Calliste stand out as exceptions in this regard. Much of this work concerns the role of the state in family formation and the discrimination that racial and ethnic minority groups face in living in family forms that they choose. As these scholars have noted, more work is needed on the experiences of women and men of colour in families and on the social organization of racialized families.

Notes

1. Twenty per cent of these women listed other reasons for returning to their husbands. In this survey, women were asked to report the main reason for returning to their husbands, and only one response was allowed. As a result, this data likely underestimates the role that financial dependence plays in women's decisions to return to their husbands.

Glossary

Cluttered nest   The situation facing parents when children return to live with them after the parents had experienced an 'empty nest' phase.

Compulsory heterosexuality   The lack of freedom that women have to decide whether they will be heterosexual or homosexual. It also refers to the pressures that confront lesbians when they are forced to act as if they were heterosexual or risk facing discriminatory actions.

Empty nest   The life stage in which all children have left their parents' home.

Fertility rate   The average number of children born to women of childbearing age.

Nuclear family   A family consisting of a husband and wife who live together with their biological or adopted children.

Sandwich generation   The generation in which adult children, usually daughters, are 'caught' between caring for their young children and their elderly parents.

Questions for Critical Thought

1. Statistics show that the total number of paid and unpaid hours of work that men and women do are similar. Some use this data to argue that there is an even split in the work that men and women do. In other words, that when it comes to 'work' the family situations for men and women are equal. Using the material presented in this chapter, develop an argument that would counter this claim.

2. Families are often described as a 'haven in a heartless world'. Use the information in this chapter to refute this claim.

3. Write a brief account of your family life when you were a child. Did your family situation seem to mirror the dominant family ideologies of the time? How did gender, age, ethnicity, race, and class structure your experience within your family?

4. Imagine your life 15 years from now. What do you think is the ideal life for someone of that age? How is this ideal influenced by family ideology? How is this ideal structured by gender, class, age, ethnicity, and race?

5. Write down the decisions that Pam made in her life. How were those decisions informed by ideas about what makes a good family? How were those decisions influenced by intersections of class, age, gender, ethnicity, and race?

Recommended Reading

Dua, Enakshi (1999). 'Beyond diversity: Exploring the ways in which the discourse of race has shaped the institution of the nuclear family'. In E. Dua and A. Robertson (eds) *Scratching the Surface: Canadian Anti-Racist, Feminist Thought*. Toronto: Women's Press. An excellent article that examines how the institution of the nuclear family has been reinforced through racist state rhetoric and policy.

Fox, Bonnie J. (ed.) (2001). *Family Patterns, Gender Relations*. 2nd edn. Toronto: Oxford University Press. An excellent collection of essays on how family life is gendered and how family relations and gender relations have changed over time.

Johnson, Holly (1996). *Dangerous Domains: Violence against Women in Canada*. Toronto: Nelson. Relying heavily on Statistics Canada data, this book provides a comprehensive account of violence against women in Canada.

Luxton, Meg, and June Corman (2001). *Getting by in Hard Times: Gendered Labour at Home and on the Job*. Toronto: University of Toronto Press. A case study of steelworkers in Hamilton. It examines how these working-class people negotiate the demands of paid and unpaid work.

Lynn, Marion (ed.) (2003). *Voices: Essays on Canadian Families*. 2nd edn. Scarborough: Nelson. A collection of essays on family diversity and experiences.

9

CAGE(s) and Paid Work

Introduction

In the mid-1990s I analyzed focus group data, industry data, key informant interviews, and archival data from the Montreal garment industry. This research confirmed what other research has shown—jobs in the garment industry are bad and garment work is hard (Das Gupta 1995). Managers and owners exploit workers in a quest to maximize productivity and profits, and there is always pressure to produce more. Managers control their workers by restricting the opportunities of those who sign grievances and by eliminating or moving 'problem' workers to different departments or jobs (McMullin 1996).

In the quest for maximum productivity and profits, bosses may also try to limit the contact that employees have with one another and to supervise their work very closely. As Isabella, one of the focus-group participants put it:

> The boss was never far away from us. He was there all day long, you couldn't speak too loudly because you soon saw him coming over. Ah yes and he would say, 'That's enough.' He was there early in the morning and he stayed with us at all times, all day. If he wanted to shock me, it would be in the morning when I arrived. You had to do a repair, he brought it to you then from the minute

you set foot in the office he kept you there and gave you an earful. He ruined my day from the start when he started to tell me off—[when he started to tell me] that I worked badly.

Although the exact words that were exchanged between Isabella and her boss in this confrontation are not discussed in detail, the excerpt illustrates how bosses attempt to control their employees by limiting their conversations with other workers and by criticizing their ability to do their job well. All of the above point to how social class shapes the production processes in garment work and how individual owners act as agents in using their power to exploit workers.

The practice of hiring the least expensive workforce in order to maximize profits has a long history in the garment industry. As a result women and immigrant workers are disproportionately represented in the industry, and in the garment industry, women and immigrant workers are paid less. At the industrial level, 82 per cent of the workers in the ladies' clothing industry in Quebec are women and jobs within the industry are segregated along gender lines. For instance, women make up between 88 per cent and 96 per cent of the three lowest-paid occupations in the garment industry. Ethnic groups are segregated in particular shops, with higher wages being paid in shops where most of the workers are French Canadian (McMullin 1996; McMullin and Marshall 2001).

One method that employers in the garment industry use to reduce labour expenses is to replace older workers who have been with a company for many years with younger, less expensive workers. Even though union regulations and Quebec law forbid the dismissal of workers on the basis of age, the owners circumvent these rules and eliminate older workers by closing their factories and then reopening them later under different names. Bankruptcy laws allow employers to close their plants, thereby terminating their debt and decreasing their labour expenses by eliminating the older workforce and the union. Several months later, many of these companies open up under different names with younger and non-unionized employees. According to Gerald Roy, the Canadian Director of the International Ladies Garment Workers' Union, companies go out of business, move on, and open a new firm in another location all within three or four months. The disgrace that once attached to bankruptcy has dissipated, states Roy, and now firms have 'hot shot' lawyers that tell them exactly how to go out of business; how to not pay their debts to the employees, landlords, machinery rental agencies, and banks; and how and when to open up another shop. Canadian bankruptcy legislation has not been changed to discourage such practices. Roy highlights the seriousness of this problem:

> It is too easy to open and close a company in the apparel industry. What is deploring is that the workers are always at the end of the process. They lose conditions of work, they lose their paycheque, they lose vacation pay, they lose their health benefits, they lose their pen-

sion benefits, they lose and lose and they are getting older. They are getting fed up, but they would like to go and work some place else maybe, but they do not have the opportunity because there are no jobs.

Thus neo-conservative state policies regarding bankruptcy favour the rights of capital over labour and serve to override legislation and union rules regarding the dismissal of older workers. Josee, a 53-year-old garment worker, described how difficult such practices are for older workers: 'You've been working for 25 years, with all your heart, all your soul. You gave up your health and you fall face to face with nothing . . . we lost part of our early retirement [pension contributions], we lost everything. . . . They [the company] changed the name, they changed the company but it is still there.'

The preceding discussion shows how production processes are structured by class, age, gender, and ethnicity in a working-class industry. Within these structures of inequality owners, managers, and workers act with agency in their daily negotiations with one another. For instance, even though garment worker's choices within production processes are constrained by the structures of class, gender, ethnicity, and age relations, garment workers make informed and strategic decisions about their work and retirement within these constraints (McMullin and Marshall 1999).

Class, gender, and racism (see chapter 4) intersect in processes of professionalization as well. Tracey Adams (2000), for instance, argues that dentistry emerged in Ontario during the early part of the 1900s as a profession that was structured as white, middle-class, and male. Students of dentistry were active in this process, as was evident from the opinion pieces submitted to student newspapers, the extracurricular activities they engaged in, their style of dress, and the ways in which some confirmed and others resisted the racial structures of their historical epoch, depending on whether they refused to treat black patients (Adams 2000).

The production processes described above in relation to garment work highlight three broad issues that may be used to classify jobs as relatively good or bad. First, the physical environments of workplaces vary considerably. People employed in good jobs experience relative comfort at work and a low risk of workplace injuries or illness. Bad jobs, on the other hand, often have physical environments that are uncomfortable and dangerous or unhealthy. Second, jobs vary in the intrinsic rewards that are derived from them. Unlike bad jobs, good jobs tend to be intrinsically rewarding because they are challenging and are characterized by high levels of **autonomy** and low levels of **alienation**. Third, extrinsic rewards, such as high pay, good benefits, job security, and promotion opportunities, are associated with good jobs (Krahn and Lowe 2002; Rinehart 1996).

Within Canada's economic system of advanced capitalism there is a wide continuum of good and bad jobs. The ideology of **capitalism** suggests that good jobs and bad jobs are distributed on the basis of individual merit. Good jobs are reserved for highly educated and skilled workers whose contributions to economic activities are considered more valuable than the contributions that others make. With this logic, inequality in the outcomes of paid work seems justified. However, many sociologists are critical of this point of view and instead recognize

that if productive processes were organized differently, the inequality associated with paid work might be reduced or eliminated (Rinehart 1996). At the most fundamental level this would require the abolition of capitalism as the predominant mode of production in industrialized societies such as Canada.

In its purest form, capitalism is an *economic* system that organizes processes of production according to the following characteristics: (1) private ownership and control of the means of production by relatively few people; (2) continuous growth, such that owners of capital continually strive to increase their profits; (3) exploitation, such that owners of capital profit at the expense of workers; (4) labour/wage exchanges, such that workers act as free agents in selling their labour power to capitalists in exchange for a wage and; (5) commodity exchange, that takes place in free markets, subject to supply and demand, which in turn, regulates economic activity (Abercrombie, Hill, and Turner 2000; Krahn and Lowe 2002; Rinehart 1996).

Karl Marx was among the first to recognize that capitalism is also a *social* system in which production processes are organized according to the social relations of production. Hence, owners, managers, and workers have various rights, privileges, power, and resources relative to one another. Unequal access to the rights and powers associated with productive resources shapes the social relations of production. In capitalist systems, class, age, gender, and ethnic relations, which are characterized by oppression, power, exploitation, and opportunity hoarding, constitute the social relations of production (see chapter 7). The social and economic organization of the processes of production results in a continuum of good and bad jobs.

Marx also argued that as capitalism evolved there would be a proliferation of bad jobs that would result from an increasing polarization of workers into two central classes, the proletariat and the bourgeoisie. This polarization would involve at least three things: (1) a reduction in the proportion of small business owners and hence a shrinking of the old middle class; (2) increasing proportions of income going to the owners of large businesses and a reduction in the earnings of middle-class workers; and (3) continued deskilling of work and corresponding increases in the alienation of workers (Conley 1999). Each of these points and related issues that classify jobs as good or bad are considered in the sections below. Specifically, this chapter examines how the social organization of production processes and the relationship between production, distribution, and reproduction lead to inequality in the intrinsic and extrinsic rewards of paid work.

Canada's Class and Occupational Structure

In Canada, as in other Western industrialized countries, the processes of production are organized by class and occupation. Clement and Myles (1994) provide what is perhaps the most comprehensive assessment of the Canadian class structure. As chapter 2 shows, they define social class through a modified, more simplified version of Wright's conceptualization in which there are four classes. The capitalist-executive class controls both the labour power of others and the means of production. The old middle class, the petite bourgeoisie in

Marxist terminology, commands the means of production but not the labour power of others. The 'new middle' class controls the labour power of others but not the means of production. And, finally, the working class commands neither the labour power of others nor the means of production (see Table 2.1).

According to this definition of social class, a slight majority of employed Canadians in the early 1980s formed the working class (57.6 per cent). Almost 25 per cent formed the new middle class, 11.3 per cent the old middle class, and 6.2 per cent were considered part of the capitalist-executive class (Clement and Myles 1994: 19). Since the early 1900s the proportion of Canada's class structure comprising small business owners declined considerably (Clement and Myles 1994). Between the 1930s and the early 1970s, for instance, the proportion of the workforce comprising small business owners declined from approximately 25 per cent to between 10 and 12 percent (Conley 1999). Much of this decline occurred in agriculture, where advances in farm technology made the business of small farming unprofitable (Conley 1999; Clement and Myles 1994).

Nonetheless, for much of the twentieth century it appeared as if Marx's prediction regarding the shrinking middle class was right. Since the mid-1970s however, this trend has reversed. Indeed, the most significant change in the class structure over the past 20 to 30 years has been the increase in the proportion of the class structure that is held by the old middle class. Clement and Myles (1994) report that non-agricultural self-employment increased from 5.8 per cent in 1975 to 7.4 per cent in 1990. When self-employed owners of incorporated businesses are included, the old middle class made up 14 per cent of the total labour force and 9 per cent of the non-agricultural labour force in the early 1980s. By 1996, 17 per cent of the total labour force were self-employed in both incorporated and unincorporated businesses (Statistics Canada 1997). More than 60 per cent of self-employed business owners do not hire paid help (Statistics Canada 2002a), and the majority have fewer than three employees (Clement and Myles 1994).

Reactions to recent increases in the proportion of employed Canadians in the old middle class have been mixed. On the one hand, some hail these changes as positive. According to this school of thought, small business owners are free of the control of large capitalist enterprises and as a result have more autonomy and other intrinsic rewards associated with their work. Their work is less alienating and this is a positive development of post-industrial capitalism. Others have argued that, far from being a positive occurrence, the rise of small business owners is the result of globalization (see Box 9.1) and workplace restructuring where workers lose their jobs and are forced to earn a living without some of the extrinsic rewards (e.g., pensions and benefits) of employment in large companies (see Clement and Myles 1994 for an overview of these views). This suggests that the conditions under which one becomes a small business owner are important considerations in discussions of the social implications of

---

Box **Globalization and Paid Work in Canada**

Globalization is a multifaceted process in which economic, political, social, and technological transformations have eroded national borders in significant ways (Giddens 2002). One of the most significant ways in which globalization has affected Canadians has been the gradual reduction in government restrictions on trade and imports. Various trade agreements reflecting the move toward globalization were put into effect during the 1980s and 1990s. These include the General Agreement on Tariffs and Trade (GATT), which resulted in a new international body known as the World Trade Organization (WTO); the Free Trade Agreement (FTA), which governs trade with the United States and was signed in early 1989 (Leach and Winson 1995); and the North American Free Trade Agreement (NAFTA), which came into effect on 1 January 1994. These trade agreements, in particular NAFTA, have facilitated economic growth by allowing Canadian companies to restructure their operations and move their production processes to Mexico or the United States. Because the cost of labour is lower in Mexico and some US states, NAFTA has enabled Canadian companies to increase their profitability.

This process of economic globalization has had devastating consequences for many working-class Canadians and particularly for women (Barndt 2002), racialized men and especially women (Ng 2002), and older workers (Winson and Leach 2002). Manufacturing jobs have been lost, unionized shops have been eliminated, full-time work has been replaced with part-time work, and income has been increasingly polarized (Winston and Leach 2002). In some cases, workers have been forced to make dramatic concessions, such as accepting pay cuts and shorter vacations, in order to keep production jobs in Canada. An example is described below.

International Truck Workers OK Package

By Simon Crouch and Jonathan Sher

Chatham—Workers at the International Truck plant here agreed overwhelmingly yesterday to concessions that might keep the facility open.

More than 90 per cent voted to accept a package that would eliminate jobs and could lead to lower wages for workers recalled from layoff.

Among the concessions by two Canadian Auto Workers locals:

The company would eliminate 48 full-time jobs for 'floaters' who fill in wherever help is needed.

Another 38 jobs would be cut as the plant eliminates its cleaning staff and contracts-out the work.

Three positions would be eliminated for employees who currently work full-time on union duties.

Wages are frozen and vacations cut back.

Of those already laid off by the plant—the total is now 1,300—only the first 210 would be recalled at full pay when an opening occurs. The rest would get paid 75 per cent and would only achieve full salary if they stay at least three years.

Workers seemed resigned but hopeful yesterday.

'We'll keep working, that's the main thing,' said Evert Wevers.

'This tells the government that this membership is willing to build trucks well into the future,' Local 127 president Doug Deneau said.

Even with concessions, Navistar Corp., the plant owner, says it will close the facility July 18 and move production to Mexico unless it gets government aid worth $30 million over three years.

'I think that Chatham-Kent definitely need to hold onto some jobs,' said Ron Newcombe, a 10-year veteran at the plant.

'I'm sure hoping the upper officials in government step in and help us out here.'

CAW president Buzz Hargrove said time is running out.

'It's a kind of a gun-at-the-head situation with a closure date of July and a deadline for reversing that just a few days away.

'The government has a lot of work to do here,' he said.

'I think there's enough people around that are sensitive enough to what this means to Chatham, to Ontario and to Canada—that this shouldn't be a major issue for us.'

Hargrove said the company has told him there isn't a specific deadline. But if there isn't something in place 'within the next few days', it will resume its plans to move to Mexico.

Unionized office and production workers voted together on the contract, an unusual move because they belong to different locals of the CAW.

The International Truck plant is Chatham's biggest industrial employer with about 900 workers.

Source: Crouch and Sher (2003).

higher proportions of workers belonging to the 'old' middle class. Notably, the old middle class is still made up of a relatively small proportion of employed workers. Workers in the new middle class and the working class encompass the overwhelming majority in the Canadian class structure (82.5 per cent according to Clement and Myles).

One of the most significant social trends of the twentieth century was the dramatic increase in female labour-force participation rates. Although the percentage of women who entered the labour force increased throughout that century, especially dramatic increases have occurred since 1961. As Figure 9.1 shows, the labour force participa-

tion rates of Canadian women between the ages of 15 and 55 have increased quite significantly since 1961. In 1961 fewer than 30 per cent of women between the ages of 25 and 35 worked for pay. By 1998 that figure was close to 80 per cent, and for all women, the labour force participation rate in 1998 was about 58 per cent (see Phillips and Phillips 2000 for a detailed discussion). But women did not enter the labour force on an equal footing with men. Rather, their social-class positions, as well as the occupations and industries they worked in, were structured by gender.

Canada's class structure is gendered. This means that production processes are

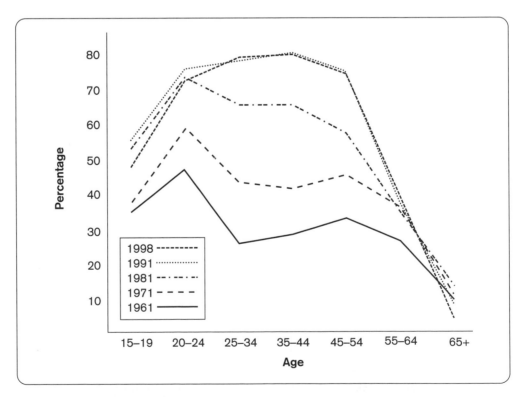

Figure 9.1 Female Labour-force Participation Rates by Age

Source: 1961–1971: *Census* (June figures); 1981–1991: Statistics Canada, *The Labour Force Annual Averages* (71–001; 71–220). Reproduced in Phillips and Phillips (2000: 80)

shaped by both class relations and gender relations (Hartmann 1981). As a result, the class structure in Canada takes a different form for women and men. Clement and Myles (1994: 129) find that although women constituted 45 per cent of the Canadian labour force in the early 1980s, only 16 per cent were part of the executive class. They were also underrepresented in the new middle class (41 per cent) and over-represented in the working class (49 per cent). Finally, women were under-represented in all occupations that involved decision making and authority, regardless of whether they work full-time or part-time.

Regarding the old middle class, the number of women who are self-employed increased by a factor of four from 1976 until 1997. Yet, in 1997, 13.9 per cent of employed women were self-employed compared to 21.1 per cent of men (Hughes 1999). Most of the gains in self-employment that women have made in relation to men have been as 'own account' workers, that is, those who do not have any employees. As Figure 9.2 shows, men far surpass women in their overrepresentation among self-employed 'employers' (Hughes 1999). Hence, although the gains that women have made in self-employment could signify improvements in women's class positions, we must be cautious about such an interpretation because the nature of work among self-employed women is different from that of men. For instance, self-employed women have lower average incomes than self-employed men ($16,814 versus $29,816) (Hughes 1999).

Women who work for pay are concentrated in particular occupations and industries. In 1961 women made up 27.3 per cent of the labour force, and they were over-represented in clerical occupations (61.5 per cent), sales (40.3 per cent), services (50.0 per cent), and professional occupations that include teachers, nurses and social workers, (43.2 per cent). Women were underrepresented in managerial occupations (10.3 per cent) and primary-sector, blue-collar jobs (19.8 per cent). By 1998, women were still underrepresented in managerial jobs (37.5 per cent versus 45.4 per cent overall representation) and primary-sector, blue-collar jobs (16.2 per cent), and they remained concentrated in clerical (74.3 per cent), professional (53 per cent), service (57.9 per cent), and sales (56.6 per cent) jobs (Phillips and Phillips 2000). Compared to men's jobs, women's jobs are more highly concentrated in health care and social assistance, services producing, and educational service industrial sectors of the economy. Men's jobs, on the other hand, are more highly concentrated in the goods-producing and manufacturing sectors (Statistics Canada 2002a).

The conceptual framework presented in this book suggests that production processes are organized not only according to class and gender relations but by ethnic and race relations as well. Historically, members of British and Jewish English-speaking groups have dominated the professional, managerial, and elite occupations and have been employed in **primary labour markets** (Krahn and Lowe 2002; Nakhaie 1995; Porter 1965). Although this dominance has declined, ethnicity still influences class and occupational structures even when education, age, and nativity are taken into account (Nakhaie 1995).

In general, ethnic and racial minority groups (with the exception of Jews) are underrepresented among the upper and middle classes and overrepresented among

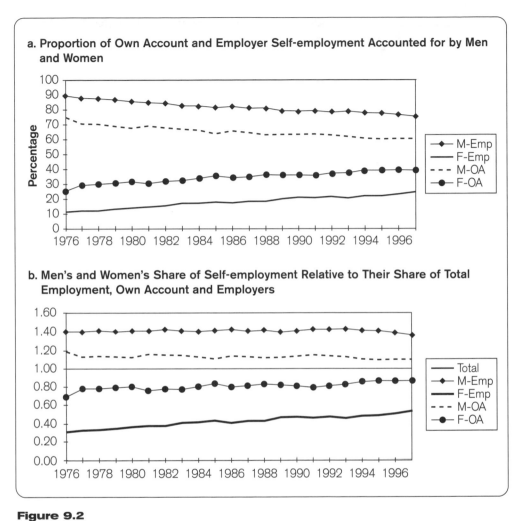

a. Proportion of Own Account and Employer Self-employment Accounted for by Men and Women

b. Men's and Women's Share of Self-employment Relative to Their Share of Total Employment, Own Account and Employers

Figure 9.2

Source: Statistics Canada, *Labour Force Historical Review CD-ROM*. Reproduced in Hughes (1999: 15)

the working class (Nakhaie 1995; 1997). Although members of visible minority groups are at least as well educated as other Canadians, they are also underrepresented in professional and managerial occupational groups (Allahar and Côté 1998: 67). With the exception of people of Arab and Chinese descent, non-white men and women are overrepresented in working-class jobs (Isajiw 1999; Kelly 2002), and racialized

women are overrepresented among domestic workers in Canada (Arat-Koc 1995).

Data on the relationship between self-employment and ethnicity or race is scarce. However, using 1989 Canadian Social Survey data, Nakhaie (1995) shows that, among men, those from German and Jewish backgrounds are much more likely to be a part of the old middle class while men of French or Italian origin are more likely to be a part of the working class. Finally, Jewish male immigrants are much more likely to be a part of the bourgeoisie than are those from any other ethnic group. Among women and compared to men, higher proportions of each ethnic group are part of the working class. As was the case among the men, women of German and Jewish backgrounds are more likely to be a part of the old middle class and those who have either French or Italian backgrounds are more likely to be a part of the working class. Li (2001a) shows that immigrants often rely on self-employment to supplement their labour-market income and that immigrants with higher educational attainment are more likely to engage in self-employment. Li also shows that immigrants from Asia, Latin America, and Africa are least likely to engage in self-employment.

Along with class, gender, ethnicity, and race, age also structures paid work. Labour-force participation rates for young adults (ages 15–24) rose throughout the 1970s and 1980s and then declined during the 1990s. In 2000, 64 per cent of young adults were working for pay (Krahn and Lowe 2002: 51). Young workers tend to be segregated in low-paid, often part-time, service sector jobs (Allahar and Coté 1998; Krahn and Lowe 2002), even though they have educational attainment rates that are higher than in previous cohorts (Lowe 2000).

Regarding older workers, labour-force participation has declined over the last few decades for men aged 55–64 while it has increased for women. In 1996, 59.3 per cent of older men were in the workforce, a nearly 20 per cent decline in 20 years. The labour-force-participation rate for women aged 55–64 has increased since the 1970s to 53 per cent among those aged 54–59 and 27

per cent among those aged 60–64 in 2000 (Krahn and Lowe 2002). This rate is a result of overall trends toward retirement before the age of 65 as well as the contrary trend of increased overall female labour-force participation. Further, statistics on women's retirement are complicated by whether they define themselves through their husband's status or whether they consider that they 'retired' 30 years ago when they left the labour market to raise their children (Connidis 1982; Street and Connidis 2001).

The class and occupational position of older workers depends a great deal on the class and occupational positions they have held throughout their working lives. Using life-course research, some scholars have examined the **cumulative advantage/disadvantage hypothesis** as it pertains to inequality in paid work. According to this hypothesis, the heterogeneity between groups of people increases over time. For the purpose of this discussion, the cumulative advantage/disadvantage hypothesis argues that individuals are born with specific class, gender, and racial or ethnic characteristics that provide them with a certain amount of advantage or disadvantage. Initially, there may be little separation between the haves and the have-nots on the basis of these distinctions. However, as time passes, the separation between the advantaged and disadvantaged grows and age groups become increasingly heterogeneous (Dannefer and Sell 1988). The reason this occurs is that the economic and social value attached to productive work depends on one's gender, race or ethnicity, class, and age (O'Rand 1996a, 1996b).

Younger and older workers are more likely to be employed in non-standard work. Non-standard employment includes part-time work, holding multiple jobs, temporary work, and own-account self-employment (Krahn and Lowe 2002: 86). In 1994, non-standard work accounted for 33 per cent of all employment, an increase of 5 per cent from 1989. Fifty-eight per cent of younger workers (aged 15–24) and 36 per cent of older workers (aged 55–64) were employed in non-standard work, compared to between 27 per cent and 30 per cent among those in the middle age groups. For women, rates of non-standard employment were higher than for men, regardless of age. The difference was greatest in the middle years (ages 35–54) (Krahn and Lowe 1998: 84), probably because of family responsibilities. These data suggest that the specific nature of non-standard work probably varies throughout the life-courses of men and women. Young workers (under the age of 15) are likely to engage in part-time work while they attend school. For older workers their non-standard work could be a choice they have made so that they can retire slowly. Or some older workers may engage in non-standard employment because they have lost their jobs and are having difficulties finding new ones (see section on unemployment below).

To understand how age relations influence production processes, we need a life-course approach that documents the age composition of the occupation and class structures with longitudinal data. Unfortunately, this kind of labour market research has not yet been done in North America. Nonetheless, in 1995 Gordon Betcherman and Norman Leckie used 1991 census data to document the age structure of employment in industries and occupations. They showed that the age structures of

industries and occupations may be classified in one of five ways: (1) uniform age distribution (age occupational/industrial distribution is the same as it is in the population as a whole); (2) youth overrepresented; (3) 'prime-age' groups overrepresented; (4) older workers overrepresented; (5) 'prime-age' groups underrepresented.

One of the most notable findings from Betcherman and Leckie's (1995) research is that only two industries (construction and wholesale trade) and no occupational groups had a uniform age distribution. Furthermore, young workers and, to a lesser extent, older workers were concentrated in 'bad-job' industrial sectors and prime-age workers were concentrated in 'good-job' sectors. Regarding industry, they showed that in 1991 older workers were overrepresented in the resource sector (e.g., agriculture and fishing), parts of the manufacturing sector (e.g., clothing and primary textile), the transportation, communication, and utilities sector, and some parts of retail services (e.g., general retail and furniture and appliances). Young workers were overrepresented in all parts of retail trade, accommodation, food and beverage services, and other services. Prime-age workers are overrepresented in some parts of the manufacturing sector, the finance, insurance, and real estate sector, and the business services sector. Regarding occupation, Betcherman and Leckie found that prime-aged workers were overrepresented in most professional and technical occupations, managerial occupations, production occupations, crafts, and trades. Younger workers were overrepresented in clerical, sales, and service occupations, whereas older workers were overrepresented in some service occupations and resource sector occupations.

Recent discussions about the 'new economy' point to the importance of social time in assessments of inequality in paid work. Tied to globalization (see Box 9.1 above) and the proliferation of information technology, the organization of work in new, knowledge-based economies is quite different than the organization of work in older industrial economies. Work in the new economy is characterized by greater individualism, job insecurity, risk, and instability. Hence, compared to workers in the industrial economy, workers in new economies are much less likely to be employed in the same job for life, and this has implications for how the life courses of individuals are organized (Marshall et al. 2001). There is increased pressure on workers to manage their own careers and to engage in life-long learning to keep pace with technological changes. Workplaces are being restructured, firms are recruiting employees with more knowledge-based skills (Adams and McQuillan 2000), and firms are placing more emphasis on flexible and non-standard employment.

In summary, this section shows how classes and occupations are organized according to gender, ethnicity, race, age, and social time. Why does this matter? Because within advanced, global capitalism, the intrinsic and extrinsic privileges and rewards that are attached to class position and occupations are different. Hence, the likelihood of being employed in a good job, a bad job, or for that matter, employed at all, depends not only on one's class, but also on gender, ethnicity, race, and age. The next three sections of this chapter consider three outcomes of inequality—unemployment, levels of income and poverty, and degree of alienation and skill—that are tied to production processes.

Unemployment

Job security has traditionally been one of the most important extrinsic rewards that employment could offer. Individuals who are employed in the primary sector and in unionized occupations have high levels of job security, whereas those who are employed in the secondary sector and in non-unionized environments have low levels of job security. Of course, unions and collective bargaining processes are gendered and racialized and have served the interests of white men at the expense of others (Creese 1996, 1999). Although labour laws in Canada are established to make it illegal to fire employees wrongfully, the extent to which these laws are upheld is questionable, especially for people in jobs that are unstable in the first place.

People who lose their jobs are more liable to experience poverty, homelessness, and distress (Avison, Wade, and Thorpe 1996). In Canada, the rates and duration of unemployment vary on the basis of region, industry, occupation, age, gender, and race. In the Atlantic provinces, unemployment rates have tended to be higher than in the rest of Canada. This is largely a result of the extent to which a particular region is economically diverse or not. In the Atlantic provinces, for instance, the heavy reliance on the fishing industry makes for high unemployment. This points to the connection between unemployment and each of occupation and industry. In industries, such as manufacturing and construction, with higher concentrations of working-class jobs, unemployment and lay-offs are more likely. Unemployment is less likely in professional and highly skilled occupations (Krahn and Lowe 2002).

Although men and women have historically had quite different unemployment rates, their relative disadvantage with unemployment varied until the mid-1980s, when some convergence occurred. During the 1950s and until about 1966, women had lower rates of unemployment than men. From 1966 until about 1990, unemployment rates for men were lower than or similar to the rates for women. Such trends defy simple explanation, but they probably have a lot to do with the types of jobs women were employed in during the 1950s and 1960s as well as the social stigma that was attached to unemployment during that time. During the 1950s and 1960s women were usually employed in teaching and service positions, which have always had lower rates of unemployment than blue-collar jobs (Krahn and Lowe 2002). Also, some women who were unemployed during this period,

may not have defined themselves as such but rather as housewives because of the social acceptability of this status. Regardless of why there was such divergence in the unemployment rates for men and women, the important point is that there has been convergence in these rates since 1990. It should be noted, however, that women and other groups who are more likely to have non-standard work patterns may be undercounted in official unemployment statistics (Pulkingham 1998).

Unemployment rates vary with ethnicity and race. As Box 9.2 shows, members of ethnic- and visible-minority groups and recent immigrants who live in Toronto have relatively high levels of unemployment. The census data reported in Box 9.2 show that the unemployment rate in 1996 for Canadian-born Torontonians was 6 per cent (for both men and women). Among recent

---

Box **Immigrants Face Underemployment in Toronto: Doctors, Lawyers, and Engineers End up Delivering Pizza, Driving Cabs or Telemarketing in Tough Job Market**
By Mark MacKinnon

The jubilation Anwar and Mubashira Khawaja felt when they came to Canada five years ago has gradually turned to despair.

The pair, doctors in their native Pakistan, were elated when they and their three sons were accepted as refugees from the religious persecution they faced as members of the Ahmadiyah sect of Islam.

Today, they're contemplating returning to Pakistan. Although they might face persecution there, at least they would be able to practise medicine.

Mr and Mrs Khawaja were practising physicians in Pakistan for 11 years, but neither has been able to work in the medical field here.

Doctors who immigrate to Canada (with the exception of Quebec) have to pass through a series of exams and internships before being allowed to practice—regardless of their previous experience. The exams alone cost thousands of dollars, and access to the internships is limited, even for those who pass the exams.

For the Khawajas, paying the exam fee is difficult to imagine, considering they missed their May rent payment at their East Toronto apartment.

'We think again and again that we should move back to our country,' Mr Khawaja said. 'If I move back now, I have a full-fledged hospital and patients. Here I have nothing.'

He and his family have been living off welfare and the small income he's earned as an occasional security guard and telemarketer. It's quite a culture shock for a family that lived in a government house with servants and a chauffeured car in Pakistan.

'We want to serve our country, but we are not allowed to,' Mr Khawaja said. 'We work as security guards. It's humiliating. My wife is a gynecologist, she has performed hundreds of cesarean sections. Here, she is nothing. She is unemployed.'

By some estimates, there are up to 1,000 doctors who have come to Canada in recent years and have ended up unemployed or working outside their field. Most of them live in Ontario.

There are similar tales of lawyers, dentists, and engineers delivering pizza or driving taxi cabs. An estimated 15,000 highly skilled professionals immigrate to Toronto each year, and few find work in the fields they have trained for.

It's a particularly sensitive issue in the fast-growing South Asian community. Among Toronto's 20,000 people of Pakistani descent in 1996, 45 per cent of those 15 and older had some sort of post-secondary education, making them one of Canada's best-educated ethnic groups. However, the unemployment rate in the community was 19.3 per cent, and almost half were classified by Statistics Canada as low-income. A family is considered below the line if it spends more than 55 per cent of its income on food, shelter, and clothing.

The picture is similar among the city's Indian population, which stood at 256,000 at the time of the last census.

Of those 15 and up, 45 per cent had some post-secondary education. The unemployment rate was 13.4 per cent, and 71 per cent of those who were earning an income made less than $30,000 the previous year.

The failure to integrate skilled immigrants is a serious issue in Toronto. In 1996, 4 in 10 members of visible minorities in Canada lived in the city. By next year it's expected that visible minorities will make up 54 per cent of Toronto's population. As of last year, they accounted for 48 per cent. It's a remarkably diverse mixture: one-quarter of the visible minority population is Chinese, one-quarter is South Asian, and one-fifth are black (a group that includes people of African and Caribbean origin).

Except for Arabs, Japanese, and West Asians, Toronto was home to the largest population of every visible minority group in Canada. Immigration to Toronto from outside Canada totalled 337,540 in 1996, down slightly from 358,405 in 1991.

Despite their diverse origins, the immigrants share a common challenge: an unfriendly job market.

In Toronto, the unemployment rate for Canadian-born men and women in 1996 was 6 per cent. Among recent immigrants, it was 14 per cent for men and 21 per cent for women.

Moy Tam, executive director of the Toronto-based Canadian Race Relations Foundation, says it's hard, looking at the statistics, not to conclude that an element of racism must be involved. Whether or not that's the case, she says the city is poorer for not putting the skills of immigrants to good use.

'This is a highly qualified group of people—the cream of their countries' crops,' she said. 'We're recruiting all this talent, but we're not taking advantage of it.'

Source: MacKinnon (1999). Reprinted with permission from the Globe and Mail.

immigrants, the unemployment rate for men was 14 per cent and for women 21 per cent. These data show that among the eight largest ethnic communities in Toronto in 1996, unemployment ranged from a low of 7.5 per cent for Ukrainians to a high of 17.9 per cent for Vietnamese. Compared to all other workers, higher proportions of racialized workers were unemployed at least once in 1999 (11.6 per cent compared to 12.4 per cent) and workers of colour worked fewer weeks per year than other workers (Jackson 2002). Unemployment is endemic for the Aboriginal population in Canada. The rate of unemployment for Aboriginals living on reserves was 31 per cent in 1991 (MacMillan et al. 1996: 1572) and 29 per cent in 1996 (Statistics Canada 2001). In 1996, almost one in four (24 per cent) Aboriginal labour-force participants was unemployed, and the rate was even higher for young Aboriginal workers (32 per cent) and for Aboriginal men (35 per cent).

Finally, unemployment varies with the age of workers. In Box 9.3, Gaile McGregor provides a detailed assessment of this situation in Canada. In particular, she notes that in the 1990s the unemployment rate increased more dramatically for older workers (those aged 55–64) than for members of any other age group. Moreover, between 1976 and 1998 the increase in unemployment rates for older workers was 30 per cent and 50 per cent for 55–9 and 60–4 year olds

respectively. However, older workers fared quite well compared to younger workers (aged 15–24), whose unemployment rate doubled during the same period (Krahn and Lowe 1998) and was higher to begin with. In 1996, youth unemployment stood at about 12.6 per cent, whereas the unemployment rate for adults aged 55–64 was only 7 per cent, which was somewhat lower than the unemployment rate for the population as a whole. However, we must be cautious in interpreting these statistics. Indeed, it is highly likely that biases in definitions of 'unemployment' lead to an under-estimation of the problem of unemployment among older people. As McGregor points out, only 67 per cent of men and 45 per cent of women between the ages of 55 and 59 and 41 per cent of men and 22 per cent of women between the ages of 60 and 64 were employed in 1996. This, combined with overall increases in unemployment rates for older workers and the rise in non-standard employment among this group, suggests that many older workers are having increasing difficulty in finding work.

Income and Poverty

The wage-exchange relationship is a crucial mechanism of distribution in capitalism and one which is intimately linked to production processes. Workers exchange their labour power for a wage that equals less

Box **(Un)Employment in Later Life**

It has become a commonplace that work has been transformed over the last decade. What is not so widely recognized is that the down side of this transformation has been disproportionately felt by older workers. Women continue to suffer more from discrimination, but men have been most impacted by recent structural changes. On the low end, they are overrepresented in the traditional primary and secondary industries which have been hardest hit by a changing global economy. On the high end, they are overrepresented in the mid-to-upper management levels which have been decimated by restructuring. The low average education of *both* genders, moreover, is a particular disadvantage given the increased premium on skills.

Older workers have also been disproportionately affected by the recent enormous burgeoning of contingent forms of work. (Almost 75 per cent of the jobs added to the economy in the nineties were non-standard types.) Between 1976 and 1998, the number of older workers in part-time jobs increased by more than 70 per cent, roughly one and one half times the rate of increase for all ages. Although some of this is a matter of choice, 15 to 20 per cent of the change in mode of participation is estimated to be involuntary. In 1993, 41 per cent of employed men and 27 per cent of employed women 45–69 who were working part-time would have preferred otherwise. The likelihood of self-employment also increases with age. Again some of this is elective, especially among better educated males. For the swelling number of women and blue-collar workers in the category, however, the shift is more likely to reflect a lack of viable alternatives. For involuntary contingent workers, the penalties may be considerable. The vast majority of jobs in this class are characterized by short tenure, irregular hours, low pay, no benefits, and a great deal of uncertainty.

If employment has changed for older workers in recent years, the *un*employment picture has changed even more so. Members of this cohort used to be protected by their experience and seniority. In the late 1970s, only about 5 per cent of employed individuals 55–64 experienced a permanent layoff, the lowest proportion of any age group. By the mid-nineties, however, the risk of a permanent layoff among older workers had risen by two full percentage points, putting it above the risk for prime-aged individuals. How did this happen? Some of it may be attributed to restructuring, particularly the tendency to leaner, meaner workplaces. The big difference between the recession of the early eighties and the recession of the early nineties was that many of the jobs lost in the later period never came back. Some of it may be attributed to the cohort disadvantages mentioned previously. Whatever the causes, the result was that the unemployment rate increased more for older workers over the nineties than for any other age group. In 1994, the percentage of unemployed in the 55–64 category jumped by 2.1 per cent, compared with an increase of 1.3 per cent for 15 to 24-year-olds and 1.7 per cent–1.8 per cent for all other cohorts. From a broader vantage, between 1976 and 1998, the relative unemployment rates of workers aged 55 to 59 increased by 50 per cent, that of those aged 60–64 by 30. But even this underrepresents the problem. Increases notwithstanding, compared with, say,

15- to 24-year-olds, strictly on the numbers older workers still seem to be doing fairly well. If one looks at those who are 'not working' rather than limiting one's purview to those who are technically unemployed, though, the figures swell enormously. In 1996, employment rates for Canadian men 55–9 and 60–4 were only 67 per cent and 41 per cent respectively. Comparable figures for women were 45 per cent and 22 per cent.

At the same time as the likelihood of unemployment has been increasing for older workers, the likelihood of *re*-employment has been plummeting. While the rising job risk factors are not to be sneezed at, the real problem for the cohort is that the *duration* of unemployment increases with age. Duration for men 45+ rose from 18 weeks in 1976 to 32 in 1985 to 35 in 1994, compared with 17 weeks for men 15–24. Duration for women has traditionally been lower than for men, but has been increasing at a faster rate. According to one government report, between 1984–6 and 1994–6 women's average jobless spells lengthened from 3.7 to 4.1 months, an increase of over 10 per cent. Duration rates for all older workers rose by 67 per cent between 1976 and 1998, compared with a 47 per cent increase for all ages. In 1998, the incidence of long-term unemployment among older workers was twice that in the labour market as a whole. In 1993, approximately 25 per cent of men and 17 per cent of women 45+ who were unemployed had been so for more than a year. This compares with 16 per cent of unemployed men and 12 per cent of unemployed women aged 15–24. To put these data in perspective, it is important to realize that high duration means more than simply a prolongation of misery. Studies show that the longer a person is jobless, the lower the probability that s/he will find work at all. More than a statistical artifact, this effect—called 'scarring'—has been related to the depreciation of human capital over the jobless spell and the stigmatization of the long-term unemployed in the eyes of employers.

Source: McGregor (2001).

than the market value of what they produce. The **surplus value** that is created in this exchange produces a profit for the owners of capital. As a result, there is a strong correlation between social class and income. Working-class jobs pay less than middle-class jobs, and owners of capital tend to have higher incomes than others (Krahn and Lowe 2002). In 1995, the average annual earnings were much higher for managers ($41,352), teachers ($35,330), and medicine and health professionals ($34,410) than for clerical workers ($21,825) and service workers ($17,160) (Krahn and Lowe 1998). These earnings stand in stark contrast to the incomes of the chief executive officers (CEOs) of large companies. In 2000, the CEOs of Canada's sixty largest corporations received an annual median compensation package of $3.7 million (Krahn and Lowe 2002: 104). However, a strong correlation between social class and income does not mean that it is a perfect correlation. There are certain jobs that, on the basis of the above definitions of social class, would be considered working-class jobs even though they command a relatively high wage. For example, assembly line workers in any of the 'big three' auto manufacturing plants are part of the working class, but because they are members of a relatively strong union they are paid a good wage and have good benefits.

From the income figures reported above we can see clearly that owners of capital and executives have much higher incomes than workers. The question that remains is whether there has been an increasing polarization of income over time. One way to answer this question is to divide Canadians into equal groups (either deciles or quintiles) on the basis of their income, calculate the proportion of the total income in Canada that each group receives, and then examine whether that proportion has changed. In 1996, 44.5 per cent of all before-tax income was concentrated in the top quintile of the Canadian population, 24.7 per cent in the fourth quintile, 16.3 per cent in the middle quintile, 10 per cent in the second quintile, and only 4.6 per cent in the lowest quintile. Between 1951 and 1996 there was a 2.9 per cent shift from the second and middle quintiles to the two highest quintiles while the proportion of income concentrated in the lowest quintile remained relatively stable. Moreover, between 1981 and 1996 the second, middle, and fourth quintiles lost 2.8 per cent of their before-tax income, a total of $14 billion, to the upper quintile (Urmetzer and Guppy 1999). These figures add support to the idea that there is increasing polarization of income in Canada.

It should be noted that the proportion of total before-tax income that is concentrated in the lowest quintile has remained relatively stable since 1951. What these figures do not tell us is that this stability has been maintained largely through government transfers such as tax credits, social assistance, and employment insurance. Indeed,

for low-income families, the proportion of their total income that comes from labour-market earnings has declined since the 1970s (Picot and Myles 1995). Hence, income polarization is not as serious as it could be because government policies ensure more equitable income distributions in Canada (Ross, Shillingon, and Lochhead 1994). But how equitable is a system in which the lowest quintile receives only 4.6 per cent of all before-tax income? And how equitable is a system in which the $14 billion gain made in the upper quintile during the 1980s and 1990s is equivalent to the amount of money it would take to eliminate poverty in Canada (Osberg 1992, cited in Urmetzer and Guppy 1999)?

Historically, women's wages have been less than men's wages. In 1931 the average wage for employed women in Canada was 60 per cent of that of an employed man's average wage. By 1997, women, on average, earned 63.8 per cent of the average employed man's salary (Phillips and Phillips 2000). Obviously, some of the variation between women's and men's incomes exists because more women (27.7 per cent) than men (10.2 per cent) work part-time (Beaujot 2000: 1996 data). Yet, even among full-year, full-time workers, women earned only about 73 per cent as much as men in 1997 (Krahn and Lowe 2002: 190).

One reason that women earn less than men is that they are disproportionately employed in low-paid occupations and industries and in occupations and industries that are considered to require little skill (see 'Canada's Class and Occupational Structure' above). But even in the 10 most highly paid occupations, occupations that are disproportionately held by men, women earn less than their male counterparts (see Table 9.1).

Table 9.1   Ten Highest-Paid Occupations by Sex, 1995

Occupation	Women as % of Total Employment	Female/Male Income Ratio
Judges	20.0	92.0
Physicians–specialists	28.3	59.4
Physicians–general practitioners	30.4	67.1
Dentists	21.9	60.4
Senior managers–goods	9.9	52.9
Senior managers–finance	19.2	61.2
Senior managers–trade	16.6	63.2
Lawyers	30.8	60.8
Primary product managers	6.6	56.0
Petroleum engineers	7.4	69.5
All occupations	46.9	63.2

Source: Statistics Canada, *Census*, 1996. Reproduced in Phillips and Phillips (2000: 64).

For instance, as Table 9.1 shows, women make up 20 per cent of the total employment among judges and earn an average of 92 per cent of what their male counterparts do. Among senior managers in the goods-producing industrial sector, women account for 10 per cent of the total employment and earn an average of only 52.9 per cent of the average male salary.

Wages are also linked to gendered processes of reproduction. Among full-time, full-year workers, parent status influences the personal incomes of both men and women but in different ways. Looking at Figure 9.3 we see that mothers with children at home have lower incomes than other women or than fathers who have children at home. The difference between the groups of women is greatest between the ages of 25 and 44. On the other hand, when compared to the average income of all men, the income of fathers with children at home is higher regardless of age. If we compare fathers and mothers who have children at home, the income difference is greatest among the 45- to 54-year-olds (a $19,550 difference). Furthermore, the responsibilities women have for raising children have a long-lasting effect on income inequality (McMullin and Ballantyne 1995), in part because their life-long pension contributions tend to be lower than for men as a result.

Wages and income also vary with ethnicity and race (see Beaujot and Kerr 2003a). Table 9.2 outlines the average incomes of various ethnic groups in Canada in 1991. The Jewish ethnic group has the highest average income ($32,826), followed by those of Canadian ethnicity. Three visible minority groups, Aboriginal peoples ($15,1990), the Vietnamese ($14,239), and those of Central and South American origin ($13,717) have particularly low average incomes. On average, workers of colour earn 16.3 per cent less than all other workers. Among men, workers of colour earn 17 per cent less than all other workers. The dif-

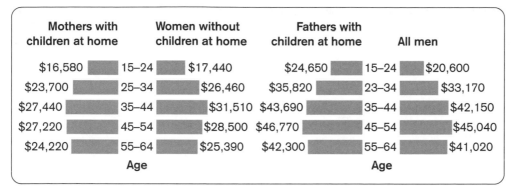

Figure 9.3 Earnings of Persons Working Full-time, by Family Characteristics, 1990

Source: Logan and Belliveau (1995: 26–27). Statistics Canada Census Data. Reproduced in (Beaujot (2000: 154). Copyright © 1999 by Roderic P. Beaujot. Reprinted by permission of Broadview Press.

ference is smaller for women, with workers of colour earning 12 per cent less than all other workers (Jackson 2002). And the income disadvantages for racialized persons remain when education and other social variables are taken into account (Lian and Matthews 1998). As is the case for women, occupational and industrial segregation of particular ethnic- and visible-minority groups accounts for much of the ethnic and racial variation in income.

Much of the research on the relationship between income and ethnic and racial minority groups has focused on poverty. If individuals have tenuous ties to labour markets or if they are employed in bad jobs, poverty often results. Poverty is a serious social problem in Canada. The National Council of Welfare reports that although poverty rates declined between 1998 and 1999 there were still more people living in poverty in 1999 than there were in 1989. Approximately 16 per cent of Canadians were poor in 1999; poverty rates are about 12 per cent for families and about 39 per cent for unattached individuals.

As a group, Aboriginal peoples in Canada suffer extreme financial deprivation and hardship and have higher rates of poverty (43.4 per cent) than non-Aboriginal peoples in Canada (19.3 per cent) (Ross, Scott, and Smith 2000). According to one study, 54 per cent of Aboriginal Canadians earned less than $10,000 per year, compared to 35 per cent among all Canadians (Armstrong 1999). Table 9.3 shows that the 'best-off' First Nations communities in Canada are more disadvantaged than the 'worst-off' non-Aboriginal areas and demonstrates that the most advantaged First Nations communities are still significantly disadvantaged when compared to the least advantaged non-Aboriginal communities (Armstrong 1999: 17). Racialized persons are more likely to live in poverty and to have a longer duration of poverty than other Canadians (Jackson 2002). Compared to the total Canadian population (29.5 per cent), higher proportions of immigrant visible minorities (42.5 per cent) and Aboriginal persons living off reserves (49.4 per cent) lived in

Table 9.2 Average Total Income of Selected Ethnic Groups, Canada, 1990

Ethnic Group(s)	Average Total Income[a] ($)
Jewish	32,826
Canadian	23,607
British	22,854
Hungarian	22,637
Balkan	22,224
Polish	22,220
Ukrainian	22,082
Italian	21,996
German	21,986
National average	**21,668**
Dutch	21,624
French	20,157
Portuguese	18,949
South Asian	18,631
Chinese	18,463
Greek	18,370
Arab	18,014
Black and Caribbean	17,613
Spanish	17,374
Philippine	17,226
West Asian	16,576
Aboriginal	15,199
Vietnamese	14,239
Central and South American	13,717

[a]*Total income* refers to the total money received by individuals 15 years of age and over during the calendar year 1990 from the following sources: wages and salaries, net non-farm self-employment income, net farm self-employment income, family allowances, federal child tax credits, old age security pension and guaranteed income supplement, benefits from Canada or Quebec pension plan, benefits from unemployment insurance, other income from governmental sources, dividends and interests on bonds, deposit and savings certificates and other investment income, retirement pensions superannuation and annuities and other.

Source: 1991 Canadian Census special tabulations. Reprinted by permission of Thompson Educational Publishing.

poverty for at least one year between 1993 and 1998. Furthermore, members of visible-minority groups and Aboriginal persons are more liable to be poor for two years or more (Jackson 2002; Ross, Scott, and Smith 2000).

Table 9.3 Comparison of Conditions in Best-off Aboriginal Communities and Poorest non-Aboriginal Regions

	Best-off Aboriginal Communities	Worst-off non-Aboriginal Regions
With less than Grade 9[a]	12%	20%
Employed	58%	57%
Number of persons per room	0.7	0.6
Average annual income	$18,200	$18,900
Speaking Aboriginal language at home	2%	n/a
Under 18 years	36%	25%

[a]As percentage of population aged 20 to 64.

Source: Statistics Canada, 1996 Census of Population. Reproduced in Armstrong (1999: 17). Catalogue 11–008.

There are significant regional variations in poverty rates in Canada. Newfoundland and Labrador has the highest poverty rate (20.7 per cent), followed closely by Quebec (19.5 per cent) and Manitoba (18.5 per cent). Ontario has the lowest poverty rate (13.5 per cent), followed by Prince Edward Island (14.7 per cent) and Alberta (15.2 per cent). Provincial variations in poverty rates are a result of regional differences in economic structures, provincial inconsistencies in government policies regarding social welfare transfers, and differential access to other social and economic resources (National Council of Welfare 2002).

Poverty rates also vary on the basis of gender, age, education, and labour-force attachment. For instance, in 1999 the poverty rate for single-parent mothers was 51.8 per cent, more than four times the poverty rate of all families. Unattached women under the age of 65 are more likely to be poor than are their male counterparts (42.3 per cent versus 33.2 per cent respectively) as are unattached women who are 65 and over (48.5 per cent compared to 31.9 per cent). Compared to all Canadians (16

per cent poverty rate), children (18.7 per cent poverty rate) and the elderly (17.7 per cent poverty rate) are somewhat more likely to be poor. Gainful employment significantly reduces poverty rates among both unattached individuals and families. Yet more than 40 per cent of families who were poor in 1999 were headed by persons who were employed. Finally, the poverty rate for single-parent mothers who worked full-time for the full year was still 19.7 per cent (National Council of Welfare 2002). Evidence also suggests that single mothers, older adults (especially women), young people (age 15–24), children (especially under age 6), and those with less than a high-school education experienced durations of poverty that lasted two years or more (Ross, Scott, and Smith 2000).

The fact that rates of poverty are higher, and that poverty lasts longer among young people, children, and older adults suggests that there is a significant relationship between income and age. Table 9.4 shows the average 'real' earnings for men and women of 'working age' in 1993, along with the percentage change in real earnings

Table 9.4 Earnings, 1993, and 1981–93 Percentage Change in Real Annual Earnings, by Sex and Age

	Men		Women	
Age	Earnings, 1993 ($)	% Change, 1981–93	Earnings, 1993 ($)	% Change, 1981–93
17–24	8,589	−33.2	7,367	−23.2
25–34	22,034	−16.3	15,761	3.0
35–44	28,620	−11.1	18,090	11.9
45–54	32,122	0.6	18,966	25.5
55–64	28,502	1.8	15,560	2.6

Source: Betcherman and Leckie (1995: 5). Calculations based on Survey of Consumer Finances data, Statistics Canada.

between 1981 and 1993. For both men and women, average earnings were larger in each successive age group until they peaked in the 45–54 year old age group. Although the average income decline for men ($3,620) was about $200 more than it is for women ($3,406), the proportional decline was greater for women (18 per cent) than for men (12.5 per cent). Of course, an average loss of $3,407 is more significant if one's average income is $18,999 (as it was among women aged 45–54) than if it is $32,122 (as it was among men aged 45–54). Average earnings are lowest among the 17–24 year age group, largely as a result of voluntary part-time work and minimum-wage legislation that allows employers to pay teenagers under the age of 18 less than those over the age of 18. It is troubling that the average real earnings in this age group have dropped by 33 per cent for men and 23 per cent for women since 1981. Beyond this age group, women made gains in average real earnings since 1981 (keeping in mind that there was not much room for a loss), whereas the average real earnings among men declined in the 25–34 and 35–44 age groups.

In the 25–54 year age groups, younger men, on average (25–34 year age group) earned 69 per cent and 89 per cent (35–44 year age group) of the average income of men who were between the ages of 45–54. For women, the 'experience gradient' is not as large. Younger women, on average, earned 83 per cent (25–34 year age group) and 95 per cent (35–44 year age group) of the average income among older women (45–54 year age group).

Although not shown in Table 9.4, average incomes of both men and women aged 65 and over are lower than they are for working-age Canadians, largely because of retirement. In 1997, adults aged 65 and over had average incomes of about $20,000. This compares with an average income of about $26,000 for persons in either the 25–34 or 55–64 age groups and with average income of $30,000 among those in the 35–54 age group (McGregor 2001). In the United States, the risk of experiencing poverty in later life is greatest for racialized women, unmarried women, and racialized men (Hardy and Hazelrigg 1995). Although research on the intersection of race and age is limited in Canada, evidence regarding the income disadvantages and poverty faced by older Aboriginal Canadians (Gyimah, White, and Maxim 2003) suggests that similar racial and age trends exist in Canada as well.

Alienation and Skill

Recall that Marx's third prediction with respect to the polarization of classes was that as capitalism developed, jobs would become increasingly deskilled and alienated. Indeed, **skill** and alienation are two characteristics of paid work that vary with social class. Generally, working-class jobs are characterized by the low levels of skill required to do the job and the often corresponding high levels of alienation, whereas jobs held by those in the new middle class and the old middle class tend to require more skill and to be more intrinsically rewarding. Therefore, for Marx's prediction to be supported, we must see evidence that middle-class jobs have become increasingly deskilled.

In 1974, Harry Braverman wrote his classic book, *Labour and Monopoly Capitalism*. Taking issue with those who argued that rising white-collar employment was a positive effect of post-industrialism that resulted in an increasingly large middle class, Braverman convincingly argued that most white-collar jobs (e.g., clerical and retail jobs) should be considered working-class, not middle-class. White-collar jobs, Braverman argued, were increasingly being deskilled and organized according to scientific management techniques that eliminated most of the control and autonomy that workers may have had over their work. Advances in new technologies contributed to this process by giving managers sophisticated tools with which they can monitor

their employees' work. Before computerized cash registers, for example, cashiers needed to know how to make change. Now cash registers tell the cashier how much change to give the customer. Furthermore, cash registers can now monitor the speed of key strokes and the number of customers that a cashier serves per minute. Managers use this information to evaluate their employees' job performance. Hence, new technology has been used both to deskill the work process and to monitor and control it.

One year before Braverman published his book, Daniel Bell also published what was to become an influential text on post-industrial society. Unlike Braverman, who argued that occupations were becoming increasingly deskilled, Bell (1973) looked to the future and argued that knowledge, and hence skill, would become a highly valued commodity in post-industrial society. Knowledge would be a basis of power much as the ownership of property had traditionally been, and knowledge workers would form a significant class (both in number and in power) in their own right. Bell argued that as the proportion of knowledge workers grew, the historical trend toward the polarization of society into two central classes, the bourgeoisie and the proletariat, would lose speed.

In the 30 years since Bell and Braverman published their books, debates have ensued over which thesis better explains the relationship between skill and class structure in post-industrial society. Although such debates are far from resolved, Clement and Myles are worth quoting at length on the issue:

We face either a postindustrial Nirvana of knowledge where everyone will be a brain surgeon, artist, or philosopher (Bell) or, alternatively, a post-industrial Hades where we shall be doomed to labour mindlessly in the service of capital (Braverman). When drawn in these terms, the historical debate is now no debate at all. Bell is the clear winner. Although much less than a knowledge revolution the net result of the shift to services has been to increase the requirements for people to think on the job (Clement and Myles 1994: 72).

In fact, in Canada 42 per cent of jobs in the post-industrial service sector are skilled, compared to only 26 per cent of those in the goods and distribution sector. And 55 per cent of new middle-class jobs are skilled, compared to only 23 per cent of working-class jobs (Clement and Myles 1994: 76). Of course, to the extent that women and members of ethnic and racial minority groups are disproportionately concentrated in the working class, the jobs that they hold are disproportionately unskilled.

Furthermore, Clement and Myles point out that the growth in the services sector has brought both skilled and unskilled jobs, but they underscore the fact that, at least in Canada and the United States, unskilled service jobs are often entry jobs for new and younger workers rather than a basis for working-class formation. This, combined with the fact that these service jobs are now often exit jobs for older workers who have been displaced, discouraged, restructured, or forced to retire early, suggests that age may play a more significant role in labour-market inequality in the years to come. It is no coincidence that during the market restructuring of the 1980s and 1990s we began to see older workers greeting us in department stores or serving us in fast food

chains. As one older worker who lost his job as a computer programmer put it, 'I can't find work. But, I'm not destitute yet so I don't need to sell running shoes and make 1/8 of the salary I was making before—like my friend is doing' (Personal correspondence, January 2003).

In short, although the conditions of work in contemporary Canadian capitalism are far from ideal, the proletarianization of labour force as predicted by Braverman has not occurred, even though skilled jobs are concentrated in the new middle and executive classes (Clement and Myles 1994). However, most of the literature on the deskilling debate has focused on class. More work must be done to consider whether and how jobs that are usually held by women or by members of racial and ethnic minority groups have been disproportionately deskilled. This requires critically examining the concept of skill itself and recognizing that gendered and racialized perceptions of skill have been driving these debates. Furthermore, when jobs are the unit of analysis (as is the case in this literature), important information regarding the 'skill mobility' of individuals over their life courses is missed.

Explaining Inequality in Paid Work

The preceding discussion shows that class, age, gender, race, and ethnicity structure the outcomes of inequality derived from paid work. And yet we know very little about how all of these structures work together in producing and reproducing market-based inequality. This points to the complexities that are associated with simultaneously considering all of these intersecting structures in analyses of paid work.

Labour-market-segmentation perspectives help to explain many of the relative disadvantages that women, people of colour, immigrants, ethnic minorities, and younger and older employees experience in paid work. According to these perspectives, good and bad jobs are located in different labour markets, the processes through which people get these jobs are different, there is little movement between these labour markets, and segregation within labour markets occurs on the basis of gender, race, ethnicity, and age. Bad jobs tend to be located in secondary labour markets and good jobs in primary labour markets.

The dual-economy perspective is one of many models of labour-market segmentation. It posits that there are a core sector and a periphery sector in the economy. The core sector comprises large companies that face little competition for their product. These firms 'exert considerable control over suppliers and markets and are also able to manipulate their political environment' (Krahn and Lowe 2002: 130). Examples of such companies are banks, telecommunication companies, automobile manufacturers, and airlines. The periphery sector of the economy, on the other hand, is dominated by smaller firms that are highly competitive with one another, are less profitable than firms in the core sector, have less political and economic power, and have lower rates of unionization. Examples of such companies are small manufacturing companies, retail outlets, and small hospitality firms. Jobs in this sector tend not to require as much skill or education as those in the core sector (Krahn and Lowe 2002: 129–31). According to this perspective, the reason that women, people of colour, immigrants, ethnic minorities, and younger and older

employees encounter labour-market disadvantages is that they are segregated in the periphery sector of the economy.

Unlike labour-market segmentation theories, which emphasize the structure of labour markets in explaining inequality, human-capital explanations of labour-market-based inequality suggest that individuals are sorted into good jobs and bad jobs on the basis of individual skill, education, and experience. Hence, those who invest more in these things will reap greater labour-market rewards, especially higher incomes. We cannot dismiss human-capital explanations, for better education does lead to better jobs and better incomes regardless of gender, age (if we only consider prime working ages), ethnicity, and race. And yet a crucial theoretical difficulty with human-capital explanations of labour-market-based inequality is that they assume that there is free and open competition for good jobs and that everyone is on a level playing field when it comes to their ability to invest in or use their education. However, research shows that racialized persons have lower returns on educational investments and that racism exists in labour markets (Kazemipur and Halli 2001; Li 2001b). A crucial methodological difficulty with human-capital approaches is that the complex multivariate models used in assessing labour market outcomes control for many variables, but do not explain, structural disadvantage.

The problem with human-capital explanations is that they often conclude that one factor accounts for more of the variation in income (as an example) than another factor, 'all else being equal'. The results of these models may suggest that a given bivariate relationship, for example, between ethnicity and income, can be explained away by human-capital variables such as education, language, experience, and so on. This then leads to the conclusion that human-capital variables account for differences in income and that ethnicity does not. Of course, what is missing in such conclusions is the fact that there are structural barriers that preclude certain ethnic and visible minority groups from attaining the human capital required for high incomes. All else is *not* equal, and adequate explanations of inequality must take that into account.

Structural barriers to good jobs and good wages feed on the logic of capitalism and its related assumptions about productive work, and they negatively affect labour-market outcomes for the working-class, women, older and younger workers, particular ethnic groups, visible minorities, and Aboriginal people. As a result, all else is not equal for persons over the age of 65, who are mostly excluded from 'productive' life as a result of mandatory retirement. All is not equal for 16-year-olds, who earn less than 18-year-olds doing the same job because of age-based minimum wages. All else is not equal for racialized persons, who face discrimination and racism in paid work and substandard education before it. And all else is not equal for women. Indeed, a second assumption under capitalism (and in human-capital theory) is that productivity increases with experience and that workers with more experience should therefore be paid higher wages. Yet experience is defined narrowly, and the skills and experience that are learned in 'non-productive' activities, such as raising children, are not considered transferable to the realm of paid work. Furthermore, as Gillian Ranson's (forthcoming) work on computer professionals and engineers shows, the combination of gender

minority status and lack of seniority makes it difficult for young women to challenge masculinist work cultures and career paths. Such difficulties are especially problematic in light of the fact that among computer professionals, women earn significantly less than men (Dryburgh 2000).

The organization of production processes does not stand in isolation from the organization of distributive and reproductive processes. For instance, some argue that because women 'choose' to work part-time, only data that compare income differences among full-year, full-time male and female employees should be considered. Yet, for many women part-time work is involuntary and for others, the choice to work part-time is conditioned by the ways in which class and gender relations structure the intersecting processes of production and reproduction.

Indeed, 'choice' is a complex word in sociology. Some women choose not to work for pay because they believe that it is better for their children to have one parent at home when they are young. The one parent who stays at home is usually a mother, in part because mothers are most often employed in jobs that pay less than fathers. Furthermore, this is often an easy choice for women because the jobs that they are employed in tend not to be 'good' jobs. From a particular family's point of view this 'choice' makes sense. Yet, the choice is structured by gendered labour markets that pay women less and employ them in jobs that are more alienating and less autonomous than the jobs that are more often held by men. Of course, this latter argument does not hold up well for working-class families. Indeed, family 'choices' are structured by both the nature of jobs held by mothers and fathers within families and by gendered ideologies which suggest that women are better caregivers than men.

The most obvious link between distributive and productive processes is through the wage (see 'Income and Poverty' above). For people who have tenuous relationships to labour markets or earn very little, state-based mechanisms of distribution help to alleviate some of the financial strain such individuals face. Welfare policy, employment insurance, maternity and parental leave, old age security, and publicly managed pension schemes are examples of state-based forms of distribution. These policies will be discussed in greater detail in chapter 12.

Beyond Statistics: Agency and Experience in Paid Work

It is clear that gender, class, age, ethnicity, and race are structural barriers to securing good, well-paid employment in Canada. But how do the choices that people make intersect with these structures in creating systems of advantage and disadvantage? How do women, the working class, older and younger workers, and racialized people experience the 'isms' that infiltrate paid work? Helen Ralston's (1996) study of immigrant women in Atlantic Canada demonstrates how racialized women experience the double-edged sword of diminished labour-market returns on their education combined with public re-employment policies that are not targeted to those who have university educations. In the words of one of Ralston's (1996: 87) informants,

> If you want to go to a programme in Manpower and Immigration, if you have a degree they are not even going to look at you. They say you have a degree. But you take that degree and go for a job and they say, 'Oh, we don't know this degree. We won't hire you.' They won't say it in so many words, but that's the implication. So I think you lose on both ends.'

Once employed, subtle and overt racism, sexism, and ageism are often experienced at work (Das Gupta 2002; McMullin and Marshall 2001).

Within the structures of class, age, gender, race, and ethnicity, people make choices about the paid work that they will do. In making these choices people often conform to structural expectations about what kind of work they should do. Women work as nurses; men work as engineers. When people resist social structures and make choices of paid work that goes against the grain, they are often required to conform to established structures and to conform to the middle-class white, male way of life. This process is illustrated through Luis M. Aguiar's choices and experiences and the difficulties he faced in becoming a professor of sociology at Okanagan University College in Kelowna, British Columbia (see Box 9.4).

Conclusion

As noted in the introduction to this chapter, some sociologists argue that the elimination of capitalism and a reorganization of work is needed in order to reduce or eliminate the 'tyranny of work' (Rinehart 1996). Although theoretically and philosophically this argument makes sense, the practicalities of revolutionizing capitalism in such a way are elusive. Nonetheless, within capitalism there

Box 9.4   Building an Academic Career

The concept of 'career' is a central part of academic life. People build their careers, change their careers, and sometimes destroy their careers by some scandal or dishonest undertaking. In addition, people participate in shaping (or not) the careers of others. Most students know the importance of a career and the need to train for it. In graduate schools students spend most of their time 'building' their careers. They take courses with specific outlines and deadlines and receive official grades that are recorded in their files in the department and the school of graduate studies. They teach courses under the supervision of faculty members, write scholarship applications with the support of a faculty member, and undergo a long period of mentoring and disciplining within the department and faculty. With many students in a department at the same time, it behooves each of them to make him/herself visible. Visibility counts when it comes to all the intangibles available in a university—for example, excellent letters of recommendation, invitations to conferences and special events and to publish, and, in some case, offers of course directorships.

But career has a class component that is often ignored. It is a foreign concept to working-class students of immigrant backgrounds. For me, the cultural capital that would communicate the importance of career was never part of my upbringing. As I grew up, my parents spoke of jobs—how to find and keep them. My father would usually go to the *canto* and wait there to be approached by a landowner, or his helping hand, to discuss the work, wages, and period of employment. '*O canto*' was the visual expression of the labour market where we lived: in a specific area of the town men advertised their willingness to work (simply by being there), and employers sought out labour power to hire. According to my father and my brother (who experienced it as a teenager for a couple of years), they had to get to the *canto* at the break of dawn in order to be able, just possibly, to select which employer to leave with. Sometimes they were lucky and were employed by the same landowners for consecutive weeks. In such cases the family was assured a steady income. More commonly, however, the men had to make daily trips to the *canto* in search of work.

I believe my father or mother never did mention the concept of career to me. The foreign nature of this concept was compounded in the new country as Portuguese immigrants joined the secondary labour market. In Montreal my father got work as a dishwasher, first at Dorval Airport and later in the Meridien Hotel, with no mention of a 'career'. It was not until I was in university that I learned that *careira* was the Portuguese equivalent.

This lack of awareness of the culture of academia was itself compounded by the relationships developed in graduate school. At York University, experiences of being the 'other', in terms of both class and ethnicity, persisted even though I had already survived McMaster University. Indeed, my class, ethnic position, and lack of knowledge about academia exacerbated my sense of dislocation. As a result I withdrew from the department, rarely communicating with anyone other than my course colleagues. I particularly disliked the pretentious relationships developed between students and some faculty members. Often I was uncomfortable with many of my classmates and their class origins and the gap between our experiences.

York University did have other students with immigrant origins, but they tended to be from bourgeois backgrounds and possessed the cultural (as well as social and financial) capital and class arrogance to persevere and do well in graduate school despite experiences of racism (Tomic and Trumper 1992). Some graduate classes were painful and intimidating. I sat through them witnessing which student would next seek to upstage the one who had just spoken. Here too, the immigrant working-class student is at a disadvantage because not everyone is equally prepared to participate in the discussion. This format silences many working-class students of immigrant background, but rarely is this recognized by bourgeois students and faculty members, who have grown up with the cultural capital of academia and thus fail to recognize its construction and reproduction via institutional and individual practices.

For these reasons I never felt at ease or secure in my sense of belonging to the sociology department at York University. In retrospect, I can see it was my self-imposed peripheralization within the department and the university that allowed me to succeed. I created my own space outside the department and most other university activities. In so doing I was able to distance myself from the climate of the department and at the same time carry on with my work at my own pace, and according to my own perception of what university education should be.

The Imposter Syndrome—Disarming the Black Student

Most working-class students in graduate training or academic posts worry about feelings of dislocation regarding their academic and cultural milieu. Their uneasiness stems from the foreignness of the culture, climate, and milieu within which they study and work. These feelings are frequently captured in the concept of the 'imposter syndrome'. That is, having no prior inside knowledge of academia, and navigating their way in uncharted waters, working-class students and academics of immigrant origin fear being 'discovered'. They fear being exposed as outsiders in a privileged and exclusive milieu in which they are not quite sure of the rules and practices of belonging.

I have not escaped this syndrome, and I often ask myself why and how I have gotten here. That question is usually followed by another set of queries. Given that I am in the university, does it mean that the system (of mobility, and merit, for instance) works? Am I an example of the system 'working for anybody'? Can one discredit a system that has benefited a working-class student from an immigrant background, enabled someone with no family history of higher education to climb to the highest level of formal education? Other important feelings also emerge to take over my psyche. I experience numerous bouts of confidence and wonder when I will finally be denounced as an imposter and revealed to be incompetent and incapable of thinking in a scholarly fashion. These feelings repeat themselves perpetually, as does the need to 'prove' over and over that I belong in academia.

Source: Aguiar (2001: 187–9). Reprinted by permission of Between the Lines.

are ways in which work could be organized that would make the experience of it better for many. On the basis of the discussion in this chapter, eliminating systemic, statistical, and other forms of discrimination, increasing wages, and reorganizing work so that it is more meaningful and autonomous are obvious places to start. Although such changes would not require the elimination of capitalism, they would require a radical shift in logic and a commitment on the part of members of business communities, governments, and individuals to redistribute wealth and to place less emphasis on capital growth. As it stands, if a company makes a $9 billion profit in one year and an $8 billion profit the next, it suffers on the stock market. Managers are then often forced to restructure and eliminate workers so that they can show, not profitability, but *increased* profitability. To eradicate inequality this logic must change, and to date, it has not done so.

Recall Marx's prediction about polarization. He argued that with advanced capitalism, work would be increasingly deskilled, the middle class would shrink, and that there would be an increasing polarization of the distribution of income and poverty. This chapter has shown that on the one hand, overall increases in the skill levels associated with many jobs and recent increases in self-employed small business owners suggests that the polarization thesis is incorrect. On the other hand, huge inequities in the distribution of income in Canada cannot be ignored. Furthermore, regardless of where one comes down on the debate about overall class polarization, the fact is that compared to middle-class jobs, working-class jobs are characterized by low levels of income and other benefits, low levels of autonomy and control in the work process, poorer working conditions, low levels of skill, and greater alienation. This chapter has also shown that discussions of polarization are incomplete unless they also consider how gender, age, ethnicity, and race influence outcomes of inequality related to paid work.

Glossary

Alienation   Marx identified four dimensions of alienation. First, workers are separated from the products of their labour. If people work on a product without knowing its purpose they are alienated from their product. Second, workers are separated from their labour process: they have little autonomy over how their work is done. Third, because to labour is part of the essence of being human, if workers are alienated from the products and processes of their labour they are also alienated from themselves. In other words, workers are unable to derive a meaningful existence from their work. The fourth dimension of alienation refers to the separation of workers from each other. This happens because work processes are set up in such a way as to minimize interaction among workers and second that capitalism establishes inherently antagonistic relationships across classes (see Rinehart 1996: 11–13).

Autonomy   The ability of workers to make their own decisions about how to do the work, how fast to do it, and what needs to be done. It refers to the control that workers have over their work processes.

Capitalism   The economic and social organization of production processes in modern industrialized countries.

Cumulative advantage/disadvantage hypothesis   The idea that social and economic advantage/disadvantage cumulates over time. The basic premise of these hypotheses may be captured by the following colloquialism: 'The rich get richer and the poor get poorer.'

Primary labour markets   A pool of good jobs that are characterized by high pay, good benefits, and job security.

Skill   In the sociological literature, the combination of job complexity and autonomy.

Surplus value   The value of surplus product that results when workers labour for more hours than would be required for them to achieve their means of subsistence. In capitalist systems of production, workers labour for themselves and for the owners of the means of production. If workers owned the product they produced and were able to sell it, they would need to work for fewer hours than they currently do in order to make the same wage. The excess time that they work and the surplus product that results from it (surplus value) is appropriated by owners.

Questions for Critical Thought

1. Consider your ideal job or the job you would like to have after you graduate. Is it a good job or a bad job? Why or why not?
2. Consider your first job. What were the advantages of having that job? What were the disadvantages of having that job? How were the advantages and disadvantages of that job related to themes discussed in this chapter? How could the job have been restructured to make it better?
3. This chapter argued that paid-work outcomes are mutually shaped by processes of production and distribution. Discuss this in relation to income disadvantages older persons face in retirement.
4. Explain labour-market-based inequality using a human capital framework. Critique that approach, paying attention to the structures of class, age, gender, ethnicity, and race.
5. Discuss the relationship between technology and skill. Will Marx's prediction about deskilling be realized in the years to come? How do gender, ethnicity, race, and age relations influence the 'deskilling' argument?

Recommended Reading

Hughes, Karen D. (1999). *Gender and Self-employment in Canada: Assessing Trends and Policy Implications*. CPRN Study No. W104. Changing Relationships Series. Ottawa: Renouf. One of the few comprehensive studies of self-employment in Canada. Although the emphasis is on gender, readers who are interested in all aspects of self-employment would do well to read this paper.

Krahn, Harvey, and Graham Lowe (2002). *Work, Industry, and Canadian Society*. 4th edn. Scarborough: ITP Nelson Canada. The most comprehensive text on paid work in Canada. Covering a wide range of topics, including class, age, race, ethnicity and gender, it is essential reading for students interested in paid work and inequality.

Luxton, Meg, and June Corman (2001). *Getting by in Hard Times: Gendered Labour at Home and on the Job*. Toronto: University of Toronto Press. This excellent book is a case study of steelworkers in Hamilton, Ontario. It examines how capital restructuring is gendered and classed and how class, gender, and race mutually constitute one another through paid and unpaid labour.

National Council on Welfare (2002). *Poverty Profile 1999*. Ottawa: Minister of Public Works and Government Services. An excellent overview of poverty in Canada. It considers class, age, gender, ethnicity, and race as well as region and other factors.

Rinehart, James W. (1996). *The Tyranny of Work: Alienation and the Labour Process*, 3rd edn. Toronto: Harcourt Brace. A Marxist account of paid work in Canada that concentrates mainly on social class.

CAGE(s) and Education

by Tammy Duerden Comeau and Julie McMullin

Introduction

In 1998 the Ontario government began mandatory testing of students in grades 3, 6, and 9. These tests are thought to evaluate students' abilities in reading, writing, and mathematics. They were established to make schools and school boards accountable for the quality of education that they provide and to identify areas that need improving. The testing is done by an office called the Educational Quality and Accountability Office (EQAO). Every year, test scores are published for each school, and individual students are given their scores so that they, their parents, and their teachers are aware of how they are doing and how they can improve (Bacigalupo 2003).

Although EQAO and school board officials stress that these scores should not be used to rank schools, the variation among the schools in their aggregate test scores makes that temptation hard to resist. In London, Ontario, and probably elsewhere, these variations do not appear random, but rather seem correlated with the socio-economic status (SES) of the neighbourhood in which a student lives. Comparing an elementary school in a low-SES neighbourhood with one in a high-SES neighbourhood, we see that only 30 per cent of the grade 6 students in the low-SES-neighbourhood school meet or exceed

provincial standards in reading whereas 66 per cent of grade 6 students in the high-SES neighbourhood do so. Comparing a high-SES neighbourhood high school with a low-SES-neighbourhood high school, reveals that there are higher proportions of students in the applied streams than in the latter (54 per cent versus 23 per cent). And in the academic stream, only 56 per cent of students at the school in the low-SES neighbourhood score at the provincial standard in math, compared to 77 per cent of the students in the high-SES-neighbourhood school who score either at or above the provincial standard (Bacigalupo 2003). Of course, this is not a systematic analysis of the relationship between SES and education. Nevertheless, a large body of literature does show that people of lower SES backgrounds tend not to be as highly educated as those from higher-SES backgrounds. It also suggests that 'universally' accessible education in Canada may vary considerably in its quality.

The pursuit of higher education is often viewed as an accessible and practical avenue for obtaining upward mobility. In a society that strongly promotes an individualistic ethos of success and failure, education is seen as an opportunity for the talented and motivated individual to move up the social ladder. Canadians would prefer not to believe that the educational system is also a place where societal inequalities are reproduced and where privileged groups solidify and maintain their advantages (Curtis, Livingstone, and Smaller 1992). This is not to deny that higher education tends to result in better life opportunities. Usually, highly educated people are employed in well-paid jobs (Little 1995) with relatively high degrees of autonomy and authority (Butlin and Oderkirk 1997). However, the chances of attaining higher education and, more specifically, of obtaining a lucrative degree that will result in substantial labour-market returns is significantly affected by one's class (Guppy and Davies 1998; Knighton and Mirza 2002), race or ethnicity (Li 2000; Mata 1997), gender (Davies, Mosher, and O'Grady 1995; Thiessen and Nickerson 1999), and age (Kapsalis, Morissette, and Picot 1999). The historical period in which we live also significantly shapes our chances for a higher education (Clark 2001). In 1996, for example, approximately 12 per cent of the Canadian population over the age of 15 had less than a grade 9 education, wheras in 1951 over half the population had less than a grade 9 education (Clark 2001: 23). At the close of the twentieth century, societal demands for an educated workforce have made a high-school education almost a compulsory requirement for sustained labour-force participation, and this marks a significant change from the popular educational expectations and aspirations of previous generations (Bowlby and McMullen 2002; Clark 2001; Statistics Canada and Council of Ministers of Education Canada 2000).

Pierre Bourdieu's work on the concepts of social and cultural capital have taken a prominent place in explaining the persistent inequalities (particularly in regard to social class) reproduced in educational systems (Wotherspoon 1998). According to Bourdieu, parents with more educational resources have richer reserves of cultural capital. **Cultural capital,** which is derived mostly from education, reflects middle- and upper-class values, attitudes, and beliefs that people hold about various aspects of social life. If education and related activities, such as reading, discussing politics, and learning about the world and music, are valued in a family and by its members, high levels of educational attainment are more likely. Working-class families tend not to expose their children to these activities to the extent that middle- and upper-class families do. Therefore, these children are often less prepared and less familiar with the knowledge that is taken for granted and drawn upon in the classroom.

The related concept of **social capital** refers to the information and social connections that are available to individuals. For example, the possession of knowledge about the workings of the educational system, such as a familiarity with the meanings of terms such as 'special education', is vital to successfully navigating through the system. The future implications of decisions made about course offerings and topics of study may also be unfamiliar to those with little experience in the educational system.

A quick look at the history of education in Canada makes it clear that achieving societal equality (even equality on the basis of 'merit') was not an overriding goal of the educational system at the outset (Curtis et al. 1992; Wotherspoon 1998). Early educational aims for the Canadian masses included the desire to create agreeable and obedient workers and a contented working class (Baldus and Kassam 1996; Curtis et al. 1992). Baldus and Kassam (1996), who analyze the predominant values found in nine-teenth-century Ontario schoolbooks, find strong prescriptive statements and moral lessons that recommend accepting one's lot in life and embracing social inequality. This is illustrated in the following excerpt from a nineteenth-century reader:

Our present lot, my parents say,

Is better for us, in every way,

Than one of our own choice could be. . . .

So now I am a little child,

Then let me try to be content;

My duty let me strive to do,

And with a thankful heart and true,

Accept the blessings heaven has sent.

(quoted in Baldus and Kassam 1996: 338)

Children were not encouraged to strive beyond their social roots, and the virtues of leading a simple and hard-working life were extolled in poems and fables (Baldus and Kassam 1996). Historically then, education-al curricula and policies have accepted, rather than challenged, societal inequalities (Curtis et al. 1992; Wotherspoon 1998).

Ng (1993) shows how the early educa-tional aims of Canadian missionaries were structured by racist, sexist, and class-based ideologies. Aboriginal men and women were taught different skills in order to reproduce European gendered societal patterns (Ng 1993). Only the men were taught how to farm, and the women were schooled in 'domestic' duties (Ng 1993). The goal was to produce a new and subordinate working class that would benefit the colonizers (Ng 1993). A strong theme of Aboriginal inferi-ority was woven through religious and edu-cational teachings (Ng 1993). The delivery

of these educational imperatives was later refined and developed in all-encompassing institutional forms (Guppy and Davies 1998; Wotherspoon 1998).

The residential school system that Aboriginals in Canada were subjected to in the late nineteenth and twentieth centuries provides a graphic illustration of the extent to which racism and class ideologies can direct 'educational' programs (Nicholas 2001; Wotherspoon 1998). Aboriginal chil-dren were cut off from their families and taught to be ashamed of their cultural her-itage (Nicholas 2001). Indeed, according to Schissel and Wotherspoon (2003: 43), 'the expressed intent of residential school policy was to destroy a culture and rebuild Indian children as active participants in the indus-trial economy, if not remove them as imped-iments to economic development'. Generations of Aboriginals are still paying the price from the humiliating, alienating, and abusive experiences endured in residen-tial schools (Jaine 1993). Indeed, the last residential school did not close until the 1980s (Nicholas 2001).

This chapter examines the barriers to educational attainment in Canada. In partic-ular, it considers the historical influence of social class, race, ethnicity, gender, and age in educational attainment, how they cur-rently affect educational attainment, and the relationship between these factors and the educational returns achieved through labour markets.

Focusing on Class: Historical Notes and Existing Patterns

The class position of our family of origin has a significant impact on our educational prospects and consequent life trajectory (Bowlby and McMullen 2002; Knighton and Mirza 2002). The effect of class on the educational attainment of Canadians has been described by Guppy and Davies (1998: 59) as a particularly 'enduring' feature of inequality. The education achieved by our parents and the kind of work that they perform have an undeniable influence on our early school experiences and on our level of educational attainment (Bowlby and McMullin 2002; Curtis et al. 1992; Guppy and Davies 1998; Nakhaie and Curtis 1998). Indeed, '**streaming**', or filtering, occurs before some children ever enter a school building (Curtis et al. 1992). Parents with enough money can choose to send their children to elite private schools, where students are groomed to attend the top universities. Within public schools, students have been classified and 'sorted' into various academic avenues or 'streams' in which some children are relegated to learning 'basic skills' and others are academically challenged and channelled to go on to higher learning (Curtis et al. 1992).

Curtis and his colleagues (1992), who have examined the practice of streaming in Ontario schools, have shown that the allocation of students to various ability levels in both elementary and secondary schools is not free of class bias. In other words, children from lower- and lower-middle-class backgrounds were found to be much more likely to end up in special education or remedial programs in elementary school and in basic streams or vocational schools in secondary school (Curtis et al. 1992). These authors cite studies from the 1970s and 1980s which show that children from families on social assistance were '60 times more likely' to be in special or remedial-education

programs than children from the families of professional workers (Curtis et al. 1992: 59). Being in special or remedial education in elementary school tended to be a permanent placement which led to a 'basic' stream in an academic high school or a vocational school. Students who attended these vocational schools were predominately of working-class and ethnic- or racial-minority backgrounds. These students faced fairly dismal job prospects, as they were not eligible for university or most college programs, and even those who achieved a vocational certificate from their high school were not actually qualified to enter many trade apprenticeship programs (Curtis et al. 1992).

Some may argue that these statistics are outdated and that streaming is no longer a predominant teaching practice in the educational system. However, recent studies indicate that children from higher socio-economic backgrounds continue to enjoy significant advantages in elementary schools (Bohatyretz and Lipps 1999; Lipps and Frank 1997). Bohatyretz and Lipps (1999) found that children from low socio-economic backgrounds were disproportionately represented in special-education programs. In addition, those children who received special education for 'problems at home' had parents with the lowest education levels (Bohatyretz and Lipps 1999). Results from the National Longitudinal Survey of Children and Youth 1994–5 showed that children from families in the highest socio-economic status were significantly less likely to be receiving remedial education (5 per cent) than those from the lowest socio-economic backgrounds (17 per cent) (Lipps and Frank 1997). Children from the highest socio-economic backgrounds were also significantly more likely to be enrolled in some form of a gifted educational program (9 per cent), when compared with children from the lowest socio-economic backgrounds (5 per cent) (Lipps and Frank 1997: 54). Children from privileged socio-economic backgrounds were also ranked considerably higher in academic ability assessments by their teachers (Lipps and Frank 1997).

Figure 10.1 shows a clear incline from the lowest socio-economic groups to the highest, with the teacher's perception of academic ability growing as the socio-economic status of the student increases. In fact, Lipps and Frank (1997: 54) found that students from the highest socio-economic status were 'two to three times as likely' to be ranked among the best in the class by their teachers in reading, writing, and math. Thus, the patterns of educational advantage and disadvantage by class discussed by

Curtis and his colleagues (1992) do not appear to have dissipated substantially over time.

Educational Attainment

The class background of students (including parental education, income, and occupation) exerts a significant influence on their chances of obtaining a high school diploma and for obtaining a post-secondary education (Ali and Grabb 1998; Bowlby and McMullen 2002; Guppy and Davies 1998; Knighton and Mirza 2002). Currently, labour-market prospects for people who do not have a high-school diploma are particularly bleak (Guppy and Davies 1998). A 1995 follow-up survey of students who dropped out of high school in 1991 found that they were more likely to be unemployed than were high school graduates

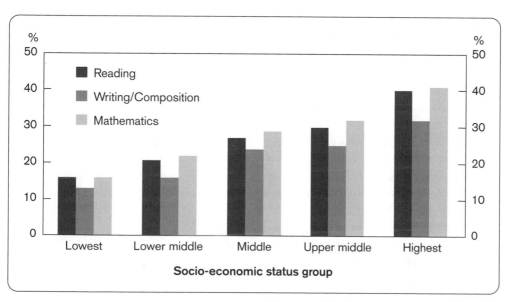

Figure 10.1 Proportion of Children Ranked near the Top of Their Class by Their Teachers, by socio-economic Status

Source: National Longitudinal Survey of Children and Youth, 1994–95. Reproduced in Lipps and Frank, (1997: 55).

(Frank 1996). Indeed, a high-school diploma is now, more than ever, seen as a requirement for stable employment prospects (Frank 1996; Guppy and Davies 1998); however, a number of students continue to leave school before acquiring their diploma (Bowlby and McMullen 2002). Still, high-school completion rates increased throughout the 1990s, such that only 12 per cent of 20-year-olds did not complete high school in 1999 as compared to 18 per cent in 1991 (Bowlby and McMullen 2002). The more highly educated parents are, the more likely their children are to complete high school (Bowlby and McMullen 2002).

Students who dropped out of high school were much less likely to have a parent with a university degree (11 per cent) than students who graduated from high school (30.6 per cent) (Bowlby and McMullen 2002). Those students who dropped out of high school were also more likely to have parents with less than a high-school education (26.9 per cent) than high-school graduates (8.7 per cent) (Bowlby and McMullen 2002). The mothers of high-school graduates were more likely to work in government, health, social science, management, business, finance, art, or culture and recreation, whereas the mothers of students who dropped out were more concentrated in sales and service, and manufacturing and trade occupations (Bowlby and McMullen 2002). Similarly, the fathers of dropouts were more likely to be employed in trades and manufacturing occupations, while the fathers of graduates were more often in management, finance, and the sciences (Bowlby and McMullen 2002). These findings suggest that it is not just family finances and income that are affecting high-school completion rates but that the mecha-

nisms of social and cultural capital in the form of the valuation of education and the exposure to educationally enhancing experiences are having an influence. More highly educated parents and those who have been 'successful' and accomplished in the educational system are more easily able to pass down the excitement of learning and to expect a certain level of education on the part of their offspring (Guppy and Davies 1998). The completion of high school is a necessary step for entrance to most types of post-secondary education, and it is here that the influence of income is seen more vividly.

The most significant barrier to post-secondary education reported by 18- to 20-year-olds in 1999 was that of finances (Bowlby and McMullen 2002). Post-secondary education, particularly university education, is becoming more and more expensive (Finnie 2002). Looker and Lowe (2001) report that post-secondary education in Canada is becoming less accessible to lower-income groups. For instance, 18- to 21-year-olds with parents in the highest income quartile were much more likely to pursue post-secondary studies (70 per cent) than those in the lowest income quartile (56 per cent) (Knighton and Mirza 2002: 26). Those from higher socio-economic backgrounds have higher educational aspirations and are more likely to go on to university and to obtain post-graduate degrees (Looker and Lowe 2001). The influence of family socio-economic status on university enrolment is outlined in Figure 10.2.

Here we see a comparison of university participation rates for 1986 and 1994. This figure shows a widening gap in accessibility for those from the lowest socio-economic status groups (Statistics Canada and CMEC 2000). Although participation has increased

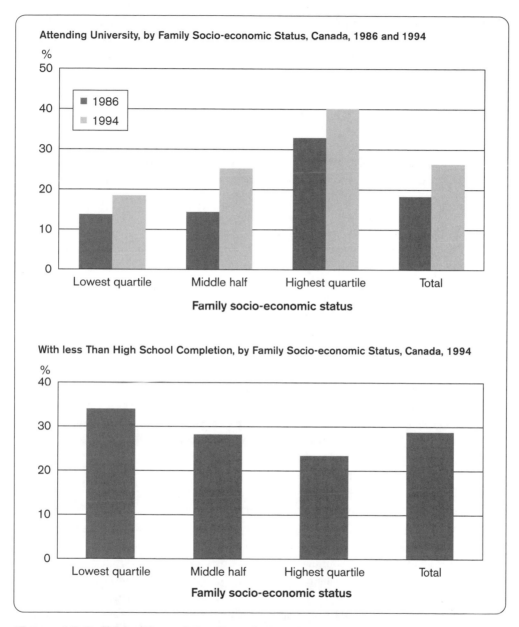

Attending University, by Family Socio-economic Status, Canada, 1986 and 1994

%

■ 1986
■ 1994

Lowest quartile   Middle half   Highest quartile   Total

Family socio-economic status

With less Than High School Completion, by Family Socio-economic Status, Canada, 1994

%

Lowest quartile   Middle half   Highest quartile   Total

Family socio-economic status

Figure 10.2 Education of the Population Aged 18 to 21

Source: General Social Survey 1986 and 1994, and Centre for Education Statistics, Statistics Canada. Reproduced in Statistics Canda and CMEC, (2000: 107).

for all groups, the participation for the lowest socio-economic group has not kept pace with that of the middle and highest income groups. A recent study by Finnic (2002) shows that Canada student loans are not being used by those with the most need, and he suggests that people from the lower socio-economic groups may forgo university and post-secondary education altogether rather than have to repay a large loan.

The multiple effects of income and education on post-secondary participation are complex. Finances are a clear factor in the ability to save for future educational goals. For instance, families with earnings under $40,000 a year have a 16 per cent participation rate in the Registered Education Savings Plan, compared to a 58 per cent participation rate for families who earn over $60,000 a year (CPRN 2002: 17). But parental education has been found to have an even larger effect on the rate of post-secondary participation (Knighton and Mirza 2002; CPRN 2002).

Knighton and Mirza (2002) found that post-secondary participation rates were significantly affected by parental education and income. Although most Canadian students (65 per cent) engage in post-secondary education of some sort, higher levels of parental income and higher levels of parental education meant higher post-secondary participation rates (Knighton and Mirza 2002: 27). Figure 10.3 shows the combined effects of parental education and income on post-secondary participation for Canadian students in 1998.

Here we see the significant influence of parents' education on whether or not their children pursue some post-secondary studies. Knighton and Mirza (2002: 29) point out that the participation of those from the lowest income quartile (68 per cent) who had at least one parent with post-secondary education outpaces the participation of those from the highest income quartile (56 per cent) with no post-secondary education. In fact, the children of university-edu-

cated parents were much more likely to engage in university studies (49 per cent) than in college studies (35 per cent) (Knighton and Mirza 2002: 28). The pattern was reversed for children of parents with a high-school diploma or less, who were much less likely to attend university (17 per cent) than college (29 per cent) (Knighton and Mirza 2002: 28). The aspirations of students are significantly affected by the aspirations that their parents have for them (Looker and Lowe 2001), and usually the aspirations of those students from more privileged socio-economic backgrounds are higher than those from less privileged backgrounds. The benefits of social capital in terms of the depth of information available about post-secondary options and the consequences of early academic decisions thus play a role in the advantages accrued for those from higher SES backgrounds (CPRN 2002).

Educational Returns in the Labour Market

The decision to attend university as opposed to college, which university or college is chosen, the program of study that students choose, and whether they pursue graduate studies have consequences for their future earnings potential (Butlin 2001; Davies and Guppy 1997; Guppy and Davies 1998). For example, in the examination by Guppy and Davies (1998) of 1990 earnings by field of study chosen for a bachelor's degree, some fields of study had definite earning advantages over others. Those who enrolled in programs such as engineering, law, and medicine reaped higher earnings than the average BA graduate, and those with more general degrees (e.g., humanities and social

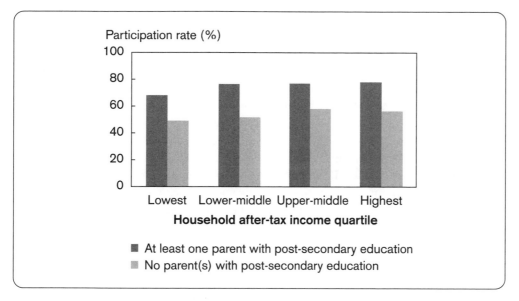

Figure 10.3 Post-secondary Participation Rates for Canadians Aged 18 to 21 and No Longer in High School, by Household Income and Parents' Education, 1998

Source: Analysis using Statistics Canada's Survey of Labour and Income Dynamics, 1993 to 1998 Knighton and Mirza (2002: 29).

sciences) earned less than the average BA graduate (Guppy and Davies 1998). The choice of what type of post-secondary or university program to enrol in depends on adequate information; however, it also increasingly depends on finances. This is particularly true in professional programs, which tend to have the highest labour-market returns. For example, the University of Toronto law program charges $20,000 a year in tuition fees, which would make it unaffordable for many students (CPRN 2002: 19).

Parental education has a significant effect on whether or not students who achieve a bachelor's degree continue on to graduate studies (Butlin 2001). Students whose parents had a high-school diploma or less were much less likely to enrol in mas-

ter's or doctoral programs than students with university-educated parents (Butlin 2001). The advantage for those students whose parents had obtained a master's or a doctoral degree was particularly pronounced, for these bachelor-degree recipients were three times more likely to pursue master's and doctoral programs than bachelor-degree recipients whose parents had only a high-school education (Butlin 2001: 28). The achievement of higher levels of education tends to result in more authoritative and higher-paying jobs (Butlin 2001; Butlin and Oderkirk 1997). Butlin (2001: 28) notes that recipients of master's degrees could expect to earn $9,000 a year more than those with only the bachelor's degree. Therefore, those students who come from more highly educated families maintain their advantage throughout university and into the labour market.

Focusing on Race/Ethnicity: Historical Notes and Existing Patterns

Issues of class and race or ethnicity are closely bound together, and many of the educational disadvantages and difficulties faced by racial and ethnic minorities stem from long-standing economic exploitation and disadvantage (as in the case of Aboriginal Canadians) and from the financial and social struggle of emigrating to a new country (Ali and Grabb, 1998; Bernhard and Freire 1999; Guppy and Davies 1998). In spite of these barriers, visible minorities in Canada tend to be more highly educated than the general population (i.e., they are more likely to have a high-school diploma and to be university-educated) (Guppy and Davies 1998). Currently, higher levels of education among visible minorities are due to the high levels of education required to gain entrance to Canada through immigration policy. Indeed, minority groups in Canada have historically faced barriers and educational obstacles based on their perceived ethnic and racial background. Individuals from racial and ethnic minority groups have historically experienced exclusions and racism in Canadian classrooms (Carr and Klassen 1995; Kelly 2002; Knight 1997; Sefa Dei 1993). This is illustrated by the history of classroom segregation and eventual 'separate' schooling for black students in Canada West in the nineteenth century (Knight 1997). This practice was instituted in spite of vigorous protests by black parents (Knight 1997). The Separate School Act of 1859 provided black students with schools that were distinctly 'separate' from the institutions attended by white children (Knight 1997). By the twentieth century, these schools no longer existed, though the act remained on the books until 1964 (Knight 1997).

These sentiments of exclusion and difference are echoed in the history of educational programs directed at Aboriginals in Canada (Wotherspoon 1998). The residential schools for Aboriginal children operated from the late nineteenth century until the 1980s, and these programs effectively stripped these children of their families and their culture (Guppy and Davies 1998). This was entirely intentional. Guppy and Davies (1998: 180) note that 'a deliberate and concerted effort was made to remove thousands of Aboriginal children from their families and communities and immerse them in European traditions, thereby assimilating or 'Canadianizing' large portions of the Aboriginal population.' These programs have had a devastating and lasting impact on Aboriginal populations (Guppy and Davies 1998).

A number of efforts have been made to promote inclusive and anti-racist education, but substantial barriers remain (Bernhard and Freire 1999; Kelly 2002; Sefa Dei 1993; Canadian Education Statistics Council 2001).Visible-minority children, children for whom English is a second language, and children from lower socio-economic backgrounds comprise the bulk of children in Canada who are defined as '**at-risk**' for educational difficulties and non-completion of high school (CESC 2001: 19). These findings are similar to those reported by Curtis and his colleagues (1992), namely, that visible-minority students, students from lower-income families, and students for whom English was a second language had a much greater chance of being placed in remedial education programs and basic or vocational high-school streams. Researchers are quick to point out that the difficulty lies not with the children concerned but rather with the school environment into which they are placed (CESC 2001). These researchers warn against stigmatizing and labelling children as 'problem students' when the problem may be the 'flawed nature of society' (CESC 2001: 19).

Bernhard and Freire (1999) give an example of the way in which the elementary schools fail students from minority backgrounds. They specifically look at the school experiences of the children of recent Latin American immigrants to Canada and the way in which these parents and teachers interact and communicate (Bernhard and Freire 1999). A primary aim was to find out how the school system could serve these families better and how these parents could be more effective advocates for their children. In spite of the high educational aspirations and valuation of education found in these Latin American families, the authors found a general pattern of academic under-performance for these children and parental alienation and confusion in their relations with educational personnel (Bernhard and Freire 1999). One of their main findings was that many parents did not understand much of the vocabulary used by the teachers. For instance, the teacher's practice of using 'positive' and complimentary descriptors when describing difficulties with a child's progress was seen by the parents to indicate a good performance. In addition, educational terms like 'special education' and 'reading clinics' were not fully understood or explained to parents. Parents expected a more compassionate and personal approach from their children's teachers and were disappointed

with the impersonal and all-business attitude on the part of Canadian teachers (Bernhard and Freire 1999). These findings illustrate that even when parents have high educational goals for their children and want to facilitate their child's education, the structures of the institution itself (e.g., institutional jargon) can pose significant barriers to a positive academic experience and effective parental involvement.

Educational Attainment

Although there is a significant body of research on the educational attainment of Aboriginals in Canada, much more information is needed on the effect that race or ethnicity and place of birth have on educational attainment (Looker and Lowe 2001). The diversity among groups designated 'visible and ethnic minorities' and the factors of nativity, the period of immigration, and the changing effect of immigration policy make these investigations complex (Guppy and Davies 1998). Much of the information that does exist does not distinguish between those born in Canada (and thus educated in Canadian schools) and those who were foreign-born and emigrated later (perhaps after completing their education) (Guppy and Davies 1998). The high educational attainments required by the current immigration regulations and the younger age of many immigrants compared to the general population may be artificially inflating the educational levels of ethnic and racial minority groups and thus underestimating the barriers encountered in the Canadian educational system (Guppy and Davies 1998). Nonetheless, a number of recent studies contend that class is a more important predictor than race and ethnicity of educational attainment (Ali and Grabb 1998; Guppy and Davies 1998).

Guppy and Davies' (1998) data show that visible minorities as a group are not collectively disadvantaged when compared to whites. In a Canadian comparison of high-school completion rates, visible minorities as a group had much higher (69.6 per cent) completion rates (69.9 per cent) than non-visible minorities (54.3 per cent) (Guppy and Davies 1998). In terms of university-degree attainment, Canadians from Chinese and Filipino backgrounds are among the top three in educational attainment according to 1991 census data (Guppy and Davies 1998). University degrees are far more common among visible-minority adults (18 per cent) than among other adults (11 per cent) (Kelly 2002). However, the educational attainments of racial and ethnic minorities are extremely variable (Guppy and Davies 1998; Kelly 2002).

Table 10.1 illustrates the diversity in educational attainment among men in Canada by ethnic group. In this table, the authors have provided an age comparison in order to account partially for potential differences between foreign-born and Canadian-born individuals. Guppy and Davies (1998) point out the significant increase in educational attainment and mobility among Greek, Italian, Polish, and Ukrainian immigrants when comparing age cohorts. The authors argue that the diversity of levels of educational attainment among ethnic and racial minorities means that specific groups (e.g., Aboriginals and blacks) face systemic obstacles in the process of educational attainment that not all racial and ethnic minority groups encounter (Guppy and Davies 1998; Simmons and Plaza 1998).

Aboriginals in Canada have encountered numerous barriers in the educational system (CPRN 2002; Guppy and Davies 1998; Mata 1997; Statistics Canada and CMEC 2000). Some of the obstacles faced in the process of obtaining a post-secondary education are 'distrust of educational institutions, lack of adequate secondary school preparation, the poverty of many Aboriginal communities, reluctance to leave their community, and perceived social discrimination' (CPRN 2002: 26). Box 10.1 shows that the government recognizes this educational deficit as a problem of structural barriers and access. Although the education ministers in this article strongly recommended action and acknowledge the extent of underrepresentation of Aboriginal students in the post-secondary system, no concrete directives or guidelines were given to ameliorate or improve the participation rate of Aboriginal students and other underrepresented minority groups.

The educational system has failed Aboriginal students, and consequently, they have much lower levels of educational attainment than the non-Aboriginal population (Statistics Canada and CMEC 2000). According to 1996 statistics, Aboriginals were much less likely to have completed high school (42 per cent) than the non-Aboriginal population (22 per cent) (Statistics Canada and CMEC 2000: 97). It is estimated that university graduates in Canada account for 13 per cent to 29 per cent of the non-Aboriginal population, whereas among Aboriginals, only 3 per cent to 10 per cent have a university degree (Statistics Canada and CMEC 2000: 98). For those Aboriginal students who do engage in post-secondary education, the attrition rate is extremely high (CPRN 2002). In Mata's

Table 10.1 Percentage of Men with a University Degree, by Ethnic Origin and Age Group, 1991

Ethnic Group	25–34		65+	
	Total Population	% with University Degree (Rank)	Total Population (Rank)	% with University Degree
Jewish	15,135	55.0 (1)	22,270	17.2 (1)
Filipino	10,230	20.8 (4)	3,865	15.8 (2)
Chinese	53,980	37.6 (2)	19,255	12.4 (3)
Hungarian	8,380	17.2 (7)	9,340	12.3 (4)
Scottish	80,255	15.7 (9)	84,855	9.7 (5)
Irish	67,545	14.8 (10)	58,325	8.0 (6)
Black	16,755	13.0 (12)	3,010	7.0 (7)
English	314,185	11.7 (16)	267,385	6.8 (8)
Spanish	6,865	11.5 (17)	1,375	6.6 (9)
Greek	12,300	24.0 (3)	4,985	5.9 (10)
Polish	23,845	18.4 (6)	24,670	5.8 (11)
Scandinavian	12,795	12.5 (15)	20,410	5.7 (12)
Dutch	38,205	12.9 (14)	21,225	5.4 (13)
French	559,650	13.0 (12)	269,830	5.2 (14)
German	85,505	13.5 (11)	63,635	4.9 (15)
Ukrainian	33,125	16.2 (8)	42,750	4.0 (16)
Italian	72,980	18.8 (5)	42,385	1.8 (17)
Portuguese	24,145	4.5 (18)	5,845	1.2 (18)
Aboriginal	40,035	1.9 (19)	8,525	0.4 (19)
Total (all groups)	**2,363,130**	**15.9**	**1,256,565**	**7.7**

Source: Census of Canada, 1991, special tabulations. Reproduced in Guppy and Davies (1998: 104).

Box **10.1**   **Open Doors for Minorities, Education Ministers Urge Aboriginal Students 'Grossly Underrepresented' in Postsecondary Institutions.**
By Paula Arab

Provincial education ministers say aboriginals and other minority groups need much better access to Canadian colleges and universities.

'We need [as institutions] to deploy our best efforts to identify and remove barriers that inhibit access to underrepresented groups,' BC Education Minister Paul Ramsay said last week after the ministers released a report on education standards.

'It's not just an issue of how many people are going to a college, university, or a vocational school, but what are we doing to get rid of systemic barriers?' said Mr Ramsey, also the chairman of the Council of Ministers of Education.

In BC, Mr Ramsey said, aboriginal people are 'grossly underrepresented at postsecondary institutions.'

A national plan detailed in the report is designed to change the situation but won't be forced onto provinces or universities. Instead, it's meant to serve as a 'first step' to improve education standards.

The plan sets out expectations and standards in six areas: quality; accessibility; mobility and portability; relevance and responsiveness; research and scholarship; and accountability. It's the first time Canadian education ministers (all but those from Quebec and Yukon, who participated only as observers) have agreed to a set of key principles, the result of two years of negotiations.

'I think what we're willing to do is we're willing to raise the standards nationally,' said Saskatchewan Education Minister Maynard Sonntag.

'When we as ministers sit around the table here, this is beneficial to all Canadians, because we learn from every other jurisdiction about what they're doing best. I think we all try to raise the levels as opposed to competing with each other.

The ministers' report provided general principles, it didn't call for specific change or set out implementation guidelines.

'This document is not concerned with how to achieve the expectations or with what level of public funding is allocated in what manner,' the report said. 'These are important issues, but they fall within the purview of individual provinces and territories.'

Funding is a legitimate barrier to accessibility, Mr Ramsey said, but it's only part of the solution.

'Sure money is one [barrier], geography is another. Let's look at the principle that says very clearly all citizens must be ensured of the opportunity to access postsecondary education and then chase down all the parameters of that and make sure we're addressing them properly.'

In Saskatchewan, for example, accessibility for out-of-province study is limited by the student-loan program. Loans are available only for study within the province unless the course is only available elsewhere. Mr Sonntag said it's systemic barriers such as those that ministers want eliminated.

Mobility is also a key issue in the report, because several provinces have criticized Quebec's two-tier tuition policy. Although Quebec charges in-provinces students fees that tend to be much lower than those in other provinces, out-of-province students studying in Quebec must pay almost double.

Recommendations

The Report on Public Expectations of Postsecondary Education in Canada outlined a framework of public expectations in six key areas: Quality: Governments and institutions are expected to work together to ensure high-quality learning environments while preparing students for satisfying employment. Accessibility: Postsecondary education should be accessible throughout life. All citizens must be assured of educational opportunities, regardless of financial need. Mobility and portability: Students should obtain credit for previous education as they transfer between programs, institutions, and the labour market. Relevance and responsiveness: Postsecondary education should promote the connection of learning, work, and civil society. Research and scholarship: These should contribute to the cultural, social, and economic development and health communities.

Source: Arab (1999). Reprinted by permission of the Canadian Press.

(1997: 8) investigation of the process of socio-economic and educational 'transmission' in Canada, Aboriginal sons and daughters experienced distinct disadvantages when compared to other ethnic and racial minority groups. While the parents in many other ethnic and racial groups were able to successfully 'transmit' their level of education to their children, in the case of highly educated Aboriginal parents, there was little success in passing on attained educational levels (Mata 1997). The only other group to face such systemic and enduring obstacles to educational attainment in Mata's (1997) study were foreign-born minority daughters.

Educational Returns in the Labour Market

The high educational attainment of many visible-minority groups and the educational mobility experienced by some ethnic and minority groups in a society that discriminates on the basis of race and ethnicity is a testament to the power of individual agents. Unfortunately, as shown in chapter 9, the true impact of racial and ethnic privilege are more starkly evident in the workings of the labour market (Basran and Zong 1998; Geschwender and Guppy 1995; Li 2001b, 2000; Mata 1997). Higher education is no guarantee of occupational and socio-economic mobility (Mata 1997). All educational credentials are not valued equally, and a number of studies have shown that visible minorities encounter systemic devaluation of their educational credentials, especially when they happen to be among Canada's more highly educated recent immigrants (Basran and Zong 1998; Li 2001b). Visible-minority professionals who emigrate to Canada have been found to experience downward mobility compared to their occupational positions in their country of origin

(Basran and Zong 1998). Geschwender and Guppy (1995) found that even among Canadian-born ethnic groups, those of British ancestry enjoyed significantly better market returns for their post-secondary education than those from many other ethnic backgrounds. Kelly (2002) notes that there are significant levels of underemployment among highly educated visible minorities and despite their higher educational attainment they are less likely to obtain employment in professional or managerial occupations when compared to the non-visible minority population.

Visible-minority immigrants who are not educated in Canada face significant barriers in obtaining jobs on par with their education (Li 2000b). Wanner (1998) notes that immigrants with foreign credentials receive essentially no labour-market compensation for their educational worth. In addition, Wanner (1998) argues that although he did not find evidence of systemic racial discrimination, immigrants from countries with lower levels of development were significantly more disadvantaged in the labour market.

Li (2001b) specifically analyzes the labour-market returns that visible-minority immigrants and non-visible minority immigrants can expect in comparison with native-born Canadians. Gender and race or ethnicity were found to have significant effects on the extent to which immigrants encountered underemployment and weak labour-market returns (Li 2001b). Visible-minority immigrants (both men and women) were penalized much more harshly in the labour market for their foreign credentials than white immigrants (Li 2001b). Visible-minority immigrant women with foreign degrees were the most disadvantaged in the labour market (Li 2001b). For example, white immigrant women with a foreign degree earned an average of $30,770 annually, in comparison to visible-minority immigrant women with a foreign degree, who earned the least of any group at $26,797 (Li 2001b: 32). These findings illustrate that the achievement of credentials and educational mobility cannot in and of themselves overcome systemic discrimination for disadvantaged groups.

Focusing on Gender : Historical Notes and Existing Patterns

Historically, women have had to fight for their right to be educated, and educational policies have tended to emphasize women's wifely and motherly roles in processes of reproduction (Ng 1993; Wollstonecraft 1792). Yet, in Canada, women's access to education and enrolments at the elementary and secondary levels have been equivalent to men's for some time (Guppy and Davies 1998; Wotherspoon 1998). In fact, the educational level of women has surpassed men's since the mid-1980s, except at the doctoral level (Butlin 2001; Wotherspoon 1998). Although alienation and 'silencing' in the classroom are still a concern for girls and women, and women continue to be underrepresented in post-secondary technical, mathematical, and engineering programs, the gender-equity issue that is gaining attention in the elementary and secondary school systems has been the relative 'under-performance' of boys in comparison to girls (CPRN 2002; Looker and Lowe 2001; Thiessen and Nickerson 1999; Wotherspoon 1998).

However, lumping all boys together as 'at-risk' may confuse the issue, because it is more specifically boys from families with low socio-economic status, Aboriginal boys, boys from some visible-minority ethnic groups, and boys for whom English is a second language who are systemically disadvantaged in the educational system (CPRN 2002: 15). This argument is supported by the research of Thiessen and Nickerson (1999:14), who found that the mathematical and problem-solving abilities of boys are much 'more variable' than the abilities of girls, and thus there are more boys scoring above and below average. As with race and ethnicity, where some minority ethnic groups attain very high levels of education and others are at a substantial disadvantage, within the 'variable' gender there are significant differences in academic performance and post-secondary participation rates among groups of boys (CPRN 2002). These findings speak to the complexity of identities and the enmeshment of the social relations of class, age, gender, and race and ethnicity, particularly when it comes to social privilege and disadvantage.

Still, a number of studies illustrate that boys comprise the majority of students 'at-risk' of educational difficulties (Bohatyretz and Lipps 1999; Bowlby and McMullen 2002; CESC 2001; CPRN 2002; Lipps and Frank 1997; Statistics Canada and CMEC 2000). Unfortunately, most of these studies do not give us more specific information about the class and race or ethnicity of boys and girls in a synthesized way (e.g., data are tabulated for these factors separately). The most recent gender-based data at the elementary-school level comes from the National Longitudinal Survey of Children and Youth, 1994–5. These data showed that boys accounted for two-thirds of the children enrolled in special education programs

and that they made up the vast majority (83 per cent) of children in special education on account of behavioural or emotional problems (Bohatyretz and Lipps 1999). Girls were also given consistently better academic ratings by their teachers (Julien and Ertl 1999).

Figure 10.4 shows the percentage of boys and girls rated near the top of the class by their teachers in various academic subjects and overall (Julien and Ertl 1999). In this figure, we see that compared to boys, girls are rated 'at the top of the class' significantly more often in writing and reading, as well as in overall ability, and that differences in the ranking of mathematical skills is negligible (Julien and Ertl 1999). In this study, teachers predicted higher educational attainment for the girls in their classes than for the boys. Furthermore, when children were rated by their teachers for various behavioural traits, boys were perceived to be more physically aggressive and more hyperactive and inattentive than girls (Julien and Ertl 1999). In contrast, girls exhibited better work habits and more **pro-social** or altruistic behaviour, although they were also perceived to exhibit more indirect aggressive behaviour. Of note, however, was that there were no perceived gender differences in anxiety and emotional disorders, and when all behavioural scores were compared, no substantial behavioural differences were found (Julien and Ertl 1999).

Overall, these findings provide few answers as to why boys encounter disadvantages in the educational process. Guppy and Davies (1998) have suggested that historically, many men have not required educational credentials to obtain well-paying, stable jobs, whereas the fields of teaching, nursing, and clerical work in which women

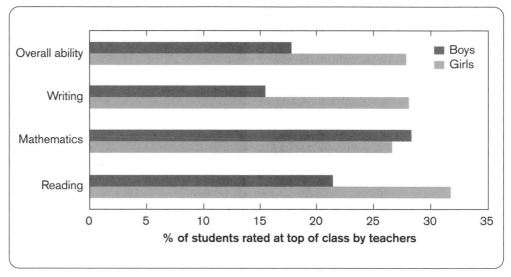

Figure 10.4 Proportion of Girls and Boys at the Top of the Class

Source: National Longitudinal Survey of Children and Youth, 1994–1995. Reproduced in Julien and Ertl (1999: 25).

found the majority of employment have required an education. Therefore, this disparity in academic performance may partially stem from lower educational aspirations on the part of boys and their families as a result of mistaken beliefs about the current demands of the labour market. Young men do tend to have somewhat lower academic aspirations than young women (Looker and Lowe 2001). Educational 'role-modelling' from our parents appears to be an important factor. Indeed, Nakhaie and Curtis's (1998) study based on the Canadian 1986 General Social Survey showed that there are sex-specific effects of the education attainment of parents. In other words, the educational attainment of mothers had a stronger influence on their daughters' educational attainment and the educational attainment of fathers had a more significant influence on their sons' educational attainment (Nakhaie and Curtis 1998).

Nancy Mandell (CPRN 2002) outlines several arguments that have been proffered to explain the lower educational performance of boys. These range from an incompatibility between boys' 'inherent nature' and classroom imperatives to a female-biased curriculum, to class and race or ethnic discrimination in the school system (CPRN 2002: 15–16). Mandell concludes that while these factors likely play a role, in order to understand boys under-achievement in school we have to stop viewing this a problem of boys versus girls. Although this may be difficult to do with the data at hand, in the future, this will require more complex and detailed information about students and their families.

Educational Attainment

The gendered trends of educational performance that are evident in elementary school appear to continue into secondary school (Bowlby and McMullen 2002; Frank 1996). Thiessen and Nickerson (1999) found that in the teen years, girls showed stronger academic performance than boys in almost all subjects. Although after the age of 16 boys do score higher on problem solving, these differences are significantly smaller than the language and reading advantage shown by girls (Thiessen and Nickerson 1999). Thiessen and Nickerson (1999) partially attribute these differences to a greater disengagement and dissatisfaction with the school environment on the part of boys. Such findings have also been reported by other researchers (Bowlby and McMullen 2002; Frank 1996). Young men are significantly less likely than young women to complete high school (Bowlby and McMullen 2002; CESC 2001; Looker and Lowe 2001). The 1991 Canadian School Leavers Survey found that dropouts were more likely to be disengaged and alienated from school, to have lower academic grades, to be Aboriginal, to be disabled, and to be working a large number of hours at a job outside of school (CESC 2001: 14). These students were also more often from single- and no-parent families. Therefore, the young men most vulnerable to high school non-completion appear to be those from lower socio-economic backgrounds and marginalized populations.

The most recent study of high-school completion among Canadian youth aged 18–20 also found marked gender disparities in high-school completion (Bowlby and McMullen 2002). In 1999, 14.7 per cent of young men dropped out of high school in comparison to 9.2 per cent of young women (Bowlby and McMullen 2002: 24) As Figure 10.5 shows, these dropout rates also vary significantly by province. Here we see that

in Prince Edward Island in 1999 the male high school dropout rate is a high 22.3 per cent for 20-year-olds (Bowlby and McMullen 2002: 25). The ratio of male to female dropouts also shows some substantial variations by province; the least gender difference was in Manitoba on account of higher-than-average female dropout rates (13.9 per cent) (Bowlby and McMullen 2002). It was also found that lower academic grades were more common among the young men who dropped out than among the young women who dropped out of high school. For young women, pregnancy and child-rearing was a contributing factor to leaving school, while labour-force participation was a more important factor for young men (Bowlby and McMullen 2002).

Clearly, academic performance in high school and high-school completion are significant determinants of whether students go on to post-secondary education. The academic 'under-performance' of young men in high school and their higher rate of high-school non-completion put them at a disadvantage in the pursuit of post-secondary education (Bowlby and McMullen 2002; Statistics Canada and CMEC 2000; Thiessen and Nickerson 1999). According to many recent studies, young men are underrepresented among post-secondary graduates and participants (with the exception of doctoral studies) (Bowlby and McMullen 2002; Looker and Lowe 2001; Thiessen and Nickerson 1999). Looker and Lowe (2001: 4) reported that in 1997, women obtained 58 per cent of university degrees and diplomas. The majority of women (61 per cent) between the ages of 25 and 29 in 1998 possessed a post-secondary degree, as did (55 per cent) of men of the same age (Statistics Canada and CMEC 2000: 21). However, in

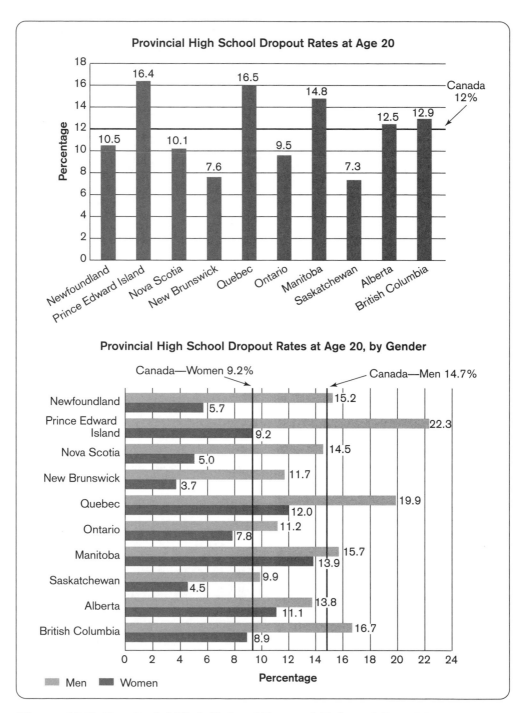

Figure 10.5 Provincial High School Dropout Rates at Age 20

Source: Bowlby and McMullen (2002: 25).

1999, among 18–20 year olds, young women made up 57.4 per cent of students who were continuing their post-secondary education, while young men comprised only 46.9 per cent of this group (Bowlby and McMullen 2002: 3). This represents a substantial change in the gendered composition of post-secondary students in a relatively short time. For example, in 1972–3 women made up 43 per cent of university undergraduates, whereas in 1992-3 they comprised 53 per cent of undergraduates (Thiessen and Nickerson 1999: 27). Change has tended to be slower in terms of the fields of university study pursued by men and women and in the number of women in full-time doctoral studies (Butlin 2001; Guppy and Davies 1998; Looker and Lowe 2001; Thiessen and Nickerson 1999). Thiessen and Nickerson (1999: 27) suggest that the lower enrolment of women in doctoral studies (35 per cent) attests to the issues of child care and family responsibilities that tend to emerge in this age group.

Despite the fact that almost equal numbers of men and women graduate from university in Canada, the educational tracks that girls and boys and men and women take in high school and university vary markedly. Even with progressive educational programs that try to eliminate these messages, as a result of socialization, the toys that girls and boys play with, and different levels of encouragement for girls and boys, few girls claim to be good at math or science regardless of their objective test scores. In university, these early trends translate into fewer women enrolling in engineering, science, or math programs. Although there have been significant improvements in the number of women who enter law and medical programs, women tend to pursue the

lower-status education streams within these programs by specializing in family law or family medicine. Men are discouraged from entering streams of education that are associated with women, such as nursing. But once in these programs, men are often viewed with greater esteem by their peers and professors.

Research suggests that the university studies that are pursued by young men and women continue to adhere to traditional gendered ideologies, with women largely concentrated in education, health, and the humanities and men in mathematics and engineering (Looker and Lowe 2001). In 1995–6, women comprised the majority of university students in the fields of education (68 per cent), the health professions (63 per cent), fine and applied arts (62 per cent), the humanities (60 per cent), agriculture and biological sciences (59 per cent), and the social sciences (56 per cent). In this same period, men made up the vast majority of students enrolled in mathematics and physical sciences (71 per cent) and in engineering and applied sciences (80 per cent) (Thiessen and Nickerson 1999: 29). The continued underrepresentation of women in these fields of study is somewhat perplexing, especially given the generally equivalent levels of mathematical performance that are emerging among young men and women. Even among women who do choose a non-traditional route in the maths and sciences, attrition rates tend to be high. Erwin and Maurutto (1998) examined the experiences of university women enrolled in science programs and found that the women most likely to leave the program were those who had to engage in significant hours of part-time work, many of whom were black working-class students. The underrepresentation of women in these well-paying scientific and technical fields and in doctoral studies further disadvantages women in the labour market—where women have tended to need much higher educational levels in order to earn wages comparable to those of men (Guppy and Davies 1998; Thiessen and Nickerson 1999).

Educational Returns in the Labour Market

In spite of being more highly educated than men, women continue to earn fewer returns on their **educational investments** than men (Finnie 2000; Guppy and Davies 1998; Thiessen and Nickerson 1999). Thiessen and Nickerson (1999: 50) report that in 1995, men with less than a grade 9 education had a higher average income than women with post-secondary education. In fact, men with less than a grade 9 education earned more than all groups of women except those with university degrees. Yet, university-educated women earned only 71.2 per cent as much as university-educated men (Thiessen and Nickerson 1999: 51). Guppy and Davies (1998) also found that men's income appears to increase more dramatically than women's over time. They attribute some of these gendered wage gaps to the fields of study in which men and women predominate (Guppy and Davies 1998). Thiessen and Nickerson (1999) suggest that **occupational segregation** and child-care responsibilities help to account for women's lower monetary returns for their educational attainment. However, it is not only in monetary ways that women are disadvantaged in the labour market (Butlin and Oderkirk 1997).

Although educational attainment usually leads to greater control and authority in the workplace, women were found to be far less likely than men to obtain significant amounts of autonomy and authority in their workplace even when education and other factors were controlled for (Butlin and Oderkirk 1997). Men were more than twice as likely as women to achieve a top management post, and among male and female supervisors, men had significantly more decision-making power in their supervisory position. Butlin and Oderkirk (1997) largely attribute these disparities to the concentration of women in occupations that differ in marked ways from those of men. For example, in 1993, 32 per cent of the female labour force was concentrated in clerical work, while the most male-concentrated occupational area was 18 per cent in management and administration (Butlin and Oderkirk 1997: 33–4). The underrepresentation of women in the educational fields of engineering and the technical sciences and the concentration of women in the educational fields of teaching and nursing have a significant influence on labour-market returns and career trajectories. However, gendered discrimination in the labour market is also a contributing factor to the difficulty that women encounter in converting their educational credentials into monetary and other labour-market rewards (Butlin and Oderkirk 1997; Muzzin, Brown, and Hornosty 1995).

Focusing on Age and Life Course

Historical Trends in Canadian Educational Attainment

The times in which we live have a profound effect on our educational opportunities

(Guppy and Davies 1998; Wanner 1999). Consequently, there are substantial differences in the educational attainment levels of different age cohorts in Canada (Guppy and Davies 1998). Younger Canadians tend to be more highly educated than older Canadians (Clark 2001; Wanner 1999). For example, in 1951, approximately 2 per cent of the Canadian population 15 years of age and older possessed a university degree, whereas in 1996, approximately 12 per cent of the same-aged population had a university degree (Clark 2001: 23). Guppy and Davies (1998) point out that before the 1950s, very few Canadians went on to university and those who did were from a distinctly elite upper class. An even greater generational contrast is evident in the percentage of Canadians with less than a grade 9 education. In 1951, over 50 per cent of Canadians 15 years of age and older had less than a grade 9 education, whereas in 1996, only about 11 per cent of the same-aged population had less than grade 9 (Clark 2001: 23).

By the mid-twentieth century, 'schooling' at the elementary and secondary levels had become an expected rite of passage for Canadian children; however, at the beginning of the century and before, school played a fleeting and sporadic role in many children's lives (Clark 2001).

The post-war baby boom and the subsequent expansion of the educational system produced some dramatic changes in the educational attainment levels of Canadians (Clark 2001; Wanner 1999). Clark (2001:19) notes that in 1901, most children were not regularly in the classroom; in fact, only 4 out of 10 children attended elementary and secondary school daily. Even later in the century, many children began school much later than they do now (Clark 2001). In 1921, 48 per cent of six-year-olds and 17 per cent of seven-year-olds did not attend school (Clark 2001: 19).

Figure 10.6 gives an indication of some of the significant shifts in school attendance over the course of the twentieth century

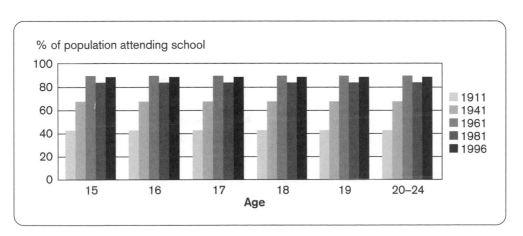

Figure 10.6 Canadians Now Leave School at Older Ages Because They Are Staying in School Longer

Source: Statistics Canada, Catalogue nos. 98–1931, vol. 1 and 98–1941, vol. 1 and special tabulations. Reproduced in Clark, (2001: 20).

(Clark 2001: 20). Here we see the percentage of Canadians between the ages of 15 and 24 who were attending school in selected years over the course of the twentieth century. This figure illustrates the strong differences between school attendance in the early part of the century in comparison to the current educational experience of Canadians. In 1941, fewer than half of 16-year-olds attended school, whereas in 1996, approximately 85 per cent attended school (Clark 2001: 20). The school attendance rates of the 20- to 24-year-olds also gives an indication of the differences in post-secondary participation. Post-secondary participation rates in 1911 and 1941 were extremely small for this group, whereas in 1996 close to 50 per cent of 20- to 24-year-olds were attending school (Clark 2001: 20).

The historical shifts in educational directives from a focus on issues of citizenship and comportment to a concern with vocational skills and the accumulation of credentials has meant a substantially different educational experience for Canadians of different age groups (Bruno-Jofre and Henley 2000; Osborne 2000; Wotherspoon 1998). Over the course of the century, some groups have experienced marked gains in their educational attainment as barriers and social norms have undergone change (Guppy and Davies 1998; Wanner 1999). For instance, women comprised only 17 per cent of university students in 1920, whereas today they make up the majority of those enrolled in university (Clark 2001; Looker and Lowe 2001).

Wanner (1999) specifically examines the changes in educational opportunity for Canadians throughout the twentieth century, in order to ascertain the effects of the **baby boom expansion** on the educational opportunities of historically disadvantaged groups (e.g., women, those with a first language other than English, and low socio-economic background). According to Wanner (1999), educational expansion has benefited some groups more than others. Analyzing age cohorts over time, he finds that the educational disadvantages experienced by women and those having English as a second language earlier in the century have largely been eliminated, except when it comes to graduate degrees, where men still have an advantage over women (Wanner 1999). In contrast, the educational disadvantage of coming from a lower socio-economic background has remained a stubborn feature of the educational landscape (Wanner 1999). In spite of the vast expansion in education, socio-economic background continues to operate as a most powerful predictor of educational attainment (Wanner 1999). The growing importance and the length of education in the lives of Canadians in the form of adult training and educational programs means that the educational disadvantage faced by those from lower socio-economic backgrounds promises to have stronger life-long economic ramifications than in the past (Clark 2001; Livingstone 2001).

Adult Education and the Changing Face of Education

The profile of students and those seeking further education has changed from the stereotypical image of the young, supposedly carefree individual (Sales, Drolet, and Bonneau 2001). The imperatives of a changing labour market, along with credential inflation have meant that a number of older adults are engaged in education and training programs (Livingstone 2001; Statistics Canada 2001e). In 1997, nearly 28 per cent of Canadians were involved in some form of adult education or training (Statistics Canada 2001e). Although adult education rates remained relatively flat throughout the 1990s, the average number of hours that participants were engaged in adult educational activities increased by 60 hours a year over the decade (Statistics Canada 2001e).

Some workers have more difficulties than others in the pursuit of adult education and training. University graduates were 7.5 times more likely to be participating in an adult learning program than those who had not completed high school (Statistics Canada 2001e). In addition, blue-collar workers received significantly less employer support for education than white-collar workers (Statistics Canada 2001e). In other words prior educational attainment levels predicted the participation rates of adult learners. In this way well-educated adults are more likely to maintain and enhance their educational advantage in the workplace. Although men and women have roughly similar participation rates in adult education men were more likely to have support and financing from their employer for their studies (Statistics Canada 2001e). Women were also more likely than men to be deterred from further educational training by family responsibilities and child care responsibilities (Statistics Canada 2001e). Thus, the women who do participate in adult education face greater financial and social costs than male participants.

The participation of adult learners in higher numbers has resulted in a much more diverse student population, particularly with regard to age (Sales et al. 2001). The average age of university students is climbing (Sales et al. 2001). Even in the 'traditional' Canadian university setting, in 1993, 'young' students (i.e., aged 18 to 21) were a minority (47.9 per cent) of those enrolled in full-time studies (Sales et al. 2001). In 1994, the average age of full-time Quebec undergraduate students was 23 and for full-time master's and doctoral students it was 28.5 and 32.5 respectively (Sales et al. 2001). Sales and his colleagues analyzed the academic routes taken by a sample of university students in Quebec and found predominately non-linear and interrupted paths in the effort to obtain a university degree (Sales et al. 2001). These academic disruptions were primarily attributable to financial difficulties, which forced students to leave their studies and seek out means of financing their education (Sales et al. 2001). The students most vulnerable to these lengthened academic pathways were those from lower socio-economic backgrounds, master's students without scholarships, and older students (Sales et al. 2001).

These findings illustrate the effects of current tuition hikes and loan policies on the educational experience of Canadians (Looker and Lowe 2001). In the span of a decade (1991–2001) the price of an undergraduate arts degree has gone up by 126 per cent, and students are borrowing more in order to finance their education (Finnie 2002; Looker and Lowe 2001: 5). Finnie (2002: 30) found that among 1995 university graduates, 44 per cent of women and 47 per cent of men had to repay university loans that averaged $13,600. Although he finds that in most cases students do manage to pay back the loans, other researchers have argued that the heavy and growing debt loads for Canadian students place a particular burden on the present generation of students and their families (CPRN 2002; Plager and Chen 1999). The grant system once in place has been largely replaced by loans that must be repaid, and a number of graduates have difficulty doing so (Plager and Chen 1999). One researcher poses the question 'why we find it acceptable that some young people, purely by an "accident of birth", are burdened by student loan debts of $20,000–30,000' (CPRN 2002: 23). The rising cost of education is making debt an increasing reality for the present generation of post-secondary graduates.

Educational Returns in the Labour Market

There have been some significant changes in the labour market returns that Canadians can expect from their educational investments (Kapsalis, Morisette and Picot 1999; Wanner 2001). Some researchers have found that younger workers in Canada experienced a drop in real wages in comparison to older age groups (Davies, Mosher and O'Grady 1996; Kapsalis et al. 1999). These relative declines in labour-market returns have affected men more dramatically than women (Kapsalis et al. 1999; Wanner 2001). Before 1960, university graduates with a bachelor's degree, particularly male graduates, could expect much higher labour-market returns on their degree than later in the century (Wanner 2001). Graduates with a high-school diploma in the first half of the twentieth century could also expect better monetary returns in the labour market than those in the latter half of the century (Wanner 2001). However, graduate and advanced degrees have brought reliable returns for men and women over the course of the century, with

men maintaining their labour market advantage among this group (Wanner 2001). Wanner suggests that the drop in the value of undergraduate degrees stems from a lowered demand for them in the labour market and not from credentialism per se, since the returns on advanced degrees have remained relatively high. In fact, Finnie (2000) argues that the concern about poor labour-market returns for younger Canadians may be overblown. He found that earnings among the most recent graduates are only moderately lower than in previous years; however, his comparison is limited to graduates in the 1980s and 1990s (Finnie 2000).

Nonetheless, many educated people in the labour force are overqualified for their jobs (Frenette 2000). Table 10.2 shows the extent to which men and women of three graduate cohorts are overqualified for their occupation. Here we see that the rates of overqualification have fallen somewhat for more recent graduates. Frenette (2000) attributes this change to a need for more educated workers in the labour force. However, it is evident from this table that the graduates of certain fields of study are more prone to be overqualified for their jobs. Graduates with degrees in fine arts and social sciences report quite high rates of over-qualification (Frenette 2000: 13). Men and women with master's degrees experienced the highest percentages of over-qualification, from 48 per cent to 72 per cent across the three age cohorts (Frenette 2000: 10). Even so, those with a master's degree maintained a wage advantage over those with a bachelor's degree (Frenette 2000). Frenette (2000) suggests that overqualified master's candidates are often hired for jobs which require only a bachelor's degree. This phenomenon may play a role in the lesser

Table 10.2 Overqualification of Bachelor's Graduates for Main Job, by Sex and Field of Study

	1982 Cohort				1986 Cohort				1990 Cohort			
	1984		1987		1988		1991		1992		1995	
	1(+) levels	2(+) levels[a]	1(+) levels	2(+) levels	1(+) levels	2(+) levels	1(+) levels	2(+) levels	1(+) levels	2(+) levels	1(+) levels	2(+) levels
					Percentage Overqualified							
Men												
Total	**32**	**26**	**29**	**25**	**34**	**28**	**28**	**21**	**29**	**23**	**27**	**21**
Education	26	19	28	24	25	19	19	15	20	17	19	15
Fine arts and humanities	54	47	44	42	54	51	41	33	55	49	53	43
Commerce	31	24	30	26	40	31	36	29	27	20	26	20
Economics	46	41	47	47	48	46	38	34	36	30	35	32
Other social sciences	54	45	50	40	62	55	48	39	52	44	46	38
Agricultural and biological sciences	41	35	46	46	43	40	35	25	40	34	36	30
Engineering and computer science	18	11	15	12	19	12	16 8	12 7	13	9		
Other health	13	9	–	–	32	17	21	18	15	6	19	2
Math and physical science	27	21	21	14	32	26	18	14	32	28	27	23
Law	6	6	3	0	18	18	17	17	13	6	21	18
Medical sciences	12	10	12	10	7	7	1	1	6	5	9	9

(continued)

Table 10.2 (continued)

	1982 Cohort				1986 Cohort				1990 Cohort			
	1984		1987		1988		1991		1992		1995	
	1(+) levels	2(+)ª levels	1(+) levels	2(+) levels	1(+) levels	2(+) levels	1(+) levels	2(+) levels	1(+) levels	2(+) levels	1(+) levels	2(+) levels
	Percentage Overqualified											
Women Total	**35**	**24**	**30**	**25**	**42**	**29**	**34**	**23**	**30**	**21**	**27**	**19**
Education	23	15	19	16	28	22	25	19	10	7	13	9
Fine arts and humanities	55	43	48	44	61	51	41	34	46	40	42	38
Commerce	29	23	27	23	42	30	42	26	32	22	27	19
Economics	39	37	–	–	47	38	33	28	50	45	–	–
Other social sciences	54	41	45	39	54	40	39	30	43	33	37	27
Agricultural and biological sciences	32	22	32	24	37	35	23	15	38	28	35	23
Engineering and computer science	17	11	9	7	23	13	19	14	15	9	19	9
Other health	24	1	22	9	50	11	46	13	32	4	28	6
Math and physical science	26	16	26	23	28	22	36	28	25	20	13	9
Law	20	16	7	7	11	11	5	5	11	10	14	14
Medical sciences	5	4	2	2	7	6	5	4	5	5	10	9

Note: – Sample too small to report (fewer than 30 subjects).

ª1+ means being overqualified by one educational level (e.g., doing a job that requires a high school diploma and having an undergraduate university degree); 2+ means being overqualified by two levels.

Source: National Graduates Surveys. (Frenette, 2000).

economic returns enjoyed by bachelor's degree graduates in comparison to previous age cohorts. The educational requirements of the labour market will probably continue to increase, and education continues to serve as an important control on access to monetary rewards and occupational autonomy (Butlin and Oderkirk 1997; Frenette 2000). Although some groups encounter more difficulty in reaping commensurable economic gains for their educational investment, the investment in education is now, more than ever, a vital requirement in the competition for jobs and occupational advancement in a global economy (Butlin and Oderkirk 1997; CPRN 2002; Guppy and Davies 1998).

Beyond the Statistics: Agency and Experience in Education

Although the preceding sections provide a statistical overview of education in Canada, they do little to show how education is experienced or what choices people make about their education. Furthermore, because statistics rely on averages and typical experiences, variation from the average and the processes involved in varying from the norm are hidden. For instance, although women are educated at similar or somewhat higher levels than men, Judith Blackwell (1998) points out women enrolled in universities sometimes experience difficulties because of overt sexism in the classroom, which is often reinforced in other aspects of university life. White privilege is perpetuated in educational institutions (Bedard 2000; Schick 2001) with racialized students feeling that their success depends on their abil-

ity to act as if they were white (Aguiar 2001). Racism runs rampant in Canadian educational institutions with racialized students being taunted and ridiculed by students and discouraged by teachers (Codjoe 2001). Henry Codjoe (2001) describes how the different experience of racism affected students in Alberta. For a minority of students racism made them strive to be the best students so that they could be labelled exceptional. For most however, racism was a barrier to success in education. As Kwame, one of Codjoe's (2001: 351) informants put it,

To this day, it [racism] still affects me. It was a big hindrance. I dropped out twice as a direct result of that and other stuff like problems in high school with security guards and principals, and when one black person does something the whole black population in the school gets to go to the principal's office and stuff like that. You get fed up and want to quit.

Whether one quits school or goes back to school after quitting is influenced not only by the structures of class, gender, age, ethnicity, and race, but by human agency. Box 10.2 describes how agency intersects with the structural difficulties of being a young single mother when one is pursuing an education in Canada. In this boxed excerpt, Sharon G. Sabourin describes the 'choices' that she made in dropping out of school, marrying and having a baby, leaving her husband, and returning to school. These choices illustrate how conformity and resistance (see chapter 7) link structure and agency as Ms Sabourin navigates through life as a young mother.

Box **10.2**   **Refusing Mediocrity: Barriers to Higher Education for Sole-Support Parents**
By Sharon G. Sabourin

No choices made in life are without their consequences, including the decision to have a child. The following is a story of the decisions I made, and the consequences that have happened since then.

No one expected that this small-town girl from Northern Ontario who was identified as being intellectually gifted in grade four and raised devoutly religious would end up begging for money to feed her and her baby before the end of her second decade. Then again, no one dreams of growing up to someday becoming a single mother either. But the reality is, it happens, and the only thing that matters afterward is how we honour the gift of becoming a mother. Let me tell you my story:

A high school dropout and expectant mother by eighteen, I often wondered if there would ever come a day when I would make my child proud to call me 'mom'. Cultural norms voiced by several people close to me led me to believe that the only penance that could be paid to free my son from bastardom would be to marry his father before the baby's birth. So, that is what I did. However, there were no guests, no cake, no rings, and certainly no gifts to commemorate the occasion. Without so much as whisper of celebration, the ceremony ended with me heading home by myself in a symbolic black dress, and the groom off to work for his afternoon shift in a food processing plant. Soon afterward, our beautiful and healthy 8-and-a-half-pound baby boy, Talon, was born . . . in wedlock.

Family grew closer as it often does with the commencement of a successive generation, but Talon's father found responsibilities surrounding parenting and family life too difficult to handle. The only thing that I had ever wanted to become was a good wife to a man that loved me and appreciated me, and I knew inside my heart that I would only ever marry once. It was my motherly duty to ensure that my marriage worked. It was a very long time, and a difficult road to realizing there is much more dignity and honour in leaving an abusive relationship, than there is in staying in one, only to be miserable for the sake of society's approval of 'intact' families.

Details that need not be mentioned here were involved and my tumultuous marriage soon began to dissolve and ultimately ended with police involvement. I was left with a newborn baby to care for, and not a glimmer of hope of becoming the confident, well-respected member of society that had been prescribed as my destiny from such a young age. The maternity-leave income that I was collecting from my job as a bartender was not enough to pay the bills, and not long after, I received an eviction notice leaving me desperate to find a home for me and my 3 month old baby. I had not completed high school, had no job, no vehicle and nowhere to go except to the local Social Service Agency. Once inside the office, I looked down at my baby sitting contentedly in his car seat, and said to myself, 'Someday I'll make you proud of me.'

Those next few days passed so slowly and numbly. I remember waking up in early morning hours to nurse a crying baby. As I sat in the dark, half lucid, I began wondering what purpose my life had. Was I only a vessel of sustenance for my baby? Whatever the purpose, my days passed by minute by minute. I would get up and diaper and dress my baby. I would put him in his car seat on the floor of the bathroom so I could shower myself. I would put on my clothes and shoes and take him outside for fresh air. I would get hungry, and wonder what I could afford to buy to eat. His babbling would fill the dead and quiet air of our world. His rattle would fall out of reach, and I'd pick it up and return it to him. His innocence and apathy for what shame I felt was condolence for my soul.

During those few weeks of complete confusion, I remember walking Talon in his stroller during midday, and seeing other young mothers playing with their children at the park. I remember looking on them with disapproval, while precluding myself from that judgment. I remember wondering if their babies had fathers who were involved, or if they were collecting welfare. I wondered what their stories were. I daresay it was the fallacy of pride, but something made me feel that I was not like them, like *those* girls who went and got knocked up by some Joe who treated them like garbage and left them to care for their kids while they went off and found new fresh meat to taint. The truth was, I wasn't any different, I was just in denial.

So there I was. Soon to be homeless, penniless, and staring down at the responsibility of caring for an entire human life. Who was this kid anyway? I mean, he didn't look like me, and he certainly wasn't much fun. I felt a tremendous amount of guilt for thinking these things that 'no self-respecting mother' would dare think. I had no idea what to do but cry, and cried I did. I cried because I felt like a failure, I cried because I felt incapable of caring for myself let alone a baby. I felt sad that I had given up my dreams for the love of a man who abandoned me and made me feel helpless. But the most heart-wrenching pain was that of seeing the disappointment in my parents' faces. They didn't understand why I did the things I did, but what was worse, neither did I.

. . .

By far, the hardest part of beginning my education was walking into my very first class the first day of college. I was terrified that I wouldn't fit in, and not surprisingly—I didn't. But not for the reasons I thought. I didn't fit in because I was a girl on a mission, I wasn't just putting in time. I knew exactly what I wanted, whereas most people in my class were there to try and figure that out. To my surprise, instead of being condemned, most students and teachers in my classes were impressed that I was a mother! One the strangest things I've learned about being a student, is that we're all afraid at first that we won't fit in. But, it never takes long to find that everyone else feels the same way, and then friendships develop from that shared fear of rejection, becoming instead a shared feeling of camaraderie among fellow students.

I was soon in the swing of things as a college student. Juggling classes, homework, part-time work, and breastfeeding were just some of the things that were priorities for my first year of post-secondary studies. Determined to make something of myself, I took extra courses during the regular semester, and attended summer classes every summer. The following year my grades were high enough to be accepted to the University of Western Ontario's Bachelor of Health Sciences program.

. . .

I knew that the cost of daycare was going to be too much for me to afford, so I applied for a city subsidy. After 3 months of paperwork shuffling, and city council meetings, I finally qualified for a subsidy from the city for the periods of time that I spent in school. It was mandatory that I provide the city with a schedule from the University for each term, outlining exactly what times I was in class, as the city will not pay a subsidy for the hours not spent in class. This meant, that when I needed to study, go to the library, or meet with other students to discuss a group project, I would be charged full price for Talon's daycare. Despite this, I knew that I would still have to work in order to help pay for schooling, so I applied to the work-study program at Western. The work-study program paid $8.50 per hour. The cheapest hourly rate I could find for daycare was $5/hr. This meant, that in essence, I was working for $3.50 an hour, almost half of the minimum wage. Well, $3.50 is better than nothing, so I began working. It was a sacrifice that paid off when I discovered my passion for academic research.

While working and continuing my studies first year, I had received some poor grades on essay style assignments, and so I decided that I should get some help with my writing skills. The Student Development Centre has an Effective Writing Program; a free service for students to offer constructive criticism on their writing skills. But, children are not welcome to attend these sessions, and I simply couldn't afford to take any extra time off work during the day to go while Talon was in daycare, so I didn't get any help with my writing.

During my first week at Western, I learned that for chemistry class, there would be an 8 o'clock lab every other week, and on the weeks there wasn't labs, there would be quizzes. Waking up at 6 a.m., I had an hour to shower, breakfast, and dress both Talon and I, 45 minutes to drive into London, 15 minutes to drop Talon off at the daycare, park the car and get onto campus and to my class by 8 a.m. This wouldn't be so bad, except that I was up until 2 in the morning the night before, because the only time I could do the preparatory lab report for the next day was after Talon was asleep. Running on four hours sleep, I made it to my first lab. I was exhausted, and didn't perform the experiment properly. There wasn't time before my next class to redo it, and so I failed my first lab.

Two weeks later, Talon is sick. He had been exposed to many new viruses at the daycare centre that he wasn't yet immune to. Public Health stipulates that if a child is sick, he/she is not permitted to go to daycare. The University Chemistry Department states that if a student misses three or more labs, they are not permitted to continue in the course. The University Policies stipulate, that if a student misses a lab/test/exam they are required to provide medical documentation. But, it doesn't matter if students had to stay home because their child was sick, that doesn't count as a valid excuse. I distinctly recall one morning while conducting one of my chemistry experiments, feeling such intense pressure that I began having visual distortions and ended up having a full-fledged migraine headache. My professor was quite empathetic and helped me find somewhere to lie down until the pain abated. Twice more, Talon was sick on lab days, and I was forced to drop out of the class. I began to feel like I might not make it.

Source: Sabourin (2003). Reprinted by permission of the author.

Conclusion

The research presented in this chapter shows that a serious obstacle to high levels of education is social class; gender, race, and ethnicity seem to matter less. Yet, what is also clear from this chapter is that much more Canadian research on educational attainment needs to be done to explore how class, age, gender, ethnicity, and race simultaneously shape educational pathways. Some of the research discussed above shows how class intersects with each of age, gender, ethnicity, and race, but rarely does research explicitly consider the complexities of all these factors. Yet the barriers to education probably vary in enigmatic ways. Consider a middle-aged, black mother who just lost her job after the factory she was working in closed down and went south. She needs to work to help support her family, but she has few marketable skills. She would like to go to school to upgrade her skills, but colleges, universities, and the like are organized with the life-course stage of a 20-year-old in mind. This hypothetical case illustrates the complex relationships among class, age, gender, ethnicity, and race as they pertain to education and potential barriers to education. It also highlights the links between education, skill, and globalized labour markets.

Policy makers are quick to point out that Canada needs to be innovative in an era of globalized markets and heightened competitiveness. Yet, the traditional education system in Canada lacks the creativity that is needed to break down the barriers to life-long learning. Although there has been some movement toward distance learning and Internet-based courses, these innovations have been slow to evolve. This is at least partly due to the overly elitist, class-based attitudes among educators in our schools of higher learning, who suggest that traditional methods of learning are superior to others.

The fact that boys are falling behind in elementary and high school also requires immediate policy attention. Again, it is not enough to examine the differences between boys and girls in this regard. The family experiences of class, gender, race, and ethnicity must also be considered. Do boys and girls employ social and cultural capital in the same way? Or do masculinities (as they vary by age, class, race, and ethnicity) influence whether and how social and cultural capital is used to one's advantage (CPRN 2002)? Obviously, agency is important here; not only the agency of parents but of the children as well. Once we have insight into these and other similar questions, Canadians will be in a better position to devise policy that will help to make education more readily accessible and useful to all.

Glossary

Baby boom expansion   The growth in the educational sector in response to the high fertility rate following the Second World War.

Children and youth 'at risk'   Students who are vulnerable to educational set-backs and or failure (e.g., high school non-completion), usually on account of social or environmental disadvantages.

Cultural capital   Bourdieu's concept of the collective dispositions, likes, dislikes, and typical recreational pursuits of the privileged classes in a given society. These activities (e.g., reading the newspaper, going to museums, golfing, etc.) are transmitted from one generation to the next through family socialization in a middle–upper-middle-class milieu. Children from mid-upper class families achieve higher levels of cultural capital and are therefore at an advantage in the educational process, where many of these activities and world views are taken for granted and are expected forms of knowledge.

Educational investment   The monetary and occupational labour-market rewards that groups can expect as a result of their level of educational attainment, their field of study, and their demographic profile (age, race or ethnicity, gender, and class)

Occupational segregation   The division of the labour force in such a way that men and women usually perform quite different tasks in their work. Men and women are generally sorted into occupations which are separate and distinct from each other (e.g., construction, truck driving, and engineering are jobs traditionally held by men, while clerical work, nursing, and child care are jobs traditionally held by women). This separation exists both in the type of work that men and women do and in the career and occupational ladders within an occupational field (e.g., within education, women tend to teach younger children, while men tend to teach older children and teenagers and are more often principals and administrators). These labour divisions also operate along ethnic and racial lines, and they tend to result in occupational advantages for the dominate social group.

Pro-social behaviour   Socially altruistic behaviour, including that which results in the inclusion of other children or that involves listening to and showing concern, comfort, or compassion to classmates.

Silencing   The practice among some students of remaining silent or not participating in response to a classroom experience that is exclusionary and does not validate their lived experience.

Social capital   Bourdieu's concept of the social networks and informational resources from which individuals are able to draw upon in their daily lives. The possession of large amounts of social capital presumes high reserves of economic and cultural capital, as it is through monied, educational, and prestige connections that valuable social networking is accomplished.

Special education   A form of educational delivery designed to address educational deficiencies and/or difficulties (e.g., social or behavioural problems, difficulty learning to read). This program may be offered directly in the classroom or it may involve separate classroom or teacher time for the student.

Streaming   The educational practice of grouping and teaching children according to different levels of ability, either informally in a classroom or more formally within secondary educational programs (e.g., basic, advanced pathways).

Questions for Critical Thought

1. Why does an identical level of educational achievement not guarantee equivalent labour-market returns? What implications does this have for agency?

2. What do you think will happen to the Canadian population's educational attainment levels over the twenty-first century?

What effect, if any, will tuition increases have on access to post-secondary education? What effect, if any, will educational debts have on future generations?

3. What processes do you think are responsible for the educational under-performance of boys? How does this phenom-

enon illustrate the enmeshment of the CAGE social relations? What can be done to improve the educational experience and attainment levels of vulnerable populations?

4. Discuss how social and cultural capital operate to advantage and disadvantage groups in the Canadian educational system.

5. What factors went into your own educational choices and opportunities? Do you think that your educational attainment and aspirations have been affected by the social relations of CAGE? If so, in what way?

Recommended Reading

Bowlby, Jeffrey W., and Kathryn McMullen (2002). *At a Crossroads: First Results for the 18- to 20-year-old Cohort of the Youth in Transition Survey*. Ottawa: Human Resources and Development Canada. Cat. no. RH64-12/2002E. A longitudinal study that examines the educational and labour-market experiences of over 22,000 18- to 20-year-olds in Canada. This study provides a good illustration of how structural factors affect educational attainment levels and labour-market experiences.

Guppy, Neil, and Scott Davies (1998). *Education in Canada: Recent Trends and Future Challenges*. Ottawa: Statistics Canada. A comprehensive Canadian compilation of how social-structural factors (i.e., gender, ethnicity, social class, and age) have affected educational and labour-market outcomes over time with recommendations for future research.

Looker, E. Diane, and Graham S. Lowe (2001). *Postsecondary Access and Student Financial Aid in Canada: Current Knowledge and Research Gaps*. Ottawa: CPRN. www.cprn.ca. The authors compile and review the existing literature on access to post-secondary education in Canada. This paper provides a valuable annotated bibliography on post-secondary education in Canada with a focus on key findings and areas for future research.

Statistics Canada and the Council of Ministers of Education Canada (2000). *Education Indicators in Canada: Report of the Pan-Canadian Education Indicators Program 1999*. <www.cmec.ca>. This website provides a wealth of information on a wide range of educational topics with up-to-date publications, statistics, indicators, and press releases on the state of education in Canada.

Wotherspoon, Terry (1998). *The Sociology of Education in Canada: Critical Perspectives*. Toronto: Oxford University Press. This book outlines the main sociological perspectives that have been used to explain educational inequalities and takes a critical approach to the analysis of education in Canada.

11

CAGE(s) and Health

by Tammy Duerden Comeau and Julie Ann McMullin

Introduction

Audre Lorde, who was born in 1934, is well known for her work as a poet and equal-rights activist. Lorde was a black woman, a feminist, and a lesbian who grew up in Harlem in the 1930s and 1940s and came of age during the 1950s. The daughter of recent Grenadian immigrants, she was raised in a working-class household. The substantive cohort in which she was born profoundly shaped her experiences in the processes of production, reproduction, and distribution—experiences which, in turn, had negative consequences for her health.

Unlike generations of black women who were born before her, Lorde did have some opportunities for paid work. This was true, in part, because of the progress made by equal-rights movements in the United States, and in part because of the prosperous economic times that New York was experiencing in the 1950s. Yet, her structural positioning as a young, working-class black woman profoundly shaped her employment options. In her search for work, Lorde's employment agency told her, 'There's not too much choice of jobs around here for Coloured people, and especially not for Negro girls. . . . [M]ost of our unskilled peoples find some sort of work in the 'hardware' factories on the other side of town' (Lorde 1982: 125). Lorde chose not to tell the employment service that she could type. In her refusal to type she acted with

agency and, in doing so, knew that she would have to work either in a factory or as a maid. Although some would no doubt question this decision, Lorde chose (at this time) to reserve her typing for the self-expression and creativity of her own writing.

Lorde found work in a factory. Her youth meant that the alternative 'option' of being a maid was not possible, for, as the employment agency told her, their clients 'usually like older women' (Lorde 1982: 125). Lorde's factory wages were somewhat better than they would have been had she been employed as a domestic worker, but the working conditions were deplorable. The following quotation from Lorde's book, *Zami: A New Spelling of My Name*, documents her harrowing experience of working at Keystone Electronics, a plant that processed the quartz crystals used in radar equipment and radios:

> It was dirty work . . . the air was heavy and acrid with the sickly fumes of carbon tetrachloride used to clean the crystals. Entering the plant after 8:00 a.m. was like entering Dante's Inferno. It was offensive to every sense, too cold and too hot, grit-ty, noisy, ugly, sticky, stinking, and dangerous. . . . Nobody mentioned that carbon tet destroys the liver and causes cancer of the kidneys. Nobody mentioned that the X-ray machines, when used unshielded, delivered doses of constant

low radiation far in excess of what was considered safe even in those days. Keystone Electronics hired Black women and didn't fire them after three weeks. We even got to join the union. (Lorde 1982: 125–6)

Every worker in the Keystone factory was either black or Puerto Rican except for the foreman and forewoman. Jobs were segregated by sex on the basis of traditional gendered ideologies, with the men cutting the crystals and doing the 'heavy' work, and the women X-raying and washing the crystals.

Before she got the job at Keystone, Lorde had worked nights as a nurse's aide and gone to school part-time. She was a part of the working poor and was not eligible for social assistance. As an unmarried woman, she did not have access to a 'family' wage distributed through an employed husband.[1] Making ends meet was a challenge, and yet Lorde redistributed her wages by providing financial support to a number of other men and women who regularly 'crashed' at her apartment. Since she could not afford nutritious food, Lorde's meals consisted of canned soup, sardines, and occasionally the treat of chicken-foot stew. Cooking was not easy, as there was no hot water (or heat) in the apartment and the kitchen was mired in years of filth and neglect from previous renters.

Regarding the processes of reproduction, high expectations of care-giving and nurturing placed upon women of colour have been well documented (Collins 1990; Glenn 1992). Lorde was unexceptional in this regard. She nurtured, fed, and sheltered her friends with what little she had, often to the detriment of her own well-being. Lorde failed the summer-school courses in

trigonometry and German that she was taking. She attributed her failure to her own capabilities and not to the mounting demands of friends on her time and money. When she eventually left New York City to find work in Stamford, Connecticut (at Keystone Electronics), she escaped many of the emotional and financial demands in her life only to encounter a physically toxic environment.

Our bodies are potent signifiers of the degree to which we experience inequality throughout our lives. Audre Lorde's exposure to toxic and dangerous working conditions was not a random event; black, working-class women were deliberately hired for jobs that no one else wanted. Some evidence suggests that this trend continues today and that black workers are exposed to more serious toxic contaminants than white workers in the same industries (Krieger et al. 1993: 88). The long-term health effects of exposure to work-place toxins, especially increased risks of cancer, have been well documented (Aragones et al. 2002; Fincham et al. 2000; Hall and Rosenman 1991; Krstev et al. 1998; Mao et al. 2000; Pollan and Gustavsson 1999). Audre Lorde developed breast cancer in the late 1970s and died, at the age of 58, in 1992.

Although Audre Lorde's health experience centred on her blatant exposure to work-place pathogens and toxic substances, health inequalities can manifest themselves in more insidious ways. Indeed, the World Health Organization (2002) defines 'health' broadly as: 'a state of complete physical, mental, and social well-being and not merely the absence of disease or infirmity.' The fact that Lorde's wages were too low to provide her with nutritious meals or a suitable environment for their preparation, probably took its toll on her physical, mental, and social health. Furthermore, the struggle to combine emotional and financial nurturing with working long hours in deplorable working conditions has been shown to negatively influence all aspects of 'health'.

Lorde's life history demonstrates that to understand inequities in health that result from the intersection of CAGEs and agency is a complex task. Yet empirical research has rarely considered these issues simultaneously. With this in mind, in the next sections we review the literature on health inequality in an effort to weave a complex tapestry of the social determinants of health in Canada.

Inequality in Health: Some Current Perspectives and Critiques

Health researchers and epidemiologists have long struggled to discover why there are inequalities in health (Anderson and Armstead 1995; House 2001; Link and Phelan 2000), and explanations for inequality in the study of health and illness have gone through numerous paradigm shifts (House 2001; Robertson 1998). In his review of the literature, House (2001) documents the overwhelming emphasis in the mid-twentieth century on a purely biomedical approach to health and illness. Inequalities in health were analyzed and examined largely through the biology of the individual and the workings of the medical system. An individual's behaviour in the form of 'lifestyle' choices (e.g., smoking, alcoholism, obesity, and physical exercise) was also believed to have a significant impact on health (House 2001: 127). Although studies that focused on individual biology, the failings of medical systems, and

lifestyle choices added to our understanding of health inequality, none of these studies explained it adequately. Rather, researchers began to recognize that factors such as socio-economic status played a significant role in health experiences and that smoking, exercise, immoderate eating, and so forth, accounted only moderately (10 to 20 per cent) for the socio-economic inequalities in health (House 2001: 134).

In the 1960s, psychosocial factors came to the forefront of health research, and social epidemiologists began to emphasize the effects of 'stress' on the physiology of the body (House 2001: 128). This led to a recognition that health is influenced by a large number of psychosocial factors, including social support, stress, and psychological or personality dispositions (House 2001: 130). Problematic however, was the fact that these **psychosocial risk factors** had been identified in the absence of an integrating theory; hence, much of the inequality in health remains unexplained (House 2001).

House (2001) draws on Link and Phelan's research (2000) to argue that if we are to understand health inequality, we need an integrated theory revolving around macro-social factors as the '**fundamental causes**' of disease risk. House (2001: 125) suggests that investigators should concentrate on factors such as socio-economic status and race or ethnicity, because these characteristics 'shape individual exposure to and experience of virtually all known psychosocial, as well as many environmental and biomedical risk factors, and these risk factors help to explain the size and persistence of social disparities in health.' House's framework is outlined in Figure 11.1. This figure shows that broader societal factors like race,

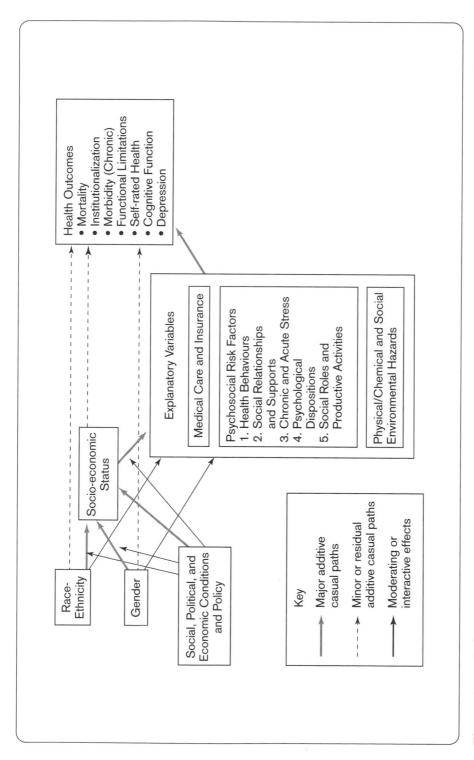

Figure 11.1 A Conceptual Framework for Understanding Social Inequalities in Health and Aging

Source: House (2001). Reprinted by permission of the American Sociological Association and the author.

ethnicity, gender, and socio-economic status are integral to health outcomes and psychosocial risk factors. Because there are complex relationships between these factors, an emphasis on psychosocial aspects alone ignores the influence that social inequities have on health. If the analytic lens is shifted to the effects of race, ethnicity, and socio-economic status on psychosocial risk factors and health outcomes, a fuller picture of health inequality emerges.

Although House's conceptual framework includes class, ethnicity, and gender, his inclusion is additive rather than interactive. A close look at Figure 11.1 reveals that gender and race or ethnicity are not considered to be related and that both race or ethnicity and gender are thought to be mediated by socio-economic status in their relation to health outcomes. Age and the influence of social time are not explicitly accounted for, and the explanatory variables (e.g., social supports and social roles) are thought to be only 'minorly' affected by gender and ethnicity. Hence, this conceptualization continues to treat gender, race, ethnicity, and socio-economic status as variables that can in some way be viewed as separate from one another.

The epidemiological literature abounds in studies that document the impact on health of the variables of class or socio-economic status (Adler et al. 1994; Humphries and van Doorslaer 2000; Marmot, Kogevinas, and Elston 1987), age (Kessler et al. 1992; Mirkowsky and Ross 1992), sex (Bird 1999; Denton and Walters 1999; Verbrugge 1989), and race or ethnicity (Leclere et al. 1997; Williams and Collins 1995) on health, both singly and in various combinations (Cooper 2002; Crimmins and Saito 2001; Curtis and Lawson 2000;

Mirkowsky and Ross 2001; O'Loughlin 1999). There is no doubt that health is shaped and moulded by these social relations, and many of the above studies point out the deficiencies and difficulties inherent in treating social relations as variables. Unfortunately, epidemiologic research rarely contextualizes and integrates these elements and critiques, and more frequently these variables are taken to signify differences located in 'biological' bodies rather than as indicators of interrelated social patterns (Inhorn and Whittle 2001; Krieger et al. 1993; Shim 2002). Given the prominent tendency of health research to treat class, age, gender, and ethnic or race relations as separate variables, the following discussion must do the same.

Mortality, Morbidity, and Mental Health

Social Class and SES

The privileged in society are those who possess more resources in the form of income, education, and social connections, enjoy better physical and mental health and longer lives than those members of society who experience want and deprivation (Cairney 1999; Humphries and van Doorslaer 2000; Jette et al. 1996; Mao et al. 2001; Williams and Collins 1995). Health education and awareness, access to prevention, and the capacity to avoid risk factors (e.g., toxic neighbourhoods), all of which are resources held by members of the middle and upper classes, contribute to health advantage (Link and Phelan 2000). People in low-income groups face more constraints on their abilities to 'look after their health', and inequitable social conditions in workplaces, neighbourhoods, and regions significantly affect health throughout the life course (Aneshensel and Sucoff 1996; Krieger et al. 1993; Mackillop et al. 2000; Williams 1990).

Beyond the simple yet strong relationships among individual income, education, occupation, and each of life expectancy and health, recent research has considered these factors in relation to geographic regions and neighbourhoods. In a recent Canadian study, for instance, socio-economic indicators explained 46 per cent of the variation in disability-free life expectancy between geographic regions, the residents of remote, rural, and Northern regions having a significant deficit in the average number of disability-free years of life (e.g., 61 years in Nunavik region compared to 73 years in Richmond, BC) (Mayer et al. 2002). In 1996, Canada's poorest neighbourhoods had infant mortality rates that were two-thirds higher than rates in the wealthiest neighbourhoods, and regions with high unemployment had lower life expectancy than regions with low unemployment (Statistics Canada 1999a: 1–2).

Figure 11.2 shows the likelihood of surviving to the age of 75 according to neighbourhood income (Wilkins et al. 2002: 9). However, this study examined urban regions only, excluding many poor rural regions in Canada which typically have higher mortality rates. Nonetheless, differences in the probability of survival to age 75 is more marked among males than among females. Slightly more than half of the men in the lowest income quintile will live until age 75, compared to nearly 70 per cent of men in the highest income quintile. Among women, nearly 80 per cent of those in the richest quintile will live until the age of 75, compared to only about 73 per cent of those

in the poorest quintile. Combining women and men and taking into account the excess deaths that occur in rural and small-town neighbourhoods, Wilkins and his colleagues conclude that 'if all income quintiles had experienced the mortality rate of the richest quintile . . . then 13,000 fewer males and 5,000 fewer females would have died before age 75 in 1996' (Wilkins et al. 2002: 9). Furthermore, eliminating these differences would be 'equivalent to eradicating one of the three leading causes of death' in Canada (Wilkins et al. 2002: 9).

The study of impoverished or disadvantaged neighbourhoods contextualizes health experiences by highlighting health risks that are often beyond the control of people who probably have no means of moving to another neighbourhood (Newbold 1998; Rosenberg and Wilson 2000; Williams and Collins 1995). This is especially problematic when neighbourhoods are polluted. The experience of residents in Sydney, Nova Scotia, provides a vivid example of how neighbourhood exposure to toxins may affect mortality and morbidity (see Box 11.1) In fact, cancer rates are higher in Sydney and Cape Breton County than in other areas in Nova Scotia (Guernsey et al. 2000).

Research on mortality and morbidity shows that health deteriorates with each incremental decline in income (Adler et al. 1994; McDonough et al. 1999; Wilkinson 1997; Wolfson et al. 1993). Research on this so-called '**socio-economic gradient**' has shown that in societies where incomes are more variable, death rates are higher (Kawachi and Kennedy 1999; Wilkinson 1997). This suggests that it is not only being poor or disadvantaged that is a health risk, but that the experience of having less than

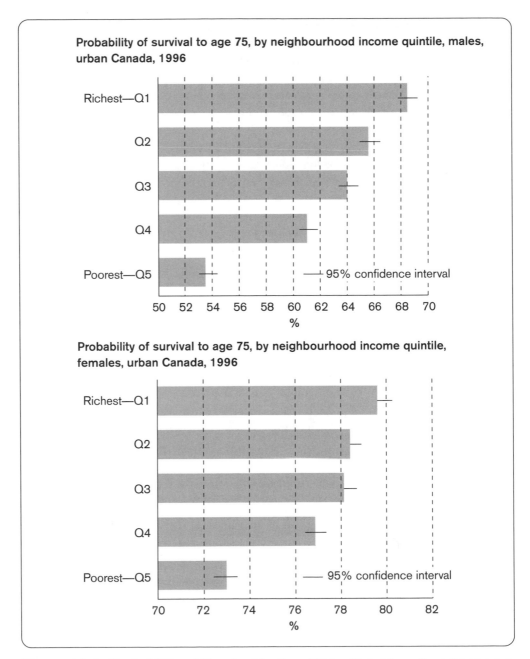

Figure 11.2 Probability of Survival to Age 75 by Neighbourhood Income Quintile, Urban Canada, 1996

Source: Russell Wilkins et al. (2002).
Data source: Canadian Mortality Data Base and supplemental address files; special tabulations of census population data. Available at: <http://www.statcan.ca/english/freepub/82-003/SIE/82-003-SIE2002007.pdf>

Box **11.1**   **The Ill Effects of Environmental Contaminants on Health: The Case of Sydney's Coke Ovens Site**

'They Don't Want Us to Know': The government says Whitney Pier is safe, but those who live near the former coke ovens site say the number of illnesses and deaths tells a different story.
By Tera Camus

Rhonda Crawford is in no mood to fight but the street where she grew up [in Sydney, Nova Scotia], the street she loves, just isn't the same anymore.

She and most of her Hankard Street neighbours learned in December that potentially hazardous levels of chemicals are in their yards and basements.

Ms Crawford's property, according to a confidential risk assessment given to each landowner who volunteered to be tested, averages 90 milligrams of arsenic per kilogram of soil. The national guideline set by the Canadian Council of Ministers of the Environment is 12.

But she doesn't know exactly what's been found or where, beyond her property line. That's one reason she was suspicious when government officials in December deemed Sydney as safe as any other urban centre, at the same time as they committed to remove tainted topsoil from dozens of properties.

Since then, some residents have been taking an unofficial inventory of diseases and deaths among loved ones in the neighbourhood. She believes that tells another story.

'You're saying you're going to clean up the area, but if my mother decides she doesn't want hers cleaned up, my neighbourhood is still not safe,' the 37-year-old federal employee said.

'Until they clean everything up, it's still a contaminated community.'

Government has shared complete details only with individual property owners to protect their privacy. Ms Crawford said if neighbours don't know, how can they stop children playing on hot properties, most of which are not fenced in? 'We should be told on Hankard Street . . . but they don't want us to know.'

The Crawford family and other property owners or renters in the Whitney Pier neighbourhood have joined a local task force and plan to hold a community meeting in March.

Government is cleaning up tested properties where chemical levels posed potential health risks. But some property owners did not volunteer to have their soil tested and others may refuse to have soil removed.

Confidential documents obtained by this newspaper show that more than a dozen homes on Hankard Street are targeted for soil removal. Properties from the top of Victoria Road where Hankard Street begins, to the bottom, three blocks down where it meets a gentle sloping blueberry hill, have high levels of chemicals like arsenic, lead, manganese, copper and cadmium, total petroleum hydrocarbons like benzene, and polycyclic aromatic hydrocarbons.

Nearly two-thirds of tested properties in the neighbourhood are to have topsoil removed because of chemical contamination. Only one property on Hankard Street had no cleanup action recommended.

Some yards on Hankard have lead levels averaging more than 1,400 milligrams per kilogram, well above the national soil quality guideline of 140 set by the Canadian Council of Ministers of the Environment. Arsenic levels there average about 90 mg/kg; the acceptable limit is 12. Arsenic and other chemicals can occur naturally at higher than CCME levels.

JDAC Environment, which tested the soil on Hankard Street and elsewhere in the area it calls North of Coke Ovens, calculated the theoretical increased risk of cancer and other diseases posed by the chemicals it found.

Ms Crawford's individual assessment says her potential additional cancer risk is 47 per 100,000 for constant exposure to the arsenic in her soil. Any result above one is considered unacceptable. JDAC Environment says its risk numbers were deliberately overestimated by a factor of at least 100 and as much as 100,000.

One Hankard Street resident was told that the family's potential exposure to elevated levels of chromium in yard soil could produce cancer in two people for every 100 exposed.

Again, JDAC said, those risks are likely much lower given their conservative assumptions, such as that residents are at home around the clock and children eat nearly a tenth of a gram of soil a day.

Laura Parris, who raised a family with husband Eddie down the street on another contaminated property, has a heart condition. She said her problems began 10 years ago and were first blamed on an overactive thyroid.

'They took it out, and things were calm for a week,' she said. 'I went to Edmonton to recuperate for a month and felt terrific. But when I was back home two weeks, that's exactly when my heart went crazy again.

'They upped my medication . . . and put the paddles on me to bring my heart back to a normal beat.'

She's still being treated.

Ms Parris said not one of her 11 siblings—who all live elsewhere in Canada—has any health or heart problems. Her parents also didn't have heart problems.

After moving into the home in the 1970s, Ms Parris gave birth to seven healthy children but had three miscarriages. Smoke from the nearby stacks stopped when the coke ovens closed in 1988. In recent years, two of her daughters—one in her 20s—had full hysterectomies.

One daughter lives on contaminated land on nearby Laurier Street. She had too much arsenic in her system when tested last year, is losing patches of her hair and is constantly tired, Ms Parris said.

'(Government officials) told me I'm going to get a new lawn but I don't want a new lawn. I want to get out of here,' she said.

Risk assessments were done for 124 properties, most of which showed chemical contamination. Each property tested had 20 samples of soil taken from various depths.

Chemical Threats to Health

These chemical can have detrimental health effects which vary according to exposure, the amount of chemical involved and the individual. The following is a list of toxic substances and their potential effects:

Acenaphthene	liver function
Arsenic	skin or lung cancer, skin lesions
Antimony	blood glucose levels
Benzene:	leukemia
Benzo(a)pyrene	cancer
Beryllium	lung cancer
Cadmium	kidney function, respiratory cancer
Chromium	respiratory tract cancer
Chrysene	cancer
Cobalt	complicates kidney problems
Dibenz(a,h)anthracene	cancer
Ethylbenzene	liver and kidney damage, developmental problems
Fluoranthene	kidney function
Indeno (1,2,3)pyrene	cancer
Lead	impairs brain development, memory
Manganese	central nervous system damage
Mercury	hand tremors
Molybdenum	uric acid in blood
Naphthalene	weight loss, nasal hyperplasia
Nickel	reproductive system damage
Pyrene	kidney function
Selenium	selenosis (silver discolouration of skin)
Thallium	liver damage
Toluene	liver and kidney damage, neurological problems
Vanadium	decreased hair cystine levels
Xylenes	liver and kidney damage, developmental problems
Zinc	weight problems

Source: JCAS Environmental, 7 Nov. 2001

Source: Camus (2002)

someone else also has negative health implications. As Adler and her colleagues (1994) note, 'there is evidence that the association of socio-economic status and health occurs at every level of the SES hierarchy, not simply below the level of poverty.' The authors refer to the classic Whitehall study, which documented the mortality risks for 17,350 British government workers and found a protective mortality effect for each successive increment in employment ranking (Adler et al. 1994). This 'gradient' effect has also been shown in studies of morbidity. For instance, analyses of data from the 1994 Canadian National Population Health Survey indicate that there are graduated declines in morbidity for each successive increase in income (see Humphries and van Doorslaer 2000).

There is considerable debate among health researchers about whether the relationship between health and SES is causal or a result of selectivity. At issue is whether low income, education, and bad jobs result in poor health and an increased risk of death, or whether those with ill and declining health consequently experience lower income and education levels (Wolfson et al. 1993). No doubt both of these explanations account for some of the SES variation in health. Nonetheless, compelling Canadian evidence for the causality argument is evident in a study by Wolfson et al. (1993: 167). This study, which examined the Canada Pension Plan records of more than 500,000 men, found that higher earnings for men aged 45 to 64 are associated with lower mortality rates at older ages (between the ages of 65 and 74). The authors show that for each increment in income there was a corresponding increase in survival rates, although this effect became less pronounced at higher income levels. These mortality gradients were evident even when retirement age was controlled, thereby taking into account those who may have retired early for health reasons. This analysis shows that the relationship between income and mortality appears to be 'real' and not an instance of 'reverse causality' (Wolfson et al. 1993).

Despite evidence of a SES gradient, conditions of poverty and the associated problems of poor health and limited access to health care cannot be ignored (MacMillan et al. 1996; Trovato 2001). The amount of time that one can expect to live is considered a critical indicator of the health and well-being of a population, and in Canada those who are poor do not live as long as the wealthy (see Box 11.2). The experience of poverty has an indelible and unmistakable effect on the condition and health of the body (Adair 2001). As Vivyan C. Adair (2001: 451) points out, 'poor children are

often marked with bodily signs that cannot be forgotten or erased', and reflecting on her own experience she says, 'In spite of my mother's heroic efforts, at an early age my brothers and sisters and I were stooped, bore scars that never healed properly, and limped with feet mangled by ill-fitting, used Salvation Army shoes' (Adair 2001: 456). Adair grew up in the United States, and many might argue that the universal health care in Canada modifies or ameliorates many of the relationships between class and health. However, in Crompton's (2000: 16) 100-year retrospective of health in Canada, she finds that even after 40 years of universal health care, low-income earners have higher rates of morbidity and lower life expectancies than those with higher incomes.

The 'poor' are, however, not a homogenous group, and attempts to treat them as such may mask important health risks (Anderson and Armstead 1995). Everyone's 'chances' of being poor are not equal, and one's marital status (Avison 1995), gender (McDonough et al. 1999), age (Mirkowsky and Ross 2001), race, and ethnicity (Williams and Collins 1995) are all integrally bound up with our class and socio-economic status. Krieger and her colleagues (1999) have shown that the study of disease must recognize the complexities of social interrelations. They investigate the incidence of five types of cancer (breast, cervix, colon, lung, and prostate) in the San Francisco Bay area in 1988–92, taking into account social class, race, ethnicity, and gender (Krieger et al. 1999). The authors found that the incidence rates varied substantially by socio-economic status; however, 'for each site, the magnitude—and even the direction—of socioeconomic gradients in inci-

Box   **Poor Dying at a Faster Rate: Report**

25-year StatsCan Study: Despite Medicare, There is Still a Gap in Life Expectancy Between Rich, Poor
By Heather Sokoloff

Poor people continue to die at a greater rate than the rich, despite rapid advances in health care and almost two decades of universal medicare, Canadian health care experts say.

Statistics Canada reported yesterday that the gap in life expectancy between high- and low-income Canadians is five years for men and two years for women. In 1971, it was six years for men and three years for women.

During that quarter-century, life expectancy improved substantially for all income levels, Statscan said, but more so for those in the lowest income neighbourhoods.

'Poverty goes along with a lot of other factors that affect health,' said John Millar, vice-president of the Canadian Institute for Health Information.

'Less education, generally higher smoking rates, higher rates of obesity, poorer housing and higher exposure to crime and antisocial behaviour.'

StatsCan said the link between premature mortality, that is death before age 75, and income is still a major concern.

'If all income groups had experienced the mortality rates of the richest group . . . 13,000 fewer men and 5,000 fewer women would have died before the age of 75 in 1996,' says the study.

Still, the agency was optimistic about the improvements.

'A year of life is a year of life,' said Russell Wilkins, a StatsCan health analyst. 'Yes, five years is still a lot of difference . . . [but] a gain in a year of life expectancy, I think that is important. I guess that's how you chose to read these things.'

More encouraging was Canada's infant mortality rate, where the gap between rich and poor declined substantially during the 25-year study period.

In 1971, the gap in infant mortality between the richest and poorest neighbourhoods was 9.8 deaths for 1,000 live births. By 1996, the gap had declined to 2.4 deaths.

Fewer poor babies die in Canada than the United States, the study also reports. Infant mortality in Canada's poorest neighbourhoods is 6.4 deaths per 1,000, compared to 7.8 per 1,000, national average in the United States.

However, Mr Wilkins said the rate in Canada's richest neighbourhoods was no better than Sweden's national average rate of four deaths per 1,000.

The survey, in line with previous studies, found that the poorer the neighbourhood, the shorter the life expectancy of its residents at birth.

'Any reduction is great news,' said John Anderson, a researcher with the Canadian Council on Social Development. 'Of course, it's in large part due to the introduction of the public health care system.

'However, we should still be angry that there is any such gap,' he said. 'Life expectancy is the most important indicator of the quality of life.

'People are still dying a lot earlier because they are poor, so we've still got a long way to go.'

Further, the report does not cover the past five years during which there were deep cuts to the health care system, a system which is increasingly underfunded, he and other analysts noted.

'We've forgotten how important medicare is,' said Ken Battle, head of the Caledon Institute of Social Policy.

'Prior to the arrival of medicare, low-income people were the least likely to see a doctor and after the arrival of medicare they showed the largest proportionate increase.'

But he too wondered whether that gap will narrow much further, especially if Canada adopts a two-tiered health care system, as is being advocated by some.

'But there are other things that account for the gap in the life expectancy between the rich and poor, including access to such basics as affordable housing, clean water, and so on,' he said. 'The homelessness problem and others do not bode well for continuing progress.'

Most causes of death related to social and economic disparities diminished markedly over time, including ischemic heart disease, a reduction of blood supply to the heart; cirrhosis of the liver; and perinatal conditions.

However, some causes of death showed little change in relation to those disparities—lung and prostrate cancers for men, and breast cancer for women.

Lung cancer in poor women dramatically increased because more of them are smoking. From 1986 on, the rates of lung cancer for women in the poorest neighbourhoods were much higher than those in other income groups.

Average annual household incomes for the rich group was $73,000 and $33,000 for the poorest. The findings are based on 1996 numbers, the latest for which the agency has data.

Money and Mortality

Socio-economic characteristics of each neighbourhood income, urban Canada, 1996:

Average household income:
  Richest: $72,944
  Poorest: $33,421
Income from gov't transfers:
  Richest: 7.3%
  Poorest: 20.3%
Housing owned:
  Richest: 84.7%
  Poorest: 30.2%
Foreign born:
  Richest: 16.2%
  Poorest: 34.0%

Recent immigrants:
    Richest: 2.7%
    Poorest: 8.6%
Unemployed:
    Richest: 6.1%
    Poorest: 14.5%
Low education (9 years):
    Richest: 5.7%
    Poorest: 15.2%
Lone parent families:
    Richest: 13.4%
    Poorest: 37.8%

Source: Statistics Canada

Source: Sokoloff (2002). Reprinted by permission of the National Post.

dence differs by race/ethnicity and gender' (Krieger et al. 1999: 532). For instance, among Asian, black, and Hispanic men the incidence of prostate cancer dropped as socio-economic status decreased; however, for white men there was no relationship between socio-economic status and the incidence of prostate cancer (Krieger et al. 1999: 530). Findings such as these illustrate that disease data must be collected in a more complete and complex way (Krieger et al. 1999: 525) .

The prevalence of mental illness also varies according to social advantage, 'the poor, the young, ethnic minorities, and blacks hav[ing] higher rates of mental illness than the well-to-do, older persons, ethnic majorities, and whites' (Muntaner et al. 1998; Simon 2000: 72). Accounts of the relationships among social factors, environmental context, and mental health have focused on stress process and vulnerability explanatory models (Simon 2000). Researchers working within the stress-

process paradigm argue that experiencing stress in various forms affects physical and mental health (Avison and Gotlib 1994). But although stress affects physical health, much of the stress-process research has concentrated on the effects of stress on mental health (Avison and Gotlib 1994).

Stress may result from significant life events (e.g., moving or losing a job), acute stressors (e.g., caring for a sick child), and chronic strains (McLean and Link 1994). McLean and Link (1994: 23) organize chronic strains into four categories:

(a) persistent life difficulties or chronically stressful situations that can be considered corollaries of life events; (b) role strain, including the strain within specific roles as well as the strain of holding multiple roles; (c) chronic strains that derive from societal responses to characteristics of a person that include him or her as part of a class of persons, such as racism or sexism; and (d) chronic community-wide strains that may operate at an ecological level, such as the chronic strain of residence in a high crime area or residence near an environmental threat.

People with less power in society are more exposed to ongoing life stresses and strains and often have fewer resources and social supports to help them cope (Simon 2000; Turner and Lloyd 1999). The development of psychosocial resources, such as mastery, self-esteem, and the perception of control over one's environment, is hindered for those who encounter ongoing structural barriers and disadvantages (McLeod and Shanahan 1996, 1993; Turner and Lloyd 1999; Turner and Roszell 1994). The experience of childhood poverty manifests itself in higher rates of depression and antisocial behaviour years later (McLeod and Shanahan 1996: 207). Psychiatric disorders, including depressed moods, anxiety, and drug and alcohol problems, are more prevalent among those from disadvantaged class backgrounds, those with fewer financial assets, and those with less control in their work environment (Muntaner et al. 1998). Even the development of schizophrenia, a psychiatric condition that is believed to have a strong genetic component, is linked to early work experience of 'noisome' occupational conditions (such as noise, temperature extremes and fluctuations, hazards, and fumes), suggesting that '**class-linked stress**' may be a predisposing factor for the disease (Link et al 1986: 242).

Race and Ethnicity

In Canada, death rates and the incidence and prevalence of physical disease and poor mental health vary across measures of 'race' and ethnicity (Dunn and Dyck 2000;

Leclere et al. 1997; O'Loughlin 1999; Sheth et al. 1999; Trovato 2001). For instance, a recent Canadian study examined the mortality rates from cardiovascular disease and cancer between 1979 and 1993 among three broad ethnic groups, those of European origin, South Asian origin, and Chinese origin (Sheth et al. 1999). Canadians of Chinese origin had very low death rates from ischemic heart disease, while Canadians of South Asian and European origin had high death rates from such heart disease (Sheth et al. 1999). Mortality rates from all causes were highest for Canadians of European origin, and this group also had the highest cancer mortality rates (Sheth et al. 1999). Canadians of South Asian origin were particularly prone to diabetes but had lower cancer mortality rates (Sheth et al. 1999).

The study of health and ethnicity is complicated by immigration screening procedures (Chen et al. 1996a; Chen et al. 1996b). Immigrants to Canada are selected partly on the basis of health, and research has shown that the 'healthy-immigrant effect' plays a significant role in studies of health and ethnicity. In other words, immigrant populations, particularly those from non-European countries, exhibit better health and live longer than Canadian-born populations (Chen et al. 1996a: 29). This is partly because immigration to Canada is dependent upon an applicant's good health. However, the 'healthy-immigrant effect' starts to dissipate after 10 years in Canada (Chen et al. 1996b; Dunn and Dyck 2000).

Table 11.1 shows the significantly lower rates of chronic illness among non-European immigrants compared to the Canadian-born population. Although it is difficult to explain, some researchers have attributed the diminishing health advantage

Table 11.1 Age-adjusted Prevalence of Chronic Conditions, by Immigrant status, Canadian-born and Immigrant, Canada, 1994-5

	Total[a]	Canadian-born	All Immigrants[b]	European Immigrants Years in Canada			Non-European Immigrants Years in Canada		
				Total[c]	0–10	11+	Total[d]	0–10	11+
				Age-adjusted Percentage					
Any chronic condition	55.5	56.8	50.3[d]	55.3	46.7	57.7	44.7[d]	37.2[d]	51.2
Sex									
Men	51.7	53.0	46.6[d]	51.1	39.8	54.7	40.8[d]	33.8[d]	46.7
Women	59	2 60	5 53.8[d]	59.3	52.3	60.5	48.1[d]	40.1[d]	55.6
Annual household income									
Less than $30,000	57.6	59.7	51.3[d]	57.4	46.3	59.5	45.8[d]	37.4[d]	55.5
$30,000 or more	53.9	54.7	49.8[d]	54.0	46.4	56.8	44.6[d]	39.0[d]	48.7
Education									
Less than secondary graduation	55.5	56.3	52.5	57.7	55.2	58.8	45.7	37.0[d]	58.3
Secondary graduation or more	54.9	56.2	49.6[d]	54.4	45.8	57.0	44.6[d]	35.8[d]	50.1
Specific chronic conditions									
Joints	23.9	24.5	21.7[d]	24.9	28.1	25.7	16.4[d]	10.9[d]	20.0
Allergy	18.9	19.5	16.4[d]	17.3	–	19.6	16.0	11.2[d]	20.0
Hypertension	9.7	9.7	9.6	10.0	–	10.2	8.9	6.8	10.3
Headaches	7.3	7.2	7.4	9.1	–	9.4	5.4	<[d]	7.0
Asthma	5.6	6.0	4.1[d]	4.6	–	5.1	3.6[d]	<[d]	–
Heart/Stroke	4.9	5.0	4.6	5.2	–	5.4	3.3	<[d]	3.9
Sinusitis	4.3	4.7	3.2[d]	3.5	–	3.9	2.7[d]	–	–
Ulcers	3.5	3.5	3.2	3.7	–	4.0	–	–	–
Diabetes	3.4	3.5	3.2	2.8	–	2.9	4.2	–	4.3
Bronchitis	3.0	3.5	1.6[d]	2.2[d]	–	2.4	<[d]	<[d]	<[d]
Cancer	1.7	1.7	1.7	2.0	–	2.1	–	–	–
Urinary incontinence	1.1	1.2	0.9	1.1	–	1.1	<[d]	–	<[d]

[a]Includes unknown immigrant status; [b]Includes unknown country of birth.
[c]Includes unknown years in Canada; [d]Difference compared with Canadian-born significant at 95% confidence level
< or > Value significantly greater or smaller than that of Canadian-born, but not shown because of large sampling error.

Source: *National Population Health Survey, 1994–95*. Reproduced in Chen et al. (1996b: 37).

of immigrant populations to lifestyle factors such as diet and physical activity (Chen et al. 1996b) and social isolation and lack of access to health care (Oxman-Martinez, Abdool and Loiselle-Leonard 2000).

Aboriginals have higher mortality rates than the non-indigenous population (MacMillan et al. 1996), and compared to Aboriginals in the United States and New Zealand, Aboriginals living in Canada are particularly disadvantaged in terms of mortality rates (Trovato 2001). For status Indians, life expectancy is approximately six to eight years shorter than for the general population in Canada (Tjepkema 2002: 1), and infant mortality rates are twice as high (Statistics Canada 1999a:1, see also MacMillan et al. 1996). Notably, homicide and suicide are prominent causes of death for Aboriginal Canadians, particularly for adults, but even for teens and young children too (Trovato 2001).

The high mortality rates of Aboriginal populations in Canada are accompanied by high rates of morbidity and poorer mental health (see Beaujot and Kerr 2003b). Compared to other racial and ethnic groups, Aboriginal populations suffer from more chronic physical illnesses and infectious diseases (MacMillan et al. 1996). For example, although tuberculosis (TB) rates have dropped in Canada, Aboriginal Canadians remain at high risk of TB (MacMillan et al. 1996: 1573). In a recent Canadian study of cardiovascular disease, Aboriginal people were much more likely to have the disease than those of European ancestry (18.5 per cent compared to 7.6 per cent) (Anand et al. 2001). Aboriginals were also more likely to have arteriosclerosis, and they had a significantly higher incidence of heath risk factors (e.g., smoking, obesity) (Anand et al. 2001).

A study of cancer trends on Manitoba reserves showed a climbing rate of cancer and deaths from cancer from 1971 to 1991, with an increase of 122 per cent between 1987 and 1991 (Rosenberg and Martel 1998).

Racism and discrimination probably have an effect on health. Although there is little Canadian research in this area, Karlsen and Nazroo (2002) document the effect that experiences of racism have on the health status of ethnic minorities in Britain. They found a substantial correlation between reporting fair or poor health and having experienced an instance of racial harassment: 'those who reported having experienced racially-motivated verbal abuse were 60 per cent more likely to report having fair or poor health compared with those who said they had experienced no racial harassment' (Karlsen and Nazroo 2002: 15). Some research has also linked the experience of racial discrimination to the incidence of high blood pressure, thus specifying one way in which discrimination can result in negative physical health (Krieger and Sidney 1996).

The daily indignities of racism and racial harassment constitute a significant risk for psychological distress and depression (Noh et al. 1999; Vega and Rumbaut 1991). Vega and Rumbaut's (1991) description of the stressors that ethnic minorities face includes perceived discrimination, constrained opportunities, and difficult life events (e.g., unemployment). Discrimination is conceptualized as a chronic strain that increases exposure to a number of stressors, such as 'unemployment, hate mail, lewd remarks, or racial epithets (McLean and Link 1994: 25). Being exposed to discrimination and unpredictable physical attacks and harassment have definite health consequences (Noh et al. 1999; Schulz et al. 2000; Vega and Rumbaut 1991; Whitbeck et al. 2001). Consider the following incident:

> I had just stormed out of the board of education offices in downtown Toronto, and joined the rush-hour stream of pedestrians on their way home. I was incensed. A woman at the board office had been rude and insulting. I was standing on the sidewalk still recovering from that encounter when out of the blue I felt something hit me hard on the chest. WHAM! For a moment I wasn't sure what had happened. Then I saw him: an old man in a rumpled suit. I heard him mutter something about immigrants, as he stomped past me. I couldn't believe it. This old man had punched me! (Author unknown, quoted in McKague 1991: 11)

The above encounter illustrates how responses or coping options are often limited (in this case the old man just 'slipped into the crowd') and confrontation is frequently not possible or desirable. Even so, subtle discrimination in the form of 'unfair treatment' or structurally blocked opportunities are often more difficult to respond to (Menaghan 1990; Noh et al. 1999; Schulz et al. 2000).

A recent Canadian study involving 647 Southeast Asian immigrants showed that depression is higher for those who had experienced racial discrimination (Noh et al. 1999). Noh and his colleagues (1999) found that depression was moderated by a forbearing coping style that was characterized by acceptance and avoidance. The authors suggest that the emphasis in the mental-health literature on problem solving as indicative of 'successful agency' may be Western-biased

(Noh et al. 1999): 'Western dichotomies, such as active versus passive or internal versus external, probably fail to capture complexities in culturally patterned responses' (202).

Gender

One persistent puzzle in the study of mortality rates has been women's mortality advantage over men. Women in industrialized countries tend to live longer than men of the same racial, ethnic, and SES backgrounds. In 1996, Canadian women could expect to live 5.7 years longer than Canadian men, and females have been found to have a longer life expectancy at all ages (Statistics Canada 1999b: 323). In Canada, the top three causes of death for men and women in 1997 were cancer, heart diseases, and cerebrovascular disease; however, more women tend to die of heart disease and more men tend to die of cancer (Statistics Canada 2001b).

Throughout the life course, men are more likely to die than women, although this difference peaks in early and middle adulthood, owing to the strong influence of external causes on men's death rate (e.g., suicide) (Wilkins 1996). Table 11.2 shows the top 10 causes of death for Canadian men and women in 1997 (Statistics Canada 2001b: 45). Eighty-three per cent of the deaths in 1997 can be attributed to the top 10 causes of death listed above (Statistics Canada 2001b). Although most of the causes of death are similar for men and women, suicide is a notable exception. Suicide is not one of the top ten causes of death for women, but it ranks seventh among men. Differences in suicide rates may point to the strong influence of external causes on the

Table 11.2 Deaths due to Top Ten Causes, 1997

	Males	Females
	Number of Deaths	
Cancer	31,555	27,148
Heart diseases	30,149	27,268
Cerebrovascular disease	6,675	9,376
Pulmonary diseases	5,607	4,011
Unintentional injuries	5,305	3,321
Pneumonia/influenza	3,749	4,283
Suicide	2,914	t
Diabetes	2,767	2,932
Diseases of arteries	2,505	2,262
Disease of central nervous system	2,104	2,945
Psychoses	?	3,084

t Did not rank in the top 10 causes for females.
? Did not rank in the top 10 causes for males.

Source: Statistics Canada (2001h: 45).

male death rate (Wilkins 1996). Boys between the ages of 10 and 19 suffer from more external causes of death than girls do, and suicide is the number-one cause of death for men between the ages of 20 and 44 (Wilkins 1996: 12–13). Although gender differences in health behaviour and the impact of gendered identities have been suggested as possible explanations for differences in rates and causes of mortality, the mortality advantage of women over men has not yet been well explained (Ballantyne 1999; McDonough et al. 1999; Verbrugge 1989).

Interestingly, measures of societal gender inequity are associated with mortality and morbidity, even after socio-economic deprivation is taken into account (Kawachi et al. 1999). For example, an examination of levels of gender inequality in 50 American states has shown that in states where women's status (measured by political participation, economic autonomy, employment, earnings, and reproductive rights) is higher, both women *and* men had lower mortality rates. However, when black women and white women were analyzed separately, only one significant correlation is found for black women (that of women in elected office), suggesting that the measures of inequality used in the study may not reflect the experiences of black women (Kawachi et al. 1999).

Historically, women have experienced a higher degree of morbidity than men (Dean 1992; Verbrugge 1989). For instance, women are much more likely to suffer from rheumatoid problems, and they are twice as likely to suffer from chronic backache as men (Messing 1997). Although Canadian women's life expectancy at birth (81.4 years) is longer than men's (75.7 years), women have more disability during their lifetime (Statistics Canada 1999a: 1). For almost all chronic health conditions (except diabetes), women are more often afflicted than men; that is particularly the case for arthritis and rheumatism (Statistics Canada 2001c).

The long-standing finding that women have more illness than men has increasingly come under fire because so much morbidity research relies on self-reported health measures (Hunt and Annandale 1999; Macintyre, Ford and Hunt 1999; Walters, McDonough, and Strohschein 2002). Hence, some believe that women's higher reported morbidity rates are due to women 'over-reporting' their symptoms. Yet, in a comparison of men and women's reporting on chronic illness, Macintyre and her colleagues found no gender differences in the initial reporting of a condition (Macintyre et al. 1999). And Arber and Cooper (1999: 61), who examined data from over 14,000 men and women over the age of 59, found that older women did experience more functional impairments than older men and considered themselves healthier than men who were less impaired.

Historically, women were thought to suffer worse mental health than men; much of the research in this regard concentrated on depression (Simon 2000; Walters 1993). More recently, research has shown that men and women experience similar levels of mental illness but that it manifests itself in different ways in men and women (Simon 2000). Hence, the previous belief in a gendered imbalance in the prevalence of mental illness has now been offset with the inclusion of certain behaviours more common to men as indicators of psychological distress, such as alcohol consumption and drug use (Menaghan 1990; Simon 2000). Women

who had one episode of depression were significantly more likely to have another (Statistics Canada 1999a: 5). While women are much more likely than men to suffer from depression, men are more prone to substance abuse (e.g., alcohol consumption, illegal drug use) and have much higher suicide rates at all ages (Statistics Canada 2001a, b, c, d).

McDonough and Walters (2001) outline the hypotheses generated from the stress literature that attempt to explain this imbalance. One explanation, called the **differential exposure hypothesis**, argues that women are subject to more stressors than men on account of their heavier domestic and caring responsibilities. The other explanation, the **differential-vulnerability hypothesis**, argues that women are more affected by stressors than men on account of a 'generalized female disadvantage in social roles and coping resources' (McDonough and Walters, 2001: 549). McDonough and Walters (2001), who tested both hypotheses with data from the Canadian National Health Population Survey for 1994, found higher distress scores and morbidity among women. However, while women were generally exposed to more stressors (specifically, chronic stress and life events) than men, this exposure accounted only for the gender differences in distress (McDonough and Walters 2001). In addition, the differential-vulnerability hypothesis did not explain any of the gendered variance in the results. The authors suggest that their results are due to the complexity in the relationship between gender and health and the inadequacy of the data to reflect this variability. They point to the impact of age on health and note that their study could not take this into account.

Women have been found to experience stress, anxiety, and depression differently depending on their socio-economic status, ethnicity, family relationships and structure, and their labour-market participation (Walters 1993). Stress was found to be more common among the women who were advantaged in terms of income and education, with competing work and family demands being a frequent cause for their increased stress (Walters 1993). In contrast, depression was common among the women who were disadvantaged in terms of education and income (Walters 1993). These women were also more likely to have English as their second language (Walters 1993). Women who suffered from anxiety were similar socio-demographically to those with depression; however, lone parents and English speakers were more likely to have anxiety (Walters 1993). Mental-health difficulties revolved around 'three main themes: the heavy workload of women, the issues of identity with which they grappled, and their social legacy' (Walters 1993: 397). The Walters (1993) study highlights the importance of daily pressures in women's mental health and the necessity to examine the differences in women's lives in relation to their mental health.

Age and Social Time

The length of time one can expect to live and the diseases one is likely to die from have varied considerably over time, partly because of historical variation in the social factors that influence health. For instance, education level is a strong predictor of health status, and whereas more than 50 per cent of Canadians had less than a grade 9 education in 1951, this rate had dropped to approximately 12 per cent by 1996 (Clark 2000: 7). Furthermore, the life expectancy and the overall health of Canadians increased over the twentieth century (Crompton 2000). Whereas an infant born in the 1920s could expect to live only 59 years, an infant born in the 1990s could expect to live 78 years (Crompton 2000). This improvement is largely attributable to public health programs, sanitation, and immunization (Crompton 2000).

In an era of globalization and 'reform' of health-care delivery and service, people born today will most likely experience different health-care services and delivery than those born before them. They will also be exposed to different and less well understood viruses. Indeed, since the 1970s more than 30 new disease-causing agents have been identified, including HIV and the Ebola virus (Lee and Patel 2003). Canadian events in the early 2000s point to the link between economic globalization and the international spread of disease. Three examples stand out. In 2002 the first human cases of West Nile virus (which is carried by mosquitoes) were identified in Ontario. In the early spring of 2003, major cities in the world, including Toronto, were 'combatting' a new disease called SARS (Severe Acute Respiratory Syndrome). In May 2003 a cow infected with mad-cow disease was discovered in Alberta.

The global health implications of mad-cow disease are worth considering in some detail. In 1986, mad-cow disease or BSE (bovine spongiform encephalopathy) was first found in a cow in the United Kingdom. It spread quickly among cattle in Britain, but the effect of BSE on humans who had eaten infected beef was unclear. Nonetheless, by the early 1990s, 15 countries, including Canada, had banned British beef imports, causing a devastating economic blow to the cattle industry in Britain. Concern over the economic impact of these bans led Britain's Ministry of Agriculture, Fisheries, and Food to minimize the potential human health risks of tainted beef consumption. However, in 1996 BSE was linked to 10 human cases of a new form of Creutzfeldt-Jakob disease (CJD), a disease of the brain that is usually fatal in less than one year. This new form of the disease (vCJD) differed from CJD in that it affected young people rather than old people and in that the duration of the illness from onset to death was shorter. By July 2002, there were 115 confirmed cases of vCJD in the UK and the disease seems to be spreading more rapidly despite radical measures to control it (Lee and Patel 2003). On 21 May 2003 the headline on the front page of the *Globe and Mail* read 'Mad-cow hits Canada hard'. After more than a decade of being free of mad-cow disease (there had been only one previous case of the disease in Canada), 'the discovery of mad-cow disease in Alberta walloped the country's multibillion-dollar cattle industry yesterday as the United States banned imports of Canadian beef and producers braced for fallout at home from frightened consumers.' The link between health, globalization, and free trade is shown in Box 11.3 as Canadian politicians react to the mad-cow crisis by eating beef.

Causes of mortality vary over the life course, with cancer posing the most significant risk for Canadians between the ages of 45 and 64 and circulatory diseases (specifically heart disease and stroke) topping the list for Canadians aged 65 and older (Wilkins 1996: 13–14). Causes of mortality differ over the life course not only because

of the aging of the body but also because of changes in socio-economic status, lifestyles, environmental stressors, life events, and surrounding social supports (Hart et al. 1998; House et al. 1994; Hunt 2002; Mustard et al. 1997). For example, on average, the level of social support available to Canadians over the age of 65 is quite low (Statistics Canada 2001c: 30). The influence of persistent poverty, fluctuations in socio-economic status, marital status, and changing conceptualizations of race, ethnicity, and gendered meanings over the life course all contribute to health status, and all have changed historically.

Studies that ignore historical context and social time may present an inaccurate picture of health risks and outcomes. Health in later life may also depend on cumulative experiences and exposures over the life course (Hunt 2002).The odds of mortality are higher for Canadians aged 65 and older who did not graduate from high school, and institutionalization is more common among seniors with low incomes (Statistics Canada 1999a: 4). Childhood experiences, such as being exposed to conflict in the household, influence adult health (Lundberg 1997). The kinds of ill health that most commonly afflict Canadians, such as heart disease, high blood pressure, arthritis, and activity limitations, have also declined substantially in the past 20 years (Chen and Millar 2000).

Rates of sickness tend to increase as people age physiologically. Many seniors, for instance, suffer from chronic pain. Long-term limitations on mental or physical activity are also prominent among those aged 65 and older. However, these limitations were often not permanent, with 60 per cent of those reporting a limitation in 1994/5 being free of it by 1998/9 (Statistics Canada

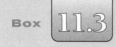
Federal officials were predicting further international trade bans on Canadian beef as they scrambled yesterday to contain damage from the discovery of mad-cow disease at a Northern Alberta ranch.

The diagnosis led to a temporary ban on Canadian exports to the US market and pressure on Ottawa to deal with potentially serious injury to Canada's multibillion-dollar industry.

'We do anticipate there will be further border closures,' said Rory McAlpine, director-general of Agriculture Canada's international trade policy directorate.

'We recognize that the markets in Asia have shown to be very sensitive about these sorts of food-safety and animal-health issues.'

Mr McAlpine said federal trade diplomats have begun immediate meetings with countries that buy Alberta beef to learn what conditions would have to be met to avoid serious injury to Canadian cattle producers.

The moves came as the United States temporarily excluded Canadian beef and cattle imports because a cow in Alberta had tested positive for mad-cow disease, also known as bovine spongiform encephalopathy (BSE). Although the United States is by far Canada's largest customer for beef and cattle, at about $3.6 billion in 2002, Canadian farmers also exported a total of almost $400 million to Mexico, Japan, South Korea, and Taiwan.

Canadian officials were also expected to meet yesterday with the International Organization for Epizootics (OIE), which establishes animal-health standards for the world.

'We will be doing everything we can to demonstrate that we've met the OIE criteria,' Mr McAlpine said. The OIE lays out criteria that it recommends countries should meet to be considered BSE-free.

Mr McAlpine added that satisfying the US government will be crucial in convincing other countries that Canada is doing all it can to ensure its beef is safe.

Alberta Premier Ralph Klein said the federal government and Prime Minister Jean Chrètien need to step in.

'If he's going to give $10 million to bring the Rolling Stones to Ontario to show there's no danger from SARS, I would certainly invite the Prime Minister to donate the same amount to have the Rolling Stones sit down to a beef dinner and gladly accept a cheque for $10 million on top of that.'

Agriculture Minister Lyle Vanclief said yesterday he didn't know whether other countries will follow the US ban. However, he said that Canada has 'the best system of surveillance in the world' and the government would work hard to convince other nations of that.

US Agriculture Secretary Ann Veneman, who announced yesterday's ban, also said Washington would send a technical team to Canada to assist in the Canadian situation.

'I have spoken with Canada's Agriculture and Agri-Food Minister, Lyle Vanclief, a short time ago about Canada's investigation, and feel that all appropriate measures are being taken in what appears to be an isolated case of bovine spongiform encephalophathy,' Ms Veneman said in a news release.

'Information suggests that risk to human health and the possibility of transmission to animals in the United States is very low.'

Pilar Bolanos, a spokeswoman for the Mexican embassy, said she expected her country would ban Canadian beef products temporarily until the situation was cleared up. However, Mr Vanclief said he did not receive any indication of a temporary ban from that country when he spoke with his Mexican counterpart yesterday.

Canadian Alliance agriculture critic Howard Hillstrom said the government must spend as much money as it needs to trace the cow's background quickly and allay international fears. He also suggested that Mr Vanclief or a designate must begin daily briefings to tell Canadians about their success in tracing the infected animal's background.

Mr Hillstrom said he expected that Canadian authorities would get the situation under control and said the Canadian surveillance system is adequate.

The diagnosis of a cow with the disease could have a devastating impact on Ontario's multibillion-dollar livestock industry, provincial Agriculture Minister Helen Johns warned at Queen's Park yesterday.

'The situation is very serious in one regard. We have a fair amount of exports, $800 million in red-meat exports from this province,' she said. Mrs Johns added: 'We have 20,000 producers in the province who have beef on their farms. . . . It could be very devastating. . . . We export a lot of beef from this province to other provinces and to other countries.'

The likelihood of mad-cow disease in Ontario is very low, she said. The province had tested more than 1,000 cows in Ontario in the past year and none showed any sign of BSE.

Source: Laghi (2003). Reprinted with permission from the Globe and Mail.

2001c: 29). In spite of an increase in overall life expectancy and, therefore, an increase in the average age of seniors, the health of seniors in terms of chronic conditions did not change significantly between 1978/9 and 1998/9 (Statistics Canada 1999a: 4). Seniors rank their health high, with the majority of those aged 65 and older (close to 80 per cent) rating their health as excellent, very good, or good in 1998/9 (Statistics Canada 1999a). Interestingly, compared to older men with the same health conditions, older women were less likely to rate their health as poor (Arber and Cooper 1999: 61).

Socio-economic status has a significant influence on morbidity as we age, and a number of studies have charted the ways in which health inequities differ over the life course and at older ages (Cairney and Arnold 1996; House et al. 1994). The impact of socio-economic status over the life course on health is substantial, and a number of researchers have found that the effects of income and education peak in middle adulthood and early older age (House et al. 1994; Mustard et al. 1997). Analyzing data from a longitudinal survey of 2,867 Americans, House and his colleagues found significant relationships between age, socio-economic status, and health, with chronic conditions and functional status impairments disproportionately afflicting those with lower socio-economic status at the early and middle ages of life (House et al. 1994). They explain the peak effect of socio-economic status on the health of those in middle and early old age as a result of a greater exposure to risk factors (e.g., negative life events, chronic stress, fewer social supports, unhealthy behaviour) and an increased vulnerability to these factors for those with low income and low education (House et al. 1994). Peek and Coward (2000) have also found that age, education, and poverty status were the most predictive for disability in older age, with low educational status and the experience of poverty indicating a greater risk for developing multiple disabilities.

Mental health varies considerably over the life course. Recently, researchers have been paying more attention to the mental health of adolescents because the emergence of disorders at this time of life is a risk factor for the development of adult mental-health disorders (Aneshensel and Sucoff 1996; Avison and McAlpine 1992; Whitbeck et al. 2001). Aneshensel and Sucoff (1996) investigated whether neighbourhood racial or ethnic segregation and socio-economic stratification were associated with the mental health of adolescents. Neighbourhoods with a lower socio-economic status were perceived by the study participants as the most hazardous and threatening. In neighbourhoods that were perceived as the most hazardous or dangerous, symptoms of depression, anxiety disorders, oppositional defiant disorders, and conduct disorders were more common.

These neighbourhood factors were more strongly associated with symptoms of mental health than was family socio-economic status. Gender significantly influenced the type of mental disorder, with girls more commonly exhibiting depression and anxiety disorders and boys more commonly exhibiting conduct and oppositional defiant disorders. A protective effect for depression was found in neighbourhoods with high levels of social cohesion, measured as communities where people knew one another (Aneshensel and Sucoff 1996). These findings suggest that studies of mental health must consider the milieu in which people live their lives (Aneshensel and Sucoff 1996).

Mental health and well-being are increasingly being conceptualized as cumulative effects, with experiences across the life course, particularly early experiences, shaping and determining later health outcomes (Lynch, Kaplan, and Salonen 1997; McLeod and Shanahan 1996; Wadsworth 1997). For example, McLeod and Shanahan (1996) have found that long-lasting poverty in childhood significantly increases antisocial behaviour later in life. Miech and Shanahan (2000) found that low levels of education predicted higher levels of depression and that this relationship intensified with age. Education levels, age, and income mutually influence each other, as our age and our cohort influence our chances of obtaining education. In addition, our income is influenced by our age, as well as by our sex. For example, women over the age of 65 are disproportionately likely to be poor (Williams 2000).

Age also influences the extent to which we are exposed to the stressors of work and family demands, the extent to which social support is available (Statistics Canada

2001c), and levels of self-esteem (McMullin and Cairney, forthcoming). Women experience higher levels of personal stress than men at every age, but men and women aged 65 and older experience significantly less stress than younger adults. However, younger men and women experience more social support than do men and women aged 65 and older (Statistics Canada 2001c: 22). Using the National Population Health Survey, McMullin and Cairney (forthcoming) show that in their early teens, boys and girls, regardless of family income, have similar levels of self-esteem. However, at each successive age, girls have lower levels of self-esteem than boys do. Once people reach their mid-forties, income levels begin to significantly affect self-esteem. From middle age on, income groups diverge in their levels of self-esteem, such that men and women from the lowest income groups have the least self-esteem. Although the level of depression in elderly men is quite low, their high rates of suicide suggest that under-diagnosis of psychological distress and disorders may be a problem, for researchers have suggested that as many as '90 per cent of people who commit suicide are suffering from depression or another mental illness, or a substance abuse disorder, which could potentially be diagnosed' (Langlois and Morrison 2001: 17).

Understanding Inequality in Health

Agency and Lifestyle Behaviour

The decisions people make about whether to smoke, how much to drink, how much physical activity they get, whether to engage in risky activities, and whether to take part in preventive health actions are all embraced under the rubric of lifestyle behaviour. These factors were once thought to account for much of the inequality that manifested itself in mortality and morbidity (House 2001; Robertson 1998). Indeed, alcohol consumption and smoking have been found to be important predictive health indicators, particularly for men (Denton and Walters 1999). And, a recent Canadian study found that drinking, smoking, and using illicit drugs could explain 21 per cent of deaths and 23 per cent of potential years lost (Single et al. 1999).

Lower socio-economic status has been associated with unhealthy behaviour (Pomerleau et al. 1997). Canadians in the highest income groups are more likely to be physically active, to take vitamins, and to eat low-fat foods than are those with lower family incomes (Pomerleau et al. 1997; Statistics Canada 2001a). Only 16 per cent of Canadians in the highest-income households smoke, compared with 30 per cent in the lowest-income households (Statistics Canada 2001a: 18). Smoking accounts for much preventable illness and death; in fact nearly 45,000 deaths in 1996 were attributed to smoking-related illness (e.g., cancer, heart disease and stroke) (Shields and Tremblay 2002:3). Besides the direct health effects of smoking, there are also confounding effects because smokers also tend to eat fewer fruits and vegetables and more fatty foods than non-smokers (Palaniappan et al. 2001). Nonetheless, when the number of cigarettes smoked is controlled for, the ill effects of smoking are greater among those from lower socio-economic groups than for those of higher socio-economic status (Mao et al. 2001: 7).

Among Aboriginal populations in Canada, high rates of smoking, obesity, and

alcohol consumption have been documented (Anand et al. 2001; Millar 1992;
Rosenberg and Martel 1998). These habits
are probably due to the poverty and discrimination experienced by Aboriginal people throughout their lives (Lynch Kaplan
and Salonen 1997; Whitbeck et al. 2001).
The marked influence of environment on
health behaviour is also evident among
immigrants. Healthful behaviour tends to be
more common among immigrants than
among Canadian-born residents (Chen et al.
1996a). Smoking rates also vary significantly by ethnic group in Canada, with Asian
and southern Europeans being the least likely to smoke (Millar 1992). Immigrants tend
to be significantly less likely to smoke than
the Canadian-born (Chen et al. 1996a;
Millar 1992). Whereas three-quarters of
recent non-European immigrants had never
smoked, only 34 per cent of the Canadian-
born population had never smoked (Chen
et al. 1996a: 41). However, after 10 years in
Canada, the number of non-European
immigrants who have never smoked
dropped to 61.7 per cent and among recent
European immigrants this number dropped
after 10 years from 55.7 per cent to 37.6 per
cent (Chen et al. 1996a: 43).

Men and women exhibit significantly
different kinds of health behaviour even
within the same socio-economic groups
(Statistics Canada 2000f, j). Although men
are more likely to be physically active than
women (Statistics Canada 2001a), the fact
that women are less likely than men to
engage in binge drinking, to smoke, or be
overweight contributes to the higher risk of
premature death from heart diseases among
men (Statistics Canada 2001d: 4). Men
engage in riskier activities than women and
are more likely to die as a result of suicide

and motor vehicle accidents (Statistics
Canada 2001j: 4). Men are also less likely
than women to visit a physician, and
women survive longer than men with the
same chronic conditions (e.g., heart disease,
lung cancer) (Rieker and Bird 2000).

Lifestyle behaviour varies significantly
over the life course. Smoking is much less
common among seniors and those aged
12–17, and vigorous leisure activity appears
to drop substantially after the age of 24.
Other kinds of behaviour, such as eating
fruit and vegetables have been found to
increase steadily with age, and seniors
report eating more fruits and vegetables
than other age groups (Statistics Canada
2001a). Aging and generational ideologies
have an effect on the health behaviour that
people engage in or ignore (Gillis and
Hirdes 1996). Graham, Carver, and Brett
(1995: 769) found that women aged 65 and
older drink less alcohol, smoke less, and use
illicit drugs less than any other age-gender
group. The authors note that changing attitudes towards drinking and smoking by
women may result in an increased risk for
future age cohorts (Graham et al. 1995).

Alcohol consumption has been found to
vary by gender, ethnicity, and changing social
roles over the life course (Johnson et al.
1998). In their American study, Johnson and
his colleagues (1998) found that whites drink
more alcohol over the course of their lives
than blacks or Hispanics; however, blacks
and Hispanics drink more in later life per
occasion than do whites. Men were found to
drink more than women, and people who
had many children or were regular churchgo-
ers drank less (Johnson et al. 1998).

Although lifestyle choices highlight the
agency that people have in their lives, the
simplicity of classifying behaviour as either

healthful or unhealthful masks the complexity of social relations and related ideologies that mediate and constrain the lifestyle choices that people make in their daily lives. For example, the increase in the number of young women smokers has been thought to stem from changes in gender ideologies (Hunt, 2002).

Health Care Access and Utilization

Access to health care, even within the 'equal-access' Canadian system, varies on the basis of class, gender, ethnicity, race, and age. Poverty, for example, can impede access to health care in very concrete ways. Roos and Mustard (1997) found that although prenatal visits made for the first-born child were not significantly different for women from the lowest and the highest income groups, the number of visits decreased for women from the lower income groups with the second birth and on: it is not hard to imagine the difficulties in arranging childcare, coping with children on public transportation, and other problems that would make it more difficult for the low-income mother who has several children to keep appointments than for a woman with greater socio-economic support (Roos and Mustard 1997: 105).

Reporting unmet health-care needs is correlated with household income: people in low-income households are 10 times more likely to report unmet health-care needs than people in middle-high income households (Chen and Hou 2002). Of particular concern for low-income households are the expense of drugs and transportation difficulties (Chen and Hou 2002). Cancer survival rates vary by community income

(Boyd et al. 1999), and access to preventive treatments is a crucial factor in the cancer survival advantage that low-income Canadians have over low-income Americans (Gorey et al. 2000).

Although some aspects of health care (e.g., preventive care) are under-used by low-income Canadians, other health services, such as hospital admissions (Glazier et al. 2000) and physician visits (Roos and Mustard 1997), are used more often by them. Higher rates of morbidity in lower-income neighbourhoods are thought to explain the higher levels of hospital utilization (Glazier et al. 2000). A recent report on the health of Canadians found that low-income individuals were more likely to use physician services, use emergency departments, be admitted to hospitals, take multiple medications, and require home-care services (Statistics Canada 1999a: 6). Paradoxically, even though people from lower-income and poorer neighbourhoods use hospitals more often than people from higher-income neighbourhoods, they undergo less surgery (Roos and Mustard 1997). Roos and Mustard (1997) argue that this is due to the underuse of specialist services by lower-income individuals, possibly owing to better access and a stronger communicative relationship on the part of individuals from higher socio-economic status. Specialists and surgeons offer more treatment to people with higher socio-economic status (Roos and Mustard 1997), perhaps as a result of a treating physician's referral decisions. A recent study based on data from the 1994 Canadian National Population Health Survey found that even though lower socio-economic groups visited physicians more often and therefore had more opportunity to be referred to specialists, they had less contact with specialists than those from higher socio-economic groups (Dunlop et al. 2000).

Access to health care is also determined by the extent to which people feel comfortable making use of the resources available (Ahmad and Walker 1997; Benoit and Carroll 2001; Newbold 1998; Oxman-Martinez et al 2000). Benoit and Carroll (2001), who interviewed urban, Aboriginal women from Vancouver, found that the most important public-health issues were those of access and availability of health care. Aboriginal women underuse preventive health-care services, and their access to prenatal care is limited. Accessibility meant encountering 'a non-judgmental, encouraging, informal environment . . . [which included] a more central service focus on Aboriginal women's health concerns' (Benoit and Carroll 2001: 6). Newbold (1998) also notes that Aboriginals living on reserves have very little access to physicians and hospitals. Geographic isolation played a large role in the difficulty of obtaining health services; however, education and greater self-governance over community issues were viewed as more vital to their health needs (Newbold 1998).

Physician visits do not appear to differ significantly by immigrant status. In fact, for both Canadian-born and immigrant populations with low incomes, the number of physician contacts is higher than among similar high-income Canadians (Chen et al. 1996a).

The actions and decisions of health-care providers are, however, influenced by the racial or ethnic backgrounds of their patients (Dunlop et al. 2000; Krieger et al. 1993; Roos and Mustard 1997). In their review of instances of racial discrimination in health care, Krieger and her colleagues (1993) discussed several studies that documented preferential treatment regimes for white patients. Geiger (2001: 1699) notes that 'disparaging racial stereotyping, not clinical data, was predictive of refusal to recommend bypass surgery for many African-American patients in one large series of cases.' These findings suggest that once a person is in the medical system, the services that are made available to them vary on the basis of race.

Although physicians are trained to be 'neutral' and to shed or ignore their own socio-demographic characteristics and those of their patients, studies indicate that in practice this is not done (Beagan 2000: 1253; van Ryn and Burke 2000). African-American patients and patients from lower-income groups are perceived in a variety of more negative ways than white patients and patients from higher-income groups. Furthermore, physicians believe that African-American and low-income patients are less compliant and less intelligent, and physicians felt less 'affiliated' with patients from minority backgrounds (van Ryn and Burke 2000). These perceptions affect the health care that racial or ethnic minorities and people of lower socio-economic status are apt to obtain. Patients sense and respond to the perceptions of the physician, so that 'when patients perceive that physicians like them, care about them, and are interested in them as a person, they are likely to volunteer more information and be more active in the encounter, more satisfied, and more compliant with medical regimens' (van Ryn and Burke 2000: 823). Patients are less likely to ask questions and be active health-care consumers when they are aware of hostility or negativity on the part of their physician (van Ryn and Burke 2000).

Interestingly enough, limited access to health care may not be at issue just when one is poor or a member of an ethnic or minority group. Wente (2002), for instance, contrasts the prostate-cancer experiences of Alan Rock (when he was the federal health minister) with that of Ralph Smith (a government worker). Both were screened for prostate cancer, and both were found to have the disease; however, despite being the same age (53) and living in the same city (Ottawa), their experiences of treatment were markedly different (see Box 11.4).

Wente's article shows that the social patterning of the relations of class, age, gender, and ethnicity can result in a privileged and

---

Box **11.4** **Socio-economic Status Influences Access to Health Care Even among the Well-to-Do**

Desperately Seeking Care
By Margaret Wente

'The beginning was not particularly ominous,' says Ralph Smith. 'I was approaching 50, I knew I should start watching out, so I asked my doctor about PSA testing and he said, "I guess it's not a bad idea."'

The PSA test is the standard screening test for prostate cancer, which is the most common cancer in men. It's the test that detected Allan Rock's cancer. After his successful surgery, Mr Rock, the former health minister, became a poster person for early detection and treatment.

Mr Smith and Mr Rock make for an interesting parallel. The two are nearly the same age; at 53, Mr Smith is a year younger. Both work for the government and live in Ottawa. Their PSA tests both turned suspicious around the same time in 2000. After that, their stories diverged.

Mr Rock, who is said not to have received any special treatment, became a glowing testimonial for a health-care system that, despite its woes, still works.

Mr Smith's story has a different lesson. Trust the system, and it could kill you.

After his first suspicious PSA result in August of 2000, Mr Smith's doctor retested him and referred him to a urologist. Waiting lists in Ottawa were long, but Mr Smith says he wasn't particularly concerned. He waited more than three months for the appointment, which was in February of 2001. 'The urologist said, "I really recommend a biopsy because your PSA levels are a little high and I detect a nodule." Then I started to get a little worried.'

The urologist, meanwhile, wrote to Mr Smith's family doctor saying he strongly suspected a malignancy—though he didn't tell his patient that.

Mr Smith had a biopsy in March. The diagnosis: cancer of the prostate. His urologist told him the good news was that they had caught it fairly early, and they agreed that surgery was the answer. Then the urologist told him the bad news. He had one of the longest waiting lists in the city. Mr Smith would have to wait for months.

Meantime, Mr Rock had been cured and was back at work. His family physician is a well-connected, high-profile doctor in Toronto, where urologists' waiting lists for surgery are often shorter than they are in Ottawa. Mr Rock had his surgery as soon as the biopsy revealed the bad news.

Back in Ottawa, more tests revealed more bad news for Mr Smith. They indicated that his cancer was the aggressive kind. He had moved from low risk to high risk.

Mr Smith is better armed than most to meet the challenges of being a cancer patient. As a policy analyst and adviser on homeless issues, he's used to doing research and dealing with complexity. He's also married to a doctor. His wife, Fionnuala O'Kelly, is a pediatrician.

But none of that did any good. They could not pull strings. They also found that there was no triage system for prostate-cancer patients; everyone had to stand in the same line. Their doctor wouldn't refer them to someone in Toronto, where, in any case, quicker treatment was not guaranteed. They were also wary of switching to a doctor whose track record was unknown to them. 'It's a long operation,' Mr Smith says. 'If it's mishandled, you could be impotent and incontinent.'

It was the end of April now, and they were helpless.

One day, Mr Smith's wife asked another cancer doctor what he would do if he were in their shoes. 'I'd get on a plane to the Mayo Clinic next week,' he said.

Instead, Mr Smith went to England, where a relative had recently been treated by one of the world's top specialists. He contacted the specialist's office on the weekend. On Monday, the office called back and told him that, if he could be in London by Friday, they would operate Saturday.

They were. The surgery was successful. Mr Smith's cancer was indeed very aggressive. He learned that it probably would have spread to his lymph nodes and surrounding tissues in a matter of weeks. When prostate cancer spreads, it can't be cured.

'I never would have thought of doing this,' Mr Smith says now. 'I come from Saskatchewan, the home of medicare. I'm a bit of a student of our big social programs.'

When Mr Smith returned home, he applied for reimbursement from the provincial health-care plan for the cost of his treatment, which was about $17,000. He was turned down, on the grounds that appropriate treatment was available in Ontario. He decided to appeal. So he and his wife began their research again, gathering facts and figures on the availability of urologists and the length of waiting times. They had to prove that further delay would have put him at significant risk, and that the long wait for treatment wasn't his fault.

Last November, they made their case before an independent appeals board. This week, they learned that they have won. The government will have to pay them back.

There are likely to be many more Ralph Smiths, because there's no quick fix for what ails cancer care. One reason for long waiting lists for surgery is that operating rooms are dark. There aren't enough nurses and anesthesiologists to staff them.

Some cancer experts say there's an even bigger problem than waiting lists—access to new drugs. Canada's health bureaucracy is slow to approve them, and the provinces are even slower to agree to pay for them because they're so costly. 'Doctors have a gag rule imposed on them if they're working in cancer centres,' said one clinical oncologist recently, before he left Canada to practice in the US. 'They can't tell patients about the newest treatments which they know are being tested and probably work, because the director will come down on their head.'

But the worst problem is probably the demographic time bomb. Mr Smith and Mr Rock belong to the first wave of baby boomers to reach the prostate cancer age. There are millions more men right behind them. The system isn't coping well now, and soon it could be overwhelmed.

'What I'd like to tell Roy Romanow is that my story is one that many cancer patients have,' says Mr Smith. As a man who makes his living studying social policy, he's got a few suggestions. 'It's not about facilitating people leaving the country to seek surgery somewhere else. And it's not about setting up a two-tier health system. It really is about ensuring that people who are at risk receive timely treatment here in Canada.'

That will be a formidable task. Meantime, don't trust the system to take care of you. As Mr Smith found out, 'It comes down to the patient having to do it himself.'

Source: Wente (2002). Reprinted with permission from the Globe and Mail.

life-saving experience in health care. As white, middle and upper-middle class, working male adults, these men largely shared positions of privilege in their age, gender, and ethnicity. Although Alan Rock claimed that there had been no 'line-jumping' and that his case had followed the normal procedure, it is clear that his political connections and prominence expedited his diagnoses and treatment. Having the 'right' physician with the shortest waiting time is not merely a matter of luck but is indicative of a milieu of privilege. Nonetheless, Ralph Smith's story also attests to the advantages of his position in the social structure. Had Smith not been a practised advocate—someone used to asking questions, challenging authority, and seeking alternative means of care, had he not been aware through his pediatrician wife and her network of other professionals of the seriousness of his case, and had he not been able to afford (even in the short term) an expensive trip for an emergency surgery, he might very well have lost his life. The prostate screening test (PSA) is not covered by OHIP, and both men asked for the test and paid for

it. The experiences of both of these men illustrate the extent to which power, knowledge, and economic and social resources can influence access to health care.

The extent to which health care is used is strongly related to gender, with women using many more health preventive and health-care services than men do (Green and Pope 1999; Statistics Canada 2001f, k). Although some of this use is explained by visits for reproductive and prenatal care (Statistics Canada 2001f), women's greater use of health care has been documented independently of these types of visits (Green and Pope 1999). Men are much less likely to visit physicians or consult a specialist (Statistics Canada 2001f). Unlike relationships among health-care access and each of class and race or ethnicity however, explanations for the underuse of health-care services by men emphasize masculine ideologies that promote unhealthy, risk-taking behaviour (Courtenay 2000; Statistics Canada 2001f, h, k; Trovato and Lalu 1995).

In an insightful study, Courtenay (2000), who examines the relationships between conceptualizations of masculinity and their consequences for men's health, suggests that different health-care utilization rates for men and women are manifestations of the gender structure. According to Courtenay, masculine imperatives to be 'strong' and self-sufficient inhibit men from attending to their health and encourage the medical establishment to under-analyze the effect of gendered beliefs on men's health behaviour (Courtenay 2000). He argues that the attributes of 'masculinity' are in contradiction to healthy behaviour, and that the way in which these attributes manifest themselves is shaped by class and ethnicity. For example, men from different social classes may take risks in varying ways. 'Demonstrating masculinities with fearless, high-risk behaviours may entail skydiving for an upper-class man, mountain climbing for a middle-class man, racing hot rods for a working-class man and street fighting for a poor urban man' (Courtenay 2000: 1390).

According to the constructs of masculinity, health-conscious behaviour fails to connote a 'strong' persona and is considered to be 'feminine' (Courtenay 2000). This is an instance where gender structures work against both men and women. On the one hand, physicians provide less information to men than women and spend less time with men, and this may jeopardize men's health (Courtenay 2000). On the other hand, the fact that physicians spend more time with women may also be the reason for the over-medicalization and pathologization of women's bodies. Hence, although women's use of the medical system is thought to be due to their greater tendency to be ill and their overuse of health services, men's utilization of health care is considered a sign that they are healthier than women. According to

Courtenay, the broader societal view of women as 'overusers' of medical services and of men as 'naturally' healthy should be reversed:

> Given that women are unquestionably less susceptible to serious illness and live longer than men, it would seem that women should provide the standard against which men's health and men's health behaviour are measured . . . if this were the case, we would be compelled instead to confront . . . men's underutilization of health care. (Courtenay 2000: 1395)

The actions and decision of health-care providers are influenced by the gender and age of patients. The medical establishment has played a critical role in defining and enforcing gendered behaviour norms on women (Lorber 1997; Mitchinson 1991). Women's bodies have been viewed as problematic, and natural processes (e.g., menstruation) have been considered to be illnesses in need of medical treatment (Lorber 1997). The construction of 'premenstrual syndrome' as a disease is a telling example of how societal imperatives are translated into medical problems. Lorber (1997: 60) argues that 'stereotypically, women suffering from PMS are said to be cranky, irritable, angry, violent and out of control . . . these characteristics assume some kind of comparison— with the same woman at other times of the month or with the way women are supposed to be.' She notes that there are no control groups in this research (either with men or with women cross-culturally or by ethnicity) (Lorber 1997). When women voice dissatisfaction or anger about their life circumstances, physicians have tended to see the problem as an internal one requiring a medical solution (e.g., psychotropic drugs) rather than as a symptom of societal inequality requiring a societal solution. The importance for women to co-operate with society's expectations is particularly evident in regard to appearance, even when women are deathly ill or recuperating from an illness.

The requirements that cancer outreach volunteers must meet demonstrates the con-

straints that women encounter on the basis of appearance. In Box 11.5, Batt (1998) describes the experience of breast-cancer survivor Darlene Betteley.

Here we see that the mandate to wear a prosthetic device in order to look 'normal' illustrates the extent to which women's bodies are medicalized and socially constructed. Still, the over-monitoring of women's bodies

Box 11.5 The Medicalization and Social Construction of Women's Bodies: The Story of Darlene Bettely

After Betteley's cancer diagnosis in 1986, she had both breasts removed. A few years later, she became a Reach to Recovery volunteer. When one of the convenors (the woman who matches visitors with patients) discovered that Betteley did not wear breast prostheses, Betteley was advised that she would have to get a bustline or give up her visits. 'We like our volunteers to look normal,' the convenor explained.

Betteley has all the letters and newspaper clippings from the dispute neatly organized in a big blue binder. The opening page has two full-length, colour photos of her, standing erect in her backyard–Before and After Surgery. 'Now I ask you, Sharon,' she prompts me, 'Do I look normal?'

An unlikely rebel, Betteley is in her mid-50s, a mother of grown children and a devout believer. She loved making hospital visits. She enjoys people and when she recovered from her two operations she was so happy to be alive that she wanted to share her zest for life with others. She had modeled as a teenager and she still loves clothes. She took pride in her ability to dress becomingly after the two mastectomies. She had been a Reach to Recovery volunteer for over a year when her convenor, who knew she didn't wear a prosthesis, called her to 'talk things over'. It happened that the head convenor for Ontario had called the local convenor in search of a suitable visitor for a woman who was having a double prophylactic mastectomy. Darlene's name was suggested. Did she wear a prosthesis? the Ontario convenor wanted to know.

'No.'

'Well,' the provincial convenor said, 'we like our volunteers to look normal.'

The local convenor, a woman Betteley knew well, presented her with the senior convenor's verdict. Faced with the prospects of losing her volunteer status, Betteley almost capitulated, but something in her rose up in protest. 'Why should I have to go against something I really believe?' she asked. 'I am happy with myself. You have to like yourself before you can share your happiness and your love with other people.'

In that case, the convenor said, Betteley could no longer make hospital visits.

'Well, there were tears and there was anger,' explained Betteley, 'because visiting was very important to me.' She began asking questions that had never occurred to her before.

'I thought, "Does the Cancer Society have anything to do with all these companies that make prostheses? And what do they do with the money they raise?"' Betteley's daughter Cathy was particularly incensed by her mother's dismissal. Cathy worked as a personnel officer and she urged her mother to complain to the Human Rights Commission. Betteley demurred. She would rather put the whole thing behind her. 'There'll be another door opening,' she said, with her characteristic aplomb.

Cathy wrote a letter to the chairman of the volunteer unit at the local Cancer Society office. Betteley also wrote to the Society, explaining that 'after discussions with my doctor and my husband, I decided, for my own physical comfort, not to wear a prosthesis.' Cathy sent yet another letter to the editor of the local newspaper and the paper decided to run a story. At a nearby university, a sociology student was so indignant when he read the article, he fired off letters to every major newspaper in the country. The first to pick up on it was the *Globe and Mail*. By now, Betteley had lost her reticence about speaking out. A male volunteer, she pointed out in the front page story, 'is not required to shove a golf ball down his pants before meeting people.' The policy, she said, was sexist ('a word I didn't even have in my vocabulary until these students brought it to mind'). 'I'm wondering how many men sit on the board of the Cancer Society who need to see a woman with a bustline,' she told the reporter. The *Globe and Mail* story opened the media floodgates. First the *Toronto Star* phoned for an interview, then a Florida tabloid, which ran its version of the story under the headline, 'Whatta Bunch of Boobs!' The same day, reporters from her local TV station crowded into her small living room with lights and cameras while another TV crew waited in the driveway to get in. Next Betteley guested on a noon hour radio phone-in program from Montreal. 'It was awesome,' she recalls.

Source: Batt (1998). Reprinted by permission of Canadian Scholars' Press Inc.

seems to pertain only to conditions that are believed to be 'female'. Some conditions that are common in women are under-treated or ignored despite women's greater contact with the medical profession. These biases have been well documented by McKinlay (1996) in his review of the under-detection of coronary heart disease in women. He notes that gender has been a primary determinant in treatment decisions on the part of physicians:

> When confronted with exactly the same presenting symptoms, vital signs, and test results depicted in a professionally acted colour videotaped patient-doctor encounter, 192 randomly sampled male internists were much less likely to arrive at a cardiac diagnosis in younger women, treat women medically, believe treatment was necessary or, for the younger women especially, to make health education and lifestyle change recommendation. (McKinlay 1996: 17)

Similarly, when older adults present physicians with their symptoms, physicians sometimes dismiss these symptoms as signs of old age and not as indicators of illness or disease.

Visits to physicians are common among those aged 65 and older, with 88 per cent of male seniors and 90 per cent of female seniors reporting they had visited a general practitioner in the last year (Statistics Canada 2001k: 33). The gender imbalances in the use of health-care services, with women having significantly more physician visits and hospitalization stays largely disappears among Canadians aged 65 and older. This shows the impact of child-bearing and reproductive concerns on health-care utilization for women in early and middle adulthood (Chen and Hou 2002). The use of home care for seniors is not significantly different for men and women; however, seniors with a low household income were significantly more likely to need home care. Unmet health-care needs in the form of accessibility and acceptability were more common for people under the age of 45 (Chen and Hou 2002). Therefore, older age per se does not appear to impede access to health care in Canada.

In fact, the process of aging, particularly for women, has led to a number of interventions which medicalize this natural process (Dinnerstein and Weitz 1998; Krieger et al. 1993; Morgan 1998;). Dinnerstein and Weitz (1998: 200) argue that 'on men, grey hair, wrinkles, even a widening waist signify experience, wisdom, maturity, and sometimes sexiness . . . on women they denote decline and asexuality.' The **medicalization** of menopause and the advent of hormone replacement therapy are developments which epitomize the quest to freeze women in a youthful mode (Lorber 1997). Vertinsky (1998: 90) notes that 'menopausal women are prime targets of medical experts, pharmaceutical companies and the media who bombard women with the message that hormones are required to cope with the "death of their ovaries".' Moreover, cosmetic surgery is becoming more of an imperative than a choice for many women in response to society's valorization of youth (Goodman 1996).

CAGE(s) and the Processes of Production, Reproduction, and Distribution

Clearly, different lifestyle choices (reflecting agency) and limited access to health care do not fully explain health inequality in Canada. To understand better why some Canadians are healthier than others, we must consider structural interpretations of the intersections among class, age, gender, ethnicity, and race alongside lifestyle and access factors. For instance, variations in levels of physical activity illustrate how class, age, gender, ethnicity, and race structure health behaviour. Gendered ideologies inhibit women from engaging in physical-fitness activities, and despite recent attempts to increase women's involvement in sport and exercise, fewer women than men are physically active (Vertinsky 1998). 'Healthy exercise is closely entwined with the social and economic status of women, disempowering stereotypes of the female body, and the issue of control over women's bodies' (Vertinsky 1998: 82). Vertinsky has identified four structural factors that contribute to the limited physical activity of women: (1) the authoritative role played by medical discourse in discouraging strenuous exercise for both younger and older women; (2) the impact of media and beauty standards which see physical fitness only as a means to reach unattainable standards, along with the perception that women are naturally weaker and less physically able; (3) ageist assumptions about the physical abilities of older women, along with the reliance on drug therapies; (4) race and ethnic bias in accounts of physical activity with young, white women idealized in sport (Vertinsky 1998). Further, women's positioning within the processes of production, reproduction, and distribution means that women of various age, racial, and ethnic backgrounds tend not to have as much money or time to spend on physical activity as men do. This suggests that ideological structures combine with material structures to influence lifestyle 'choices'.

The ways in which processes of production, reproduction, and distribution are organized contribute to health inequalities. The nature of the productive labour that people perform may involve exposures to toxins, a lack of control over the work process, and discriminatory or oppressive treatment, all of which make an imprint on the physical and mental health of bodies. Similarly, individuals with higher degrees of control in productive processes and positive work experiences likely enjoy better health.

Of course, our place in the productive realm and the related health consequences are not randomly assigned, but are strongly influenced by our class, age, gender, and race or ethnicity (Tomiak, Gentleman, and Jette 1997; Walters et al. 1996). Even when men and women share the same occupation in paid work, they often experience differing work realities, which manifest themselves in differing health consequences (Messing 1997). For example, in Messing's (1997: 3) review of the literature on women's occupational health, she says, 'Women and men with the same job titles can have very different exposures—male cleaners mop and female cleaners dust.' Furthermore, women's occupational illnesses are likely underrepresented because waitresses, supermarket clerks, and cleaners (female-dominated jobs) are under-studied in the occupational literature (Messing 1997). Although employment is associated with better overall

health for women (Elstad 1995; Walters, McDonough, and Strohschein 2002), some researchers have observed that the combination of caregiving and paid employment can take a toll (Dean 1992; Pavalko and Woodbury 2000), suggesting that processes of production and reproduction must be considered simultaneously.

Similarly, the organization of reproductive processes leads to variations in health. Social ties and contacts are not always health-protective and may in fact be stressful. Thus, to the extent that women's primary responsibility for reproductive processes engages them in vast social networks, there may be a 'cost of caring' that produces ill health effects. Moreover, marriage is health-protective for many men, but the effect of marriage for women on health is more complex: 'Marriage may at once improve economic and social support opportunities, while diminishing control over paid and unpaid work—potentially increasing as well as compromising the health status of women' (Ballantyne 1999: 27).

Unpaid work includes domestic work in the form of meal preparation, cleaning, clothing care, repairs and maintenance, child care, adult care, financial management, shopping, transportation, and volunteer work (Jackson 1996). Women perform the majority of unpaid labour; in fact, Canadian women in 1992 spent 78 per cent more time than men doing unpaid work (1,482 hours a year compared to 831) (Jackson 1996). In spite of the importance of domestic work for women's health, Walters and her colleagues (2002: 687) note the 'striking omission' that the 1994 Canadian National Population Health Survey still contains no information on the domestic conditions in the home. Dean

(1992) argues that a more equitable division of caregiving and child-raising in the family would benefit both men and women's health.

Walters and her colleagues (1996) look at the health of 2,285 male and female registered nurses in Ontario through a proportional random sample and compares their health in relation to paid work, unpaid work, and social support. They found that unpaid work substantially affected health, particularly for women (Walters et al. 1996).Women were much more affected by caregiver burden and time constraints and had to contend with 'having to divide themselves up in pieces and juggle things' (Walters et al. 1996: 1633). Walters and her colleagues (1996) view this as indicative of the burden of the 'double day' for women who must contend with additional responsibilities in the home. Among men, the only significant unpaid-work variable was 'disliking housework'. The occupational concerns of 'overload' and 'hazard exposure' were relevant to both male and female nurses, and the authors did not find discrimination or harassment in the workplace to be significant (Walters et al. 1996). However, male nurses were much more likely than their female counterparts to be concerned with issues of sexual harassment (Walters et al. 1996). This may indicate the importance of context and the experience of being in the minority in a male- or female-dominated profession.

The preceding discussion of the processes of production, distribution, and reproduction illustrates the tendency in the health literature to treat race, ethnicity, gender, social class, and age as separate entities. Yet, the intersections of race/ethnicity, gender, class, and age influence health in a par-

ticular historical context and over time (Kreiger et al. 1993). The confusion and contradictions in the study of gendered patterns of morbidity discussed in the preceding sections attest to the need for integrating class, ethnicity, and age into these investigations (Ballantyne 1999; Cooper 2002; Curtis and Lawson 2000; Matthews, Manor and Power 1999). For instance, some research has shown that in early adulthood, few socio-economic health inequalities were found for men and women. However, over time the impact of reproductive processes and the 'cost of caring' appeared to have greater health consequences for women, while occupational concerns seemed to have greater health consequences for men (Matthews et al. 1999).

Cooper (2002) addresses the lack of research that incorporates considerations of ethnicity in studies investigating gender and health relationships. In her examination of data from the Health Survey for England, 1993–6, she finds that ethnic minorities report significantly poorer health than whites (Cooper, 2002). In addition, ethnic-minority women experience much more morbidity than men of the same ethnicity. Cooper (2002) also found that much of the health disparities could be accounted for by taking socio-economic status into consideration; however, the impact of ethnicity on illness experience could not be explained solely by class.

The health status and length of life of Aboriginals can often be attributed to poverty and geographic isolation (MacMillan et al. 1996; Newbold 1998; Trovato 2001: 81), adding further support to the idea that multiple bases of inequality must be considered simultaneously if we are to understand disparities in health. Indeed, research in the

United States has revealed substantial racial differences in health that can be largely attributed to socio-economic factors (Anderson and Armstead 1995; Leclere et al. 1997; Williams and Collins 1995); however, even within socio-economic groups there are disadvantages stemming from the effects of discrimination. Anderson and Armstead (1995: 217) have found that poor whites and poor blacks in the United States experience different levels of deprivations and therefore are exposed to different health risks. The 'hypersegregation' or 'housing discrimination that blacks face at every level of socio-economic status but especially at the low end . . . may partially explain the disparity in health outcomes between poor blacks and poor whites' (Anderson and Armstead 1995: 217). This 'hypersegregation' means that more poor blacks live in more impoverished neighbourhoods than poor whites (Anderson and Armstead 1995), and this leads to increased health risks, as these neighbourhoods are more often used as toxic waste dump sites (Krieger et al. 1993; Maher 1998; Williams and Collins 1995). In fact, mortality rates are higher for black Americans at nearly every SES level (Anderson and Armstead 1995). Krieger and her colleagues (1993: 87) suggest that these disparities may be due to the fact that socio-economic class is experienced differently by blacks and whites. They point to studies which show that the 'economic return for the same level of education is lower for blacks than whites (and also for women than men within each racial group).' In summary, although we know a lot about how gender, class, age, ethnicity, and race influence health separately, the mutual structural 'coalescence' of class, age, gender, race, and ethnicity found in only a handful

of studies suggests that this issue should be further explored in health research (Krieger et al. 1993).

Conclusion

Our experience of health is located squarely in the body, and this embodiment permeates every aspect of our lives. Health is not a haphazard phenomenon. As Audre Lorde's life history and the various sections of this chapter demonstrate, our experiences and opportunities within productive, reproductive, and distributive processes, as they are shaped by structural CAGEs, influence our physical and mental health. Our class, age, gender, ethnicity, and race may work to constrain or facilitate our experiences in the processes of production, reproduction, and distribution. These processes, in turn, significantly shape both the degree of health we enjoy over the life course and the very length of our lives. Of course, biology, genetics, and physiological aging processes also play a part in determining health outcomes. So too, does agency. People often make informed and conscious decisions about their health. They decide whether to exercise or whether a symptom warrants a visit to the physician, or they decide what type of treatment is best suited for them, including something as simple as deciding whether they need to take a pill for a headache. The extent to which people are informed or financially able to seek a physician's advice or to take a pill are, however, influenced by structural CAGE(s) as well.

Yet, health research rarely considers how the structures of class, age, gender, ethnicity, and race mutually constitute inequality in health outcomes. Furthermore, the focus in the health literature on individual causes of disease outcomes precludes adequate consideration of how the processes of reproduction, distribution, and production as they are structured by class, age, gender, ethnicity, and race influence health. Even in the literature on occupational health, which is located squarely in production processes, the emphasis is on occupations that are more commonly held by men rather than women. We know little about the health effects of waitressing or of being a secretary or a teacher. And, with the possible exception of mental health, we know very little about how gendered processes of reproduction influence inequality in physical health. We also know very little about how the processes of distribution within families influences health. In poor families, for instance, do mothers or fathers go without medicine so that they can afford to buy it for their children? When parents sacrifice good nutrition so that their children can eat well, does their health suffer?

Health care is a social-policy issue that the majority of Canadians are passionate about. In the fall of 2002, Roy Romanow, a former NDP premier of Saskatchewan, was commissioned by the federal government to write a report on the health care system in Canada. Romanow talked with Canadians from across the country and examined the provincial health-care systems to assess what changes and improvements were needed. One strong message he received from Canadians was that we valued our publicly funded health-care system and that most of us wanted to keep it. Romanow recommended that the federal government direct more money to health services and that reform of health services required investment in three areas: home care, primary patient care, and 'catastrophic' drug care, such as the treatment necessary for people with HIV/AIDS. Although these recommendations are commendable, basic health-care services are also in need of more funding because they deteriorated significantly throughout the 1990s. Furthermore, equal access to health care, although recommended in the Romanow report, has taken a back seat to other issues, such as those listed above. Whether disadvantaged groups of Canadians will be better able to access health care services through current reforms remains to be seen.

Notes

1   Lorde was married in the 1960s for eight years.

Glossary

Class-linked stress   Stress exposures that are largely dependent on social status. For example, working-class and lower-income individuals are more frequently employed in physically stressful jobs (e.g., where there are extreme temperatures, high noise levels, shift work, noxious fumes, or where the worker has to work at an assembly-line pace).

Differential-exposure hypothesis   The argument that women experience more morbidity because they are exposed to more chronic and daily stressors in their lives.

Differential-vulnerability hypothesis   The argument that women experience more morbidity because their caregiving role makes them more susceptible to emotional stress;

this may also involve vulnerabilities due to women's internalized coping styles when dealing with stress.

Fundamental causes explanations Link and Phelan's (2000: 40) sociologically informed theory of the reasons for the strong associations between social factors and disease. They recommend a focus on macro-factors like 'access to knowledge, money, power, prestige, and social connections' and the ways in which these factors can influence the exposure to health risks and preventive measures in order to explain long-time associations between inequality and health. As new risk factors and new technologies are discovered, those people in society with better resources and connections are more able to benefit from new knowledge and avoid health risks.

Hypersegregation The disproportionate number of minority groups located in impoverished, dangerous, and environmentally polluted neighbourhoods. Poor African-Americans more often live in extremely disadvantaged neighbourhoods than do poor non-Hispanic whites.

Medicalization The defining of a natural biological event or progression as a form of illness requiring medical intervention and treatment. (For example, menopause has been treated with hormone replacement therapy).

Psychosocial risk factors A system of exposures, resources, and situational variables believed to have an impact on health; they include mastery or sense of control, self-esteem, ease or availability of social supports, negative life events, and daily exposure to stress or exposure to traumatic events.

Socio-economic gradient The finding that for each successive increase in income, there appears to be an increase in health-protective effects. In other words, mortality and morbidity are lower for those with higher income (all the way up the scale). This suggests that it is not deprivation or poverty alone that affects health but the experience of inequality itself.

Questions for Critical Thought

1. In what ways could an individual's psychosocial resources (e.g., mastery, self-esteem, social support) be shaped by his or her class, age, gender, race, and ethnicity?

2. How can we explain persistent health inequality in spite of a system of 'universal health-care access' in Canada?

3. How do class, age, gender, and ethnicity or race contribute to the development of a healthy or unhealthy lifestyle?

4. Describe how societal ideologies of gender, race, ethnicity, age, and class affect patterns of health care utilization and delivery.

5. In what ways does the historical period in which we live influence our health? What do you think the major health problems will be in the future?

Recommended Reading

Courtenay, Will H. (2000). 'Constructions of masculinity and their influence on men's well-being: A theory of gender and health'. *Social Science and Medicine* 50 (10): 1385–401. The author examines how socially constructed forms of masculinity (e.g., shaped by ethnicity, social class, sexuality, etc.) influence men's health behaviour and their consequent health risks.

House, James S. (2001). 'Understanding social factors and inequalities in health: 20th century progress and 21st century prospects'. *Journal of Health and Social Behavior* 43 (June): 125–42. An important article that chronicles the main ways in which health inequalities have been explained and outlines the current state of research with future directions.

Inhorn, Marcia C., and K. Lisa Whittle (2001). 'Feminism meets the "new" epidemiologies: Toward an appraisal of antifeminist biases in epidemiological research on women's health'. *Social Science and Medicine* 53 (5): 553–67. The authors examine gender biases in current epidemiologic approaches to women's health research (e.g., biological essentialism) and suggest more feminist-friendly research directions.

Kawachi, Ichiro, Bruce P. Kennedy, and Richard G. Wilkinson (1999). *The Society and Population Health Reader: Income Inequality and Health.* New York: New Press. A large collection of articles with an international focus on how income inequalities and economic policies affect the health of various populations.

Krieger, N., D.L. Rowley, A.A. Herman, and Avery B. Phillips (1993). 'Racism, sexism, and social class: Implications for studies of health, disease, and well- being'. *American Journal of Preventive Medicine* 9(6): 82–122. The authors provide a comprehensive critical review of US epidemiologic literature, including detailed recommendations on how to overcome racism, sexism, and class biases in future health studies.

Link, Bruce G., and Jo Phelan (1995). 'Social conditions as fundamental causes of disease'. *Journal of Health and Social Behavior* 35: 80–94. An important article in which the authors argue that health policy and research must shift from the focus on individual risk factors to more *fundamental* causes of disease (e.g., SES).

Lynch, J.W., G.A. Kaplan, and J.T. Salonen (1997). 'Why do poor people behave poorly? Variation in adult health behaviours and psychosocial characteristics by stages of the socioeconomic lifecourse'. *Social Science and Medicine* 44(6): 809–19. A population-based study of Finnish men which found that socio-economic conditions in childhood were significantly associated with adult health behaviours. This life-course approach illustrates how health or 'lifestyle' behaviour is influenced by socio-structural factors.

McDonough, Peggy, and Vivienne Walters (2001). 'Gender and health: Reassessing patterns and explanations'. *Social Science and Medicine* 52 (4): 547–59. The authors use a Canadian national-probability sample to examine the relationship between gender and health, particularly with reference to the explanatory roles of differential exposure to stress and differential vulnerability to stress. Many health measures are included (e.g., self-rated health, chronic conditions, heavy drinking, distress, and restricted activity). The results illustrate the complexity of the relationship between health and gender.

Simon, Robin (2000). 'The importance of culture in sociological theory and research on stress and mental health: A missing link?' Chapter 5 in Chloe E. Bird, Peter Conrad, and Allen M. Fremont (eds), *Handbook of Medical Sociology,* 5th edn. New Jersey: Prentice-Hall. This chapter outlines the three main approaches to explaining the relationship between stress and mental health; it argues that cultural context (e.g., norms, values, etc.) and meanings deserve a more prominent place in sociological theories of stress and mental health.

Wadsworth, M.E.J. (1997). 'Health inequalities in the life course perspective'. *Social Science and Medicine* 44(6): 859–69. The author outlines the value of a life-history approach to research by explaining how social factors (particularly those associated with poverty) may affect an individual's health trajectory. For example, nutrition in childhood may influence adult blood pressure levels, height, etc.)

12

CAGE(s) and the State

by Tammy Duerden Comeau and Julie McMullin

Introduction

In January 2003, André Le Corre, a retired medical lab technician, was in court presenting a $3 billion class-action suit against the Government of Canada for not informing him and 380,000 other seniors that they are eligible for the Guaranteed Income Supplement (GIS). The GIS is a federal social assistance program that tops up Old Age Security (OAS) benefits for seniors who earn less that $12,648 a year. This figure does not include the OAS benefits (approximately $5,000 a year in 2003), which is a point of confusion for some seniors. Mr Le Corre, who was 76 years old, had thought he was ineligible for the top-up because his combined pension income and OAS was greater than $12,648 a year. In fact, he had been eligible for the GIS benefits since 1994, but had never made a claim. Mr Le Corre's court case argues that Ottawa was negligent in not informing seniors who were eligible for benefits, even though it could have used Revenue Canada data banks to identify these people. For Mr Le Corre, the GIS benefits would have made a big difference in the quality of his life, including 'the awful events that could have been prevented, the rent that could have been paid, the medications that could have been bought'. But for Mr Le Corre, the 'lawsuit is a matter of principle. It's more about the sad-ness I feel for the poorer people' (Thuanh Ha 2003: A7).

This tiny glimpse into Mr Le Corre's life tells us a lot about the role the **state** plays in processes of distribution and in distributive outcomes of inequality for older adults living. Without social assistance Mr Le Corre's income would be less than $12,648 per year, well below official poverty lines. If he had claimed all the benefits for which he was eligible the quality of his life would have been greatly enhanced. But in acknowledging the 'poorer people' Mr Le Corre recognizes that, while he is poor, there are many older Canadians who are worse off than he is. Although significant gains have been made in eradicating poverty among older Canadians, 17.5 per cent are still poor and most of these people are women (National Council on Welfare 2000). Hence, the ways in which gender relations shape the interrelated processes of production, reproduction, and distribution (see chapters 8 and 9) intersect with age relations in determining income inequality in later life. Of course, class, ethnicity, and race matter too. If Mr Le Corre were a member of the capitalist executive class, he would not likely have to worry about GIS. And yet, his ethnicity and race put him in a position of privilege according to the Canadian state because recent immigrants to Canada are ineligible for OAS regardless of whether they become Canadian citizens.

Indeed, the state encompasses a vast range of institutions, policies, and programs that have a profound effect on the individuals living in a society. The workings of the state provide a strong example of the overlapping and intertwining nature of the processes of production, reproduction, and distribution. For instance, the Canadian state's influence on the processes of production and the labour market as discussed in chapter 9 are evident in the management of immigration policy, anti-strike legislation, pay-equity policies, maternity benefits, and unemployment insurance (Pupo 2001). The processes of reproduction and the work of caring discussed in chapter 8 are directly shaped and affected by maternity benefits, pensions, and immigration policy, particularly in the realm of paid reproductive work (Stasiulis and Bakan 1995). Governments dictate education and health policy, which influences the outcomes of health and education inequality discussed in chapters 10 and 11. Indeed, health and education policy have come under intense scrutiny in recent years as conservative policies led to significant service cutbacks. All of these policies concern largely distributive processes, and the form in which wages and benefits are distributed in the family comprise another process through which inequality is manifested. While the state can act to ameliorate or mend unequal relations, and agents have used the state for retribution, its actions are often ambiguous and contradictory (Armstrong and Connelly 1999). Armstrong and Connelly (1999) point out that the beneficiaries of state actions, such as pay equity, are often the most privileged in the first place and there is considerable difficulty in predicting the effects of even well-intentioned policies. Pupo (2001: 136) argues that the state's policy of treating men and women as the 'same' in divorce and child custody legislation disadvantages women by discounting their care work in the family. The state's undervaluation of caregiving and nurturing puts women in a losing position even though the policy is ostensibly equitable.

According to Pupo (2001: 129), the state's main tasks are those of 'accumulation, legitimation, and coercion or social control', and these tasks are played out in the arenas of the economy, in the labour market, and among individuals and families. To carry out these tasks involves the establishment of a **'citizenship regime'** consisting of boundaries, rules, definitions, and geographic boarders (Jenson and Papillon 2000: 246). Citizenship rights are defined, and avenues for obtaining access to these rights are made clear. A complex bureaucracy establishes the 'democratic rules of the game' and determines things such as acceptable ways in which to make claims. Nations are defined on the basis of historical claims and conceptualizations of nationality. Finally, states establish 'the geographical borders of the political community' as an exclusionary principle of citizenship (Jenson and Papillon 2000: 246).

One way to examine the reach of the state on groups and individuals is to look at the state's role in denoting who is deemed a **citizen** and what it is that citizens are entitled to in Canadian society. T.H. Marshall's concept of citizenship organizes the rights and responsibilities of citizens into three groups: **civil citizenship**, which includes basic human rights, such as the right to individual freedom and justice in the courts of law; **political citizenship**, which includes the franchise and the right to participate in the political process; and **social citizenship** (perhaps the broadest concept), which includes financial well-being, social heritage, and access to social services (Marshall 1950). Marshall's typology has been criticized for its generalization of the experience of white, European men to represent the process of citizenship in general (Walby 1997). In fact, Walby (1997) notes that the means by which white, European men achieved citizenship does not represent the experience of most other groups. However, in Walby's (1997: 168) analysis she argues that there are 'degrees' of citizenry and that Marshall's conceptualization is a useful one for considering how portions of citizenship were meted out to different groups at different historical times. It is important to note that although the state has a substantial amount of power with which to structure and constrain the lives of its citizens, state institutions have also been successfully mobilized by agents for the purposes of social justice (Pupo 2001). Individuals and groups can use state institutions (e.g., the legal system) and programs to their own ends (e.g., to seek redress or to monopolize resources).

In this chapter, 'social citizenship' will be a main point of discussion, because the state programs of unemployment insurance, parental benefits or maternity leave, social welfare, pensions, and old-age security in many ways reproduce the existing inequalities and shore up long-standing advantages among the privileged. Although aid and assistance for the disadvantaged groups in Canadian society are desperately needed, the form that this aid has frequently taken has had mixed and often negative results. The current climate of cutbacks and the

reappearance of '**workfare**' are examples of the individualization of what are predominantly social problems (Brodie 1999). Furthermore, Canadian citizens are experiencing more and more infringements on their civil liberties with the enforcement of welfare 'snitch lines' and advances in surveillance technology (Brodie 1999: 44).

This chapter will take a critical view of the role of the state, focusing on the state's role in social regulation and the social reproduction of the relations of class, gender, race, ethnicity, and age. The division of the chapter into separate sections on class, age, gender, and race and ethnicity is in some ways arbitrary and is done largely for the purposes of organization. The state's conceptualization of these social relations are integral to the way in which policies are conceived and developed and in the effects that they have on groups and individuals. Notions of who is counted as a citizen shape the penalties, constraints, and privileges meted out to Canadians.

Focusing on Class: Making Citizens, Making 'Class'[1]

Poverty

The face of poverty and social class is deeply gendered, racialized, and age-based. Canadians living in poverty are predominately women, particularly elderly women and lone women raising children (Evans 1997). Women and men who have recently immigrated, particularly visible-minority immigrants and Aboriginal men and women, are also at increased risk of being poor (Armstrong 1999; Kazemipur and Halli 2001). Aboriginals in Canada have been described as a 'colonized' people, existing as a reserve labour army and kept dependent on the economic imperatives of the Canadian state (Frideres 1988). Immigration policies in Canada have historically favoured workers who could be more easily exploited, both by the manufactured vulnerability of their citizenship status and through overtly racist practices (Bolaria and Li 1988; Calliste 1996). For example, immigrants were allowed entry to Canada specifically to fill the need for cheap labour (e.g., Chinese workers were paid less than European workers in the construction of the Canadian Pacific Railway) and to toil at jobs that no one else wanted. For example, Caribbean black women were brought in to perform domestic labour (Calliste 1996; Li 1988). Thus, immigration practices constructed classes, because immigrants were desired largely for their labour. Furthermore, strict limitations have often accompanied the entry of immigrants into the country (Calliste 1996). This was illustrated by the exclusion 'in July 1911, [of] eight Guadeloupean domestics when it was judged that they were likely to become a public charge because they were single parents . . . the immigration officer surmised that they were likely to become pregnant again and would probably become a drain on the public purse' (Calliste 1996: 73). Calliste (1996: 72) argues that these actions show the Canadian state's racialization of Caribbean women as 'immoral' because of the belief that they are 'likely to become single parents'. Assumptions about who was likely to be 'poor' and who would be supported in such a circumstance are evident in Canadian social assistance policy.

The Canadian state has a long history of policies designed to aid those who are poor,

but the state's conceptualization of the 'deserving' poor has largely incorporated the image of the 'white, working-class, breadwinner' who is momentarily out of work (Scott 1996). The poor of Canadian society are not all viewed as entitled to the rights of economic well-being and social security. The poor are sorted and classified on the basis of their age, race and ethnicity, and gender in order to determine their measure of entitlement. Traditionally, the white, working-class breadwinner has been seen as the 'real' citizen, deserving of the guarantee of the rights of social citizenship. The conflation of the 'deserving worker-citizen' with the white, male, working-class worker engaged in paid work has long shaped policy making (Evans 1997; Scott 1996).

Tracing the history of social assistance, Scott (1996) analyzes how the assistance for single mothers originated from the notion of entitlement owed to the 'worker,' ostensibly the 'white, male, middle-aged, family supporter'. Thus, the 'deserving' mother-recipient of social citizenship is fundamentally racialized as well, since 'racial' homogeneity in families (in particular the quest to reproduce a 'sanitized' white, Northern citizen) was strongly encouraged (Mackey 1999; McLaren 1991; Valverde 1991). Consider the moral panics over the 'corruption' of young, white women by Chinese men (Valverde 1991), the exclusion of current and 'potential' Caribbean black mothers (Calliste 1996), and the effect that the Indian Act had on unions between Aboriginals and white settlers. (Aboriginal women who married a non-Indian were stripped of their Indian status) (Nelson 2002). The very possibility of existing in a family itself was also strongly controlled and racialized. For example, Chinese men who emigrated were not allowed to bring their families with them, and in this way the number of non-white families was limited (Bolaria and Li 1988; Das Gupta 1995).

Mother's Allowance (which evolved into Family Benefits) was introduced in 1920 and was only for First World War widows, who were deemed to be entitled to support from the government, since it wasn't their own 'fault' that they were single mothers' (Scott 1996: 17). Evans (1997: 99) calls this the 'breadwinner/dependent model of the family'. In this case, the 'mother-citizen' was owed a stake in social citizenship; however, she had to adhere to the prevailing gender norms and strict behavioural guidelines (Little 1999; Scott 1996: 18). The gendering of social policy is noted by Scott (1996), who argues that women were not granted state support for their role as paid workers or even for their reproductive labour but only as a proxy for their relationship to a bona fide and entitled 'worker'. Scott (1996: 18) points to the 'man about the house rule', which prohibits any woman living with a man from collecting government support. This prohibition is imbued with assumptions about men's presumed support of women. The family-class immigration status is yet another example of the state's construction of women as dependent on a male provider, for women more commonly enter under this status, which effectively denies them the language training and social programs that are available to the 'independent' sponsor (Abu-Laban 1998). The notion of the 'deserving' recipient and the moral regulation and monitoring of those receiving state support illustrate the state's role in constructing gendered and racialized ideologies and in perpetuating class inequalities.

The penalization of women for existing as single heads of families is evident in Kilkey and Bradshaw's (1999) contemporary international comparative analysis of mothers in lone- and two-parent families. The countries studied were the Nordic countries, France, Germany, Austria, the United States, the United Kingdom, Ireland, the Netherlands, Australia, and Canada. In their comparison, Canada is grouped with the UK and Australia as a country where lone mothers have 'an above average rate of poverty whether in paid work or not' (Kilkey and Bradshaw, 1999: 176). There are few incentives or legitimate opportunities for women in these circumstances to engage in paid work, and, the authors argue, in most cases, the policies designed to support lone mothers do not make it possible to escape poverty, even if they do join the labour force (Kilkey and Bradshaw 1999). This paradox is evident in Box 12.1, where we see that leaving the welfare system is not synonymous with leaving poverty.

Single mothers such as Jill McLean (see Box 12.1) have simply joined the leagues of the working poor. In fact, many of the lone mothers in the UK, Australia, and Canada were found to live in multi-generational households. Kilkey and Bradshaw (1999) suggest that the poverty rate (as measured by household income) may underestimate the extent of poverty and that those lone mothers who have paid jobs may be able to do so only because of support from their families. The lack of support from the state fuels the perpetuation of poverty for lone mothers and creates these women and their families as an 'underclass' in Canadian society.

Box **12.1** **Child Poverty Rate Won't Budge: Provincial Welfare Reform Fails to Ease Growing Problem in Canada's Largest City**
By Margaret Philp

The rate of child poverty in Canada's largest city has remained stubbornly fixed even as provincial welfare rolls have shrunk, a new report says.

One in three children were living in poverty in 1998, says Report Card on Child Poverty in Toronto, written by Colin Hughes for Campaign 2000, a group that advocates for the elimination of child poverty. And poor families slid deeper into poverty from 1995 to 1998.

'The rate of child poverty in Toronto is scary enough, but when you look at the depth of poverty–the severity of poverty getting worse–that gets very, very scary,' said Mr Hughes, a community worker with the Children's Aid Society of Toronto. 'I just don't think people get it how severe and bad poverty is in this city. It really is more than numbers.'

What the numbers show is that, while the population of Toronto children 18 rose by 2 per cent from 1995 to 1998, the latest year for which figures are available, the count of poor children jumped 7 per cent.

There were 152,250 poor children in the city the year Premier Mike Harris came to power–31 per cent of children. Three years later, 163,010 children–32 per cent of those in the city–were considered poor.

In measuring poverty, the report relies on Statistics Canada's Low Income Measure, which sets the threshold for poverty at half the median income for families of the same size.

For a single parent with one child, that's $17,080.

But most poor families are living on incomes that fall thousands of dollars shy of the poverty line. And since 1995, the report shows, most poor families have drifted only further from the threshold.

While the median income for poor Toronto families fell $4,728 below the threshold in 1995, the shortfall swelled to $5,980 in 1998. The evidence lies in the growing number of children staying in homeless shelters and waiting for hampers at food banks, Mr Hughes said.

The number of children with parents on social assistance in Ontario has plunged from about 145,000 in 1994 to roughly 72,000 now. But as the face of poverty has changed from people on welfare to those juggling low-wage and part-time jobs, child poverty rates have barely budged.

'You can't equate declining caseloads with an assumption that families are automatically better off,' Mr Hughes said. 'This report card certainly raises questions about that.'

Few would argue that Jill McLean is better off for leaving the welfare system last fall.

The single mother of two girls, Jenna, 9, and Phoebe, 7, works part-time in a community centre for about $400 a month and baby sits for friends whenever she can, surviving thanks to hand-me-downs from friends and a rent subsidy on her two-bedroom apartment in a public-housing project that costs her $121 a month. Still, she routinely falls behind.

> A month after leaving social assistance, one of her daughters was diagnosed as need-ing glasses—an expense that would have been covered by the welfare system. 'Maybe I would have been better off, but is it worth the hassle?' Ms McLean asks.
>
> Her daughters know they are poor.
>
> A few weeks ago, when one of the girls was invited to a birthday party and there was no money to buy a present, she decided to part with a Beanie Baby from her stuffed-ani-mal collection.
>
> 'My girls know there isn't enough money. And they understand.' At food banks across Toronto, a soaring number of working-poor families are turning up for hampers.
>
> A study just conducted by the Daily Bread Food Bank found that 18.9 per cent of the families receiving food in late February and early March held down jobs. A year earlier, 12.6 per cent of people using food banks were working.
>
> Source: Philp (2001). Reprinted with permission from the Globe and Mail.

Social Regulation: Class and the Law

Civil citizenship includes the right to justice and redress in a society's legal system. Class relations have an impact on the prosecution of crime and on who is considered a crim-inal. Some members of society, by virtue of their class, enjoy a certain amount of pro-tection from criminalization and moral reg-ulation. Visibility can make some popula-tions more vulnerable, as in the case of young people living on the streets. Schissel (1997), who undertook a study of 179 young people living on the street in Saskatoon, found that over half of them had been arrested at least once, an arrest rate that is much higher than for suburban youth. The law targets individuals and processes them differentially on the basis of their class, age, race or ethnicity, and gender (Schissel 1997). For example, Aboriginal youth comprise only 5 per cent of youth in Canada; however, they make up almost a quarter of the young people who have been sentenced to serve time in custody (Marinelli 2002: 5).

In fact, structural disadvantages are built into the fabric of the law itself. The state does not usually view harm inflicted by companies and corporations as 'crime'. Snider (1993) notes that crimes committed by corporations are not taken seriously by the state, despite the fact that the costs of these crimes in terms of environmental damage, financial loss, and loss of human life are often higher than those from 'street crime'. **Corporate crime** includes a wide range of illegal activities that carry serious consequences for their victims. Consider the harm inflicted by inadequately tested drugs, such as thalidomide and DES (Peppin 1995). According to Snider (1993: 1), a worker in Canada dies on the job every six hours, and these statistics may be a significant underes-timate. The state's complicity in corporate crime may stem partly from the involvement of the government with big business. For example, McMullan and Smith (1997) doc-ument the devastating environmental and health effects of steel production in Sydney, Nova Scotia, where government bureaucra-cies were intimately connected with the offending corporations.

Re-manufacturing Class: Workfare

Some observers suggest that the rights of Canadian citizens are in jeopardy (Broadbent 1999; Mooers 1999). Mooers (1999: 288) argues that as with the idea of 'lean production' in the global workplace, there has been a shift in the notion of citizenship, such that social citizenship rights are being pared down and citizens are increasingly being required to 'earn' their right to social benefits. The requirement that Canadians perform labour for the right to economic survival can be seen as one example of the move to 'lean citizenship'. 'Workfare' has been described by some as a harking back to the era of the workhouses for the poor, who were required, to 'pay' in one way or another for a minimal amount of aid (Shragge 1997). Shragge (1997: 26) notes that the Canadian governments' endorsement and development of workfare reflects the view that 'able-bodied individuals' who are collecting welfare do so simply because of their own lack of skills and lack of initiative. These recipients will now be required to work and or take training in order to receive government aid. The wider societal shifts in the labour market and the difficulty in finding work are discounted as explanations for receiving welfare. The assumption is that if workers are sufficiently qualified, they will be able to find a job that adequately supports themselves and by extension, their family. In fact, Shragge (1997) argues that workfare is calculated more to use the unemployed and the vulnerable to perform work for less than a job would normally pay. Workfare is a 'coercive' method of government control over the most underprivileged in society (deRouche 2001: 329). The right to social citizenship is being eroded in the face of demands that citizens must demonstrate that they deserve support.

DeRouche (2001) describes the effects of a workfare-type program in Cape Breton, Nova Scotia. This program is not compulsory and is promoted as a voluntary. DeRouche (2001) argues that, although those involved in the project reap some benefits from it, the main beneficiary is the state itself. Cape Breton is an economically depressed area with '23 per cent of families and 50 per cent of "unattached individuals" classified as low-income (i.e., below the poverty line)' (deRouche 2001: 318). The project, which is called the 'Cape Breton Community Employment and Innovation Project' and was established in 1999, aimed to encourage 1,500 Cape Bretoners on social assistance to take part in an 'experiment' in which half of those involved would be given the option of performing paid community work for up to three years instead of collecting social assistance or employment insurance (deRouche 2001: 320).

The community wages for participants in the Cape Breton project were $280 per week (or $14,560 a year), which is still below the poverty line; however, the added costs of working (transportation, child care, and wardrobe) are not taken into account in the program (deRouche 2001). In addition, income is not contingent upon family size. DeRouche (2001) calculates that for a single parent with two children under the age of six, the program would leave the family worse off financially. Hence, deRouche's (2001) analysis underscores how government programs may not alter the nature of inequality and in fact may worsen the circumstances of some families.

The Cape Breton project also illustrates the inconsistency and contradictions inherent in state policies. For instance, despite the fact that historically some women have been able to obtain social assistance on the basis of their rights as mothers, the advent of 'workfare' programs has largely ignored gender and 'mother-status' (Evans 1997). In this case, the class status of individuals as welfare-recipient appears to take precedence. In Alberta's social assistance program, single mothers are considered 'employable once the youngest child is six months old', and in the expansion of Ontario's workfare program, single mothers with children over the age of three will be required to participate (Evans 1997: 100). Therefore, Evans (1997: 100) argues, in the area of social assistance, there has been a move to define 'mothers' as 'workers' simultaneously with the increasing inaccessibility of child care. The rather opportunistic 'gender-neutrality' (Evans 1997: 100) of current workfare programs appears to be repeated in the Cape Breton program.

The claim that the community-involvement requirement in the Cape Breton project will upgrade skills and train workers for jobs which they are currently unqualified for is also suspect. DeRouche (2001: 325) notes that 'enhanced employability' is a buzz word of the program but that government officials have conceded that 'the project will offer no skills-training or education'. Thus, participants will be performing 'low-skilled or unskilled' work that they are likely already qualified to do (deRouche 2001: 325). The assumption that individuals on social assistance and employment insurance are predominately unskilled also belies the circumstances in Cape Breton, namely that there are few work opportunities for skilled workers in this province. For recipients of social assistance and employ-

ment insurance who are unskilled, the program is not improving their skills or even their income; however, the social assistance payments required of the province will be reduced, thus benefiting the state (deRouche 2001).

Agents in Action: Dissent and Co-optation

Although the preceding sections have emphasized the significant reach of the state into people's lives, this does not mean that individuals and groups in Canadian society do not exercise agency with regard to the state. Mooers (1999) uses Gramsci's idea of hegemony to discuss the co-optation of workers in the state's renewed emphasis on 'self-reliance' and 'active citizenship' (e.g., workfare). Certainly, these programs have had both widespread public support and strident opposition (e.g., the Days of Action), thus illustrating the contradictory and complex nature of hegemony (Mooers 1999). Mooers (1999) claims that the state's recruitment of public support and community input for government privatization projects have been recent tactics in the attempt to minimize opposition. Still, citizens have continued to mobilize against the state's welfare reforms and attempts to privatize various public enterprises (e.g., health care). Mr Le Corre's decision to sue the federal government for not making people aware of their eligibility for GIS is another case in point.

Indeed, class actions against governments are quite common. In the last few years, gay- and lesbian-rights activists have challenged provincial and federal governments on various human-rights and family issues. Louise Gosselin brought a class action against the Quebec government for its new 'coercive' welfare policies. These policies substantially reduced payments to able-bodied welfare recipients under the age of 30 who do not participate in 'schooling, job training, or community work' (Seeman 2001). Gosselin contends that the welfare reforms are unconstitutional and that they violate basic citizenship rights. However, Neil Seeman, a journalist with the *Globe and Mail*, trivialized and condemned Gosselin's law suit, claiming that granting 'protected "rights" . . . would spiral the country into debt . . . [and] would also reverse political priorities established by voters at the ballet box' (Seeman 2001). Seeman's response and portrayal of Gosselin and workfare is an apt example of the hegemonic control of the state. Citizen protest and dissent exist, but they are often harshly challenged by those who support the ideologies of the ruling regime.

Focusing on Race: Making Citizens, Making 'Race'

The often oppressive nature of government policy and state action is evident in the history of policies concerning aboriginals in Canada. The outright denial of basic citizenship rights and the intricate and totalitarian declaration of the Indian Act (1876) have wreaked havoc on Aboriginal communities and crafted a perpetual cycle of poverty and dysfunction for many (Armstrong 1999; Boyko 1995; Frideres 1988). Political citizenship has been historically denied to Aboriginal groups by the Canadian government (Borrows 2001). The civil and social citizenship rights of Aboriginals have also been strongly curtailed by the Indian Act and its legacy. If social citizenship includes

the right to one's social heritage, than this entitlement has been severely compromised for Aboriginal Canadians. Heritage and social relations were ignored because Indian status was defined by the government on the basis of where one lived (e.g., on a reserve) and on the basis of band registration (Boyko 1995; Smith 1975). The Indian Act effectively denied people their social heritage, for Aboriginal women who married non-Indians were stripped of their Indian status, as were their children (Boyko 1995). These women were forced to leave the reserve and live apart from their families. This aspect of the policy illustrates that the Indian Act was both a racial and a gender project. Although Aboriginal women who married non-Indians were subsumed under their husband's status, this stipulation did not apply to Aboriginal men who married non-Indians. The policy is dehumanizing because it treats a person's identity and social heritage as a set of clothes that can be taken on and off (at will or by force). This approach is evident in the government's scheme of location tickets, by which Aboriginals were granted a plot of reserve land in exchange for their right to Indian status (Boyko 1995). Of course, these government acts and initiatives have recently been met with strong resistance on the part of Aboriginals in Canada (Anderson 1992; Borrows 2001; Jenson and Papillon 2000). Aboriginal groups have made citizenship claims and demanded that the Canadian government honour the historical land treaties and pacts (Borrows 2001). Jenson and Papillon (2000), who trace the citizenship claims and mobilization of the James Bay Cree, argue that they have mounted challenges to the Canadian 'citizenship regime' in all of its four dimensions (Jenson and Papillon 2000). These challenges will be discussed in more depth in the sections to follow.

Re-manufacturing 'Race'/Ethnicity: Immigration

Citizenship in Canada has long been a racial project. Race affects who is allowed to enter Canada, what work people are allowed to perform, what 'class' of citizenship they are granted, and whether this citizenship can be revoked (Bolaria and Li 1988; Comeau and Allahar 2001; Jakubowski 1997). The experience of Chinese-Canadians is a poignant example of the extent to which citizenship rights can be denied and diluted. The history of immigration policies concerning Chinese immigrants also illustrates how policy is shaped by class-based and capitalistic imperatives policy, and the way in which gendering and racialization are built into these objectives. Bolaria and Li (1988: 106) contend that 'from the outset, the whole Chinese question in Canada was in essence a question of labour exploitation.' In the late nineteenth and early twentieth centuries, Chinese immigrants did the labour-intensive work that 'white' Canadians would not do, and they did so for a lesser wage. They worked on the railway, in salmon canneries, and until they were barred from doing so, in mines (Bolaria and Li 1988). As soon as the exigencies of labour passed, citizenship infringements were imposed on Chinese immigrants. Head taxes were imposed as early as 1885, and by 1903 they were as high as $500 per person (Bolaria and Li 1988). The federal government required all Chinese in Canada to be registered and to have a certificate (Bolaria and Li 1988). The province of British Columbia barred the Chinese from voting in provincial and municipal elections, and they were legally excluded from numerous professions (e.g., law, pharmacy, public works, skilled jobs in coal mines). The 'second-class' citizenship status of Chinese Canadians (both naturalized and immigrant) was upheld by the Supreme Court of Canada in 1903 despite the fact that it conceded that the prohibitions enacted by the province 'were in truth devised to deprive the Chinese, naturalized or not, of the ordinary rights of the inhabitant of British Columbia' (Bolaria and Li 1988: 109).

The government's immigration policy significantly shaped social relations within Chinese communities, because women were effectively excluded for many years (Abu-Laban 1998; Bolaria and Li 1988). Although the vast majority of Chinese men who emigrated were married and had families, the head tax intentionally prevented most of them from bringing their families to Canada (Bolaria and Li 1988). Table 12.1 shows the impact of government immigration policies and the subsequent sex ratios of Chinese immigrants over the course of the twentieth century.

Chinese men were treated preeminently as 'last-resort' and expendable workers who were not entitled to the rights of white workers. Abu-Laban (1998: 17) notes that 'racialized immigrant minorities' were 'active[ly] discouraged from permanent settlement.' Chinese women were largely excluded from Canadian society, and those who were in Canada were also treated as 'second-class' citizens in the gendering of legislation. Like the Indian Act, the 1914 Naturalization Act made certain that a woman's status was that of her husband's; therefore, any Chinese woman with Canadian citizenship lost it if she married a

Table 12.1 Number and Sex Ratio of Chinese Immigrants Admitted to Canadaᵃ, and Major Immigration Legislation Affecting Chinese Immigration, 1906–1976

Period	Total # of Chinese Immigrants Admitted to Canada	Males per 100 Females	Major Immigration Legislation	Impact on Chinese Immigrants
1906–24[b]	43,470	3,578	Chinese Immigration Act, 1903	Head tax raised
1924–46[c]	7	–	Chinese Immigration Act, 1923	Exclusion of Chinese
1947–62[d]	21,877	98	Repeal of 1923 Act, 1947; Immigration Act, 1952	Repeal of exclusion, limited sponsored immigrants permitted
1963–67	18,716	72	Immigration Act, 1962	Independent and sponsored immigrants permitted
1968–76	91,490	98	Immigration Act, 1967	Universal point system applied

[a]Source: Annual Reports of the Department of the Interior (1906–17); Department of Immigration and Colonization (1918–36); Department of Mines and Resources(1936–49); Department of Citizenship and Immigration (1950–65); Department of Manpower and Immigration (1966–76). Figures from 1907–25 are based on reported nationality (China); 1926–8, racial origin (Chinese); 1929, nationality (China); 1930–1, racial origin (Chinese); 1932, nationality (China); 1933-49, racial origin (Chinese); 1950–1, nationality (China); 1952–4, racial origin (Chinese); 1956–61, ethnic origin (Chinese); 1962–6, country of last permanent residence (China, Hong Kong, Taiwan); 1967–71, country of former residence (China, Hong Kong, Taiwan); and 1972–6, country of last permanent residence (China, Hong Kong, Taiwan). Figures for 1905–55 are computed on fiscal year ending 31 March; for 1956–76, on calendar year ending 31 December.

[b]The Canada Yearbook, 1931 (Table 15, p. 184), provides somewhat different figures of Chinese immigration to Canada, which add up to 44,911 for the period of 1906–24. The sex ratio for this period is estimated from the sex distribution of the adult population, based on figures from the reports indicated in footnote a. (approximate years). The figures for 1907 are based on a nine-month period.

[c]Six of the seven immigrants were male.

[d]Figures for the entire year of 1955 were not available, due to a change in reporting on calendar-year statistics from fiscal-year statistics in 1955.

Source: Abridged from B. Singh Bolaria and Peter Li, *Racial Oppression in Canada*, Garamond Press, Toronto, 1988. Reprinted with the permission of Garamond Press.

man who was not a Canadian citizen (Bolaria and Li 1988).

It has not only been men who have been targeted as 'cheap' labour through Canadian immigration policy. Domestic labour has a long history of being done by the most vulnerable members of any society (Glenn 1992). Immigrant women have historically been used to fill the need for domestic labour and child care in Canada (Calliste

1996; Jakubowski 1997; Stasiulis and Bakan 1997; 1995). In the first half of the twentieth century, young, white, single women were targeted both for domestic labour and for 'nation-building' imperatives and were regarded as needed permanent propagators of a 'white, Canadian nation' (Abu-Laban 1998; Calliste 1996; Ng 1993). Significant restrictions were placed upon the entry of women from non-European countries (Bolaria and Li 1988; Calliste 1996). In the early twentieth century, Caribbean black women were recruited for Canadian domestic work only in the face of severe labour shortages, and their arrival was often opposed on racist perceptions of their 'unfitness' and 'undeservedness' for motherhood (Calliste 1996: 80). Unlike the view of white, European women as future 'mothers of the nation', black Caribbean women were not wanted for their biological reproductive capabilities but for their reproductive labour. The classification of minority women as 'workers' and not as 'mothers' has a long history, and the desire to separate migrant domestic workers from a 'motherhood' role continues to be evident in contemporary immigration policies (Glenn 1992).

The current immigration policy concerning domestic labour, which was crafted in 1992, is called the **Live-In Caregiver Program** (Jakubowski 1997; Stasiulis and Bakan 1997). The overt discrimination in immigration policies have been replaced by more insidious forms of differentiation and preference. Jakubowski (1997) argues that the Live-In Caregiver Program has been 'deracialized' by removing specified 'race' preferences of caregivers in exchange for specified 'educational requirements' that are by and large available more readily in First World countries. In this way, applicants from First World countries can be given preferential treatment. Still, the majority of live-in domestic workers in Canada are women from Third World countries, and these workers are classified as temporary workers and are required to live in their employer's home for two years (Stasiulis and Bakan 1997). Their status as 'non-Canadian citizens' and their employment within a 'private' household leave them vulnerable to exploitation and abuse with little recourse (Stasiulis and Bakan 1997). Arat-Koc (1997: 431) notes the irony that immigrant women are effectively denied their right to 'motherhood' and femininity and have been classified as 'individual workers' similar to the male conceptualization of 'worker' and yet, they are still excluded from citizenship.

According to Arat-Koc (1997: 432), there is a sharp difference between the nature of the domestic work expected and the classification of caregivers from the First World and the Third World. Domestic workers from Western Europe are conceptualized as 'deserving immigrants'. She argues that they are 'generally employed as 'nannies', expected to be involved only in childcare. . . . They are likely to get higher pay, better treatment, and recognition for their work' (Arat-Koc 1997: 432). In contrast, caregivers from the Philippines or the Caribbean are seen as 'undeserving immigrants', are required to do more for less, and are expected to be grateful for the 'opportunity' to do so (Arat-Koc 1997: 432). The poor working conditions and non-citizenship status of migrant domestic workers in Canada are considered justified on the basis of 'where they've come from'. Thus, a complex of intersection of social relations dictates the rights and privileges that people are thought to deserve. In this sense, the possession of a 'devalued social identity' is used as a justification for exclusion from basic citizenship rights and infringements.

Social Regulation: 'Race'/Ethnicity and the Law

Systemic discrimination in the Canadian justice system is evident in the disproportionate number of Aboriginal Canadians in the penal system (Schissel 1997; Thomas 2000). In 1998/99, 17 per cent of those admitted to correctional services were Aboriginal, although Aboriginals make up only 2 per cent of the population of Canada (Thomas 2000: 9). Aboriginals have been targeted, monitored, and regulated by the legal system as a potential disruptive force, and many miscarriages of justice have resulted (Boyko 1995). Schissel (1997: 83) documented the significantly higher arrest rate for Aboriginal street youths than for youths from other backgrounds. He found that 77 per cent of Aboriginal street youth have been arrested in comparison to 44.2 per cent of non-Aboriginal street youth. He also found that Aboriginal youths are treated more harshly for relatively minor offences than other youth (Schissel 1997). This treatment may also lead to subsequently harsher sentences for any future offences, since they would now have a record and any prior offences would affect future sentences.

At the same time that Aboriginals are targeted for surveillance, crimes against Aboriginals have historically been treated lightly and many have gone unsolved (Boyko 1995). In fact, Aboriginal people in Canada are much more likely to be victims of crime, particularly of violent crime, than non-aboriginals (Statistics Canada 2001).

Boyko (1995: 202) recounts the case of Helen Betty Osborne, a Cree teenager who was brutally raped and murdered in 1971 in The Pas, Manitoba. The white men who had raped and murdered her bragged about their crime and 'whispers around town indicated that everyone deemed to know who the four were' (Boyko 1995: 202). In spite of this, the police did little to investigate and the crime went unpunished. Still, Osborne's family did not give up, and eventually one of the four murderers was convicted. The Osborne case was specifically investigated in 1991 by a study examining the treatment of Aboriginals in the Manitoba justice system, the conclusion being that Helen Betty Osborne was attacked and her case was allowed to languish because she was Aboriginal (Boyko 1995). Clearly, the identity of the victim, as well as her attackers structured the response of the police and the justice system.

Agents in Action: Citizenship Claims

Many groups have made claims on the government to recognize their citizenship rights and to uphold the government's promise of democratic equality. Some of the descendants of Chinese immigrants who were forced to pay the head tax in order to enter Canada have taken legal action against the government for compensation. Box 12.2 outlines the history of the government's discriminatory treatment of the Chinese.

Unfortunately, the courts have ruled that these claimants have no right to compensation, contending that the 'standards' of today cannot be applied to the past. Still, the claimants are going to appeal and will continue to pursue some compensation through the courts.

Box **12.2**   **The Unfinished Business of the Chinese Head Tax**

Canada has a nasty record of discrimination against people considered 'others', a practice it has worked hard to correct over the past half-century.

From 1885 to 1974, it took particular aim at Chinese immigrants. After benefiting from their labour in building the Canadian Pacific Railway, it levied a head tax on any other Chinese entering the country, effectively preventing the labourers' families from joining them. The tax rose from a then-formidable $50 in 1885 to $500 by 1923, at which point Parliament passed the Chinese Immigration Act, known as the Chinese exclusion act, to bar Chinese from entering the country at all. The act remained in force until 1947, when Chinese-Canadians were finally allowed to vote.

Modern Canadian may well wince at this discrimination and persecution, but the story isn't over. Those of us who were discriminated against, or whose fathers and grandfathers were charged the head tax and effectively denied companionship for decades, are asking Ottawa for redress. The Chinese Canadian National Council has been pressing the federal government for 17 years to compensate those who paid the tax (a group that numbered in the thousands in 1984 and has dwindled to several hundred today) or their survivors and descendants.

Since the council was rebuffed in 1984 by Sheila Finestone, who as multiculturalism minister rejected compensation because the government 'cannot rewrite history', it took its case to the courts. It asked to bring a class-action lawsuit against Ottawa on behalf of those forced to pay the head tax and relegated by the 1923 act to the ministry of isolation.

This week, Mr Justice Peter Cumming of Ontario's Superior Court of Justice dismissed the suit. He agreed that the goal was worthy, and took pains to suggest that those seeking redress continue to pursue the political route. But he ruled that the Charter of Rights, which came into force in 1982 and whose equality section took effect in 1985, cannot be applied retroactively. If it could, 'just about every instance of past discrimination since the turn of the century could be reviewed.'

He is right in law, and right in spirit: that the claim belongs in the political arena. Unhappily, as the Chinese-Canadian council turned its face back to Ottawa, Ottawa was there with a fresh slap. Immigration Minister Elinor Caplan, channelling the spirit of Sheila Finestone, said, 'The government has a very clear policy on this issue'—no compensation for the head tax. 'The courts have spoken and I think it's time to move on.'

It is true that to open the door to compensation for all grievances of the past, however intangible the monetary damage, would be bad public policy: amorphous, open-ended and offering a blank cheque written by today's taxpayers for the sins of politicians generations ago. As well, to expand any scheme of direct compensation from victims who are still alive to relatives of descendants of the victims would make it all but impossible to draw a line. Where would the cutoff be for past wrongs? A century ago? Two? The expulsion of the Acadians in the 1760s?

But two realistic avenues are open to the government. The first is, where there is specific evidence of financial harm caused by a deliberate and indefensible action by the government, Ottawa may provide at least symbolic compensation to those victims who are still alive. It did so with the Japanese-Canadians interned during the Second World War, whose goods and property were confiscated when they were forcibly relocated and prevented from returning to the West Coast until well after the war; they were offered $21,000 a person. (The United States paid $20,000 [US] to the survivors of its internment camps.) It could do so now with the Chinese-Canadians, by agreeing to repay the head tax to those who are alive to accept the money.

Calculating the figure would take some finesse. A simple cheque for $50 or $500 would be insultingly low, even for a symbolic gesture. A cheque for $105,000—a rough estimate of what $500 in 1923 might have become, not accounting for inflation, if it earned interest of 4 per cent a year—would be unaffordably high. Something closer to $5,400—an estimate of what $500 in 1923 would be, with inflation but without accumulated interest—might be about right. And—no small point—the money should be paid out quickly, and not delayed until, one by one, the remaining survivors died off.

There would be arguments that such a sum does not come close to compensating Chinese-Canadians for the injustice of the tax and the pain of the exclusion act that followed. No, it doesn't. No amount could. That leads us to the second avenue.

As part of the redress to Japanese-Canadians, Ottawa provided money for a Canadian race-relations foundation. It could rededicate itself to that pursuit, or, for more direct effect, fund special chairs at Canadian universities to focus attention on past and present discrimination, and to study the ways in which present policies improve on or repeat the errors of past ones.

And the government should express sincere regret for the official discrimination practised by the Canadian governments of the first half of the 20th century. Something a bit more graceful than, 'The courts have spoken and I think it's time to move on.'

Source: The *Globe and Mail* (2001). Reprinted with permission from the Globe and Mail.

The James Bay Cree have had success in the courts and in mobilizing and using **transnational action** through human-rights and environmental organizations to make citizenship claims. Jenson and Papillon (2000) document the success of the James Bay Cree in contesting the infringements on their territories and asserting their citizenship rights on the basis of 'nationhood' rather than as individual citizens. The Cree have fought the attempts of the Quebec government to subsume them into questions of sovereignty through the Quebec referendum, arguing that they already exist as a sovereign nation (Jenson and Papillon 2000). Their first success came in 1971 when they opposed the attempts of the Quebec government to build an enormous hydroelectric project on the Cree's traditional hunting grounds. The James Bay Cree won their court challenge, which contended that they had title and rights to the land and the Quebec government was required to engage in negotiations (Jenson and Papillon 2000). 'This was the first, and until very recently the only, comprehensive land claim settlement in Canada . . . beyond that, it was the first time in modern history that

Canadian governments, in this case both federal and provincial, recognized that Canadian citizenship included collective rights for aboriginal peoples' (Jenson and Papillon 2000: 251). The rarity of success in the courts for aboriginal rights demonstrates the frequent need for aboriginal groups to seek international support for the validity of their citizenship claims. The James Bay Cree have found widespread international support for their opposition to the Quebec government's plans for hydroelectric projects and have had considerable success in staving off encroachments and in defending their rights (Jenson and Papillon 2000).

Focusing on Gender: Engendering Citizens

In Canada, women's access to the rights of citizenship have been (and continue to be) compromised by the state's adoption of the 'breadwinner' policy scheme with all of its racialized and gendered implications (McDaniel 2002; Pulkingham 1998; Sainsbury 1999). Women who do not have access to '**breadwinner wages**', either because their 'breadwinners' are low-income earners or because they are unmarried or lesbians, are disadvantaged in this policy system. The state's 'ideal family type' consists of a husband engaged in paid productive labour and a wife engaged in unpaid reproductive labour and dependent on the distribution of the 'family wage'. Again, it is important to note the ideology wrapped up in the package of the 'family' (Das Gupta 1995). Historically, the Canadian government's policies towards Aboriginal families, immigrant families, and visible-minority families (e.g., residential schools, 'family' class immigration limitations and prohibi-

tions) belie the valuation of the 'family' as specific to the 'white, Canadianized family' (Das Gupta 1995). Thus, the privileges of the breadwinner wage are largely limited to racial and ethnic majorities. Although the breadwinner-policy formula is a familiar one, it is not the only way in which to distribute the rights of social citizenship. Sainsbury (1999:78) compares three different 'genderized' approaches to policy in democratic welfare states in Table 12.2.

We can see that in Table 12.2 caring work is given a monetary valuation from the state in the 'separate gender roles' regime; however, women and men are explicitly divided and viewed as either productive or reproductive workers (Sainsbury 1999). The 'individual earner-carer' is a more equitable option or 'ideal', as women and men are viewed equally as potential earners and/or carers, and carework is valued on par with 'productive' labour. In contrast, the characteristics of the typical 'male breadwinner policy regime' are considered to be predicated upon gender inequality and differential responsibilities (Sainsbury 1999). Social citizenship and benefits in the form of income security are designed and distributed with the ideology of the 'patriarchal' family in mind. In this schema, caring work in the household is unpaid, it is predominately performed by and expected of women, and these responsibilities penalize women in a citizenship regime which preferentially rewards paid work (particularly, work that does not involve caring) (Evans 1997; Sainsbury 1999).

Historically, the imperatives of the breadwinner policy have worked to exclude and limit the participation of women (especially married women) in the labour force (Pulkingham 1998). Pulkingham (1998)

Table 12.2 Three Gender Policy Regimes

Regime Attributes	Male Breadwinner	Separate Gender Roles	Individual Earner-Carer
Ideology	Strict division of labour	Strict division of labour	Shared tasks
	Husband = earner	Husband = earner	Father = earner-carer
	Wife = carer	Wife = carer	Mother = earner-carer
Entitlement	Unequal among spouses	Differentiated by gender role	Equal
Basis of entitlement	The principle of maintenance	Family responsibilities	Citizenship or residence
Recipient of benefits	Head of household Supplements for dependants	Men as family providers Women as caregivers	Individual
Taxation	Joint taxation Deductions for dependants	Joint taxation Deductions for dependants for both spouses	Separate taxation Equal tax relief
Employment and wage policies	Priority to men	Priority to men	Aimed at both sexes
Sphere of care	Primarily private	Primarily private	Strong state involvement
Caring work	Unpaid	Paid component to caregivers in the home	Paid component to caregivers in and outside the home

Source: Sainsbury (1999: 78). Reprinted by permission of Oxford University Press.

charts the evolution of unemployment and employment insurance in Canada to illustrate the way in which social policy is gendered and the extent to which women were encouraged and expected to be dependent on a male breadwinner. From its beginnings in 1940, unemployment insurance was intended for the male breadwinner and married women could not receive direct compensation on the basis of their own work history (Pulkingham 1998). Instead, they were eligible for state support only through their status as a dependant of their husband. In 1950, the impact of gendered ideologies on policy inequality becomes even more apparent, as a woman who married was rendered ineligible to claim unemployment insurance benefits for a period of two years following her marriage (Pulkingham 1998). This effectively barred '12,000 to 14,000 women each year' from collecting unemployment insurance until this stipulation was withdrawn in 1957 (Evans 1997: 102). In fact, in order to obtain unemployment insurance a woman was required to 'prove her attachment to the labour force' in a number of ways (Pulkingham 1998: 15). Women who refused to take low-paying jobs that they were overqualified for were also denied benefits (unlike men in similar circumstances) (Pulkingham 1998). Thus, women's access to the 'first-track' citizenship benefits of unemployment insurance (as opposed to the 'second-track' benefits of social assistance) was made exceptionally difficult (Pulkingham 1998: 10). Here we see that 'claims made through social assistance on the basis of "citizen-mother"' are accorded neither the degree of legitimacy nor the level of benefits that accompanies "worker" claims through social insurance' (Evans 1997: 98).

Women continue to be disadvantaged in their access to social insurance on the basis of their paid productive and reproductive labour. Child-bearing and caring responsibilities mean that women have more frequent departures and absences from the formal labour force than men do (Evans 1997). In spite of the introduction of a 'parental' leave policy in 1990, the vast majority of its claimants are women (97 out of 100 claimants (Evans 1997: 102). Women make up the majority of part-time workers, and they are more likely to have more than one job (Evans 1997). The argument that women's overrepresentation among part-time workers is a matter of choice is inaccurate, as 'fully one-third of them work part-time because they cannot find full-time work' (Evans 1997: 103). Even when women work full-time and all year (as the majority of employed women do) and 'conform' to the 'male' worker formula, they have not received equal pay for their efforts and this too affects the level of compensation they are eligible to receive (Pulkingham 1998: 30).

As chapter 9 shows, there is considerable occupational segregation by sex, and the work that women have disproportionately performed has been devalued and paid less than the work done by men (Armstrong

1997). The job-evaluation schemes which determine levels of pay under the Pay Equity Act in Ontario have tended to reinforce traditional gender ideologies of 'valued' work (Armstrong: 1997). For instance, 'garbage removal is considered more onerous than cleaning dirty diapers; police work more dangerous than dressing the wounds of patients with contagious diseases. . . . The stress created by working outdoors or in excessive heat is often counted, but the stress of working with dying patients or demanding children does not get counted' (Armstrong 1997: 261). Thus, the combination of domestic responsibilities, devalued work, and lower wages all work to make employment insurance a predominately 'male' benefit (Evans 1997). Although the recent revisions of 'employment insurance' purport to be more equitable, because part-time workers are included, Pulkingham (1998) says this inclusion is illusory. She shows that 18 per cent of part-time workers who will now be paying for coverage will never actually be able to qualify for benefits under the 'hours worked' requirement. She argues that those who work 15 to 35 hours a week (78 per cent of whom are women) will have a more difficult time qualifying for employment insurance under the new system (Pulkingham 1998).

Social Regulation: Reproductive Rights

There are ironic contradictions in the state's regulation and control of aspects of women's lives. Historically, women's reproductive potential has been closely watched by the state, while in the areas of sexual assault and 'domestic' violence the state has been less willing to intervene on women's behalf

(Walby 1997). For instance, women's sexuality and reproductive potential have been controlled in varying degrees by the state, from the outlawing of birth control until 1969 to the practice of sterilization for reproducers deemed 'unfit' (Findlay and Miller 2002; McLaren and McLaren 1997). While some women have been financially and ideologically supported for their reproductive potential (e.g., with baby bonuses and nationalistic rhetoric), other women have been penalized and degraded for it (Comacchio 1993; Valverde 1991). The right to have control over one's own body has not been a guaranteed right for women in general, and especially for women of colour and working-class women (Egan and Gardner 1999). Greschner (1990, 1998) points to the case of Chantal Daigle in Quebec as an example of the extent to which fetal and paternal rights take precedence over a woman's right to autonomy. Daigle was forced to carry on with a pregnancy against her will by an abusive ex-boyfriend who obtained a court injunction to halt her attempt to end the pregnancy (Greschner 1990). Only in the Supreme Court was this injunction overturned. The discourse of fetal and paternal rights frequently emerge without an examination of the threats that they entail for women's personhood (Casper 1998; Greschner 1990, 1998; Martin and Coleman 1995). Greschner (1990) argues that the notion of 'fetal rights' represents a concerted effort to enforce traditional gender roles. The question of control over a woman's conduct during her pregnancy has also been contested, and the potential for coercive action on the part of the state is looming. For example, Martin and Coleman (1995) point out that in New Brunswick, child protection extends to unborn children and that this legislation has been used to 'supervise' a pregnant woman in at least one case. The most disadvantaged women in society would be the most likely to be targeted and prosecuted under such a law. This tendency is illustrated in an American study of court-ordered caesarian sections occurring in a teaching hospital where close to 90 per cent of the women involved were visible minorities, nearly half were unmarried, and all were welfare recipients (Martin and Coleman 1995).

Agents in Action: Violence Against Women

As discussed in chapter 8, sexual assault is a weapon by which the relations of power and domination are reproduced and reinforced. McIntyre and Scott (2000) note that the act of sexual assault is strongly gendered, being predominately committed by men against women. Some women are more vulnerable than others to the threat of violence. Aboriginal women report much higher rates of spousal violence, and they run the greatest risk of being killed by their spouse (Johnson and Hotton 2001). Feminist groups and grass-roots organizations have lobbied provincial and federal governments to take action against the violence in women's lives (Ursel 1998). Ursel (1998) argues that feminist action has made a difference in the way in which the state confronts domestic violence. She takes the case of Manitoba and shows that the changes in the courts have resulted in a system that takes domestic violence seriously and has a more positive result for the women who are abused (Ursel 1998). In 1990, a specific Family Violence Court (FVC) was instituted to handle all cases of spouse, child, and elder abuse (Ursel 1998). And in 1993 the police department adopted a 'zero tolerance policy' by which a charge was laid for any domestic complaint (Ursel 1998: 143). Figure 12.1 shows the dramatic difference in spousal assault charges after the changes came into effect.

The increase in charges also made a difference in how domestic cases were viewed by crown attorneys (Ursel 1998). Before the establishment of a specialized court to hear domestic cases, these cases were shuffled off to the least experienced prosecutors because they were regarded as 'a messy, low-profile case with a minimal chance of conviction' (Ursel 1998: 147). In the new system, these

cases were redefined as requiring the legal experts who were adept at handling complex cases (Ursel 1998). The 'battered women's movement' has resulted in effective and more compassionate reforms in the legal system for victims of violence (Ursel 1998). Still, the problem is far from solved, and the serious consequences and wide reach of violence in Canada are apparent in Box 12.3.

Here we can see that although there has been government action, there are still not enough resources to meet the demands. Over the course of the 1990s, violent assaults against wives as measured by the

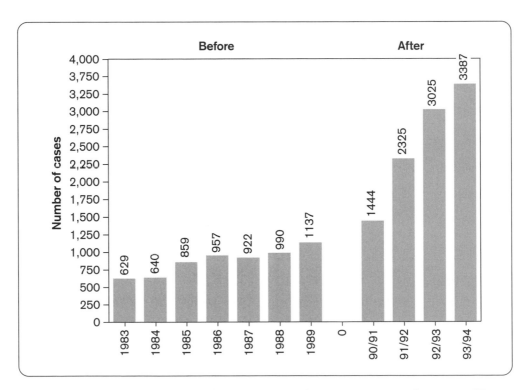

Figure 12.1 Number of Spousalᵃ Assault Cases in Which Charges Were Laid—Winnipeg Before and after Family Violence Court

ᵃSpousal assault includes those cases in which a spouse and child were assaulted.

Source: Ursel (1998: 144). Reprinted by permission of Fernwood Publishing.

1999 General Social Survey and the 1993 Violence Against Women Survey have declined; however, police reporting and use of social services by female victims of spousal violence have risen (Johnson and Hotton 2001). The researchers attribute both the decline in incidence and the increase in reporting to the various social and policy shifts that have occurred, such as better police training and restructured support services (Johnson and Hotton 2001).

Box **Battered Women Have Help Just a Phone Call Away**
By Gay Abbate

Gillian Hadley was one of 40 Ontario women who died at the hands of an intimate partner in 2000.

That's the average number of women killed by their spouses, boyfriends, or live-in companions in any given year in Ontario.

When Ms Hadley wanted to escape from her abusive, estranged husband, there was no safe place for her to seek shelter.

Today, help for female victims of domestic violence is just a phone call away, regardless of where they live in Ontario.

What made the young mother's death all the more tragic is that she lived in Durham Region, just east of Toronto, close to all the support services for battered women that the country's largest metropolis provides. Close in one sense, yet so far in another because her area's lone women's shelter was not accessible for her disabled child.

Consequently, she was still in the matrimonial home when Ralph Hadley broke in. Naked and screaming, she nearly escaped into the street before he forced her back inside and shot her to death. He then turned the weapon on himself.

The new province-wide service for battered women is the Assaulted Women's Helpline. Beth Jordan, its director of programs and services, said she hopes it will help save the lives of potential Gillian Hadleys in the province.

The helpline has operated in Toronto for 16 years. Now, with a five-year commitment of $4.5 million from the Ontario government, the service is accessible in every community, no matter how rural.

All calls are kept confidential and anonymous, Ms Jordan said, because the telephones do not have call display.

The expanded helpline was officially unveiled on 10 April. Within hours, women were calling from Ottawa, Sudbury, Thunder Bay, and Lindsay.

When the help line was limited to Toronto, it received 25,000 calls a year. Ms Jordan said she expects that number to double over the next year with the additional service.

It will take time to evaluate the helpline's success, but she hopes it will exceed expectations so that the province will be forced to provide permanent funding.

Ms Jordan predicts that the extra demand for help will severely test a shelter system that is already straining at the seams.

But that may be a good thing, she said, because it will make the province realize that a need for more shelters exists and that the 101 women's shelters that the Ministry of Community and Social Services currently funds require more resources. According to ministry figures, 15,000 women and 13,000 children use those shelters annually.

The Ontario government is already aware that funding still does not meet the increasing province-wide needs of abused women.

In the 2001 audit, the provincial auditor told the ministry that its practices and procedures did not ensure that services being provided were of an acceptable and consistent standard across the province.

The auditor noted that one shelter turned away more than 1,000 women and children in 2000.

According to the auditor, battered women have to wait an unacceptable three to six months to get counselling help.

The province has also heard the recommendations of the jury at the coroner's inquest held earlier this year into Ms Hadley's death. That jury called for more support services for abused women, including subsidized housing, which the government no longer finances.

In anticipation of receiving the funding, which was announced last October, the helpline staff have been visiting and collecting information on the various services available to women across Ontario.

Their database now has more than 2,000 agencies and support groups from which the professional counsellors who staff the telephones can draw to assist callers. The wide range of resources includes shelters, rape crisis centres, legal services, child-protection agencies, police and hospitals.

The help line can provide service in 154 languages, with interpreters available within seconds, Ms Jordan said.

The toll-free helpline operates 24 hours a day, seven days a week. The number outside Toronto is 1-866-863-0511. In the Toronto area, call 416-863-0511. The number for the hearing impaired is 1-866-863-7868. Domestic violence.

- About 70 women are killed each year in Canada by an intimate partner.
- 1,468 women were killed by their partners in the past two decades.
- 470 shelters for abused women existed across Canada in 1998. They were used by 47,962 women and 42,830 children.
- 11 per cent of female victims of violence reported having used a shelter in the past five years.
- 690,000 women report experiencing at least one incident of violence in the past five years.
- Of 23,502 incidents of spousal violence reported to police in 1999, 523 women were either killed or received major physical injuries (based on a sampling of 164 police departments).
- Women under 25 reported the highest rate of domestic violence—5 per cent—compared with 1 per cent for women 45 and older.

Source: Canadian Centre for Justice Statistics, Family Violence in Canada, 2000 statistical report
Rates of abuse. These are the estimated provincial rates of spousal violence against women over a
five-year period:

PEI	12%
Alberta	11%
Sask.	11%
BC	10%
Manitoba	9%
N.B.	9%
N.S.	8%
Quebec	8%
Ontario	7%
Nfld.	4%

Source: Abbate (2002). Reprinted with permission from the Globe and Mail.

Focusing on Age: Citizenship over the Life Course

The examination of citizenship shows how the historical period and the socio-historical circumstances in which we live have a powerful impact on the structures of inequality (McDaniel 2001). Citizenship, in all its forms, has historically been denied to various groups on the basis of race, ethnicity, and gender. Consider that in the 1960s, employers in Canada had the legal right to fire women if they married or became pregnant (Sangster 1995). Individuals and groups have struggled and triumphed over inequality throughout history; however, in some ways we are fated to grapple with the socio-historical milieu into which we are born. This milieu has changed especially for those whose lives have spanned the twentieth century, particularly in regard to citizenship in Canada.

Still, the expectation that women will perform most of the tasks involved in reproductive labour have remained fairly stable.

As we have seen throughout this chapter, women's involvement in caring work over the life course puts them at a disadvantage in their ability to gain the rights of citizenship. And the life chances of women and men of different ethnic and racial groups and of different ages are shaped by the substantive birth cohort in which they were born. In this regard, McDaniel (2001) discusses 'gendered generations', pointing out, among other things, that state benefits are influenced by the historical time in which one was born. These benefits must also be considered within the context of changes in gender relations that have occurred over the last three generations. McDaniel cautions, however, that we should not be overly optimistic about the opportunities for the youngest generation of women. Post–baby boom women (born between 1965 and 1975), according to McDaniel (2001: 204), 'although benefitting from the legacies of previous generations of women in struggling for rights and job equity, are finding jobs difficult to find and family formation/dissolution economically challenging.'

Women's contributions to society go largely unrecognized and unrewarded. In spite of the devaluation and artificial separation of caring work in the home from the 'productive' realm, unpaid caring work is vital to the workings of the state (McDaniel 2002). McDaniel (2002: 136) argues that 'caring is central to welfare states, not because they are inherently caring (abundant evidence calls this into question), but because care (for the young, old, sick and infirm, and those who cannot work) leads to more productive, less discontented, workers and consumers for capitalist economies.' As was outlined earlier, the weight of this imbalance in caring work penalizes women through increased work absences, more departures from and entries into the labour force, and consequently, lower lifetime wages (Gough 2001; Marshall 2000). The successive effects of wage inequality, marginalized work status, and interrupted or unstable work histories exact a specific toll for women in older age (Gough 2001; Hill and Tigges 1995). Gower (1998) points out that women's pre-retirement incomes are significantly lower than men's. In 1992, for example, 41 per cent of women reported pre-retirement incomes of less than $20,000, while only 16 per cent of men did so (Gower 1998: 18). On the other hand, nearly half of men reported earnings of $40,000 and up, whereas only 16 per cent of women earned this amount (Gower 1998: 18). All of the inequalities and discriminatory practices experienced in the labour force (e.g., the creation of 'reserve armies of labour' and the exclusion of groups through racism and sexism) have consequences for the class status of aging adults.

In the mid-twentieth century, the poverty of Canadian seniors sparked the enactment of a number of distributive policies designed to ameliorate this situation (Myles 2000). The Canadian government instituted a network of financial coverage for elderly citizens, including Old Age Security, the Guaranteed Income Supplement, the Canada/Quebec Pension Plan, and incentives for retirement savings in the form of Registered Retirement Savings Plans (Marshall 2000). Although the financial coverage of the Canada/Quebec Pension Plan is dependent upon labour force earnings and RRSPs require individual contributions, the other policies were intended to improve the situation of low-income seniors (Marshall 2000). All seniors receive Old Age Security (OAS) regardless of their employment history. In addition, there is the Guaranteed Income Supplement (GIS) and a Spouse's Allowance, which are intended to improve the financial situation of those seniors with low or no pre-retirement incomes (Marshall 2000). Myles (2000) shows that these policies have had success in alleviating extreme poverty among seniors. For instance, 40 per cent of seniors were in the very lowest income quintile in 1980, whereas in 1995, only 17 per cent were (Myles 2000: 18). Poverty among unattached female seniors was also reduced over this period, moving from 70 per cent in the lowest income quintile in 1980 to 42 per cent by 1995 (Myles 2000: 18). Still, the fact that 42 per cent of unattached female seniors remain in the lowest income quintile highlights the magnitude of poverty and illustrates that these 'safety nets' continue to be inadequate. So too, does the fact that Aboriginal Canadians who live on reserves were not allowed to contribute to the Canadian Public Pension plan until 1988. Thus, Canadians are differentially protected from the vulnerabilities of old age.

Older Canadians who have immigrated recently are also more vulnerable because they are ineligible for social security benefits. And evidence from Britain indicates that all ethnic minorities may have smaller pensions in later life. Ginn and Arber (2001), who document the extent of pension inequality in Britain by gender and ethnicity, find significant disadvantages for minorities in comparison to whites. After controlling for a number of other factors, they found that both minority men and women were significantly less likely to have private pensions (Ginn and Arber 2001). Discriminatory labour-market practices, shorter employment histories, and gendered ideologies are among the variables which disadvantage ethnic minority groups in the accumulation of private pensions (Ginn and Arber 2001). Hence, at least in Britain, the likelihood of having a significant pension and financial stability in older age is not a matter of chance. The experience of inequality throughout the life course casts a long shadow in old age.

Although secure and stable employment has long been denied to many groups, researchers have recently highlighted the lack of significant employment opportunities and citizenship participation for today's youth (Allahar and Côté 1994; Kapsalis et al. 1999; Wanner 2001). Although this crisis may be somewhat overestimated, young men in particular have seen some losses in their labour-market returns from educational investments (Wanner 2001). In general, today's youth are experiencing 'negative mobility compared to their parents and grandparents', and this means that the parents of these young people will encounter longer periods when they will be supporting their children financially (McDaniel 2002:

141). For today's youth, the pension prospects and life-course earnings appear to be less promising than for previous generations. The Canadian state's retreat from the tasks of caring has resulted in further 'intergenerational inequities' between women, as women responsible for children and elderly parents face additional burdens (McDaniel 2002: 141). The intensification of private caring responsibilities means that youth and elderly people from the middle and upper classes will be protected and sheltered against the contingencies of market imperatives, while those from lower-income groups will be further disadvantaged (McDaniel 2002).

Social Regulation: Child Welfare Legislation

The state's intervention in the lives of its citizens starts in childhood (Ursel 1990). Although the protection of children and young people would appear to be desirable, Ursel (1990) shows that the roots of the Canadian child-welfare laws established in the late nineteenth and early twentieth centuries were paternalistic and punitive rather than supportive. The welfare agencies aimed strongly for the regulation of reproductive processes and were quick to remove children and make them wards of the state, rather than working with parents to improve the family situation (Ursel 1990). Kline (1993, 2000) shows that this legacy is evident in present-day child-welfare practices. She examines how the ideology of motherhood, with its attendant racialized and bourgeois meanings, is applied in contemporary legal discourse to Aboriginal women who are then found to be 'lacking'. Kline (1993) argues that Aboriginal women have been construed by child welfare agencies as inadequate and uncooperative mothers who violate the dominant definitions of 'good' mothering. According to Kline (1993), the moralizing dictates of the good-mother ideology include an ethic of selflessness, whereby a mother is ready and able to provide her children with a stable and enriched environment. All of the expectations of 'good mothering' are judged without any consideration of the impact of the broader socio-structural factors of inequality (Kline 1993, 2000).

Kline (1993, 2000) points to several cases involving Aboriginal women and child welfare agencies to show that the courts individualize and personalize the societal inequalities stemming from colonization and racism that are present in the lives of Aboriginal women. For instance, Aboriginal women who were being abused have had their children taken from them with the rationale that the 'choices' these women made were unstable (Kline 1993). This is a classic case of 'blaming the victim' and reducing social issues to individual problems. In this sense, the reduction of violent abuse to a 'lifestyle' carries strong elements of blame for the mothers involved (Kline 1993). The difficulties inherent in providing basic sustenance and adequate living conditions while living in poverty are subsequently ignored in assessments by the courts. In fact, Aboriginal women run a much greater risk of being the victims of spousal violence, with 25 per cent of Aboriginal women reporting abuse compared to 8 per cent of non-Aboriginal women in the same period (Johnson and Hotton 2001). Kline (1993) notes that the colonialism and government policies toward Aboriginal groups have constructed a system in which Aboriginal women live disproportionately in poverty with all of its disadvantages and hardships. This leaves many Aboriginal women (in addition to other poor women) much more vulnerable to state intervention and the potential dissolution of their families.

Agents in Action: Mandatory Retirement

The regulative force of the state stretches and intertwines through the life course and into the domains of reproduction, production, and distribution. At the end of the life course, the inequalities that have manifested themselves throughout these processes do not disappear, but rather crystallize and extend their reach. Privileged adults who have weathered little in the way of inequality or disadvantage are often introduced at this point to the experience of age discrimination in the processes of production. The virtual exclusion of aging adults from the world of productive labour by the mechanism of mandatory retirement has increasingly been challenged by older workers in Canada (Shellenbarger 2001). The right to remain active in the labour force and to re-enter the labour force have both been points of contention for the growing numbers of older workers. Box 12.4 shows that opposition is mounting.

Ontario Human Rights Commissioner Keith Norton notes that this practice is particularly disadvantageous for women who have worked in the home. It would also hurt those workers who enter the workforce later in life and find it necessary to continue working. Although several court cases have challenged mandatory retirement as a human-rights violation (i.e., age discrimination), none have been successful.

Box **12.4** **End to Forced Retirement Urged**
By Richard Mackie

People who want to avoid mandatory retirement and continue to work after the age of 65 should be protected under the Human Rights Code, says Ontario Human Rights Commissioner Keith Norton.

'There are lots of people who are vigorous at the age of 80,' he told a news conference at Queen's Park yesterday. 'If they want to continue to work, why shouldn't they have the choice, as opposed to being arbitrarily dismissed at 65?'

Mr Norton, who himself is 60, said that Ontario laws should be changed to ban mandatory retirement ages in contracts or imposed by companies. As it stands, Ontario law does not establish a mandatory retirement age but allows it to be established in union contracts and in other ways, he said.

'The person making the decision [on retirement] ought to be the older person,' Mr Norton said.

But he said the law could allow companies to require employees to retire at 65 'if you can demonstrate that they can't do the job any more.'

He complained that age discrimination is not taken seriously in Ontario society and predicted it will become a more important issue as the population ages. Demographic forecasts project that the province will have three million residents aged 65 or over by 2021.

'We don't view discrimination based on age as seriously as we view race discrimination or gender or any of the other grounds in the code.'

The lack of concern about discrimination based on age results in part from 'the assumptions with respect to aging that people become forgetful, less adaptable, they're less vigorous,' he said.

The general acceptance of forcing retirements at 65 also is based on the assumption that it benefits older people, Mr Norton said. 'People would look at retirement as sort of like a gift to older people—"You don't have to work any more."'

But he stressed that the realities unearthed in consultations about age discrimination show that mandatory retirement often is harmful to people. 'Those things are based on stereotypes.'

The consultations conducted by the Human Rights Commission in the past year revealed that forcing someone to retire can be unfair and discriminatory. Yet the law doesn't allow the commission to look at discrimination in the workplace against anyone over 65.

'Things like mandatory retirement often disproportionately impact upon women, especially women who have taken time out to be a homemaker and raise a young family.'

Forced retirement also is a problem for those who start families later in life and find their income cut to pension level at a time when their need for money is peaking.

Source: Mackie (2001). Reprinted with permission from the Globe and Mail.

Conclusion

The meanings of the term 'citizen' have a significant effect on the development and delivery of policy, and these meanings are intimately structured by the social relations of
class, gender, race, ethnicity, and age. Jenson
(1997: 632) argues that there are a number
of different citizenship 'identities', including
the 'model citizen', the 'second-class citizen',
and the 'non-citizen'. A 'model citizen' can
expect to receive the full entitlements of citizenship, whereas those groups and individuals that are considered 'second-class' or 'non-
citizens' are offered few, if any, of the benefits
of citizenship. This chapter has shown that
the fragility of citizenship is produced and
reproduced through state policy and legislation that are shaped by the intersections of
class, age, gender, ethnic, and race relations.

Regarding social welfare, for instance,
there are clear distinctions between model
citizens and second-class citizens or those
who are deemed deserving or undeserving
of social assistance. Consider the extremely
high rates of poverty among single mothers
and old women. Because welfare policies are
often based on narrow ideas of 'productive'
citizenship, the work that women do in the
processes of reproduction are often unacknowledged in social welfare policy. This
leads to state distributive processes that

reproduce the gendered structures of
inequality. In old age, when many adults are
not allowed to work, pension schemes are
established on the basis of a 'typical' labour-
force career, or a secure and stable relationship with someone who has had such a
career. Yet, even if an Aboriginal Canadian
has had a stable career, they will have very
small pensions after retirement because of
pre-existing biases in pension-contribution
rules. Hence, state distributive processes are
not only gendered, but are also structured
by age and race relations. And as the preceding sections of this chapter show, race,
ethnicity, and class are implicated in state
distributive processes as well. Indeed, views
of morality and idealized traditional families
still frame much of the political rhetoric
around poverty; governments are committed to reducing child poverty, not poverty
among single mothers, and of course they
are part of the same thing.

To alleviate social inequality in Canada,
state policy and legislation must evolve so
that the complexities of inequality that
result from coalescent CAGE(s) are its heart.
This requires radical social change, and the
process will be slow even if policy makers
have the best intentions. The value of 'neutral' social policy must be challenged if such
change is to take place. It is to this issue that
we turn in chapter 13.

Notes

1. Scott (1996).

Glossary

Breadwinner wage The 'family-supporting'
wages that some men (especially, white
European men) were considered to be entitled
to over the course of the twentieth century.
State laws and support systems reinforced and

sustained this gendered division of labour in
the family, thereby reproducing an ideology
of female economic dependence for some
groups of women.

Citizen A citizen of a society should be entitled

to all the benefits of being a member of society (e.g., rights, political voice, social welfare); however, many individuals and groups within societies are denied the full rights of citizenship and are treated as second-class citizens (perhaps granted some rights but denied others e.g., granted welfare benefits but not allowed to vote) (Jenson 1997). Those who are treated as 'non-citizens' are denied virtually all of the benefits of citizenship and are left extremely vulnerable to exploitation with little recourse.

Civil citizenship   T.H. Marshall's citizenship conceptualization of an individual's basic human rights. These include the right to sign a legal contract, the right to freedom of person and freedom of speech, and the right to seek redress in the courts for any violation of property or person.

Corporate crime   Illegal activities undertaken by businesses. In the course of procuring financial gain and minimizing economic losses, businesses (or rather the agents within them) have the potential to engage in numerous criminal acts (e.g., environmental contamination, health and safety violations, fraud, etc.)

Live-In Caregiver Program   An immigration policy that gives temporary work permits to women coming to fill the Canadian need for live-in caregivers (e.g., nannies). This policy aims to fill a demand for child care, while at the same time severely restricting the activities and the duration of stay for the women involved in the program.

Political citizenship   T.H. Marshall's conceptualization of an individual's right to political involvement in their society. This guarantees a political voice for citizens in the form of voting and/or by seeking out political office.

Social citizenship   T.H. Marshall's conceptualization of an individual's right to full social inclusion in a society's wealth. This means that citizens should be guaranteed economic well-being, educational and health services, and participation or inclusion in the culture and heritage of their society.

State   A complex array of governing institutions in a society. Includes national-security, parliamentary, judicial, and bureaucratic institutions just to name a few. For this reason, the state itself cannot be said to act either consciously or uniformly; however, agents (both internally and externally) can use the tools of the state to acquire, monopolize, or distribute resources and services, and to maintain social order. This diversity of institutions means that dissent and conflict within and between institutions are a feature of democratic states. Clearly, some individuals and groups in a society are more vulnerable to punitive action on the part of state institutions, whereas individuals and groups with more power are better equipped to attempt to use the state to their advantage.

Transnational action   The mobilization of international agencies, non-governmental organizations (e.g., environmental, human-rights) to generate support for the protection of aboriginal lands and land claims

Workfare   A social-assistance program that requires the recipients to take certain paid work or enrol in educational or training courses as a condition for receiving welfare benefits. Although some recipients, notably mothers of young children, have been exempt from this requirement, some of these exemptions are being revised or abolished.

Questions for Critical Thought

1. What do you see as the advantages and disadvantages of the 'three gender policy regimes'? What implications do these various regimes have for class, age, gender,

ethnic, or race relations?

2. How have immigration policies affected the processes of production, reproduction, and distribution in various families and communities? What type of compensation or redress, if any, should governments offer to individuals and groups that have been discriminated against and denied citizenship rights in the past?

3. How would you characterize the role of the state? Does the state primarily ameliorate or exacerbate societal inequities? Give examples to make your case.

4. How have the social relations of class, age, race or ethnicity, and gender affected the achievement of citizenship rights in Canada? What rights do you think should be included in the notion of full citizenship? Explain why.

5. How has the state's intervention and regulation of the processes of reproduction changed over time (e.g., reproductive rights, child welfare, and social welfare)? Do you support more intervention or less on the part of the state? What implications would this have for different groups in society?

Recommended Reading

Armstrong, Pat, and M. Patricia Connelly (1999). *Feminism, Political Economy and the State: Contested Terrain.* Toronto: Canadian Scholars Press. An anthology that looks at how welfare, health, and education policies have been shaped by feminist struggles, as well as examining how women's lives have been affected by the state. The countries examined include Canada and Latin American and European countries.

Broad, Dave, and Wayne Antony (1999), *Citizens or Consumers? Social Policy in a Market Society.* Halifax: Fernwood. This anthology takes a critical approach to social welfare policy with a focus on Canadian citizenship issues and social activism.

Orloff, Ann (1996). 'Gender in the welfare state'. *Annual Review of Sociology* 22: 51–78. An accessible theoretical look at how gender relations influence welfare-state policies with an explanation of existing approaches and future trends.

Pupo, Norene (2001). 'The role of the state in a restructured economy'. Chapter 4 in Dan Glenday and Ann Duffy (eds), *Canadian Society: Meeting the Challenges of the Twenty-First Century.* Toronto: Oxford University Press. In this book chapter, the author succinctly reviews theories of the state and explains the influence of the Canadian state in the economy, the labour market, and the lives of individuals and families.

Sainsbury, Diane (ed.) (1999). *Gender and Welfare State Regimes.* New York: Oxford University Press. A valuable collection which provides international comparisons of welfare policies in a broad range of areas (e.g., child care, taxation, the labour market, employment equality) with an emphasis on gender issues.

Stasiulis, Daiva, and Abigail B. Bakan (1997). 'Negotiating citizenship: The case of foreign domestic workers in Canada'. *Feminist Review* 57 (Autumn): 112–39. The authors challenge predominant conceptualizations of 'citizenship', arguing that citizenship is a 'negotiated relationship' that is shaped by numerous societal axes of inequality. They illustrate this negotiation through the experience of foreign domestic workers in Canada.

Epilogue

The first four chapters of this book discussed influential theoretical contributions to the study of class, gender, ethnicity, race, and age. After outlining the strengths and weaknesses of these theories, each of the chapters concluded with a working definition of the concept in question. These working definitions incorporated many elements of the theories previously assessed. Yet, a crucial reason for formulating these concepts was to ensure that they would be compatible with one another in a conceptual framework that combined them all. Thus it was important to identify a nucleus around which class, age, gender, ethnicity, and race could be grouped. Three elements of this nucleus were identified: processes of production, processes of distribution, and processes of reproduction (see chapter 2 for definitions). These processes were chosen because they are essential for the survival of individuals and societies. Class, age, gender, ethnicity, and race are structured sets of social relations that organize the interrelated processes of production, distribution, and production in Canada. As such, class, age, gender, ethnicity, and race are characterized by power, oppression, opportunity hoarding, and exploitation.

Whereas chapters 2 to 5 discussed the structural dimensions of inequality, chapter 6 considered the idea that individuals are agents in the social construction of class, age, gender, ethnic, and race relations. Chapter 7 introduced a conceptual framework of social inequality that brought together many of the ideas discussed in the previous chapters into a cohesive whole. Besides organizing concepts that have traditionally been studied in research on social inequality, this framework contributes to our understanding of social inequality by explicitly considering social time and agency.

Part II of this book examined various outcomes of inequality in five social domains. Chapters 8 and 9 considered outcomes of inequality that came about primarily through families and paid work, such as differences in the division of household labour, caregiving, violence, occupations, and income. Chapters 10 and 11 discussed inequalities in education and health, and chapter 12 examined the role the Canadian state plays in producing and reproducing various forms of inequality through its ideas of what constitutes citizenship. Each chapter considered examples or case studies that demonstrated the relevance of inequality in the social domain in question. These chapters also provided an overview of the Canadian literature on social inequality.

The purpose of Part II was twofold. In the first place, the chapters showed how outcomes of inequality in Canada are shaped by class, age, gender, and ethnicity, and race. In doing so, the chapters showed how certain groups of Canadians are disadvantaged in relation to others in various domains of social life. These chapters also identified issues that require further research. The ideas presented in the conceptual framework of the book were often captured most explicitly through the examples and case studies presented in the chapters. Although my goal was to organize the chapters in Part II with these ideas in mind, much of the available research was deficient in three important ways. First, very little of it had considered whether and how class, age, gender, and ethnicity/race work together simultaneously in creating systems of advantage and disadvantage. Second, and related to the first, there is a dearth of research on inequality that considers whether and how age and social time influence outcomes of inequality. Third, more research is needed into the strategies that agents use in conforming to or resisting the social-structural influences in their lives. Although a picture of inequality in Canada has evolved from the material presented, it remains incomplete.

Many aspects of social life need to change if inequality is to be eradicated in Canada. Widely held ideologies about gender, class, ethnicity, race, and age need to be challenged, and the processes through which the activities of production, distribution, and reproduction are organized need to change. Another avenue through which such changes may begin to take place is the reform of social policy. Although it would take another book to outline the specific policies needed to address all of the issues identified in this book, some general ideas about how such policies should evolve are worth considering. First and foremost, given what we know about how class, age, gender,

ethnicity, and race work together in structuring inequality, it is useful to consider how policy makers might better integrate these structures of inequality into their programs. They will need to give up the idea that gender, class, age, ethnic, or racial 'neutrality' is desirable in social policy and, instead, recognize that such neutrality actually reproduces systems of inequality.

The goal of 'neutral' social policy is to treat everyone the same way. Neutral social policy emerged in response to policies that explicitly treated certain groups of people unfairly. For example, in the latter part of the nineteenth century, laws and policies changed so that women were entitled to own property. Before that, women had to relinquish control of anything that was theirs—land, money, furniture, and so on—to their husbands when they married. The law became neutral so that both men and women were eligible to control their own possessions. Why then is neutral social policy that assumes formal equality problematic? Because 'strict adherence to the principle of formal equality in the absence of substantive equality leads to inequality; treating unalikes in the same way simply perpetuates differences' (Chunn, 2000: 242). As an example, consider Canadian family law. Under the guise of equality, Canadian family law assumes that mothers and fathers are both able to contribute to the financial support of their children. Technically, of course, this is true. As a result, spousal support payment schemes are generally short-term and work on the assumption that an individual will and should be able to support themselves economically after a short time. The 'substantive' problem with such assumptions is that women are at a disadvantage in labour markets and are unlikely to be able to support themselves financially to the same extent as men (Chunn 2000). Clearly, such policy leads to the reproduction of inequality.

Equality means different things to different people. Consider, for instance, the version of equality that is presented by the Canadian Alliance party. Equality is one of the basic political principles that have guided the party since it was originally established as the Reform Party of Canada in 1987. The preamble to the Canadian Alliance's official policy document states that its vision of Canada includes 'true equality of citizens' (www.canadianalliance.ca). Yet, curiously missing from Canadian Alliance policy statements are explicit views on the groups of Canadians that have been identified as disadvantaged in this book (i.e., women, the old and young, and members of visible minorities). Box 13.1 compares the policies and issues that are identified by the Liberal Party of Canada and the Canadian Alliance. Here we see differences between the parties in their views of equality. The Liberal platform identifies disadvantaged groups and outlines what it has done or is trying to do in order to improve the quality of life for these groups. The Canadian Alliance platform, on the other hand, does not mention women, and with respect to multiculturalism, Aboriginal peoples, and seniors, it suggests that their policies will treat these groups equally under Canadian law and encourage their individualism in ensuring their well-being. While this language may seem innocuous, the fact that groups are not treated equally under Canadian law and policy in the first place goes unacknowledged (see chapter 12). Furthermore, and as noted above, treating everyone as 'equal' under policy and law reinforces substantive inequality. Clearly, the

Canadian Alliance Party's understanding of equality is different from that of the Liberal Party's and from the ideas of equality that are adopted in this book.

This brief discussion of the Canadian Alliance and Liberal Party platforms shows two different understandings of equality. For the Canadian Alliance, equality reflects both the ontological view that 'all people are created equal' and the idea of equal opportunity. It assumes that individuals, regardless of their class, age, gender, ethnicity, or race, are on a level playing field and that with similar levels of intelligence and ambition they will have equal chances of success. The Liberal Party takes the idea of equality one step further. Along with an ontological view of equality, the Liberal Party promotes equality through social-policy attempts to make the playing field more level. Equal opportunities are not assumed, and social programs are established to help produce situations that treat groups equally. Such views of equality have led to equal-opportunity policies and legislation which have helped to open doors to paid work for women and members of ethnic and visible minority groups in Canada and the United States.

Neither the Canadian Alliance nor the Liberal views of equality go far enough, however. For social policy to eradicate social inequality it must rely on a definition of equality that also considers the outcomes of inequality discussed in this book (e.g., income, occupation, and health). In other words, social policy must be established with the goal of equality of outcomes in mind. To do so, such policy must simultaneously consider the intersecting structures of inequality and not simply focus on one particular disadvantaged group at a time. An example of how such policy might be formulated is reproduced here in Appendix A. On the basis of their research on gender inequality and poverty, Davies, McMullin, and Avison (2001) make policy recommendations that are informed by gender, class, and age. The guiding assumption in this work is that public policy must be situated within a life-course framework and must be developed in a way that does not penalize individuals for their responsibilities in processes of reproduction. Another assumption is that men and women should divide equally the work involved in production, reproduction, and distribution. The problem with the policies described in Appendix A is that it will be a long time before that is done in Canadian society (see chapter 8). Indeed, to achieve equality of outcomes, changes to social policy will not suffice. Rather, Canadians will need to challenge the ways in which the processes of production, distribution, and reproduction are organized and the dominant ideologies that shape such organization.

Box **Comparison of Liberal and Canadian Alliance Platforms on Women, Aboriginals, Multiculturalism, and Seniors**

Liberals on Women

We improved the way Canada monitors gender equality:
- by pioneering new forms of analysis to ensure that our policies treat women equally;
- by developing tools to show the difference between men and women in their income, in their learning and in their work—both paid and unpaid work.

We supported women as decision makers and entrepreneurs:
- by supporting women who choose to run for Parliament;
- by ensuring that women have a voice at the federal Cabinet table;
- by helping small business with a seven per cent cut in small business taxes—women start twice the number of small businesses that men do.

We worked to enhance women's health:
- by creating five Centres of Excellence for research into women's health;
- by taking a close look at women's experiences with the health care system;
- by funding research into heart disease and breast cancer.

We worked to ensure safer communities for women;
- by amending the criminal code so that it is easier to obtain Peace Bonds—or protective court orders—and so that peace bonds are more effective;
- by supporting actions to combat family violence, and by helping communities tackle the root causes of crime.

We helped seek equality through the courts:
- by restoring the Court Challenges Program, which helps with legal costs that Canadians face when they pursue their rights through the courts.

We'll keep supporting a woman's equal right to respect, safety and health:
- by recognizing what Canada owes its unpaid caregivers—mostly women—and giving them special tax benefits, while studying their needs to inform future policies;
- by creating concrete strategies to fight family violence;
- by enhancing research into women's health needs, with $45 million for the fight against breast cancer.

We're helping women strengthen their families:
- by investing in children through the Canada Child Tax Benefit, which helped 3.2 million families in 2000;
- by funding the National Child Benefit—a comprehensive system of support for low income families;
- by helping mothers go to school, with Canada Study Grants for Students with Dependants.

Canadian Alliance on Women

No explicit statement about women. Indeed, the word does not appear in their policy document. There is a general statement of equality that is as follows: 'We recognize that all human beings possess the fundamental human rights of life, freedom, and the right to own and enjoy property.'

Liberals on Aboriginal Peoples

Many Aboriginal Canadians face daily challenges to healthy and productive lives, rooted in problems like:
- high unemployment;
- housing shortages;
- a lack of basic services, like a safe water supply;
- high rates of infant mortality and youth suicide.

All Canadian have the right to participate fully in our society.

We started with a long-term strategy called Gathering Strength—Canada's Aboriginal Action Plan, founded on four themes:
- renewing partnerships;
- strengthening Aboriginal governance;
- developing a new fiscal relationship between the federal government and Aboriginal communities;
- and supporting strong communities, people and economies.

We undertook a process of healing:
- by recognizing a series of historical grievances, including physical and sexual abuse at residential schools;
- by investing $350 million in a Healing Foundation;
- by finding new ways to collaborate with Aboriginal peoples and communities on joint programs;

- by creating new financial arrangements between the federal government and Aboriginal communities that foster self-reliance;
- by working towards a better quality of life for Aboriginal people.

We supported Aboriginal self-government:
- by recognizing that inherent right under the existing Constitution;
- by participating in negotiations for over 80 self-government agreements across Canada;
- by finalizing a treaty with the Nisga'a people of British Columbia, which brought certainty to issues like land access, resource and wildlife management, governance, funding, and taxes.

We worked to help Aboriginal Canadians become self-sufficient:
- by putting their organizations in charge of federally funded job training programs;
- by working with Canadian employers on strategies to recruit, retain and promote Aboriginal people;
- by helping 23,500 Aboriginal youth find secure jobs with a future.

We supported Aboriginal arts:
- by adding $2 million over six years to programs that train young Aboriginal artists.

We strengthened our support for Aboriginal economic development:
- by boosting the budget for Aboriginal economic development to $200 million in 2001, up from $25 million in 1999;
- by investing $1.6 billion over five years on Aboriginal programs that focus on the individual, like:
  - labour-market programs;
  - youth programs;
  - child care programs;
  - programs for Aboriginal people living in urban centres;
  - and programs for those living with disabilities.

We'll keep helping Aboriginal Canadians realize self-government:
- by supporting communities as they develop effective, stable and accountable, governments.

We'll continue our focus on youth and children:
- with programs that give youth the education and opportunities they need to succeed;
- with increased funding for the Aboriginal Head Start program to foster the spiritual, emotional, intellectual and physical growth of Aboriginal children;
- by continuing to support aboriginal children and youth learning.

We'll continue to help build dynamic Aboriginal economics:
- by seeking more opportunities to work with communities, provincial and territorial governments, and the private sector to foster the development of economic skills and prosperous First Nation and Inuit communities.

We'll help Aboriginal communities prevent disease and injuries and promote wellness. We'll keep helping Aboriginal children and youth learn about their languages and cultures in natural settings rather than exclusively in classrooms.

Canadian Alliance on Aboriginal Peoples

Our commitment to individual freedom and equality before and under the law is the key principle from which we will approach aboriginal affairs policy. We affirm the right of aboriginal Canadians to mange their own affairs subject to the laws of Canada and the provinces. Aboriginal self-government will be a delegated municipal level of government rather than a sovereign third order of government. We will not support race-based allocation of harvest rights to natural resources.

Aboriginal Canadians should have the same rights and responsibilities as all other Canadians. Transfer of powers to aboriginal governments will include measures to ensure democratic accountability and the responsibility to fund services through the tax dollars of those being served.

Our position in land claims negotiations will be to ensure respect for existing private property rights, affordable and conclusive settlement of all claims, and an open and transparent process involving all stakeholders. We will protect the democratic rights and freedoms of individual Aboriginals, and establish their right to private ownership of property.

Liberals on Multiculturalism

All of Canada deserves to reap the benefits of Canada's multicultural society.

We revitalized Canadian multiculturalism:
- by revamping our Multiculturalism Program, launched 29 years ago, with a new focus on social justice, identity, and civic participation;
- by recognizing the strong links between our multiculturalism policy and our strategy for trade in foreign markets.

We worked to eliminate intolerance:
- by stiffening sentences on hate crimes;
- by launching national youth programs to fight racism;
- by establishing the Canada Race Relations Foundation to help resolve race relations issues.
- by launching a national strategy to fight hate and bias activities.

We helped all Canadians seek equality through the courts:
- by restoring the Court Challenges Program, which helps with the legal costs faced by equality-seeking Canadians who pursue their rights through the courts.

And we renewed Canada's commitment to immigration:
- by abolishing a fee that refugees had to pay when they arrived in Canada;
- by continuing to welcome citizens from around the world who seek a better life in Canada.

We helped seek equality through the courts:
- by restoring the Court Challenges Program, which helps with the legal costs that Canadians face when they pursue their rights through the courts.

We're renewing Canada's commitment to immigration:
- by moving Canada's immigration levels closer to 1 per cent of the population;
- by ensuring there are sufficient resources to allow families to settle properly;
- by making it easier to bring high skilled foreign workers and families to Canada;
- by cracking down on the criminals who exploit people trying to come to Canada;
- by streamlining the refugee application process, so applicants can know as soon as possible whether they are eligible to stay in Canada—allowing us to protect those in genuine need.

And we will foster the development of official language minorities across Canada by:
- expanding efforts to better reflect Canada's two languages in the public service;
- increasing funding for French immersion schools.

Canadian Alliance on Multiculturalism

We affirm Canada as a society where people of different races and cultural backgrounds live and work together as Canadians, and we welcome the resulting cultural enrichment and enhanced economic prosperity. We will therefore uphold the freedom of individuals and families to nurture aspects of culture that are important to them. While cherishing our diversity, we believe that multiculturalism is a personal choice and should not be publicly funded.

Liberals on Seniors

All Canadians have the right to participate fully in our society.

And, as Canada's society ages, we must make the right decisions today for future generations.

We ensured that policies affecting seniors respect their rights to:
- dignity
- independence
- fairness
- participation
- security

We protected seniors' public pensions:
- by sheltering benefits from inflation;
- by maintaining the retirement age;
- by improving the way the government invests retirement funds, to generate greater revenues, and cut administrative costs.

We will support seniors and their families:
- by increasing tax credits for caregivers;
- by promoting active living;
- by making seniors feel safer in their communities;
- by creating a plan to increase appropriate housing for seniors.

We'll continue to ensure that federal policies protect seniors' dignity and independence.

We'll continue to work for a society in which seniors participate actively, and which treats seniors fairly.

Canadian Alliance on Seniors

We value retirement security as a vital element of independence. We will honour obligations under current state-run programs to retired Canadians and those close to retirement, and will maintain support for low-income seniors. We will provide future retirees with a greater choice between a government-managed pension plan and mandatory personal plans. We will eliminate the foreign investment restriction for retirement investments and allow individuals greater opportunity to save for their own retirement, giving Canadians greater control over their own affairs.

Appendix A

Excerpt from Davies, Lorraine, Julie Ann McMullin, and William R. Avison (2001). *Social Policy, Gender Inequality and Poverty.* Ottawa: Status of Women Canada, 73–80.

The introduction of the Canada Health and Social Transfer (CHST) in 1995 resulted in sweeping changes to the administration and funding of social programs across Canada. These changes jeopardized income security by providing provinces with greater autonomy over spending decisions (thereby reducing national standards for social assistance) and by limiting the availability of funds. The consequences of these changes affect women's economic circumstances in ways that are distinct from those of men. The analyses presented above examined the predictors of low income among women using both quantitative and qualitative data at the national and community level. In combination, our results suggest that in order to reduce low income among women, social policy changes are needed that target individuals at various points in the life cycle, beginning in childhood. The underlying goal of these policy changes should be to make it easier for women to acquire the education and job training that would ensure their economic independence *regardless of their marital and parental status*. In outlining the policy implications of our findings, we address the following questions:

- How can children's needs be better met to ensure greater opportunities to become economically independent adults?
- How can the frequency of unplanned teenage pregnancies be reduced? And how can we ensure that young mothers continue with their schooling and/or acquire life and job skills?
- What changes need to be implemented to social assistance programs to improve economic security and economic independence?
- What do our results reveal about the importance of maternity benefits and employment insurance for the economic security of low income women?
- What other changes should be made to social policies to enhance the economic security of women?

These questions reflect the life course perspective of the study and we address them below in turn.

5.2 Childhood

Although our quantitative results do not reveal a significant relationship between early adversities and low income in adulthood, other research does find that exposure to adversities in childhood and adolescence increases the likelihood of single parenthood.

Given that economic disadvantages of single motherhood are widely documented both here and elsewhere, there is additional support for our qualitative findings that family background characteristics portend economic difficulties in adulthood. Specifically, our qualitative results suggest that parental absence is an adversity that makes it very difficult for children to acquire the social capital necessary to obtain life skills and human capital. Thus, within our community are children who, for example, witness and experience violence within their homes, and/or who have alcohol or drug dependent parents; in short, children whose parents for these or various other reasons are unwilling or unable to provide the time and effort necessary to build trusting relationships with their children.

Consequences for children include poor school performance, dropping out of school, running away from home, drug or alcohol dependency, and teenage pregnancy, each of which reduce educational attainment. And as our quantitative results underscore, lack of education increases the risk of low income. Thus, interventions that compensate for parental absence in childhood may significantly reduce economic insecurity in adulthood.

5.2.1 Recommendations

a. Increase the visibility of and access to organizations with a non- punitive mandate that will fill gaps left by parental absence (e.g., respite centres for families and/or Big Sisters, Big Brothers).
   - the creation of family respite care centres that would also serve as a sounding board for families experiencing economic and social stress, and would provide a place where parents could temporarily leave children, and obtain information about other available resources within their community to deal with their particular circumstances
   - organizations such as Big Sisters foster a mentoring relationship between adult and child, thereby providing important support that may be absent in her home

b. Incorporate education about family violence, sex education, birth control, drug and alcohol abuse within public and high school curriculums.
   - educators must be trained to break down resistance to discussing these topics and to encourage open communication among students and teachers
   - students must be made aware of agencies and community groups that can provide information and assistance to those who need it

c. Increase government funding to shelters and second stage housing for abused women and children and improve awareness of these options.
   - Ensure that women and children who experience violence have a place to go and assistance to start a new life

Contrary to the common view of families as private refuges, economic and social conditions affect family relationships, and, in particular, the well-being of children. Investing in children has long-term implications for the health of a community. Thus, as we recommend above, it is important for government to support communities so that they can assume greater responsibility for the health of their children.

5.3 Young Adulthood

When faced with pregnancy (regardless of whether or not it is accompanied by marriage) the typical response of women is to leave school. While this is risky at any age, it is particularly consequential for young women because they have accumulated fewer years of schooling by the time of their pregnancy. Yet, pregnancy outside of marriage or a cohabiting union is rarely planned. Nonetheless, young girls grow up believing that marriage and motherhood should take precedence over education and careers. Social programs that dismantle the relationship among motherhood, education, and low income promise to improve women's economic security.

The Ontario government has clearly recognized the economic benefits that young mothers would accrue if they stayed in school. In March of this year, the Community and Social Services Minister revealed the details of a new mandatory program, Learning, Earning, and Parenting (LEAP), whose goal is to encourage teen mothers to stay in school. It falls under OntarioWorks and makes enrollment in school mandatory for mothers between the ages of 16 and 17 in order to receive welfare, and provides for transportation costs and offers child care subsidies. An additional requirement is participation in parenting workshops. The program also provides opportunities to develop employment skills and/or transitions to education beyond high school. The government should be commended for its efforts to improve the education of young mothers. Based on the results of our qualitative study, however, we recommend the following changes to this program, and propose an additional intervention that would increase accessibility of education to mothers generally.

5.3.1 Recommendations

1. Inject flexibility into the program by not tying eligibility for General Welfare Assistance to participation in LEAP

Teen mothers will vary with respect to their readiness to combine schooling and parenting. There is evidence to suggest that teen mothers are selected into this status because of adverse family backgrounds. For those who had trouble managing school before they became pregnant, combining courses and a baby is unlikely to enhance human capital. Thus, LEAP delivery agents should be trained to evaluate the readiness of teen mothers to continue with their schooling, rather than enforce legislation that makes going to school a requirement of General Welfare Assistance.

2. Eliminate day care costs for all teen mothers rather than providing subsidies.
    *   make more fully subsidized daycare spots available
    *   provide additional funds to accommodate extra caregiving costs when children are sick, when schools are not operating etc. (i.e., professional development days, spring break)

Current LEAP childcare subsidies fall short of need and are problematic because any child care costs reduce the income available for food and shelter.

3. Provide on-site daycare facilities at all adult learning centres, colleges and universities

- provide services to parents of infants as well as toddlers and preschool children

This will increase accessibility of education by reducing time, cost and stress of taking children first to daycare before going to school, and provide greater contact between children and parents during the day. We view the above recommendations as changes that would eventually be encompassed within a national childcare system.

5.4 Adulthood

5.4.1 Social Assistance

As others have noted and predicted our qualitative data confirm that changes to Ontario General Welfare Assistance since the introduction of the CHST have undermined the economic security of women. Two examples are the cuts to rates and the repeal of the three-year cohabitation rule. As a consequence of the 21.6 percent reduction in welfare rates, many women in our study report moving to less adequate housing, an increase in food bank use, as well as greater personal debt. For example, Carrie (#15) was a single mother with a 5 year old and a 3 year old when her cheque was reduced because of the cuts to General Welfare Assistance. As she explains,

> When they took that $300 off me, it was just brutal, absolutely brutal. . . . I couldn't make ends meet. There was no way, I was not going to not have food in my kids mouths. So bills suffered a great deal. I got into financial trouble. I had bill collectors coming after me. I moved out of that apartment because I couldn't

afford it. It was a cheap place anyway but I had to move out of there.

The intense stress involved in trying to manage on an inadequate income reduces mothers' real and perceived control over their lives, contributing to a state of helplessness rather than empowerment.

Another example of how changes to Ontario General Welfare Assistance jeopardize women's economic security is the decision to revoke the three-year cohabitation rule. On the one hand, marriage or cohabitation is an obvious pathway off of social assistance. On the other hand, marriage or cohabitation guarantee neither safety nor economic security. Understandably, many women have serious reservations about entering into a marital or cohabiting relationship again. Furthermore, equitable distribution of financial resources does not characterize all relationships. In describing a live-in relationship with a man during the period when the three-year cohabitation rule was in place, Martha (#35) says, 'The thing that made me mad . . . was that he got a really good job and he didn't give me rent. Because he figured he was on the road a lot that he didn't need to give me rent. And I kept asking for money.' The relationship did not last beyond three years and her social assistance was not compromised. Having a period where one can ' try out' relationships and still continue to receive assistance gives women more control over their ability to find a stable, equitable long-term relationship.

5.4.1.1 Recommendations

1. The Federal government should reinstate an open-ended federal- provincial

cost-sharing arrangement like the Canada Assistance Plan and, in response, the Ontario government should revoke the changes it has made to General Welfare Assistance since 1995.

While this would be a start, our data underscore the importance of providing mothers on assistance with financial support that better reflects their expenses. Raising the standard of living for low income families would improve their health and well-being, reduce their stress, and therefore improve their ability to parent their children. In essence, governments need to recognize and value the work that mothers do; for example:

2. The Federal government should require that all low income families receive the Canada Child Tax Benefit and encourage provinces to allow those receiving social assistance benefits to keep the full amount.
3. The financial costs of post-secondary education should be reduced for mothers on social assistance by allowing them to receive student assistance in addition to their benefits.

This will ensure that the student loans cover only their educational costs and thus minimize their debt accumulation.

4. Childcare should be free to all parents receiving social assistance or those with comparable incomes.

This would enable women to better their lives by giving them the freedom to explore work and educational opportunities.

While decreasing financial constraints is critical, it must be accompanied by a social support system that recognizes and effectively confronts the disadvantages mothers face as they venture to improve their economic situation. Two problems with the current and previous social assistance systems is that first, they do not recognize the heterogeneity that exists among recipients, and mothers are no exception to this. Second, they do not understand that most women do not need incentives to be independent of assistance, they need opportunities. By emphasizing 'incentives' they grossly underestimate the barriers that exist between incentive and welfare independence and therefore maintain or even undermine the economic insecurity of women.

Many of the barriers facing mothers on social assistance are linked directly to their limited knowledge of available options and resources that would facilitate their entry into the labour force or educational system. Our qualitative results confirm previous research that finds 'information support . . . [to be] the type of support mothers are least likely to receive and with which they are least satisfied'. Limited knowledge of community supports and resources restrict women's ability to help themselves. For example, without up-to-date information, women who have been removed from the workforce for a significant period of time will be unaware of recent changes in the job search process; therefore, they will be less competitive in the job market. Additionally, women are often not aware of the opportunities for upgrading that are available to them. The ability of current social assistance case workers to help clients is limited because of their enormous caseloads and administrative duties. As such, they are unable to offer the individual support, disseminate information or provide the individualized assistance that would more effectively increase opportunities to become employment reliant.

5. Specialized workers are needed to give individualized help to women attempting to become self sufficient.

Communication among these workers, and then between workers and government officials, would convey information about programs that are not achieving their goals, would alert policy makers to program restrictions that limit accessibility and effectiveness, and would identify needs for other services that would enhance exit strategies and simultaneously improve economic security.

5.4.2 Employment Insurance and Maternity Benefits

It is revealing that only three of the women in this sample had ever received employment benefits, and in each instance receiving EI was followed by the receipt of social assistance. This reflects a national pattern whereby men are more likely than women to collect EI benefits, and points to the inapplicability and inaccessibility of EI for women. One of ways in which EI inadvertently excludes women is illustrated by a recent change to the policy that makes employees ineligible if they quit their jobs. This stipulation assumes that there is no valid reason for leaving one's employment. Yet, women in our sample described 'quitting' jobs because of sexual harassment and problems with

childcare— situations that reflect broader disadvantages of women in society.

Further, EI is virtually inaccessible to low income mothers. As a monitoring report for Human Resources Development Canada finds, women are disproportionately represented in non-standard jobs and as such often do not accumulate enough hours to qualify for benefits. Further, because EI benefits only replace 55 percent of earnings, they do not offer enough assistance to support a family.

5.4.2.1 Recommendations

1. Consideration should be given to the reasons for quitting a job making allowances for exceptional circumstances.
2. Low income employees should receive 100 per cent of their earnings in employment benefits.
3. Lower the number of hours one has to work in a year to qualify for benefits.
4. Make allowances for repeat users who have family care responsibilities, thereby increasing the value of unpaid labour.

All of the preceding points regarding EI apply to maternity benefits as well because curiously, this program is tied to Employment insurance. Consequently, only those mothers who are strongly attached to the labour market (excluding self-employed women) qualify for benefits. In addition to the above recommendations we argue that:

5. Maternity benefits should be replaced by parental benefits and should be available to everyone, regardless of their labour

force attachment. This would require disassociating maternity and paternity benefits from the EI system.

This would compensate women for the economic costs of child-bearing while encouraging a more equitable division of labour among couples. This would also reduce the barriers that prevent men from taking an employment leave to care for their infants, ultimately increasing gender equality and the value of unpaid work.

5.5 General Recommendations

In addition to the recommendations made above, we have also addressed divorce laws, and policies related to workplace flexibility that would further benefit women's economic security. The data from our study lead us to conclude that a concerted effort must be made on various fronts to make women economically independent. All of our suggested changes reflect this view. However, if we had to identify the change that is most necessary, it would be the implementation of a universal childcare system.

There has been a great deal of political rhetoric over the issue of providing stay-at-home mothers with tax relief. This is simply not an issue for low income mothers and such tax-relief would not have an impact on their lives. Further, this proposal is problematic for middle-class women because of the individual nature of the tax filing system. Tax credits would more directly benefit fathers because it is they who have the tax-

able earnings. Regardless of social class, married mothers who are not economically independent are at risk for low income if their marriages end. Consequently, any policies aimed at implementing tax credits should be critically reviewed.

More important, in our view, is the necessity for a universal child care system. In addition to the child care system recommendations we have made earlier, we suggest the following:

1. After parental leave, quality child care should be available and affordable to all parents.
2. Transportation of children should be provided by child care centres.
3. Workplaces and educational institutions should receive incentives to implement on-site child care centres.
4. Recognize and support a diversity of child care arrangements to provide parents with as much choice and flexibility as possible concerning their children's needs.

In closing, Canadians should be not underestimate the negative consequences of reducing social spending in favour of tax cuts. By undermining the economic security of women, these cuts put all families at risk of experiencing social, economic, mental and physical health hardships. The effects of these hardships on children are particularly worrisome because they will resonate throughout their lives, impairing their potential to be productive citizens of Canadian society.

References

Abbate, Gay (2002). 'Battered women have help just a phone call away'. The *Globe and Mail*, 24 April.

Abercrombie, Nicholas, Stephen Hill, and Bryan S. Turner (2000). *The Penguin Dictionary of Sociology*. 4th edn. London: Penguin.

Abu-Laban, Yasmeen (1998). 'Keeping 'em out: Gender, race, and class biases in Canadian immigration policy'. In Veronica Strong-Boag, Sherrill Grace, Avigail Eisenberg, and Joan Anderson (eds), *Painting the Maple: Essays on Race, Gender, and the Construction of Canada*. Vancouver: UBC Press.

Acker, Joan (1988). 'Class, gender and the relations of distribution'. *Signs 13*, 473–97.

———— (1989). 'The Problem with Patriarchy'. *Sociology 23*, 2: 235–40.

———— (2000). 'Rewriting class, race, and gender: Problems in feminist rethinking'. Chapter 2 in Myra Marx Ferree, Judith Lorber, and Beth Hess (eds), *Revisioning Gender*. New York: Altamira Press.

Adair, Vivyan C. (2001). 'Branded with infamy: Inscriptions of poverty and class in the United States'. *Signs 27*(2): 451–71.

Adams, T. L. (2000). *A Dentist and a Gentleman: Gender and the Rise of Dentistry in Ontario*. Toronto: University of Toronto Press.

————, and K. McQuillan (2000). 'New jobs, new workers? Organizations, restructuring, and management hiring decisions'. *Relations Industrielles/Industrial Relations 55*(3): 39–412.

Adler, Nancy E., Thomas Boyce, Margaret A. Chesney, Sheldon Cohen, Susan Folkman, Robert L. Kahn, and S. Leonard Syme (1994). 'Socioeconomic status and health: The challenge of the gradient'. *American Psychologist 49*(1): 15–24.

Aguiar, L. (2001). 'Race, privilege, and challenges', in Carl E. James and Adrienne Shadd (eds), *Talking about Identity*. Toronto: Between the Lines, 187–9.

Ahmad, Waqar I.U., and Reg Walker (1997). 'Asian older people: Housing, health and access to services'. *Ageing and Society 17*: 141–65.

Ali, Jennifer, and Edward Grabb (1998). 'Ethnic origin, class origin and educational attainment in Canada: Further evidence on the mosaic thesis'. *Journal of Canadian Studies 33*(1): 3–21.

Allahar, Anton (1995). *Sociology and the Periphery: Theories and Issues*. 2nd edn. Toronto: Garamond Press.

———— (1998). 'Race and racism: Strategies of resistance'. Chapter 15 in Vic Satzewich (ed.), *Racism, and Social Inequality in Canada: Concepts, Controversies, and Strategies of Resistance*. Toronto: Thompson Educational.

————, and James E. Côté (1994). *Generation on Hold: Coming of Age in the Late Twentieth Century*. Toronto: Stoddart.

————, and James E. Côté (1998). *Richer and Poorer: Social Inequality in Canada*. Toronto: Lorimer.

Anand, Sonia S., Salim Yusuf, Ruby Jacobs, A. Darlene Davis, Quilong Yi, Hertzel Gerstein, Patricia A. Montague, and Eva Lonn (2001). 'Risk factors, atherosclerosis, and cardiovascular disease among aboriginal people in Canada: The Study of Health Assessment and Risk Evaluation in Aboriginal Peoples (SHARE-AP)'. *The Lancet 358*: 1147–53.

Andersen, Margaret (1988). *Thinking about Women: Sociological Perspectives on Sex and Gender.* 2nd edn. New York: Macmillan.

Anderson, Alan (1992). 'Policing native people: native militancy and Canadian militarianism'. Chapter 19 in Vic Satzewich (ed.), *Deconstructing a Nation: Immigration, Multiculturalism and Racism in '90s Canada.* Halifax: Fernwood and Saskatoon: Social Research Unit, Department of Sociology, University of Saskatchewan.

Anderson, Norman B., and Cheryl A. Armstead (1995). 'Toward understanding the association of socioeconomic status and health: A new challenge for the biopsychosocial approach'. *Psychosomatic Medicine 57*: 213–25.

Aneshensel, Carol S., and Clea A. Sucoff (1996). 'The neighbourhood context of adolescent mental health'. *Journal of Health and Social Behavior 37*(4): 293–310.

Angus Reid Group (1991). *Multiculturalism and Canadians: Attitude Study 1991: National Survey Report.* Submitted to Multiculturalism and Citizenship Canada.

Anthias, Floya (1992). 'Connecting "race" and ethnic phenomena'. *Sociology 26*(3): 421–38.

Arab, Paula, (1999). 'Open doors for minorities, education ministers urge Aboriginal students "grossly underrepresented" in postsecondary institutions'. The *Globe and Mail,* 4 March.

Aragones, N., M. Pollan, and P. Gustavsson (2002). 'Stomach cancer and occupation in Sweden: 1971–89'. *Occupational, and Environmental Medicine 59*(5): 329–37.

Arat-Koc, Sedef (1995). 'The politics of family and immigration in the subordination of domestic workers in Canada'. In E.D. Nelson and B.W. Robinson (eds), *Gender in the 1990s: Images, Realities and Issues.* Toronto: Nelson.

———— (1997). 'Immigration policies, migrant domestic workers, and the definition of citizenship in Canada', in Veronica Strong-Boag, and Anita Clair Fellman (eds), *Rethinking Canada: The Promise of Women's History,* 3rd edn. Toronto: Oxford University Press, 224–36.

———— (2001). 'The politics of family and immigration in the subordination of domestic workers in Canada'. Chapter 23 in Bonnie J. Fox (ed.), *Family Patterns, Gender Relations.* Toronto: Oxford University Press, 401–19.

Arber, Sara, and Helen Cooper (1999). 'Gender differences in health in later life: The new paradox?' *Social Science and Medicine 48*(1): 61–76.

Archer, Margaret (1995). *Realist Social Theory: The Morphogenetic Approach.* Cambridge: Cambridge University Press.

———— (2000). *Being Human: The Problem of Agency.* Cambridge: Cambridge University Press.

Armstrong, Pat (1997). 'The state and pay equity: Juggling similarity and difference, meaning, and structures'. Chapter 10 in Patricia M. Evans and Gerda R. Wekerle (eds), *Women and the Canadian Welfare State: Challenges and Change.* Toronto: University of Toronto Press.

————, and M. Patricia Connelly (1999). 'Introduction: Feminism, political economy and the state: Contested terrain'. Chapter 1 in Pat Armstrong and M. Patricia Connelly (eds), *Feminism, Political Economy and the State: Contested Terrain.* Toronto: Canadian Scholars Press.

————, H. Armstrong, J. Choiniere, G. Feldberg, and J. White (1994). *Take Care: Warning Signals for Canada's Health System.* Toronto: Garamond Press.

Armstrong, Robin (1999). 'Mapping the conditions of First Nations communities'. *Canadian Social Trends,* Winter: 14–18.

Aronson, Jane (1992). 'Women's sense of responsibility for the care of old people: But who else is going to do it?' *Gender and Society 6*: 8–29.

Aronson, J., C. Thornewell, and K. Williams (1995). 'Wife assault in old age: Coming out of obscurity'. *Canadian Journal on Aging 14* (supplement 2): 72–88.

Askam, Janet (1995). 'The married lives of older people', in Sara Arber and Jay Ginn (eds),

Connecting Gender and Ageing: A Sociological Approach. Buckingham, UK: Open University Press, 86–97.

Avison, William R. (1995). 'Roles and resources: The effects of family structure and employment on women's psychosocial resources and psychological distress'. *Research in Community and Mental Health* 8: 233–56.

———, and Ian H. Gotlib (1994). 'Introduction and overview'. Chapter 1 in William R. Avison and Ian H. Gotlib (eds), *Stress and Mental Health: Contemporary Issues and Prospects for the Future*. New York: Plenum Press.

———, and Donna McAlpine (1992). 'Gender differences in symptoms of depression in adolescents'. *Journal of Health and Social Behavior* 33(2): 77–96.

———, Terrance J. Wade, and Cathy F. Thorpe. (1996). 'Families' experiences of unemployment: Mental health consequences for husbands and wives'. Paper presented at the American Sociological Association, New York.

Bacigalupo, Mardy (2003).'How did your school do?: Overall tests results show improvement for city'. *The Londoner*, 30 January.

Baldus, Bernhard, and Meenaz Kassam (1996). ' "Make me truthful, good and mild": Values in nineteenth-century Ontario schoolbooks'. *Canadian Journal of Sociology* 21(3): 327–57.

Ballantyne, Peri J. (1999). 'The social determinants of health: A contribution to the analysis of gender differences in health and illness'. *Scandinavian Journal of Public Health* 27: 290–5.

Barndt, Deborah (2002). 'Fruits of injustice: Women in the post–NAFTA food system'. *Canadian Woman Studies* 21/22 (4/1): 82–8.

Barnes, Barry (2000). *Understanding Agency: Social Theory and Responsible Action*. London: Sage.

Basran, Gurcharn S., and Li Zong (1998). 'Devaluation of foreign credentials as perceived by visible minority professional immigrants'. *Canadian Ethnic Studies* 30(3): 6–23.

Batt, Sharon (1998). ' "Perfect people": Cancer charities' in *Patient No More: The Politics of Breast Cancer*. Toronto: Canadian Scholars Press.

Beagan, Brenda L. (2000). 'Neutralizing differences: Producing neutral doctors for (almost) neutral patients'. *Social Science and Medicine* 51(8): 1253–65.

Beaujot, Roderic (2000). *Earning and Caring in Canadian Families*. Toronto: Broadview Press.

———, and Don Kerr (2003a). 'Socio-cultural and socio-economic composition'. Chapter 10 in *Population Change in Canada*. Toronto: Oxford University Press.

——— (2003b). 'The demography of the Aboriginal population of Canada'. Chapter 11 in *Population Change in Canada*. Toronto: Oxford University Press.

Bedard, Gabriel (2000). 'Desconstructing whiteness: Pedagogical implications for anti-racism education'. In G.J.S. Dei, and A. Calliste (eds), *Power, Knowledge, and Anti-racism education*. Halifax: Fernwood.

Bell, Daniel (1973). *The Coming of Post-industrial Society*. New York: Basic Books.

Bengtson, V.L., T.M. Parrott, and E.O. Burgess. (1994). 'The third generation of theories in social gerontology'. Paper presented at the Annual Scientific Meeting of the Gerontological Society of America, 18–22 November, Atlanta.

Benoit, Cecilia, and Dena Carroll (2001). 'Marginalized voices from Vancouver's downtown eastside: Aboriginal women speak about their health care experiences'. Centres of Excellence for Women's Health Research Bulletin 1(2): 6–7.

Berger, P.L., and T. Luckmann (1967). *The Social Construction of Reality*. New York: Doubleday.

Bernhard, Judith K., and Marlinda Freire (1999). 'What is my child learning at elementary school? Culturally contested issues between teachers and Latin American families'. *Canadian Ethnic Studies* 31(3): 72–94.

Betcherman, Gordon, and Norman Leckie (1995). 'Age structure of employment in industries and occupations'. Ottawa: Applied Research Branch, Human Resources Development Canada (R- 96–7E).

Bird, Chloe E. (1999). 'Gender, household labor and psychological distress: The impact of the amount and division of housework'. *Journal of Health and Social Behavior* 40(1): 32–45.

Black, S.M., and C.E. Hill (1984). 'The psychological well-being of women in their middle years'. *Psychology of Women Quarterly* 8: 282–91.

Blackwell, Judith (1998). 'Making the grade against the odds: Women as university undergraduates'. In J. Stalker and S. Prentice (eds), *Illusion of Inclusion: Women in Post-secondary Education*. Halifax: Fernwood.

Bohatyretz, Sandra, and Garth Lipps (1999). 'Diversity in the classroom: Characteristics of elementary students receiving special education'. *Education Quarterly Review* 6(2): 7–19. Statistics Canada catalogue 81-003.

Bolaria, B. Singh, and Peter Li (1988). 'Capitalist expansion and immigrant labour: Chinese in Canada'. Chapter 5 in B. Singh Bolaria and Peter S. Li (eds), *Racial Oppression in Canada*, 2nd edn. Toronto: Garamond Press.

Bonilla-Silva, Eduardo (1997). 'Rethinking racism: Toward a structural interpretation'. *American Sociological Review* 62 (June): 465–80.

——— (1999). 'The essential social fact of race'. *American Sociological Review* 64: 899–906.

Borrows, John (2001). 'Domesticating doctrines: Aboriginal peoples after the Royal Commission'. *McGill Law Journal* 46: 615–61.

Bourdieu, Pierre (1977). *Outline of a Theory of Practice*. Cambridge: Cambridge University Press.

——— (1998). *Practical Reason: On the Theory of Action*. Stanford: Stanford University Press.

Bowlby, Jeffrey W., and Kathryn McMullen (2002). *At a Crossroads: First Results for the 18 to 20 year old cohort of the Youth in Transition Survey*. Ottawa: Human Resources and Development Canada. Catalogue RH64-12/2002E.

Boyd, Chris, Jina Y. Zhang-Salomons, Patti A. Groome, and William J. Mackillop (1999). 'Associations between community income and cancer survival in Ontario, Canada, and the United States'. *Journal of Clinical Oncology* 17(7): 2244–55.

Boyko, John (1995). *Last Steps to Freedom: The Evolution of Canadian Racism*. Winnipeg: Watson and Dwyer.

Braverman, H. (1974). *Labor and Monopoly Capital: The Degradation of Work in the Twentieth Century*. New York: Monthly Review Press.

Broadbent, Ed (1999). 'Citizenship today: is there a crisis?' Chapter 1 in Dave Broad and Wayne Antony (eds), *Citizens or Consumers? Social Policy in a Market Society*. Halifax: Fernwood.

Brodie, Janine (1999). 'Neo-liberalism and the rise of the citizen as consumer'. Chapter 2 in Dave Broad and Wayne Antony (eds), *Citizens or Consumers? Social Policy in a Market Society*. Halifax: Fernwood.

Bruno-Jofre, Rosa, and Dick Henley (2000). 'Public schooling in English Canada: Addressing difference in the context of globalization'. *Canadian Ethnic Studies* 32(1): 38–54.

Burton, Clare (1985). *Subordination: Feminism and Social Theory*. Sydney: Allen and Unwin.

Butlin, George (2001). 'Bachelor's graduates who pursue further postsecondary education'. *Education Quarterly Review* 7(2): 22–42. Statistics Canada catalogue 81-003.

———, and Jillian Oderkirk (1997). 'Educational attainment: A key to autonomy and authority in the workplace'. *Education Quarterly Review* 4(1): 32–52. Statistics Canada catalogue 81-003.

Cain, Leonard (1964). 'Life course and social structure', in R.E.L. Faris (ed.), *Handbook to Modern Sociology*. Chicago: Rand McNally, 272–309.

Cairney, John (1999). 'Socio-economic status and self-rated health among older Canadians'. *Canadian Journal on Aging* 19(4): 456–77.

————, and Robert Arnold (1996). 'Social class, health and aging: Socioeconomic determinants of self-reported morbidity among the non-institutionalized elderly in Canada'. *Canadian Journal of Public Health* 87(3): 199–203.

Calasanti, Toni M. (1996). 'Incorporating diversity: Meaning, levels of research, and implications for theory'. *The Gerontologist* 36: 147–56.

————, and Kathleen E. Slevin (2001). *Gender, Social Inequalities, and Aging*. Walnut Creek, Calif.: Altamira Press.

Calliste, Agnes (1996). 'Race, gender and Canadian immigration policy: blacks from the Caribbean, 1900–1932', in Joy Parr and Mark Rosenfeld (eds), *Gender and History in Canada*. Toronto: Copp Clark, 70–87.

———— (2001). 'Black families in Canada: Exploring the interconnections of race, class, and gender'. Chapter 26 in Bonnie J. Fox (ed.), *Family Patterns, Gender Relations*. Toronto: Oxford University Press.

Camus, Tera (2002). 'They don't want us to know'. *The Halifax Herald*, 26 February.

Canadian Education Statistics Council (2001). 'Children and youth at risk: Symposium report'. *Pan-Canadian Education Research Agenda*. Ottawa: Statistics Canada and Human Resources Development Canada. Statistics Canada catalogue 81-589-XIE.

Canadian Policy Research Network (2002). *Access to Postsecondary Education in Canada: Facts and Gaps*. Ottawa: Sussex Circle Inc. <www.cprn.ca>.

Cancian, F.M., and S. Oliker (2000). *Caring and Gender*. Walnut Creek, Calif.: Altamira Press.

Carr, Paul R., and Thomas R. Klassen (1996). 'The role of racial minority teachers in anti-racist education'. *Canadian Ethnic Studies* 28(2): 126–38.

Casper, Lynne M., Sara S. McLanahan, and Irwin Garfinkel (1994). 'The gender-poverty gap: what we can learn from other countries'. *American Sociological Review* 59: 594–605.

Casper, Monica J. (1998). *The Making of the Unborn Patient: A Social Anatomy of Fetal Surgery*. New Brunswick, NJ: Rutgers University Press.

Cassell, Philip (ed) (1993). *The Giddens Reader*. Stanford: Standford University Press.

CESC see Canadian Education Statistics Council (2000).

Chafetz, Janet Saltzman (1990). *Gender Equity: An Integrated Theory of Stability and Change*. Newbury Park: Sage.

Charness, N., Dykstra, K., and Philips, C. (1995). *Luminance and legibility in the workplace*. Canadian Aging Research Network 5th Annual Colloquium. Toronto.

Chen, Jiajian, and Feng Hou (2002). 'Unmet needs for health care'. *Health Reports* 13(2): 23–33. Statistics Canada catalogue 82-003.

————, and Wayne Millar (2000). 'Are recent cohorts healthier than their predecessors?' *Health Reports* 11(4): 9–23. Statistics Canada catalogue 82-003.

————, Edward Ng, and Russell Wilkins (1996b). 'The health of Canada's immigrants in 1994–95. *Health Reports* 7(4): 33–45. Statistics Canada catalogue 82-003.

————, Russell Wilkins, and Edward Ng (1996a). 'Health expectancy by immigrant status, 1986 and 1991'. *Health Reports* 8(3): 29–37. Statistics Canada catalogue 82-003.

Chunn, D.E. 2000. '"Politicizing the personal:" Feminism, law, and public policy,' in Nancy Mandell and Ann Duffy (eds). *Canadian Families, Diversity, Conflict, and Change* 2nd edition. Toronto: Harcourt, Brace and Company Canada, 225–59.

Church, Elizabeth, 'Managing working life'. *The Globe and Mail*, 28 June 2000, B8.

Citizen and Immigration Canada (1999). *Citizen and Immigration Statistics, 1996*. Ottawa: Minister of Public Works and Government Services.

Clark, Warren (2000). '"Education" in 100 Years of . . .' *Canadian Social Trends* 58: 3–6. Statistics Canada catalogue 11-008.

———— (2001). '100 years of education'. *Education Quarterly Review* 7(3): 18–24. Statistics Canada catalogue 81-003.

Clement, W., and J. Myles (1994). *Relations of Ruling: Class and Gender in Postindustrial Societies*. Montreal: McGill-Queen's University Press.

CMEC see Statistics Canada and Council of Ministers of Education, Canada.

Codjoe, Henry M. (2001). 'Fighting a "public enemy" of Black academic achievement: The persistence of racism and the schooling experiences of Black students in Canada'. *Race, Ethnicity, and Education* 4: 343–75.

Collins, Patricia Hill (1990). *Black Feminist Thought: Knowledge, Consciousness, and the Politics of Empowerment*. Boston: Unwin Hyman.

Coltrane, Scott (2000). *Gender and Families*. Walnut Creek, CA: Altamira Press.

Comacchio, Cynthia (1993). *Nations Are Built of Babies: Saving Ontario's Mothers and Children, 1900–1940*. Montreal: McGill-Queen's University Press.

Comeau, Tammy Duerden, and Anton Allahar (2001). 'Forming Canada's ethnoracial identity: Psychiatry and the history of immigration practices'. *Identity: An International Journal of Theory and Research* 1(2): 143–60.

Conley, James (1999). 'Working-class formation in twentieth century Canada'. Chapter 3 in James E. Curtis, Edward G. Grabb, and Neil L. Guppy (eds), *Social Inequality in Canada: Patterns, Problems, and Policies*. Scarborough: Prentice Hall Allyn and Bacon Canada.

Connidis, Ingrid Arnet (1982). 'Women and retirement: The effect of multiple careers on retirement adjustment'. *Canadian Journal on Aging* 1(3, 4): 17–27.

——— (2001). *Family Ties and Aging*. Thousand Oaks: Sage.

———, and Julie Ann McMullin (1994). 'Social support in older age: assessing the impact of marital and parent status'. *Canadian Journal on Aging* 13(4): 510–27.

———, and Julie Ann McMullin (2002). 'Sociological ambivalence and family ties: A critical perspective'. *Journal of Marriage and Family* 64(3): 558–67.

Cooper, Helen (2002). 'Investigating socio-economic explanations for gender and ethnic inequalities in health'. *Social Science and Medicine* 54(5): 693–706.

Cott, Nancy F. (2001). 'Domesticity'. Chapter 9 in Bonnie J. Fox (ed.), *Family Patterns, Gender Relations*. Toronto: Oxford University Press.

Courtenay, Will H. (2000). 'Constructions of masculinity and their influence on men's well-being: A theory of gender and health'. *Social Science and Medicine* 50(10): 1385–401.

CPRN. *See* Canadian Policy Research Network

Craig, Gerald. (1968). *Upper Canada: The Formative years—1784-1841*. Toronto: McClelland and Stewart.

Creese, Gillian (1996). 'Gendering collective bargaining: from men's rights to women's issues'. *Canadian Review of Sociology and Anthropology* 33 (4): 437–56.

——— (1999). *Contracting masculinity: Gender, Class, and Race in a White-collar Union, 1944–1994*. Toronto: Oxford University Press.

Crimmins, Eileen M., and Yasuhiko Saito (2001). 'Trends in healthy life expectancy in the United States, 1970–1990: Gender, racial, and educational differences'. *Social Science and Medicine* 52(11): 1629–41.

Crompton, Susan (2000). '"Health" in 100 Years of . . .' *Canadian Social Trends,* Winter, 12–17. Statistics Canada catalogue 11-008.

Crouch, Simon, and Jonathan Sher (2003). 'International Truck workers OK package'. *The London Free Press*, 14 May.

Curtis, Bruce, D.W. Livingstone, and David Smaller (1992). *Stacking the Deck: The Streaming of Working-Class Kids in Ontario Schools*. Toronto: Our Schools/Our Selves Education Foundation.

Curtis, Sarah, and Kim Lawson (2000). 'Gender, ethnicity and self-reported health: The case of

African-Caribbean populations in London'. *Social Science and Medicine* 50(3): 365–85.

Dannefer, D. (1984). 'Adult development and social theory: A paradigmatic reappraisal'. *American Sociological Review* 49: 100–16.

———, and R.R. Sell, (1988). 'Age structure, the life course, and aged heterogeneity: Prospects for research and theory'. *Comprehensive Gerontology* B 2(1988): 1–10.

Das Gupta, Tania (1995). 'Families of native peoples, immigrants, and people of colour', in Nancy Mandell and Ann Duffy (eds), *Canadian Families: Diversity, Conflict and Change*. Toronto: Harcourt, Brace, 141–74.

——— (1996). *Racism and Paid Work*. Toronto: Garamond Press.

——— (2000). 'Families of native peoples, immigrants and people of colour', in Barbara A. Crow and Lise Gotell (eds), *Open Boundaries: A Canadian Women's Studies Reader*. Toronto: Prentice-Hall, 215–30.

——— (2002). 'Racism in nursing'. Chapter 5 in Merle Jacobs (ed.), *Is Anyone Listening? Women, Work, and Society*. Toronto: Women's Press.

Davies, Lorraine, and Donna D. McAlpine (1998). 'Gendered work and family relations: The impact of unemployment'. Paper presented at Restructuring Work and the Life Course: An International Symposium, Toronto, May 1998.

———, Julie Ann McMullin, and William R. Avison (2001). *Social Policy, Gender Inequality and Poverty*. Ottawa: Status of Women Canada.

Davies, Scott, and Neil Guppy (1997). 'Fields of study, college selectivity, and student inequalities'. *Social Forces* 73(4): 131–51.

———, Clayton Mosher, and Bill O'Grady (1996). 'Educating women: Gender inequalities among Canadian university graduates'. *Canadian Review of Sociology and Anthropology* 33(2): 127–43.

Davis, Kingsley, and Wilbert E. Moore. (1945). 'Some principles of stratification'. *American Sociological Review* 10: 242–9.

Dean, Kathryn (1992). 'Double burdens of work: The female work and health paradox'. *Health Promotion International* 7(1): 17–25.

Dei, George Sefa (1996). 'The intersections of race, class, and gender in the anti-racism discourse', in G.S. Dei, *Anti-racism Education: Theory and Practice*. Halifax: Fernwood, 55–74.

DeKeseredy, W.S., and M.D. Schwartz (1998). *Women Abuse on Campus: Results from the Canadian National Survey*. Thousand Oaks: Sage.

deRouche, Constance P. (2001). 'Workfare's cousin: exploring a labour-force enhancement experiment in Cape Breton'. *The Canadian Review of Sociology and Anthropology* 38(3): 309–35.

State: Challenges and Change. Toronto: University of Toronto Press.

Dekkers, Midas (2000). *The Way of All Flesh*, trans. Sherry Marx-Macdonald. New York: Farrar, Straus, and Giroux.

Denton F.T., and B.G. Spencer (1995). 'Demographic change and the cost of publicly funded health care'. *Canadian Journal on Aging* 14: 174–92.

Denton, Margaret, and Vivienne Walters (1999). 'Gender differences in structural and behavioural determinants of health: An analysis of the social production of health'. *Social Science and Medicine* 48(9): 1221–35.

Dinnerstein, Myra, and Rose Weitz (1998). Chapter 14 in Rose Weitz (ed.), *The Politics of Women's Bodies: Sexuality, Appearance, and Behavior*. New York: Oxford University Press.

Dowd, J. J. (1987). 'The reification of age: Age stratification and the passing of the autonomous subject'. *Journal of Aging Studies* 1: 317–35.

Dryburgh, H. (2000). 'Women and computer science: Alternative routes to computing careers'. Doctoral dissertation, McMaster University.

Dua, Enakshi (1999). 'Beyond diversity: Exploring the ways in which the discourse of race has shaped the institution of the nuclear family'. In E. Dua and A. Robertson (eds). *Scratching the*

Surface: Canadian, Anti-Racist, Feminist Thought. Toronto: Women's Press.

Dunlop, Sheryl, Peter C. Coyte, and Warren McIsaac (2000). 'Socio-economic status and the utilization of physican's services: results from the Canadian National Population Health Survey'. *Social Science and Medicine* 51(1): 123–33.

Dunn, James R., and Isabel Dyck (2000). 'Social determinants of health in Canada's immigrant population: Results from the National Population Health Survey'. *Social Science and Medicine* 51(11): 1573–93.

Easterlin, R.A. (1987). *Birth and Fortune: The Impact of Numbers on Personal Welfare*, 2nd edn. Chicago: University of Chicago Press.

Egan, Carolyn, and Linda Gardner (1999). 'Racism, women's health, and reproductive freedom'. In E. Dua and A. Robertson (eds), *Scratching the Surface: Canadian, Anti-racist, Feminist Thought*. Toronto: Women's Press.

Ehrenreich, B., and J. Ehrenreich (1979). 'The professional managerial class'. In P. Walker (ed.), *Between Labor and Capital*. Boston: South End.

Elder, G.H., Jr (1974). *Children of the Great Depression: Social Change in Life Experience.* Chicago: University of Chicago Press.

——— (1985). *Life Course Dynamics: Trajectories and Transitions, 1968–80*. Ithaca: Cornell University Press.

——— (1994). 'Time, human agency, and social change: Perspectives on the life course'. *Social Psychology Quarterly* 57: 4–15.

——— (1995). 'The life course paradigm: Historical, comparative, and developmental perspectives'. In P. Moen, G.H. Elder, Jr, and K. Luscher (eds), *Examining Lives and Context: Perspectives on the Ecology of Human Development*. Washington, DC: American Psychological Association Press.

———, and A.M. O'Rand (1995). 'Adult lives in a changing society', in K. Cook, G. Fine, and J.S. House (eds), *Sociological Perspectives on Social Psychology*. New York: Allyn and Bacon, 452–75.

———, and R.C. Rockwell (1976). 'Marital age in life patterns'. *Journal of Family History* 1, 34–53.

Elstad, Jon Ivar (1995). 'Employment status and women's health: Exploring the dynamics'. *Acta Sociologica* 38: 231–49.

Erwin, Lorna, and Paula Maurutto (1998). 'Beyond access: Considering gender deficits in science education. *Gender and Education* 10(1): 51–69.

Essed, Philomena (1991). *Understanding Everyday Racism: An Interdisciplinary Theory*. Newbury Park: Sage.

Estes, C.L. (1979). *The Aging Enterprise*. San Francisco: Jossey-Bass.

——— (1991). 'The new political economy of aging: introduction and critique'. Chapter 2 in M. Minkler and C. Estes (eds), *Critical Perspectives on Aging: The Political and Moral Economy of Growing Old*. Amityville, NY: Baywood.

——— (1999). 'The new political economy of aging: introduction and critique'. Chapter 1 in M. Minkler and C. Estes (eds), *Critical Gerontology*. Amityville, NY: Baywood .

———, K.W. Linkins, and E.A. Binney (1996). 'The political economy of aging'. Chapter 18 in R.H. Binstock and L.K. George (eds), *Handbook of Aging and the Social Sciences,* 4th edn. San Diego: Academic Press.

———, J.H. Swan, and L.E. Gerard. (1982). 'Dominant and competing paradigms in gerontology: Towards a political economy of ageing. *Aging and Society* 12, 151–64.

Evans, Patricia M. (1997). 'Divided citizenship? Gender, income security, and the welfare state'. Chapter 4 in Patricia M. Evans and Gerda R. Wekerle (eds), *Women and the Canadian Welfare State: Challenges and Change*. Toronto: University of Toronto Press.

Fallo-Mitchell, L., and C.D. Ryff (1982). 'Preferred timing of female life events: Cohort differences. *Research on Aging 4*, 249–67.

Fast, Janet, J. Frederick, N. Zukewich, and S. Franke (2001). 'The time of our lives . . .'. *Canadian social trends,* Winter: 20–3.

Finch, Janet (1989). *Family Obligations and Social Change.* Cambridge, UK: Basil Blackwell.

Fincham, S.M., A.M. Ugnat, G.B. Hill, N. Krieger, and Y. Mao (2000). 'Is occupation a risk factor for thyroid cancer?' *Journal of Occupational and Environmental Medicine* 42(3): 318–22.

Findlay, Deborah A., and Leslie J. Miller (2002). 'Through medical eyes: The medicalization of women's bodies and women's lives'. In B. Singh Bolaria and H. Dickinson (eds), *Health, Illness, and Health Care in Canada.* Toronto: Nelson.

Finn, Anne, Shelley Trevethan, Gisele Carriere, and Melanie Kowalski (1999). 'Female inmates, Aboriginal inmates, and inmates serving life sentences: A one day snapshot'. *Juristat* 19(5) Statistics Canada, Canadian Centre for Justice Statistics. Catalogue 85-002.

Finnie, Ross (2000). 'Holding their own: Employment and earnings of postsecondary graduates'. *Education Quarterly Review* 7(1): 21–37. Statistics Canada catalogue 81-003.

——— (2001). '"Graduates" earnings and the job skills-education match'. *Education Quarterly Review* 7(2): 7–21. Statistics Canada catalogue 81-003.

——— (2002). 'Student loans: Borrowing and burden'. *Education Quarterly Review* 8(4): 28–42. Statistics Canada catalogue 81-003.

Firestone, Shulamith (1971). *The Dialectic of Sex.* New York: Bantam Books.

Foner, A. (1974). 'Age stratification and age conflict in political life'. *American Sociological Review* 39, 187–96.

——— (1986). *Aging and Old Age: New Perspectives.* Englewood Cliffs, NJ: Prentice-Hall.

———, and K. Schwab (1981). *Aging and Retirement.* Monterey, CA: Brooks/Cole.

Fox, B.J. (1988). 'Conceptualizing "patriarchy"'. *Canadian Review of Sociology and Anthropology* 25: 163–81.

——— (1989). 'The feminist challenge: A reconsideration of social inequality and economic development'. Chapter 5 in R.J. Brym and B.J. Fox (eds), *From Culture to Power: The Sociology of English Canada.* Toronto: Oxford University Press.

——— (1997). 'Reproducing difference: Changes in the lives of partners becoming parents', in Meg Luxton (ed.), *Feminism and Families: Critical Policies and Changing Practices.* Halifax: Fernwood, 142–61.

——— (2001). 'The formative years: How parenthood creates gender'. *Canadian Review of Sociology and Anthropology* 38(4): 373–90.

Fox, Bonnie and Meg Luxton (2001). 'Conceptualizing family'. Chapter 3 in Bonnie Fox (ed.), *Family Patterns, Gender Relations*, 2nd edn. Toronto: Oxford University Press.

Frank, Jeffrey (1996). *After High School: The First Years.* First report of the School Leavers Follow-up Survey, 1995. Ottawa: Human Resources Development Canada and Statistics Canada.

Frenette, Marc (2000). 'Overqualified? Recent graduates and the needs of their employers'. *Education Quarterly Review* 7(1): 6–20. Statistics Canada catalogue 81-003.

Frideres, James S. (1988). 'Institutional structures and economic deprivation: Native people in Canada'. Chapter 4 in B. Singh Bolaria and Peter S. Li (eds), *Racial Oppression in Canada,* 2nd edn. Toronto: Garamond Press.

Fry, C.L. (1976). 'The ages of adulthood: A question of numbers'. *Journal of Gerontology* 3, 199–217.

——— (1980). 'Cultural dimensions of age: A multidimensional scaling analysis'. In C.L. Fry (ed.), *Aging in Culture and Society.* New York: Praeger.

——— (1985). 'Culture, behavior, and aging in the comparative in perspective'. In V.E. Birren and V.W. Schaie (eds), *Handbook on the Psychology of Aging.* New York: Van Nostrand Reinhold.

——— (1986). 'Emics and age: Age differentiation and cognitive anthropological strategies'. Pp. 105–130 in C.L Fry and J. Keith (eds), *New*

Methods for Old Age Research. South Hadley, MA: Bergin and Garvey.

Frye, Marilyn (1983). *The Politics of Reality: Essays in Feminist Theory*. Freedom, Calif.: Crossing Press.

Gardiner-Barber, Pauline T. (2003). 'The "culture of making do": Gender, work, and family in Cape Breton working class life'. In M. Lynn (ed.), *Voices: Essays on Canadian Families*, 2nd edn. Scarborough: Thomson Nelson.

Gazso-Windle, Amber, and Julie McMullin (2003). 'Doing domestic labour: Strategising in a gendered domain'. *Canadian Journal of Sociology* 28(3): 341–66.

Gee, Ellen (2000a). 'Voodoo demography, population aging, and social policy'. In Ellen Gee and G.M Gutman (eds), *The Overselling of Population Aging: Apocalyptic Demography, Intergenerational Challenges, and Social Policy*. Toronto: Oxford University Press.

Gee, Ellen (2000b). 'Contemporary diversities'. Chapter 3 in Nancy Mandell and Ann Duffy (eds), *Canadian Families: Diversity, Conflict, and Change*, 2nd edn. Toronto: Harcourt Brace.

Geiger, H. Jack (2001). 'Racial stereotyping and medicine: The need for cultural competence'. *Canadian Medical Association* 164(12): 1699–704.

Gerson, Judith M., and Kathy Peiss (1985). 'Boundaries, negotiation, consciousness: reconceptualizing gender relations'. *Social Problems* 32(4): 317–31.

Geschwender, James A., and Neil Guppy (1995). 'Ethnicity, educational attainment, and earned income among Canadian-born men and women'. *Canadian Ethnic Studies* 27(1): 67–83.

Giddens, Anthony (1971). *Capitalism and Modern Social Theory: An Analysis of the Writings of Marx, Durkheim, and Max Weber*. Cambridge, UK: Cambridge University Press.

——— (1979). *Central Problems in Social Theory*. London: Macmillan.

——— (1984). *The Constitution of Society: Outline of the Theory of Structuration*. Berkeley: University of California Press.

——— (1993). *New Rules of Sociological Method: A Positive Critique of Interpretative Sociologies*, 2nd edn. Stanford Stanford University Press.

——— (2002). *Runaway world: How globalisation is reshaping our lives*. London: Profile Books.

———, and Christopher Pierson (1998). 'Interview Three: Structuration Theory'. In *Conversations with Anthony Giddens*. Cambridge, UK: Polity Press.

Gillis, Kelly J., and John P. Hirdes (1996). 'The quality of life implications of health practices among older adults: evidence from the 1991 Canadian General Social Survey'. *Canadian Journal on Aging* 15(2): 299–314.

Ginn, Jay, and Sara Arber (2001). 'Pension prospects of minority ethnic groups: inequalities by gender and ethnicity'. *British Journal of Sociology* 52(3): 519–39.

Glazier, Richard H., Elizabeth M. Badley, Julie E. Gilbert, and Lorne Rothman (2000). 'The nature of increased hospital use in poor neighbourhoods: findings from a Canadian inner city'. *Canadian Journal of Public Health* 91(4): 268–73.

Glenn, Evelyn Nakano (1992). 'From servitude to service work: historical continuities in the racial division of paid reproductive labour'. *Signs* 18(1): 1–43.

——— (2000). 'The social construction and institutionalization of gender and race: An integrative framework', in Myra Marx Feree, Judith Lorber, and Beth B. Hess (eds), *Revisioning Gender*. New York: Altamira Press, 3–43.

The Globe and Mail (2001). 'The Unfinished Business of the Chinese Head Tax'. Editorial. 13 July.

Goffman, Erving (1983). 'The interaction order'. *American Sociological Review* 48, Feb.: 1–17.

Goodman, Marcene (1996). 'Culture, cohort, and cosmetic surgery'. *Journal of Women and Aging* 8(2): 55–73.

Gorey, Kevin M., Eric J. Holowaty, Gordon Fehringer, Ethan Laukkanen, Nancy L. Richter, and Cynthia M. Meyer (2000). 'An international comparison of cancer survival: Relatively poor areas of Toronto, Ontario and three US metropolitan areas'. *Journal of Public Health Medicine* 22(3): 343–9.

Gough, Orla (2001). 'The impact of the gender pay gap on post-retirement earnings'. *Critical Social Policy* 21(3): 311–34.

Gower, Dave (1998). 'Income transition upon retirement'. *Perspectives on Labour and Income* 10:4: 18–23. Statistics Canada catalogue 75-001-XPE.

Grabb, Edward (2002). *Theories of Social Inequality,* 4th edn. Toronto: Harcourt Canada.

Graham, Kathryn, Virginia Carver, and Pamela J. Brett (1995). 'Alcohol and drug use by older women: Results of a national survey'. *Canadian Journal on Aging* 14(4): 769–91.

Gramsci, Antonio (1971). *Selections from the Prison Notebooks.* Quintin Hoare and Geoffrey Nowell Smith (eds and trans). New York: International.

Greaves, L., Hankivsky, O., and Kingston-Riechers, J. (1995). *Selected Estimates of the Costs of Violence Against Women.* London, ON: Centre for Research on Violence Against Women and Children.

Green, Carla A., and Clyde R. Pope (1999). 'Gender, psychosocial factors and the use of medical services: A longitudinal analysis'. *Social Science and Medicine* 48(10): 1363–72.

Greschner, Donna (1990). 'Abortion and democracy for women: A critique of Tremblay v. Daigle'. *McGill Law Journal* 35: 633–69.

———— (1998). 'Pregnant with meaning: Discourse, democracy, and the Daigle decision'. Chapter 8 in Les Samuelson and Wayne Antony (eds), *Power and Resistance: Critical Thinking about Canadian Social Issues,* 2nd edn. Halifax: Fernwood.

Grimes, Michael, D. (1991). *Class in Twentieth-Century American Sociology: An Analysis of Theories and Measurement Strategies.* New York: Praeger.

Guernsey, Judith Read, Ron Dewar, Swarna Weerasinghe, Susan Kirkland, and Paul J. Veugelers (2000). 'Incidence of cancer in Sydney and Cape Breton County, Nova Scotia 1979–1997'. *Canadian Journal of Public Health* 91(4): 285–92.

Guillemard, A. (1982). 'Old age, retirement, and the social class structure: Toward an analysis of the structural dynamics of the later stage of life'. In T.K. Hareven and K. Adams (eds), *Aging and the Life Course Transition: An Interdisciplinary Perspective.* New York: Guildford Press.

———— (1983). 'The making of old age policy in France'. In A.M. Guillemard (ed.), *Old Age and the Welfare State,* Beverly Hills: Sage.

Guppy, Neil, and Scott Davies (1998). *Education in Canada: Recent Trends and Future Challenges.* Ottawa: Statistics Canada, Catalogue 96-321.

Gyimah, Stephen Obeng, Jerry White, and Paul Maxim (2003). 'Income and first nations elderly: policies for a better future'. Unpublished manuscript.

Habermas, Jürgen (1984). *The Theory of Communicative Action,* vol. 1. Boston: Beacon Press.

———— (1987). *The Theory of Communicative Action,* vol. 2, *Lifeworld and System: A Functionalist Critique.* Cambridge, UK: Polity Press.

Hagestad, G. (1990). 'Social perspectives on the life course', in R.H. Binstock and L. K. George (eds), *Handbook of Aging and the Social Sciences,* 3rd edn. Toronto: Harcourt Brace Jovanovich, 151–68.

————, and B. Neugarten (1985). 'Age and the life course', in E. Shanas and R. Binstock (eds), *Handbook of Aging and the Social Sciences,* 2nd edn. New York: Van Nostrand-Reinhold, 36–61.

Hall, N.E., and K.D. Rosenman (1991). 'Cancer by industry: Analysis of a population-based cancer registry with an emphasis on blue-collar workers'. *American Journal of Industrial Medicine* 19(2): 145–59.

Hardy, Melissa, and Lawrence E. Hazelrigg (1995). 'Gender, race/ethnicity, and poverty in later life'. *Journal of Aging Studies* 9(1): 43–63.

Hart, Carole L., George Davey Smith, and David Blane (1998). 'Social mobility and 21 year mortality in a cohort of Scottish men'. *Social Science and Medicine* 47(8): 1121–30.

Hartmann, H. (1981). 'The unhappy marriage of Marxism and feminism: Towards a more progressive union'. In L. Sargent (ed.), *The Unhappy Marriage of Marxism and Feminism: A Debate on Class and Patriarchy*. London: Pluto Press.

Hill, Dana, Carol Davis, and Leann M. Tigges (1995). 'Gendering welfare state theory: a cross-national study of women's public pension quality' *Gender and Society* 9(1): 99–119.

Hochschild, Arlie (1989). *The Second Shift: Working Parents and the Revolution at Home*. New York: Viking.

——— (1997). *The Time Bind: When Work Becomes Home and Home Becomes Work*. New York, NY: Metropolitan Books.

House, James S. (2001). 'Understanding social factors and inequalities in health: 20th century progress and 21st century prospects'. *Journal of Health and Social Behavior* 43(2): 125–42.

———, James M. Lepkowski, Ann M. Kinney, Richard P. Mero, Ronald C. Kessler, and A. Regula Herzog (1994). 'The social stratification of aging and health'. *Journal of Health and Social Behavior* 35(3): 213–34.

Hughes, Karen D. (1999). *Gender and Self-employment in Canada: Assessing Trends and Policy Implications*. CPRN Study No. W104. Changing Relationships Series. Ottawa: Renouf.

Humphries, Karin H., and Eddy van Doorslaer (2000). 'Income-related health inequality in Canada'. *Social Science and Medicine* 50(5): 663–71.

Hunt, Kate (2002). 'A generation apart? Gender-related experiences and health in women in early and late mid-life'. *Social Science and Medicine* 54(1): 663–76.

———, and Ellen Annandale (1999). 'Relocating gender and morbidity: Examining men's and women's health in contemporary Western societies'. Introduction to Special Issue on Gender and Health. *Social Science and Medicine* 48: 1–5.

Hunter, Alfred A. (1981). *Class Tells: On Social Inequality in Canada*. Toronto: Butterworths.

Immen, Wallace, and James Rusk. (2002). 'Toronto's tent city sealed off, squatters ejected'. The *Globe and Mail*, 25 September.

Inhorn, Marcia C., and K. Lisa Whittle (2001). 'Feminism meets the "new" epidemiologies: Toward an appraisal of antifeminist biases in epidemiological research on women's health'. *Social Science and Medicine* 53(5): 553–67.

Isajiw, Wsevolod W. (1999). *Understanding Diversity: Ethnicity and Race in the Canadian Context*. Toronto: Thompson Educational.

Jackson, Andrew (2002). *Is Work Working for Workers of Colour?* Research paper #18, Canadian Labour Congress. <www.clc-ctc.ca>.

Jackson, Chris (1996). 'Measuring and valuing: Households' unpaid work'. *Canadian Social Trends*, Autumn, 25–9. Statistics Canada catalogue 11-008.

Jaine, Linda (1993). *Residential Schools: The Stolen Years*. Saskatoon: University Extension Press.

Jakubowski, Lisa Marie (1997). *Immigration and the Legalization of Racism*. Halifax: Fernwood.

Jenson, Jane (1997). 'Fated to live in interesting times: Canada's changing citizenship regimes' *Canadian Journal of Political Science* 30(4): 627–44.

Jenson, Jane, and Martin Papillon (2000). 'Challenging the citizenship regime: The James Bay Cree and transnational action'. *Politics and Society* 28(2): 245–64.

Jette, Allan M., Sybil L. Crawford, and Sharon L. Tennstedt (1996). 'Toward understanding ethnic differences in late-life disability'. *Research on Aging* 18(3): 292–309.

Johnson, Fred W., Paul J. Gruenewald, Andrew J. Treno, and Gail Armstrong Taff (1998). 'Drinking over the life course within gender and ethnic groups: A hyperparametric analysis'. *Journal of Studies on Alcohol* 59: 568–80.

Johnson, Holly (1996). *Dangerous Domains: Violence against Women in Canada*. Toronto: Nelson.

————, and Tina Hotton (2001). *Spousal Violence. Family Violence in Canada: A Statistical Profile*. Statistics Canada catalogue 85-224. Ottawa: Statistics Canada.

————, and Vincent Sacco (1995). 'Researching violence against women: Statistics Canada's national survey'. *Canadian Journal of Criminology* 37(3): 281–304.

Johnson, Karen L., Donna Lero, and Jennifer Rooney (2001). *Work-life Compendium 2001: 150 Canadian Statistics on Work, Family, and Well-being*. Guelph: Centre for Families, Work, and Wellbeing and Human Resources Development Canada.

Julien, Ann-Marie, and Heidi Ertl (1999). 'Children's school experiences in the NLSCY, 1994–1995'. *Education Quarterly Review* 6(2): 20–34. Statistics Canada catalogue 81-003.

Kalbach, Madeline A., and Warren E. Kalbach (eds) (2000). *Perspectives on Ethnicity in Canada*. Toronto: Harcourt Canada.

Kamo, Y. (1988). 'Determinants of household division of labour'. *Journal of Family Issues 9*: 177–200.

Kapsalis, C., R. Morissette, and Garnett Picot (1999). *The Returns to Education, and the Increasing Wage Gap between Younger and Older Workers*. Statistics Canada catalogue 11F0019MPE No. 131. Ottawa: Statistics Canada.

Karlsen, Saffron, and James Y. Nazroo (2002). 'Relation between racial discrimination, social class, and health among ethnic minority groups'. *American Journal of Public Health* 92: 624–31.

Katz, S. (1996). *Disciplining Old Age: The Formation of Gerontological Knowledge*. Charlottesville: University Press of Virginia.

Katz, Stephen, and Barbara Marshall (2003). 'New sex for old: Lifestyle, consumerism, and the ethics of aging well'. *Journal of Aging Studies* 17(1): 3–16.

Kawachi, Ichiro, and Bruce P. Kennedy (1999). 'The relationship of income inequality to mortality'. Chapter 13 in Ichiro Kawachi, Bruce P. Kennedy, and Richard G. Wilkinson (eds), *The Society and Population Health Reader: Income Inequality and Health*. New York: New Press.

————, Bruce P. Kennedy, Vanita Gupta, and Deborah Prothrow-Stith (1999). 'Women's status and the health of women and men: A view from the States'. *Social Science and Medicine* 48(1): 21–32.

Kazemipur, Abdolmohammad, and Shiva S. Halli (2001). 'The changing colour of poverty in Canada'. *Canadian Sociological and Anthropological Review* 38(2): 217–38.

Kelly, Karen (2002). *Visible Minorities: A diverse Population*. Statistics Canada catalogue 1-008-XIE. <http://statcan.ca/english/ads/11-008-XIE/vismin.html>. Accessed December 2002.

Kessler, Ronald C., Cindy Foster, Pamela S. Webster, and James S. House (1992). 'The relationship between age and depressive symptoms in two national surveys'. *Psychology and Aging* 7(1): 119–26.

Kilkey, Majella, and Jonathan Bradshaw (1999). 'Lone mothers, economic well-being, and policies'. Chapter 5 in Diane Sainsbury (ed.), *Gender and Welfare State Regimes*. New York: Oxford University Press.

Kline, Marlee (1993). 'Complicating the ideology of motherhood: Child welfare law and First Nation women'. *Queen's Law Journal* 18: 310–19.

———— (2000). 'Complicating the ideology of motherhood: Child welfare law and First Nation women', in Barbara A. Crow and Lise Gotell (eds), *Open Boundaries: A Canadian Women's Studies Reader*. Toronto: Prentice-Hall, 194–204.

Knight, Claudette (1997). 'Black parents speak: Education in mid-nineteenth-century Canada West'. *Ontario History* 89(4): 269–84.

Knighton, Karen, and Sheba Mirza (2002). 'Postsecondary participation: The effects of parent education and income'. *Education Quarterly Review* 18(3): 25–32. Statistics Canada catalogue 81-003, June.

Knowles, Valerie (1992). *Strangers at Our Gates: Canadian Immigration and Immigration Policy, 1540–1990*. Toronto: Dundurn Press.

Koretz, Gene (2001). 'Why married men earn more'. *Business Week*, 17 September.

Kohli, M. (1988). Ageing as a challenge for sociological theory. *Ageing and Society* 8: 367–94.

Krahn, Harvey, J. and Graham S. Lowe (1998). *Work, Industry, and Canadian Society*, 3rd edn. Toronto: ITP Nelson.

————, and Graham S. Lowe (2002). *Work, Industry, and Canadian Society*, 4th edn. Toronto: ITP Nelson.

Krieger, Nancy, Charles Quesenberry, Tiffany Peng, Pamela Horn-Ross, Susan Stewart, Susan Brown, Karen Swallen, Tessie Guillermo, Dong Suh, Luz Alvarez Martinez, and Felicia Ward (1999). 'Social class, race/ethnicity, and incidence of breast, cervix, colon, lung, and prostate cancer among Asian, black, Hispanic, and white residents of the San Francisco Bay Area, 1988–92 (United States)'. *Cancer Causes and Control 10*: 525–37.

————, D.L. Rowley, A.A. Herman, and Avery B. Phillips (1993). 'Racism, sexism, and social class: Implications for studies of health, disease, and well-being'. *American Journal of Preventive Medicine* 9(6): 82–122.

————, and S. Sidney (1996). 'Racial discrimination and blood pressure. The CARDIA study of young black and white adults'. *American Journal of Public Health* 86:1370–8.

Krstev, S., D. Baris, P.A. Stewart, R.B. Hayes, A. Blair, and M. Dosemeci (1998). 'Risk for prostate cancer by occupation and industry: A 24-state death certificate study'. *American Journal of Industrial Medicine* 34(5): 413–20.

Krug, Etienne G., Linda L. Dahlberg, James A. Mercy, Anthony B. Zwi, and Rafel Lozano (eds), (2002). *World Report on Violence and Health*. Geneva: World Health Organization.

Laghi, B. (2003). 'Ottawa fears further bans on beef trade'. The *Globe and Mail*, 21 May.

Langlois, Stephanie, and Peter Morrison (2001). 'Suicide deaths and suicide attempts'. *Health Reports* 13(2): 9–21. Statistics Canada catalogue 11-008.

Langton, Nancy, and Jeffrey Pfeffer (1994). 'Paying the professor: Sources of salary variation in academic labor markets'. *American Sociological Review* 59: 236–56.

Laslett, B., and J. Brenner (1987). 'Gender and social reproduction: historical perspectives'. *Annual Review of Sociology* 15: 381–404.

Laurence, Margaret (1964). *The Stone Angel*. Toronto: McClelland and Stewart.

Layder, D. (1994). *Understanding Social Theory*. Thousand Oaks, CA: Sage.

Leach, Belinda, and Anthony Winson (1995). 'Bringing 'globalization' down to earth: restructuring and labour in rural communities'. *Canadian Review of Sociology and Anthropology.* 32: 341–64.

Leclere, Felicia B., Richard G. Rogers, and Kimberley D. Peters (1997). 'Ethnicity and mortality in the United States: individual and community correlates'. *Social Forces* 76(1): 169–98.

Lee, K., and P. Patel (2003). 'Far from the maddening cows: The global dimensions of BSE and vCJD' . Chapter 4 in K. Lee (ed.), *Health Impacts of Globalization: Towards Global Governance*. New York: Palgrave.

Leisering, Lutz, and Leibfried, Stephan (1999). *Time and Poverty in Western Welfare Studies*. Cambridge: Cambridge University Press.

Li, Peter S. (1988). *Ethnic Inequality in a Class Society*. Toronto: Wall and Thompson.

———— (1998). 'The Market Value and Social Value of Race' Chapter 5 in Vic Satzewich (ed.) *Racism and Social Inequality in Canada*. Toronto: Thompson Educational.

———— (2000). 'Earning disparities between immigrants and native-born Canadians'. *The Canadian Review of Sociology and Anthropology* 37(3): 289–311.

———— (2001a). 'Immigrants' propensity to self-employment: evidence from Canada'. *International Migration Review* 35(4): 1106–28.

———— (2001b). 'The market worth of immigrants' educational credentials'. *Canadian Public Policy* 27(1): 23–38.

Lian, Jason Z. and David Ralph Matthews (1998). 'Does the vertical mosaic still exist? Ethnicity and income in Canada, 1991. *Canadian Review of Sociology and Anthropology* 35(4), 461.

Link, Bruce G., Bruce P. Dohrenwend, and Andrew E. Skodol (1986). 'Socio-economic status and schizophrenia: Noisome occupational characteristics as a risk factor'. *American Sociological Review* 51: 242–58.

———, and Jo Phelan (2000). 'Evaluating the Fundamental Cause Explanation for Social Disparities in Health'. Chapter 3 in Chloe E. Bird, Peter Conrad, and Allen M. Fremont (eds), *Handbook of Medical Sociology,* 5th edn. New Jersey: Prentice-Hall Inc.

Lipps, Garth, and Jeffrey Frank (1997). 'The National Longitudinal Survey of Children and Youth, 1994–95: initial results from the school component'. *Education Quarterly Review* 4(2): 43–57. Statistics Canada catalogue 81-003-XPB.

Little, Don (1995). 'Earnings and labour force status of 1990 graduates'. *Education Quarterly Review* 2(3): 10–20. Statistics Canada catalogue 81-003.

Little, Margaret (1999). 'The Blurring of Boundaries: Private and public welfare for single mothers in Ontario'. Chapter 6 in Pat Armstrong and M. Patricia Connelly (eds), *Feminism, Political Economy and the State: Contested Terrain.* Toronto: Canadian Scholars Press.

Livingstone, David W. (2001). 'Public Education at the Crossroads: Confronting Underemployment in a Knowledge Society'. Chapter 5 in Dan Glenday and Ann Duffy (eds), *Canadian Society: Meeting the Challenges of the Twenty-First Century.* Oxford: Oxford University Press.

Looker, E. Diane, and Graham S. Lowe (2001). *Postsecondary Access and Student Financial Aid in Canada: Current Knowledge and Research Gaps.* Ottawa: CPRN <www.cprn.ca>.

Lorber, Judith (1994). *Paradoxes of Gender.* New Haven: Yale University Press.

——— (1997). *Gender and the Social Construction of Illness,* 2nd edn. Thousand Oaks, CA: Sage.

Lorber, Judith (2000) 'Believing is seeing: biology as ideology'. Chapter 1 in Maxime Baca Zinn, Pierrette Hondagneu-Sotelo, and Michael A. Messner (eds), *Through the prism of difference,* 2nd edn. Needham Heights, MA: Allyn and Bacon.

Lorde, Audre (1982). *Zami: A New Spelling of My Name.* Freedom, Calif.: Crossing Press.

Loveman, Mara (1999). 'Is "race" essential?' *American Sociological Review* 64: 891–8.

Lowe, Graham S. (2000). *The Quality of Work: A People-centred Agenda.* Toronto: Oxford University Press.

Lukes, S. (1974). *Power, A Radical View.* London: MacMillan.

Lundberg, Olle (1997). 'Childhood conditions, sense of coherence, social class and adult ill health: Exploring their theoretical and empirical relations'. *Social Science and Medicine* 44(6): 821–31.

Luxton, Meg (1980). *More than a Labour of Love: Three Generations of Women's Work in the Home.* Toronto: Women's Press.

———, and June Corman (2001). *Getting by in hard times: Gendered labour at home and on the job.* Toronto: University of Toronto Press.

Lynch, J.W., G.A. Kaplan, and J.T. Salonen (1997). 'Why do poor people behave poorly? Variation in adult health behaviours and psychosocial characteristics by stages of the socioeconomic lifecourse'. *Social Science and Medicine* 44(6): 809–19.

MacBride-King, J., and K. Bachmann (1999). *Is work-life balance still and issue for Canadians and their employers? You bet it is.* Ottawa: Conference Board of Canada.

Macintyre, Sally, Graeme Ford, and Kate Hunt (1999). 'Do women 'over-report' morbidity? Men's and women's responses to structured prompting on a standard question on long standing illness'. *Social Science and Medicine* 48(1): 89–98.

Mackey, Eva (1999). *The House of Difference: Cultural Politics and National Identity in Canada.* London: Routledge.

Mackie, Richard (2001). 'End to forced retirement urged'. The *Globe and Mail*, 18 May.

Mackillop, W.J., J. Zhang-Salomons, C.J. Boyd, and P.A. Groome (2000). 'Associations between community income and cancer incidence in Canada and the United States'. *Cancer* 89(4): 901–12.

MacKinnon, Mark (1999). 'Immigrants Face Underemployment in Toronto'. The *Globe and Mail*, 24 May.

MacMillan, Harriet L., Angus B. MacMillan, David R. Offord, and Jennifer L. Dingle (1996). 'Aboriginal health'. *Canadian Medical Association Journal* 155(11): 1569–78.

Maddox, G.L., and J. Wiley (1976). 'Scope, concepts and methods in the study of aging'. In R.H. Binstock and E. Shanas (eds), *Handbook of Aging and the Social Sciences*. New York: Van Nostrand Reinhold.

Maher, Timothy (1998). 'Environmental oppression: Who is targeted for toxic exposure?' *Journal of Black Studies* 28(3): 357–67.

Makin, Kirk (2002). 'Head-tax judge no stranger to controversy.' The *Globe and Mail*, 19 September.

Mannheim, K. ([1928] 1952). 'The problem of generations'. In P. Kecskemeti (ed.), *Essays on the Sociology of Knowledge*. London: Routledge and Kegan Paul.

Mao, Yang, Jinfu Hu, Anne-Marie Ugnat, Robert Semenciw, and Shirley Fincham (2001). 'Socioeconomic status and lung cancer risk in Canada'. *International Journal of Epidemiology* 30: 809–17.

Mao, Y., J. Hu, A.M. Ugnat, and K. White (2000). 'Non-Hodgkin's lymphoma and occupational exposure to chemicals in Canada'. *Annals of Oncology* 11 (Supplement 1): 69–73.

Margolis, Maxine (2001). 'Putting mothers on the pedestal'. Chapter 10 in Bonnie J. Fox (ed), *Family Patterns, Gender Relations*. Toronto: Oxford University Press.

Marinelli, Julie (2002). 'Youth custody and community services in Canada, 2000/01'. *Juristat*

22(8): 1–18. Statistics Canada catalogue 85-002-XIE.

Marmot, M.G., M. Kogevinas, and M.A. Elston (1987). 'Social/Economic Status and Disease'. *Annual Review of Public Health* 8: 111–35.

Marshall, Barbara L. (2000). *Configuring Gender: Explorations in Theory and Politics*. Peterborough, Ont.: Broadview Press.

———, and Stephen Katz (2002). 'Forever functional: Sexual fitness and the ageing male body'. *Body and Society* 8(4): 43–70.

Marshall, Katherine (1993a). 'Employed parents and the division of housework'. *Perspectives on labour and income* 5(3): 23–30.

——— (1993b). 'Dual earners: Who's responsible for housework?' *Canadian Social Trends* 31: 11–14.

——— (2000). 'Incomes of younger retired women: the past 30 years'. *Perspectives on Labour and Income* 12 (4): 9–17. Statistics Canada catalogue 75-001-XPE.

Marshall, T.H. (1950). *Citizenship and Social Class*. Cambridge: Cambridge University Press.

Marshall, Victor W. (1983). 'Generations, age groups, and cohorts: Conceptual distinctions'. *Canadian Journal on Aging* 2: 51–61

——— (1995). 'The micro-macro link in the sociology of aging'. In C. Hummel and C. Lalive D'Epinay (eds), *Images of Aging in Western Societies*, in Proceedings of the 2nd Images of Aging conference. Geneva, Switzerland. Centre for Interdisciplinary Gerontology, University of Geneva, 337–71.

———, Heinz, H. Krueger, and A. Verma (eds) (2001). *Restructuring Work and the Life Course*. Toronto: University of Toronto Press.

———, Fay Lomax Cook, and Joanne Gard Marshall (1993). 'Conflict over intergenerational equity: rhetoric and reality in a comparative context', in Vern L. Bengtson and W.A. Achenbaum (eds), *The Changing Contract Across Generations*. New York: Aldine de Gruyter, 119–40.

———, and B.D. McPherson (1994). 'Introduction: Aging: Canadian perspectives'. In

V.W. Marshall and B.D. McPherson (eds), *Aging: Canadian Perspectives*. Peterborough: Broadview Press/Journal of Canadian Studies.

————, and J. Tindale, J. (1978). 'Notes for a radical gerontology'. *International Journal of Aging and Human Development* 9: 163–75.

Martin, Sheilah, and Murray Coleman (1995). 'Judicial intervention in pregnancy'. *McGill Law Journal* 40: 947–91.

Martin-Matthews, Anne (2000). 'Intergenerational caregiving: How apocalyptic and dominant demographies form the questions and shape the answers, in Ellen M. Gee and Glori M. Guttman (eds), *The Overselling of Population Aging: Apocalyptic Demography, Intergenerational Challenges, and Social Policy*. Don Mills, ON: Oxford University Press, 80–79.

Marx, Karl ([1893–94] 1956). 'Capital Vol. III', in T.B. Bottomore (ed.), *Karl Marx: Selected Writings in Sociology and Social Philosophy*. New York: McGraw-Hill, 178–9.

———— (1969). *Selected Works*. Vol. I. Moscow: Progress Publishers.

———— ([1848] 1983). *The Portable Karl Marx*. New York: Penguin.

————, and F. Engels ([1848] 1970). *The Communist Manifesto*. New York: Washington Square Press.

Mata, Fernando (1997). 'Intergenerational transmission of education and socio-economic status: A look at immigrants, visible minorities and Aboriginals'. Income and Labour Dynamics Working Paper Series: Statistics Canada product number 75F0002M, catalogue 97-07.

Matthews, Sharon, Orly Manor, and Chris Power (1999). 'Social inequalities in health: Are there gender differences?' *Social Science and Medicine* 48 (1): 49–60.

May, Martha (1993). 'Bread before roses: American workingmen, labour unions and the family wage'. Chapter 11 in B. Fox (ed.), *Family Patterns, Gender Relations*. Toronto: Oxford University Press.

Mayer, Francine, Nancy Ross, Jean-Marie Berthelot, and Russell Wilkins (2002).

'Disability-free life expectancy by health region'. *Health Reports* 13(4): 49–60. Statistics Canada catalogue 82-003.

Mayer, L.U., and W. Muller (1986). 'The State and the Structure of the Life Course'. Chapter 10 in A.B. Sorensen, F.E. Weinert and L.R. Sherrod (eds), *Human Development and the Life Course: Multidisciplinary Perspectives*. Hillsdale, NJ: Lawrence Erlbaum Associates, 217–45.

McAll, C. (1990). *Class, Ethnicity and Social Inequality*. Montreal: McGill-Queen's University Press.

McCourt, Frank (1996). *Angela's Ashes: A Memoir*. New York: Touchstone.

McDaniel, Susan A. (2001). 'Born at the right time? Gendered generations and webs of entitlement and responsibility'. *Canadian Journal of Sociology*, 26(2): 193–214.

———— (2002). 'Women's changing relations to the state and citzenship: caring and intergenerational relations in globalizing western democracies'. *Canadian Review of Sociology and Anthropology* 39 (2): 125–50.

McDonald, L., J. Hornick, G. Robertson, and J. Wallace (1991). *Elder Abuse and Neglect in Canada*. Toronto: Butterworths.

McDonald, L., and B. Wigdor (1995). 'Taking stock: Elder abuse research in Canada'. *Canadian Journal on Aging* 14 (supplement 2): 1–6.

McDonough, Peggy, and Vivienne Walters (2001). 'Gender and health: Reassessing patterns and explanations'. *Social Science and Medicine* 52(4): 547–59.

————, Vivienne Walters, and Lisa Strohschein (2002). 'Chronic stress and the social patterning of women's health in Canada'. *Social Science and Medicine* 54 (5): 767–82.

————, David R. Williams, James S. House, and Greg J. Duncan (1999). 'Gender and the socioeconomic gradient in mortality'. *Journal of Health and Social Behavior* 40 (1): 17–31.

McGregor, Gaile (2001). *A Fact Sheet on the Economics of Aging in Canada*. London: Terraconnaissance.

McIntyre, Sheila, and Jennifer Scott (2000). 'Submissions to the Committee on Justice and Legal Affairs Review of Bill C-46', in Barbara A. Crow and Lise Gotell (eds), *Open Boundaries: A Canadian Women's Studies Reader.* Toronto: Prentice-Hall, 348–56.

McKague, Ormond (ed.) (1991). 'Racial harassment: Two individual reflections', of *Racism in Canada.* Saskatoon: Fifth House, 11–14.

McKinlay, John B. (1996). 'Some contributions from the social system to gender inequalities in heart disease'. *Journal of Health and Social Behavior* 37 (1): 1–26.

McLaren, Angus (1991). *Our Own Master Race: Eugenics in Canada, 1885–1945.* Toronto: McClelland and Stewart.

——, and Arlene Tigar McLaren (1997). *The Bedroom and the State: The Changing Practices and Politics of Contraception and Abortion in Canada, 1880–1997*, 2nd edn. Toronto: Oxford University Press.

McLean, Diane E., and Bruce G. Link (1994). 'Unraveling Complexity: Strategies to refine concepts, measures, and research designs in the study of life events and mental health'. Chapter 2 in William R. Avison and Ian H. Gotlib (eds), *Stress and Mental Health: Contemporary Issues and Prospects for the Future.* New York: Plenum Press.

McLeod, Jane D., and Michael J. Shanahan (1993). 'Poverty, parenting, and children's mental health'. *American Sociological Review* 58(3): 351–66.

McLeod, Jane D., and Michael J. Shanahan (1996). 'Trajectories of poverty and children's mental health'. *Journal of Health and Social Behavior* 37(3): 207–20.

McMahon, Martha (1995). *Engendering Motherhood: Identity and Self-transformation in Women's Lives.* New York: Guilford Press.

McMullan, John L., and Stephen Smith (1997). 'Toxic steel: State-corporate crime and the contamination of the environment'. Chapter 3 in John McMullan, David Perrier, Stephen Smith, and Peter Swan (eds), *Crimes, Laws and Communities.* Halifax: Fernwood.

McMullin, Julie Ann (1996). 'Connecting age, gender, class, and ethnicity: A case study of the garment industry in Montreal'. Doctoral dissertation, University of Toronto.

—— (2000). 'Diversity and the state of sociological aging theory'. *The Gerontologist* 40: 517–30.

—— (2002). 'Negotiating mothering and caring in an inflexible paid work environment: A case study of older garment workers'. *Hayllm International Journal on Aging* 4(2): 141–60.

——, and Peri Ballantyne (1995). 'Employment characteristics and income: Assessing gender and age group effects for Canadians aged 45 years and over'. *Canadian Journal of Sociology* 20 (4): 529–55.

——, and John Cairney (Forthcoming). *Journal of Aging Studies.*

——, and Victor W. Marshall (1999). 'Structure and agency in the retirement process: A case study of Montreal garment workers'. Chapter 11 in C.D. Ryff and V.W. Marshall (eds), *The Self and Society in Aging Processes.* New York: Springer.

——, and Victor W. Marshall (2001) 'Ageism, age relations and garment industry work in Montreal'. *The Gerontologist* 41: 111–22.

Menaghan, Elizabeth G. (1990). 'Social stress and individual distress'. *Research in Community and Mental Health* 6: 107–41.

Messing, Karen (1997). 'Women's occupational health: a critical review and discussion of current issues'. *Women and Health* 25 (4): 39–68.

Middlesex-London Health Unit (2000). *Final Report of the Task Force on the Health Effects of Women Abuse.* London, Ont.: Middlesex-London Health Unit.

Miech, Richard Allen, and Michael J. Shanahan (2000). 'Socioeconomic status and depression over the life course'. *Journal of Health and Social Behavior* 41 (2): 162–76.

Miles, Robert (1989). *Racism.* London: Routledge.

——, and Rudy Torres (2000). 'Does race matter? Transatlantic perspectives on racism after "race relations"'. Chapter 2 in Madeline A. Kalbach and Warren E. Kalbach (eds), *Perspectives on Ethnicity in Canada*. Toronto: Harcourt Canada.

Millar, Wayne (1992). 'Place of birth and ethnic status: Factors associated with smoking prevalence among Canadians'. *Health Reports* 4(1): 7–24. Statistics Canada catalogue 82-003.

Millett, Kate (1969). *Sexual Politics*. New York: Avon Books.

Mirkowsky, John, and Catherine E. Ross (1992). 'Age and depression'. *Journal of Health and Social Behavior* 33 (3): 187–205.

———— (2001). 'Age and the effect of economic hardship on depression'. *Journal of Health and Social Behavior* 42 (2): 132–50.

Mitchell, B. 2000. 'The refilled "nest": Debunking the myth of families in crisis', in E.M. Gee and G. M. Guttman (eds), *The Overselling of Population Aging: Apocalyptic Demography, Intergenerational Challenges, and Social Policy*. Don Mills, ON: Oxford University Press, 80–99.

————, and E.M. Gee 1996. 'Boomerang kids and midlife parental marital satisfaction'. *Family Relations* 45 (Oct).: 442–8.

Mitchinson, Wendy (1991). *The Nature of their Bodies: Women and their Doctors in Victorian Canada*. Toronto: University of Toronto Press.

Mooers, Colin (1999). 'Can we still resist? Globalization, citizenship rights and class formation'. Chapter 20 in Dave Broad and Wayne Antony (eds), *Citizens or Consumers? Social Policy in a Market Society*. Halifax: Fernwood.

Morgan, D.H.J. (1985). *The Family, Politics, and Social Theory*. London: Routledge and Kegan Paul.

Morgan, Kathryn Pauly (1998). 'Women and the knife: Cosmetic surgery and the colonization of women's bodies'. Chapter 11 in Rose Weitz (ed.), *The Politics of Women's Bodies: Sexuality, Appearance, and Behavior*. New York: Oxford University Press.

Morris, Martina, Bernhardt, Annette D., and Handcock, Mark S. (1994). 'Economic inequality: New methods for new trends'. *American Sociological Review* 59(2): 205–19.

Muntaner, C., W.W. Eaton, C. Diala, R.C. Kessler and P.D. Sorlie (1998). 'Social class, assets, organizational control and the prevalence of common groups of common groups of psychiatric disorders'. *Social Science and Medicine* 47 (12): 2043–53.

Mustard, Cameron A., Shelley Derkson, Jean-Marie Berthelot, Michael Wolfson and Leslie L. Roos (1997). 'Age-specific education and income gradients in morbidity and mortality in a Canadian province'. *Social Science and Medicine* 45 (3): 383–97

Muzzin, Linda, Greg Brown, and Roy Hornosty (1995). 'Gender, educational credentials, contributions and career advancement: Results of a follow-up study in hospital pharmacy'. *Canadian Review of Sociology and Anthropology* 32(2): 151–68.

Myles, J.F. (1980). 'The aged, the state, and the structure of inequality', in J. Harp and J. Hofley (eds), *Structural Inequality in Canada*. Toronto: Prentice Hall, 317–42.

———— (1981). 'Income inequality and status maintenance'. *Research on Aging* 3: 123–41.

———— (1984). *The Political Economy of Public Pensions*. Boston: Little Brown.

———— (1989). *Old Age in the Welfare State: The Political Economy of Public Pensions*, rev. edn. Lawrence, Kan: University Press of Kansas.

———— (1995). 'The market's revenge: Old age security and social rights'. Paper presented at the Wilson Abernathy Distinguished lecture. University of Toronto, April.

———— (2000). 'The maturation of Canada's retirement income system: Income levels, income inequality and low-income among the elderly'. *Statistics Canada and Florida State University*. Statistics Canada catalogue 11F0019MPE #147.

————, and D. Street (1995). 'Should the economic life course be redesigned? Old age security in a time of transition'. *Canadian Journal on Aging* 14: 335–59.

Nakhaie, M. Reza (1995). 'Ownership and management positions of Canadian ethnic groups in 1973 and 1989'. *Canadian Journal of Sociology* 20 (2): 167–92.

————— (1997). 'Vertical mosaic among the elites: The new imagery revisited'. *Canadian Review of Sociology and Anthropology* 34 (1): 1–24.

—————, and James Curtis (1998). 'Effects of class positions of parents on educational attainment of daughters and sons'. *Canadian Review of Sociology and Anthropology* 35 (4): 483–515.

National Advisory Council on Aging (NACA) (1991). *Intergovernmental relations and the aging of the population.* Ottawa: Minister of Supply and Services.

National Council of Welfare (2000). *Poverty Profile: A Report.* Ottawa: Minister of Public Works and Government Services Canada.

————— (2002). *Poverty Profile 1999.* Ottawa: Minister of Public Works and Government Services.

Nelson, E.D., and Barrie W. Robinson (1999). *Gender in Canada.* Scarborough: Prentice-Hall Allyn and Bacon.

Nelson, Jay (2002). '"A strange revolution in the manners of the country": Aboriginal-settler intermarriage in nineteenth-century British Columbia'. Chapter 1 in John McLaren, Robert Menzies, and Dorothy E. Chunn (eds), *Regulating Lives: Historical Essays on the State, Society, the Individual and the Law.* Vancouver: UBC Press.

Neugarten, B.L. (1970). 'The old and the young in modern societies'. *American Behavioral Scientist* 4, 13–24.

—————, and G.O. Hagestad (1976). 'Age and the life course'. In R. H. Binstock and E. Shanas (eds), *Handbook of Aging and the Social Sciences.* New York: Van Nostrand Reinhold.

—————, J.W. Moore, and J.C. Lowe (1965). 'Age norms, age constraints, and adult socialization'. *American Journal of Sociology* 70: 710–17.

Newbold, K. Bruce (1998). 'Problems in search of solutions: Health and Canadian Aboriginals'. *Journal of Community Health* 23 (1): 59–73.

Ng, Roxanna (1993). 'Racism, sexism and nation-building in Canada', in Cameron McCarthy and Warren Crichlow (eds), *Race, Identity and Representation in Education.* New York: Routledge, 50–9.

————— (2002). 'Freedom for whom? Globalization and trade from the standpoint of garment workers'. *Canadian Women's Studies* 21 (22): 74–81.

Nicholas, Andrea Bear (2001). 'Canada's colonial mission: The great white bird'. Chapter 1 in K.P. Binda (ed.) with Sharilyn Calliou, *Aboriginal Education in Canada: A Study in Decolonization.* Mississauga, Ont.: Canadian Educators' Press.

Nicholson, Linda (1994). 'Interpreting gender'. *Signs* 20 (1): 79–105.

Noh, Samuel, Morton Beiser, Violet Kaspar, Feng Hou, and Joanna Rummens (1999). 'Perceived racial discrimination, depression, and coping: a study of Southeast Asian refugees in Canada. *Journal of Health and Social Behavior* 40 (3): 193–207.

O'Brien, Mary (1981). *The Politics of Reproduction.* Boston: Routledge and Kegan Paul.

Offe, C., and V. Ronge 1982. 'Thesis on the theory of the state'. In A. Giddens and D.Held (eds), *Classes, Power and Conflict.* Berkeley, CA: University of California Press.

O'Loughlin, Jennifer (1999). 'Understanding the role of ethnicity in chronic disease: A challenge for the new millennium'. *Canadian Medical Association Journal* 161 (2): 152–5.

—————, Gilles Paradis, Lise Renaud, Garbis Meshefedjian, and Katherine Gray-Donald (1998). 'Prevalence and correlates of overweight among elementary schoolchildren in multiethnic, low income, inner-city neighbourhoods in Montreal, Canada'. *AEP* 8 (7): 422–32.

Omi, Michael, and Howard Winant (1994). *Racial Formation in the United States from the 1960s to the 1990s* , 2nd edn. New York: Routledge.

O'Rand, Angela (1996a). 'The cumulative stratification of the life course', in R.H. Binstock and L.K. George (eds), *Handbook of Aging and the*

Social Sciences, 4th edn. New York: Academic Press, 188–207.

―――― (1996b). 'The precious and the precocious: understanding cumulative disadvantage and cumulative advantage over the life course'. *The Gerontologist* 36: 230–8.

―――― , and John C. Henretta (1999). *Age and Inequality: Diverse Pathways through Later Life.* Boulder, CO: Westview Press.

Orloff, Ann Shola (1993). 'Gender and the social rights of citizenship: The comparative analysis of gender relations and welfare states'. *American Sociological Review* 58 (June): 303–28.

―――― (1996). 'Gender in the welfare state'. *Annual Review of Sociology* 22: 51–78.

Osberg, Lars (1992). 'Canada's economic performance: Inequality, poverty, and growth', in Allen and Rosenbluth (eds), *False Promises, the Failure of Conservative Economics.* Vancouver: New Star Books, 39–52.

Osborne, Ken (2000). 'Public schooling and citizenship education in Canada'. *Canadian Ethnic Studies* 32 (1): 8–37.

Oxford English Dictionary Oxford: Clarendon Press, 1989.

Oxman-Martinez, Jacqueline, Shelly N. Abdool, and Margot Loiselle-Leonard (2000). 'Immigration, women and health in Canada'. *Canadian Journal of Public Health* 91(5): 394–5.

Palaniappan, U., L. Starkey Jacobs, J. O'Loughlin, and K. Gray-Donald (2001). 'Fruit and vegetable consumption is lower and saturated fat intake is higher among Canadians reporting smoking'. *Journal of Nutrition* 131 (7): 1952–8.

Pampel, Fred C. (1998). *Aging, Social Inequality, and Public Policy.* Thousand Oaks, CA: Pine Forge Press.

Parkin, Frank (1979). *Marxism and Class Theory: A Bourgeois Critique.* London: Tavistock.

Parsons, Talcott (1929). 'Capitalism in recent German literature'. *Journal of Political Economy* 37: 40.

―――― (1942). 'Age and sex in the social structure of the United States'. *American Sociological Review* 7: 604–16.

―――― (1949). *The Structure of Social Action: A Study in Social Theory with Reference to a Group of Recent European Writers.* Glencoe IL: Free Press.

―――― (1951). *The Social System.* Glencoe, IL: Free Press.

―――― ([1937] 1968). *The Structure of Social Action: A Study in Social Theory with Special Reference to a Group of Recent European Writers.* Glencoe, IL: Free Press.

Passuth, P.M., and V.L. Bengtson (1988). 'Sociological theories of aging: Current perspectives and future directions', in J.E. Birren and V.L. Bengtson (eds), *Emergent Theories of Aging.* New York: Springer, 335–55.

Pavalko, Eliza K., and Shari Woodbury (2000). 'Social roles as process: Caregiving careers and women's health'. *Journal of Health and Social Behavior* 41 (1): 91–105.

Peek, M. Kristen, and Raymond T. Coward (2000). 'Antecedents of disability for older adults with multiple chronic health conditions'. *Research on Aging* 22(4): 422–44.

Peppin, Patricia (1995). 'Feminism, law, and the pharmaceutical industry'. Chapter 5 in Frank Pearce and Laureen Snider (eds), *Corporate Crime: Contemporary Debates.* Toronto: University of Toronto Press.

Perkel, Colin (2000). 'Ontario's black guards want probe into workplace racism'. The *Globe and Mail*, 7 April.

Pheasant, Valerie Bedassigae (2001). 'My mother used to dance', in Carl E. James and Adrienne Shadd, *Talking about Identity.* Toronto: Between the Lines, 38–43.

Phillips, Paul, and Erin Phillips (2000). *Women and Work: Inequality in the Canadian Labour Market.* Toronto: James Lorimer.

Phillips, L.R. (1986). 'Theoretical explanations of elder abuse: competing hypotheses and unresolved issues', in K.A. Pillemer and R.S. Wold (eds), *Elder Abuse: Conflict in the Family.* Dover, MA: Auburn House, 197–217.

Phillipson, C. 1982. *Capitalism and the Construction of Old Age.* London: Macmillan.

Philp, Margaret (2001). 'Child poverty in Canada won't budge: Provincial welfare reform fails to ease growing problem in Canada's largest city'. The *Globe and Mail*, 26 April.

Picot, Garnett, and John Myles (1995). *Social Transfers, Changing Family Structure, and Low Income Among Children*. Ottawa: Statistics Canada. Catalogue 11F0019MPE No. 82

Plager, Laurie, and Edward Chen (1999). 'Student debt from 1990–91 to 1995–96: An analysis of Canada student loans data'. *Education Quarterly Review* 5(4): 10–35. Statistics Canada catalogue 81-003.

Podnieks, E. (1992). 'National survey on abuse of the elderly in Canada'. *Journal of Elder Abuse and Neglect* 4: 5–58.

Pollan, M., and P. Gustavsson (1999). 'High-risk occupations for breast cancer in the Swedish female working population'. *American Journal of Public Health* 89(6): 875–81.

Pomerleau, Joceline, Linda L. Pederson, Truls Ostbye, Mark Speechley, and Kathy N. Speechley (1997). 'Health behaviours and socio-economic status in Ontario, Canada'. *European Journal of Epidemiology* 13: 613–22.

Popenoe, David (1993). 'American family decline, 1960–1990: A review and appraisal'. *Journal of Marriage and the Family* 55 (August): 527–55.

Porter, J. (1965). '*The vertical mosaic: An analysis of social class and power in Canada*'. Toronto: University of Toronto Press.

Poulantzas, N. (1975). *Classes in Contemporary Capitalism*. London: New Left Books.

Pulkingham, Jane (1998). 'Remaking of the social divisions of welfare: Gender, "dependency", and UI reform'. *Studies in Political Economy* 56 (Summer): 7–48.

Pupo, Norene (2001). 'The role of the state in a restructured economy'. Chapter 4 in Dan Glenday and Ann Duffy (eds), *Canadian Society: Meeting the Challenges of the Twenty-First Century*. Toronto: Oxford University Press.

Ralston, Helen (1996). *The Lived Experience of South Asian Immigrant Women in Atlantic Canada: the Interconnections of Race, Class, and Gender.* New York: Edwin Mellen Press.

Ranson, Gillian (2003). 'Beyond gender differences: A Canadian study of women's and men's careers in engineering'. *Gender, Work, and Organization* 10(1): 22–41.

Reiter, Ester (1996). *Making Fast Food*. Montreal: McGill-Queen's University Press.

Renzetti, Elizabeth (1998). 'War of independents: battle of the bookstores'. The *Globe and Mail*, 20 June.

Reynolds, L.T. (1992). 'A retrospective on "race": The career of a concept'. *Sociological Focus* 25 (1): 1–14.

Rich, Adrienne (1980). 'Compulsory heterosexuality and lesbian existence'. *Signs* 5: 631–60.

Rieker, Patricia P., and Chloe E. Bird (2000). 'Sociological explanations of gender differences in mental and physical health'. Chapter 7 in Chloe E. Bird, Peter Conrad, and Allen M. Fremont (eds), *Handbook of Medical Sociology,* 5th edn. Englewood Cliffs, NJ: Prentice Hall.

Riley, M.W. (1971). 'Social gerontology and the age stratification of society'. *The Gerontologist* 11: 79–87.

——— (1985). 'Age strata in social systems'. In R.H. Binstock and E. Shanas (eds), *Handbook of Aging and the Social Sciences*. New York: Van Nostrand Reinhold.

——— (1988). 'On the significance of age in sociology'. In M.W. Riley in association with B. J. Huber and B.B. Hess, *Social Structures and Human Lives*. Newbury Park, CA: Sage.

——— (1994). 'Aging and society: past, present and future'. *The Gerontologist* 34, 436–46.

———, A. Foner, and J. Waring (1988). 'Sociology of age', in N.J. Smelser (ed.), *Handbook of Sociology*. Newbury Park, CA: Sage, 243–90.

———, M. Johnson, and A. Foner (1972). *Aging and Society,* vol. 3: *A Sociology of Age Stratification*. New York: Russell Sage Foundation.

———, and J.W. Riley, Jr (1994a). 'Age integration and the lives of older people'. *The Gerontologist* 34, 110–15.

————, and J.W. Riley, Jr (1994b). 'Structural lag: Past and future'. In M.W. Riley, R.L. Kahn,, and A. Fonner (eds), *Age and Structural Lag: Society's Failure to Provide Meaningful Opportunities in Work, Family, and Leisure.* New York: John Wiley.

Rinehart, James W. (1996). *The Tyranny of Work: Alienation and the Labour Process,* 3rd edn. Toronto: Harcourt Brace.

Risman, Barbara J. (1998). *Gender Vertigo: American Families in Transition.* New Haven: Yale University Press.

Robertson, Ann (1998). 'Shifting discourses on health in Canada: From health promotion to population health'. *Health Promotion International* 13 (2): 155–66.

Rodgers, Karen (1994). 'Wife assault in Canada'. *Canadian Social Trends*, Autumn. Ottawa: Statistics Canada.

Roos, Noralou P., and Cameron A. Mustard (1997). 'Variation in health and health care use by socioeconomic status in Winnipeg, Canada: Does the system work well? Yes and no'. *Milbank Quarterly* 75 (1): 89–111.

Rose, David, and Gordon Marshall (1986). 'Constructing the (W)right classes'. *Sociology* 20: 440–55.

Rosenberg, Mark W., and Kathleen Wilson (2000). 'Gender, poverty and location: How much difference do they make in the geography of health inequalities?' *Social Science and Medicine* 51 (2): 275–87.

Rosenberg, T., and S. Martel (1998). 'Cancer trends from 1972–1991 for registered Indians living on Manitoba reserves'. *International Journal of Circumpolar Health* 57 (Supplement 1): 391–8.

Rosenthal, C. J., Matthews, S.H., and Marshall, V.W. (1989). 'Is parent care normative? The experiences of a sample of middle-aged women'. *Research on Aging* 11 (2): 244–60.

Ross, David P., E. Richard Shillingon, and Clarence Lochhead (1994). *The Canadian Fact Book on Poverty.* Ottawa: Canadian Council on Social Development.

————, Katherine J. Scott, and Peter J. Smith (2000). *The Canadian Fact Book on Poverty.* Ottawa: Canadian Council on Social Development.

Royson, James (2002). 'Poverty statistics tell startling truth', *The Toronto Star*, 15 March.

Ryan, Darlene (2003). 'Lessons from stay at home dads'. *Mochasofa, Women Connecting for Solutions.* 29 January.

Ryder, N. (1965). 'The cohort as a concept in the study of social change'. *American Sociological Review* 30: 834 61.

Sabourin, S. (2003). 'My story—A narrative: Refusing mediocrity: Barriers to higher education for sole support parents'. Unpublished manuscript.

Sainsbury, Diane (1999). 'Gender and social-democratic welfare states'. Chapter 3 in Diane Sainsbury (ed.), *Gender and Welfare State Regimes.* New York: Oxford University Press.

Sales, Arnaud, Rejean Drolet, and Isabelle Bonneau, (2001). 'Academic paths, ageing, and the living conditions of students in the late 20th century'. *The Canadian Review of Sociology and Anthropology* 38 (2): 167–88.

Sangster, Joan (1995). 'Doing two jobs: the wage-earning mother, 1945–70', in Joy Parr (ed.), *A Diversity of Women: Ontario, 1945–1980.* Toronto: University of Toronto Press, 98–134.

Satzewich, Vic (1998). 'Race, racism and racialization: Contested concepts'. Chapter 1 in Vic Satzewich (ed.), *Racism and Social Inequality in Canada.* Toronto: Thompson Educational.

Schick, Carol (2001). 'Keeping the ivory tower white: Discourse of racial domination'. In S.H. Razack (ed.), *Race, Space and the Law.* Toronto: Between the Lines.

Schissel, Bernard (1997). *Blaming Children: Youth Crime, Moral Panics and the Politics of Hate.* Halifax: Fernwood.

Schissel, Bernard and Terry Wotherspoon (2003). *The Legacy of School for Aboriginal People: Education, Oppression and Emancipation.* Don Mills, ON: Oxford University Press.

Schulz, Amy, David Williams, Barbara Israel, Adam Becker, Edith Parker, Sherman A. James, and James Jackson (2000). 'Unfair treatment, neighbourhood effects, and mental health in the Detroit Metropolitan area'. *Journal of Health and Social Behavior* 41(3): 314–32.

Scott, Katherine (1996). 'The dilemma of liberal citizenship: Women and social assistance reform in the 1990s'. *Studies in Political Economy* 50 (Summer): 7–36.

Seeman, Neil (2001). 'A right to welfare is a loss of democracy'. The *Globe and Mail,* 31 October.

Sefa Dei, George J., (1993). 'The challenges of anti-racist education in Canada'. *Canadian Ethnic Studies* 25(2): 36–51.

Sewell, William H.J., Jr (1992). 'A theory of structure: Duality, agency, and transformation'. *American Journal of Sociology* 98: 1–29.

Shellenbarger, Sue (2001). 'Anger over age discrimination grows as baby boomers hit 55'. The *Globe and Mail*, 4 June.

Sheth, Tej, Cyril Nair, Mukund Nargundkar, Sonia Anand, and Salim Yusuf (1999). 'Cardiovascular and cancer mortality among Canadians of European, south Asian and Chinese origin from 1979 to 1993'. *Canadian Medical Association Journal* 161(2): 132–43.

Shields, Margot, and Stephane Tremblay (2002). The health of Canada's communities. Supplement to *Health Reports 13*: 1–24. Statistics Canada catalogue 82-003.

Shim, Janet K. (2002). 'Understanding the routinised inclusion of race, socioeconomic status and sex in epidemiology: The utility of concepts from technoscience studies'. *Sociology of Health and Illness* 24(2): 129–50.

Shragge, Eric (1997). 'Workfare: An overview'. Chapter 1 in Eric Shragge (ed.), *Workfare: Ideology for a New Underclass.* Toronto: Garamond Press.

Simmons, Alan B., and Dwaine E. Plaza, (1998). 'Breaking through the glass ceiling: The pursuit of university training among African-Caribbean migrants and their children in Toronto'. *Canadian Ethnic Studies* 30(3): 99–120.

Simon, Robin (2000). 'The importance of culture in sociological theory and research on stress and mental health: A missing link?' Chapter 5 in Chloe E. Bird, Peter Conrad, and Allen M.

Fremont (eds), *Handbook of Medical Sociology,* 5th edn. Englewood Cliffs, NJ: Prentice-Hall.

Single, Eric, Lynda Robson, Jurgen Rehm, and Xiaodi Xi (1999). 'Morbidity and mortality attributable to alcohol, tobacco, and illicit drug use in Canada'. *American Journal of Public Health* 89: 385–90.

Small, Stephen (1998). 'The contours of racialization: Structures, representation, and resistance in the United States'. Chapter 3 in *Racism and Social Inequality in Canada: Concepts, Controversies, and Strategies of Resistance*. Toronto: Thompson Educational.

Smith, Derek G. (1975). *Canadian Indians and the Law: Selected Documents, 1663–1972.* Toronto: McClelland and Stewart.

Smith, Dorothy E. (1987). *The Everyday World as Problematic: A Feminist Sociology*. Toronto: University of Toronto Press.

Smith, Graeme (2001) 'Spanking puts power over safety, court told'. *The Globe and Mail*, 11 September.

Snider, Laureen (1993). *Bad Business: Corporate Crime in Canada*. Nelson Canada.

Sokoloff, Heather (2002). 'Poor dying at a faster rate: Report, 25 year Stats Can study'. The *National Post*, 27 September.

Stackhouse, John (2001a). 'Canada's apartheid'. Part 1, 'Welcome to Harlem on the Prairies'. The *Globe and Mail*, 3 November.

——— (2001b). 'Canada's apartheid'. Part 2, 'Crystal's choice: The best of both worlds'. The *Globe and Mail*, 5 November.

Stasiulis, Davia (1999). 'Feminist intersectional theorizing'. Chapter 12 in Peter Li (ed.), *Race and Ethnic Relations in Canada,* 2nd edn. Toronto: Oxford University Press.

———, and Abigail B. Bakan (1995). 'Making the match: Domestic placement agencies and the racialization of women's household work'. *Signs* 20(2): 303–35.

———, and Abigail B. Bakan (1997). 'Negotiating citizenship: The case of foreign domestic workers in Canada'. *Feminist Review* 57 (Autumn): 112–39.

Statistics Canada (1997). 'A profile of the self-employed'. *Canadian Economic Observer*. Ottawa: Minister of Industry. Statistics Canada catalogue 11-010-XPB.

——— (1999a). 'How healthy are Canadians? A special issue'. *A Summary of Health Reports* 11 (3): 1–8. Statistics Canada catalogue 82-003. Accessed at <www.statcan.ca/english/ads/82-003-XPB/toc.htm>. October 2002.

——— (2001a). *Family Violence in Canada: A Statistical Profile, 2001*. Ottawa: Minister of Industry. Statistics Canada catalogue 85-224.

——— (2001b). *Annual Demographic Statistics*. Ottawa: Minister of Industry. Statistics Canada catalogue 91-213XPB.

——— (2001c). *Spousal Violence after Marital Separation*. Ottawa: Minister of Industry. Statistics Canada catalogue 85-002-XIE.

——— (2001d). *Aboriginal Peoples in Canada*. Profile Series. Ottawa: Minister of Industry. Statistics Canada catalogue 85F0033MIE.

——— (2001e). *A Report on Adult Education and Training in Canada: Learning a Living*. Ottawa: Minister of Industry. Statistics Canada catalogue 81-586-XPE.

——— (2001f). 'Taking risks/ taking care'. *Health Reports* 12(3): 11–20. Statistics Canada catalogue 82-003.

——— (2001h). 'Death-shifting trends'. *Health Reports* 12(3): 41–6. Statistics Canada catalogue 82-003.

——— (2001i). 'Stress and well-being'. *Health Reports* 12(3): 21–32. Statistics Canada catalogue 82-003.

——— (2001j). 'The health divide: How the sexes differ'. *The Daily*. Ottawa, Minister of Industry. 26 April.

——— (2001k).'Health care/self-care'. *Health Reports* 12(3): 33–40. Statistics Canada catalogue 82-003.

——— (2001l). *Census: Age and Sex Highlight Tables*. Statistics Canada catalogue 97F0024XIE2001001. <www.statcan.ca>.

——— (2002a). CANSIM II, Table 282-0008. <www.statcan.ca>.

——— (2002b). *Family Violence in Canada: A Statistical Profile, 2002*. Ottawa: Minister of Industry. Statistics Canada catalogue 85-224.

——— (2003). *Canada's Ethnocultural Portrait: The Changing Mosaic*. Ottawa: Minister of Industry. Statistics Canada catalogue 96F0030XIE2001008.

——— and the Council of Ministers of Education Canada (CMEC) (2000). *Education Indicators in Canada: Report of the Pan-Canadian Education Indicators Program 1999*. <www.cmec.ca>.

——— and Health Canada (1999b). *Statistical Report on the Health of Canadians*. Statistics Canada catalogue 82-570-XIE. Prepared by the Federal , Provincial, and Territorial Advisory Committee on Population Health for the meeting of Ministers of Health 16–17 September 1999. Accessed at <www.statcan.ca/english/freepub/82-570-XIE/partb/htm>. October 2002.

Street, Debra, and Ingrid Connidis (2001). 'Creeping selectivity in Canadian women's pensions', in Jay Ginn, Debra Street, and Sara Arber (eds), *Women, Work and Pensions*. Buckingham, England: Open University Press, 158–78.

Strong-Boag, Veronica, Sherrill Grace, Avigail Eisenberg, and Joan Anderson (1998). *Painting the Maple: Essays on Race, Gender, and the Construction of Canada*. Vancouver: UBC Press.

Sullivan, Oriel (2000). 'The division of domestic labour: 20 years of change?' *Sociology* 34(3): 437–56.

Thiessen, Victor, and Christy Nickerson (1999). *Canadian Gender Trends in Education and Work*. Ottawa: Applied Research Branch, Strategic Policy, Human Resources Development Canada (T-00-4E). Catalogue MP32-30/00-4E.

Thomas, Jennifer (2000). 'Adult correctional services in Canada, 1998–99'. *Juristat* 20(3): 1–17. Statistics Canada catalogue 85-002-XIE.

Thompson, E.P. (1963). *The Making of the English Working Class*. New York: Vintage.

Thuanh Ha, Tu (2003). 'Senior seeks to sue Ottawa over unpaid supplement'. The *Globe and Mail,* 31 January.

Tilly, Charles (1998). *Durable Inequality*. Berkeley: University of California Press.

Tindale, J., and V.W. Marshall (1980). 'A generational-conflict perspective for gerontology'. Pp. 43–50 in V.W. Marshall (ed.), *Aging in Canada: Social Perspectives*. Toronto: Fitzhenry and Whiteside.

Tjaden, P., and N. Thoennes (2000). 'Extent, nature and consequences of intimate partner violence: Findings from the National Violence against Women Survey'. Ottawa: National Institute of Justice and the Centre for Disease Control Prevention. July.

Tjepkema, Michael (2002). 'The health of the off-reserve Aboriginal population'. Supplement to *Health Reports* 13: 1–16. Statistics Canada catalogue 82-003.

Tomiak, Monica, Jane F. Gentleman, and Maurice Jette (1997). 'Health and gender differences between middle and senior managers in the Canadian public service'. *Social Science and Medicine* 45(10): 1589–96.

Townsend, P. (1981). 'The structured dependency of the elderly: A creation of social policy in the twentieth century'. *Ageing and Society* 1: 5–28.

Trovato, Frank (2001). 'Aboriginal mortality in Canada, the United States and New Zealand'. *Journal of Biosocial Science* 33: 67–86.

———, and N.M. Lalu (1995). 'The narrowing sex differential in mortality in Canada since 1971'. *Canadian Studies in Population* 22(2): 145–67.

Tumin, Melvin (1953). 'Some principles of stratification: A critical analysis'. *American Sociological Review* 18 (August): 387–93.

Turner, Jonathan H. (1988). *A Theory of Social Interaction*. Stanford, CA: Stanford University Press.

———, and L. Beeghley (1981). *The Emergence of Sociological Theory*. Homewood, IL: Dorsey Press.

Turner, R. Jay, and Donald A. Lloyd (1999). 'The stress process and the social distribution of depression'. *Journal of Health and Social Behavior* 40(4): 374–404.

———, and Patricia Roszell (1994). 'Psychosocial resources and the stress process'. Chapter 7 in William R. Avison and Ian H. Gotlib (eds), *Stress and Mental Health: Contemporary Issues and Prospects for the Future*. New York: Plenum Press.

Ujimoto, Victor K. (1994). 'Aging, ethnicity and health'. In B.S. Bolaria and H. D. Dickinson (eds), *Health, Illness and Health Care in Canada*, 2nd edn. Toronto: Harcourt Brace.

Urmetzer, Peter, and Neil Guppy (1999). 'Changing income inequality in Canada'. Chapter 5 in James E. Curtis, Edward G. Grabb, and Neil L. Guppy (eds), *Social Inequality in Canada: Patterns, Problems, and Policies*. Scarborough, ON: Prentice Hall Allyn and Bacon.

Ursel, Jane (1990). 'The state and the maintenance of patriarchy: A case study of family, labour, and welfare legislation in Canada', in Arlene Tigar McLaren (ed.), *Gender and Society: Creating a Canadian Women's Sociology*. Toronto: Copp Clark Pitman, 108–45.

——— (1998). 'Eliminating violence against women: Reform or co-optation in state institutions?' Chapter 7 in Les Samuelson and Wayne Antony (eds), *Power and Resistance: Critical Thinking about Canadian Social Issues*, 2nd edn. Halifax: Fernwood.

Valverde, Mariana. (1991). *The Age of Light, Soap, and Water: Moral Reform in English Canada, 1885–1925*. Toronto: McClelland and Stewart.

van Ryn, Michelle, and Jane Burke (2000). 'The effect of patient race and socio-economic status on physicians' perceptions of patients'. *Social Science and Medicine* 50(6): 813–28.

Vega, William A., and Ruben G. Rumbaut (1991). 'Ethnic minorities and mental health'. *Annual Review of Sociology* 17: 351–83.

Verbrugge, Lois M. (1989). 'The twain meet: Empirical explanations of sex differences in health and mortality'. *Journal of Health and Social Behavior* 30(3): 282–304.

Vertinsky, Patricia (1998). '"Run, Jane, run": Central tensions in the current debate about enhancing women's health through exercise'. *Women and Health* 27(4): 81–115.

Vinograd, Julia (1997). *Dead People Laughing.* Berkeley, Calif.: Zeitgeist.

Wadsworth, M.E.J. (1997). 'Health inequalities in the life course perspective'. *Social Science and Medicine* 44(6): 859–69.

Walby, Sylvia (1989). 'Theorizing patriarchy'. *Sociology* 23: 213–34.

——— (1990). *Theorizing Patriarchy.* Oxford: Basil Blackwell.

——— (1997). *Gender Transformations.* London: Routledge.

Walker, Alan (1981). 'Towards a political economy of old age'. *Ageing and Society* 1: 74–94.

Walters, Vivenne (1993). 'Stress, anxiety and depression: Women's accounts of their health problems'. *Social Science and Medicine* 36(4): 393–402.

———, Rhonda Lenton, Susan French, John Eyles, Janet Mayr, and Bruce Newbold (1996). 'Paid work, unpaid work and social support: A study of the health of women and men nurses'. *Social Science and Medicine* 43(11): 1627–36.

———, Peggy McDonough, and Lisa Strohschein (2002). 'The influence of work, household structure, and social, personal and material resources on gender differences in health: An analysis of the 1994 Canadian National Population Health Survey'. *Social Science and Medicine* 54(5): 677–92.

Wanner, Richard A. (1998). 'Prejudice, profit, or productivity: Explaining returns to human capital among male immigrants to Canada'. *Canadian Ethnic Studies* 30(3): 24–55.

——— (1999). 'Expansion and ascription: trends in educational opportunity in Canada,

1920–1994'. *The Canadian Review of Sociology and Anthropology* 36(3): 409–42.

——— (2001). 'A matter of degree(s): Twentieth-century trends in occupational status returns to educational credentials in Canada'. *Canadian Review of Sociology and Anthropology* 37(3): 313–43.

Weber, Max ([1922] 1978). *Economy and Society: An Outline of Interpretive Sociology,* vol. 1 Guenther Roth and Claus Wittich (eds), Berkeley, CA: University of California Press.

Welsh, Sandy (1999). 'Gender and sexual harassment'. *Annual Review of Sociology* 25: 169–90.

Wente, Margaret (2002). 'Prostate cancer: Desperately seeking care'. The *Globe and Mail,* 23 March.

West, Candace, and Don Zimmerman, (1987). 'Doing gender'. *Gender and Society* 1: 125–51.

Whitbeck, Les B., Dan R. Hoyt, Barbara J. McMorris, Xiaojin Chen, and Jerry D. Stubben (2001). 'Perceived discrimination and early substance abuse among American Indian children'. *Journal of Health and Social Behavior* 42(4): 405–24.

Wilkins, Kathryn (1996). 'Causes of death: How the sexes differ'. *Canadian Social Trends* (Summer): 11–17. Statistics Canada catalogue 11-008.

Wilkins, Russell, Jean-Marie Berthelot, and Edward Ng (2002). 'Trends in mortality by neighbourhood income in urban Canada from 1971 to 1996'. Supplement to *Health Reports* 13: 1–27. Statistics Canada catalogue 82-003.

Wilkinson, Richard G. (1997). 'Comment: Income, inequality, and social cohesion'. *American Journal of Public Health* 87(9): 1504–6.

Williams, Cara (2000). 'Income and expenditure', in '100 years of . . .' *Canadian Social Trends* 58 (Winter): 7–11. Statistics Canada catalogue 11-008.

——— (2002). 'Time or money? How high and low income Canadians spend their time'. *Canadian Social Trends,* Summer: 7–11.

Williams, Christine L. (1992). 'The glass escalator: Hidden advantages for men in the 'female' professions'. *Social Problems* 39(3): 253–67.

Williams, David R. (1990). 'Socioeconomic differentials in health: A review and redirection'. *Social Psychology Quarterly* 53(2): 81–99.

———, and Chiquita Collins (1995). 'US socioeconomic and racial differences in health: patterns and explanations'. *Annual Review of Sociology* 21: 349–86.

Willis, Paul (1977). *Learning to Labour.* Farnborough, UK: Saxon House.

Winson, Anthony, and Belinda Leach (2002). *Contingent Work, Disrupted Lives: Labour and Community in the New Rural Economy.* Toronto: University of Toronto Press.

Wolfson, Michael, Geoff Rowe, Jane F. Gentleman, and Monica Tomiak (1993). 'Career earnings and death: A longitudinal analysis of older Canadian men'. *Journal of Gerontology* 48(4): S167–79.

Wollstonecraft, Mary (1792). *A Vindication of the Rights of Woman: With Strictures on Political and Moral Subjects.* London.

World Health Organization (WHO) (1996). *Violence: A Public Health Priority.* Geneva: WHO.

Catalogue WHO/EHA/SPI.POA.2.

——— (2002) Preamble to the Constitution of the World Health Organization. <http://www.who.int/about/definition/en>. Accessed September 2002.

Wotherspoon, Terry (1998). *The Sociology of Education in Canada: Critical Perspectives.* Toronto: Oxford University Press.

Wright, E.O. (1985). *Classes.* London: Verso.

——— (1997). *Class Counts: Comparative Studies in Class Analysis.* Cambridge: Cambridge University Press.

——— (1999). 'Foundations of class analysis: a Marxist perspective'. Paper presented at the annual meeting of the American Sociological Association, Chicago.

Yezierska, Anzia (1979). 'A window full of sky' in *The Open Cage* by Anzia Yezierska. New York: Persea Books, Inc.

Young, Iris (1981). 'Beyond the unhappy marriage: a critique of the dual systems theory', of Lydia Sargent (ed.), *The Unhappy Marriage of Marxism and Feminism: A Debate on Class and Patriarchy.* London: Pluto Press, 43–69.

Zeitlin, I.M. (1990). *Ideology and the Development of Sociological Theory* , 4th edn. Englewood Cliffs, NJ: Prentice Hall.

Index

Aboriginal people: and citizenship, 287; and crime, 284; and education, 203, 210, 211, 213–15; and health, 261–2, 273–4; and justice system, 291; land claims, 69, 293–4; mortality rates, 252; and pension plans, 302, 306; perceptions of, 62–3, 71–3; policies towards, 287, 304; and poverty, 187–8, 189, 280–1; and racism, 58, 71–3; in Saskatoon, 60–1; self-government, 314, 315; violence against, 297; women, 264, 281, 287, 303–4

Acker, Joan, 49–50

action, 104, 118; in Archer, 108; Habermas's types of, 105–6; individual, 117, 128–9; rational and non-rational components, 106; vs. social action, 104; and structure, 110

actors, 104–6

Adair, Vivyan C., 246

Adams, Tracey, 169

adaptation, 55, 79, 131

Adler, Nancy, 245

affectual action, 105

age: and education, 222–9; and health, 256–61; and income, 189–90; norms, 89–90, 95; and paid work, 176; and personal experience, 90; privileges, 82; as relational, 100–1; Riley and, 85–90; social categories and, 99; and stress, 260–1; and theory of inequality, 100–1; and workforce, 169

age and society paradigm, 85, 87–8, 89, 101; diachronic view of, 87–8; synchronic view of, 87

age-based roles, 95

age categories, 90

age distribution: in Canada, 85; and occupations, 178

age groups, 99, 100, 101

ageism, 83–4

agency, 6, 13–14, 106–8, 120; and age inequality, 100; and citizenship claims, 291–4; and conceptual framework of social inequality, 130; corporate, 115; and education, 233; and gender, 54; Grabb and, 29; and health, 262–3, 274; and racialization, 75; reification, 89; Sewell and, 117; and the state, 286–7; and structure, 108–18, 130–1; and violence, 158, 297–300

agency and structure, dualism of, 112–16

agents, 104; in Archer, 107–8, 114; and autonomy, 112; primary, 115

age relations, 10–11, 13, 100; and labour force, 176

age strata, 89–90, 91, 95, 101

age stratification theory, 85–9, 90–5, 100

aging: as biopsychosocial process, 86; and class, 84; and health behaviours, 262; medicalization of, 271; naturalizing, 100; physical signs of, 83–4; political economy of, 95–9; and social time, 127; social security, 96; synchronic view, 86

aging enterprise, 96, 99

aging population, 10–11, 84, 99

'Agnes', 51

agriculture, 171

Aguiar, Luis M., 195, 196–7

Alberta, and social assistance, 286

alcohol consumption, 261, 262

alienation, 170, 171, 191–2, 198, 216

Allahar, Anton, 65, 66

allocation, 86, 87, 101

altruistic behaviour, 217

ambivalence, and social relations, 161–2

analytic dualism, 112–16, 130–1

Anderson, Norman, 274

Aneshensel, Carol S., 260

Angela's Ashes (McCourt), 18–19
'Anna', 3, 121–3, 131–4
appropriation principle, 21
Arat-Koc, Sedef, 290
Arber, Sara, 303
Archer, Margaret, 107–8, 114–16, 118, 126
Arendt, Hannah, 76
Armstead, Cheryl A., 274
Armstrong, Pat, 279
Assaulted Women's Helpline, 299–300
assimilation, 66
authority, 22, 26, 222
auto manufacturing industry, 173, 184–5
autonomy: of agents, 112; for women, 222; in work, 170, 198
Avison, William R., 312; policy recommendations, 318–24
Axworthy, Lloyd, 11

baby boom expansion, 224, 233
Bachmann, Kimberley, 146
Bachmann, Richard, 36
bankruptcy legislation, 169
battered women, 298, 299–300; *see also* intimate partner violence (IPV)
Beaujot, Rod, 143–4
Bell, Daniel, 191
Benoit, Cecilia, 264
Berger, Peter, 108–9
Bernhard, Judith K., 211
Betcherman, Gordon, 178
'Beth', 41
Bettely, Darlene, 269–70
Big Sisters/Big Brothers, 319
Bigsky, Marvin, 60
biological families, 45
biology: and aging, 100; gender differences, 42–4; and race, 59–61
biopsychosocial processes, 86, 100, 101, 123
birth control, 297
Bohatyretz, Sandra, 204
Bonilla-Silva, Eduardo, 73–4, 74–5
bookstores, competition amongst, 36–9
Bourdieu, Pierre, 113–14, 118, 202
bourgeoisie, 20, 39, 171
bovine spongiform encephalopathy (BSE). See mad-cow disease
Bradshaw, Jonathan, 282
Braverman, Larry, 191

breadwinner policy, 294–5, 306
Butlin, George, 222

CAGE(s), 130–1, and health, 274–5; and social processes, 271–4
Cain, Leonard, 85
Calliste, Agnes, 281
Campaign 2000, 283
Canada Assistance Plan, 322
Canada Child Tax Benefit, 322
Canada Health and Social Transfer (CHST), 318, 321
Canada Pension Plan/Quebec Pension Plan (C/QPP), 84, 97, 302; *see also* public pension plans
Canadian Alliance, 311; on Aboriginal people, 315; and multiculturalism, 316; on seniors, 317; on women, 313
Canadian Auto Workers, 173
Canadian Council on Social Development (CCSD), 4
Canadian Incidence Study of Reported Child Abuse and Neglect (CIS), 154–6
Cape Breton Community Employment and Innovation Project, 285–6
Capital III (Marx), 19–20
capitalism, 198; and alienation, 191; and authority, 22; and class, 19, 21; global, 179; ideology of, 170; and means of production, 20; and work, 194, 195–8; and patriarchy, 46–9; race and ethnicity, 68; and skill, 198
capitalist-executive class, 25, 171
Caplan, Elinor, 292
caregivers, 195, 237, 273, 290
Caribbean black women, 281, 290
caring, 141–2, 144–5, 147; economic support for, 141–2; for elderly parents, 149–50; retreat from, 303; work, 294
'Carrie', 321
Carroll, Dena, 264
causality argument, health and socio-economic relationship, 246
charismatic authority, 26
chemicals, and health, 244–5
child abuse, 154–6
childbirth, 46, 160–1, 296
child care, 145, 322, 324; class and, 150; and educational returns in labour market, 222; men and, 147–8; negotiations, 162; race and

ethnicity, 150; and teenage mothers, 320–1; women and, 286, 296

child care benefits, 147

children: academic performance and gender, 216–17, 217–18, 233; 'at-risk,' 210–11, 216–17, 233; policy recommendations for, 318–19; rights of, 155

child homicide, 156

child poverty, 7, 283–4; and mental illness, 250

children and youth 'at-risk,' 210–11, 216–17, 233

child welfare legislation, 303–4

Chinese Canadian National Council, 292

Chinese immigrants, 58–9, 281, 288–9, 291, 292–3

Chinese Immigration Act, 292

choices: and health, 238; of individuals, 103, 106, 109, 162–5; and social actors, 108; and work, 194

chronic strains, 249–50, 252

citizen: definition, 306–7

citizenship, 15, 279–80, 306; Chinese women and, 288–9; civil, 279, 284, 307; claims, 291–4; and exclusion, 290–1; and gender, 294–5; over life course, 301–5; political, 279–80, 287, 307; social, 280, 285, 307

citizenship regime, 279, 287–8

civil citizenship, 279, 284, 307

Clark, Warren, 222

class, 35–8, 171–9; and aging, 84, 99; and career, 196; and domestic labour, 150; and education, 203–10, 211–12; exploitation, 21; and gender, 174–5; Grabb and, 29–31; and income, 184–5; and the law, 284; Marx and, 26–7; and poverty, 280–2; and production, 20, 34–5; and social processes, 128; and social structures, 10; Weber and, 24, 26–7; Wright and, 21

class actions, 286–7

Class Counts (Wright), 39n

Classes (Wright), 39n

class-linked stress, 275

class locations, 22, 39n

class typology: Clement and Myles's, 23–4, 25; Grabb's, 29–31; Weber's, 24; Wright's, 22, 23

Clement, Wallace, 22–4, 25, 171, 175, 191–2

cluttered nest, 145, 166

cohort centrism, 89

cohort flow, 86, 88, 90

cohorts, 86, 87, 90, 100, 101; and education, 222–4

Coke Ovens (Sydney), 243–4

Coleman, Murray, 297

communicative action, 106

Communist Manifesto (Marx), 19

Comparative Project on Class Structure and Class Consciousness (Wright), 22–3

compulsory heterosexuality, 159, 166

computer professionals, 194

conflict: class, 10, 19, 21, 120; and power, 12; and structural functionalists, 9

conformation, 131, 135

Connelly, M. Patricia, 279

consent, 68

Constitution of Society, The (Giddens), 110–11

Cooper, Helen, 273

core sector, 193

corporal punishment, 154, 155

corporate agents, 115

corporate crime, 284, 307

corrections workers, and race, 69–70

Côté, James E., 65, 66

Courtenay, Will H., 267–8

Coward, Raymond T., 260

credentialism, 27

Creutzfeldt-Jakob disease (CJD), 257; *see also* mad-cow disease

crime, 156, 284, 291

Crompton, Susan, 246

cultural capital, 202, 233–4

cultural pluralism, 66

culture, 64–7

Cumming, Peter, 292

cumulative advantage/disadvantage hypothesis, 176, 198–9

Curtis, Bruce, 204, 210–11

Daigle, Chantal, 297

date rape, 160

dating experience, 159–60

Davies, Lorraine, 312; policy recommendations, 318–24

Davies, Scott, 204, 208–9, 212

Davis, K., 32–3

Decade in Decline, A, 7

deep social structures, 54, 73, 75

dentistry, 169–70

dependant care benefits, 147

deRouche, Constance P., 285

'deserving' poor, 281, 282

diachronic, 101; view of aging and society, 87, 89

Different Drummer Books, 36–7

differential exposure hypothesis, 255, 275

differential-vulnerability hypothesis, 255, 275–6

discrimination, 80; and health, 252; in production processes, 79; and race, 76

disease, 246, 263; and Aboriginal people, 252; epidemiological research, 240; fundamental causes of risk, 238; and gender, 253; and life course, 257; race and ethnicity, 250; and social time, 256; women's bodies and, 268–9

distance learning, 233

distribution: ideologies of, 310; and marital relations, 50; of resources, 24, 27; state relations of, 50

division of labour: and age, 96; in families, 161; gendered, 49, 54, 141, 143–4

divorce rates, 139

'Doing Gender' (West and Zimmerman), 51–3

domestic labour, 141–51; Beaujot's study, 143–4; division of, 165; gender and, 44; immigrant women, 289–90; and policy, 290; race and ethnicity, 150; see also unpaid work

domestic violence, 297, 300–1; charges for, 298; help for victims, 299–300, 319; and the state, 296; see also intimate partner violence (IPV)

dominant groups, 77

domination, 26, 98, 109, 297

door-opening rituals, 112–13

double morphogenesis, 115

dramaturgical action, 106

drugs, 261

dual-closure strategy, 28

dual-economy perspective, 193

duality of structure, 107, 116

dual-system theory, 46–7, 56

dynamism, 88

Economy and Society (Weber), 24, 64

education, 202–3; adult, 224–5; agency and experience within, 229; barriers to, 15, 138, 210–11, 233; and class, 29; curricula, 203; and gender, 138, 216–22; graduate, 221; high school, 205–6, 207, 220; investment into, 234; parental education, 206, 208, 209–10, 218; paying for, 207–8; post-secondary, 206, 207, 212; 'problem students',

211; and social problems, 319; special, 202, 204, 211, 234; streaming, 204; and technology, 233; and work, 193, 195, 202, 205–6

educational attainment, 15; and Aboriginal people, 211; and class, 29, 205–8; cohorts and, 222–3; and ethnicity, 212, 213; and gender, 218–22

educational expansion, 224

Educational Quality and Accountability Office (EQAO), 201

EI. See employment insurance (EI)

Eichler, Margrit, 142, 141

Elder, Glenn, 123–4

elder abuse, 156–8

elderly parents: caring for, 149–50

employees, 22, 168

employment: barriers to, 138, 194; and experience, 194; job security, 179; and new economy, 179; overqualification, 226–9, 227–8; part-time, 194, 296; in post-industrial society, 191–2; and racism, 79; re-employment, 184; and services sector, 192; youth, 91; see also paid work

employment benefits, 323

employment insurance (EI), 195, 296, 323; gendered, 295; and maternity benefits, 323–4

empty nest, 145, 166

emulation, 55, 79, 131

enmeshed approaches, to structure and agency, 108–12

environmental contaminants, 243–4

equality, 310, 311–12

Erwin, Lorna, 221

Essed, Philomena, 75, 77, 78

Estes, C.L., 99; and social class, 98

ethnicity, 64–7; and assessment, 65–6; and exclusion, 64–5; and health, 273–4; and income, 188; and social disadvantage, 66; see also race

Evans, Patricia M., 286

'Eve', 156, 157–8

everyday racism, 76–7, 78

exclusion: blatant and subtle, 77; and education, 210; race and ethnicity, 64–5, 67, 77, 78; and the state, 279

exclusion principle, 21

experience gradient, 190

exploitation, 21, 39, 39n, 129; gender-based, 128; racial, 77, 79; Tilly and, 55

expressive action, 105
externalization process, 109

families: agency and experience within, 162–5; and age stratification, 91–5; biological, 45; decline of, 139–40; defining, 140–1, 142; and education, 206; feminist research on, 151; and inequality, 14, 91–5, 161–2, 165–6; low-income, 142; nuclear, 140; and power imbalances, 95; race and ethnicity, 150–1; racialization, 281–2; and social processes, 139; and sociological ambivalence, 161–2; violence in, 139, 151–9, 319
Family Benefits, 282
family law, 310
family respite care centres, 319
Family Violence Court (FVC), 297
family wage, 47, 237, 294
feminist sociologists, 44
femininity, 268
fertility rate, 139, 140, 166
fetal rights, 297
Finnie, Ross, 207–8, 225, 226
Firestone, Shulamith, 45, 46
food banks, 284
Fox, Bonnie, 141, 142, 162
Freire, Marlinda, 211
Frenette, Marc, 226
Fry, Christine, 89–90
Frye, Marilyn, 113
functionalism, 85–6
fundamental causes explanations, 238, 276

garment industry, 168–9, 170
Garrick, Anthony, 70
gender, 42, 53, 54–6; and academic performance, 216–17; and agency, 54; and breadwinner policy, 294–5; and class, 50; and division of domestic labour, 143–4; and education, 138, 216–22; and family roles, 146–8; and health, 253–6, 260, 262, 267–8; and meaning, 129; and mental health, 255–6, 260; policy regimes, 294–5; roles, 294, 297; social categories, 43; social construction of, 51–3, 54; as social structure, 44, 52–3; and unemployment, 180; West and Zimmerman, 51, 52
gendered generations, 301
gendered identities, 51–3, 57
gendered power relationship, 45

gender inequality, 13, 54–6; and biology, 42–4; and radical feminism, 45; social construction of, 52; and socialist-feminism, 46; and sports, 43–4; structured accounts of, 44
gender relations, 42, 128
Gender Transformations (Walby), 49
General Social Study (1999), 156–7, 299
General Welfare Assistance, 320, 321, 322
generation, 14, 126, 135
generational equity, 11
generational location, 126
Giddens, Anthony: and agency, 106–7; and families, 165; and Marx, 20; structuration theory, 109–12
gifted educational programs, 205
Ginn, Jay, 303
glass ceiling, 42
globalization, 165, 172–3, 179, 256–7
Goffman, Erving, 52, 112–13, 131
Gosselin, Louise, 286–7
Goudge, Stephen, 155
Gower, Dave, 302
Grabb, Edward, 29–31, 79
Gramsci, Antonio, 68
Greschner, Donna, 297
Grimes, Michael D., 33–4
group elaboration, 114
Guaranteed Income Supplement (GIS), 278, 302
Guppy, Neil, 204, 208–9, 212

Habermas, Jürgen, 105–6
habitus, 113–14, 116, 117, 131, 134
Hadley, Gillian, 299
'Hagar Shipley', 82
Hands On Ministry, 61
Hargrove, Buzz, 173
Hartmann, Heidi, 46–7
head taxes, 288, 291, 292–3
health, 237; and age, 256–61; and agency, 261–3; and CAGE(s), 274–5; chemicals, 244–5; and geographic regions, 241, 264; inequality in, 15, 238–40; low-income groups, 240–1; race and ethnicity, 250–3; and social class, 240–50; and socio-economic status, 240–50, 245–6
health benefits, 96
health care: and Aboriginal women, 264; access to, 263–71; in Canada, 246; cuts to, 248; experience of, 265–7; gender and, 267–8;

and low-income individuals, 263–4; policy, 275; race and ethnicity, 264–5; and social time, 256; and socio-economic status, 263

Health Survey for England, 1993-6, 273

healthy-immigrant effect, 250

hegemony, 68, 80

heterosexuality, 159

high school education: dropout rates, 220; and job opportunities, 205–6; and socio-economic status, 207

historical time, 89, 90, 126–7

home care, 271

homelessness, 8–9

House, James S., 238, 240, 259–60

households, 26, 141–2

housework, 55, 141–2, 150; *see also* unpaid work

human action, 104–6; Parkin and, 29; *see also* agency

human agency. *See* agency

human capital, 193–4

human resources, 116, 129

Hunter, Alfred A., 21

hypersegregation, 274, 276

ideal family type, 294

ideal types, 118

identity: ethnicity and culture, 64–7; formation, 38–9

ideology: 79–80; and Marxism, 80; and race, 74–5, 79–80; and radical feminism, 80

immigrants: Chinese, 58–9, 281, 288–9, 291, 292–3; 'deserving,' 290–1; and education, 215–16; and head taxes, 288, 291, 292–3; and health, 250–2, 262; Japanese, 58–9; and labour, 67–8; older, 303; and social assistance, 278–9; and underemployment, 180–2; women, 289–90

immigration: and citizenship, 288–91; and educational requirements, 210, 211; and labour, 289–90; and Liberal Party of Canada, 315; policies, 281; and poverty, 11–12; and racism, 58–9

income, 4; and age, 97, 99, 185, 189–90; and class, 184–5; and educational attainment, 206–8, 208–9; and mental health, 261; mortality and morbidity, 241–5; and older women, 260; and poverty, 182–91; sex and, 190; and socio-economic status, 248–9; and

unpaid work, 150

income class, 24

Indian Act, 281, 287

individual earner-carer, 294, 295

individualism, 139

individuals: and action, 104, 128–9; and agency, 120; and choice, 103, 10 109, 162–5; in families, 162; and power, 28; and socialization, 109; and social roles, 10; and social structures, 13–14

in-group/out-group dynamic, 65

institutional level of analysis: of gender, 53

instrumental action: Habermas's, 105–6; Parsons's, 105; Weber's, 105

interactional level of analysis, of gender, 53

interaction order, 52

internalization, 109

Internet-based education, 233

intimate partner violence (IPV), 151–2, 152–3; and elder abuse, 157–8; leaving, 159

inverse interdependence principle, 21

'Isabella', 168

Jakubowski, Lisa Marie, 290

James Bay Cree, 293

Japanese Canadians, 58–9, 293

Jenson, Jane, 287

jobs, good vs. bad, 170, 171, 178, 179, 193; *see also* employment; paid work

Jordan, Beth, 299–300

Karlsen, Saffron, 252

Khawaja, Anwar and Mubashira, 180–2

Kilkey, Majella, 282

Kline, Marlee, 303–4

Knighton, Karen, 208

knowledge, as commodity, 191

knowledge-based economies, 179

Krieger, Nancy, 246–9, 274

Labour and Monopoly Capitalism (Braverman), 191

labour expenses, 168, 169

labour force participation: and age, 91; and women, 294–5

labour markets: and class, 196, 208–10; core vs. periphery, 193; and age/life-course, 226–9; and visible minority groups, 215–16; and young men, 303; gender and, 41–2, 44,

194–5, 222; and immigrants, 281; inequality in, 15; and racism, 69, 77; and the state, 279
labour-market-segmentation perspectives, 193
labour-power, 19, 28–9, 39; and new middle class, 23; and wage-exchange, 182–4; women's, 46, 47
land claims, 69, 293–4, 315
Lastman, Mel, 8
law, 284, 291, 311
Learning, Earning, and Parenting (LEAP), 320
Leckie, Norman, 178
Le Corre, André, 278, 286
legislation, child welfare, 303–4
Li, Peter S., 176, 216
Liberal Party of Canada, 311; on Aboriginal people, 313–15; and multiculturalism, 315–16; on seniors, 316–17; on women, 312–13
life course: and education, 222–9; and lifestyle behaviours, 262; and skill, 192; and social time, 123
life-course approach, 14, 98, 123, 178
life-course fallacy, 89
life expectancy, 246, 247–8; female, 253; for status Indians, 252
lifestyle choices, and health, 238, 261–3
Link, Bruce G., 249–50
Lipps, Garth, 204
Live-In Caregiver Program, 290, 307
lives in time and place, 124–6, 135
loose coupling, 112, 114, 131
Lorde, Audre, 236–8, 274
Loveman, Mara, 67
Low Income Cut-Offs (LICO), 4
low-income families, 142
Low Income Measure (LIM), 4
low-income neighbourhoods, 260, 263, 274
Luckmann, Thomas, 108–9
Lukes, Steven, 76; and power, 111–12
Luxton, Meg, 141, 142, 151

McCourt, Frank, 18–19, 103
McDaniel, Susan A., 301
McDonough, Peggy, 255–6
McGregor, Gaile, 182
Macintyre, Sally, 255
McKinlay, John B., 270
Mclean, Diane E., 249–50
McLean, Jill, 282, 283–4
McMillan, Keldon, 60

McMullan, John L., 284
McMullin, Julie Ann, 312; policy recommendations, 318–24
mad-cow disease, 256–7, 258–9
'making ends meet', 141–2, 151
male dominance, 46; see also patriarchy
managers, 22
mandatory retirement, 101, 194, 304
Mandell, Nancy, 218
Mannheim, Karl, 126
Man's Most Dangerous Myth (Montagu), 59
marital relations, and distribution, 50
marital status, and poverty, 11
markers: of age, 83, 85, 99; of race and ethnicity, 65–6, 77–9
Market Basket Measure (MBM), 4
marriage, 138, 139; sex and, 160; and teenage pregnancy, 160–1; and violence, 153
marriage premium, 56
Marshall, T.H., 279–80
'Martha', 321
Martin, Sheilah, 297
Marx, Karl, 19–21, 34; and capitalism, 170; and human action, 104; and power, 26; and skill, 198
Marxism, 10, 19–21; and ideology, 80; race and ethnicity, 67–8; and social class, 20; and socialist-feminism, 46
'Mary', 139
masculinity, 143, 268
material oppression, 35
maternity benefits, 161, 195, 323–4
Maurutto, Paula, 221
meaning: and age, 89; and inequality, 129; and structures, 117; and racism, 76
medicalization, 271, 276
membranes, 112, 113, 131, 134
men: death rate, 253; and domestic labour, 146–8, 149; and health care, 268; and intimate partner violence (IPV), 153–4; and labour markets, 41–2; and parenting, 162, 324; and power, 55; and reproduction, 45; and wages, 56
mental health: and life course, 260; racism and, 252–3; and socio-economic status, 249–50; and women, 255–6
Messing, Karen, 272
middle-aged people, 83
middle classes: in Canada, 36; expansion of,

171–2; Grabb's, 29–31; new and old, 23, 25;
Parkin and, 28; shrinking of, 7, 171; Wright
and, 22
Miech, Richard Allen, 260
Milne, Cheryl, 155
minimum wage, 101, 190; *see also* wages
Mirza, Sheba, 208
Montagu, Ashley, 59
Montreal garment industry, 168
Mooers, Colin, 285, 286
Moore, W.E., 32–3
moral action, 105
morbidity: gendered patterns of, 273; and gradient effect, 245; and income, 241–5
morphogenesis, 114, 115, 118
morphostasis, 114, 118
mortality: and income, 241–5; women and, 253–4
motherhood, 45, 138, 139; and Aboriginal women, 303–4; and family responsibilities, 138
mothers: and employment insurance (EI), 323; and labour-force participation, 145–6; and social assistance, 322; and tax relief, 324; teenage, 160–1, 320–1
Mother's Allowance, 282
motivation, 105
multiculturalism, 315–16
multiplicity of structures, 117
Murdock, George, 141, 142
Mustard, Cameron A., 263
Myles, John, 22–4, 25, 97; and Canadian class structure, 171; and social class, 98–9; women in work force, 175; and work, 191–2

National Longitudinal Survey of Children and Youth 1994–5, 204–5, 217
National Population Health Survey, 261
Native people, perceptions of, 62–3; *see also* Aboriginal people
Nazroo, James Y., 252
neo-Marxism, 21–4
neo-Weberianism, 27–31
Neugarten, Bernice, 85
'neutral' social policy, 310
New Brunswick, child protection in, 297
new economy, 179
new middle class, 23, 25, 171, 175
new technologies, and work, 191

Ng, Roxanna, 203
Night, Darrell, 58, 60
Nisga'a, 314
Noh, Samuel, 253
non-family living, 139
non-human resources, 116–17, 129
non-standard employment, 178
normatively regulated action, 106
North American Free Trade Agreement (NAFTA), 172
Norton, Keith, 304
nuclear families, 140, 141, 150–1, 166

objectivation process, 109
O'Brien, Mary, 45
occupations: academic, 196–7; and age distribution, 178; and class, 29; and illness, 272; low-income, 185; middle-class, 184; and poverty rates, 11; professional, 27; and research on inequality, 34
occupational health, 275
occupational segregation, 222, 234, 296
Oderkirk, Gillian, 222
old age: social construction of, 99–100; security, 195
Old Age Security (OAS), 10, 97, 278, 302
older people: bodies of, 83–4; caring for, 143; as commodity, 99; immigrants, 303; and inequality, 92–5; and political-economy theory, 95–9; and poverty, 11, 15n, 302; and re-employment, 184; and sickness, 257–9; and social assistance, 278, 302; and unemployment, 183–4; work in service sector, 192
old middle class, 25, 171, 172, 175
Omi, Michael, 58, 64, 67, 68, 68–9, 73; and ideology, 75, 80
opportunity hoarding, 55, 79, 129
oppression, 129; and age, 100–1; and gender relations, 54–5; material, 35; racial, 79; women's, 45, 48, 54; of workers, 169
Osborne, Helen Betty, 291
ownership, and class, 22, 29

paid work: agency and experience within, 195; and housework, 143–4; inequality in, 192–5; and resistance to social structures, 195; vs. unpaid work, 47, 143–4; and women, 180
'Pam', 162–5
Papillon, Martin, 287

parental benefits, 195, 323–4

parental education, 206, 218

parenting, 145; and absence, 319; life-long, 145; men and, 148–9, 162

Parkin, Frank, 27–9

Parsons, Talcott, 9, 105, 106

parties, 24–6, 39

part-time work, 194, 296

patriarchy, 45–6, 57; material base of, 46; public vs. private, 48–9; Walby's theory, 47–9

Pay Equity Act, 296

Peek, M. Kristen, 260

pension plans, 97, 302, 303, 306; *see also* public pension plans

'People Who Slipped thru the Cracks' (Vinograd), 5

periphery sector, 193

personal relations of distribution, 49–50

petite bourgeoisie, 39, 171

Pheasant, Valerie Bedassignae, 62–3

physical activity, and health, 271–2

physicians: and aging, 99, 270–1; race and ethnicity, 265–7; specialists, 263; visits to, 264, 267, 270–1

plural-system theory, 48–9

polarization, 198

policies: for adulthood, 321–2; and age, 11; anti-racism, 70; bankruptcy, 169; of Canadian Alliance, 311; and caregivers, 290; for childhood, 318–19; equality and, 311–12; gender, 282, 294–6; health and education, 279; immigration, 210; 'neutral,' 310; and old age, 96; for poor people, 281; sexism, 15; unemployment, 185; welfare, 286–7; and women, 279

policing, and racism, 60–1

policy makers, 310

political citizenship, 279–80, 287, 307

political-economy perspective: and age groups, 99; on aging, 95–9, 99–100; and state, 96–8

Politics of Reproduction, The (O'Brien), 45

pollution, and health, 241

poor people, and health, 246, 247–9; *see also* health; poverty

Popenoe, David, 139–40

population structure, 86

post-industrial society, and work, 191

post-secondary education: Aboriginal people and, 213, 214; barriers to, 206; and cohorts, 222; disruption of, 225; gender and, 219–21; graduate, 221; and income, 208–9; and mothers on social assistance, 322; and parental education, 209–10; and sole-support parents, 230–2; value of, 226; and women, 224

poverty, 4, 187: and gender, 11; and immigration, 11–12; and income, 182–91; and marital status, 11; and mothers, 138, 139, 282, 306; and occupation, 11; Pam's case study, 162–5; regional variations, 189; and seniors, 302; and social class, 280–2; in Toronto, 7; transitions in, 121–2

poverty line, 7

power, 39, 129; and action, 112; and age, 100–1; and attractiveness, 83; economic, 98; Essed and, 76; in families, 139, 151; gender and, 45, 55; Giddens and, 111–12; Grabb and, 29, 31; and inaction, 76; marital, 161; and old age, 98; and oppression, 129; Parkin and, 27, 28, 29; political-economy perspective, 98; and social change, 115; of the state, 96–7; and violence, 152, 154, 297; and wages, 151; Weber and, 12, 26

power imbalances, 154, 165–6; in families, 95

pregnancy, 46, 160–1, 297

prejudice, 76, 80

premenstrual syndrome, 268

prenatal care, 263, 264

primary agents, 108, 115

primary labour markets, 175, 193, 199

privacy, and age, 82

processes of distribution, 34, 127–8; and gender, 54, 49–50; and health, 275; and racism, 79; state-based mechanisms, 195; and wage-exchange, 182; *see also* social processes

processes of production, 34, 127–8; class and occupation structure, 171; garment work, 170; ideologies of, 310; means of, 20, 31; and older people, 98; race and ethnicity, 68; and racism, 79; and working-class industry, 169; *see also* social processes

processes of reproduction, 34, 127–8, 141; and health, 272; and racism, 79; and the state, 279; and wages, 186; and women of colour, 237; *see also* social processes

professionalization, 169–70

professionals, 27, 36, 38, 179, 194

proletariat, 20, 39, 171

property class, 24

property ownership, 27

pro-social behaviour, 217, 234

prostate screening tests (PSA), 265, 267

psychosocial risk factors, 238, 276

public pension plans, 84, 97, 99, 195, 316, 317; and Aboriginal people, 302, 306

Pulkingham, Jane, 294–5

Quebec: and James Bay Cree, 293–4; tuition in, 215

race, 59, 68, 73; abandoning concept of, 59–64; African slavery, 68–9; ambiguity, 61; and biology, 59–61; as deep social structure, 73, 75; and force, 68–9; and ideology, 75; political structures of, 68; and power, 74; reification, 59; significance of, 64; social construction of, 64, 75; in social sciences, 61–4; 'subordinate' and 'superior', 74; in United States, 58, 68

race and ethnicity, 77–80; and citizenship, 288–91; class and structure, 175–6; and education, 210–16; and health, 237, 250–3, 264–5; and inequality, 13; markers of, 65–6, 77–9; in Marxism, 67–8; social construction of, 67; and unemployment, 180–2; and wages, 186–8; and work, 196–7

racial contestation, 74

racial formation, 68–74

Racial Formation in the United States (Omi and Winant), 58

racialized persons, 193, 194, 229

racialized social systems, 74–5

racial projects, 68, 69; and citizenship, 288; individual, 71; interactional, 71–3; racist and non-racist, 73; structural, 69

racial 'strife', 74

racism: in Canada, 58–9, 60–1; and educational institutions, 229; Essed and, 75–6; everyday, 75–7, 78; and health, 252; and ideology, 74–5; material base of, 75, 77; and meaning, 76; and mental illness, 252–3; in school, 71–3; structural, 74–5; tolerance, 76, 77

radical feminism, 45, 46, 57; and ideology, 80; and patriarchy, 48

Ralston, Helen, 195

Ramsay, Paul, 214

Ranson, Gillian, 194

realist social ontology, 114–15, 118

reality, and social construction, 109

Reform Party of Canada, 311

Registered Education Savings Plan, 208

registered nurses, 273

Registered Retirement Savings Plans, 302

reification, 59, 80; of age, 89; of historical time, 89; of race, 73–4; of social order, 109

Reisman, Heather, 38

relational oppression, 129

remedial education, 204

reproduction: feminist perspectives, 39n; ideologies of, 310; and patriarchy, 45–6; and power, 45–6; regulation of, 296–7

residential schools, 58, 203, 210

resistance, 131, 135

resources, 112, 116–17

retirement: mandatory, 101, 194, 304; women and, 176

reverse causality, 246

Rich, Adrienne, 159

Richards, Renee, 43

Riley, Matilda White, 85

Risman, Barbara, 53

Rock, Alan, 265–7

role incumbents, 108

Romanow, Roy, 275

Roos, Noralou P., 263

'Rosa N.', 76–7

Rosen, Sam, 8

Roy, Gerald, 169

rules, 116

Ryder, Norman, 90

Sabourin, Sharon G., 229–32

Sales, Arnaud, 225

Samms, Crystal, 69–73

Sampson, Rob, 70

sandwich generation, 149–50, 166

SARS (Severe Acute Respiratory Syndrome), 256, 258

Saskatchewan, tuition in, 214

Saskatoon: racism in, 60–1; social agencies, 61

scarring, 184

schemas, 116, 117, 128–9, 131

schools: older students in, 223; in Ontario, 201, 204; private and public, 204; residential, 58, 203, 210; under-performance of boys, 216–17; vocational, 204, 211

Scott, Katherine, 281, 282
secondary labour markets, 193
Seeman, Neil, 287
self-employment, 36, 175; 176-177, 176
seniors: benefits for, 278; and Canadian Alliance, 317; and Liberal Party of Canada, 316–17; *see also* older people
separate gender roles regime, 294, 295
Sewell, William, 116–18, 131
sex, 42–4, 51, 52
sex categorization, 51, 52
sexual abuse, 160, 297
sexuality, 159–61; women's, 296–7
Shanahan, Michael J., 260
shelters, women's, 300, 319
silencing, 216, 234
singlehood, 139
single mothers, 282, 283–4; and poverty, 306
skill, 191–2, 199; and capitalism, 198; mobility, 192; and professional occupations, 27; and stratification, 32; Wright and, 22
slavery, 68–9
small business owners, 171, 172–4
Smith, Ralph, 265–7
Smith, Stephen, 284
smoking, 261, 262
Snider, Laureen, 284
social action, 104–5, 118
social actors, 115, 117
social agency, 108
social assistance: and adulthood, 321–2; and Canada Health and Social Transfer (CHST), 318; case workers, 322–3; and childhood, 318–19; history of, 281–2; and immigrants, 278–9; and morality, 282; and older people, 278; for women, 139, 322
social capital, 202, 208, 234
social change, 114, 124, 131
social citizenship, 280, 285, 307
social class, 10, 12–13, 20, 34, 171; age relations and, 100; conceptualizing, 19, 20–1, 34–9; and gender relations, 50; and health, 240–50; indicators of, 35; and Marx, 19–20; and political-economy theories of aging, 98; pre-retirement, 98; relational terms, 20; Weber and, 24
social class relations, 128
social closure, 27–8
social construction: of age, 100; race as, 59–61;

of women's bodies, 269–70
social constructionism, 80
Social Construction of Reality, The (Berger and Luckmann), 108–9
social gerontologists, 95–9
social inequality, 6–9, 16; abstract and concrete dimensions of, 134–5; conceptual framework for, 120, 125, 130, 309; critical approaches to, 10, 16; economic, 12; and families, 91–5; feminist approaches, 13; in health, 239; individual experience of, 6–7; and learned behaviours, 55; outcomes of, 309–10; race and ethnicity, 13; sites of, 14–15; stratification approaches to, 31–4; structures of, 10–13; transitions in, 4–6
social institutions, 9, 44, 86
social interaction, 113, 120; Archer and, 114–15; and gender, 52; and rules, 116
socialist feminism, 46, 57
socialization, 76, 86, 101, 109
social life, 110, 112, 120
social mobility, 103, 118, 123; and education, 201–2
social order, 109; reification, 109
social power, 24–6
social processes, 127–8, 309; in Anna's life, 132–3; and CAGE(s), 271–4; families and, 139; and health inequalities, 272–4; and social relations, 34, 49, 128
social reality, 109
social relations, 12, 16; and class, 50; of distribution, 49; Essed and, 75; of production, 49; and social processes, 34, 49, 128
social reproduction, 45, 46
social roles, 9, 86
social strata, 10
social structures, 9–10, 16, 128–30; and action, 106; of aging, 86–7; critical approaches to, 10; Riley and, 86; of Western nations, 120
social time, 6–7, 14, 123–7; and health, 256–61; and life-course research, 123
socio-economic gradient, 241–5, 276
socio-economic status (SES): and aging, 259–60; and education, 204–5, 206–8, 224; and health, 238, 240–50, 261, 263; and intimate partner violence (IPV), 154; and school test results, 201
Sonntag, Maynard, 214
spanking, 155

special education, 202, 204, 211, 234

sports, gender in, 43–4

spousal assault: and Aboriginal women, 304; charges for, 298; *see also* intimate partner violence (IPV)

spousal homicides, 154

spousal support payments, 310

Spouse's Allowance, 302

Stairway of Life, The (Anonymous), 123, 124

Stasiulis, Daiva, 77

state, 15, 307; and agency, 286–7; and families, 141, 166; institutions, 96; and political-economy theory, 96–8; and power, 96–7; and reproduction, 296–7; and social processes, 278, 279; and workfare, 285

state relations of distribution, 50

status groups, 24–6, 39

status situations, 26

'stay-at-home' dads, 148–9

sterilization, 297

Stevenson, Larry, 38

St Francis Xavier School, 71–2

Stone Angel, The (Laurence), 82

strata: age, 85; Marx and, 19; social, 10

strategic action, 105–6

stratification, 9–10, 16, 31–4; vs. class, 33–4

streaming, 204

stress, 238, 249–50; class-linked, 275; women and, 256

structural effects, 111

structural functionalists, 9

structural lag, 89, 101–2

structural racism, 74–5

structuration theory, 13–14, 107, 110–11

structure: Giddens and, 109–11; and meaning, 117

structure and agency, 108–18; and Anna, 131–4; and family inequality, 161–2; and habitus, 113–14; and power, 111–12; Sewell and, 116–18; and time, 114

structures of inequality, 6, 16

student loans, 207–8, 214, 225–6, 322

students: adult, 224–5; diversity of, 225; English as second language, 210–11; mandatory testing, 201; with minority backgrounds, 211; 'problem students', 211

subordinate classes, 28–9

subordination, 77, 78

substantive birth cohorts, 126, 127, 132, 135

Sucoff, Clea A., 260

suicide, 253–4

surplus value, 184, 199

Sydney, Nova Scotia, 243–4, 284

symbolic interactionism, 52, 57, 104, 118

synchronic, 102; view of aging and society, 87–8, 89

technology, and work, 191

teenage mothers: and child care, 320–1; pregnancy, 160–1

teenagers: and sex, 159, 160–1; and wages, 190

Tent City (Toronto), 8–9

Theorizing Patriarchy (Walby), 48, 49

Tilly, Charles, 10, 55

time, 108, 114

timing of lives, 123, 127, 135

Toronto: and poverty, 7, 283–4; Tent City, 8–9

toxic contaminants, 237

toys, and gender, 221

trade agreements, 172

traditional action, 105

traditional authority, 26

transnational action, 307

transposability, 131

tuberculosis (TB), 252

tuition, 207–8, 215, 225

Tumin, M., 32–3

underemployment, 216

Understanding Everyday Racism (Essed), 75

unemployment, 179–82; and age of workers, 182; and women, 180

unions, 28, 169, 173, 179

university education, 206, 207, 212

unpaid work, 47, 55; average weekly hours, 144; in families, 161; gendered oppression in, 55; and health, 272–3; men and, 149; and the state, 302; wives and, 56

upper classes: in Canada, 35; Grabb's, 29, 31

usurpation strategies, 28

value-rational action, 105

Vanier Institute of the Family, 141, 142

Vertinsky, Patricia, 271

victims: child and youth, 156; of familial abuse, 158; services for, 159

Vinograd, Julia, 5
violence, 151: date rape, 160; in families, 151–9, 165, 297, 319; against men, 153–4; as punishment, 154; against women, 297–300; *see also* intimate partner violence (IPV)
Violence Against Women Survey, 299
visible minority groups: in Canada, 66; class and structure, 175–6; and education, 210, 212; students, 210–11; women and, 290; *see also* race and ethnicity; immigrants
vocational schools, 204, 211
volunteers, cancer outreach, 269–70

wages, 47, 49; breadwinner, 294, 306; and education, 226; into food, 151; and marital status, 56; minimum wage, 101; and social processes, 195; women's, 185–6
Walby, Sylvia, 47–8, 280
Walters, Vivienne, 255, 256, 273
Wanner, Richard A., 216, 224, 226
Weber, Max, 24–7; and ethnicity, 64–5; and patriarchy, 57; and power, 12, 26–7; and social action, 104–5
Weekes, Anthony, 69–70
welfare, 96, 195; coercive policies, 286–7; individual experience of, 92–5
Wente, Margaret, 265–7
wertrational action, 105
West, Candace, 51–3, 54
West Nile virus, 256
white-collar employment, 191
Whitehall study, 245
wife assault, 153; *see also* intimate partner violence (IPV)
Wilkins, Russell, 241, 247
Winant, Howard, 58, 64, 67, 68, 68–9, 73; and ideology, 75, 80
Wolfson, Michael, 246
women, 6, 141, 315; and adult education, 225; and aging, 83–4; and social barriers 138; biological capacity, 45; and caring work, 195, 301; and child care, 145; and citizenship, 294; and control of sexuality, 160; and education, 221–2, 224, 229, 322; and employment insurance (EI), 323; and illness, 254–5, 270, 272; immigrant, 289–90; and intimate partner violence (IPV), 151–3; and labour, 55; and labour-force participation, 145–6, 174;

and labour markets, 310–11; and labour power, 46, 47; and low income, 318; and mental health, 255–6; and middle class, 175; mortality, 253–4; older, 302; and oppression, 45; and paid work, 42, 175, 180, 194–5; and part-time work, 296; and physical activity, 271–2; and policy, 279; retirement, 176; roles of, 141; and social assistance, 282, 286; and social insurance, 296; and stress, 261; traditional belief systems, 138–9; and unemployment insurance, 295–6; and unpaid work, 56; violence against, 151–2, 297–300; wages, 185–6
women's bodies: as problematic, 268–9; social construction of, 269–70
work. *See* employment; paid work
workers: age and, 194; in auto manufacturing industry, 184–5; in Canada, 174; deaths of, 284; full-time earnings, 187; older, 183–4; older vs. younger, 91; and power, 28–9; race and ethnicity, 67–8; and unions, 28; young, 91, 176, 192, 226
workfare, 280, 285–6, 287, 307
working class, 6, 25; in Canada, 35–6; Clement and Myles's, 171; Grabb's, 31; occupations, 184, 191, 198; Parkin's, 28; race and ethnicity, 68; and wages, 47
working-class families, and cultural capital, 202
working-class industry, 169
work-life balance, 146–7
Work-Life Balance, Are Employers Listening? (Bachmann), 146–7
workplace, 42, 70 170, 237
Wright, Erik Olin, 21–2, 22–3; and class locations, 39n; old middle class, 23; and power, 28

York University, 196–7
younger workers, 176, 192, 226
youth: Aboriginal, 284; favour of, 83, 101; funding for, 11; income and, 190; negative mobility, 303; and outcomes of inequality, 320–1; and racism, 71–3; and unemployment, 182; and work, 91, 176, 192, 226

Zami: A New Spelling of My Name (Lorde), 236–7
Zimmerman, Don, 51–3, 54
zweckrational action, 105